Praise for *Child*

MW01014855

"Reed and Warner-Rogers have made a sub child neuropsychology, which has suffere broad-ranging, well-conceived and authoritative volume. Balanced, extensively referenced, and sufficiently 'international', this very readable book addresses both theoretical and practical aspects of the discipline. It will be an invaluable resource for neuropsychologists working with children suffering from neurological injury and disease, those training for this role, and clinicians in cognate disciplines."

Professor J Graham Beaumont, Department of Clinical Psychology,
Royal Hospital for Neuro-disability, London

"The authors have supplied their 'missing textbook'. For me, they have more than succeeded in meeting their goals for combining science and practice, staying academically grounded but accessible, and powerfully presenting the case for the necessary focus on developmental variables in the investigation of the neuropsychology of the child, both in health and disease. The organization of their volume as a whole – key concepts, focus on principles of normal development within and across behavioral domains, clinical practice with children developing atypically – is reinforced chapter by chapter in the interweaving and integration of these three themes by a team of high caliber thinkers and writers. The contributions are consistent in range and quality. The text is both fascinating and readable throughout."

Jane Holmes Bernstein PhD, Department of Psychiatry,
Children's Hospital Boston/Harvard Medical School

"The book will be a valuable addition to the libraries of pediatric/child neuropsychologists. It takes a somewhat different and refreshing approach as compared to existing texts, focusing on neurobehavioral functions rather than clinical disorders. The book places a strong emphasis on clinical translation and application that should appeal to practitioners, but is firmly grounded in state-of-the-art theory and research."

Professor Keith Yeates, Department of Pediatrics,
Children's Research Institute, Ohio State University

"Here in a single volume, the reader will find summaries (some written by experts in the field) of current theory and knowledge regarding nearly all of the most common disorders seen by pediatric neuropsychologists. Whether read as the textbook for a course, or bought as a self-study aid, those new to the field will find this information to be invaluable. More experienced professionals are sure to appreciate well-edited chapters that will quickly bring them 'up to speed' on recent advances. In any case, *Child Neuropsychology* is unlikely to spend time collecting dust on the shelf. This is an immensely useful book that should be a part of every pediatric neuropsychologist's library."

Steve Hughes, PhD, LP, ABPdN,
Director of Education and Research, The TOVA Company

For Mandy and our children, Luke, Simon, Poppy, and Kitty
For my brothers and sisters and for Mum and Dad –
wish you could be here to see it. *J.R.*

To Marcus – for helping me to be. *J.W.-R.*

CHILD NEUROPSYCHOLOGY

CONCEPTS, THEORY, AND PRACTICE

Edited by

Jonathan Reed and Jody Warner-Rogers

A John Wiley & Sons, Ltd., Publication

Library of Congress Cataloging-in-Publication Data

Child neuropsychology: concepts, theory, and practice / edited by Jonathan Reed and Jody Warner-Rogers.
    p. ; cm.
    Includes bibliographical references and index.
    ISBN 978-1-4051-5266-2 (pbk.: alk. paper) 1. Child neuropsychology. I. Reed, Jonathan, 1965–
II. Warner-Rogers, Jody. [DNLM: 1. Child Development. 2. Neuropsychology. 3. Child. 4. Developmental
Disabilities–physiopathology. 5. Developmental Disabilities–psychology. 6. Neuropsychological Tests. WL
103.5 C5356 2008]

RJ486.5.C46 2008
618.92'8–dc22

2007049204

A catalogue record for this book is available from the British Library.

Contents

Contents

Plate section falls between pages 238 and 239

Illustrations

List of Figures

List of Plates

Notes on Contributors

Ruksana Ahmed is a chartered clinical psychologist with specialist experience in providing assessments and interventions for children with neurodevelopmental disorders and their families. She currently works at the Centre for Interventional Paediatric Psychopharmacology (CIPP) within the Child and Adolescent Mental Health Department of Great Ormond Street Hospital for Children, London. As a member of the CIPP team, she is involved in a number of research projects which are continuing to inform pharmacological and psychological practice for children with a range of highly complex needs and their families.

Mike Anderson is Director of the Neurocognitive Development Unit of the School of Psychology at the University of Western Australia. He took his undergraduate degree in psychology at the University of Edinburgh and his PhD at the University of Oxford under the supervision of Pat Rabbitt. He was a lecturer at the University of Edinburgh and a senior scientist at the Medical Research Council's Cognitive Development Unit in London before moving to Western Australia in 1990. His research interests are in developmental psychology, particularly in understanding the mechanisms underlying individual differences and developmental changes in intelligence.

Dagmara Annaz is a Lecturer in Developmental Psychology at the University of Edinburgh and Honorary Research Fellow at Birkbeck, University of London. She is part of the team that was awarded the Queen's Anniversary Prize for Higher and Further Education in 2006. She studies cognitive abilities in developmental disorders.

Janette Atkinson gained her PhD from the University of Cambridge, followed by post-doctoral research at the Behavioral Genetics Institute, Colorado, and the Johns Hopkins University, Baltimore. In Cambridge, she jointly started the Visual Development Unit supported by the Medical Research Council, the first interdisciplinary team in developmental vision, combining psychology, ophthalmology, neuroscience, and neurology. She is recognized internationally as a leading researcher in neurobiological models of visual brain development, pioneering innovative techniques for assessing vision, visual disability, and blindness in infants and children. She has over 300 scientific publications to her name and is a Fellow of the Academy of Medical Sciences, a member of the Williams Syndrome Foundation Professional Advisory Panel, and a founder of the International Child Vision Research Society. She holds a professorship in psychology at University College London (UCL) and a visiting professorship at the University of Oxford. She is UCL Pro-Provost for North America, Coordinator for Athena SWAN (careers for women in SET), and continues to direct the Visual Development Unit at University College London and the University of Oxford.

Simon Baron-Cohen is Professor of Developmental Psychopathology at the University of Cambridge and Fellow of Trinity College, Cambridge. He is Director of the Autism Research Centre in Cambridge. He holds degrees in human sciences from New College, Oxford, a PhD in psychology from University College London, and an MPhil in clinical psychology from the Institute of Psychiatry, London. He held lectureships in both of these departments in London before moving to Cambridge in 1994. He is also Director of the Cambridge Lifespan Asperger Syndrome Service. Among his publications, he is the author of *Mindblindness* (1995), *The Essential Difference: Men, Women and the Extreme Male Brain* (2003), and *Prenatal Testosterone in Mind* (2005), and the editor of *Understanding Other Minds* (1993, 2001), *The Maladapted Mind* (1997), and *Synaesthesia* (1997). He has also written books for parents and teachers, such as *Autism: The Facts* (1993), *Tourette Syndrome: The Facts* (1998), and *Teaching Children with Autism to Mind Read* (1998). He is the author of the DVD-ROM *Mind Reading: An Interactive Guide to Emotions* (2003), which was nominated for a BAFTA award for Best Off-line Learning. He has been awarded prizes from the American Psychological Association, the British Association for the Advancement of Science (BA), and the British Psychological Society (BPS) for his research into autism. In 2007 he was President of the Psychology Section of the BA and Vice President of the National Autistic Society, and he received the 2006 Presidents' Award for Distinguished Contributions to Psychological Knowledge from the BPS. His current research is testing the "extreme male brain" theory of autism at the neural, endocrine, and genetic levels.

Brian Butterworth is Professor of Cognitive Neuropsychology at the Institute of Cognitive Neuroscience of University College London. He taught at Cambridge for eight years and is Professorial Fellow at the University of Melbourne, and has held visiting appointments at Padua, Trieste, MIT, and the Max Planck Institute at Nijmegen. He was elected Fellow of the British Psychological Society in 1993 and of the British Academy in 2002. He has been the coordinator of two European networks to research the neural basis of mathematical abilities, Neuromath: Mathematics and the Brain (2000–3) and Numbra: Numeracy and Brain Development (2004–7). He is currently working with colleagues around the world on the neuropsychology and genetics of mathematical abilities.

Bhismadev Chakrabarti is the Charles and Katharine Darwin Research Fellow at Darwin College, University of Cambridge. He holds a degree in chemistry from the

University of Delhi, India, and a degree in natural sciences from the University of Cambridge. His doctoral research with Simon Baron-Cohen focused on genetic, neuro-imaging, and behavioral studies of emotion processing and empathy. He is currently a Senior Research Associate at the Cambridge Autism Research Centre.

Frederic Dick is a Senior Lecturer at the Centre for Brain and Cognitive Development of the School of Psychology at Birkbeck, University of London, and Assistant Research Scientist at the Center for Research in Language at the University of California, San Diego. Much of his work focuses on the acquisition of spoken language and other complex auditory skills, and the way in which these processes shape functional and structural organization in the brain.

Hans J. ten Donkelaar studied medicine at the University of Nijmegen in The Netherlands, where he received his MD (1974) as well as his PhD (1975). In 1978, he was appointed Associate Professor of Neuroanatomy in the Department of Anatomy and Embryology of that university. His research interests are developmental and comparative aspects of motor systems, developmental disorders of the CNS, and neuro-degenerative diseases. He is co-author of *The Central Nervous System of Vertebrates* (with Rudolf Nieuwenhuys and Charles Nicholson, 1998), *Clinical Neuroembryology: Development and Developmental Disorders of the Human Central Nervous System* (with Martin Lammens and Akira Hori, 2006), and an anatomy and embryology textbook in Dutch, which is now in its third edition (with Anthony Lohman and Antoon Moorman, 2007). In 1998, he joined the Department of Neurology of the Radboud University Nijmegen Medical Center to do research in developmental and neurodegenerative diseases. He is currently working on a book on brain circuitry and its disorders.

Ian Frampton trained in the Clinical and Community Psychology Doctoral Program of the University of Exeter and held the postdoctoral Fellowship in Developmental Neuropsychology at the Institute of Psychiatry, London, from 1996 to 1998. During this time, he worked with children with cerebral palsy and other neurodevelopmental disorders, including obsessive compulsive disorder and Tourette syndrome. He is currently Consultant in Paediatric Psychology in Cornwall and Clinical Co-Director of the Centre for Clinical Neuropsychology Research at the University of Exeter. He is a Visiting Research Consultant to the Regional Eating Disorders Research Team at Ulleval University Hospital, Oslo, Norway.

Usha Goswami is Professor of Education at the University of Cambridge and a Fellow of St. John's College, Cambridge. She is also Director of the university's Centre for Neuroscience in Education, which uses EEG techniques to study the neural basis of dyslexia and dyscalculia. Previously, she was Professor of Cognitive Developmental Psychology at the Institute of Child Health, University College London (1997–2003), and University Lecturer in Experimental Psychology at the University of Cambridge (1990–7). She received her PhD from the University of Oxford in 1987. Her current research examines relations between phonology and reading, with special reference to the neural underpinnings of rhyme and rhythm in children's reading. She has received a number of career awards, including the British Psychological Society Spearman Medal, the Norman Geschwind-Rodin Prize for Dyslexia Research, and Fellowships from the National Academy of Education (USA) and the Alexander von Humboldt Foundation (Germany).

Andrew Graham is a consultant neurologist at Addenbrooke's Hospital, Cambridge, with a specialist interest in cognitive and behavioral neurology. He contributes to the Addenbrooke's Memory and Cognitive Disorders Clinic, and his research interests include developing novel neuropsychological tasks to detect early frontal lobe dysfunction.

Sue Harrison is a clinical pediatric neuropsychologist working at Great Ormond Street Hospital for Children, London. She is also a fully qualified teacher and an educational psychologist. She has worked in mainstream and special schools with pupils from nursery to secondary age, including those with neurological, learning, and behavior problems. She is interested in meeting the educational needs of children with neurological issues, and is actively researching in the area of epilepsy and its effect on cognitive abilities and educational outcome.

Sarah Helps is a consultant clinical psychologist working both within the UK National Health Service and in private practice. She has a special interest in working with children and young people with neuropsychological and neurodevelopmental difficulties and the impact of these on the individual and their family and social context.

Jane Hood is a consultant pediatric neuropsychologist in pediatric neurosciences at Guy's and St. Thomas' Hospital, London. She is also a qualified educational psychologist and has recently completed a CPD doctorate in educational psychology. She worked as an educational psychologist for several years before training in pediatric neuropsychology. Prior to that, as a qualified teacher, she taught in a number of special schools, working with children with severe emotional and behavioral difficulties, and moderate through to profound learning difficulties. She has published papers on memory disorders in children and the cognitive effects of stimulant medication on children with attention deficit hyperactivity disorder.

Arthur MacNeill Horton, Jr. received his EdD degree in counselor education from the University of Virginia in 1976. He also holds diplomas in clinical psychology and behavioral psychology from the American Board of Professional Psychology and the American Board of Professional Neuropsychology. He is the author or editor of over 15 books, more than 50 book chapters, and over 150 journal articles. He is a past president of the American Board of Professional Neuropsychology and the National Academy of Neuropsychology. He previously worked as a Program Administrator at the National Institute on Drug Abuse of the National Institutes of Health, with responsibilities for neuropsychology.

Claire Hughes is a Reader in Developmental Psychology in the Department of Social and Developmental Psychology of the University of Cambridge. She also heads the

Social Development Research Group of the Centre for Family Research and is a Fellow of Newnham College, Cambridge. Her current research interests include cognitive development (with a special focus on executive functions and theory of mind) and social development (with a special focus on developmental psychopathology).

Annette Karmiloff-Smith is a Professorial Research Fellow at Birkbeck, University of London. She has a doctorate from the University of Geneva, where she worked with Piaget, and is a Fellow of the British Academy and Academy of Medical Sciences. She was awarded the 1995 British Psychological Society Book Award for *Beyond Modularity*. In 2002, she won the European Science Foundation Latsis Prize for Cognitive Sciences. She has honorary doctorates from Louvain and Zhejiang Universities. In 2004, she was awarded a CBE. She is the author of seven books and 200 book chapters and journal articles; her writings have been translated into 17 languages.

Yulia Kovas is a Lecturer at Goldsmiths College, London, and an Honorary Visiting Lecturer at the Institute of Psychiatry, King's College, London. She received her PhD in 2007 from the Social, Genetic and Developmental Psychiatry Centre of the Institute of Psychiatry. She received her first degree in 1996 in world literature, linguistics, and pedagogy from the University of St. Petersburg, Russia, and taught children of all ages for six years. She received a BSc in psychology from Birkbeck, University of London, in 2003, and an MSc in social, genetic, and developmental psychiatry from King's College, London, in 2004. Her current interests include the genetic and environmental etiology of individual differences in mathematical ability and disability and the etiology of covariation and comorbidity between different learning abilities and disabilities. She is also involved in research into the etiology of common psychopathology, including depression, anxiety, addiction, and post-traumatic stress disorder.

Robert Leech is a postdoctoral researcher in the School of Psychology at Birkbeck, University of London. His research focuses on the development of linguistic and auditory processing and analogical reasoning, using behavioral, neuroimaging, and computational methodologies.

Susan C. Levine is a Professor in the Department of Psychology, the Department of Comparative Human Development, and the Committee on Education of the University of Chicago. Her research focuses on mathematical, spatial, and language development, and how variations in input affect the development of typically developing children and children with early brain injury.

Marc D. Lewis is a Professor of Human Development and Applied Psychology at the University of Toronto. He specializes in the study of personality development as it relates to emotion and emotion regulation. His work is informed by developmental psychology, affective neuroscience, and a dynamic systems perspective on brain and behavior. His research has focused on transitions in emotional development and, in collaboration with Isabela Granic, he has developed a state space grid methodology for analyzing socioemotional behavior as a dynamic system. More recent work utilizes EEG methods for identifying the neural underpinnings of emotion regulation in normal and clinically referred children and for assessing neural changes corresponding with successful treatment. His papers on the contribution of dynamic systems theory and affective neuroscience to understanding human development have appeared in such journals as *Behavioral and Brain Sciences, Child Development, Development and Psychopathology*, and the *Journal of Abnormal Child Psychology*.

Marko Nardini studied psychology and philosophy at the University of Oxford, and gained a PhD in psychology from University College London. His doctoral work, supervised by Janette Atkinson, was on normal and atypical development of spatial cognition. He has continued his postdoctoral research at Oxford, University College London, and Birkbeck, University of London.

Ruth Nass is a pediatric neurologist at New York University Medical Center. Her clinical interests include dyslexia, attention deficit hyperactivity disorder, and autism. Her research interests are in the cognitive consequences of congenital stroke and risk factors for autism in tuberous sclerosis.

Robert Plomin is Medical Research Council Research Professor and Director of the Social, Genetic and Developmental Psychiatry Centre of the Institute of Psychiatry in London. He received his PhD in psychology from the University of Texas at Austin in 1974. He was then at the Institute for Behavioral Genetics in Boulder, Colorado (1974–86) and at Pennsylvania State University (1986–94) until he moved to London and launched the Twins' Early Development Study. His current research combines quantitative genetic and molecular genetic analyses of learning abilities and disabilities in childhood.

Jonathan Reed is a clinical psychologist in private practice specializing in child neuropsychology. He is a director and co-founder of a community child neuropsychology rehabilitation service, Recolo UK Ltd. He has worked as a child neuropsychologist at Guy's Hospital, London, and at the Royal London Hospital, and as a developmental psychologist in East Kent. He was also a researcher on the National Traumatic Brain Injury Study. His major interest is in applying scientific knowledge from the rapidly expanding field of child neuroscience to clinical practice.

Judy S. Reilly is a developmental psycholinguist. She is a Professor of Psychology at San Diego State University and the University of Poitiers in France. Her research focuses on the development of language and literacy as well as emotion in typically developing children and those with neurodevelopmental disorders.

Fiona Richardson received her PhD in cognitive science from the University of Hertfordshire. She integrates a range of different approaches, such as brain imaging, computational modeling, and behavioral testing, to explore general mechanisms of development, and in particular the development of language skills across the lifespan.

Paramala J. Santosh is a consultant child and adolescent neuropsychiatrist who is the Head of the Centre for Interventional Paediatric Psychopharmacology at Great

Ormond Street Hospital for Children, London. He is recognized as an international expert in developmental neuropsychiatry and pediatric psychopharmacology. He has published widely and has conducted research in neuroimaging, pediatric psychopharmacology, comorbidity of autism, ADHD and bipolar disorders, and childhood dementias. He is an Honorary Senior Lecturer at both the Institute of Child Health and the Institute of Psychiatry in London, and is the Joint Programme Director for the Great Ormond Street Hospital and Royal London Hospital Child and Adolescent Psychiatry Training Scheme. He is a member of the Neurosciences Subcommittee of the Medicines for Children Research Network.

Peta Sharples studied medicine at St. Mary's Hospital, London. She trained in pediatric neurology at Great Ormond Street Hospital, Oxford and Newcastle, where she was an Action Research Training Fellow and First Assistant in Paediatric Neuroscience. Her PhD, which described the relationship between clinical outcome and cerebral metabolism in children with severe traumatic brain injury, was awarded the Michael Blacow Prize of the Royal College of Paediatrics and Child Health and the Ronnie MacKeith Prize of the British Paediatric Neurology Association. She is a consultant pediatric neurologist in Bristol. As well as leading the pediatric neuro-rehabilitation service at Frenchay Hospital, she heads a clinical and experimental program of research, funded by grants from national bodies including the Department of Health, the British Brain and Spine Foundation, the Royal College of Surgeons, and Cancer and Leukaemia in Childhood.

Maxine Sinclair is a clinical child psychologist at South London and Maudsley Foundation Trust and Honorary Tutor at the Institute of Psychiatry, London. Her research interests are in developmental neuropsychology and childhood hyperkinesis.

Henry Soper is a faculty member of the Clinical Psychology Program at The Fielding Graduate University in Santa Barbara, California. He developed and is the Director of the Neuropsychology Concentration at Fielding, and teaches a certificate program in school neuropsychology. He is also the Director of the Developmental Neuropsychology Laboratory in Ventura, California. He is known internationally for his work on autism, attention deficit hyperactivity disorder, handedness, schizophrenia, experimental and clinical neuropsychology, experimental psychology, and language development. For many years he directed the clinical neuropsychology internship program at Camarillo State Hospital. His current research includes investigations into cognitive hemispheric specialization and the bases of different forms of intellectual functioning. He is also investigating the neuropsychology of expressive and receptive prosody. He is the author of over 70 scientific articles, chapters, and presentations in the basic and clinical neurosciences, and has held several National Institutes of Health and other research fellowships.

Joan Stiles is Professor of Cognitive Science and the Director of the Center for Human Development and the Human Development Program at the University of California, San Diego. Her research employs both behavioral and functional neuroimaging methodologies to explore the relation between brain and cognitive development in typically developing children and children with neurodevelopmental disorders.

Eric Taylor is a child neuropsychiatrist. He is Head of the Child and Adolescent Psychiatry Department of the Institute of Psychiatry at King's College, London, and chairs an interdisciplinary research group on the childhood problems that lead to poor adult mental health. His personal research interests are in childhood hyperkinesis, psychopharmacology, and neuropsychiatric conditions in childhood. This currently takes him (usually in collaboration) into neuroimaging and experimental psychological studies, molecular genetics, clinical nosography, longitudinal epidemiology, treatment trials, and community surveys of needs for treatment. He is lead clinician for the outpatient teams at the Maudsley Hospital, has been Vice-Dean and Deputy Registrar of the Royal College of Psychiatrists, and chairs the Paediatric Psychopharmacology Group, the Child Psychiatry Research Society, and a guidelines development group for the National Institute for Clinical Excellence. He is past editor of the *Journal of Child Psychology and Psychiatry*, an editor of *European Child and Adolescent Psychiatry*, and serves on several journal editorial boards.

Michael C. S. Thomas is a Reader in Cognitive Neuropsychology at Birkbeck, University of London, and the Director of the Developmental Neurocognition Laboratory at the Centre for Brain and Cognitive Development. He studies cognitive variability and developmental disorders, using behavioral, computational, and neuroimaging methods.

Rebecca M. Todd is a doctoral candidate in developmental science and neuroscience at the University of Toronto. Her research lies within the domain of developmental social cognitive neuroscience, an emerging field that bridges developmental psychology and cognitive and affective neuroscience. Specific research interests include the consolidation of the neural correlates of self-regulation processes over development, and individual differences in regulatory patterns associated with anxiety and response to trauma.

Jody Warner-Rogers is a consultant clinical psychologist and pediatric neuropsychologist. Together with Jonathan Reed, she ran the Paediatric Neuropsychology Service for several years at Guy's Hospital, London. She now divides her time between the Paediatric Neurodisability Service at Guy's and St. Thomas' NHS Foundation Trust and her private practice.

Ingram Wright has a long-standing interest in children's development. After completing a first degree in psychology at the University of Cambridge, he took a PhD in developmental psychology at the University of Warwick, followed by a doctorate in clinical psychology at the University of Leeds. He then undertook work in clinical neuropsychology at several UK centers and specialist training at Great Ormond Street Hospital in London before continuing with applied research and clinical practice at the University of Sheffield and Sheffield Children's Hospital. He now works as a consultant neuropsychologist at North Bristol NHS Trust where he is engaged in teaching, research, and clinical work in child neuropsychology. He has particular research and clinical interests in the cognitive development and rehabilitation of children with acquired brain injury.

Acknowledgments

We would like to thank all the contributors who gave their time and energy to make this book possible. Our initial ideas for the book were shaped in conversation with Mike Coombs, and we would like to thank him for his help in this and for introducing us to Blackwell. Our thanks go to Andrew McCleer for commissioning the book, and to Elizabeth Johnston, our editor at Blackwell, for her constant support, advice, and help, which has been invaluable. Also many thanks go to Sue Ashton, our copy-editor, for her excellent practical support and guidance. A number of people made helpful suggestions, and we would particularly like to thank Keith Yeates, Howard Fine, Mark Pertini, and Katie Byard, and also Steve Hughes and Cecil Reynolds for helping us out of a corner.

We would also like to thank Professor Richard Robinson, who saw the value of pediatric neuropsychology to the practice of neurology and fought to create the first pediatric neuropsychology post at Guy's Hospital over a decade ago. Thanks are also due to Melinda Edwards, who argued for the first job-share post in the psychology department, a post that allowed us to collaborate professionally and combine our ideas, enthusiasm, and clinical experience in a manner that eventually led to the publication of this book.

1

Introduction

Jonathan Reed and Jody Warner-Rogers

If "child neuropsychology is the study of brain-behaviour relationships within the dynamic context of the developing brain" (Anderson, 2001, p. 3), then in order to understand the field and practice within it, one must possess a thorough understanding of what a brain does and how it develops. The process of change is key in child neuropsychology. This differs from adult neuropsychology, where the focus of study is on damage to an already developed brain. Robust models of adult brain–behavior relationships have developed over the past hundred years. Child neuropsychology is, in contrast, an emerging discipline. It requires the creation of new models based on the process of development. We need to understand how brains and behavior develop, what contributions genes make, and what happens when there are deviations from typical development. Many people from different backgrounds, including researchers in child development, neuroscientists, and clinicians, are developing their understanding of these processes. We felt that there was a need to bring together different voices to begin to define what a comprehensive theory of child neuropsychology should encompass.

The idea for this book came from our experiences as clinicians. As practicing neuropsychologists, we recognized that a clear formulation is the key to understanding and supporting children's brain-based difficulties. For children, a neuropsychologically informed formulation requires a thorough understanding of how brain–behavior relationships develop over time (see Chapter 21). But how does one acquire this understanding? We realized that something was missing from our bookshelf, and it was at this point that the idea for the book began to materialize. By their very nature, textbooks can date very quickly, particularly in a fast-moving field. They can never reflect the most contemporary research findings; one must hit the journals for that level of recency. Yet textbooks can provide the conceptual framework within which newly acquired knowledge can be organized, understood, and integrated. This textbook aims to provide that architecture for child neuropsychology. We saw the need for a book that bridged cutting-edge science and clinical practice, a book that was developmentally focused and not disorder based, a book that was academically grounded, but accessible to a range of students, clinicians, and researchers. We hope that this textbook addresses this need.

The first part of the book looks at key theoretical concepts and research evidence that underpins our current understanding of brain development and function. Dagmara Annaz, Annette Karmiloff-Smith, and Michael C. S. Thomas operationalize the term "developmental approach" by stressing the need to trace normal developmental trajectories. Hans J. ten Donkelaar describes basic brain development from conception onward, and discusses the influence of specific aberrations that occur throughout this process, each capable of producing a wide range of deviations from the expected trajectories. Yulia Kovas and Robert Plomin discuss the contribution of genes in relation to learning disability and provide insight into the possible impact of genes on neuropsychological development. Judy S. Reilly and colleagues outline the fallout of early traumatic brain injury, highlighting the concept and constraints of neural plasticity. Brain imaging has brought forward our understanding of brain–behavior relationships, and Paramala J. Santosh and Ruksana Ahmed provide a helpful review of the technologies of brain imaging and their use with children. One key concept that is often missing from neuropsychology textbooks is that of general intellectual ability (IQ). Mike Anderson explores the concept of IQ and how this broad-based marker of brain functioning may develop.

Undoubtedly, a firm grounding in "normal" child neuropsychological development is the foundation for any efforts to evaluate and (most importantly) to improve those situations in which developmental progress has not proceeded smoothly. The field of child neuropsychology relies heavily on the theories and research of developmental and cognitive psychologists. Part II of the book gives an overview of current research regarding normal neuropsychological development and provides examples of deviations from these processes. Within the domain of cognitive development, Frederic Dick and colleagues take us through the emergence of language skills and the effect of different disorders on language development. Janette Atkinson and Marko Nardini look at visuospatial and visuomotor development; Arthur MacNeill Horton and Henry Soper outline the key factors that are important in understanding the development of memory; Maxine Sinclair and Eric Taylor discuss the development of attention; and Claire Hughes and Andrew Graham examine the development of executive function. But neuropsychological development is not confined to basic information processes: social, behavioral, and emotional development are key factors in clinical practice. Rebecca M. Todd and Marc D. Lewis provide a fascinating discussion of the development of the self-regulation of emotions and behavior. Simon Baron-Cohen and Bhismadev Chakrabarti review the state of our understanding in social neuroscience and, in particular, how empathy develops. No discussion of normal development would be complete without reference to education. The last two chapters of Part II are devoted to the development of academic skills: Usha Goswami summarizes the acquisition of reading, and Brian Butterworth provides insight into the often neglected areas of numeracy and dyscalculia.

Building on the first two parts of the book, Part III focuses on clinical practice. Ingram Wright and Peta Sharples discuss neuropsychological practice with neurological disorders. Ian Frampton illustrates the applicability of neuropsychological thinking to child and adolescent mental health issues. Sue Harrison and Jane Hood highlight the value of neuropsychological assessment in education. Sarah Helps demonstrates how the field can contribute to the understanding and management of other physical illnesses. The book concludes with an approach to neuropsychological assessment and formulation, based on the themes of this book and on our clinical experiences.

We hope that this book will enhance the clinical practice of our colleagues, and help to stimulate ideas and discussion for the next stage of research and practice within the exciting field of child neuropsychology.

Reference

Anderson, V., Northam, E., Hendy, J., & Wrennall, J. (2001). *Developmental neuropsychology: A clinical approach*. Hove, East Sussex: Psychology Press.

Part I
Key Concepts

The Importance of Tracing Developmental Trajectories for Clinical Child Neuropsychology

Dagmara Annaz, Annette Karmiloff-Smith, and Michael C. S. Thomas

Children change. Despite the truism of this statement, the dynamics of developmental change are frequently absent from studies of child disorders. Why is this? We believe that the reason lies in the strong influence of *adult* neuropsychology, in which researchers and clinicians focus on brains that have developed normally and become consolidated by adulthood prior to the brain insult. Since the adult brain is highly specialized, it is unsurprising that models of adult brain function focus on special purpose, independently functioning modules, whose components could be damaged or left intact by a specific brain trauma: the metaphor of boxes in the brain to be crossed through when damaged. While the adult framework can be informative about the end-state of development, it is inappropriate for understanding developmental disorders or even typical development because it ignores the dynamics of developmental change (Karmiloff-Smith, 1997, 1998). Indeed, the start-state of development is very different from the adult end-state.

The normal infant cortex is initially highly interconnected (Huttenlocher & Dabholkar, 1997; Neville, 2006), and it is only with time and with the processing of different kinds of inputs that the child brain becomes increasingly specialized and localized for function (Johnson, 2001). In other words, the brain does not start out with independently functioning modules: Modules are emergent from a gradual and complex process of modularization (Karmiloff-Smith, 1992). This means that a tiny impairment early on in, say, the developing visual system might have cascading effects on the subsequent acquisition of, say, number or vocabulary. Such impairments may or may not be compensated for, depending on the severity and the specialization of the impairment in question. It also means that one cannot take a single snapshot of, say, middle childhood, describe the phenotype of a developmental disorder, and from that suggest an intervention program. This would not only be clinically imprecise for a given child, but likely to be inappropriate for the syndrome in general. In our view, to assist clinical diagnosis and subsequent intervention, it is crucial to ascertain how the current phenotype originated at the beginning of a developmental trajectory, as well as knowing where it will lead in the future of that developmental trajectory.

This chapter will therefore concentrate on the importance of tracing and tracking full developmental trajectories, as well as focusing on associations between domains and between syndromes, rather than the current focus on dissociations. For illustrative purposes, we will concentrate mainly on autism spectrum disorder (ASD), Down syndrome (DS), fragile-X syndrome (FXS), and Williams syndrome (WS).

Prenatal Learning

Fetal development starts very early, at the onset of zygote formation, with the first neurons of the human forebrain present at a very early stage (Bystron, Rakic, Molnár, & Blakemore, 2006). Moreover, for the cognitive neuroscientist, learning also starts very early. From about the seventh month of pregnancy onward, the healthy fetus is actively processing various forms of auditory input (Hepper, 1995; Moore, 2002). Fetuses who hear a specific piece of music in the womb will discriminate that particular music from other pieces at birth. Newborns also recognize their mother's voice at birth, despite the fact that in the womb it was filtered through the amniotic fluid and sounds very different ex utero. Yet, during intrauterine life the fetus forms some abstract representation of mother's voice and is able to distinguish her voice from other female voices at birth (Kisilevsky et al., 2003).

Furthermore, fetuses also learn the beginnings of the speech patterns of their mother tongue while in the womb. Research using acoustic spectroscopy has shown that, at 27 weeks, a fetus's cry already contains some features of his or her mother's speech, such as rhythms and voice characteristics. Also, DeCasper and colleagues showed that fetuses at 33–37 weeks' gestation demonstrated memory of children's rhyme, while still in the womb, in response to mothers repeatedly reading a certain rhyme to their unborn baby (DeCasper, Lecaunet, Busnel, Granier-Deferre, & Maugeais, 1994).

For the moment, we lack any knowledge about the learning capacities of the atypically developing fetus. However, for a truly full understanding of the developmental trajectory of a child with a disorder, this is where we should in the future be grounding our field of enquiry. For the time being, we must begin with postnatal development.

Neuroconstructivism and Postnatal Learning

From the moment the child is born, he or she is bombarded with interesting stimuli—faces, voices, objects, and so forth—and, as a result of the repeated processing of these different stimuli, the infant brain becomes slowly but increasingly specialized (Johnson, 2001). Elsewhere, we have argued that a middle way is needed between staunch nativism, on the one hand, in which the infant brain is thought to be prespecified for each of its modular abilities, and behaviorism, on the other, in which a single, general purpose learning mechanism is invoked. Neuroconstructivism, an intermediate way between nativism and behaviorism, holds that a small number of domain-relevant learning algorithms jump-start the infant brain (Elman et al., 1996). Initially, all algorithms attempt to process all inputs, but with time the one that is most domain-relevant (say, to rapid sequential processing) wins out in the competition between algorithms and *becomes* domain-specific over developmental time (Karmiloff-Smith, 1998). We speculate that this is the case for the typically developing infant. However, we do not know whether the atypically developing infant brain displays the same level of interconnectivity early on, and whether subsequent pruning leads to specialization and localization of function in children with developmental disorders. But, theoretically, we can already ask what the implications of early interconnectivity would be for the atypically developing brain.

Within the theoretical assumptions of neuroconstructivism, the interconnectivity of early cortical development means that a tiny deficit could permeate all parts of the cortex. But, given the interaction between different algorithms and different structures in the environmental input, some parts of the brain would be more seriously affected by the deficit than others. This could give rise, over developmental time, to a seemingly isolated domain-specific impairment and the apparent preservation of other domains (i.e., scores "in the normal range"). In other words, what seems in the end-state to be a domain-specific deficit may have originated in the start-state as a more domain-general deficit (Annaz & Karmiloff-Smith, 2005; Karmiloff-Smith, 1997, 1998; Karmiloff-Smith et al., 2004). We therefore strongly advocate the importance of investigating not only domains of weaknesses, but also domains in which individuals show proficiency; that is, reach scores comparable to controls. Indeed, if changes to domain-relevant properties are initially widespread, and some properties are less relevant to a given domain, then that domain might exhibit lesser, more subtle impairments (Karmiloff-Smith, 1998; Karmiloff-Smith, Scerif, & Ansari, 2003). Ideally, then, an explanation of developmental deficits consists in identifying how these initial domain relevancies have been altered in the disorder, and then how the subsequent process of emergent modularization has been perturbed.

"Spared" versus "Impaired" Processing?

In the literature on developmental disorders, one frequently encounters terms such as "spared," "intact," and "preserved" when describing atypical development (e.g., Hoffman, Landau, & Pagani, 2003; Rouse, Donnelly, Hadwin, & Brown, 2004; Tager-Flusberg, Plesa-Skwerer, Faja, & Joseph, 2003). The notion of a selective deficit implies the impairment of a single process or domain together with the preservation (i.e., normal development and functioning across time) of others. When a brain has developed normally, resulting over time in specialized, localized functions, it is possible that after consolidation subsequent brain injury may produce selective damage(s) while other components continue to operate normally. Hence, it might be appropriate to consider them as spared, intact, or preserved.

However, in the case of a developmental disorder of genetic origin, the use of such terms is questionable. They imply that the purported intact function has *developed normally* from infancy, through childhood to adulthood, with no interactions with other developing parts of the brain. Yet, as we mentioned above, the infant brain starts out highly interconnected (Neville, 2006), so it is unlikely that one part of the brain can develop normally in total isolation, without being affected (even subtly) by other parts of the atypically developing brain. The use by clinicians of the intact–impaired dichotomy in characterizing developmental aspects of functioning has problematic implications for intervention (A = intact, no intervention required; B = impaired, intervention required). Such dichotomies, then, could actually hinder rather than enhance the study of the dynamics of atypical development. By contrast, if one considers development as a dynamic process of interactions and competition, it could be, for instance, that training in rapid sequential movements in the assumed "preserved" motor system could impact another nonmotor domain which is impaired, rather than direct training in that nonmotor domain.

Concrete Examples from Developmental Cognitive Neuroscience

Studies that have taken the neuroconstructivist developmental approach to behavioral phenotypes have shown, for instance, that areas of purported relative strength at one stage of development (middle childhood or adolescence) were not necessarily stronger at earlier stages of development (Paterson, Brown, Gsödl, Johnson, & Karmiloff-Smith, 1999). For example, Paterson and colleagues (1999) showed that infant cognitive profiles in Williams syndrome and Down syndrome cannot be predicted from the adult end-state pattern of their cognitive functioning. One of the most compelling examples is vocabulary learning in toddlers with Williams syndrome, which is very poor and as delayed as vocabulary acquisition in toddlers with Down syndrome. By contrast, when individuals with Williams syndrome reach adolescence or adulthood, their language vastly outstrips that of their counterparts with Down syndrome. The same differences between the infant start-state and the adult end-state exist for number (Paterson et al., 1999; Paterson, Girelli, Butterworth, & Karmiloff-Smith, 2006). Infants and toddlers with Williams syndrome are sensitive to differences in small numbers, whereas those with Down syndrome perform even more poorly than younger mental age-matched infant controls. By contrast, in adulthood, scores for Down syndrome in the number domain outstrip those for Williams syndrome (Paterson et al., 2006). This highlights the importance of examining an entire developmental trajectory rather than a snapshot of development in childhood or adulthood.

Another example comes from studies of children with unusual genetic mutations. We have for several years been examining the cognitive phenotypes of children with deletions within the Williams syndrome critical region but which are smaller than the typical Williams syndrome deletion on chromosome 7 (Karmiloff-Smith et al., 2003; Tassabehji et al., 1999). Our aim is to delineate the functions of various genes in expressing the full Williams syndrome phenotype. Here again, developmental trajectories have played a crucial role. In the case of one partial deletion child (HR), we found on initial testing that she did not differ from normal controls on the Bayley Scales of Infant Development. We could have concluded that the genes deleted in her case played no role in the Williams syndrome phenotype. However, as we began to trace her trajectory over developmental time, we found that, although she had a milder phenotype, she none the less progressively approximated the Williams syndrome phenotype and drew away from the typical trajectory. This was true at both the level of facial dysmorphology (Hammond et al., 2005) and that of her cognitive phenotype (Karmiloff-Smith, 2004). Figure 2.1 provides an illustration of this changing pattern.

Another example from developmental cognitive neuroscience is provided by Scerif and colleagues (2004) who investigated visual search in toddlers with fragile-X syndrome and those with Williams syndrome. These researchers demonstrated how important it is to go beyond mere scores to examine patterns of errors. While both groups of atypically developing toddlers reached a similar overall level compared to mental age-matched controls, their pattern of errors was very different. Toddlers with Williams syndrome made the highest number of erroneous touches on distractors. They were more affected than the other groups by the combination of larger display size and target–distractor similarity (conjointly increasing the perceptual load of the search task). By contrast, the toddlers with fragile-X syndrome made more errors of perseverance to targets already visited. In other words, where performance scores did not distinguish between the two syndromes, their respective patterns of error did.

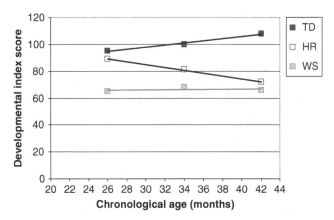

Figure 2.1 Changes in scores on the Bayley Scale of Infant Development over time for a child (HR) with Williams syndrome with deletion on chromosome 7, compared to typically developing (TD) children and children with Williams syndrome (WS).

A third example comes from face processing in Williams syndrome. There is no doubt that face processing is a relative strength in this syndrome: On some standardized tests, individuals with Williams syndrome achieve scores in the normal range (Bellugi, Marks, Bihrle, & Sabo, 1988; Udwin & Yule, 1991). However, it would be erroneous to maintain that face processing *develops* normally in this clinical group. Several behavioral and electrophysiological studies point to atypical development of face processing in Williams syndrome compared to controls (Grice et al., 2003; Karmiloff-Smith et al., 2004). The general consensus (but see Tager-Flusberg et al., 2003, who continue to maintain that Williams syndrome face processing is no different from healthy controls) is that the behavioral proficiency in Williams syndrome face processing (and in autism spectrum disorder face processing) is underpinned by different cognitive processes (Annaz, 2006; Deruelle, Mancini, Livet, Cassé-Perrot, & de Schonen 1999; Karmiloff-Smith, 1997, 1998; Karmiloff-Smith et al., 2004; Rossen, Bihrle, Klima, Bellugi, & Jones, 1996). This was further corroborated by our event-related potential (ERP) study comparing the brain processes of healthy controls versus adolescents and adults with Williams syndrome when processing faces and cars (Grice et al., 2003), as well as in another study of cerebral integration (Grice et al., 2001). The face-processing findings highlighted the fact that although healthy controls processed both human and monkey faces in a relatively similar way, their brains treated cars very differently. By contrast, the brains of participants with Williams syndrome displayed no differences between faces and cars.

Moreover, unlike the healthy controls, who showed a right hemisphere dominance for upright faces, the clinical group failed to display any difference in hemispheric activation (Karmiloff-Smith et al., 2004). This highlights two facts about the deviant trajectory of Williams syndrome face processing, despite their behavioral proficiency. First, there is a lack of specialization: Individuals with Williams syndrome show similar electrophysiological responses for both faces and cars; that is, they have not progressively restricted the brain circuits responsible for face processing uniquely to face stimuli, but process all manner of visual stimuli in a similar way. Second, there is a lack of localization: Healthy controls show stronger processing for faces in the right hemisphere, whereas the clinical population displayed equivalent bilateral activation. The lack of specialization and localization in Williams syndrome face processing indicates that, despite enormous daily experience with faces, a face-processing module fails to emerge over developmental time in this clinical population. In other words, their proficiency on some standardized tasks is achieved through different cognitive and brain processes than in normal development. It follows that clinicians need to be cautious when they encounter scores in the normal range, given that these may camouflage different cognitive and brain processes from healthy controls.

The sensitivity of standardized tests is, as we saw above, open to discussion, raising the risk that scores in the normal range may be achieved by atypical brain and cognitive processes. It also raises questions about what is being matched when researchers do group or individual mental age matching. Annaz (2006) illustrated these problems by testing children with Williams syndrome and those with high functioning autism (HFA) on the Benton Facial Recognition Test (Benton, Hamsher, Varney, & Spreen, 1983). Figure 2.2 illustrates how both groups score within the normal range on this

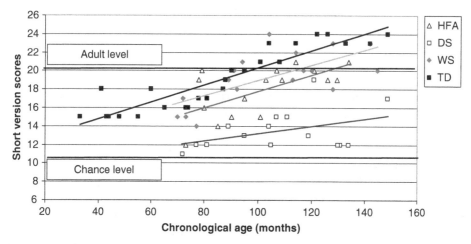

Figure 2.2 Performance of children with Down syndrome (DS), Williams syndrome (WS), and high functioning autism (HFA) compared to typically developing (TD) children on the Benton Facial Recognition Test.

face-processing task. However, to examine whether both groups were processing faces like their typically developing (TD) counterparts, Annaz carried out an in-depth examination of their face-recognition skills. She found that both clinical groups performed significantly more poorly on face-specific tasks in which configural processing was manipulated, suggesting that the Benton task can be solved by featural processing and does not require the configural processing used by normal controls.

We have illustrated in the case of face processing just how crucial it is to differentiate "normal" scores at the behavioral level from underlying cognitive and brain processes. It is also obvious that the choice of a matched control group has theoretical implications. If one matches on IQ, it implies that intelligence affects the domain in question, say, language. If one matches, say, Williams syndrome with Down syndrome, this is not theory neutral because a match on their overall IQ camouflages the fact that in one case the score is brought down by the spatial component and in the other case by the verbal component. These differences will clearly affect all subsequent measures. So, what is the best way to gain a deeper understanding of developmental disorders? We believe that it is by building task-specific, full developmental trajectories.

The Need for Developmental Trajectories

Of course, the most informative way of gaining an insight into how developmental changes occur over time in clinical groups (or, in fact, typically developing children also) is to conduct longitudinal studies. However, these studies are highly time-consuming and may put parents, children, and teachers under unnecessary pressure. Drop-out rates are indeed high in longitudinal studies. An alternative to the longitudinal method is to build *developmental trajectories* by means of a cross-sectional design. This approach has been successfully used in recent studies (Annaz, 2006; Karmiloff-Smith et al., 2004; Thomas et al., 2001). The developmental trajectories approach seeks to build a task-specific typical developmental trajectory by first measuring performance across a wide range of ages in the normal population. Then, given an individual with a disorder, one can next establish whether his or her performance fits *anywhere* on the typical trajectory. Unlike the use of matched controls, this comparison is theory neutral.

Secondly, one can assess whether the individual fits on the trajectory at the position predicted by his or her chronological or mental age. Additionally, one can use a variety of other predictors (for example, language age, nonverbal reasoning age, and so on) to assess whether the individual fits on the normal trajectory according to *any* aspect of their cognitive profile. Indeed, one will often discover that predictors differ between healthy controls and the clinical group. So, for instance, whereas language predicts scores in numerical cognition in Williams syndrome, it is spatial scores that predict numerical outcome in the typical group (Ansari et al., 2003; Ansari & Karmiloff-Smith, 2002).

Tracing developing trajectories is not only possible for the normal population. Given a group of individuals with a certain disorder, with a wide age range, it is also possible to construct atypical task-specific developmental trajectories for a particular disorder and contrast this with the typically developing group. So, rather than comparing scores at a single point in development, the trajectories approach offers a more direct way of addressing the question "Does the target behavior *develop normally or atypically* in the disorder?" Such an approach also makes it possible to reconsider the notions of delay versus deviance.

An illustration comes from a cross-syndrome study (WS, DS, and ASD) by Annaz (2006). She and her colleagues investigated the development of featural and configural face recognition using the Jane Faces Task that had been extensively tested on the normal population (Mondloch, Le Grand, & Maurer, 2002). In the low functioning ASD group, atypical U-shaped performance was observed on the inverted featural face trials: Younger children with autism displayed better performance on inverted trials, followed by a decrease in accuracy at around 9 years of age (Figure 2.3). Yet for the whole developmental period, accuracy on upright featural trials continued to increase. However, performance on the configural trials did not significantly increase with chronological age or when assessed against other predictors (such as language). Had the research used the traditional mental age-matched individual or group comparisons, these effects would actually have been masked.

The use of the trajectories approach makes it possible to go beyond describing behavior as delayed. In other words, it becomes possible to provide more in-depth descriptors in terms of a *delayed onset*, which implies a normal rate (not statistically different from a normal trajectory); a *delayed rate* of developmental trajectory, which implies a normal onset but a slower rate of increase in performance; a *delayed rate and onset*; or, finally, a *zero rate* (a gradient not significantly different across time; Thomas et al., in press). It is also possible to examine intra- and intergroup variability using the trajectories approach.

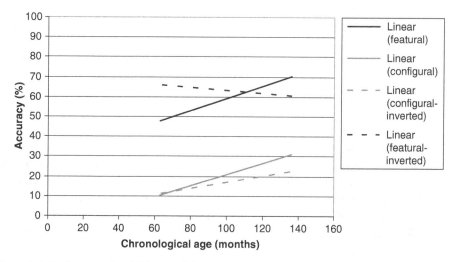

Figure 2.3 Performance by children with low functioning autism on a featural and configural face recognition task. *Note.* From *The development of visuo-spatial processing in children with autism, Down syndrome and Williams syndrome*, by D. Annaz, 2006, unpublished PhD thesis, Birkbeck College, University of London.

The use of developmental trajectories is not only necessary at the behavioral level but it also needs to be complemented at the neuroanatomical level (Shaw et al., 2006). Shaw and colleagues used a longitudinal design to examine the relationship between cortical development and cognitive variation. They found a marked developmental shift from a predominantly negative correlation between intelligence and cortical thickness in early childhood to a positive correlation in late childhood and beyond. This study indicates that the neuroanatomical expression of intelligence in children is dynamic. Many other studies also indicate that IQ levels are not static but change with brain development and are impacted by environmental factors. Indeed, environmental factors may play a more important role than research often grants them (Mareschal et al., 2007). A child must always be considered within the environment that he or she lives because, as soon as parents are told that their child has a developmental disorder, their behavior changes subtly. They may unwittingly impede their child from freely exploring the environment and/or they may help the child avoid making mistakes, whereas the natural process of learning actually involves erroneous overgeneralizations and so forth.

Conclusion

No approach to developmental disorders is without its inherent problems, and neuro-constructivism is no exception. For example, Thomas (2005) highlights two unan-swered problems associated with the theoretical assumptions of neuroconstructivism.

First, a clearer picture is needed of the initial domain relevancies that predate a particular domain and of the nature of the process that eventually delivers domain-specific functional structures. The second difficulty is related to methodological issues of building developmental trajectories from infancy through to adulthood. It cannot be assumed that the same task is treated in the same way across developmental time (i.e., using the same brain and cognitive mechanisms at very different ages). Clearly, these questions need to be at the heart of new research within the developmental trajectories approach.

In our view, the notions of interactivity, competition, compensation, redundancy, specialization, localization, and modularization will be key in characterizing in more depth how atypical development proceeds at the cognitive level, notions that have significant implications for the formation and functioning of mechanisms over developmental time (Karmiloff-Smith, 1992, 1998; Karmiloff-Smith & Thomas, 2003; Scerif & Karmiloff-Smith, 2005; Thomas, 2003, 2005), and as yet these mechanisms have in the main been neglected in developmental cognitive neuroscience.

We reiterate the importance of examining more closely "scores in the normal range." It is also important to recall that phenotypic outcomes at the cognitive level could stem from much lower level deficits. Indeed, a very small difference in developmental timing, gene expression, neuronal formation, migration, and density, and many other genetic and biochemical factors, can impact on development over time and result in much greater deficits in the phenotypic outcome. This is why we contend that the task-specific developmental trajectories approach, starting wherever possible at the very outset of infant development, constitutes a first but important step toward gaining a deeper understanding of both the dissociations and associations across different syndromes.

References

Annaz, D. (2006). *The development of visuo-spatial processing in children with autism, Down syndrome and Williams syndrome*. Unpublished PhD thesis, Birkbeck College, University of London.

Annaz, D., & Karmiloff-Smith, A. (2005). Cross-syndrome, cross-domain comparisons of development trajectories: Commentary on Mile, Swettenham and Campbell. *Cahiers de Psychologie Cognitive/Current Psychology of Cognition, 23*(1–2), 44–48.

Ansari, D., Donlan, C., Thomas, M., Ewing, S., Peen, T., & Karmiloff-Smith, A. (2003). What makes counting count? Verbal and visuo-spatial contributions to typical and atypical number development. *Journal of Experimental Child Psychology, 85*(1), 50–62.

Ansari, D., & Karmiloff-Smith, A. (2002). Atypical trajectories of number development. *Trends in the Cognitive Sciences, 6*(12), 511–516.

Bellugi, U., Marks, S., Bihrle, A., & Sabo, H. (1988). Dissociation between language and cognitive functions in Williams syndrome. In D. Bishop & K. Mogford (Eds.), *Language development in exceptional circumstances* (pp. 177–189). Hillsdale, NJ: Lawrence Erlbaum.

Benton, A., Hamsher, K. deS., Varney, N., & Spreen, O. (1983). *Benton test of facial recognition.* New York: Oxford University Press.

Bystron, I., Rakic, P., Molnár, Z., & Blakemore, C. (2006). The first neurons of the human cerebral cortex. *Nature Neuroscience, 9*, 880–886.

DeCasper, A. J., Lecaunet, J., Busnel, M., Granier-Deferre, C., & Maugeais, R. (1994). Fetal reactions to recurrent maternal speech. *Infant Behavior and Development, 17*, 159–164.

Deruelle, C., Mancini, J., Livet, M., Cassé-Perrot, C., & de Schonen, S. (1999). Configural and local processing of faces in children with Williams syndrome. *Brain and Cognition, 41*, 276–298.

Elman, J. L., Bates, E. A., Johnson, M., Karmiloff-Smith, A., Parisi, D., & Plunkett, K. (1996). *Rethinking innateness: A connectionist perspective on development.* Cambridge, MA: MIT Press.

Grice, S. J., de Haan, M., Halit, H., Johnson, M. H., Csibra, G., & Karmiloff-Smith, A. (2003). ERP abnormalities of illusory contour perception in Williams syndrome. *NeuroReport, 14*, 1773–1777.

Grice, S. J., Spratling, M. W., Karmiloff-Smith, A., Halit, H., Csibra, G., de Haan, M., et al. (2001). Disordered visual processing and oscillatory brain activity in autism and Williams syndrome. *NeuroReport, 12*(12), 2697–2700.

Hammond, P., Hutton, T. J., Allanson, J. E., Buxton, B., Campbell, L. E., Clayton-Smith, J., et al. (2005). Discriminating power of localized three-dimensional facial morphology. *American Journal of Human Genetics, 77*, 999–1010.

Hepper, P. G. (1995). The behavior of the fetus as an indicator of neural functioning. In J.-P. Lecanuet, W. Fifer, N. Krasnegor, & W. Smotherman (Eds.), *Fetal development: A psychobiological perspective* (pp. 405–417). Hillsdale, NJ: Lawrence Erlbaum.

Hoffman, J. E., Landau, B., & Pagani, B. (2003). Spatial breakdown in spatial construction: Evidence from eye fixations in children with Williams syndrome. *Cognitive Psychology, 46*, 260–301.

Huttenlocher, P. R., & Dabholkar, A. S. (1997). Regional differences in synaptogenesis in human cerebral cortex. *Journal of Comparative Neurology, 387*, 167–178.

Johnson, M. H. (2001). Functional brain development in humans. *Nature Reviews Neuroscience, 2*, 475–483.

Karmiloff-Smith, A. (1992). *Beyond modularity: A developmental approach to cognitive science.* Cambridge, MA: MIT Press.

Karmiloff-Smith, A. (1997). Crucial differences between developmental cognitive neuroscience and adult neuropsychology. *Developmental Neuropsychology, 13*, 513–524.

Karmiloff-Smith, A. (1998). Development itself is the key to understanding developmental disorders. *Trends in Cognitive Sciences, 2*, 389–398.

Karmiloff-Smith, A. (2004). *Modules, genes and evolution: What have we learned from developmental disorders?* Inaugural lecture at the Kavli Institute for Brain and Mind, University of California, San Diego.

Karmiloff-Smith, A., Grant, J., Ewing, S., Carette, M. J., Metcalfe, K., Donnai, D., et al. (2003). Using case study comparisons to explore genotype-phenotype correlations in Williams–Beuren syndrome. *Journal of Medical Genetics, 40*(2), 136–140.

Karmiloff-Smith, A., Scerif, G., & Ansari, D. (2003). Double dissociations in developmental disorders? Theoretically misconceived, empirically dubious. *Cortex, 39*, 161–163.

Karmiloff-Smith, A., & Thomas, M. (2003). What can developmental disorders tell us about the neurocomputational constraints that shape development? The case of Williams syndrome. *Development and Psychopathology, 15*, 969–990.

Karmiloff-Smith, A., Thomas, M. S. C., Annaz, D., Humphreys, K., Ewing, S., Grice, S., et al. (2004). Exploring the Williams syndrome face processing debate: The importance of building developmental trajectories. *Journal of Child Psychology and Psychiatry and Allied Disciplines, 45*(7), 1258–1274.

Kisilevsky, B. S., Hains, S. M., Lee, K., Xie, X., Huang, H., Ye, H. H., et al. (2003). Effects of experience on fetal voice recognition. *Psychological Science, 14*(3), 220–224.

Mareschal, D., Johnson, M., Sirios, S., Spratling, M., Thomas, M. S. C., & Westermann, G. (2007). *Neuroconstructivism: How the brain constructs cognition.* Oxford University Press.

Mondloch, C. J., Le Grand, R., & Maurer, D. (2002). Configural face processing develops more slowly than featural face processing. *Perception, 31*(5), 553–566.

Moore, J. K. (2002). Maturation of human auditory cortex: Implications for speech perception. *Annals of Otology, Rhinology, and Laryngology, 189*(Suppl.), 7–10.

Neville, H. J. (2006). Flexibility and plasticity in cortical development. In Y. Munakata & M. H. Johnson (Eds.), *Attention and performance, XXI* (pp. 287–314). Oxford University Press.

Paterson, S. J., Brown, J. H., Gsödl, M. K., Johnson, M. H., & Karmiloff-Smith, A. (1999). Cognitive modularity and genetic disorders. *Science, 286* (5448), 2355–2358.

Paterson, S. J., Girelli, L., Butterworth, B., & Karmiloff-Smith, A. (2006). Are numerical impairments syndrome specific? Evidence from Williams syndrome and Down's syndrome. *Journal of Child Psychology and Psychiatry, 47*(2), 190–204.

Rossen, M., Bihrle, A., Klima, E. S., Bellugi, U., & Jones, W. (1996). Interaction between language and cognition: Evidence from Williams syndrome. In J. H. Beitchman, N. Cohen, M. Konstantareas, & Tannock, R. (Eds.), *Language learning and behaviour* (pp. 367–392). New York: Cambridge University Press.

Rouse, H., Donnelly, N., Hadwin, J. A., & Brown, T. (2004). Do children with autism perceive second-order relational features? The case of the Thatcher illusion. *Journal of Child Psychology and Psychiatry, 45*(7), 1246–1257.

Scerif, G., Cornish, K., Wilding, J., Driver, J., & Karmiloff-Smith, A. (2004). Visual search in typically developing toddlers and toddlers with fragile X or Williams syndrome. *Developmental Science, 7,* 116–130.

Scerif, G., & Karmiloff-Smith, A. (2005). The dawn of cognitive genetics? Crucial developmental caveats. *Trends in Cognitive Sciences, 3,* 126–135.

Shaw, P., Greenstein, D., Lerch, J., Clasen, L., Lenroot, R., Gogtay, N., et al. (2006). Intellectual ability and cortical development in children and adolescents. *Nature, 440,* 676–679.

Tager-Flusberg, H., Plesa-Skwerer, D., Faja, S., & Joseph, R. M. (2003). People with Williams syndrome process faces holistically. *Cognition, 89,* 11–24.

Tassabehji, M., Metcalfe, K., Karmiloff-Smith, A., Carette, M. J., Grant, J., Dennis, N., et al. (1999). Williams syndrome: Use of chromosomal microdeletions as a tool to dissect cognitive and physical phenotypes. *American Journal of Human Genetics, 64,* 118–125.

Thomas, M. S. C. (2003). Multiple causality in developmental disorders: Methodological implications from computational modelling. *Developmental Science, 6*(5), 537–556.

Thomas, M. S. C. (2005). Characterising compensation. *Cortex, 41,* 434–442.

Thomas, M. S. C., Annaz, D., Ansari, D., Scerif, G., Jarrold, S., & Karmiloff-Smith, A. (in press). Using developmental trajectories to understand developmental disorders. *Journal of Speech, Language, and Hearing Research.*

Thomas, M. S. C., Grant, J., Barham, Z., Gsödl, M., Laing, E., Lakusta, L., et al. (2001). Past tense formation in Williams syndrome. *Language and Cognitive Processes, 16*(2/3), 143–176.

Udwin, O., & Yule, W. (1991). A cognitive and behavioural phenotype in Williams syndrome. *Journal of Clinical and Experimental Neuropsychology, 13*(2), 232–244.

3

Child Brain Development

Hans J. ten Donkelaar

The development of the human brain may be divided into several phases, each of which is characterized by particular developmental disorders (ten Donkelaar, Lammens, & Hori, 2006; see Table 3.1). After implantation, formation and separation of the three germ layers occur, followed by dorsal and ventral induction phases, and phases of neurogenesis, migration, organization, and myelination. With the transvaginal ultrasound technique, a detailed description of the living embryo has become possible (Blaas, 1999; Blaas & Eik-Nes, 2002; Pooh, Maeda, & Pooh, 2003), and, with magnetic resonance imaging (MRI), fetal development of the brain can be studied from about the beginning of the second half of pregnancy (Garel, 2004).

In recent years, much progress has been made in elucidating the mechanisms by which the central nervous system (CNS) develops, and also in our understanding of its major developmental disorders, such as neural tube defects, holoprosencephaly, microcephaly, and neuronal migration disorders. Molecular genetic data, which explain the programming of development etiologically, can now be incorporated (Barkovich, Kuzniecky, Jackson, Guerrini, & Dobyns, 2001; Sarnat, 2000). This chapter presents an overview of the major stages in the development of the human CNS, embryonic and fetal development of the human brain, some developmental disorders of the brain, the cerebral cortex in particular, and, briefly, the postnatal development of the brain.

Major Stages in the Development of the Human Brain

The *embryonic period* in man (i.e., the first eight weeks of development) can be divided into 23 stages, the *Carnegie stages* (O'Rahilly & Müller, 1987). In the embryonic period, postfertilization or postconception age is estimated by assigning an embryo to a developmental stage using a table of norms. The term *gestational age* is commonly used in clinical practice, beginning with the first day of the last menstrual period. Usually, the number of menstrual or gestational weeks exceeds the number of postfertilization weeks by two.

Hans J. ten Donkelaar

Table 3.1 Major Stages of Human Central Nervous System Development.

Stage	Time of occurrence (weeks)	Major morphological events in the brain	Main corresponding disorders
Embryonic period			
Formation and separation of germ layers	2	Neural plate	Enterogeneous cysts and fistulas; split notochord syndrome
Dorsal induction: primary neurulation	3–4	Neural tube, neural crest and derivatives; closure of rostral and caudal neuropores; paired alar plates	Anencephaly, encephalocele, myeloschisis, myelomeningocele
Ventral induction: telencephalization	4–6	Development of forebrain and face; formation of cerebral vesicles; optic and olfactory placodes; rhombic lips appear; "fusion" of cerebellar plates	Holoprosencephaly, Dandy–Walker malformation
Fetal period			
Neuronal and glial proliferation	6–16	Cellular proliferation in ventricular and subventricular zones; early differentiation of neuroblasts and glioblasts; cellular death (apoptosis); migration of Purkinje cells and external granular layer in cerebellum	Microcephaly, megalencephaly
Migration	12–24	Migration of cortical neurons; formation of corpus callosum	Neuronal migration disorders (lissencephalies, polymicrogyria, schizencephaly, heterotopia)
Perinatal period			
Organization and maturation	24 to postnatal	Late migration; organization and maturation of cerebral cortex; synaptogenesis; formation of internal granular layer in cerebellum	Minor cortical dysplasias
Myelination	24 to 2 years postnatally		Myelination disorders, destructive lesions (secondarily acquired injury of normally formed structures)

Note. From *Clinical neuroembryology: Development and developmental disorders of the human central nervous system* by H. J. ten Donkelaar, M. Lammens, & A. Hori, 2006, Berlin: Springer Verlag.

During week 1 (stages 2–4), the blastocyst is formed; during week 2 (stages 5 and 6), implantation occurs, followed by the formation of the notochord and the beginning of neurulation (stages 7–10). The neural folds begin to fuse at stage 10, and the rostral and caudal neuropores close at stages 11 and 12, respectively. The first four embryonic weeks are also described as the period of blastogenesis, and the fifth to eighth weeks as the period of organogenesis (Opitz, 1993; Opitz, Wilson, & Gilbert-Barnes, 1997). The *fetal period* cannot be divided into a series of morphologically defined stages. It is the period of phenogenesis (Opitz, 1993). In the clinical literature, a subdivision of the prenatal period into three trimesters of 13 weeks each is commonly used. At the junction of trimesters 1 and 2, the fetus of about 90 days has a greatest length of 90 mm, whereas at the junction of trimesters 2 and 3, the fetus is about 250 mm in length and weighs approximately 1,000 g (O'Rahilly & Müller, 2001). The newborn brain weighs 300–400 g at full term.

The embryonic period includes three phases overlapping in time: formation and separation of the germ layers, dorsal induction, and ventral induction (Table 3.1). During the first phase, the neural plate is formed. In the *dorsal induction* phase (primary neurulation), the neural tube is formed and closed, and the three primary divisions of the brain (the prosencephalon, mesencephalon, and rhombencephalon) appear. In the *ventral induction* phase (telencephalization), the cerebral hemispheres, the eye vesicles, the olfactory bulbs and tracts, the pituitary gland, and part of the face are formed. In the sixth week of development, strong proliferation of the ventral walls of the telencephalic vesicles gives rise to the ganglionic or ventricular eminences. These elevations do not only form the basal ganglia but also give rise to many neurons for the cerebral cortex. Neurogenesis starts in the spinal cord and brain stem. Neurogenesis in the cerebellum and cerebral cortex occurs largely in the fetal period. The fetal period may be divided into a *fetal period proper* (9–24 gestational weeks), characterized by the formation of the cortical plate, and a *perinatal period*, extending from the 24th week of gestation to the time of birth (Marín-Padilla, 1990). This period is characterized by neuronal maturation. The 24th week of gestation approximates roughly the lower limit for possible survival of the prematurely born infant. Disorders of migration are more likely to occur in the fetal period, whereas abnormalities affecting the architectonic organization of the cerebral cortex are more likely to occur in the perinatal period.

Each of the developmental phases of the brain is characterized by particular developmental disorders (Table 3.1). In the dorsal induction phase, neural tube defects occur. Developmental disorders in the ventral induction phase, in which the prosencephalon is normally divided into the diencephalon and the two cerebral hemispheres, are characterized by a single, incompletely divided forebrain (holoprosencephaly). This very heterogeneous disorder may be due to disorders of ventralization of the neural tube, such as the underexpression of the ventralizing gene *Sonic hedgehog* (SHH). During neurogenesis of the forebrain, malformations due to abnormal neuronal proliferation or apoptosis may occur, leading to microcephaly or megalencephaly. During the migration of the cortical neurons, malformations due to abnormal neuronal migration may appear, varying from classic lissencephaly ("smooth brain"), several types of neuronal

heterotopia, polymicrogyria to minor cortical dysplasias. For many of these malformations, disorders of secretory molecules and genes that mediate migration have been
found. Many of these malformations are characterized by the presence of mental retardation and epilepsy. Cerebellar disorders are more difficult to fit into this scheme. The
Dandy–Walker malformation is thought to arise late in the embryonic period, whereas
cerebellar hypoplasia presumably occurs in the fetal period.

Embryonic Development of the Brain

The first indication of the *neural plate* in human embryos is a median sulcus around 23
days of development. About two days later (stage 9), this *neural groove* is deeper and
longer. Its rostral half represents the forebrain where neural folds are conspicuous, its
caudal half mainly the hindbrain (Plate 1). The appearance of the mesencephalic
flexure allows a first subdivision of the brain into three major subdivisions in the still
unfused neural folds (Jirásek, 2001): the forebrain or *prosencephalon*, the midbrain or
mesencephalon, and the hindbrain or *rhombencephalon*. Closure of the neural tube is
initiated at multiple sites as in mice and other animals (Nakatsu et al., 2000). Rostrally
and caudally, the cavity of the developing neural tube communicates via the rostral and
caudal neuropores with the amniotic cavity. The rostral neuropore closes at about
30 days (stage 11), and the caudal neuropore about one day later (stage 12).

Neural tube defects (NTDs) are among the most common human malformations, with
an incidence of 1–5 per 1,000 live births. NTDs are a group of defects in which the neural
tube has failed to complete neurulation, and one or more of the neural tube coverings are
incomplete (Naidich et al., 1996; Norman, McGillivray, Kalousek, Hill, & Poskitt, 1995;
ten Donkelaar et al., 2006). Four main types of NTDs are found at the cranial and spinal
level: (a) the neural plate remains open (anencephaly and myeloschisis, respectively);
(b) the neural tube is exteriorized (encephalomeningocele and myelomeningocele);
(c) only meninges are exteriorized (cranial and spinal meningoceles); and (d) merely a
skeletal defect is evident (cranium bifidum occultum and spina bifida occulta).

The embryonic development of the human brain is shown in Figure 3.1. The
neural tube becomes bent by three flexures: (a) the mesencephalic flexure at the
midbrain level; (b) the cervical flexure at the junction between the rhombencephalon
and the spinal cord; and (c) the pontine flexure in the hindbrain. The three main
divisions of the brain (prosencephalon, mesencephalon, and rhombencephalon) can
already be recognized when the neural tube is not yet closed. The forebrain soon
divides into an end region, the *telencephalon*, and the *diencephalon*, which gives rise
to the optic vesicles. With the development of the cerebellum and the pons, the division of the hindbrain into a rostral part, the *metencephalon*, and a caudal part, the
medulla oblongata or *myelencephalon*, becomes evident. By stage 15, the future cerebral hemispheres can be recognized. The cerebral hemispheres enlarge rapidly so that by
the end of the embryonic period they completely cover the diencephalon. Frontal,
temporal, and occipital lobes, the insula, and the olfactory bulb become recognizable
(Figure 3.1a).

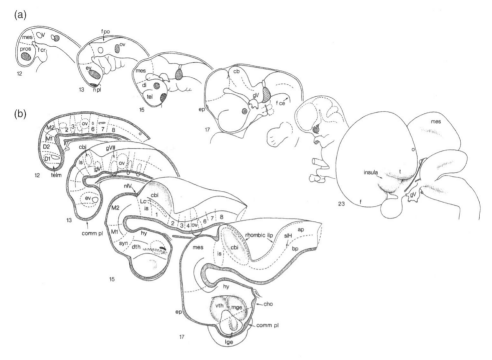

Figure 3.1 Lateral (a) and medial (b) views of the developing brain in Carnegie stages 12, 13, 15, and 17, and a lateral view of the brain at the end of the embryonic period (i.e., at stage 23). *Abbreviations.* ap, alar plate; bp, basal plate; cb, cerebellum; cbi, internal cerebellar bulge; cho, chiasma opticum; comm pl, commissural plate; di, diencephalon; D1, D2, diencephalic neuromeres; dth, dorsal thalamus; ep, epiphysis; ev, eye vesicle; f, frontal lobe; f ce, flexura cervicalis; f cr, flexura cranialis; f po, flexura pontina; gV, trigeminal ganglion; gVII, facial ganglion; hy, hypothalamus; is, isthmus; Lc, locus coeruleus; lge, lateral ganglionic eminence; lterm, lamina terminalis; mes, mesencephalon; M1, M2, mesomeres; mge, medial ganglionic eminence; npl, nasal placode; nIV, trochlear nerve; o, occipital lobe; ov, otic vesicle; pros, prosencephalon; slH, sulcus limitans of His; syn, synencephalon; t, temporal lobe; tel, telencephalon; telm, telencephalon medium; vth, ventral thalamus; 1–8, rhombomeres 1–8. Note. Adapted from *The embryonic human brain: An atlas of developmental stages* (2nd ed.) by R. O'Rahilly and F. Müller, 1999, New York: Wiley-Liss; and *Clinical neuroembryology: Development and developmental disorders of the human central nervous system* by H. J. ten Donkelaar, M. Lammens, and A. Hori, 2006, Berlin: Springer Verlag.

Neuromeres

Morphological segments of the brain or *neuromeres* have been known since their first description by von Baer in 1828. Neuromeres are segmentally arranged transverse bulges along the neural tube, particularly evident in the hindbrain (Figure 3.1b). Each neuromere has alar (dorsal) and basal (ventral) components. Six primary neuromeres already appear at stage 9 when the neural folds are not fused: prosencephalon, mesencephalon, and four rhombomeres. Sixteen secondary neuromeres can be recognized from about stage 11 (Müller & O'Rahilly, 1997). They gradually fade after stage 15. Eight rhombomeres (Rh1–8), an isthmic neuromere (I), two mesomeres (M1, M2) of the midbrain, two diencephalic neuromeres (D1, D2), and one telencephalic neuromere (T) can be distinguished. The diencephalic neuromere D2 can be further subdivided into the synencephalon, the parencephalon caudalis, and the parencephalon rostralis. Neuromere D1 gives rise to the eye vesicles and the medial ganglionic eminence (Müller & O'Rahilly, 1997). In mice, the prosencephalon was originally divided into six prosomeres, numbered P1–P6 from caudal to rostral. The prosomeres P1–P3 form the diencephalon: P1 is the synencephalon, P2 the parencephalon caudalis, and P3 the parencephalon rostralis. The alar component of the synencephalon forms the pretectum, that of the caudal parencephalon the dorsal thalamus and the epithalamus, and that of the rostral parencephalon the ventral thalamus. The basal components form the prerubral tegmentum. The prosomeres P4–P6, together known as a protosegment, form the secondary prosencephalon, from which the hypothalamus, both optic vesicles, and the telencephalon arise (Puelles & Rubinstein, 2003; Rubinstein, Shimamura, Martinez, & Puelles, 1998). The basal parts of the secondary prosencephalon give rise to the various subdivisions of the hypothalamus, whereas from the alar parts the cerebral cortex and the basal ganglia arise.

Pattern formation

Prospective subdivisions of the brain are specified through *pattern formation* which takes place in two directions: from medial to lateral, and from rostral to caudal (Jessell & Sanes, 2000; Lumsden & Krumlauf, 1996; Rubinstein & Beachy, 1998). Neural patterning involves a series of inductive interactions by which the neural tube is divided into distinct regions that form the different areas of the nervous system. Mediolateral or ventrodorsal pattern formation generates longitudinal areas, such as the alar and basal plates, and rostrocaudal pattern formation generates transverse zones (one or more neuromeres). Developmental gene expression studies show that the vertebrate CNS can be divided into three regions (Figure 3.2): (a) an anterior region, comprising the forebrain and most of the midbrain, and characterized by expression of the homeobox genes *Emx* and *Otx*; (b) a middle division, formed by the posterior part of the midbrain and most of the first rhombomere, and known as the midbrain–hindbrain boundary (MHB); and (c) a posterior region, composed of the rhombencephalon and spinal cord, and characterized by *Hox* gene expression.

Longitudinal patterning centers are present along the ventral (notochord and prechordal plate, and later the floor plate) and dorsal (epidermal-neuroectodermal junction, and later the roof plate) aspects of the neural plate and early neural tube. Medial (i.e., *ventralizing*) signals such as SHH play an important role during the formation of the primordia of the basal plate. SHH induces the formation of motoneurons in the spinal cord and brain stem. Lateral (i.e., *dorsalizing*) signals such as the bone morphogenetic proteins (BMPs) from the adjacent ectoderm induce the formation of

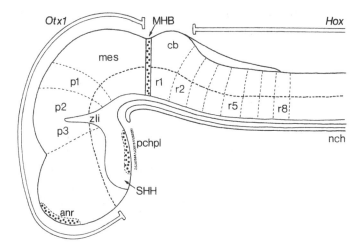

Figure 3.2 Overview of regional patterning of the neural tube. FGF8 expression at the level of the anterior neural ridge, the midbrain–hindbrain boundary, and above the prechordal plate is indicated by dots. *Abbreviations*. anr, anterior neural ridge; cb, cerebellum; *Hox*, expression of *Hox genes* in the hindbrain; mes, mesencephalon; MHB, midbrain–hindbrain boundary; nch, notochord; *Otx1*, expression of *Otx1* genes in the forebrain and midbrain; p1–p3, prosomeres; pchpl, prechordal plate; r1–r8, rhombomeres; SHH, Sonic hedgehog expression; zli, zona limitans interthalamica. *Note.* Adapted from "Development: The Decade of the Developing Brain," by T. M. Jessell and J. R. Sanes, 2000, *Current Opinion in Neurobiology, 10,* 599–601.

the alar plate and the dorsal part of the forebrain. The entire cerebral cortex as well as the basal ganglia appear to be derived from the alar plate territory.

Specialized, *transverse patterning centers* are present at specific anteroposterior locations of the neural plate such as the anterior neural ridge, the MHB, and above the prechordal plate (Figure 3.2). They provide a source of secreted factors, such as the fibroblast growth factor FGF8, that establish the regional identity in adjacent domains of the neural tube. The MHB or *isthmic organizer* is responsible for specifying the fate of the midbrain and cerebellum. FGF8 signaling from the anterior neural ridge regulates the expression of *Foxg1*, a transcription factor that is required for the normal development of the telencephalon and cerebral cortex (Monuki & Walsh, 2001; Rubinstein & Beachy, 1998).

An example of a defect in brain patterning is *holoprosencephaly* (Plate 2). Holoprosencephaly (HPE) is the most common structural anomaly of the developing forebrain and is usually associated with specific craniofacial anomalies (DeMyer, Zeman, & Palmer, 1964; Golden, 1998; Muenke & Beachy, 2000; Sarnat & Flores-Sarnat, 2001). HPE is etiologically very heterogeneous with an incidence in liveborn children of 0.48–0.88 per 10,000. In contrast, the rate among human abortuses has been estimated at 40 per 10,000 (Shiota, 1993). It can be associated with chromosomal abnormalities, single gene mutations, polygenic mechanisms, and environmental factors such as diabetes mellitus and alcohol.

The brain malformations in HPE range from the *alobar, complete form* with one single ventricle, undivided thalami and corpora striata, and absence of the olfactory bulbs and corpus callosum, to the *semilobar, incomplete form*, in which hypoplastic cerebral lobes with an interhemispheric posterior fissure and a hypoplastic corpus callosum may be present, to the *lobar type*, in which a distinct interhemispheric fissure is present with some midline continuity and the olfactory bulbs may vary from normal to absent. The facial abnormalities in HPE are usually categorized into four main types (Cohen & Sulik, 1992; DeMyer et al., 1964): (a) cyclopia with a single eye and various degrees of doubling of the eye anlage, with or without a proboscis; (b) ethmocephaly with ocular hypotelorism and a proboscis located between the eyes; (c) cebocephaly with ocular hypotelorism and a single nostril; and (d) median cleft lip and palate and ocular hypotelorism. Less severe facial dysmorphism and even HPE without facial malformations are also found.

Pallium

At first, each cerebral hemisphere consists of a thick basal part, the *subpallium*, giving rise to the basal ganglia, and a thin part, the *pallium*, which becomes the future cerebral cortex. The subpallium appears as medial and lateral *ganglionic* or *ventricular eminences*, two intraventricular protusions or bulges. The caudal part of the ventricular eminences is also known as the caudal ganglionic eminence, and primarily gives rise to parts of the amygdala. The medial ganglionic eminence is derived from the diencephalon, and is involved in the formation of the globus pallidus. The larger lateral ganglionic eminence is derived from the telencephalon, and gives rise to the caudate nucleus and the putamen. Both the lateral and medial ganglionic eminences are also involved in the formation of the cerebral cortex (see Figure 3.6 below). The pyramidal cells of the cerebral cortex arise from the ventricular zone of the pallium, but the cortical GABAergic interneurons arise from both ganglionic eminences, the medial eminence in particular (Marín & Rubinstein, 2001; Parnavelas, 2000).

Fetal Development of the Brain

The most obvious changes in the brain in the fetal period are: (a) the development of the cerebellar hemispheres and of their median part, the vermis; (b) the continuous expansion of the cerebral hemispheres, the formation of the temporal pole, and the formation of sulci and gyri; and (c) the formation of commissural connections, the corpus callosum in particular.

Development of the cerebellum

The cerebellum largely develops in the fetal period. The cerebellum arises bilaterally from the alar layers of the first rhombomere which form the cerebellar primordium or tuberculum cerebelli (Figure 3.3). The development of the cerebellum occurs in four basic steps:

1. Characterization of the cerebellar territory at the midbrain–hindbrain boundary.
2. Formation of two compartments for cell proliferation: First, the Purkinje cells and the deep cerebellar nuclei arise from the ventricular zone of the metencephalic alar plate; second, granule cell precursors are formed from a second compartment of proliferation known as the upper rhombic lip.
3. Inward migration of the granule cells: Granule cell precursor cells form the external granular layer, from which (and continuing into the first postnatal year) granule cells migrate inward to their definite position in the internal granular layer.
4. Formation of cerebellar circuitry and further differentiation (ten Donkelaar et al., 2003, 2006; Wang & Zoghbi, 2001). The precerebellar nuclei, such as the pontine nuclei and the inferior olive, arise from the lower rhombic lip.

Developmental malformations of the cerebellum are mostly bilateral and may be divided into: (a) malformations of the vermis; and (b) malformations of the vermis as well as of the hemispheres (Ramaeckers, Heimann, Reul, Thron, & Jaeken, 1997; ten Donkelaar et al., 2003, 2006). Agenesis or hypoplasia of the vermis may occur in a great variety of disorders, most frequently in the *Dandy–Walker malformation*. The Dandy–Walker malformation is characterized by cystic dilatation of the fourth ventricle and an enlarged posterior fossa, varying degrees of vermian aplasia or hypoplasia, and hydrocephalus, usually developing just after birth. Mental retardation and seizures have been reported in up to 50% of cases with a Dandy–Walker malformation (Pascual-Castroviejo, Velez, Pascual-Pascual, Roche, & Villarejo, 1991). Vermis anomalies have also been reported in neurobehavioral disorders such as autism and developmental dyslexia. The *pontocerebellar hypoplasias* form a large group of disorders characterized by a smaller volume of the pons and varying degrees of cerebellar hypoplasia up to near total absence of the cerebellum (Gardner et al., 2001; Ramaeckers et al., 1997).

Development of the cerebral cortex

The cerebral hemispheres are composed of structures derived from the pallium and the subpallium. The *pallium* can be divided into a medial or archipallium, a dorsal or neopallium, a lateral or paleopallium, and a recently added ventral pallium. The medial or archipallium forms the hippocampal cortex, the three-layered allocortex. Parts of the surrounding cingulate and entorhinal cortex, the four- to five-layered mesocortex, may have the same origin. The dorsal or neopallium forms the six-layered isocortex or neocortex. The lateral pallium forms the olfactory cortex and the ventral pallium the claustroamygdaloid complex. The *subpallium* consists of two progenitor domains, the lateral and medial ganglionic eminences, generating the striatum and the pallidum, respectively. Dorsal and ventral domains of the developing telencephalon are

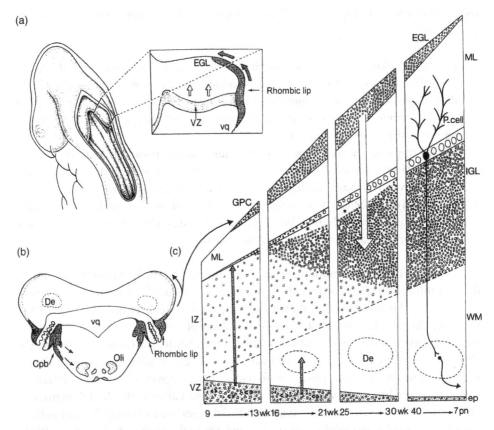

Figure 3.3 Overview of the histogenesis of the cerebellum. In (a) a dorsolateral view of a human embryo is shown and part of the cerebellar anlage (the tuberculum cerebelli with an inverted V-shape) is enlarged, showing the two proliferative compartments: the ventricular zone, giving rise to Purkinje cells and the deep cerebellar nuclei, and the external germinal or granular layer, giving rise to the granule cells. In (b) the position of the rhombic lip is shown in a transverse section at the level of the lateral recess of the fourth ventricle. The upper rhombic lip is found lateral to the lateral recess, and the lower rhombic lip medial to the recess. In (c) the formation of the layers of the cerebellum is shown in four periods from the early fetal period till 7 weeks postnatally. The asterisks mark the transient lamina dissecans. The arrows in (a)–(c) show the migration paths. *Abbreviations.* Cpb, corpus pontobulbare; De, dentate nucleus; EGL, external granular layer; ep, ependyma; GPC, granule precursor cells; IGL, internal granular layer; IZ, intermediate zone; ML, molecular layer; Oli, oliva inferior; P-cell, Purkinje cell; vq, ventriculus quartus; VZ, ventricular zone; WM, white matter. *Note.* Reproduced with permission from "Development and Developmental Disorders of the Human Cerebellum," by H. J. ten Donkelaar, M. Lammens, P. Wesseling, H. O. M. Thijssen, and W. O. Renier, 2003, *Journal of Neurology, 250,* 1025–1036.

(a)

(b)

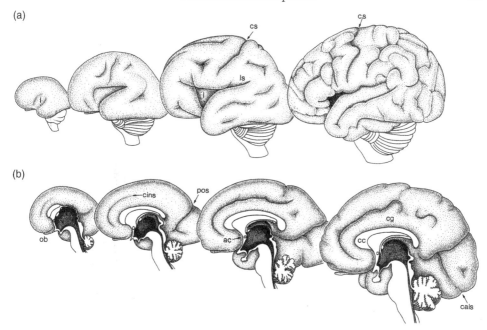

Figure 3.4 (a) lateral views of the developing human brain in the fourth, sixth, and eighth gestational months, and in a neonate; (b) medial views at the end of the fourth, sixth, and eighth gestational months, and in a neonate. *Abbreviations.* ac, anterior commissure; cals, calcarine sulcus, cc, corpus callosum; cg, cingulate gyrus; cins, cingulate sulcus; cs, central sulcus; I, insula; ls, lateral sulcus; ob, olfactory bulb; pos, parieto-occipital sulcus. *Note.* Adapted from *Clinical neuroembryology: Development and developmental disorders of the human central nervous system* by H. J. ten Donkelaar, M. Lammens, and A. Hori, 2006, Berlin: Springer Verlag.

distinguished by distinct patterns of gene expression. *Emx1* and *Emx2* are among the earliest expressed pallial markers, whereas the *Dlx* genes are expressed in the developing subpallium (Rubinstein et al., 1998; Zaki, Quinn, & Price, 2003).

The outgrowth of the cerebral cortex and the proliferation and migration of cortical neurons largely takes place in the fetal period. Each hemisphere first grows caudalwards, and then bends to grow into ventral and rostral directions (Figure 3.4). In this way, the temporal lobe with the hippocampus and amygdala arises. During this outgrowth, the so-called retrocommissural part of the hippocampus becomes situated in the temporal lobe. The supracommissural part of the hippocampus above the corpus callosum disappears, sometimes leaving rudiments on top of the corpus callosum. During the fetal period, the complex pattern of sulci and gyri arises. On the lateral surface of the brain, the sulcus lateralis and the sulcus centralis can be recognized from four months onward (Figure 3.4a), whereas on its medial surface first the parieto-occipital and cingulate sulci appear, followed by the calcarine and central sulci (Figure 3.4b). The formation of sulci and gyri in the right hemisphere usually precedes that in the left one.

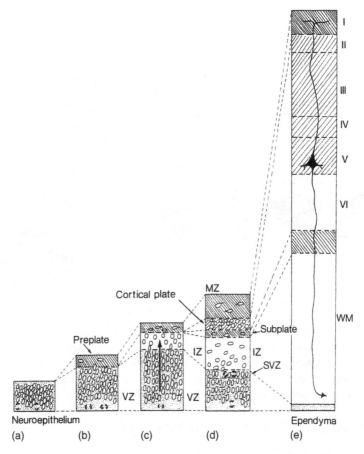

Figure 3.5 Histogenesis of the cerebral cortex. In (a)–(c) the neuroepithelium forms three zones, the ventricular zone (VZ), the intermediate zone (IZ), and the preplate. During the 8th–18th weeks of development, neurons migrate from the ventricular zone and form the cortical plate (d). The preplate becomes divided into the marginal zone (MZ) and the subplate. A second compartment for cell division, the subventricular zone (SVZ), is mainly involved in the production of glial cells. Finally (e), the marginal zone forms the molecular layer (layer I) and the cortical plate layers II–VI. The intermediate zone forms the subcortical white matter (WM). The subplate disappears. *Note.* Adapted from *The embryonic human brain: An atlas of developmental stages* (2nd ed.) by R. O'Rahilly and F. Müller, 1999, New York: Wiley-Liss.

During the *histogenesis* of the six-layered cerebral cortex, the developing cerebral wall contains several transient embryonic zones (Figure 3.5):

1. The *ventricular zone*, which is composed of dividing neural progenitor cells.
2. The *subventricular zone*, which acts early in corticogenesis as a secondary neuronal progenitor compartment, and later in development as the major source of glial cells.
3. The *intermediate zone*, through which migrating neurons traverse along radial glial processes.

4. The *subplate*, thought to be essential in orchestrating thalamocortical connectivity and pioneering corticofugal projections.
5. The *cortical plate*, the initial condensation of postmitotic neurons that will become layers II–VI of the mature cortex.
6. The *marginal zone*, the superficial, cell-sparse layer that is important in the establishment of the laminar organization of the cortex.

Cortical neurons are generated in the ventricular zones of the cortical walls and ganglionic eminences, and reach their destination by radial and tangential migration, respectively. The first postmitotic cells form the *preplate* or *primordial plexiform layer* (Marín-Padilla, 1998; Meyer & Goffinet, 1998; Meyer, Schaaps, Moreau, & Goffinet, 2000). Then, cells from the ventricular zone migrate to form an intermediate zone and, toward the end of the embryonic period, the cortical plate. This plate develops within the preplate, thereby dividing the preplate into a small superficial component, the marginal zone, and a large deep component, the subplate. The marginal zone is composed largely of *Cajal–Retzius cells*, secreting the extracellular protein reelin, and the subplate contains pioneer projection neurons. Reelin is required for the normal inside-to-outside positioning of cells as they migrate from the ventricular zone.

The formation of the cortical plate takes place from approximately 7 to 16 weeks. The first cells to arrive will reside in the future layer VI. Later born cells migrate past the already present cortical cells to reside in progressively more superficial layers. In this way, the cortical layers VI–VII are subsequently formed. The marginal zone becomes layer I; that is, the molecular or plexiform layer. The subplate gradually disappears. The ventricular zone becomes the ependyma and the intermediate zone the subcortical white matter. A transient cell layer, the *subpial granular layer* (SGL) of Ranke, originates from the basal periolfactory subventricular zone (Meyer & Wahle, 1999). It migrates tangentially beneath the pia to cover the neocortical marginal zone from the 14th gestational week onward. The SGL provides a constant supply of reelin-producing cells during the critical period of cortical migration, keeping pace with the dramatic growth and surface expansion during corticogenesis. Hippocampal neurons are generated over a longer period than neocortical neurons: pyramidal neurons up to the 24th gestational week, granule cells of the dentate gyrus mostly during the second half of pregnancy and continuing to be born during the first postnatal year (Seress, Ábrahám, Tornóczky, & Kosztolányi, 2001).

In the cerebral cortex, *radial migration* is the primary mechanism by which developing neurons reach their final position (Rakic, 1972). The newly born neuroblasts associate with specialized glial cells known as radial glial cells. Radial glial cells are bipolar cells with one short process extended to the adjacent ventricular surface and a second projecting to the pial surface. A two-way signaling process between the migrating neuron and the radial glial fiber permits the neuroblast to migrate, and provides a signal to maintain the structure of the radial glial fiber (Hatten, 1999). This process requires known receptors and ligands such as neuregulin, cell adhesion molecules, putative ligands with unknown receptors such as astrotactin, and extracellular matrix molecules

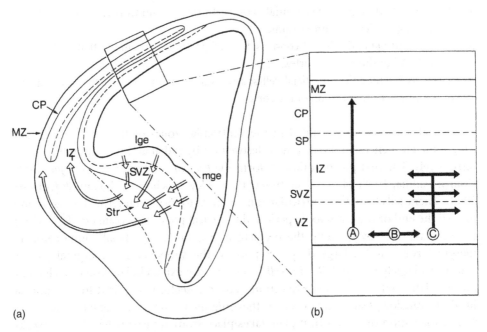

Figure 3.6 Radial and tangential migration of cortical neurons. In (a) the proliferative compartments of the murine telencephalon are shown: the ventricular zone (VZ) and the subventricular zone (SVZ). Postmitotic GABAergic neurons leave the lateral (lge) and medial (mge) ganglionic eminences and reach the striatum (Str) and, through tangential migration, the marginal zone (MZ) and the intermediate zone (IZ). In (b) part of the cortex is enlarged in which radial migration of neurons (A) through the subplate (SP) to the cortical plate (CP) and tangential migration, occurring in the ventricular, subventricular, and intermediate zones (B and C) is indicated. *Note.* Adapted from "New Directions for Neuronal Migration," by A. L. Pearlman, P. L. Faust, M. E. Hatten, and J. E. Brunnstrom, 1998, *Current Opinion in Neurobiology, 8,* 45–54.

and their surface receptors. Blocking any of these components can slow or even prevent radial cell migration (Pilz, Stoodley, & Golden, 2002), resulting in neuronal migration disorders.

Cell migration perpendicular to the radial axis (i.e., *tangential migration*; Figure 3.6) differs from radial cell migration in the direction of movement and in the mechanism of cell guidance. Instead of radial glia, axons appear to be the substrate for at least some nonradial cell migration (Pearlman, Faust, Hatten, & Brunnstrom, 1998). Nonradial cell migration provides most, if not all, GABAergic interneurons of the cerebral cortex. This population of cortical neurons migrates from the ganglionic eminences along nonradial routes to reach the cerebral cortex (Anderson, Marín, Horn, Jennings, & Rubinstein, 2001; Anderson, Mione, Yun, & Rubinstein, 1999; Lavdas, Grigoriou, Pachnis, & Parnavelas, 1999; Marín & Rubinstein, 2001). The medial ganglionic eminence is the source of most cortical interneurons, and is also a major source of striatal interneurons (Marín, Anderson, & Rubinstein, 2000). The tangential migration of postmitotic interneurons from the ganglionic eminences to the neocortex occurs along multiple paths, and is directed in part by members of the Slit and semaphorin families of guidance molecules (Marín & Rubinstein, 2001).

Shortly after the formation of the cortical plate, the afferent and efferent fiber connections of the cerebral cortex arise. Axons from the first preplate neurons form a kind of scaffold along which corticofugal axons from the cortical plate and thalamocortical fibers to the cerebral cortex find their way to the targets. Important roles in the guidance of these fibers are played by the subplate and, also mostly transient, cell populations in the internal capsule and ventral thalamus. The human *capsula interna* can be distinguished late in the embryonic period (O'Rahilly & Müller, 1999). The development of the pyramidal tract also starts late in the embryonic period (see ten Donkelaar et al., 2004), whereas the development of the corpus callosum starts around the 11th week of gestation (Rakic & Yakovlev, 1968). *Thalamocortical fibers* reach the internal capsule late in the embryonic period, and early fetally reach the subplate. After a rather long waiting period, they enter the cortical plate. The human *pyramidal tract* reaches the level of the pyramidal decussation at the end of the embryonic period (O'Rahilly & Müller, 1999). Pyramidal decussation is complete by 17 weeks of gestation, and the rest of the spinal cord is invaded by 19 weeks gestational age (lower thoracic cord) and 29 weeks gestational age (lumbosacral cord). Myelination of the pyramidal tract starts at the pyramidal decussation as early as 25 weeks of gestation, but is not completed until about two years postnatally (Yakovlev & Lecours, 1967).

Development of the cerebral commissures

Cerebral commissures arise in a thin plate, the embryonic lamina terminalis, situated just rostral to the chiasmatic plate. At approximately 5 weeks of development (stage 16), the *commissural plate* appears as a thickening in the embryonic lamina terminalis (O'Rahilly & Müller, 1999). The commissural plate gives rise to: (a) the anterior commissure, which appears at the end of the embryonic period and connects the future temporal lobes; (b) the hippocampal commissure, which appears several weeks later and connects the crura of the fornix; and (c) the corpus callosum, which appears early in the fetal period and connects the cerebral hemispheres. The *corpus callosum* is first identified at 11–12 weeks of development, and gradually extends considerably caudalwards (Rakic & Yakovlev, 1968; see Figure 3.4b). The overlying part of the commissural plate becomes thinned to form the septum pellucidum. Within the septum, a narrow cavity appears, the cavum septi pellucidi. The corpus callosum appears to be fully formed by the middle of prenatal life. Partial or complete absence of the corpus callosum is not uncommon (Barkovich, 2003; Raybaud & Girard, 1998, 1999). Every disorder that influences the development of the commissural plate may lead to this malformation. Dysgenesis of the corpus callosum occurs in approximately 20% of cases as an isolated disorder, but in about 80% in combination with other malformations of the brain such as lissencephalies, polymicrogyria, schizencephaly, and trisomies.

Developmental Disorders of the Cerebral Cortex

The introduction of modern imaging techniques (CT, MRI) and recent discoveries in the molecular biology of malformations of cortical development have led to a revised classification of such malformations (Barkovich et al., 2001; Guerrini, Sicca, & Parmeggiani, 2003). This classification follows the stage of development (cell proliferation, neuronal migration, cortical organization) at which cortical development is first affected, and is based on known developmental steps, pathological features, genetics, and neuroimaging data (Plate 3). Identified genes for disorders of cortical development are summarized in Table 3.2. In many cases, however, the precise developmental and genetic features of cortical developmental disorders are still uncertain. Many disorders of cortical development are associated with severe, often intractable epilepsy and mental retardation.

Abnormal cell proliferation or abnormal apoptosis may lead to congenital microcephaly, megalencephaly, and malformations with abnormal cell types, such as tuberous sclerosis, hemimegalencephaly, and neoplastic forms such as dysembryoplastic neuroepithelial tumors. The etiology of *microcephaly*, usually defined as a condition in which the occipitofrontal circumference of the head is more than two standard deviations below the mean, can be broadly divided into environmental and genetic causes (Mochida & Walsh, 2001). Common environmental causes are congenital infections such as cytomegalovirus, intrauterine exposure to teratogenic agents, and hypoxic/ischemic injury in the fetal and perinatal periods. Abnormal proliferation may lead to cortical hamartomas of tuberous sclerosis, cortical dysplasias with balloon cells and hemimegalencephaly.

The *tuberous sclerosis complex* (TSC) is a multisystem, autosomal dominant syndrome that most commonly affects the brain, the eyes, the skin, the kidneys, and the heart in 1 in 10,000 births. The characteristic brain lesions with a potato-like or root-like (therefore tubers) consistency are hamartomas; that is, benign tumors composed of cellular elements normally present in a tissue. The CNS manifestations of TSC include tubers in the cerebral cortex and subependymal nodules protruding into the ventricular system (Plate 3A). These regions of cortical dysplasia likely result from aberrant neuronal migration during corticogenesis, and are static lesions, directly related to the neurological manifestations observed, including epilepsy, mental retardation, and autism. These symptoms are highly variable in age of onset and severity. Two TSC genes have been identified. *Hemimegalencephaly* (Plate 3B) may occur isolated or as part of neurocutaneous disorders (Flores-Sarnat, 2002). It forms a major but rare hamartomatous congenital malformation of the brain, remarkable for the often extreme brain asymmetry.

Malformations due to abnormal cortical migration form a rather heterogeneous group of cortical malformations. The *neuronal migration disorders* (NMDs) comprise disorders such as the lissencephaly/subcortical band heterotopia spectrum, the cobblestone complex, and various forms of heterotopia. From a pathogenetic point of

Table 3.2 Identified Genes for Malformations of Cortical Development.

Cortical malformation	Trait	Locus	Gene/protein	Clinical manifestations
Abnormal proliferation				
Cortical hamartomas of tuberous sclerosis		9q32 16p13.3	TSC1/hamartin TSC2/tuberin	Epilepsy, mental retardation, autism ibid.
Neuronal heterotopia in white matter				
Bilateral periventricular nodular heterotopia (lethal in boys)	XL	Xq28	FLM1/filamin-1	Epilepsy
Classic lissencephalies				
Miller–Dieker syndrome	AD	17p13.3	Several contiguous genes/ PAFAH1B1 (LIS1)	Severe mental retardation, epilepsy, spasticity
Isolated lissencephaly	AD	17p13.3	LIS1/PAFAH1B1 (LIS1)	Mental retardation, epilepsy
X-linked lissencephaly (SBH in girls)	XL	Xq22.3–q23	XLIS (DCX)/doublecortin	Mental retardation (less severe in girls), epilepsy
Lissencephaly with cerebellar hypoplasia				
Lissencephaly with cerebellar hypoplasia	AR	7q22	RELN/reelin	Severe mental retardation, epilepsy, hypotonia
Cobblestone lissencephalies				
Walker–Warburg syndrome	AR		POMT1/O-mannosyltransferase	Severe mental retardation, hypotonia, hydrocephalus, eye malformations, cerebellar malformations
Muscle-eye-brain disease	AR	1p32–34	POMGnT1	Usually severe mental retardation, epilepsy, hypotonia, and glaucoma

(continued)

Table 3.2 (*continued*)

Cortical malformation	Trait	Locus	Gene/protein	Clinical manifestations
Fukuyama congenital muscular dystrophy	AR	9q31–33	FCMD/Fukutin	Severe mental retardation, epilepsy (in 20%), hypotonia, mild spasticity
Polymicrogyrias				
Aicardi syndrome	XL	Xp22		Severe mental retardation, chorioretinopathy, agenesis of corpus callosum, infantile spasms
Zellweger syndrome	AR	At least 10 different genes	Peroxisomal enzymes	Cerebrohepatorenal syndrome: mental retardation, epilepsy, hypotonia, hepatomegaly, cardiac malformations, polycystic kidneys

Note. From "Classification System for Malformations of Cortical Development: Update 2001," by A. J. Barkovich, R. I. Kuzniecky, G. D. Jackson, R. Guerrini, & W. B. Dobyns, 2001, *Neurology, 57,* 2168–2178; and "Epilepsy and Malformations of the Cerebral Cortex," by R. Guerrini, F. Sicca, & L. Parmeggiani, 2003, *Epileptic Disorders,* 9(Suppl. 2), S9–S26.

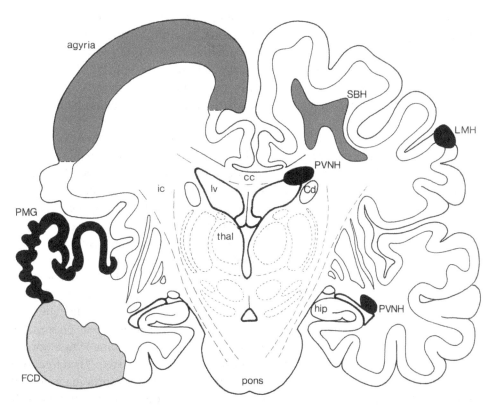

Figure 3.7 Overview of neuronal migration disorders. *Abbreviations.* cc, corpus callosum; Cd, caudate nucleus; FCD, focal cortical dysplasia; hip, hippocampus; ic, internal capsule; LMH, leptomeningeal heterotopia; lv, lateral ventricle; PMG, polymicrogyria; PVNH, periventricular nodular heterotopia; SBH, subcortical band heterotopia; thal, thalamus. *Note.* Adapted from "Neuronal Migration Disorders in Humans and in Mouse Models: An Overview," by A. J. Copp and B. N. Harding, 1999, *Epilepsy Research, 36,* 133–141.

view, disorders of at least four distinct steps in cortical neuronal migration may lead to NMDs (Barkovich et al., 2001; Copp & Harding, 1999; Pilz et al., 2002; Ross & Walsh, 2001; see Figure 3.7): (a) disorders at the onset of neuronal migration (neuronal heterotopia); (b) disorders of the ongoing process of migration (classic, type 1 lissencephaly, double cortex syndrome); (c) problems in the penetration of the subplate (reeler mouse; human lissencephaly with cerebellar hypoplasia); and (d) disruption of the architecture of the developing cerebral wall, leading to an overmigration of neurons (cobblestone, type 2 lissencephaly). Some examples are shown in Plate 3; the identified genes and clinical manifestations are summarized in Table 3.2.

Disorders at the start of migration result in nodular heterotopia such as the X-linked *bilateral periventricular nodular heterotopia* (BPNH; Plate 3C). Cortical neurons are unable to leave their position in the ventricular zone owing to the absence of *Filamin 1* (FLM1). Boys with BPNH usually die before birth (Dubeau et al., 1995), whereas in normally intelligent girls a large proportion of patients suffer from seizures that begin in the second or third decade of life (Huttenlocher, Taravath, & Mojtahedi, 1994). The brain in the *classic, type 1 lissencephaly* ("smooth brain") has a macroscopically smooth surface and a thick, usually four-layered cortex. Classic lissencephaly (Miller–Dieker syndrome, isolated lissencephaly), caused by mutations in the *lissencephaly-1* (LIS1) gene, is characterized by severe mental retardation, epilepsy, feeding problems, and a shortened lifespan.

A second, *X-linked form of lissencephaly* (XLIS) is expressed in different ways in males and females (Dobyns et al., 1996, 1999). In boys, the phenotype is comparable to that of classic lissencephaly, but with a different location: In cases with LIS1 mutations, the malformations are predominantly expressed in the parietal and occipital lobes (Plate 3D), whereas in the XLIS forms the frontal lobes are more involved (Dobyns et al., 1999). Girls with the XLIS form of lissencephaly are less retarded and have less severe epilepsy. They show *subcortical band heterotopia* (SBH) in which below the cerebral cortex a second cortex is found (Plate 3E). The causative gene for XLIS, *doublecortin* (DCX), is located on the long arm of the X-chromosome (des Portes et al., 1998; Gleeson 2000; Gleeson et al., 1998). The assumed mechanism for this different expression is the normal and random X-chromosome inactivation that occurs in females. When the chromosome carrying a mutated copy of DCX is inactivated, that neuron will presumably behave normally and migrate to the cortical plate. If the chromosome with a normal copy of DCX is inactivated, only the mutant allele will be expressed. Therefore, two populations of neurons are present in the ventricular zone, one expressing a normal copy of DCX and giving rise to the cortical plate, the other expressing the mutant DCX copy and forming a band of heterotopic neurons in the white matter. Despite its epileptogenic activity, SBH seems to be responsible for part of the functional activity of the brain, as was shown with functional MRI (Pinard et al., 2000). Several other syndromes with lissencephaly as a component have been identified. The best characterized of these is lissencephaly with cerebellar hypoplasia, at least in some cases caused by mutations in the *reelin* (RELN) gene (Hong et al., 2000; Ross, Swanson, & Dobyns, 2001).

Type 2 or *cobblestone lissencephaly* is a complex brain malformation that consists of cobblestone cortex, abnormal white matter, enlarged ventricles, and a small brain stem and cerebellum. The cerebral cortex is chaotically organized by a combination of agyria, pachygyria, and polymicrogyria with a pebbled surface ("cobblestones"), and largely without lamination. The pathogenesis of cobblestone lissencephaly may be overmigration. Cobblestone lissencephaly is usually associated with ocular manifestations and muscular dystrophy, and occurs in various forms including Walker–Warburg syndrome (Dobyns, Kirkpatrick, Hittner, Roberts, & Kretzer, 1985; Dobyns et al., 1989), muscle-eye-brain disease found in Finland (Santavuori et al., 1989), and Fukuyama-type congenital muscular dystrophy, almost restricted to the Japanese (Fukuyama, Osawa, & Suzuki, 1981; Toda et al., 2003).

Malformations due to abnormal cortical organization and late migration include the polymicrogyrias and schizencephalies. *Schizencephaly* (Plate 3F) means a brain cleft, unilateral or bilateral, extending from the pial surface of the cerebral cortex to the ventricular surface. It is usually accompanied by polymicrogyria. *Polymicrogyria* may result from a developmental disorder or injury that occurs toward the end of the period of neuronal migration and the early phase of cortical organization (Barkovich et al., 2001). Polymicrogyria occurs in several forms such as the bilateral perisylvian (Kuzniecky, Andermann, & Guerrini, 1993) and frontal (Guerrini, Barkovich, Sztriha, & Dobyns, 2000) forms. Polymicrogyria or schizencephaly may also occur in association with other brain malformations or as part of several multiple congenital anomaly–mental retardation syndromes, such as Aicardi syndrome and Zellweger syndrome, and are rather common.

Developmental disorders of the cerebral cortex may lead to mental retardation. *Mental retardation* is characterized by global deficiency in cognitive and social abilities and onset during childhood. In the majority of cases, the cause of mental retardation is unknown, especially in "mild" cases with an IQ > 50. In this group, interaction between genetic and environmental factors is thought to play the most important role, whereas in "severe" mental retardation (IQ ≤ 50) more often a single recognizable factor is present which is of genetic origin in at least 50% of cases (Chiurazzi & Oostra, 2000). Among patients with mental retardation, males outnumber females. This male excess is partially explained by the existence of mutations in X-linked genes, causing X-linked mental retardation. In males, Down syndrome (trisomy 21) and fragile-X syndrome are the most common causes of mental retardation. In females, Down and Rett syndromes are the leading causes of mental retardation. Mental retardation is associated with abnormalities in dendritic branching and spines (Huttenlocher, 1974, 1991; Kaufmann & Moser, 2000; Marín-Padilla, 1972, 1976; Purpura, 1974).

Recent studies suggest that altered interneuron development may underlie at least part of the pathophysiological process of *neurobehavioral disorders* (Buxhoeveden & Casanova, 2002; Levitt, Eagleson, & Powell, 2004; Powell et al., 2003). Selectivity in interneuron disruption appears to be one of the neuroanatomical hallmarks of prefrontal cortical circuitry in individuals with schizophrenia (Lewis & Levitt, 2002). In *autism*, a regional disruption of interneuron development in the cerebral cortex has been suggested (Levitt et al., 2004). Postmortem studies suggest that the number of GABAergic interneurons is reduced (Benes & Berretta, 2001; Benes, Taylor, & Cunningham, 2000). The brains of individuals with autism are initially larger than normal (Courchesne, Carper, & Akshoomoff, 2003; Courchesne & Pierce, 2005), possibly owing to changes in the patterns of neuropil maturation and white matter development. The likelihood of altered interneuron development is also supported by the location of several genes involved in interneuron development, such as those of the *Dlx* family, at autism-susceptibility loci (Gutknecht, 2001; Levitt et al., 2004).

Postnatal Development

At birth, the weight of the brain is about one quarter of its adult size. The neonatal brain continues to grow and specialize according to the precise genetic program started in the embryonic period and modified by environmental influences. Around the time of birth, most neurons have migrated to their appropriate locations within the cerebral cortex, hippocampus, cerebellum, and other regions of the brain. Some neurogenesis continues in the first postnatal year in the hippocampus, olfactory bulb, and cerebellum. New granule cells are produced throughout adulthood in the dentate gyrus of mammals from rodents to man (Cameron & McKay, 2001; Eriksson et al., 1998; Gould et al., 1999).

The dendritic branching of neurons and the number of synaptic connections greatly increase. The overproduction of brain connections is followed by dendritic pruning and synapse elimination. Huttenlocher (1979) was one of the first to study the time-course for synaptic development and pruning in the human brain. He showed that in the visual cortex, synaptic overproduction reaches a maximum at about the fourth postnatal month. Then synapse elimination starts, and this continues until preschool age, by which time synaptic density has reached the adult level. In the prefrontal cortex, however, the peak occurs at 3–4 years of age, and substantial decline does not occur until mid- to late adolescence (Huttenlocher, 1990; Huttenlocher & Dabholkar, 1997). Human brain maturation is a complex, lifelong process that can now be examined in detail using neuroimaging techniques (Giedd et al., 1999; Toga, Thompson, & Sowell, 2006).

Myelination in the CNS is carried out by oligodendrocytes, and is a very slow process. The presence of myelin has been noted in the spinal cord at the end of the first trimester and proceeds caudorostrally (Yakovlev & Lecours, 1967). In the CNS, afferent tracts become myelinated earlier than the motor pathways. The vestibulospinal tracts become myelinated at the end of the second trimester, whereas the pyramidal tracts begin at the end of the third trimester, and myelination is not completed in them until about 2 years. Cortical association fibers are the last to become myelinated. The appearance of myelin in MRI lags about one month behind the histological timetables (van der Knaap & Valk, 1995). At birth, the human brain is rather immature with regard to the extent of its myelination. The rate of deposition of myelin is greatest during the first two postnatal years. Age-related changes in white matter myelination continue during childhood and adolescence (Paus et al., 2001).

References

Anderson, S. A., Marín, O., Horn, C., Jennings, K., & Rubinstein, J. L. R. (2001). Distinct cortical migrations from the medial and lateral ganglionic eminences. *Development, 128,* 353–363.

Anderson, S. A., Mione, M., Yun, K., & Rubinstein, J. L. R. (1999). Differential origins of neocortical projection and local circuit neurons: Role of Dlx genes in neocortical interneuronogenesis. *Cerebral Cortex, 9,* 646–654.

Barkovich, A. J. (2003). Anomalies of the corpus callosum and cortical malformations. In P. G. Barth (Ed.), *Disorders of neuronal migration* (pp. 83–103). London: MacKeith.

Barkovich, A. J., Kuzniecky, R. I., Jackson, G. D., Guerrini, R., & Dobyns, W. B. (2001). Classification system for malformations of cortical development: Update 2001. *Neurology, 57,* 2168–2178.

Benes, F. M., & Berretta, S. (2001). GABAergic interneurons: Implications for understanding schizophrenia and bipolar disorder. *Neuropsychopharmacology, 25,* 1–27.

Benes, F. M., Taylor, J. B., & Cunningham, M. C. (2000). Convergence and plasticity of monoaminergic systems in the medial prefrontal cortex during the postnatal period: Implications for the development of psychopathology. *Cerebral Cortex, 10,* 1014–1027.

Blaas, H.-G. (1999). *The embryonic examination: Ultrasound studies on the development of the human embryo.* Unpublished thesis, Norwegian University of Science and Technology, Trondheim, Norway.

Blaas, H.-G., & Eik-Nes, S. H. (2002). The description of the early development of the human central nervous system using two-dimensional and three-dimensional ultrasound. In H. Lagercrantz, M. Hanson, P. Evrard, & C. H. Rodeck (Eds.), *The newborn brain: Neuroscience and clinical applications* (pp. 278–288). Cambridge University Press.

Buxhoeveden, D. P., & Casanova, M. F. (2002). The minicolumn hypothesis in neuroscience. *Brain, 125,* 935–961.

Cameron, H. E., & McKay, R. D. G. (2001). Adult neurogenesis produces a large pool of new granule cells in the dentate gyrus. *Journal of Comparative Neurology, 435,* 406–417.

Chiurazzi, P., & Oostra, B. A. (2000). Genetics of mental retardation. *Current Opinion in Pediatrics, 12,* 529–535.

Cohen, M. M., Jr., & Sulik, K. K. (1992). Perspectives on holoprosencephaly: Part II. Central nervous system, craniofacial anatomy, syndrome commentary, diagnostic approach, and experimental studies. *Journal of Craniofacial Genetics and Developmental Biology, 12,* 196–244.

Copp, A. J., & Harding, B. N. (1999). Neuronal migration disorders in humans and in mouse models: An overview. *Epilepsy Research, 36,* 133–141.

Courchesne, E., Carper, R., & Akshoomoff, N. (2003). Evidence of brain overgrowth in the first year of life in autism. *Journal of the American Medical Association, 290,* 337–344.

Courchesne, E., & Pierce, K. (2005). Why the frontal cortex in autism might be talking to itself: Local over-connectivity but long-distance disconnection. *Current Opinion in Neurobiology, 15,* 225–230.

DeMyer, W. E., Zeman, W., & Palmer, C. (1964). The face predicts the brain: Diagnostic significance of median anomalies for holoprosencephaly (arhinencephaly). *Pediatrics, 34,* 256–263.

des Portes, V., Pinard, J. M., Billuart, P., Vinet, M. C., Koulakoff, A., Carrié, A., et al. (1998). A novel gene required for neuronal migration and involved in X-linked subcortical laminar heterotopia and lissencephaly syndrome. *Cell, 92,* 51–61.

Dobyns, W. B., Andermann, E., Andermann, F., Czapansky-Beilman, D., Dubeau, F., Dulac O., et al. (1996). X-linked malformations of neuronal migration. *Neurology, 47,* 331–339.

Dobyns, W. B., Kirkpatrick, J. B., Hittner, H. M., Roberts, R. M., & Kretzer, F. L. (1985). Syndromes with lissencephaly: Part II. Walker–Warburg and cerebro-oculo-muscular syndromes and a new syndrome with type II lissencephaly. *American Journal of Medical Genetics, 22,* 157–195.

Dobyns, W. B., Pagon, R. A., Armstrong, D., Curry, C. J., Greenberg, F., Grix, A., et al. (1989). Diagnostic criteria for Walker–Warburg syndrome. *American Journal of Medical Genetics, 32,* 195–210.

Dobyns, W. B., Truwit, C. L., Ross, M. E., Matsumoto, N., Pilz, D. T., Ledbetter, D. H., et al. (1999). Differences in the gyral pattern distinguish chromosome 17-linked and X-linked lissencephaly. *Neurology, 53,* 270–277.

Dubeau, F., Tampieri, D., Lee, N., Andermann, E., Carpenter, S., Leblanc, R., et al. (1995). Periventricular and subcortical nodular heterotopia: A study of 33 patients. *Brain, 118,* 1273–1281.

Eriksson, P. S., Perfilieva, E., Björk-Eriksson, T., Alborn, A. M., Nordborg, C., Peterson, D. A., et al. (1998). Neurogenesis in the adult human hippocampus. *Nature Medicine, 4,* 1313–1317.

Flores-Sarnat, L. (2002). Hemimegalencephaly: Part 1. Genetic, clinical, and imaging aspects. *Journal of Child Neurology, 17*, 373–384.

Fukuyama, Y., Osawa, M., & Suzuki, H. (1981). Congenital progressive muscular dystrophy of the Fukuyama type: Clinical, genetic and pathological considerations. *Brain and Development, 3*, 1–29.

Gardner, R. J. M., Coleman, L. T., Mitchell, L. A., Smith, L. J., Harvey, A. S., Scheffer, I. E., et al. (2001). Near-total absence of the cerebellum. *Neuropediatrics, 32*, 62–68.

Garel, C. (2004). *MRI of the fetal brain: Normal development and cerebral pathologies.* Berlin: Springer Verlag.

Giedd, J. N., Blumenthal, J., Jeffries, N. O., Castellanos, F. X., Liu, H., Zijdenbos, A., et al. (1999). Brain development during childhood and adolescence: A longitudinal MRI study. *Nature Neuroscience, 2*, 861–863.

Gleeson, J. G. (2000). Classical lissencephaly and double cortex (subcortical band heterotopia): LIS1 and doublecortin. *Current Opinion in Neurology, 131*, 121–125.

Gleeson, J. G., Allen, K. M., Fox, J. W., Lamperti, E. D., Berkovic, S. F., Scheffer, I. E., et al. (1998). Doublecortin, a brain-specific gene mutated in human X-linked lissencephaly and double cortex syndrome, encodes a putative signaling protein. *Cell, 92*, 63–72.

Golden, J. A. (1998). Holoprosencephaly: A defect in brain patterning. *Journal of Neuropathology and Experimental Neurology, 57*, 991–999.

Gould, E., Reeves, A. J., Fallah, M., Tanapat, P., Gross, C. G., & Fuchs, E. (1999). Hippocampal neurogenesis in adult Old World primates. *Proceedings of the National Academy of Sciences, USA, 96*, 5263–5267.

Guerrini, R., Barkovich, A. J., Sztriha, L., & Dobyns, W. B. (2000). Bilateral frontal polymicrogyria: A newly recognized malformation syndrome. *Neurology, 54*, 909–913.

Guerrini, R., Sicca, F., & Parmeggiani, L. (2003). Epilepsy and malformations of the cerebral cortex. *Epileptic Disorders, 9*(Suppl. 2), S9–S26.

Gutknecht, L. (2001). Full-genomic scans with autistic disorder: A review. *Behavior Genetics, 31*, 113–123.

Hatten, M. E. (1999). Central nervous system neuronal migration. *Annual Review of Neuroscience, 22*, 511–539.

Hong, S. E., Shugart, Y. Y., Huang, D. T., Al Shahwan, S., Grant, P. E., Hourihane, J. O., et al. (2000). Autosomal recessive lissencephaly with cerebellar hypoplasia is associated with human *RELN* mutations. *Nature Genetics, 26*, 93–96.

Huttenlocher, P. R. (1974). Dendritic development in neocortex of children with mental defect and infantile spasms. *Neurology, 24*, 203–210.

Huttenlocher, P. R. (1979). Synaptic density in human frontal cortex: Developmental changes and effects of aging. *Brain Research, 163*, 195–205.

Huttenlocher, P. R. (1990). Morphometric study of human cerebral cortex development. *Neuropsychologia, 28*, 517–527.

Huttenlocher, P. R. (1991). Dendritic and synaptic pathology in mental retardation. *Pediatric Neurology, 7*, 79–85.

Huttenlocher, P. R., & Dabholkar, A. S. (1997). Regional differences in synaptogenesis in human cerebral cortex. *Journal of Comparative Neurology, 387*, 167–178.

Huttenlocher, P. R., Taravath, S., & Mojtahedi, S. (1994). Periventricular heterotopia and epilepsy. *Neurology, 44*, 51–55.

Jessell, T. M., & Sanes, J. R. (2000). Development: The decade of the developing brain. *Current Opinion in Neurobiology, 10*, 599–601.

Jirásek, J. E. (2001). *An atlas of the human embryo and fetus*. New York: Parthenon.

Kaufmann, W. E., & Moser, H. W. (2000). Dendritic anomalies associated with mental retardation. *Cerebral Cortex, 10*, 981–991.

Kuzniecky, R., Andermann, F., & Guerrini, R. (1993). Congenital bilateral perisylvian syndrome: A study of 31 patients (The Congenital Bilateral Perisylvian Syndrome Multicenter collaborative study). *Lancet, 1*, 608–612.

Lavdas, A. A., Grigoriou, M., Pachnis, V., & Parnavelas, J. G. (1999). The medial ganglionic eminence gives rise to a population of early neurons in the developing cerebral cortex. *Journal of Neuroscience, 19*, 7881–7888.

Levitt, P., Eagleson, K. L., & Powell, E. M. (2004). Regulation of neocortical interneuron development and the implications for neurodevelopmental disorders. *Trends in Neurosciences, 27*, 400–406.

Lewis, D. A., & Levitt, P. (2002). Schizophrenia as a disorder of neurodevelopment. *Annual Review of Neuroscience, 25*, 409–432.

Lumsden, A., & Krumlauf, A. R. (1996). Patterning the vertebrate neuraxis. *Science, 274*, 1109–1115.

Marín, O., Anderson, S. A., & Rubinstein, J. L. R. (2000). Origin and molecular specification of striatal interneurons. *Journal of Neuroscience, 20*, 6063–6076.

Marín, O., & Rubinstein, J. L. R. (2001). A long, remarkable journey: Tangential migration in the telencephalon. *Nature Reviews Neuroscience, 2*, 780–790.

Marín-Padilla, M. (1972). Structural abnormalities of the cerebral cortex in human chromosomal aberrations: A Golgi study. *Brain Research, 44*, 625–629.

Marín-Padilla, M. (1976). Pyramidal cell abnormalities in the motor cortex of a child with Down's syndrome: A Golgi study. *Journal of Comparative Neurology, 167*, 63–82.

Marín-Padilla, M. (1990). Origin, formation, and prenatal maturation of the human cerebral cortex: An overview. *Journal of Craniofacial Genetics and Developmental Biology, 10*, 137–146.

Marín-Padilla, M. (1998). Cajal–Retzius cells and the development of the neocortex. *Trends in Neurosciences, 21*, 64–71.

Meyer, G., & Goffinet, A. M. (1998). Prenatal development of reelin-immunoreactive neurons in the human neocortex. *Journal of Comparative Neurology, 397*, 29–40.

Meyer, G., Schaaps, J. P., Moreau, L., & Goffinet, A. M. (2000). Embryonic and early fetal development of the human neocortex. *Journal of Neuroscience, 20*, 1858–1868.

Meyer, G., & Wahle, P. (1999). The paleocortical ventricle is the origin of reelin-expressing neurons in the marginal zone of the foetal human neocortex. *European Journal of Neuroscience, 11*, 3937–3944.

Mochida, G. H., & Walsh, C. A. (2001). Molecular genetics of human microcephaly. *Current Opinion in Neurobiology, 14*, 151–156.

Monuki, E. S., & Walsh, C. A. (2001). Mechanisms of cerebral cortical patterning in mice and humans. *Nature Neuroscience, 4*, 1199–1206.

Muenke, M., & Beachy, P. A. (2000). Genetics of ventral forebrain development and holoprosencephaly. *Current Opinion in Genetics and Development, 10*, 262–269.

Müller, F., & O'Rahilly, R. (1997). The timing and sequence of appearing of neuromeres and their derivatives in staged human embryos. *Acta Anatomica (Basel), 158*, 83–99.

Naidich, T. P., Zimmerman, R. A., McLone, D. G., Raybaud, C. A., Altman, N. R., & Braffmann, B. H. (1996). Congenital anomalies of the spine and spinal cord. In S. W. Atlas (Ed.), *Magnetic resonance imaging of the brain and spine* (2nd ed., pp. 1265–1337). New York: Lippincott-Raven.

Nakatsu, T., Uwabe, C., & Shiota, K. (2000). Neural tube closure in human initiates at multiple sites: Evidence from human embryos and implications for the pathogenesis of neural tube defects. *Anatomica Embryologica (Berlin), 201*, 455–466.

Norman, M. G., McGillivray, B. C., Kalousek, D. K., Hill, A., & Poskitt, K. J. (1995). *Congenital malformations of the brain: Pathological, embryological, clinical, radiological and genetic aspects.* New York: Oxford University Press.

Opitz, J. M. (1993). Blastogenesis and the "primary field" in human development. *Birth Defects, 29*, 3–37.

Opitz, J. M., Wilson, G. N., & Gilbert-Barnes, E. (1997). Abnormalities of blastogenesis, organogenesis, and phenogenesis. In E. Gilbert-Barnes (Ed.), *Potter's pathology of the fetus and infant* (pp. 65–105). St. Louis, MO: Mosby.

O'Rahilly, R., & Müller, F. (1987). *Developmental stages in human embryos* (Publication 637). Washington, DC: Carnegie Institution of Washington.

O'Rahilly, R., & Müller, F. (1999). *The embryonic human brain: An atlas of developmental stages* (2nd ed.). New York: Wiley-Liss.

O'Rahilly, R., & Müller, F. (2001). *Human embryology and teratology* (3rd ed.). New York: Wiley-Liss.

Parnavelas, J. G. (2000). The origin and migration of cortical neurones: New vistas. *Trends in Neurosciences, 23*, 126–131.

Pascual-Castroviejo, I., Velez, A., Pascual-Pascual, S.-I., Roche, M. C., & Villarejo, F. (1991). Dandy–Walker malformation: An analysis of 38 cases. *Child's Nervous System, 7*, 88–97.

Paus, T., Collins, D. L., Evans, A. C., Leonard, G., Pike, B., & Zijdenbos, A. (2001). Maturation of white matter in the human brain: A review of magnetic resonance studies. *Brain Research Bulletin, 54*, 255–266.

Pearlman, A. L., Faust, P. L., Hatten, M. E., & Brunnstrom, J. E. (1998). New directions for neuronal migration. *Current Opinion in Neurobiology, 8*, 45–54.

Pilz, D., Stoodley, N., & Golden, J. A. (2002). Neuronal migration, cerebral cortical development, and cerebral cortical anomalies. *Journal of Neuropathology and Experimental Neurology, 61*, 1–11.

Pinard, J.-M., Feydy, A., Carlier, P., Perez, N., Pierot, L., & Burnod, Y. (2000). Functional MRI in double cortex: Functionality of heterotopia. *Neurology, 54*, 1531–1533.

Pooh, R. K., Maeda, K., & Pooh, K. (2003). *An atlas of fetal central nervous system diseases: Diagnosis and treatment.* Boca Raton, FL: Parthenon.

Powell, E. M., Campbell, D. B., Stanwood, G. D., Davis, C., Noebels, J. L., & Levitt, P. (2003). Genetic disruption of cortical interneuron development causes region- and GABA cell type-specific deficits, epilepsy, and behavioral dysfunction. *Journal of Neuroscience, 23*, 622–631.

Puelles, L., & Rubinstein, J. L. R. (2003). Forebrain gene expression domains and the evolving prosomeric model. *Trends in Neurosciences, 26*, 469–476.

Purpura, D. P. (1974). Dendritic spine "dysgenesis" and mental retardation. *Science, 186*, 1126–1128.

Rakic, P. (1972). Mode of cell migration to the superficial layers of fetal monkey neocortex. *Journal of Comparative Neurology, 145*, 61–84.

Rakic, P., & Yakovlev, P. I. (1968). Development of the corpus callosum and cavum septi in man. *Journal of Comparative Neurology, 132*, 45–72.

Ramaeckers, V. T., Heimann, G., Reul, J., Thron, A., & Jaeken, J. (1997). Genetic disorders and cerebellar structural abnormalities in childhood. *Brain, 120*, 1739–1751.

Raybaud, C. A., & Girard, N. (1998). Études anatomique par IRM des agénésies et dysplasies commissurales télencéphaliques. *Neurochirurgie, 44*(Suppl. 1), 38–60.

Raybaud, C. A., & Girard, N. (1999). The developmental disorders of the commissural plate of the telencephalon: MR imaging study and morphological classification. *Nervous System in Children, 24*, 348–357.

Ross, M. E., Swanson, K., & Dobyns, W. B. (2001). Lissencephaly with cerebellar hypoplasia (LCH): A heterogeneous group of cortical malformation. *Neuropediatrics, 32*, 256–263.

Ross, M. E., & Walsh, C. A. (2001). Human brain malformations and their lessons for neuronal migration. *Annual Review of Neuroscience, 24*, 1041–1070.

Rubinstein, J. L. R., & Beachy, P. A. (1998). Patterning of the embryonic forebrain. *Current Opinion in Neurobiology, 8*, 18–26.

Rubinstein, J. L. R., Shimamura, K., Martinez, S., & Puelles, L. (1998). Regionalization of the prosencephalic neural plate. *Annual Review of Neuroscience, 21*, 445–447.

Santavuori, P., Somer, H., Sainio, K., Rapola, J., Kruus, S., Nikitin, T., et al. (1989). Muscle-eye-brain disease (MEB). *Brain and Development, 11*, 147–153.

Sarnat, H. B. (2000). Molecular genetic classification of central nervous system malformations. *Journal of Child Neurology, 15*, 675–687.

Sarnat, H. B., & Flores-Sarnat, L. (2001). Neuropathologic research strategies in holoprosencephaly. *Journal of Child Neurology, 16*, 918–931.

Seress, L., Ábrahám, H., Tornóczky, T., & Kosztolányi, G. (2001). Cell formation in the human hippocampal formation from mid-gestation to the late postnatal period. *Neuroscience, 105*, 831–843.

Shiota, K. (1993). Teratothanasia: Prenatal loss of abnormal conceptuses and the prevalence of various malformations during human gestation. *Birth Defects, 29*, 189–199.

ten Donkelaar, H. J., Lammens, M., & Hori, A. (2006). *Clinical neuroembryology: Development and developmental disorders of the human central nervous system.* Berlin: Springer Verlag.

ten Donkelaar, H. J., Lammens, M., Wesseling, P., Hori, A., Keyser, A., & Rotteveel, J. (2004). Development and malformations of the human pyramidal tract. *Journal of Neurology, 251*, 1429–1442.

ten Donkelaar, H. J., Lammens, M., Wesseling, P., Thijssen, H. O. M., & Renier, W. O. (2003). Development and developmental disorders of the human cerebellum. *Journal of Neurology, 250*, 1025–1036.

Toda, T., Kobayashi, K., Takeda, S., Sasaki, J., Kurahashi, H., Kano, H., et al. (2003). Fukuyama-type congenital muscular dystrophy (FCMD) and α-dystroglycanopathy. *Congenital Anomalies, 43*, 97–104.

Toga, A. W., Thompson, P. M., & Sowell, E. R. (2006). Mapping brain maturation. *Trends in Neurosciences, 29*, 148–159.

van der Knaap, M. S., & Valk, J. (1995). *Magnetic resonance of myelin, myelination and myelin disorders* (2nd ed.). Berlin: Springer Verlag.

Wang, V. Y., & Zoghbi, H. Y. (2001). Genetic regulation of cerebellar development. *Nature Reviews Neuroscience, 2*, 484–491.

Yakovlev, P. I., & Lecours, A. R. (1967). The myelogenetic cycles of regional maturation of the brain. In A. Minkowski (Ed.), *Regional development of the brain in early life* (pp. 3–70). Oxford: Blackwell.

Zaki, P. A., Quinn, J. C., & Price, D. J. (2003). Mouse models of telencephalic development. *Current Opinion in Genetics and Development, 128*, 193–205.

4

Genetics of Learning Abilities and Disabilities: Implications for Cognitive Neuroscience and Translational Research

Yulia Kovas and Robert Plomin

Genetic research methods can help to address the question of why children differ in their ability to read, to use language, and to understand mathematics. Two decades of research into genetic and environmental causes of individual differences in cognitive abilities make it clear that genetics is a surprisingly large part of the answer both for learning abilities and learning disabilities. Twin studies, comparing identical and fraternal twins, consistently show substantial genetic influence on individual differences in learning abilities, such as reading and mathematics, as well as other cognitive abilities, such as spatial ability and memory.

Genetic research has moved beyond merely demonstrating the importance of genetic influence to ask more interesting questions. One of the most important examples is multivariate genetic analysis, which makes it possible to ask questions about the genetic and environmental links between and within learning abilities and disabilities. This research has produced surprising findings with far-reaching implications. The purpose of this chapter is to review these results and to consider their implications for neuroscience and translational research. We begin with a brief description of multivariate genetic analysis.

Multivariate Genetic Analysis

Multivariate genetic analysis is best understood in contrast to univariate genetic analysis. Univariate genetic analysis uses methods such as the twin method to estimate genetic and environmental contributions to individual differences (variance) on a single variable (univariate). If monozygotic (MZ) twins are more similar than dizygotic (DZ) twins for a trait, this suggests that genetic differences account for some of the observed (phenotypic) differences on the trait. Heritability estimates the extent to which genetic variance accounts for phenotypic variance. In contrast, multivariate genetic analysis focuses on the covariance (correlation) between two traits (bivariate) or multiple traits (multivariate) and uses the twin method to estimate genetic and environmental contributions to their covariance as well as the variance of each trait. In other words, multivariate genetic analysis estimates the extent to which genetic and environmental factors that affect one trait also affect another trait.

The gist of the method lies in cross-trait twin correlations. Just as univariate genetic analysis compares MZ and DZ correlations for a single trait, multivariate genetic analysis compares MZ and DZ correlations across traits. If MZ cross-trait cross-twin (CTCT) correlations are greater than DZ CTCT correlations, this suggests that genetic differences account for some of the phenotypic correlation between the traits. Multivariate genetic analysis yields two distinct statistics: the genetic correlation and bivariate heritability. The genetic correlation indexes the extent to which genetic effects on one trait correlate with genetic effects on another trait independent of the heritability of the two traits. A genetic correlation of 1.0 indicates that the same genes affect both traits, and a genetic correlation of 0.0 signifies that completely different genes affect the traits. The important point is that the genetic correlation can be high even if the heritabilities of the two traits are low and vice versa. Bivariate heritability weights the genetic correlation by the heritabilities of the two traits in order to estimate the extent to which genetic factors account for the phenotypic correlation between the traits. Multivariate genetic analyses also yield estimates of shared and non-shared environmental parameters analogous to the genetic correlation and bivariate heritability.

Generalist Genes for Learning Abilities and Disabilities

Multivariate genetic research on learning abilities consistently yields high genetic correlations. In a recent review, genetic correlations varied from 0.67 to 1.0 for reading versus language (5 studies), 0.47 to 0.98 for reading versus mathematics (3 studies), and 0.59 to 0.98 for language versus mathematics (2 studies; Plomin & Kovas, 2005). The average genetic correlation is about 0.70. The first study to conduct a multivariate genetic analysis of reading, language, and mathematics together in a single trivariate analysis reported genetic correlations of 0.64 between reading and language, 0.71 between reading and mathematics, and 0.59 between language and mathematics for nearly three thousand 7-year-old twin pairs based on a year-long assessment by their teachers using UK National Curriculum criteria (Plomin & Kovas, 2005).

These analyses are based on unselected samples and address the origins of individual differences throughout the distribution. Few multivariate genetic studies of disabilities have been reported because they require large samples of twins for both types of disabilities in order to investigate comorbidity between the disabilities. In general, genetic research comparing abilities and disabilities suggests that what we call "learning disability" is merely the low end of the same genetic and environmental factors responsible for the normal distribution of learning ability. In other words, the abnormal is normal (Plomin & Kovas, 2005). The implication is that when large multivariate genetic studies of disabilities are conducted they will yield similarly high genetic correlations.

These high genetic correlations indicate that there is substantial genetic overlap between different types of learning abilities and disabilities. That is, the genes that affect reading are to a surprising extent the same genes that affect mathematics. In order to highlight this general effect of genes, we refer to them as generalist genes. When DNA research identifies genes responsible for genetic influence on reading ability and disability, for example, we predict that most of these genes will also be associated with mathematics ability and disability because the genetic correlation between reading and mathematics is 0.70. Because we tend to square correlations when considering effect sizes, it is worth mentioning that the genetic correlation itself, not the squared correlation, indicates the degree of genetic overlap between genetic effects on the two traits.

A common reaction to these results is disbelief because they go against the common observation that there are specific disabilities. That is, some children with reading problems have no problem with mathematics and vice versa. If genes are generalists, why do specific disabilities occur? There are three reasons. First, genes are also specialists— genetic correlations are not 1.0. Second, environments of a certain type are largely specialists, a point to which we shall return. Third, there is less specificity than it might seem. Even though reading and mathematics correlate phenotypically 0.65, some children with reading problems have no problems with mathematics and vice versa. However, this so-called double-dissociation is to be expected on statistical grounds alone and has no bearing on the extent to which different causal processes affect reading and mathematics. A related issue is that, although genetic correlations between learning abilities are greater than their phenotypic correlations, we cannot see genetic correlations in the population in the way that we can see phenotypic associations and dissociations.

If genetic correlations are so high between learning abilities, it makes sense to expect that components within each learning domain are also highly correlated genetically, and that is the case. Genetic correlations range between 0.60 and 0.90 within each of the domains of language, reading, and mathematics (Plomin & Kovas, 2005). The most recent study used web-based testing to assess five components of mathematics, including computation, application, and interpretation, in a study of more than a thousand 10-year-old twin pairs (Kovas, Haworth, Petrill, & Plomin, 2007). The average genetic correlation between the five components of mathematics was 0.91.

Generalist Genes for Other Cognitive Abilities

Much multivariate genetic research has focused on cognitive abilities such as verbal, spatial, and memory abilities rather than learning abilities. This research consistently finds genetic correlations greater than 0.50 and often near 1.0 across diverse cognitive abilities (Deary, Spinath, & Bates, 2006). Similar results suggesting substantial genetic overlap have been found for more basic information-processing measures such as speed of processing as well as measures of brain volume (Deary et al., 2006). This genetic overlap across cognitive abilities becomes stronger across the lifespan (Petrill, 2002).

Phenotypic correlations among diverse tests of cognitive abilities led Charles Spearman in 1904 to call this general factor *g* in order to avoid the many connotations of the word "intelligence." To what extent do generalist genes for *g* overlap with generalist genes for learning abilities? A review of about a dozen such studies concludes that genetic correlations between *g* and learning abilities (mostly reading) are substantial but somewhat lower than the genetic correlations among learning abilities (Plomin & Kovas, 2005). For example, a study of nearly three thousand pairs of 7-year-old, same-sex twins reported genetic correlations of 0.74 between reading and mathematics, 0.58 between reading and *g*, and 0.67 between mathematics and *g* (Kovas, Harlaar, Petrill, & Plomin, 2005). This result suggests that most (but not all) generalist genes that affect learning abilities are even more general in that they also affect other sorts of cognitive abilities included in the *g* factor.

Specialist Genes and Specialist Environments

Although genetic correlations among learning abilities and disabilities are substantial, they are less than 1.0 in most cases, which means that genes also contribute to making children better at some abilities than others. As mentioned earlier, when DNA research identifies genes responsible for genetic influence on reading ability, we predict that most of the genes will also be associated with mathematics ability. However, we also predict that some of these genes will not be associated with mathematics. Because genetic influence on learning abilities is substantial, such specialist genes contribute importantly to dissociations among learning abilities and disabilities even though most genes are generalists.

Multivariate genetic research also has an interesting story to tell about environmental influences on learning abilities and disabilities. Genetic research distinguishes two types of environmental influences. Environmental influences that make family members similar are called shared environment. The rest of environmental influences, those that do not contribute to resemblance among family members, is called non-shared environment, which also includes error of measurement. In childhood, shared environment accounts for 15–25% of the variance of learning and cognitive abilities. Multivariate genetic analyses indicate that these shared environmental influences are generalists: Shared environmental correlations among learning and cognitive abilities are as high as genetic correlations. For example, in the two recent studies mentioned earlier, the shared environmental correlation was 0.74 between reading and mathematics at 7 years as assessed by teachers (Kovas et al., 2005), and the average shared environmental correlation was 0.86 between five components of mathematics at 10 years as assessed by web-based testing (Kovas, Petrill, & Plomin, 2007). An obvious hypothesis that has not yet been rigorously tested is that some monolithic factors, such as the socioeconomic status of the family or school quality, might be responsible for these generalist shared environmental effects (Walker, Petrill, & Plomin, 2005).

In contrast to these generalist effects of shared environment, non-shared environmental effects are specialists: Non-shared environmental correlations are low. For example, in the same two studies, the non-shared environmental correlation was 0.39 between reading and mathematics at 7 years as assessed by teachers (Kovas et al., 2005), and the average non-shared environmental correlation was 0.24 between five components of mathematics at 10 years as assessed by web-based testing (Kovas, Petrill, & Plomin, 2007).

Unlike shared environment, for which it is easy to point to influences with general effects such as socioeconomic status or school quality, it is more difficult to imagine non-shared environmental influences that might affect siblings differently—even for clones (MZ twins) growing up in the same family, attending the same schools, and sitting in the same classrooms. We are aware of no measures of the school environment that are child-specific other than measures of children's perceptions of their environments. Perceptions of the environment may be an important direction for research on non-shared environments because experience is the environment as perceived and such perceptions incorporate appetites and attitudes as well as aptitudes that filter the way in which children view their experiences. A recent study of three thousand 9-year-old twin pairs found that children's perceptions of school experiences were significantly but modestly influenced by genetic factors (20% of the variance), but most of the variance (65%) was due to non-shared environment (Walker & Plomin, 2005).

Implications of Generalist Genes for Neuroscience

Definitive proof of the importance of generalist genes will come from molecular genetic research that identifies DNA associated with learning and cognitive abilities and disabilities, which is beginning to happen as new techniques make it possible to study hundreds of thousands of DNA sequences (Butcher, Kennedy, & Plomin, 2006). The multivariate genetic research reviewed here leads to a clear prediction: Most (but not all) genes found to be associated with a particular learning ability or disability (such as reading) will also be associated with other learning abilities and disabilities (such as mathematics). In addition, most (but not all) of these generalist genes for learning abilities (such as reading and mathematics) will also be associated with other cognitive abilities (such as memory and spatial ability). When these generalist genes are identified, they will greatly accelerate research on general mechanisms at all levels of analysis from genes to brain to behavior.

One major implication of generalist genes is the way we think about the brain. We suggest that two genetic concepts are key: pleiotropy (a gene affects many traits) and polygenicity (many genes affect a trait). In our opinion, these two key genetic concepts of pleiotropy and polygenicity suggest that the genetic input into brain structure and function is general not modular.

Pleiotropy, which refers to the manifold, cascading effects of genes, is one of the reasons to expect that genes have general effects in the brain. Pleiotropy is common in complex organisms and can be expressed at various biological levels, from a gene that mediates several intracellular signal transduction pathways to a gene that is expressed in different tissues (Dudley, Janse, Tanay, Shamir, & McDonald Church, 2005). As one of hundreds of examples, most of the genes responsible for the 185 proteins involved in the NMDA receptor complexes are widely expressed throughout the central nervous system (Grant, Marshall, Page, Cumiskey, & Armstrong, 2005). A powerful new tool for seeing pleiotropy in the brain is gene expression mapping. Gene expression can be indexed by the presence of RNA that is transcribed from DNA. A critical development in gene expression mapping throughout the brain is the microarray, which can detect the expression of thousands of genes simultaneously (Greenberg, 2001), which is the genetic equivalent of neuroimaging. Gene expression is not limited to traditional genes, that is, the 2% of DNA called coding DNA that is transcribed into mRNA and translated into amino-acid sequences. There is great interest recently in noncoding DNA that is transcribed into RNA but not translated; such noncoding DNA has been shown to regulate the transcription of other DNA (Mattick, 2005).

In the present context, the key question is the relative specificity or generality of gene expression across brain regions. The generalist genes hypothesis predicts that gene expression is distributed widely throughout the brain rather than being localized in a specific region. Although in its early stages, gene expression mapping so far supports the generalist genes hypothesis in that most genes are expressed throughout the brain, not just in one specific region. For example, two genes most often studied in human cognition are catechol-O-methyltransferase (COMT) and brain-derived neurotrophic factor (BDNF; Plomin, Kennedy, & Craig, 2006). COMT is one of the major metabolic pathways of the catecholamine transmitters; BDNF is a member of the nerve growth family and is induced by cortical neurons. Because both genes have such basic neural functions, it seems likely that their effects in the brain are widespread both in terms of structure and function, an expectation supported by gene expression brain maps. In humans as well as mice, both COMT and BDNF are expressed in cortex, cerebellum, caudate nucleus, amygdala, thalamus, corpus callosum, dorsal root ganglia, and spinal cord (see www.geneatlas.org; www.brainatlas.org; Su et al., 2004).

Like early neuroimaging research, this early genetic neuroimaging work focuses on structural localization, for example, in the transcriptome mapping project in humans (Yamasaki et al., 2005). Structural brain maps of gene expression are fundamental because genes can only function if they are expressed (i.e., transcribed from DNA into RNA). The next goal will involve the much more difficult task of functional genetic neuroimaging: studying changes in gene expression as a function of interventions such as learning and memory tasks or drugs. One problem is that in the human species, localization of gene expression can only be studied using postmortem brain tissue, which limits research to structural genetic neuroimaging. (Although gene expression can be studied in peripheral tissues such as white blood cells as a model system, such studies cannot address the question of localization in the brain.)

Functional genetic neuroimaging needs to rely on mice and other animal models. Mouse research is obviously not useful as a behavioral model of uniquely human behaviors such as language, reading, and mathematics. However, mouse model research will play an important role in charting the functional expression of genes in the brain, even for learning abilities and disabilities, because nearly every human gene can be found in only slightly altered form in mice. Research on mice is underway that aims to create an atlas of patterns of gene expression throughout the brain during learning and memory tasks (Grant, 2003) in the Genes to Cognition Research Consortium (see www.genes2cognition.org). The generalist genes hypothesis predicts that functional genetic neuroimaging will also show general effects of genes across brain regions and across tasks.

Structural and functional genetic neuroimaging using gene expression mapping is only the first step toward understanding pleiotropic effects of generalist genes on the brain. Gene transcripts are translated into proteins and form protein complexes by attaching themselves to other proteins, setting up the possibility for even greater pleiotropy as genetic effects cascade throughout the brain (Grant et al., 2005), leading to "generalist brains."

The key question is how generalist genes for cognitive abilities work pleiotropically in the brain. One possibility is that a generalist gene affects a single brain area or function that in turn influences several cognitive processes (Figure 4.1, Mechanism 1).

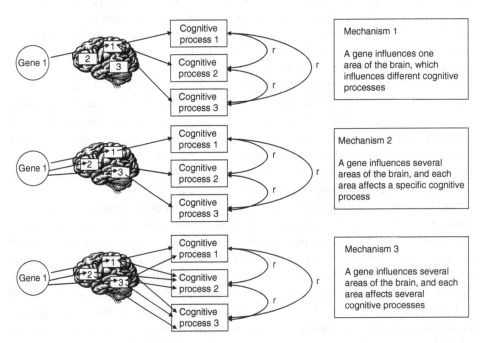

Figure 4.1 Three hypothesized mechanisms of the effects of a single gene on the brain and associated cognitive processes (pleiotropy). In our opinion, Mechanism 3 is the most likely. This figure can be extended by replacing the single gene shown for each mechanism with multiple genes to illustrate polygenicity (the involvement of many genes). Polygenicity will greatly multiply and magnify the effects of pleiotropy. *Note.* Adapted from "Generalist Genes: Implications for Cognitive Sciences," by Y. Kovas and R. Plomin, 2006, *Trends in Cognitive Science, 10,* 198–203, with permission from Elsevier.

The effect of this gene would be general at the cognitive level, but specific at the level of localization in the brain. That is, the brain structures and functions are uncorrelated genetically because they are influenced by different genes. We believe that this possibility is unlikely because pleiotropy suggests that any gene is likely to be expressed in more than one structure or function.

A second possibility is that cognition-related generalist genes pleiotropically affect multiple brain structures and functions, but each of these structures and functions affects a specific cognitive process (Figure 4.1, Mechanism 2). Structure and function of these specialized areas are correlated genetically because the same genetic polymorphism affects these different regions. Even though each brain structure and function is associated with one specific cognitive process, these cognitive processes will be correlated genetically because the brain processes are correlated genetically.

The most likely possibility in our opinion is that generalist genes affect multiple brain structures and functions and that each of these affects multiple cognitive processes (Figure 4.1, Mechanism 3). This mechanism would lead to genetic correlations in the brain as well as in the mind. Several general candidate processes, such as neural plasticity (Garlick, 2002), dendritic complexity, myelinization, and speed of nerve conduction (Deary, 2000) have been proposed. A gene that affected a general process of this type would be specific to that brain process, but the gene would have general effects structurally and functionally throughout the brain because the fundamental brain process it influences has diffuse effects. Such generalist brain processes would be compatible with either Mechanism 2 or 3 (see Kovas & Plomin, 2006, for more discussion).

Clearly, we are a long way from understanding the mechanisms by which generalist genes for cognition have their effects on the brain, but it is interesting to view current research in cognitive neuroscience from the perspective of generalist genes that operate pleiotropically throughout the brain, creating genetic correlations among brain processes (Mechanisms 2 and 3). For example, one trend in much recent neuroscience research is a focus on functional circuits, pathways, and networks in the brain rather than individual specific areas (David et al., 2005). Such "functional networks" could reflect the generalist effects of genes.

Despite the challenges and complexities of generalist genes, when such genes are identified, they will provide opportunities for empirical research on brain pathways between genes and cognition in three ways. First, these genes will be identified on the basis of their prediction of differences in cognitive function. In other words, no matter how complex the brain pathways are between genes and cognition, these genes will be anchored to a functional effect at the level of cognition. Second, each of these generalist genes will provide a window through which we can view brain mechanisms that are functionally related to cognitive function. Third, although there are likely to be many genes of small effect, rather than fractionating the view of brain processes, these generalist genes will together provide glimpses of processes that are all united functionally in terms of cognition, which we hope will promote research on the integration of brain processes.

The strongest evidence for generalist genes operating in the brain will come when specific DNA variations are identified that are associated with cognitive and brain processes, which will make it possible to investigate the extent to which these genes have general or specific effects. However, progress has been slow in identifying these genes, in part because abilities and common disabilities are likely to be affected by many genes (polygenicity) of much smaller effect size than previously expected (Butcher et al., 2006). Polygenicity has a much more direct relevance to our thesis than merely making it difficult to find generalist genes: Polygenicity amplifies the generalist effects of pleiotropy, as discussed earlier.

For common disorders and complex traits, genetic research has undergone a revolution that has radically altered molecular genetic strategies. Instead of thinking about rare genetic disorders caused by a single-gene mutation of the sort that Mendel investigated in the pea plant, it is now generally accepted that common disorders are caused by many genes (polygenicity) which implies that each of these genes will have only a small effect (Plomin, Owen, & McGuffin, 1994). To emphasize the contrast with single-gene disorders, these multiple genetic variants of small effect are called *quantitative trait loci* (QTLs).

QTLs are more than a metaphor in terms of brain function: If the set of generalist genes that affects common cognitive disabilities involves many QTLs of small effect, this suggests that there are likely to be many brain mechanisms of small effect as well. The possibility that many QTLs are involved in the links between genes, brain, and cognition greatly multiplies and magnifies the pleiotropic effects of generalist genes.

QTLs lead to a prediction that common disorders are likely to be the quantitative extremes of normally distributed dimensions, at least at the level of genetic etiology. In other words, disorders are part of normal variation, rather than etiologically distinct entities. This is the reason why QTLs refer to quantitative traits even in the case of common disorders: If many genes affect a disorder, it necessarily follows that there will be a quantitative distribution rather than a dichotomy. This is another way in which genes are generalists: Genes that affect disabilities also affect normal variation in abilities.

This prediction that the abnormal is normal has important implications for cognitive neuroscience. For example, this view predicts that learning disabilities are the extremes of the same brain and cognitive processes responsible for normal variation, not a broken brain caused by abnormal events such as lesions. We offer the acronym QTNs (quantitative trait neural processes) to highlight the need for a revolution in cognitive neuroscience similar to the QTL revolution in molecular genetics. That is, just as cognitive disabilities are influenced by many genes of small effect (QTLs), many neural processes of small effect (QTNs) mediate the effects of QTLs on cognition. The QTL prediction that the abnormal is normal is likely to have a QTN parallel in that cognitive disabilities are merely the quantitative extreme of the same neural processes that are responsible for normal variation. This view suggests a shift from thinking about diagnosed cases versus controls to thinking about normal variation. A QTN revolution would also follow the QTL direction of heeding the exorbitant demands for large sample sizes that enable adequate power to detect QTNs of small effect size.

Implications of Generalist Genes and Specialist Environments for Translational Research

Implications of generalist genes for translational research are also far-reaching. For example, genetic "diagnoses" of learning disabilities differ from traditional diagnoses, which are based on symptoms rather than causes. From a genetic perspective, learning disabilities are not distinct diagnostic entities: The same set of generalist genes affects learning abilities and disabilities. When these generalist genes are identified, they will radically alter diagnostic schemes. Moreover, as discussed in the previous section, if generalist genes are QTLs, this suggests that there are no common disorders, just the quantitative extreme of the same genetic and environmental factors that affect variation throughout the distribution. Identifying generalist genes is also likely to contribute to the trend in translational research toward individually tailored treatments and to early prediction and, eventually, preventive interventions.

Just as important for translational research and education are the multivariate genetic findings about the environment. Discrepancies in children's profiles of performance are largely due to specialist environments. Even though we have a long way to go to understand the non-shared environmental influences that are the source of specialist environments, there are important implications now of thinking about specialist environments in relation to education. Almost all work on school environments focuses on shared environmental factors, such as family background and school and teacher quality. However, such shared environmental influences have modest effects and, at least for cognitive abilities, decline sharply in importance from childhood to adolescence (Deary et al., 2006). Moreover, shared environmental influences act as generalists. More important, and of increasing importance during development, are non-shared environmental influences. As we have described, multivariate genetic research shows that these environmental factors primarily work as specialists, contributing to differences in children's performances in different areas. One implication is that educational influences might have their greatest impact on remediating discrepant performances among learning abilities (such as differences in reading and mathematics) and discrepancies between learning abilities and cognitive abilities, which is one way to view the topic of over- and underachievement.

Acknowledgments

The writing of this chapter and some of the research it describes were supported in part by grants from the UK Medical Research Council (G0500079), the UK Wellcome Trust (GR75492), and the US National Institutes of Health (HD46167, HD44454, HD49861).

References

Butcher, L. M., Kennedy, J. K. J., & Plomin, R. (2006). Generalist genes and cognitive neuroscience. *Current Opinion in Neurobiology, 16*, 141–151.

David, S. P., Munafó, M. R., Johansen-Berg, H., Smith, S. M., Rogers, R. D., Matthews, P. M., et al. (2005). Ventral striatum/nucleus accumbens activation to smoking-related pictorial cues in smokers and nonsmokers: A functional magnetic resonance imaging study. *Biological Psychiatry, 58*, 488–494.

Deary, I. (2000). *Looking down on human intelligence: From psychometrics to the brain.* Oxford University Press.

Deary, I. J., Spinath, F. M., & Bates, T. C. (2006). Genetics of intelligence. *European Journal of Human Genetics, 14*, 690–700.

Dudley, A. M., Janse, D. M., Tanay, A., Shamir, R., & McDonald Church, G. (2005). A global view of pleiotropy and phenotypically derived gene function in yeast. *Molecular Systems Biology*, doi: 10.1038/msb4100004, E1–E11.

Garlick, D. (2002). Understanding the nature of the general factor of intelligence: The role of individual differences in neural plasticity as an explanatory mechanism. *Psychological Review, 109*, 116–136.

Grant, S. G. N. (2003). An integrative neuroscience program linking genes to cognition and disease. In R. Plomin, J. C. DeFries, I. W. Craig, & P. McGuffin (Eds.), *Behavioral genetics in the postgenomic era* (pp. 123–138). Washington, DC: American Psychological Association.

Grant, S. G. N., Marshall, M. C., Page, K.-L., Cumiskey, M. A., & Armstrong, J. D. (2005). Synapse proteomics of multiprotein complexes: A route from genes to nervous system diseases. *Human Molecular Genetics, 14*(2), R225–R234.

Greenberg, S. A. (2001). DNA microarray gene expression analysis technology and its application to neurological disorders. *Neurology, 57*(5), 755–761.

Kovas, Y., Harlaar, N., Petrill, S. A., & Plomin, R. (2005). "Generalist genes" and mathematics in 7-year-old twins. *Intelligence, 5*, 473–489.

Kovas, Y., Haworth, C. M. A., Petrill, S. A., & Plomin, R. (2007). Mathematical ability of 10-year-old boys and girls: Genetic and environmental etiology of typical and low performance. *Journal of Learning Disabilities, 40*(6), 554–567.

Kovas, Y., Petrill, S. A., & Plomin, R. (2007). The origins of diverse domains of mathematics: Generalist genes but specialist environments. *Journal of Educational Psychology, 99*(1), 128–139.

Kovas, Y. & Plomin, R. (2006). Generalist genes: Implications for cognitive sciences. *Trends in Cognitive Science, 10*, 198–203.

Mattick, J. S. (2005). The functional genomics of noncoding RNA. *Science, 309*, 1527–1528.

Petrill, S. A. (2002). The case for general intelligence: A behavioral genetic perspective. In R. J. Sternberg & E. L. Grigorenko (Eds.), *The general factor of intelligence: How general is it?* (pp. 281–298). Mahwah, NJ: Lawrence Erlbaum.

Plomin, R., Kennedy, J. K. J., & Craig, I. W. (2006). Quest for quantitative trait loci associated with intelligence. *Intelligence, 34*, 513–526.

Plomin, R. & Kovas, Y. (2005). Generalist genes and learning disabilities. *Psychological Bulletin, 131*, 592–617.

Plomin, R., Owen, M. J., & McGuffin, P. (1994). The genetic basis of complex human behaviors. *Science, 264*, 1733–1739.

Su, A. I., Wiltshire, T., Batalov, S., Lapp, H., Ching, K. A., Block, D., et al. (2004). A gene atlas of the mouse and human protein-encoding transcriptomes. *Proceedings of the National Academy of Sciences, USA, 101*(16), 6062–6067.

Walker, S. O., Petrill, S. A., & Plomin, R. (2005). School environment and socio-economic status are associated with teacher-assessed academic achievement at 7 years old after controlling for genetics. *Educational Psychology, 25,* 55–73.

Walker, S. O., & Plomin, R. (2005). The nature–nurture question: Teachers' perceptions of how genes and the environment influence educationally relevant behavior. *Educational Psychology, 25,* 509–515.

Yamasaki, C., Koyanagi, K. O., Fujii, Y., Barrero, R., Tamura, T., Yamaguchi-Kabata,Y., et al. (2005). Investigation of protein functions through data-mining on integrated human transcriptome database, H-invitational database (H-InvDB). *Gene, 364,* 99–107.

5

Brain Plasticity: Evidence from Children with Perinatal Brain Injury

Judy S. Reilly, Susan C. Levine, Ruth Nass, and Joan Stiles

Until very recently, our understanding of brain organization in humans has relied primarily on the classical neuropsychological approach of associating a specific lesion site with a behavioral deficit. Using this approach, studies of adults with strokes have informed our understanding of the neural underpinnings of various cognitive systems in the adult steady state, that is, after the brain has already acquired critical cognitive systems and the individual is an "expert user." Functional imaging studies have broadly confirmed these findings, while adding to and refining our understanding of adult brain organization. However, how the brain reaches this mature state is a topic of significant interest and rich debate.

The development of the young brain is a dynamic process (Stiles, Paul, & Hesselink, 2006) and children's brains continue to develop well into adolescence (e.g., Blakemore & Choudhury, 2006). A corollary of this protracted development is that children with early localized brain injury suffer less severe effects than adults with comparable lesions (e.g., Basser, 1962; Lenneberg, 1967), suggesting that this dynamic developmental process continues even in the presence of an early injury. For example, in language studies, children's impressive development after early stroke led Lenneberg (1967) to propose that both hemispheres of the child's brain were *equipotential* for language. Such plasticity, first systematically studied by Kennard in the 1930s (Kennard, 1940), has led to the widely held view that the brain is remarkably malleable or plastic early in life, and that, over development, there is a decrease in this flexibility. However, development is neither linear nor unidimensional, and different cognitive systems develop on distinctive timetables. For example, whereas children are generally producing short sentences by their second birthday, they do not draw recognizable objects, such as houses, until about the age of 4.

In this chapter on brain plasticity, the principal questions we pose concern the degree to which particular brain regions may be privileged for certain functions, and the degree to which there is neuroplasticity for differing cognitive systems as they develop. The context for this discussion will be prospective studies of children's development following a perinatal (PL) injury (i.e., before higher cognitive systems have developed). This will permit us to witness how the developing brain adapts; that is, how the brain generates alternative organizations for behavioral functions. Following such children will illuminate both the degree to which initial biases exist, as well as the extent to which the developing brain is flexible in adapting and acquiring behavioral functions in the face of early injury and an overall, decreased capacity. Investigating development both within and across cognitive systems will permit us to identify gradients of plasticity for various systems as well as their component processes.

The chapter begins with an introduction to the population and then an overview of general intellectual functioning in children with perinatal stroke. We then turn to profiles of development within cognitive systems that in the adult model reflect distinct neural profiles: language, spatial cognition, and emotion processing. We close by exploring two contexts where these systems intersect: labeling emotions and the development of literacy in the PL group. As a framework to evaluate cognitive development in the PL group, we propose four questions that have guided our research over the past 20 years:

1. Do children show specific deficits early in development?
2. Do such profiles of deficit map onto those of adults with comparable lesions?
3. Do these deficits persist or is there development over time?
4. If they persist, do these deficits remain stable or change with development?

Children with Perinatal Brain Injury: Lesion Characterization

Perinatal strokes occur in 1 in 4,000 term infants (Nelson & Lynch, 2004). Stroke in the full-term infant can occur during the third trimester, during labor and delivery, or during the neonatal period (birth to the end of the first month of life)—in other words, the pre-perinatal period. Term infants generally have large strokes involving the middle cerebral artery, damaging both cortical and subcortical regions (Bax, Tydeman, & Flormark, 2006; Kirton & deVeber, 2006; Wu, Croen, Shah, Newman, & Najjar, 2006). Thus, this population provides an opportunity to examine issues of specialization and plasticity in children with large lesions that compromise much of one cerebral hemisphere.

Most pre-perinatal strokes involve the left hemisphere (LH), a finding attributable to anatomic or hemodynamic differences between the left and right common carotid artery (Volpe, 2000). The majority of the strokes have an embolic etiology and the placenta (Pathan & Kittner, 2003) is probably the most common source of these emboli. About three-quarters of term infants with stroke present with seizures in the neonatal period. However, some children with perinatal stroke do not present until several months of age when decreased hand use is noted and imaging (CT or MRI) reveals an old stroke which is presumed to have occurred in the pre-perinatal period. Because proximal arm and leg muscles have bilateral innervation and because infants do not really start to use their hands until a few months of age, the hemiparesis is not imme-diately apparent. Newborns whose injury occurs during labor and delivery have acute signs of brain insult like seizures, while those whose stroke occurred even a few days before birth have "recovered" and are usually asymptomatic as newborns.

Neonatal seizures are routinely evaluated with an EEG and a CT and/or an MRI scan. Imaging of children presenting with a hemiparesis during the first year docu-ments the extent of the lesion and confirms the unilaterality of the pathology. The medical workup at all ages includes an assessment of the heart, studies of blood clot-ting, ruling out infection, and studies evaluating for metabolic/genetic problems which can cause stroke (Kirton & deVeber, 2006). This workup assures exclusion of a child with bilateral involvement. Between 30% and 50% of children who have had a neonatal stroke appear neurologically normal (Lee, Croen, & Lindan, 2005; Nelson & Lynch, 2004). Hemiparetic cerebral palsy (which rarely prevents walking) occurs in 40–60% of cases, epilepsy in about 40%, visual problems in 25%, and behavior problems in 20%. About 80% have a problem in at least one domain. Risk factors for poor outcome include: abnormal examination at discharge from the nursery, neonatal seizures, abnor-mal initial EEG, blood clotting abnormalities, and late presentation of hemiparesis (Bax et al., 2006; Mercuri et al., 1999; Sreenan, Bhargava, & Robertson, 2000; Wu et al., 2004). Imaging data about site, side, and timing of stroke (pre- versus perinatal) pro-vides additional information predictive of outcome (Kirton & deVeber, 2006; Kwong & Wong, 2004; Nass, Peterson, & Koch, 1989; Staudt et al., 2004).

Epilepsy is associated with poorer cognitive outcomes in children with early unilat-eral brain injury (Carlsson, Hagberg, & Olsson, 2003; Isaacs et al., 1996; Muter, Taylor, & Vargha-Khadem, 1997; Vargha-Khadem, Isaacs, Van der Werf, Robb, & Wilson, 1992). Consistent with these findings, an abnormal neonatal EEG predicts poorer outcomes at 15 months (Mercuri et al., 1999). When neonatal seizures occur concurrently with the stroke, they are generally few in number and easy to control. Moreover, the majority of children who have seizures as newborns never have them again; about 25–40% have recurrent seizures later in life that are easily controlled with medication. A small pro-portion of children with early unilateral brain injury have persistent seizures, and a small proportion of these children develop intractable seizures. Rarely, surgery is required to control the seizures.

Overall Intellectual Performance: Performance IQ and Verbal IQ

While is it is well known that focal brain lesions incurred early in life have very different functional consequences than apparently similar lesions incurred later in life, our knowledge of early functional plasticity comes mainly from studies that examine the functioning of PL children at only one developmental time-point. Such studies provide only a snapshot of how an early lesion affects behavioral outcomes. With respect to the IQ of PL children, the majority of studies are based on assessments that were obtained at only a single time-point. These studies leave us with a somewhat mixed pattern of results: Some studies report that the average IQ of children in this population is more than one standard deviation below that of control children (e.g., Levine, Huttenlocher, Banich, & Duda, 1987; Perlstein & Hood, 1955; St. James-Roberts, 1981; Woods, 1980), whereas other studies report that there is no significant IQ deficit (e.g., Aram & Ekelman, 1986; Bates, Vicari, & Trauner, 1999; Nass et al., 1989). These apparent discrepancies may reflect differences in the age of the children at the time of assessment as the studies that report little or no impact on IQ tend to assess children at earlier time-points than those that report IQ deficits.

Animal studies indicate that the functional consequences of early lesions change over the course of development (Goldman, 1971, 1974; Goldman-Rakic, Isseroff, Schwartz, & Bugbee, 1983; Kolb & Wishaw, 1985). For example, a series of studies of monkeys with early bilateral lesions of the dorsolateral frontal lobe revealed *no* impairment on a delayed response task at 12–18 months but a marked impairment at 2 years of age, in both cases in comparison to age-matched control monkeys (Goldman, 1971, 1974). Goldman-Rakic et al. (1983) suggest that this pattern reflects maturational changes in the frontal lobe. That is, deficits are only apparent in the lesioned monkeys when the dorsolateral frontal cortex, the region that is damaged in the lesioned monkeys, becomes sufficiently mature in the intact monkeys to contribute to the target behavior, their delayed response behavior. This level of frontal lobe maturity is apparently attained by 2 years of age, but not yet by 12–18 months of age. Thus, a comparison of performance between lesioned and intact monkeys reveals a deficit at the later but not at the earlier time-point.

A recent study examining the IQ level of PL children uncovered a similar developmental pattern (Levine, Brasky, & Nikolas, 2005). In this study, a group of children with pre- or perinatal unilateral brain injury was administered a standardized IQ test both before and after the age of 7. The results showed that PL children had significantly lower verbal and performance IQ levels at the later time-point than at the earlier time-point (*M*pre-7 verbal IQ = 95.13; *M*post-7 verbal IQ = 85.73; *M*pre-7 performance IQ = 94.67; *M*post-7 performance IQ = 87.87). Importantly, the lower IQ levels at the later assessment time-point do not reflect a loss of knowledge, but rather, a slower rate of development than occurred in the normative sample (Banich, Levine, Kim, & Huttenlocher, 1990). Individual subtest scaled scores were compared across time to examine whether the decline in IQ level was specific to particular subtests. Although all of the subtests that were administered at both time-points showed a decline, the decline was significant for Arithmetic, Vocabulary, Picture Completion, and Block Design, but not for Similarities or Information. Overall, this analysis revealed a rather broad decline that was not specific to verbal or spatial subtests. Levine and colleagues also examined whether the degree of falloff on subtests tapping visuospatial skills was greater for those tests with a motor requirement (Levine, Kraus, Alexander, Suriyakham, & Huttenlocher, 2005). We viewed this as a possibility since most of our PL children had some degree of hemiparesis. This question was addressed by comparing the degree of falloff on two performance subtests, Block Design, which requires some dexterity in manipulating pieces, and Picture Completion, which has minimal or no motor demands. This comparison revealed that the degree of decline did not significantly differ on these two subtests, suggesting that the falloff on performance subtests is not attributable solely to motor difficulties.

As in the monkeys with early frontal lesions whose deficits were only apparent at the later assessment time-point, it is possible that the increasing IQ gap between PL and typically developing children reflects maturational changes in the developing brains of non-brain-injured children. That is, particular brain regions may only contribute to task performance in typically developing children once they have reached a sufficient level of maturity. If such regions are damaged and fail to develop normally in the PL children, the IQ gap between typically developing and brain-injured children will become increasingly apparent over time. The falloff in IQ level in brain-injured children can also be viewed as reflecting limitations that early lesions place on the brain's overall processing capacities. Assuming that these processing capacities are increasingly taxed as task demands augment, the gap between the IQ level of typical and brain-injured children would be expected to widen over time. Thus, the degree of functional plasticity observed after an early lesion may vary with the age of the child at the time of assessment. It may also vary depending on the specific task and domain of functioning being examined. Since IQ tests were designed to assess overall levels of intellectual functioning rather than functioning in particular cognitive domains, it is critical to examine performance using more specific tasks in order to address this question; thus, we begin with an overview of language acquisition in the PL group.

Language Development in Children with Perinatal Stroke

In mapping brain–language relations, 160 years of research in a broad range of languages, including sign languages, has confirmed the original findings of Paul Broca: For the vast majority of adults, the formal and core aspects of language (phonology, morphology, and syntax) are mediated by the left hemisphere of the brain. With respect to the development of such relations, early observations of both Basser (1962) and Lenneberg (1967) noted that children who suffered brain injury did not display the same persistent and marked deficits as did adults with injuries to homologous regions. In the past 40 years, a number of studies have investigated language development in both typically developing children and in children with different neurodevelopmental disorders to better understand the process of language development and its neural substrates. A growing literature attests to Lenneberg's observation: Children with brain injury fare much better than adults on tasks of language performance (Bates et al., 1999, 2001; Eisele & Aram, 1995; Feldman, 2005; Reilly, Losh, Bellugi, & Wulfeck et al., 2004; Vargha-Khadem, Isaacs, & Muter, 1994; Vicari et al., 2000, Weckerly, Wulfeck, & Reilly, 2004; Wulfeck, Bates, Krupa-Kwiatkowski, & Saltzman, 2004). For those studies that included children who have suffered lesions *after* their first birthday, that is, once the process of language acquisition is underway, the findings are mixed: Some studies show no significant differences in language performance according to lesion site (e.g., Vargha-Khadem, Gorman, & Watters, 1985), whereas others have noted subtle persistent deficits for children with left hemisphere injury or hemidecortication (Dennis & Kohn, 1975; Dennis & Whitaker, 1976; Eisele & Aram, 1995; Riva & Cazzaniga, 1986; Vargha-Khadem et al., 1985). Here we address these issues by focusing on children who incurred their lesions in the perinatal period, before the onset of higher cognitive functions.

Traditionally, neuropsychologists have used standardized language tests (such as the Clinical Evaluation of Language Function [CELF]; Semel, Wiig, & Secord, 1995) to assess language proficiency. Such tests are designed to evaluate specific aspects of both receptive and productive language: vocabulary, morphology, and specific syntactic structures. Others subtests, rather than testing individual linguistic structures, ask children to use language to solve problems. For example, in the subtest Formulating Sentences (CELF), the child is shown a picture and given two words. His or her job is to make a coherent sentence about the picture using those two words. Such subtests are similar to those that constitute the verbal IQ score where language is a tool to solve problems, rather than testing mastery of specific grammatical structures. Two studies of PL children that used the CELF (Ballantyne, Spilkin, & Trauner, in press; MacWhinney, Feldman, Sacco, & Valdes-Perez, 2000) found that the performance of the PL group was significantly worse than age-matched controls. MacWhinney et al. (2000) also reported that the children with left hemisphere injury had particular difficulty on the subtests of formulating sentences and oral directions, similar to studies looking at overall intellectual performance (Carlsson et al., 2003; Isaacs et al., 1996; Muter et al., 1997; Vargha-Khadem et al., 1992). Ballantyne et al. (in press) reported that children with seizures performed significantly more poorly than the rest of the PL group on the standardized language measures. Seizure status has also been noted by other researchers as a factor in mediating language performance (e.g., Dall'Oglio, Bates, Volterra, Di Capua, & Pezzini, 1994). To complement these studies using standardized tests, below we present studies targeting the acquisition of core aspects of language and their development. The vast majority of studies have been conducted with English-speaking children, but studies of children acquiring other languages are included where available.

Early communication and language in children with perinatal brain injury

Early development of language in the PL group has been the focus of several research groups: All have noted initial delay in the emergence of language with subsequent progress following the typical developmental trajectory. Importantly, delay in the PL group is characteristic of children with lesions to *either* the left or the right hemisphere and thus does not map onto the language profile of adults who incur strokes later in life.

Several investigators have asked whether language development proceeds in the same way in brain-injured and in typically developing children by focusing on the relation of early gesture use and language development. As in typically developing children, early gesture milestones predate and predict subsequent vocabulary and syntactic milestones in the PL group (e.g., Bates & Dick, 2002; Sauer, Gripshover, Harden, Meanwell, & Levine,

2006). For example, the number of gestures produced at 14 months of age predicts subsequent word production and comprehension in both typically developing and PL children (Sauer et al., 2006). Similarly, gesture–speech combinations (e.g., "Mommy" + point to shoe) predict the subsequent emergence of parallel argument structures in speech (Levine, Özçaliskan, & Goldin-Meadow, 2007). Such findings are particularly noteworthy in that the integral relationship between language and gesture is maintained even though children with PL are frequently hemiparetic. Another early study (Marchman, Miller, & Bates, 1991) followed a small group of PL children, and found delay in the onset of babbling, gesture, and first words in the PL group regardless of lesion site.

With the advent of the MacArthur Communicative Inventory, a parental report form (MCDI; Fenson et al., 1993), tracking children's lexical development became more convenient and efficient. Bates and colleagues (1997) used the MCDI to chronicle early language development in a group of 40 PL children aged between 8 and 30 months. They found overall delay in the PL group as a whole, both for comprehension and for the production of first words. However, within this general context of delay, site-specific deficits emerged: In the group of PL children between 10 and 17 months, children with early right hemisphere injury (RPL) demonstrated greater delays in word *comprehension* than the rest of the PL group; between the ages of 19 and 31 months, children with left temporal damage (LPL) showed the greatest delays for *productive* vocabulary; a transient bilateral frontal effect appeared from 19 to 31 months. To directly evaluate children's language production, Bates and colleagues also collected and analyzed language data from spontaneous parent–child interactions from 30 children with PL aged 19–44 months of age. Focusing on mean length of utterance (MLU), they found that children with left posterior damage on average used shorter utterances than controls or children with injury to other brain regions. This production profile is consistent with that of the parental reports, but is at odds with the typical adult profile of deficits in comprehension after left temporal injury.

Several longitudinal studies have also focused on early lexical development: Feldman and colleagues (Feldman, 1994; Feldman, Holland, Kemp, & Janosky, 1992) found both initial delay and wide variability in performance. In this smaller group of PL children, some performed in the normal range whereas others were delayed. However, after an initial delay, in most of the children progress was steady. Looking at morphological and syntactic development, they analyzed free-speech language samples using the IPSYN (Index of Productive Syntax; Scarborough, 1990). Again, they found wide variability in performance with half of those with LH injury and half of those with RH injury falling well below the norm. A longitudinal study of PL children by Thal and colleagues (Thal, Reilly, Seibert, Jeffries, & Fenson, 2004) also analyzed language samples using the IPSYN, and they too found wide variability in performance with delay in PL children with either RPL or LPL. These data are consistent with, and complemented by, a large longitudinal study of 40 PL children conducted by Levine and colleagues (Brasky, Nikolas, Meanwell, Levine, & Goldin-Meadow, 2005; Levine, Kraus et al., 2005) where the investigators found overall delay in the onset of language, but that lesion size rather than site modulated the developmental trajectory for both productive vocabulary and syntactic development.

These findings are broadly consistent with those of other groups, including those studying languages other than English. Using the Italian MCDI, Vicari et al. (2000) also noted early delay in language onset with some site-specific profiles: Children with LH injury were more delayed in lexical and grammatical production than those with RH injury. Chilosi's studies (Chilosi, Cipriani, Bertuccelli, Pfanner, & Cioni, 2001; Chilosi et al., 2005) of Italian PL children report similar findings. Further, as in typically developing children (Hart & Risley, 1995), Rowe and Levine (2007) found that the language a child hears (i.e., caregiver input) mediates language development of children with PL. This effect is sufficiently significant that children with lesions who have high language input from parents (more than 1 *SD* above the mean) have more rapid vocabulary development than control children with low language input from parents (more than 1 *SD* below the mean) at least until 3 years of age. In sum, as in typically developing children, input modulates language development; however, early brain injury to either the right *or* the left hemisphere will delay the onset of language. These findings suggest that the process of acquiring a language is different from maintaining an already functional system, as in adults, and, further, acquiring language draws on both the right and left cerebral hemispheres.

Language performance during the school years

By the age of 4–5 years, typically developing children have access to the majority of the morphosyntactic structures of their language (Slobin, 1985, 1992, 1995). None the less, conversations with a 5-year-old are markedly different from those with a child of 10. How do they differ? Whereas we assume a larger and more diverse vocabulary with older children, there are structural differences as well (Nippold, 1998). Language development from kindergarten onward entails refining particular components; for example, complex auxiliary verb morphology (for English) and developing the knowledge and facility to use structures effectively in various discourse contexts, such as telling a story, giving directions, or persuading one's parents. Rather than focusing on morphology intraclausally (e.g., noun–verb agreement), children during the school years acquire more and diverse logical connectives (e.g., "although"), and they are learning how to exploit these elements to establish both cross-clausal connections ("If I *had known* you were coming, I *would have baked* a cake") and hierarchical relationships (as in integrating the local episode of a narrative with its overarching theme (e.g., "While he was searching for his lost frog, he climbed up the tree to look into the hole and an owl swooped out and frightened him"; Bamberg, 1987; Berman & Slobin, 1994; Reilly et al., 2004). Researchers have proposed that this entails a re-organization in which old forms now assume new discourse functions (Berman & Slobin, 1994; Slobin, 1973) or a re-representation of particular structures (Karmiloff-Smith, 1992). To illustrate discourse development in the PL group, below we present data from two discourse genres: a biographical interview and a storybook narrative.

An interview is a locally organized interaction: The experimenter poses a question and the child responds using the vocabulary and grammatical structures of his or her own choosing. Such quasi-naturalistic measures permit us to capture not only the child's everyday language, but also how he or she uses the language; for example, the appropriateness or relevance of a response. In one of the few studies directly comparing language performance of PL children (aged 5–8) to that of adults with comparable lesions, Bates et al. (2001) report data from a biographical interview. Unsurprisingly, the adults displayed the predicted adult profile: Those with LHD displayed contrastive profiles of impairment (including classic differences between fluent and nonfluent aphasia); those adults with RHD (and three nonaphasic adults with LHD) showed fluent but disinhibited, and sometimes empty speech. In contrast, the spontaneous language of the children with PL did not differ from the typically developing (TD) group. Both groups made very few morphological errors, and they used complex sentences with comparable frequency and diversity. As such, the earlier site-specific differences noted above were resolved. With respect to lexical production and diversity, morphology and syntax, that is, core aspects of language, the language of the PL group was comparable to their age-matched typically developing peers in this conversational context.

In this same data set of biographical interviews, we also examined anaphora, or the use of pronouns, as adults with RHD often have difficulty with the coherence of their discourse. Since a pronoun can function as a link to a preceding noun phrase, pronouns represent one linguistic means to connect utterances (Halliday & Hasan, 1976). Interestingly, in examining the children's use of pronouns (Dardier, Reilly, Bates, Delaye, & Laurent-Vannier, 2005), we found that both PL and TD children had many pronouns for which the referent was unclear. However, in the younger group (ages 5–6), those with RPL had a significantly greater frequency of ambiguous pronouns than either those with LPL or the TD group (see Figure 5.1).

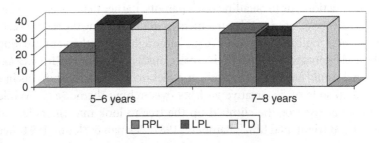

Figure 5.1 Pronominal use in biographical interviews: proportion of non-ambiguous pronouns used in interview. In the younger group, children with RPL use significantly fewer pronouns for which the referent is clear than either children with LPL or the control group. However, by the age of 7–8 years, there are no longer differences between groups.

By the age of 7–8 years, this side-specific difference had resolved, even though both PL and TD children still have many unspecified referents for their pronouns. Considered together, these findings suggest that toddlers and preschoolers with PL are making good progress by school age in acquiring the structures of language, and, unlike the profile for adults with later acquired lesions (e.g., Rasmussen & Milner, 1977; Strauss, Satz, & Wada, 1990), a bilateral brain network is implicated in acquiring language functions. In contrast, as the PL children reach school age, RH injury appears to be associated with difficulties in discourse cohesion; this is true for both children with early lesions and adults with later acquired lesions. However, for the PL children, this deficit appears to resolve with development.

Continuing to investigate language production in school-aged children with PL, Reilly and colleagues (Reilly, Bates, & Marchman, 1998; Reilly et al., 2004) studied spoken narratives by asking children to tell the story from Mayer's wordless picture book, *Frog, where are you?* (Mayer, 1969). Narratives constitute a more challenging discourse genre because they are monologic, as opposed to the interview (above) which is a dialogue. In telling a picture story, the child must choose what information to convey and then use appropriate linguistic structures to organize and convey the significant events in the story. The child must infer the motivations of the characters as well as the theme of the story; and these must be integrated linguistically into the recounting of the narrative. Reporting data from 52 children with PL, Reilly and colleagues found that the younger PL group (4–6 years) told shorter stories, and made significantly more morphological errors than age-matched controls. They also used complex syntax less frequently and used fewer distinct complex syntactic constructions than controls. Overall, there were no significant side-specific differences. As children reach the age of 8–9 years, performance by the PL group was in the low normal range for all linguistic measures (morphology and syntax) as well as those of narrative structure: the number of episodes included in the stories and explicit mention and integration of the theme of the story.

It is important to note that the types of morphological errors of the PL children were similar to those made by younger controls; that is, we did not find any extraordinary errors in the stories of the PL group. These findings suggest that the language acquisition process in the PL group follows a similar developmental course to that of TD children despite being mediated by different underlying brain structures. The findings for productive morphosyntax in this quasi-naturalistic narrative task are mirrored in experimental data reported by Weckerly et al. (2004). They tested English verb morphology using a Tag Question task ("He loves chocolate, *doesn't he?*") and reported performance in the low normal range for the PL group with no left–right differences. To summarize so far, with respect to the acquisition of morphology and syntax in naturalistic and experimental contexts, the PL group as a whole, regardless of lesion side, is performing in the low normal range by mid-school age. Further, to illustrate the degree to which children with PL have mastered English, and how children with LPL do not mirror adults with acquired LH injury, given below are some expressive language samples from the Frog narrative and biographical interview from a child with a large perinatal, left hemisphere, middle cerebral infarct that involves frontal, temporal, parietal, and occipital regions.

Frog story (4 years, 11 months)
The boy is looking at the f'og.
The dog is looking at the frog too.
The ... the boy was s'eeping and the f'og comed out. Then he woked up and he didn't see the f'og.

Biographical interview (7 years)
Oh we really had fun ...
[there's] a dragon ride that's fun and it goes um fast but it doesn't go as fast as a roller coaster.

Returning to the pragmatic use of language, in addition to the pronominal use mentioned above, another index of discourse cohesion is how one uses complex sentences, as these make the relations between propositions explicit. For example, it is grammatical to say: "The boy was sleeping. The frog escaped." However, by adding a subordinate conjunction—for example, "*While* the little boy was sleeping, the frog escaped!"—the simultaneous relation between the events is clear. As they get older, typically developing children use complex syntax more frequently and with more diversity. In the cross-sectional data, the results show a trend wherein the TD and LPL group use more complex syntax in the older groups, but those with RPL appear to plateau and use complex syntax less frequently than those with LPL or the TD group. Complementing their cross-sectional narrative data, Reilly and colleagues (Reilly, Stiles, Wulfeck, & Nass, 2005) reported corroborating longitudinal narrative data from children at three data points (see Figure 5.2): Those with RPL use significantly less complex syntax than those with

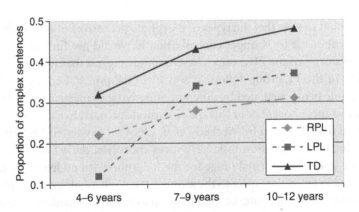

Figure 5.2 Use of complex syntax in narratives: a longitudinal study. In the youngest group, the children with both LPL and RPL are significantly below the TD group in their use of complex sentences. However, the children with LH injury make impressive developmental progress, and at the two older data points, only the differences between the RPL and TD group are significant.

LPL or controls. Why might this be the case? One function of complex sentences in a narrative is to tie or link different episodes in the story or to integrate the ongoing local event with the theme of the narrative, searching for the lost frog; for example: "When the boy climbed the rock to call for his frog, he grabbed the branches, but they were a deer."

Thus, we propose that, similar to the increased use of ambiguous pronouns of the younger children with RPL in the interview data, this decrease in the use of complex syntax in narratives reflects an impairment in *using* language for discourse cohesion. Problems in discourse cohesion are also reported in adults with RHD (Gardner, Brownell, Wapner, & Michelow, 1983; Hough, 1990; Joanette, Goulet, & Hannequin, 1990; Kaplan, Brownell, Jacobs, & Gardner, 1990). However, just as the early pronominal impairment appears to resolve with age for the children, we expect a similar profile of development in the use of complex syntax as well. In responding to questions in an interview or telling a story from pictures, it is the child who chooses the words and structures he or she uses.

Online measures represent an alternative means of assessing language comprehension and grammaticality knowledge. Since online measures not only assess accuracy but also reaction time, they may be more sensitive measures of morphosyntactic abilities. Such tasks provide a measure of processing time and thus provide another dimension to our understanding of children's linguistic abilities. MacWhinney et al. (2000) administered an online battery of detection, recognition and word repetition, and picture-naming tasks and found that, overall, the PL group showed slight impairments and slower reaction times, although these differences resolved with age. Dick and colleagues (Dick, Wulfeck, Krupa-Kwiatkowski, & Bates, 2004) focused on complex syntax and assessed sentence comprehension in PL children; they focused their investigation on active and passive sentences as well as subject and object cleft sentences. For the easier sentences, active and subject clefts, the performance of the PL group was comparable to controls, but they were less accurate on the passive sentences, and their accuracy was significantly lower for the object clefts; reaction times mirrored accuracy. Wulfeck et al. (2004) investigated what school-aged children know about their language—that is, grammatical sensitivity—by asking children to make grammaticality judgments on sentences, half of which included determiner or auxiliary verb violations. The PL group showed lower grammatical sensitivity than controls, but they scored well above chance. Further, both the controls and the PL group improved with age.

In sum, these findings suggest subtle impairments in the processing of complex language for the children with PL; however, the differences largely resolve with age. As in the language production data, the children appear to catch up in individual aspects of language learning, and performance overall resembled that of younger, healthy controls. The similarity of the error patterns in both language production and the online interpretation tasks to those of younger, typically developing children suggests two notable points: (a) the process of language acquisition itself is fairly rigid and constrained, and (b) children with PL are approaching the problem of acquiring a language in a similar manner to typically developing children despite the recruitment of different brain areas.

To summarize: First, in the *acquisition* of grammatical structures, children with early focal brain injury do surprisingly well; their functional everyday use of language is in the normal range by the age of 8–9 years. The trajectory of language development in these children does not map onto that for adults with comparable damage; rather, we see initial delay in children with *either* right or left hemisphere injury, suggesting that acquiring language as opposed to maintaining the system, requires a bilateral cerebral network. After the early delay, language development in the PL group follows the same trajectory as seen in TD children: Early site-specific profiles largely resolve, and by mid-school age, the PL group performs in the low normal range. It is important to note that acquisition is not just "catching up;" rather, at each new level of linguistic challenge, we see initial delay and then subsequent development in mastering grammatical structures.

Second, in contrast to acquiring language, if we focus on how the PL group *uses* language, a different picture is emerging. Evidence is accruing that the right hemisphere mediates discourse integration in children, as is typical of adults. Thus, pragmatically—that is, in recruiting and employing language structures for discourse purposes—the PL children with RH injury subtly mirror the profile of adults with RH injury. Moreover, as in the acquisition of linguistic structures, an iterative profile is apparent with development: Early deficits resolve with age to appear again in new guises in more challenging discourse contexts.

Visuospatial Cognition in Children with Perinatal Brain Injury

Visual pattern processing

The ability to understand and interpret a visually presented pattern requires assessment of both the parts and the overall configuration, and analysis of how the parts are related to form a whole. In adults, the neural system for processing visual pattern information is organized bilaterally in the ventral occipitotemporal lobes (OT). The two cerebral hemispheres work cooperatively, but contribute differently to visual pattern processing. Within this bilateral network, the left OT region is dominant for processing parts or features, and right OT is dominant in processing pattern configuration. Studies with adults have shown that localized injury to this region results in specific disorders of visuospatial functioning (e.g., Arena & Gainotti, 1978; Delis, Kiefner, & Fridlund, 1988; Delis, Robertson, & Efron, 1986; Lamb & Robertson, 1988; McFie & Zangwill, 1960; Piercy, Hecaen, & De Ajuriaguerra, 1960; Ratcliff, 1982; Robertson & Delis, 1986; Robertson, Lamb, & Knight, 1988; Swindell, Holland, Fromm, & Greenhouse, 1988; Wasserstein, Zappulla, Rosen, & Gerstman, 1987). Injury to left OT brain regions results in disorders involving difficulty in defining the parts of a spatial array. Patients with left injury tend to oversimplify spatial patterns and to rely upon overall configural cues while ignoring specific elements. By contrast, patients with right OT lesions have difficulty with the configural aspects of spatial analysis.

They fail to maintain a coherent organization among the elements, focusing on the parts of the pattern without attending to the overall form.

Children in the PL population present with a similar pattern of deficit as those observed among adult stroke patients (Stiles et al., 2006; Stiles, Reilly, Moses, & Paul, 2005; Stiles, Trauner, Engel, & Nass, 1997; Stiles-Davis, Janowsky, Engel, & Nass, 1988; Vicari, Stiles, Stern, & Resca, 1998). Specifically, children with right-sided injury have impairments of configural processing that are evident on a wide variety of tasks, while children with left-sided injury have difficulty with pattern detail. However, their deficits are milder than those observed among adults, and children appear to be able to compensate for their deficits to a degree that adults do not. The fact that children with PL manifest specific deficits of visuospatial processing suggests that the basic organization of the OT system is established early. But the subtle nature of their deficits and their capacity for compensation suggest that the neural system is also capable of adaptive organization. Studies examining visual pattern processing among children ranging in age from the preschool period through adolescence provide supporting evidence for subtle, persistent, but lesion site-specific deficits (Stiles & Nass, 1991; Stiles, Stern, Trauner, & Nass, 1996; Stiles-Davis, 1988; Stiles-Davis et al., 1988; Stiles-Davis, Sugarman, & Nass, 1985).

Studies of visual pattern processing have used "hierarchical" stimuli to examine part–whole processing in both typical and atypical populations (Figure 5.3, model). Hierarchical stimuli are large "global level" forms composed of appropriately arranged "local level" elements (e.g. a global level "H" made up of smaller local level "S"s). When asked to copy such patterns from memory, adults with right OT injury have difficulty with the global level form, while local level processing is impaired by left OT. Children with right or left hemisphere injury show similar patterns of deficit. Among children with right-sided injury, accuracy scores for the local level are comparable to those of age- and IQ-matched control children, but their global level accuracy is significantly lower (Stiles, 2008; Stiles et al., 2006). The children with left-sided injury showed the reverse pattern. These data suggest a dissociation in global–local processing deficits associated with early lateralized brain injury that is similar to that observed with adult onset injury. Further, data from a smaller cohort of children studied longitudinally confirmed the persistence of subtle processing deficits lasting into early adolescence.

Other studies of visuospatial processing confirm the early patterns of impairment, but also suggest that children may compensate for their deficits by developing alternative processing strategies. For example, at the age of 5 years, children with right-sided injury have difficulty with the simple task of drawing a house (Stiles et al., 1997). With development, they master the task but notably the houses they produce are very similar from year to year, suggesting that they have developed a graphic formula. Moreover, when the task is made more challenging, the limitations of that strategy emerge. When typical school-aged children, or children with LH injury, are asked to draw "an impossible house, a house that could not be," the most common response is to alter the spatial configuration of the parts of the house. However, children with right-sided injury

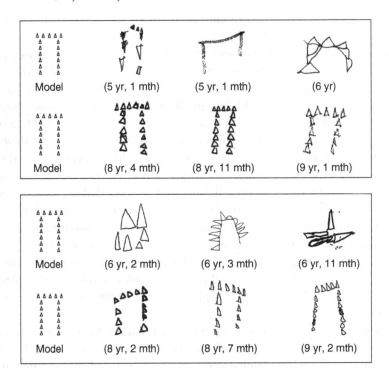

Figure 5.3 Hierarchical forms: the model and longitudinal data from children with LPL and RPL. Top: three children with left hemisphere stroke showing local processing deficit; bottom, three children with right hemisphere stroke showing global processing deficit.

rarely respond in that manner. Rather, they draw a house using their graphic formula, and provide verbal descriptions about why this house is impossible ("the kitchen is so hot you can't go in"; "it is on the moon"), or they draw a dot and say it is a tiny house, or they hand back a blank sheet of paper and say it is invisible. Altering the configuration of the house to make it "impossible" taxes a spatial weakness for which the graphic formula provided compensation. Their solutions to the task of making a house "impossible," while all reasonable and appropriate, diverge from that of typically developing children who most commonly employ a spatial solution.

Evidence for the use of alternative strategies is observed among older children using a more difficult construction task, the Rey–Osterrieth Complex Figure (ROCF; Plate 4, model). The ROCF was originally developed to examine spatial planning in adult patients with neurological disorders. The ROCF is a complex 2-D geometric pattern which is organized around a central rectangle that is symmetrically divided by a set of three bisecting lines. Additional pattern details are positioned both within and surrounding the core rectangle.

In the standard administration, patients are first asked to copy the ROCF with the model present; later, they are asked to reproduce the form from memory. The most efficient strategy for copying the ROCF, the one adopted by most typical adults, is to begin with the core rectangle and bisectors, and then add pattern details. Studies of typically developing children (Akshoomoff & Stiles, 1995) have documented that they do not regularly use this advanced copying strategy until about 10–12 years of age. Younger children parse the figure into smaller units, but the size of the unit increases with age. Six-year-olds typically use a very piecemeal strategy, drawing each small sub-division separately, while older children use progressively larger subunits (quadrants, halves), until finally, by about 10–12 years, their organization strategy centers around the core rectangle.

Children with PL, regardless of side of brain injury, have particular difficulty with the ROCF (Akshoomoff, Feroleto, Doyle, & Stiles, 2002). On the copying version of the task, the performance of all the children in the PL group was worse than normal age-matched controls. Deficits were particularly evident among the 6 to 7-year-olds, the youngest age tested. Their drawings were more poorly organized and included less detail than those of typical controls. Interestingly, there were few notable differences between the drawings of the children with left-sided injury and those with right-sided injury. Data were collected from this sample of children longitudinally between the ages of 6 and 12 years. Across the developmental period, the performance of all children improved considerably, such that by the age of 10 these children produced accurate copies of the ROCF. However, the strategies children used did not change significantly over the developmental period. At 10–12 years of age, the children with early injury persisted in using the piecemeal, immature strategy to generate their copy of the ROCF (see Plate 4, for example). The fact that the left and right lesion groups did not differ in their performance was interesting and unexpected. The ROCF is a challenging task, even for adults. It is likely that the underlying task demands tax both segmentation and integration processes. Thus, a deficit in either process would disrupt performance on the task.

Interestingly, while the copying task did not differentiate the lesion groups, the memory task did. Examination of the copy and memory data obtained when the children were 11–14 years old revealed a striking difference in performance on the two tasks for the children with left- but not right-sided lesions. The memory and copy reproductions for the children with right-sided injury were remarkably similar. For both tasks, children produced accurate copies of the ROCF using a piecemeal process-ing strategy. The memory data from the children with left-sided injury differed dra-matically from their copy data. While the children produced accurate reproductions on the copying task by using a piecemeal strategy, in their memory reproductions the chil-dren organized their drawings around the core rectangle and provided relatively few additional details. The particular processing demands of the memory task thus revealed a characteristic left hemisphere visuospatial processing deficit. Specifically, the children encoded the core, global form but very few other details. By contrast, the copying task captured the children's strategies for compensating for that deficit. With a model avail-able, the children adopted the most immature drawing strategy, but with that approach were able to produce relatively accurate copies of the target form.

Coding of spatial location in children with early focal lesions

Much less work has been done on the processing of dorsal stream spatial information in PL children. A number of studies that have been carried out on normal adults and children indicate that there are hemispheric differences in the coding of locational information. These lateralization studies indicate that the left hemisphere is advantaged at coding categorical spatial relations (e.g., *above/below*), whereas the right hemisphere is advantaged in coding coordinate spatial relations that retain precise metric information about the location of objects and the distance between objects (e.g., Hellige & Michimata, 1989; Koenig, Reiss, & Kosslyn, 1990). Consistent with these findings, Laeng (1994) reports that adult patients with right hemisphere damage are more impaired on coordinate spatial tasks and those with left hemisphere damage are more impaired on metric spatial tasks.

In a recent study, Lourenco and Levine (2007) asked whether young children with pre- or perinatal unilateral lesions show this same pattern. On their task, 3-, 4-, and 5-year-old PL children were shown the locations of different toys on a long, narrow rug, 5 ft (1.5 m) by 8 in (20 cm). Each toy was placed on the rug, and then removed by the experimenter. The child (who stood in different positions relative to the rug) was then asked to place that toy in the location that it had been previously placed. On a similar location reproduction task, typically developing 16 to 24-month-olds showed evidence of hierarchical coding of spatial location information (Huttenlocher, Newcombe, & Sandberg, 1994). That is, not only did they represent information about the exact location of the target object (e.g., fine-grained distance information), they also incorporated information about the larger spatial region (e.g., categorical information) in which the target was located. While the responses of typically developing children are generally highly accurate on this location reproduction task, the responses are also consistently biased toward the center of the space. The bias would only occur if children treated the long, narrow space as a single category with a prototypic location at the center. Although such hierarchical coding leads to bias in responses, when there is uncertainty about the fine-grained distance information, using information about a prototypic location within a category has the effect of increasing overall accuracy (for review, see Huttenlocher & Lourenco, 2007).

Studies of 3 to 5-year-old typically developing children show that they are highly accurate on this task. They show category effects, but unlike younger children, they divide the space into two categories (the left half and the right half), each with a prototype at the center. Thus, they show bias toward the center of each of these categories for object locations within each half (see Huttenlocher & Lourenco, 2007). Similar to typically developing children, 3 to 5-year-olds with early left hemisphere injury showed very accurate performance. However, rather than reflecting two prototypic centers (one for the left half of the space and one for the right half), their category effects were similar to those shown by typically developing 16 to 24-month-olds (i.e., bias toward the center of a single category). Three- and 4-year-old children with RH injury showed much less accurate performance than those with LH injury, but also showed marked category effects of the kind shown by typically developing 16 to 24-month-olds. By 5 years of age, the RH children, like the LH children, were highly accurate and they, too, continued to show the kind of category effects shown by typically developing toddlers. Interestingly, even at 5 years of age, neither the LH nor the RH children showed the more complex category effects that were apparent in the typical 3 to 5-year-old children. We are currently exploring whether this more complex kind of hierarchical coding emerges later in development in the brain-injured children. Thus, similar to the pattern processing deficits described above, children with early brain injury show site-specific deficits in the coding of spatial location. There is also evidence of plasticity as children with RH injury are initially delayed in coding the locations of objects in space, but show improvement across age. It remains an open question whether there is plasticity in the nature of the hierarchical coding used.

Lourenco and Levine (2007) also gave these same PL children a mapping task. On this task, the children were given a strip of paper indicating the location of a toy and were asked to place the toy on the larger rug in the corresponding location. Interestingly, the results obtained on this mapping task were markedly different from those obtained on the spatial location task. In particular, 3- and 4-year-old children with left and right hemisphere injury showed evidence of contralateral neglect. That is, they placed the objects on the side of the rug that was ipsilateral to their lesions, regardless of the location indicated on the map. By 5 years of age, this neglect had resolved in children with RH and LH lesions. Again, resolution of an initial deficit provides evidence of plasticity. However, the symmetrical neglect evident on the mapping task differs from the preponderance of neglect following right hemisphere lesions in adult patients (see also Trauner, 2003). Further, the neglect observed on the mapping task was not observed on the object location task, suggesting a dissociation that depends on how the locations were initially coded.

In summary, these longitudinal data on spatial location coding and visual pattern processing indicate that, with development, children with left- and right-sided injury show both early deficits and considerable behavioral improvement, eventually achieving ceiling level performance on many spatial tasks, at least when accuracy is used as the measure of performance. However, the time course over which this improvement occurs is often protracted. Further, when process is used as the metric of performance, it becomes evident that the PL children frequently adopt compensatory strategies to facilitate performance, and when those strategies are taxed, persistent deficits in performance are again observed (Akshoomoff & Stiles, 2003).

Emotion Processing

Studies of patients with unilateral lesions acquired during adulthood, as well as those from healthy adults, overwhelmingly find that the right hemisphere, especially frontoparietal regions, are critical for emotion recognition (e.g., Adolphs, Tranel, & Damasio, 2003; Blonder, Bowers, & Heilman, 1991; Borod, 1992, 1993; Borod et al.,

1998; Damasio, Adolphs, & Damasio, 2003; De Renzi, Perani, Carlesimo, Silveri, & Fazio, 1994; Ley & Bryden, 1979; Stone & Valentine, 2003). Moreover, models of face and emotion processing propose dissociations in the neural systems responsible for processing face identity from other aspects of face processing, namely, discrimination, labeling, and recognition of facial affect (Bowers, Bauer, Coslett, & Heilman, 1985; Bowers & Heilman, 1984; Bruce & Young, 1986; Haxby, Hoffman, & Gobbini, 2000; Tranel, Damasio, & Damasio, 1988). Such findings have been largely confirmed by structural and functional imaging (e.g., Adolphs, Damasio, Tranel, Cooper, & Damasio, 2000). In this section, we first present findings on facial recognition in school-aged children and adolescents; we then look at the emergence of emotional expression in infants with PL.

Face processing

Faces are critical in both conveying and interpreting emotional signals. As such, how one processes faces per se can influence the processing of emotional information on the face. Typically, face processing is mediated by occipitotemporal regions of the brain, including the fusiform gyrus: As a spatial pattern, such processing relies more on holistic and configural processing than featural processing, at least by school age (Carey & Diamond, 1977; de Haan, 2001). As such, many studies report an RH bias for face processing; in fact, infants have shown an RH bias for face processing as early as 4 months of age (de Schonen & Mathivet, 1990). A study of face processing in a small sample of children with PL (Mancini, de Schonen, Deruelle, & Massoulier, 1994) suggests long-term face-processing deficits. In a larger sample of PL children and adolescents, Paul et al. (2007) conducted a reaction-time study of face matching to examine whether the ability to identify faces might be differentially affected in children with PL. Children were presented with a series of three black-and-white face photographs, then two memory set items, followed by a probe. Participants were asked to indicate whether the probe face matched one of the faces in the memory set. Data from 42 participants between 9 and 23 years of age matched for age and IQ were studied (RH = 11; LH = 15; controls = 16). The groups differed significantly on both accuracy and reaction time. Children with RH injury were significantly less accurate and slower than controls, while children with LH injury were marginally less accurate than controls, but did not differ in speed. The two lesion groups did not differ from one another in accuracy or reaction time. These data suggest a face-processing deficit in both groups, which is somewhat more severe in the RH group.

Expression of emotion in infants and toddlers with perinatal brain injury

As typically developing children approach their first birthday, they produce their first words and use facial expressions both to convey and to interpret emotions. To characterize emotional expression in infants and toddlers with PL, we have conducted naturalistic studies of emotional facial expression and vocalizations using videotaped

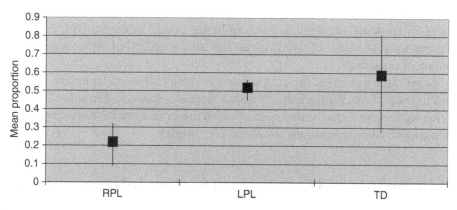

Figure 5.4 Expressing positive emotions: smiles in response to maternal bids for interaction. Typically developing children and children with LPL smile significantly more often than children with RPL. Note also the range of expressivity in the TD group compared to the children with brain injury. Both the LPL and the RPL groups demonstrate more homogeneous profiles than their typically developing controls.

recordings of mother–infant dyads in free play (Reilly, Stiles, Larsen, & Trauner, 1995). Focusing on facial expressions, 24 infants (6–22 months; 6 with RPL; 6 with LPL; and 12 age- and gender-matched controls) were videotaped. The Facial Action Coding System (FACS; Ekman & Friesen, 1978) was used to code infant and maternal facial expressions. As an index of expressivity, infants' and toddlers' positive responses to their mothers' bids for interaction were coded. All children smiled in response to their mothers; however, those with left posterior injury and controls smiled easily and often, but those with right posterior injury smiled infrequently (Figure 5.4). These data were further confirmed by longitudinal case studies; together they suggest that the right hemisphere mediates emotional expression from as early as 6 months of age and that valence (positive/negative) is a significant factor in the early organization of emotions. Such findings are consistent with infant perceptual data that show a right hemisphere bias for face perception from 4–9 months of age (de Schonen & Mathivet, 1990).

Infants and toddlers use not only the face, but also the vocal channel to express emotions. Reilly and colleagues (Reilly, Anderson, & Martinez, 2007) have used free-play mother–infant interactions as a context to collect infant vocalizations from 23 infants with PL (13 LPL, 10 RPL) aged 9–16 months. Listening to 2,200 vocalizations extracted from videotapes, independent judges evaluated the children's vocal productions as positive, negative, or ambiguous in quality. As in the facial-expression data, control infants and infants with LPL produced more positive than negative vocalizations. The RPL group produced significantly more negative vocalizations than either of the other groups. The children with RPL who also had basal ganglia involvement were most responsible for this profile. These findings are complemented by a study of temperament in the PL group that found increased negative affect in infants and toddlers with RH injury (Nass & Koch, 1987). In sum, the expressive data are consistent across productive channels for emotion: face and voice. They suggest that the neural sub-strates for emotion are established at least by the middle of the first year of life, and, importantly, that profile of deficit is not modality specific, but rather general to the domain of emotion.

The previous sections of this chapter were devoted to the developmental profiles in the PL group of specific cognitive domains: language, space, and emotion. In the fol-lowing sections, we examine two areas in which two or more of these cognitive systems are recruited: labeling emotions and developing literacy.

Language, Spatial Cognition, and Emotion: Labeling Emotions

A traditional measure of evaluating emotion processing involves supplying emo-tional labels for static photographs of people's faces conveying different emotional expressions. As such, this task draws on three cognitive systems, requiring (a) spatial analysis, (b) recognition of the emotion, and (c) recruiting the appropriate linguistic form. Free labeling data from 24 PL and 24 TD children aged 4–8 demonstrate how characteristic behavioral profiles in each of these systems play a role (Reilly, Charten, Stiles, del Guercio, & Nass, 2005b). In this task, the stimuli included photographs of the same woman demonstrating the following emotional expressions: happy, sad, angry, afraid, surprised, and neutral. For the TD children, there is a slight improve-ment in overall performance with age, and, to our surprise, the children with RPL generally perform like controls. Interestingly, it is the younger children (aged 4–5) with LPL who fare the worst (see Figure 5.5) in labeling emotional expressions. Even though those children with RPL appear to have deficits in producing emotional facial expressions in infancy, it is the young children with LPL who are impaired in labeling emotional expressions.

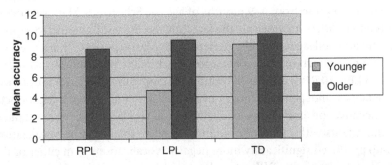

Figure 5.5 Labeling facial expressions: all emotions together. In the younger age group (4:00–5:11 years), the children with RPL perform comparably to controls, but those with LPL perform signifi-cantly worse than either children with RPL or TD. However, at the older data point (age 6:00–7:11 years) performance is comparable in all groups.

Several possible explanations come to mind: The performance of the LPL group may reflect a subtle deficit in lexical production as noted above, or perhaps it may be a reflection of their problems with isolating and identifying features within a spatial array, as discussed above (Stiles et al., 2006). Importantly, the early deficit evident at 4–5 years is no longer apparent in the older group (ages 6–7), again demonstrating the plasticity of development following early lesions.

Literacy: The Intersection of Language and Space

Literacy is the major academic challenge for school-aged children. A traditional definition of literacy includes the ability to read and write. Thus, the acquisition of literacy involves learning to map spoken language onto its visual counterpart. For beginning readers, the task involves learning letter forms, learning letter–sound correspondences, and using these skills, along with language comprehension skills, to decode and understand written texts. Overall, reading involves the coordination of orthographic, phonologic, semantic, syntactic, metalinguistic, and comprehension skills (e.g., Snow, Burns, & Griffin, 1998). Thus, reading achievement is related to both the acquisition of code-related skills (letter–sound correspondences) and also to oral language comprehension skills (e.g., Gough & Tunner, 1986; Joshi, Williams, & Wood, 1998; NICHD Early Child Care Research Network, 2005; Storch & Whitehurst, 2002). Code-related skills in the preschool years, including phonologic awareness and letter identification, are significant predictors of later reading achievement (e.g., Whitehurst & Lonigan, 1998) as are early language skills, including lexical, syntactic, and narrative skills (e.g., Dickinson & Tabors, 2001; NICHD, 2005; Storch & Whitehurst, 2002).

Whereas a large body of literature exists on reading and its development in typically developing youngsters, much less is known about the development of reading in children with early unilateral brain injury. The vast majority of studies have focused on the development of language skills, mainly in the toddler and preschool years, whereas literacy acquisition occurs during primary school. The little information that exists about the development of literacy skills in this population presents a mixed picture, perhaps due to the variety of different kinds of reading assessments that have been used. Using the Woodcock–Johnson Psycho-Education Battery, Aram and Ekelman (1988) found that children with right hemisphere lesions performed significantly lower than control children on the Reading and Math Clusters as well as the Written Language Cluster (dictation and proofing), whereas children with left hemisphere lesions performed significantly lower than control children only on the Written Language Cluster. Woods and Carey (1979) administered a reading test (Sentence Completion test from Boston Diagnostic Aphasia Examination) and a spelling test to children with pre- or perinatal left hemisphere injury. Relative to controls, the children with early left hemisphere injury were significantly impaired on the spelling test, but not on the reading test. Of note, the reading comprehension tests used by Aram and Ekelman and Woods and Carey involved reading a sentence and selecting the best completion from multiple alternatives. This type of "cloze" procedure has been shown to load more heavily on word recognition/decoding skills than on language comprehension skills, whereas the reverse loading pattern is found for measures involving passage reading followed by comprehension questions (e.g., Bowey, 1986; Cutting & Scarborough, 2006; Francis, Fletcher, Catts, & Tomblin, 2005). Thus, it is possible that children with PL have greater difficulty with the kind of reading tasks that load more heavily on oral language comprehension skills, but this issue is in need of investigation.

Booth et al. (2000) found that children with large pre- or perinatal left hemisphere lesions scored lower on reading decoding tasks (e.g., Woodcock–Johnson Word Identification and Word Attack) than those with smaller lesions, even though the receptive vocabularies of the children with large lesions were in the normal range. Based on this finding, Booth et al. suggest that early developmental plasticity may be of more benefit to earlier developing language skills than to reading. Consistent with this possibility, Levine and Fisher (2007) have found that school-aged children with early brain injury (*n* = 17; 13 with left hemisphere injury, 4 with right hemisphere injury) performed significantly below age norms on reading decoding and compre-hension tests even when they performed within the normal range on verbal IQ tests at 6–9 years of age.

Whereas reading is the recognition of language in the visual modality, writing requires its creation and production. In typically developing children, preschoolers already distinguish writing from drawing and numerals (Tolchinsky, 2003), but it is not until the age of 5–6 that they acquire the alphabetic principle (Tolchinsky, 2003; Treiman & Bourassa, 2000). This is the concept that letter strings (words) have particu-lar meaning, and specifically that graphemes (letters) represent the phonemes of a word. Typically, children map the sounds of English onto their graphic forms (letters) in a series of stages (Sprenger-Charolles & Bechennec, 2004) wherein, first, entire syllables are represented by one letter (e.g., *car* may be written as *k*), then by multiple consonants (*car* is now *kr*); next, vowels appear, (*kar*); and, finally, English spelling conventions emerge: *car*. Unlike Spanish or Turkish, where sound–letter correspondences are regu-lar with one-to-one mapping, the English spelling system is a holdover from the pro-nunciation of fifteenth-century English. Our pronunciation has changed dramatically, but our spelling has not. The result is an opaque relationship between the spoken and written forms (consider *knife, lamb, phone, ghost, wreath* vs *read, where* vs *wear*, and *box* vs *socks* or *weight* vs *wait*).

Earlier studies investigating writing in PL groups have used standardized achieve-ment tests to assess writing. As noted above, on standardized tests, both the Aram and Ekelman (1988) and Woods and Carey (1979) studies found that children with left hemisphere injury had more difficulty with dictation and spelling than those with right hemisphere injury or controls. A more recent study by Frith and Vargha-Khadem (2000) looked at both French- and English-speaking children with unilateral brain injury (both early and during childhood). They found no significant differences in spelling performance according to lesion site, or the age at which the lesion was acquired; however, they did identify a sex-by-side interaction. Boys with left hemisphere injury performed more poorly than those with right hemisphere injury (who performed like controls), whereas girls showed the reverse profile but did not differ significantly from controls. Such findings suggest that sexual dimorphism may play a role in literacy skills from early in life.

Taking a broader view of written discourse, we have begun to trace writing development in a group of PL children aged 8–16 (Reilly, Stiles, Fenson, & Nass, 2005) by asking them first "to tell about a time when they had a problem either at home or at school, how it started, what happened, and how it ended." After the child has told a story, the child is asked to write the same story. Constructing a narrative spontaneously is a more challenging task than telling a story from pictures (as in the frog story above). As in the frog story data, in this older group of children, there were no significant right–left differences; moreover, in the spoken personal narratives there were *no* significant differences between the stories of the PL and TD groups with respect to story length (in propositions), frequency of complex sentences, diversity of complex syntax, nor in the structure of the narratives, although the children with PL required more prompts to provide a resolution to their spoken narrative.

The most striking differences in the profiles of PL and TD children become apparent when spoken and written narrative texts are compared. Whereas the spoken stories do not differ significantly across groups with respect to linguistic measures, in the written form, the stories of both groups are shorter than the spoken form, but those of the PL group are significantly shorter than those of the TD group. With respect to recruiting complex sentences, we found that written stories from the PL group have proportions of complex syntax that are in the low normal range. Interestingly, when we calculated the *types* of complex syntactic structures recruited by both groups, we found no differences across groups in either spoken or written forms.

An analysis of narrative structure (that is, the degree to which children include basic components of narrative: setting, problem, complication, and resolution) reveals no site-specific differences. Moreover, neither group, PL or TD, tells or writes narratives that include all components. However, in the spoken modality, the stories from the PL group do not differ significantly from those of the TD children. In contrast, in the written modality, the TD group performs slightly better than in the oral modality, while the PL group fares worse in the written than the oral, reflecting the challenges that writing presents to these children. Thus, whereas writing as a process permits planning and revision, without the online pressures of spoken language, it appears that only the typically developing children were able to take advantage of the possibilities offered by the written modality.

Gradients of Plasticity: Language, Space, and Emotion

Looking across the three behavioral domains discussed above—language, spatial cognition, and emotion—the profiles of the PL group are distinctive, and responses to our original questions will differ for each of the domains.

For *language acquisition* (that is, acquiring the morphology and syntax of language), children with either right *or* left hemisphere injury are initially delayed, and a bilateral network is implicated for the acquisition of language. Their profile is unlike adults with late acquired strokes. Site-specific profiles evident early in development resolve, and by mid-school age, language performance for the PL group overall is in the low normal range. Importantly, children with early left hemisphere injury do not mirror the pattern for adults with acquired left hemisphere injury. However, if we consider *how language is used* in discourse, children with RPL are more likely to resemble the pattern seen in patients with right hemisphere injury acquired in adulthood, albeit more subtly. At different developmental stages, there is evidence of impairment with subsequent development in the integration of discourse. Although the basic nature of the integrative deficit appears to be persistent, how it manifests is dependent on the child's level of development.

In the *domain of spatial cognition*, although we see clear evidence of development, the children's profiles much more closely mirror that of adults with similar injury. This profile is evident for spatial analysis of patterns and for the coding of spatial location. The profile is one of deficit and subsequent development to achieve specific spatial milestones; however, the characteristic deficits are again revealed with increasingly challenging tasks.

Similar to the visuospatial profile, for the domain of *face processing and emotion*, the PL children again follow the adult path for both simple face matching and for processing emotions. Children with right hemisphere injury are significantly more impaired on simple face-matching tasks than controls, although it is notable that children with LH injury also have subtle face-processing deficits. Early RH injury also impacts at least the early development of affective processing as is evident in a decrease in the production of positive and an increase in the production of negative facial expressions and vocalizations in this group of children.

Finally, considering tasks that tap multiple cognitive systems (e.g., labeling emotions), if we probe at the particular developmental point at which the necessary skill is still developing, deficits within the individual domains become apparent. Decrements in later developing tasks drawing on multiple cognitive systems, such as reading and writing, may reflect declining plasticity and/or the result of decreased functional neural tissue to handle increased processing demands. By looking at development across several cognitive systems, we see strong evidence for development in all three cognitive domains. None the less, the three functional systems reflect differing degrees of developmental flexibility with language acquisition showing delay regardless of lesion site and then developing fairly rapidly; in contrast, spatial cognition and emotion mirror the adult model, albeit more subtly. Such contrastive behavioral profiles suggest differing degrees of brain plasticity: The findings for language acquisition, but not language use, provide clear evidence that, although perhaps not optimal, multiple brain regions can assume core language functions. This does not appear to be the case for either visuospatial cognition or for emotion processing.

Several possible explanations come to mind for these differential profiles. The first is an evolutionary perspective: Emotion and space are older systems, whereas language represents an evolutionarily newer invention. As our late colleague, Elizabeth Bates often noted, "language is a new system invented from old parts." It may also be the case that systems that are dependent on a particular sensory modality (e.g., face perception) are by definition less flexible than those, such as language, that are amodal (language exists in spoken, signed, or written forms). Another finding that emerged from a cross-domain perspective is the possibility of a more general characterization of the children with RH injury. If we consider their recurrent problems with discourse cohesion and their visuospatial impairments, both might be characterized as an integrative deficit that persists across cognitive domains, reflecting the global processing of the right hemisphere.

In sum, children with PL provide a unique context for investigating neuroplasticity. Tracing development across cognitive systems in the PL group has demonstrated that neuroplasticity is not a unidimensional construct. Rather, a gradient of plasticity exists, both across, as well as within, cognitive systems. For example, for language acquisition, the developing brain shows impressive flexibility; however, even within language, if we focus on its use in discourse, we see differential degrees of adaptive flexibility. As such, chronicling behavior in the PL group provides us with important clues as to which specific brain areas might be privileged for specific cognitive functions, as well as those for which the developing brain is more flexible.

Acknowledgments

This work was partially supported by grants: NIH-NINDS Grant P50 NS22343, NIH-NIDCD Grant P50-DC01289, NIH-NICHD Grant R01-HD25077, and NIH-NICHD Grant PO1 HD040605. We are especially grateful to the many families who have participated in these studies and to S. F. Lourenco for her helpful comments.

References

Adolphs, R., Damasio, H., Tranel, D., Cooper, G., & Damasio, A. R. (2000). A role for somatosensory cortices in the visual recognition of emotion as revealed by three-dimensional lesion mapping. *Journal of Neuroscience, 20*(7), 2683–2690.

Adolphs, R., Tranel, D., & Damasio, A. R. (2003). Dissociable neural systems for recognizing emotions. *Brain and Cognition, 52*(1), 61–69.

Akshoomoff, N. A., Feroleto, C. C., Doyle, R. E., & Stiles, J. (2002). The impact of early unilateral brain injury on perceptual organization and visual memory. *Neuropsychologia, 40*, 539–561.

Akshoomoff, N. A., & Stiles, J. (1995). Developmental trends in visuospatial analysis and planning: I. Copying a complex figure. *Neuropsychology, 9*, 364–377.

Akshoomoff, N. A., & Stiles, J. (2003). Children's performance on the ROCF and the development of spatial analysis. In J. A. Knight & E. Kaplan (Eds.), *The handbook of Rey-Osterrieth complex figure usage: Clinical and research applications* (pp. 393–409). Lutz, FL: Psychological Assessment Resources.

Aram, D. M., & Ekelman, B. L. (1986). Cognitive profiles of children with early onset unilateral lesions. *Developmental Neuropsychology, 2,* 155–172.

Aram, D. M., & Ekelman, B. L. (1988). Scholastic aptitude and achievement among children with unilateral brain lesions. *Neuropsychologia, 26*(6), 903–916.

Arena, R., and Gainotti, G. (1978). Constructional apraxia and visuoperceptive disabilities in relation to laterality of cerebral lesions. *Cortex, 14*(4), 463–473.

Ballantyne, A. O., Spilkin, A., & Trauner, D. (in press). Language outcome after perinatal stroke: Does side matter?

Bamberg, M. (1987). *The acquisition of narratives.* Berlin: Mouton de Gruyter.

Banich, M. T., Levine, S. C., Kim, H., & Huttenlocher, P. (1990). The effects of developmental factors on IQ in hemiplegic children. *Neuropsychologia, 28,* 35–47.

Basser, L. S. (1962). Hemiplegia of early onset and the faculty of speech with special reference to the effects of hemispherectomy. *Brain, 85,* 427–460.

Bates, E., & Dick, F. (2002). Language, gesture and the developing brain. *Developmental Psychobiology, 40*(3), 293–310.

Bates, E., Reilly, J., Wulfeck, B., Dronkers, N., Opie, M., Fenson, J., et al. (2001). Differential effects of unilateral lesions on language production in children and adults. *Brain and Language, 79*(2), 223–265.

Bates, E., Thal, D., Trauner, D., Fenson, J., Aram, D., Eisele, J., et al. (1997). From first words to grammar in children with focal brain injury. In D. Thal & J. Reilly (Eds.), Special Issue on Origins of Communication Disorders. *Developmental Neuropsychology, 13*(3), 275–343.

Bates, E., Vicari, S., & Trauner, D. (1999). Neural mediation of language development: Perspectives from lesion studies of infants and children. In H. Tager-Flusberg (Ed.), *Neurodevelopmental disorders: Developmental cognitive neuroscience* (pp. 533–581). Cambridge, MA: MIT Press.

Bax, M., Tydeman, C., & Flormark, O. (2006). Clinical and MRI correlates of CP. *Journal of the American Medical Association, 296,* 1602–1608.

Berman, R., & Slobin, D. (1994). *Relating events in narrative.* Hillsdale, NJ: Lawrence Erlbaum.

Blakemore, S.-J., & Choudhury, S. (2006). Development of the adolescent brain: Implications for executive function and social cognition. *Journal of Child Psychology and Psychiatry, 47*(3–4), 296–312.

Blonder, L. X., Bowers, D., & Heilman, K. M. (1991). The role of the right hemisphere in emotional communication. *Brain, 114*(3), 1115–1127.

Booth, J. R., MacWhinney, B., Thulborn, K. R., Sacco, K., Voyvodic, J. T., & Feldman, H. M. (2000). Developmental and lesion effects in brain activation during sentence comprehension and mental rotation. *Developmental Neuropsychology, 18,* 139–169.

Borod, J. C. (1992). Interhemispheric and intrahemispheric control of emotion: A focus on unilateral brain damage. *Journal of Consulting and Clinical Psychology, 60,* 339–348.

Borod, J. C. (1993). Cerebral mechanisms underlying facial, prosodic, and lexical emotional expression: A review of neuropsychological studies and methodological issues. *Neuropsycholoy, 4,* 445–463.

Borod, J. C., Cicero, B. A., Obler, L. K., Welkowitz, J., Erhan, H. M., Santschi, C., et al. (1998). Right hemisphere emotional perception: Evidence across multiple channels. *Neuropsychology, 12*(3), 446–458.

Bowers, D., Bauer, R. M., Coslett, H. B., & Heilman, K. M. (1985). Processing of faces by patients with unilateral hemisphere lesions. *Brain and Cognition, 4,* 258–272.

Bowers, D., & Heilman, K. M. (1984). Dissociation between the processing of affective and nonaffective faces: A case study. *Journal of Clinical Neuropsychology, 6,* 367–379.

Bowey, J. (1986). Syntactic awareness in relation to reading skill and ongoing reading comprehension monitoring. *Journal of Experimental Child Psychology, 41,* 282–299.

Brasky, K., Nikolas, M., Meanwell, C., Levine, S., & Goldin-Meadow, S. (2005). *Language development in children with unilateral brain injury: Effects of lesion size*. Poster presented at the Symposium on Research in Child Language Disorders, Madison, Wisconsin.

Bruce, V., & Young, A. (1986). Understanding face recognition. *British Journal of Psychology, 77*(3), 305.

Carey, S., & Diamond, R. (1977). From piecemeal to configurational representation of faces. *Science, 195*(4275), 312–314.

Carlsson, M., Hagberg, G., & Olsson, M. (2003). Clinical and aetiological aspects of epilepsy in children with cerebral palsy. *Developmental Medicine and Child Neurology, 45*(6), 371–376.

Chilosi, A. M., Cipriani, P., Bertuccelli, B., Pfanner, P. L., & Cioni, P. G. (2001). Early cognitive and communication development in children with focal brain lesions. *Journal of Child Neurology, 16*(5), 309–316.

Chilosi, A. M., Cipriani, P., Brovedani, P., Brizzolara, D., Ferretti, G., & Pfanner, P. L. (2005). Atypical language lateralization and early linguistic development in children with focal brain lesions. *Developmental Medicine and Child Neurology, 47*, 725–730.

Cutting, L. E., & Scarborough, H. S. (2006). Prediction of reading comprehension: Relative contributions of word recognition, language proficiency, and other cognitive skills can depend on how comprehension is measured. *Scientific Studies of Reading, 10*(3), 277–299.

Dall'Oglio, A. M., Bates, E., Volterra, V., Di Capua, M., & Pezzini, G. (1994). Early cognition, communication and language in children with focal brain injury. *Developmental Medicine and Child Neurology, 36*, 1076–1098.

Damasio, A. R., Adolphs, R., & Damasio, H. (2003). The contributions of the lesion method to the functional neuroanatomy of emotion. In R. J. Davidson, K. R. Scherer, & H. H. Goldsmith (Eds.), *Handbook of affective sciences* (pp. 66–92). Oxford University Press.

Dardier, V., Reilly, J., Bates, E., Delaye, C., & Laurent-Vannier, A. (2005). La cohesion du discours de chez les enfants et les adolescents cerbroleses: Analyse de l'usage des pronoms et des connecteurs. *Cahiers d'Acquisition et Pathologie du Langage (CALAP), 24*, 101–114.

Delis, D. C., Kiefner, M. G., & Fridlund, A. J. (1988). Visuospatial dysfunction following unilateral brain damage: Dissociations in hierarchical hemispatial analysis. *Journal of Clinical and Experimental Neuropsychology, 10*(4), 421–431.

Delis, D. C., Robertson, L. C., & Efron, R. (1986). Hemispheric specialization of memory for visual hierarchical stimuli. *Neuropsychologia, 24*(2), 205–214.

Dennis, M., & Kohn, B. (1975). Comprehension of syntax in infantile hemiplegics after cerebral hemidecortication. *Brain and Language, 2*, 472–482.

Dennis, M., & Whitaker, H. A. (1976). Language acquisition following hemidecortication: Linguistic superiority of the left over the right hemisphere. *Brain and Language, 3*, 404–433.

De Renzi, E., Perani, D., Carlesimo, G. A., Silveri, M. C., & Fazio, F. (1994). Prosopagnosia can be associated with damage confined to the right hemisphere: An MRI and PET study and a review of the literature. *Neuropsychologia, 32*(8), 893–902.

Dick, F., Wulfeck, B., Krupa-Kwiatkowski, M., & Bates, E. (2004). The development of complex sentence interpretation in typically developing children compared with children with specific language impairments or early unilateral focal lesions. *Developmental Science, 7*, 360–377.

Dickinson, D. K., & Tabors, P. O. (Eds.). (2001). *Beginning literacy with language: Young children learning at home and school*. Baltimore: Paul H. Brookes.

Eisele, J., & Aram, D. (1995). Lexical and grammatical development in children with early hemisphere damage: A cross-sectional view from birth to adolescence. In P. Fletcher & B. MacWhinney (Eds.), *The handbook for child language* (pp. 664–689). Oxford: Blackwell.

Ekman, P., & Friesen, W. V. (1978). *Facial action coding system: Investigator's guide* (Vol. 2). Palo Alto: Consulting Psychologists Press.

Feldman, H. M. (1994). Language development after early brain injury: A replication study. In H. Tager-Flusberg (Ed.), *Constraints on language acquisition: Studies of atypical children* (pp. 75–90). Hillsdale, NJ: Lawrence Erlbaum.

Feldman, H. M. (2005). Language learning with an injured brain. *Language Learning and Development, 1*(3&4), 265–288.

Feldman, H. M., Holland, A. L., Kemp, S. S., & Janosky, J. E. (1992). Language development after unilateral brain injury. *Brain and Language, 42*, 89–102.

Fenson, L. D., Dale, P., Reznick, J. S., Thal, D., Bates, E., Hartung, J., et al. (1993). *MacArthur–Bates communicative development inventories: User's guide and technical manual.* San Diego, CA: Singular.

Francis, D. J., Fletcher, J. M., Catts, H. W., & Tomblin, J. B. (2005). Dimensions affecting the assessment of reading comprehension. In S. G. Paris & S. A. Stahl (Eds.), *Children's reading comprehension and assessment* (pp. 369–394). Mahwah, NJ: Lawrence Erlbaum.

Frith, U., & Vargha-Khadem, F. (2000). Are there sex differences in the brain basis of literacy related skills? Evidence from reading and spelling impairments after early unilateral brain damage. *Neuropsychologia, 39*, 1485–1488.

Gardner, H., Brownell, H., Wapner, W., & Michelow, D. (1983). Missing the point: The role of the right hemisphere in the processing of complex linguistic materials. In E. Perceman (Ed.), *Cognitive processing in the right hemisphere* (pp. 169–191). New York: Academic Press.

Goldman, P. (1971). Functional development of the prefrontal cortex in early life and the problem of neuronal plasticity. *Experimental Neurology, 32*, 366–387.

Goldman, P. (1974). An alternative to developmental plasticity: Heterology of CNS structures in infants and adults. In D. G. Stein, J. J. Rosen, & N. Butters (Eds.), *Plasticity and recovery of function in the central nervous system* (pp. 149–174). New York: Academic Press.

Goldman-Rakic, P., Isseroff, A., Schwartz, M., & Bugbee, N. (1983). The neurobiology of cognitive development. In M. Haith & J. Campos (Eds.), *Handbook of child psychology.* Vol. 2: *Infancy and developmental psychobiology* (pp. 281–344). New York: Wiley.

Gough, P. B., & Tunner, W. E. (1986). Decoding reading and reading disability. *Remedial and Special Education, 7*, 6–10.

de Haan, M. (2001). The neuropsychology of face processing during infancy and childhood. In C. A. Nelson & M. Luciana (Eds.), *Handbook of developmental cognitive neuroscience* (pp. 3831–3398). Cambridge, MA: MIT Press.

Halliday, M. A. K., & Hasan, R. (1976). *Cohesion in English.* London: Longman.

Hart, B., & Risley, T. (1995). *Meaningful differences.* Baltimore: Brookes.

Haxby, J. V., Hoffman, E. A., & Gobbini, M. I. (2000). The distributed human neural system for face perception. *Trends in Cognitive Sciences, 4*, 223–233.

Hellige, J. B., & Michimata, C. (1989). Categorization versus distance: Hemispheric differences for processing spatial information. *Memory and Cognition, 17*, 770–776.

Hough, M. (1990). Narrative comprehension in adults with right and left hemisphere brain damage: Theme organization. *Brain and Language, 38*, 253–277.

Huttenlocher, J., & Lourenco, S. F. (2007). Using spatial categories to reason about location. In J. Plumert & J. Spencer (Eds.), *The emerging spatial mind* (pp. 3–24). New York: Oxford University Press.

Huttenlocher, J., Newcombe, N., & Sandberg, E. H. (1994). The coding of spatial location in young children. *Cognitive Psychology, 27*, 115–147.

Isaacs, E. B., Christie, D., Vargha-Khadem, F., & Mishkin, M. (1996). Effects of hemispheric side of injury, age at injury, and presence of seizure disorder on functional ear and hand asymmetries in hemiplegic children. *Neuropsychologia, 34,* 127–137.

Joanette, Y., Goulet, P., & Hannequin, D. (1990). *Right hemisphere and verbal communication.* New York: Springer Verlag.

Joshi, R. M., Williams, K. A., & Wood, J. R. (1998). Predicting reading comprehension from listening comprehension: Is this the answer to the IQ debate? In C. Hume & R. M. Joshi (Eds.), *Reading and spelling: Development and disorders* (pp. 319–327). Mahwah, NJ: Lawrence Erlbaum.

Kaplan, J., Brownell, H., Jacobs, J., & Gardner, H. (1990). The effects of right hemisphere damage on the pragmatic interpretation of conversational remarks. *Brain and Language, 38,* 315–333.

Karmiloff-Smith, A. (1992). *Beyond modularity: A developmental perspective on cognitive science.* Cambridge, MA: MIT Press.

Kennard, M. (1940). Relation of age to motor impairment in man and in subhuman primates. *Archives of Neurology and Psychiatry, 44,* 377–397.

Kirton, A., & deVeber, G. (2006). Cerebral palsy secondary to perinatal ischemic stroke. *Clinics in Perinatology, 33*(2), 367–386.

Koenig, O., Reiss, L. P., & Kosslyn, S. M. (1990). The development of spatial relation representations: Evidence from studies of cerebral lateralization. *Journal of Experimental Child Psychology, 50,* 119–130.

Kolb, B., & Wishaw, I. Q. (1985). Neonatal frontal lesions in hamsters impair species-typical behaviors and reduce brain weight and neocortical thickness. *Behavioral Neuroscience, 99,* 691–706.

Kwong, K., & Wong, Y. C. (2004). MRI in 127 children with spastic cerebral palsy. *Pediatrics, 21,* 172–176.

Laeng, B. (1994). Lateralization of categorical and coordinate spatial functions: A study of unilateral stroke patients. *Journal of Cognitive Neuroscience, 6,* 189–203.

Lamb, M. R., & Robertson, C. R. (1988). The processing of hierarchical stimuli: Effects of retinal locus, locational uncertainty, and stimulus identity. *Perception and Psychophysics, 44*(2), 172–181.

Lee, J., Croen, L. A., & Lindan, C. (2005). Predictors of outcome in perinatal arterial stroke: A population study. *Annals of Neurology, 58,* 301–308.

Lenneberg, E. H. (1967). *Biological foundations of language.* New York: John Wiley.

Levine, S. C., Brasky, K., & Nikolas, M. (2005). *The role of gesture in language development in brain injured children.* Paper presented to the International Association for the Study of Child Language, Berlin, Germany.

Levine, S. C., & Fisher, J. (2007). *Reading skills in children with early unilateral brain injury.* Manuscript in preparation.

Levine, S. C., Huttenlocher, P. R., Banich, M. T., & Duda, E. (1987). Factors affecting cognitive functioning of hemiplegic children. *Developmental Medicine and Child Neurology, 27,* 27–35.

Levine, S. C., Kraus, R., Alexander, E., Suriyakham, L. W., & Huttenlocher, P. R. (2005). IQ decline following early unilateral brain injury: A longitudinal study. *Brain and Cognition, 59,* 114–123.

Levine, S. C., Özçaliskan, S., & Goldin-Meadow, S. (2007). *Conveying linguistic constructions in gesture and speech: Plasticity after early unilateral lesions.* Manuscript in preparation.

Ley, R. G., & Bryden, M. P. (1979). Hemispheric differences in processing emotions and faces. *Brain and Language, 7*(1), 127–138.

Lourenco, S. F., & Levine, S. C. (2007). *Early hemispheric specialization for distance coding: Evidence from children with pre- or perinatal lesions.* Manuscript in preparation.

MacWhinney, B., Feldman, H., Sacco, K., & Valdes-Perez, R. (2000). Online measures of basic language skills in children with early focal brain lesions. *Brain and Language, 71,* 400–431.

Mancini, J., de Schonen, S., Deruelle, C., & Massoulier, A. (1994). Face recognition in children with early right or left brain damage. *Developmental Medicine and Child Neurology, 36,* 156–166.

Marchman, V. A., Miller, R., & Bates, E. A. (1991). Babble and first words in children with focal brain injury. *Applied Psycholinguistics, 12,* 1–22.

Mayer, M. (1969). *Frog, where are you?* New York: Dial Press.

McFie, J., & Zangwill, O. L. (1960). Visual-constructive disabilities associated with lesions of the left cerebral hemisphere. *Brain, 83,* 243–259.

Mercuri, E., Cowan, F., & Gupte, G. (2001). Prothrombotic disorders and abnormal neurodevelopmental outcome in infants with neonatal cerebral infarction. *Pediatrics. 107,* 1400–1404.

Mercuri, E., Rutherford, M., Cowan, F., Pennock, J., Counsell, S., Papadimitriou, M., et al. (1999). Early prognostic indicators of outcome in infants with neonatal cerebral infarction: A clinical, electroencephalogram, and magnetic resonance imaging study. *Pediatrics, 103,* 39–46.

Muter, V., Taylor, S., & Vargha-Khadem, F. (1997). A longitudinal study of early intellectual development in hemiplegic children. *Neuropsychologia, 35*(3), 289–298.

Nass, R., & Koch, D. (1987). Differential effects of early left versus right brain damage on temperament. *Developmental Neuropsychology, 3,* 93–99.

Nass, R., Peterson, H., & Koch, D. (1989). Differential effects of early left versus right brain injury on intelligence. *Brain and Cognition, 9,* 258–266.

Nelson, K., & Lynch, J. (2004). Stroke in newborn infants. *Lancet Neurology, 3,* 150–158.

NICHD Early Child Care Research Network. (2005). Pathways to reading: The role of oral language in the transition to reading. *Developmental Psychology, 41,* 428–442.

Nippold, M. (1998). *Later language development: The school-age and adolescent years* (2nd edn.). Austin, TX: Pro-Ed.

Pathan, M., & Kittner, S. J. (2003). Pregnancy and stroke. *Current Neurology and Neuroscience Reports, 3,* 27–31.

Paul, B., Carapetian, S., Hesselink, J., Nass, R., Trauner, D., & Stiles, J. (2007). *Face and location processing in children with early unilateral brain injury.* Manuscript in preparation.

Perlstein, M. A., & Hood, P. N. (1955). Infantile spastic hemiplegia. *American Journal of Physical Medicine, 34,* 391–407.

Piercy, M., Hecaen, H., & De Ajuriaguerra, J. (1960). Constructional apraxia associated with unilateral cerebral lesions: Left and right sided cases compared. *Brain, 83,* 225–242.

Rasmussen, T., & Milner, B. (1977). The role of early left brain injury in determining lateralization of cerebral speech functions. *Annals of the New York Academy of Sciences, 299,* 355–369.

Ratcliff, G. (1982). Disturbances of spatial orientation associated with cerebral lesions. In M. Potegal (Ed.), *Spatial abilities: Development and physiological foundations* (pp. 301–331). New York: Academic Press.

Reilly, J., Anderson, D., & Martinez, R. (2007). *Pre-linguistic vocalizations in infants with early focal brain injury.* Manuscript in preparation.

Reilly, J. S., Bates, E. A., & Marchman, V. A. (1998). Narrative discourse in children with early focal brain injury. *Brain and Language, 61*(3), 335–375.

Reilly, J., Charten, V., Stiles, J., del Guercio, C., & Nass, R. (2005). *Labeling emotional facial expressions in children with early brain damage.* Poster session presented at the annual meeting of the Cognitive Neuroscience Society, New York.

Reilly, J., Losh, M., Bellugi, U., & Wulfeck, B. (2004). "Frog, where are you?" Narratives in children with specific language impairment, early focal brain injury, and Williams syndrome. *Brain and Language, 88*(2), 229–247.

Reilly, J., Stiles, J., Fenson, J., & Nass, R. (2005). *Speaking and writing: Later language development in children with early brain damage*. Paper presented at the Tenth International Congress for the Study of Child Language, Berlin.

Reilly, J. S., Stiles, J., Larsen, J., & Trauner, D. A. (1995). Affective facial expression in infants with focal brain damage. *Neuropsychologia, 33*(1), 83–99.

Reilly, J. S., Stiles, J., Wulfeck, B., & Nass, R. (2005). Language development in children with early focal brain damage: Is there a right hemisphere profile? *Journal of Cognitive Neuroscience* (Suppl.), 229.

Riva, D., & Cazzaniga, L. (1986). Late effects of unilateral brain lesions sustained before and after age one. *Neuropsychologia, 24*(3), 423–428.

Robertson, L. C., & Delis, D. C. (1986). "Part-whole" processing in unilateral brain-damaged patients: Dysfunction of hierarchical organization. *Neuropsychologia, 24*(3), 363–370.

Robertson, L. C., Lamb, M. R., & Knight, R. T. (1988). Effects of lesions of temporal-parietal junction on perceptual and attentional processing in humans. *Journal of Neuroscience, 8*(10), 3757–3769.

Rowe, M., & Levine, S. C. (2007). *The joint effects of biology and input on vocabulary growth in brain-injured children*. Manuscript in preparation.

St. James-Roberts, I. (1981). A reinterpretation of hemispherectomy data without functional plasticity of the brain. *Brain and Language, 14*, 292–306.

Sauer, E., Gripshover, S., Harden, K., Meanwell, C., & Levine, S. (2006). *Gesture development in children with early unilateral brain injury*. Madison, WI: Symposium on Research in Child Language Disorders.

Scarborough, H. S. (1990). Index of productive syntax. *Applied Psycholinguistics, 11*(1), 1.

de Schonen, S., & Mathivet, E. (1990). Hemispheric asymmetry in a face discrimination task in infants. *Child Development, 61*, 1192–1205.

Semel, E., Wiig, E., & Secord, W. (1995). *Clinical evaluation of language fundamentals*. San Antonio, TX: Psychological Corporation.

Slobin, D. I. (1973). Cognitive prerequisites for the development of grammar. In C. A. Ferguson & D. I. Slobin (Eds.), *Studies of child language development* (pp. 175–208). New York: Holt, Reinhart and Winston.

Slobin, D. I. (1985/1992/1995). *Cross-linguistic studies of language acquisition* (Vols. 1, 3, 4). Hillsdale, NJ: Lawrence Erlbaum.

Snow, C. E., Burns, M. S., & Griffin, P. (1998). *Preventing reading difficulties in young children*. Washington, DC: National Academy Press.

Sprenger-Charolles, L., & Bechennec, D. (2004). Variability and invariance in learning alphabetic orthographies. *Written Language and Literacy, 7*(1), 9–33.

Sreenan, R., Bhargava, & Robertson, C. M. (2000). Cerebral infarction in the term newborn: Clinical presentation and long-term outcome. *Journal of Pediatrics, 137*, 351–355.

Staudt, M., Gerloff, C., Grodd, W., Holthausen, H., Niemann, G., & Krageloh-Mann, I. (2004). Reorganization in congenital hemiparesis acquired at different gestational ages. *Annals of Neurology, 56*(6), 854–863.

Stiles, J. (2008). *The fundamentals of brain development: Integrating nature and nurture*. Cambridge, MA: Harvard University Press.

Stiles, J., & Nass, R. (1991). Spatial grouping activity in young children with congenital right or left hemisphere brain injury. *Brain and Cognition, 15*(2), 201–222.

Stiles, J., Paul, B., & Hesselink, J. (2006). Spatial cognitive development following early focal brain injury: Evidence for adaptive change in brain and cognition. In Y. Munakata (Ed.), *Processes of change in brain and cognitive development* (pp. 533–560). New York: Oxford University Press.

Stiles, J., Reilly, J., Moses, P., & Paul, B. M. (2005). Adaptive brains: Alternative developmental trajectories following early brain injury. *Trends in Cognitive Science, 9*(3), 136–143.

Stiles, J., Stern, C., Trauner, D., & Nass, R. (1996). Developmental change in spatial grouping activity among children with early focal brain injury: Evidence from a modeling task. *Brain and Cognition, 31*(1), 46–62.

Stiles, J., Trauner, D., Engel, M., and Nass, R. (1997). The development of drawing in children with congenital focal brain injury: Evidence for limited functional recovery. *Neuropsychologia, 35,* 299–312.

Stiles-Davis, J. (1988). Developmental change in young children's spatial grouping activity. *Developmental Psychology, 24*(4), 522–531.

Stiles-Davis, J., Janowsky, J., Engel, M., & Nass, R. D. (1988). Drawing ability in four young children with congenital unilateral brain lesions. *Neuropsychologia, 26*(3), 359–371.

Stiles-Davis, J., Sugarman, S., & Nass, R. (1985). The development of spatial and class relations in four young children with right cerebral hemisphere damage: Evidence for an early spatial constructive deficit. *Brain and Cognition, 4*(4), 388–412.

Stone, A., & Valentine, T. (2003). Perspectives on prosopagnosia and models of face recognition. *Cortex, 39*(1), 31–40.

Storch, S. A., & Whitehurst, G. J. (2002). Oral language and code-related precursors to reading: Evidence from a longitudinal structural model. *Developmental Psychology, 38,* 934–947.

Strauss, E., Satz, P., & Wada, J. (1990). An examination of the crowding hypothesis in epileptic patients who have undergone the carotid amytal test. *Neuropsychologia, 28*(11), 1221–1227.

Swindell, C. S., Holland, A. L., Fromm, D., & Greenhouse, J. B. (1988). Characteristics of recovery of drawing ability in left and right brain-damaged patients. *Brain and Cognition, 7*(1), 16–30.

Thal, D. J., Reilly, J., Seibert, L., Jeffries, R., & Fenson, J. (2004). Language development in children at risk for language impairment: Cross-population comparisons. *Brain and Language, 88,* 167–179.

Tolchinsky, L. (2003). *The cradle of culture and what children know about writing and numbers before being taught.* Mahwah, NJ: Lawrence Erlbaum.

Tranel, D., Damasio, A. R., & Damasio, H. (1988). Intact recognition of facial expression, gender, and age in patients with impaired recognition of face identity. *Neurology, 38*(5), 690–696.

Trauner, D. A. (2003). Hemispatial neglect in young children with early unilateral brain damage. *Developmental Medicine and Child Neurology, 45,* 160–166.

Treiman, R., & Bourassa, D. (2000). The development of spelling skill. *Topics in Language Disorders, 20*(3), 1–18.

Vargha-Khadem, F., Gorman, A.-M., & Watters, G. V. (1985). Aphasia and handedness in relation to hemispheric side, age at injury and severity of cerebral lesion during childhood. *Brain, 108,* 677–696.

Vargha-Khadem, F., Isaacs, E., & Muter, V. (1994). A review of cognitive outcome after unilateral lesions sustained during childhood. *Journal of Child Neurology, 9*(Suppl. 2), 67–73.

Vargha-Khadem, F., Isaacs, E., Van der Werf, S., Robb, S., & Wilson, B. (1992). Development of intelligence and memory in children with hemiplegic cerebral palsy: The deleterious consequences of early seizures. *Brain, 115*(1), 315–329.

Vicari, S., Albertoni, A., Chilosi, A. M., Cipriani, P., Cioni, G., & Bates, E. (2000). Plasticity and reorganization during language development in children with early brain injury. *Cortex, 36*(1), 31–46.

Vicari, S., Stiles, J., Stern, C., & Resca, A. (1998). Spatial grouping activity in children with early cortical and subcortical lesions. *Developmental Medicine and Child Neurology, 40,* 90–99.

Volpe, J. (2000). *Neurology of the newborn*. Philadelphia: J. B. Saunders.

Wasserstein, J., Zappulla, R., Rosen, J., & Gerstman, L. (1987). In search of closure: Subjective contour illusions, Gestalt completion tests, and implications. *Brain and Cognition, 6*(1), 1–14.

Weckerly, J., Wulfeck, B., & Reilly, J. (2004). The development of morphosyntactic ability in atypical populations: The acquisition of tag questions in children with early focal lesions and children with specific-language impairment. *Brain and Language, 88*(2), 190–201.

Whitehurst, G. J., & Lonigan, C. J. (1998). Child development and emergent literacy. *Child Development, 69,* 848–872.

Woods, B. T. (1980). The restricted effects of right-hemisphere lesions after age one: Wechsler test data. *Neuropsychologia, 18,* 65–70.

Woods, B. T., & Carey, S. (1979). Language deficits after apparent clinical recovery from childhood aphasia. *Annals of Neurology, 6,* 405–409.

Wu, Y. W., Croen, L. A., Shah, S. J., Newman, T. B., & Najjar, D. V. (2006). Cerebral palsy in a term population: Risk factors and neuroimaging findings. *Pediatrics, 118*(2), 690–697.

Wu, Y. W., March, W. M., Croen, L. A., Grether, J. K., Escobar, G. J., & Newman, T. B. (2004). Perinatal stroke in children with motor impairment: A population-based study. *Pediatrics, 114,* 612–619.

Wulfeck, B., Bates, E., Krupa-Kwiatkowski, M., & Saltzman, D. (2004). Grammaticality sensitivity in children with early focal brain injury and children with specific language impairment. *Brain and Language, 88,* 215–228.

6

Neuroimaging in Child and Adolescent Psychiatric Disorders

Paramala J. Santosh and Ruksana Ahmed

Neuroimaging in child psychiatry is a rapidly developing field and the number of different techniques being used is increasing quickly. During the past 20 years, technological advances have provided and refined a variety of neuroimaging methods based on different physical phenomena. There is now a considerable literature on the application of neuroimaging to children with neurodevelopmental disorders. At this stage in the field's development, replicable findings are sufficient to permit an appraisal of the progress made so far, while attempting to outline potential pitfalls and difficulties faced.

One of the most significant points to date is that no specific and consistent abnormality has been detected in childhood psychiatric disorders: Although research into some disorders has shown more consistent findings, progress has been slow. Obsessive compulsive disorder has shown the most consistent findings so far, with orbitofrontal cortex and the caudate nucleus being implicated. It is suggested that better understanding of the corticostriatal neural networks will shed more light on the neurodevelopmental disorders of childhood. The following review aims to describe the current status of neuroimaging in childhood psychopathology and to discuss some of the limitations of the various studies that have been conducted.

Brain Imaging Techniques

There are a number of well-established brain-imaging techniques that allow the examination of both healthy and "damaged" brains without any known risks. The range of techniques available will be described, and the advantages and disadvantages of these different techniques will be presented. Structural imaging measures anatomic structure (radiographs, computed tomography [CT], magnetic resonance [MR] imaging), while functional imaging measures the intrinsic physical properties of tissues (e.g., metabolism, blood flow) and changes that occur in disease (magnetic resonance spectroscopy [MRS], functional MR imaging [fMRI], positron emission tomography [PET], single photon emission CT [SPECT], magnetic encephalography [MEG]). The nature of the connection between the physical property measured (e.g., radioactivity in some areas) and the underlying physiological phenomenon (e.g., metabolism) establishes and limits the utility of different methods, and the technical constraints of each technique. Anderson and Gore (1997) give a very detailed account of the physical basis of the various neuroimaging techniques.

Brain imaging may be performed for a variety of reasons: to address needs in clinical research, patient management, or diagnosis. In clinical practice, structural neuroimaging is indicated when one suspects intracranial pathology, if the patient exhibits focal neurological signs on examination, or when there is a history of significant head trauma (i.e., with extended loss of consciousness, enduring neurologic sequelae of any kind, or when there is a close temporal relation to the onset of psychopathology), refractory epilepsy, childhood-onset psychoses, and when the disorder is refractory to an extensive array of conventional treatments. Apart from being indicated in complicated epilepsy, functional neuroimaging is currently only a research tool in psychiatry. Functional abnormalities are often picked up in subjects with negative structural scans.

Although structures may show group differences, they need not show the same degree of difference in, for example, electron density (CT), phosphorylation (MRS), or oxygenation of blood (fMRI). Thus, the fMRI cerebral activation may not equate to the PET activation, and both may differ from the anatomy depicted by visual inspection or tissue typing.

Neurophysiological imaging refers to the use of cerebral blood flow radiotracers (^{15}O-labeled water, ^{133}Xe) or metabolic radiotracers (^{18}F-flurodeoxyglucose) to spatially resolve the hemodynamic and metabolic correlates of neural circuit activity. *Neuroreceptor imaging* refers to the use of PET or SPECT radionuclides bound to ligands possessing a high and selective affinity for neurotransmitter receptors or transporters. Tracer kinetic models are used to convert local positron annihilations into estimates of receptor or transporter density, distribution, or occupancy. *Neurochemical imaging* refers to the use of PET or SPECT radionuclides bound to precursors (for example, tryptophan, dihydroxyphenylalanine [DOPA]) of enzymatic reactions that support neurotransmitter synthesis.

Electroencephalography (EEG) is an imaging technique that measures brain function by analyzing the scalp electrical activity generated by brain structures. Local current flows are produced when brain cells (neurons) are activated. However, only electrical activity generated by large populations of neurons concurrently active can be recorded on the head surface. The small electrical signals detected by the scalp electrodes are amplified thousands of times, then displayed on paper or stored to computer memory. Clinical applications include the diagnosis of epilepsy, sleep disorders, stroke, head trauma, and so on. The EEG procedure is currently being widely used to study the brain organization of cognitive processes such as perception, memory, attention, language, and emotion in normal adults and children. For this purpose, the most useful application of EEG recording is the *event-related potential* technique.

Event-related potentials (ERPs) are small voltage fluctuations resulting from evoked neural activity. These electrical changes are extracted from scalp recordings by computer averaging epochs (recording periods) of EEG time-locked to repeated occurrences of sensory, cognitive, or motor events. The spontaneous background EEG fluctuations, which are random relative to when the stimuli occurred, are averaged out, leaving the event-related brain potentials. These electrical signals reflect only the activity that is consistently associated with the stimulus processing in a time-locked way. The ERP thus reflects, with high temporal resolution, the patterns of neuronal activity evoked by a stimulus. Due to their high temporal resolution, ERPs provide timing information about brain processing. As a result, ERPs represent the natural complement of PET and fMRI to study human cognition. Whereas PET and fMRI can localize regions of activation during a given mental task, ERPs can help in defining the time course of these activations. As ERP is noninvasive, it is particularly useful in infant and child brain–behavior research.

Comparison of Different Neuroimaging Techniques

Computed tomography

The mechanism in this type of imaging involves collimated beams of X-rays being rotated around the head and passed through the brain where they lose energy in proportion to the density of the various tissues (gray matter, white matter, and cerebrospinal fluid [CSF]). The advantages of this type of imaging include the provision of excellent images of the skull, sulci, and ventricles. Moreover, volumetric and dynamic images can be obtained if spiral CT is used. However, a disadvantage of this technique is that artifacts often arise in regions containing very dense structures, especially in posterior fossa and areas close to bony interfaces. The patient is exposed to ionizing radiation and only transverse slices are obtained.

Magnetic resonance imaging

The mechanism in this type of imaging involves brief radiofrequency pulses activating the inherent distribution of hydrogen atoms in the brain, following which the hydrogen atoms align themselves in the strong magnetic field generated by the superconducting magnet around the head. The different realignment times after the burst of radiofrequency perturbation are used to delineate the different tissues of the brain. The advantages of this type of imaging make it the primary method of choice for brain imaging. This is because it produces superior images with high spatial resolution (Figure 6.1); it is a safe technique with no exposure to radiation. As a result, repeated scans are possible even in very young children, and arbitrary planes, transverse, coronal, and sagittal images can be generated. However, pacemakers, shell injury, plates, screws, and metallic implants are contraindications. Subjects also have to remain relatively still and can find the scanner noise quite loud and find that it is a constrained environment within the receiver coil.

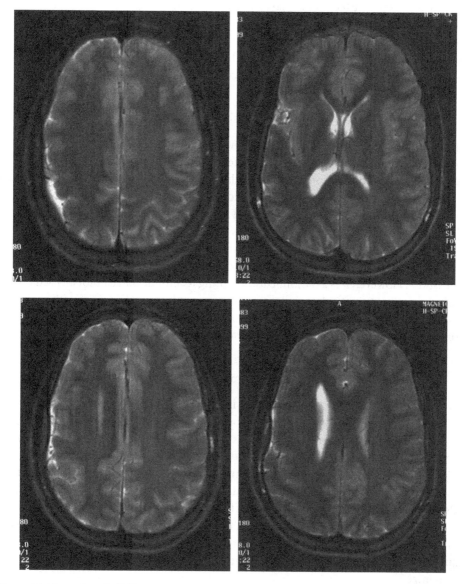

Figure 6.1 Examples of MRI images.

Functional magnetic resonance imaging

The mechanism in this type of imaging involves the detection of changes in blood flow (characterized by altered levels of oxygen or oxygenated blood) which establish a new equilibrium of the oxygen-dependent magnetic properties of hemoglobin, which are then detected through high field magnets. The main advantages of this type of imaging include its ability to map the brain's functional responses to specific stimuli. It is a noninvasive and safe technique that can help us to learn about neurophysiology in both disease and health. It also provides reference anatomic images that are simultaneously acquired with the functional data. However, image analysis techniques need to improve in children. Also, artifacts near the skull base limit its use, and again there is a constrained environment within the receiver coil.

Positron emission tomography

The mechanism in this type of imaging involves the detection of annihilation photons arising from the decay of injected radiotracer. Arrays of scintillation detectors are used as an electronic collimation system, which transforms the photons into visible light; this is ultimately filtered and reconstructed to form the image, showing blood flow or glucose metabolism, receptor occupancy, or neurochemical binding in the brain (depending on the tracer). The advantages of this type of imaging include the fact that it provides exact quantification of cerebral blood flow and metabolism. Also whole head imaging is more reliable, and neuroreceptor concentration and affinity can be measured. However, it is a radionuclide scanning technique and cannot be used repeatedly or in pregnancy. Cyclotron is necessary to provide the radiotracers with very short half-life. Its use is also constrained by the need to inject isotope for each new task, and anatomic data needs to be obtained separately.

Single photon emission tomography

The mechanism in this type of imaging is similar to positron emission tomography where it measures changes in blood flow and receptor activity using appropriate radiotracers. In this technique, detectors specialized for localizing photons (γ-rays) emitted by positron annihilation are used. The data are processed to create images of slices of the brain in the transaxial, coronal, and sagittal planes. An advantage of this technique is that it is available in most departments of nuclear medicine. There are also a larger number of radiotracers available for use, and as a result of these factors it is a cost-effective technique. However, it is a radionuclide scanning technique and cannot be used repeatedly or in pregnancy. In addition, in this technique absolute quantification is not possible, and bilateral symmetrical reduction is difficult to recognize.

Magnetic resonance spectroscopy

The mechanism in this type of imaging involves the exploitation of the slight differences in resonant frequency of protons (usually ^1H and ^{31}P) bound to different cell-associated structures. It characterizes the molecular state of both bound and free tissue water and the chemical microenvironment of cells and provides a profile of the status of intermediary metabolism within a selected tissue volume. The advantage of this technique is that it provides a direct investigation of phosphorylated intermediate metabolites and neurotransmitters such as GABA and glutamate. However, it is a long procedure if one is interested in quantification at the molecular level and only limited substrates are measurable.

Magnetic encephalography

The mechanism in this type of imaging involves the use of specialized superconducting detectors and sensory coils to measure magnetic fields that surround the currents that give rise to EEGs and ERPs. The magnetic fields reflect currents induced within the dendrites of neurons oriented parallel to the sulci. Advantages of this technique include the fact that it can help to locate and measure the strength of electrical impulses from the brain. ERP recordings provide a millisecond by millisecond reflection of evoked brain activity. For this reason, ERPs are an ideal methodology for studying the timing aspects of both normal and abnormal cognitive processes. It is a safe procedure with no exposure to radioactive compounds. However, it can result in a bias that favors only some neurons and not all in a particular field and hence may not be accurate. ERP data provide less accurate spatial information than positron emission tomography (PET) or functional magnetic resonance imaging (fMRI), which lack fine temporal resolution. Structural scans are necessary separately to transpose findings onto a brain map.

Normal Neurodevelopmental Changes that Influence Pediatric Neuroimaging

Knowledge of the normal patterns of brain development in the clinically relevant ages of 4–18 years is necessary to interpret the subtle brain imaging findings reported in the literature. Giedd and colleagues report the best data to date from the ongoing NIMH pediatric neuroimaging project (Giedd, Snell, et al., 1996). Cortical gray matter decreases with age, while white matter and CSF volumes (to a lesser extent) gradually increase with age. Lateral ventricles, corpus callosum, basal ganglia, amygdalae, and the hippocampus also increase in size with age. Although total brain volume appears to approach adult size by school age, this belies an active and sex-specific dynamic balance achieved between growth and regression of certain brain structures throughout childhood and adolescence. Similarly, brain metabolism (as shown by PET studies) rapidly increases during the first years of life, peaks during childhood, and then declines to adult levels during adolescence.

Speculatively, the observed gender differences in incidence, age of onset, and symptom profiles of developmental neuropsychiatric disorders could arise from the complex interactions between the gender-specific differences in brain development and the child's environment. For example, the lower incidence of attention deficit hyperactivity disorder (ADHD) in girls might be related to having a relatively larger caudate nucleus than boys. Also, the male-only adolescent increase in lateral ventricular volume (Giedd,

Rumsey, et al., 1996; Giedd, Snell, et al., 1996) is intriguing in light of consistent findings of enlarged ventricular volume in adolescent-onset schizophrenia, which is more
predominant in boys.

Current Status of Neuroimaging in Childhood Psychopathology

Despite accumulating neuroimaging research in children, findings are often inconsistent and not replicable across centers. Many problems exist in the application of neuroimaging to children, and these are detailed later in this chapter. The important
findings in childhood disorders are summarized below.

Language impairment and reading disability

Children with specific language impairment have been reported to have a significantly
smaller left pars triangularis, with rightward asymmetry of language structures (Gauger,
Lombardino, & Leonard, 1997). Similarly, in those with specific reading disability, the
degree of left cerebral asymmetry has been found to correlate with both reading skills
and skills in phonemic analysis of spoken language (Dalby, Elbro, & Stodkilde-
Jorgensen, 1998). Cao and colleagues (Cao, Bitan, Chou, Burman, & Booth, 2006) further investigated the issue of children with these difficulties having problems mapping
orthographic representations onto phonological representations. They found that
normal children showed greater activity in brain regions concerned with phonology
and orthography in response to the more difficult judgment in which there was conflict. These increases in activity were not observed in children with dyslexia. Therefore,
children with dyslexia are not observed to show compensation for task difficulty associated with increased activity (Grady, McIntosh, & Craik, 2005). Therefore, imaging
studies have provided interesting points of consideration for both structural and functional differences in children with language impairment and reading disabilities.

Attention deficit hyperactivity disorder

Although methodological problems remain, there is increasing agreement on the role
of the prefrontal-striatal-thalamocortical circuit in attention deficit hyperactivity disorder (ADHD), with a preponderance of the evidence suggesting that the right-sided
circuit is primary, at least at the level of the basal ganglia. Reviews in this field include
those by Castellanos (1997) and Filipek (1999). Neuroimaging in ADHD has advanced
greatly to unpick the neural subsystems involved in its pathophysiology. Hyperactive
adolescents have been shown to have different functional brain abnormalities when
tested on two tasks, a motor inhibition task and a motor timing task (Rubia et al.,
1996). Adolescents with ADHD, in comparison to matched controls, show lower power
of response in the right mesial prefrontal cortex during both tasks, and in the right
inferior prefrontal cortex and left caudate during the stop task. Dickstein and colleagues

(Dickstein, Bannon, Castellanos, & Milham, 2006) conducted a meta-analysis of functional imaging studies of ADHD, and their results were consistent with previous studies' findings of hypoactivity in specific regions, as stated above, but also suggested that future work should aim to identify what might be going wrong with the control normally exerted by these systems.

Autism

Despite the presence of numerous brain-imaging studies attempting to isolate brain regions or pathways specifically implicated, the literature remains inconclusive. Autism has been associated with increased regional brain volume, with the occipital, parietal, and temporal lobes (in decreasing frequency) being enlarged (Filipek, 1996; Piven, Arndt, Bailey, & Andreasen, 1996). A report that cerebellar vermis lobules VI and VII are specifically affected in autism (either being hypoplastic or hyperplastic) remains controversial because few others have been able to replicate it (Courchesne et al., 1994). Recently, the ability to attribute independent mental states to self and others (theory of mind) has been associated with the activation of the left medial frontal gyrus (Broadmann's area 8) and the posterior cingulated cortex, areas that are not activated in Asperger's syndrome during similar tasks (Fletcher et al., 1995; Happé et al., 1996). Using the recently developed voxel-based whole brain analysis of structural MRI, Abell and colleagues (1999) report structural abnormalities in a distributed system centered on the amygdala in autism. They report decreases of gray matter in anterior parts of this system (right paracingulate sulcus, left inferior frontal gyrus) and increases in posterior parts (amygdala/peri-amygdaloid cortex, middle temporal gyrus, inferior temporal gyrus) and in the regions of the cerebellum. These findings are appealing because the structures involved have been previously implicated in social cognition by animal and histopathological studies. Using neurochemical imaging, an increased serotonin synthesis capacity in autistic children (using α-^{11}C-methyl-L-tryptophan PET) has been reported, and is hypothesized to be related to the disruption of the normal developmental pattern of brain serotonin synthesis (Chugani et al., 1999).

More recent research has considered the link between behavioral abnormalities associated with autism and electrocortical activation. Children with autism and pervasive developmental disorder (PDD) show abnormalities in gaze and face processing. In particular, Kemner, Schuller, and Engeland (2006) conducted a study measuring brain activity related to face and gaze processing in children with PDD. Their study provided evidence that children with PDD have normal brain activity associated with face processing in certain conditions (i.e., older children with PDD). In addition, they showed that brain activity in relation to attentional orienting in response to gaze change is also normal in high functioning children with PDD. These recent studies may add to the growing literature that indicates normal capabilities for the processing of social cues in PDD (Pierce, Haist, Sedaghat, & Courchesne, 2006), but overall there is a need for further investigation of the complex neural circuitry involved in social processing (Wang, Lee, Sigman, & Dapretto, 2006).

Tourette syndrome

Increased dopamine transporter availability in the caudate in ^{123}I-BZM SPECT studies (Malison et al., 1995; Wolf et al., 1996), and fMRI-based activation of the orbitofrontal cortex, bilateral premotor regions, and the head of the right caudate, and decreased activation of the bilateral globus pallidus and thalamus during tic-suppression tasks have been reported (Peterson et al., 1998). Plessen et al. (2006) also found that Tourette syndrome is associated with reduced cross-sectional area of the corpus callosum, which may also reflect a mechanism for reducing the frequency of tics. However, it cannot be said with certainty that a reduction in the area of the corpus callosum is associated with reduced connectivity. Plessen et al. (2006) used diffusion tensor imaging as a direct measure of connectivity in the corpus callosum, and this measure confirmed that there was reduced connectivity in the corpus callosum of patients with Tourette syndrome.

Obsessive compulsive disorder

Obsessive compulsive disorder (OCD) has been extensively studied, and subjects show orbitofrontal and anterior cingulated hypermetabolism at rest. Successful attenuation of OCD symptoms results in the attenuation of the hypermetabolism of the orbito-frontal cortex, caudate nucleus, and anterior cingulated cortex, irrespective of whether the treatment used is behavior therapy or medication. Subjects with OCD show increased activation in the bilateral orbitofrontal cortex, right caudate nucleus, and anterior cingulated cortex during symptom induction procedures, with the degree of induced obsessionality being positively correlated with the magnitude of activation within an anterior orbitofrontal locus. Furthermore, individuals with OCD fail to recruit normally the corticostriatal system during cognitive behavioral activation paradigms, and instead activate the medial temporal lobe system (involved in conscious information processing). Rauch, Bates, and Grachev (1997) have provided an in-depth review of the subject.

Childhood-onset schizophrenia

Childhood-onset schizophrenia (COS) is defined as schizophrenia with onset by 12 years of age, and provides a unique research opportunity to test the neurodevelop-mental hypothesis of schizophrenia. Children meeting strict criteria for COS show smaller cerebral volume and thalamic area and increased basal ganglia and lateral ventricular volumes (Frazier, Giedd, Hamburger, et al., 1996), the size of the effect being similar to that observed for adult populations (Greenstein et al., 2006). In adolescents with COS, caudate enlargement appears to be secondary to exposure to typical neuroleptics (Frazier, Giedd, Kaysen, et al., 1996). Smaller volumes of cerebellar vermis (inferior posterior lobe) have also been reported, which is consistent with the observations in adult schizophrenia (Jacobsen et al., 1997). Patients with COS are reported to have a fourfold greater decrease in cortical gray matter volume during adolescence, with a disease-specific reduction in the frontal and temporal regions (Rapoport et al., 1999).

Affective and depressive disorders

Reviews on affective disorders implicate the prefrontal cortex (especially orbital), basal ganglia, thalamus, and amygdala with possible dopamine and serotonin underpinnings (Drevets et al., 1992; Mayberg, 1993). Decreased frontal lobe volume and increased ventricular volume have been reported in children with depressive disorders, with a significant inverse relation between age and frontal lobe volume (Steingard et al., 1996). Temporal horn enlargement and deep white matter hyperintensities, with the absence of normal frontal asymmetry, have been reported in children and adolescents with bipolar illness. These findings in childhood affective disorders have largely been replicated in adults with similar disorders.

Post-traumatic stress disorder

MRI-based hippocampal atrophy and PET-based failure of hippocampal activation during the performance of memory tasks have been reported in women with child-hood sexual abuse-related post-traumatic stress disorder (PTSD; Bremner, 1998). Children and adolescents with PTSD resulting from child maltreatment have been shown to have smaller intracranial and cerebral volumes than matched controls (De Bellis et al., 1999). Brain volume positively correlated with age of onset of PTSD trauma and negatively correlated with the duration of abuse. This suggests that intense stress in childhood can lead to long-term structural and functional changes in the brain. On the other hand, in anorexia nervosa, the observed morphological and func-tional cerebral alterations (enlarged CSF spaces especially of cortical sulci) are inter-preted to be consequences of the anorexic state, which is at least partially reversible with weight gain (Herholz, 1996).

After reviewing the neuroimaging findings in the various disorders, it seems pos-sible that some symptoms (irrespective of diagnosis) have common underlying pathophysiology (e.g., inattention in mania has been shown to be associated with prefrontal dysfunction, which is similar to that reported in ADHD; Table 6.1). This is in keeping with the model proposed by Santosh & Baird (1999) for the management of psychopathology in neurodevelopmental disorders. Tourette syndrome, OCD, depression, and ADHD frequently co-occur clinically, which may be related in part to common elements in their pathophysiologies, which at the level of the brain organi-zation may involve particular cortical-subcortical circuits. It is possible that putamen dysfunction leads to the sensorimotor symptoms of Tourette syndrome, ventral caudate nuclear dysfunction leads to obsessions and compulsions, dorsolateral caudate nuclear involvement leads to hyperactivity and inattention, and predomi-nant involvement of the nucleus accumbens results in affective or anxiety disorders (Rauch et al., 1997).

Table 6.1 Brain Regions Suggested from Neuroimaging Data to be Involved in Childhood Psychiatric Disorders.

Disorder	Frontal	Parieto-occipital	Temporal	Caudate	Putamen	Limbic	Corpus callosum	Cerebellum	Altered laterality
ADHD	Probable	Possible	Possible	Probable	Likely		Likely	Possible	Possible
Autism	Possible	Possible	Probable	Possible		Probable		Likely	
Tourette syndrome	Probable			Possible	Probable	Possible			Likely
OCD	Probable			Probable				Likely	Likely
Schizophrenia	Possible		Probable			Possible	Likely	Likely	Possible
Mania	Possible					Possible			
Depression	Possible					Possible			
Dyslexia	Possible	Probable	Probable						Possible

Limitations of Neuroimaging Studies in Childhood

The limitations of neuroimaging techniques and therefore studies and the impact on obtaining consistency in neuroimaging findings in children and adolescents cannot be emphasized enough. Therefore, one must be cautious in generalizing findings because the existing published literature reflects a publication bias toward studies with positive findings. With an increasing number of centers becoming involved in neuroimaging research, findings being reported are not uniform. The result is that a number of different variables and factors need to be taken into consideration when reviewing studies relating to neuroimaging in children and adolescents. These factors and variables are summarized below.

Subject variables

Gender
Cerebral volume is approximately 9% larger in males, and lateral ventricular volume increases at about twice the rate per year in males, occurring mostly after 11 years of age (important when ventricular to brain ratios are calculated). While boys have larger globus pallidi, girls have larger caudate nuclei than boys. Similarly, while amygdala volumes increase sharply in boys (about six to seven times that of girls), hippocampal volume increases more rapidly in girls (at about three times that of boys).

Handedness
As symmetry differences are often the key features in discriminating controls from patients with disorders such as ADHD, dyslexia, or Tourette syndrome, it is necessary to control for handedness in pediatric neuroimaging studies (Castellanos, Giedd, & March, 1996; Hynd et al., 1993; Pine, 2006).

Body size
This is a very poor indicator of brain size in humans. Children have larger head to height ratio than adults, with large interindividual variations (Harvey & Krebs, 1990).

Intelligence
Intelligence has been reported to have a statistically significant relation to brain size (Andreasen et al., 1993). Socioeconomic status and education have also been reported to relate to brain size, although the interdependence with factors such as prenatal care, nutrition, and IQ is not clear.

Inherent variability in children
A striking feature of brain morphometric data on normal children and adolescents is the high degree of variability of brain structure size, even in well-screened healthy cohorts, leading to the need for larger sample sizes to detect significant differences. Most of the studies to date do not meet the projected numbers necessary to rule out type II errors.

Developmental age
Cortical and subcortical gray and white matter and CSF volumes change rapidly during childhood and adolescence, resulting in problems when children of a wide age range are studied.

Cognitive style
Cognitive strategies being used to solve tasks during functional imaging may be different at different ages, leading to different activation patterns in subjects.

Ethical issues
Ethical issues that need to be addressed include the possibility of overprotection by policy-makers and institutional review boards arising from the recognition of children's special vulnerability, without equal recognition of their need for research; assessment of the risk–benefit ratio; the difficulty of justifying risk for normal controls; the development and use of age-graded consent; the development of child-friendly imaging procedures; and disposition of unwanted or unexpected knowledge about individuals, including the subject's right not to know and the parent's right not to tell, among other things (Arnold et al., 1995).

Study variables

Subject selection
As subtle neuroimaging findings have been reported in many childhood disorders, it is important to have good normative data from a control group. Ideally, normative data should be acquired from scans of community-recruited subjects who have been assessed prior to the scan.

Sample size/study design
The high variability of brain sizes and the nonlinear pattern of most developmental curves call for large samples and longitudinal study designs in order to adequately characterize neuroanatomic patterns of development in children.

Lack of hypothesis-driven neuroimaging research
It needs to be recognized that investigations using new techniques in the absence of guiding hypotheses can lead to confusion. Chance associations are bound to occur from exhaustive analysis of small numbers of subjects, receiving a disproportionate emphasis in the literature.

Imaging variables

Image acquisition and anxiety
Many children become anxious during scanning and become uncooperative, leading to inflated drop-out rates and difficulty in unpicking the anxiety-related findings

(artifacts) during functional neuroimaging. Familiarity and comfort with the people acquiring the scan, undergoing scanning in the evening when natural sleep is more likely, reading a bedtime story or bringing in a favorite blanket or stuffed toy, and being allowed to stop the procedure at any time for any reason can all increase the chances of acquiring adequate scans and make the experience more pleasant for the child.

Movement artifacts
Movement during scanning produces significant artifacts and needs to be monitored and adjusted for. The advent of new collars to prevent movement will help improve the quality of the scans.

Scanning parameters
Thicker slices result in less spatial resolution and greater partial volume effects, a critical consideration for quantifying small but clinically pertinent structures, such as the caudate nucleus, putamen, or globus pallidus.

Image analysis
Analysis of MR images has benefited enormously from advances in computer technology. However, the absence of a "gold standard" hampers the validation of these techniques, and comparison with results obtained from manual tracing by expert human raters remains the best standard. Developmentally correct child brain maps are not yet freely available, resulting in the use of adult brain maps–Talairach space for analysis. This could result in computerized programs picking up wrongly identified areas during analysis. Statistical threshold adjustments for multiple comparisons, and uncertainty regarding the heterogeneity of the condition under study, also affect the reliability of results. None the less, imaging offers distinct advantages over nonimaging methods in assessing function and structure.

Interpretation of data
The interpretation of data using "subtraction paradigms" has major limitations. It assumes that successive cognitive tasks lead to linear cerebral activation, and discounts the current understanding that the process is clearly more complex. Problems of averaging results across groups of subjects and unreliable identification of boundaries, structures, sites of activation, and their changes over time further lower reliability.

Measured parameter versus inference
The measured changes of physical parameters in the various methods (e.g., nuclear MR signal decay time triggered by changes in the electron structure of iron in MRI) are often quite distant from the biological event that induced the change. This introduces doubt into the assumption that neuroimaging accurately measures brain structure or function. It is possible that there is no clear quantitative relation between the biological change and the magnitude of the signal acquired for imaging.

Implication of abnormality

The demonstration of abnormality does not necessarily indicate that it is of current etiological significance. Abnormalities in brain structure can result from various early experiences encountered by the subject, shaping its development, including unstimulating environments, physical insults, and genetic alterations. Neuroimaging studies often neglect to appreciate the brain-based adaptive capacity and compensatory responses that accompany chronic childhood psychiatric disorders, when attributing findings to disease process, even though this may only be compensatory.

Future Trends and Implications for Neuroimaging in Child Psychiatry

The future will probably see the increasing use of functional neuroimaging in treatment planning and monitoring response in psychiatry. The functional methods will continue to evolve, and the primary challenge will be to develop better computerized image analysis techniques capable of handling the wealth of anatomic and functional neuroimaging data in children. Some of the important developments in the field are detailed below.

Research into new radiopharmaceuticals has opened up the possibility of using SPECT and PET to study a wider range of clinically relevant neurotransmitters and receptors (for example, D_1 antagonists in prefrontal cortex, hippocampus, and amygdala; a D_2 receptor agonist which localizes mainly in the striatum; $5HT_{1A}$, $5HT_{2A}$, $5HT_{2c}$ receptor ligands). Ligands which help quantify receptors, such as N-methyl-D-aspartate (NMDA), α-amino-3-hydroxy-5-methyl-4-isoxazolepropionate (AMPA), ion channels, γ-aminobutyric acid B (GABA-B), and so on, will help the understanding of neurodevelopmental disorders.

The ability to study in vivo pharmacokinetics of agonists and antagonists of dopaminergic, serotoninergic, noradrenergic, GABA, opioid, and muscarinic receptors has opened up new research avenues. PET activation studies using radioligand tagged drugs (for example, ^{11}C-methylphenidate) will increasingly be used to predict drug response. Probes investigating the clinically relevant neuroreceptor subsystems will help in etiological understanding of disorders such as ADHD, leading to more targeted treatments. Appropriate pre- and post-drug treatment receptor occupancy data using neuroreceptor scanning techniques, will help predict side-effect propensity (e.g., tardive dyskinesia) and clinical response. Dynamic PET studies using receptor ligands (e.g., opioid or dopamine receptor ligands) will help in understanding the site and the neurochemical basis of neuronal activity, leading to designing innovative pharmacological strategies.

Judicious combination of complementary methodologies (multimodal imaging) is necessary to understand the relation between structure and function, and will at the very least be necessary to explore whether altered regional metabolism or receptor densities arise due to an underlying change in the volume of that structure.

Studies of normal children will shed new light on neurological underpinnings of normal cognitive and emotional processes, helping us to understand the deficits of children with specific problems (for example, the localization of brain regions involved in phonologic processing, providing compelling evidence that disturbances in phonologic processing is a core deficit in reading disability).

The recent findings in PTSD have aroused interest in the interrelation of psychosocial stressors, brain function, and structure. It would be possible to harness functional neuroimaging techniques to test hypotheses based on the biopsychosocial models of childhood psychopathology. Understanding the mechanism of trauma-related alteration of brain function (and probably structure) is important to plan appropriate preventive strategies, and to improve long-term outcome in traumatized children.

Genetic information will increasingly be used to leverage the probability of locating brain abnormalities, as the effects of genetic lesions can be mapped with reasonable certainty to specific brain regions. This powerful methodology remains largely untapped to date. Knowing where in the brain these genes will express themselves will in the future permit studies of the secondary effects of these genes on maturation, development, and adaptation of brain structure and function. The approach of studying specific genetic/chromosomal disorders (e.g., fragile-X syndrome, William syndrome, Rett syndrome) will also help elucidate the manner in which gene–brain–behavior associations develop and vary across developmental disability.

Transcranial magnetic stimulation (TMS) is a new, noninvasive technique for directly stimulating cortical neurons, with the hope of a therapeutic effect (George, Wassermann, & Post, 1996). This technique is closely related to the MRI technique. Preliminary investigations using rapid-rate TMS to improve motor speed in Parkinson's disease and mood in depression have been encouraging. This could soon prove to be an important neuropsychiatric tool in the assessment and management of neurodevelopmental disorders.

As in utero brain development is abnormal in many neurodevelopmental disorders, methods of assessing brain development in utero will become a priority to understand the relation between observed in utero brain development and the subsequent development of neuropsychiatric disorders. Ultrasound-based mild ventriculomegaly in utero (in the absence of other abnormalities) is associated with mild developmental delay in about 20% of children (Patel, Filly, Hersh, & Goldstein, 1994).

Developments in Imaging Technology

This will be ongoing and the areas of focus will be the acquisition of ever faster images, improvement of activation paradigms, such as event-related task designs, which offer more flexibility than block design paradigms, and examining data beyond averaging. Co-registration of scan data across time will help define the differences in subjects over time, leading to longitudinal changes being picked up. The future of brain imaging in child neuropsychiatry will probably be different for each technique.

In structural MR imaging, faster image-acquisition techniques may help improve the cooperation of distressed children, and better head restraint systems, combined with software and hardware development that corrects each acquisition for motion artifacts, will help greatly and allow the study of developmentally delayed children and those with movement disorders. Higher field strength magnets used in MR imaging could improve image quality, but may need to go through ethical committees and may need the demonstration that higher fields are a minimal risk for younger subjects. Voxel-based whole brain analysis and connectivity analysis will increasingly be used to understand neural activity.

Functional MR imaging will increasingly be used, with improvements in technology tackling the problem of movement artifacts, imaging data reduction, and postimaging data processing (Patel et al., 1994). The sound of the scanner will also possibly decrease significantly, helping to reduce the effect of noise on functional MR imaging. Rapid MR scanning (including gradient echo, fast spin echo, and planar sequences), the recently developed event-related fMRI, contrast-based fMRI techniques, diffusion MR imaging, arterial spine labeling (ASL) techniques, and dynamic susceptibility MR perfusion imaging of the brain offer clinically relevant physiological data not obtainable by conventional MR imaging, and may be used in child psychiatric disorders in the near future. They are likely to be at least as sensitive and specific as radionuclide-based techniques, and offer the added advantage of higher intrinsic resolution, convenient co-registration with conventional MR imaging, as well as time- and cost-effective imaging in patients who require routine MR imaging.

MR spectroscopy involving ^{31}P for the evaluation of membrane lipids and ^{13}C for the evaluation of glutamate neurotransmission and excitoxicity will be increasingly used. MRS technology has already improved to include approaches voxel tailored to the needs of each individual and disorder.

In PET, the progress will probably involve improved scanning resolution with newer tracers requiring lower radiation dose. An important step in understanding cerebral function will be the increasing use of "autoradiography" helping to understand the time-course of minute differences between subjects, to differentiate acquired from developmental abnormalities, and to understand cerebral reorganization. Fluid attenuated inversion recovery (FLAIR), diffusion anisotropy imaging, and event-related PET scanning (e.g., EEG spike-related PET changes) are all strategies that will have a role in the near future in understanding complex neural mechanisms in neuropsychiatry (especially the epilepsies).

In SPECT, there will be an improvement in image resolution; more novel radiotracers will become available and will become widely used as a cost-effective technique to which most departments will have access.

Conclusion

Neuroimaging in child psychiatry is a rapidly developing field, and the different techniques being used are increasing so quickly that no single individual will be able to be conversant in all methodologies. As yet, no specific and consistent abnormality has been detected in childhood psychiatric disorders. Findings have frequently been inconsistent owing to various factors that affect neuroimaging in children. Obsessive compulsive disorder has shown the most consistent findings so far, with orbitofrontal cortex and the caudate nucleus being implicated. Better understanding of the cortico-striatal neural networks will shed more light on the neurodevelopmental disorders in childhood (Frith, 2006; Zametkin & Liotta, 1997).

The design of developmentally correct pediatric brain maps for computerized analysis of pediatric neuroimaging data should become a priority. Identification of homogeneous subgroups in pediatric research using genetics, molecular biology, or immunology could improve the specificity of neuroimaging findings. Despite all the pitfalls of pediatric neuroimaging, refinements in techniques and improvements in the field could help in diagnosis, triage, and in predicting and monitoring medication response and side-effects.

References

Abell, F., Krams, M., Ashburner, J., Passingham, R., Friston, K., Frackowiak, R., et al. (1999). The neuroanatomy of autism: A voxel-based whole brain analysis of structural scans. *Neuroreport, 10,* 1647–1651.

Anderson, A. W., & Gore, J. C. (1997). The physical basis of neuroimaging techniques. *Child and Adolescent Psychiatric Clinics of North America, 6,* 213–264.

Andreasen, N. C., Flaum, M., Swayze, V., O'Leary, D. S., Alliger, R., Cohen, G., et al. (1993). Intelligence and brain structure in normal individuals. *American Journal of Psychiatry, 150,* 130–134.

Arnold, L. E., Stoff, D. M., Cook, E., Jr., Cohen, D. J., Kruesi, M., Wright, C., et al. (1995). Ethical issues in biological psychiatric research with children and adolescents. *Journal of the American Academy of Child and Adolescent Psychiatry, 34,* 929–939.

Bremner, J. D. (1998). Neuroimaging of posttraumatic stress disorder. *Psychiatric Annals, 28,* 445–450.

Cao, F., Bitan, T., Chou, T. L., Burman, D. D., & Booth, J. R. (2006). Deficient orthographic and phonological representations in children with dyslexia revealed by brain activation patterns. *Journal of Child Psychology and Psychiatry, 47*(10), 1041–1050.

Castellanos, F. X. (1997). Toward a pathophysiology of attention-deficit/hyperactivity disorder. *Clinical Pediatrics, 36,* 381–393.

Castellanos, F. X., Giedd, J. N., & March, W. L. (1996). Quantitative brain magnetic resonance imaging in attention-deficit/hyperactivity disorder. *Archives of General Psychiatry, 53,* 607–616.

Chugani, D. C., Muzik, O., Behen, M., Rothermel, R., Janisse, J. J., Lee, J., et al. (1999). Developmental changes in brain serotonin synthesis capacity in autistic and nonautistic children. *Annals of Neurology, 45,* 287–295.

Courchesne, E., Saitoh, O., Townsend, J. P., Yeung-Courchesne, R., Press, G. A., Lincoln, A. J., et al. (1994). Cerebellar hypoplasia and hyperplasia in infantile autism [Letter]. *Lancet, 343,* 63–64.

Dalby, M. A., Elbro, C., & Stodkilde-Jorgensen J. H. (1998). Temporal lobe asymmetry and dyslexia: An in vivo study using MRI. *Brain and Language, 62,* 51–69.

De Bellis, M. D., Keshavan, M. S., Clark, D. B., Casey, B. J., Giedd, J. N., Boring, A. M., et al. (1999). Developmental traumatology: Part II. Brain development. *Biological Psychiatry, 45,* 1271–1284.

Dickstein, S. G., Bannon, K., Castellanos, F. X., & Milham, M. P. (2006). The neural correlates of attention deficit disorder: An ALE meta-analysis. *Journal of Child Psychology and Psychiatry, 47*(10), 1051–1062.

Drevets, W. C., Videen, T. O., Price J. L., Preskorn, S. H., Carmichael, S. T., & Raichle, M. E. (1992). A functional anatomical study of unipolar depression. *Journal of Neuroscience, 12,* 3628–3641.

Filipek, P. A. (1996). Structural variations in measures in the developmental disorders. In R. W. Thatcher, G. R. Lyon, G. Rumsby, & K. Krasnegor (Eds.), *Developmental neuroimaging: Mapping the development of brain and behavior* (pp. 169–186). San Diego, CA: Academic Press.

Filipek, P. A. (1999). Neuroimaging in the developmental disorders: The state of the science. *Journal of Child Psychology and Psychiatry, 40,* 113–128.

Fletcher, P. C., Happé, F., Frith, U., Baker, S. C., Dolan, R. J., Frackowiak, R. S. J., et al. (1995). Other minds in the brain: A functional imaging study of "theory of mind" in story comprehension. *Cognition, 57,* 109–128.

Frazier, J. A., Giedd, J. N., Hamburger, S. D., Albus, K. E., Kaysen, D., Vaituzis, A. C., et al. (1996). Brain anatomic magnetic resonance imaging in childhood-onset schizophrenia. *Archives of General Psychiatry, 53,* 617–624.

Frazier, J. A., Giedd, J. N., Kaysen, D., Albus, K., Hamburger, S., Alaghband-Rad, J., et al. (1996). Childhood-onset schizophrenia: Brain MRI rescan after 2 years of clozapine maintenance treatment. *American Journal of Psychiatry, 153,* 564–566.

Frith, C. D. (2006). The value of brain imaging in the study of development and its disorders. *Journal of Child Psychology and Psychiatry, 47*(10), 979–982.

Gauger, L. M., Lombardino, L. J., & Leonard, C. M. (1997). Brain morphology in children with specific language impairment. *Journal of Speech, Language and Hearing Research, 40,* 1272–1284.

George, M. S., Wassermann, E. M., & Post, R. M. (1996). Transcranial magnetic stimulation: A neuropsychiatric tool for the twenty-first century. *Journal of Neuropsychiatry and Clinical Neurosciences, 8,* 373–382.

Giedd, J. N., Rumsey, J. M., Castellanos, F. X., Rajapakse, J. C., Kaysen, D., Vaituzis, A. C., et al. (1996). A quantitative MRI study of the corpus callosum in children and adolescents. *Developmental Brain Research, 91,* 274–280.

Giedd, J. N., Snell, J. W., Lange, N., Rajapakse, J. C., Casey, B. J., Kozuch, P. L., et al. (1996). Quantitative magnetic resonance imaging of human brain development: Ages 4–18. *Cerebral Cortex, 6,* 551–560.

Grady, C. L., McIntosh, A. R., & Craik, F. I. (2005). Task-related activity in prefrontal cortex and its relation to recognition memory performance in young and old adults. *Neuropsychologia, 43,* 1466–1481.

Greenstein, D., Lerch, J., Shaw, P., Clasen, L., Giedd, J., Gochman, J., et al. (2006). Childhood onset schizophrenia: Cortical brain abnormalities as young adults. *Journal of Child Psychology and Psychiatry, 47*(10), 1003–1012.

Happé, F., Ehlers, S., Fletcher, P., Frith, U., Johansson, M., Gillberg, C., et al. (1996). "Theory of mind" in the brain: Evidence from a PET scan study of Asperger syndrome. *Neuroreport, 8,* 197–201.

Harvey, P. H., & Krebs, J. R. (1990). Comparing brains. *Science, 249,* 140–146.

Herholz, K. (1996). Neuroimaging in anorexia nervosa. *Psychiatry Research, 62,* 105–110.

Hynd, G. W., Hern, K. L., Novey, E. S., Eliopulos, D., Marshall, R., Gonzalez, J. J., et al. (1993). Attention deficit hyperactivity disorder and asymmetry of the caudate nucleus. *Journal of Child Neurology, 8,* 339–347.

Jacobsen, L. K., Giedd, J. N., Berquin, P. C., Krain, A. L., Hamburger, S. D., Kumra, S., et al. (1997). Quantitative morphology of the cerebellum and fourth ventricle in childhood-onset schizophrenia. *American Journal of Psychiatry, 154,* 1663–1669.

Kemner, C., Schuller, A.-M., & Engeland, H. V. (2006). Electrocortical reflections of face and gaze processing in children with pervasive developmental disorder. *Journal of Child Psychology and Psychiatry, 47*(10), 1063–1072.

Malison, R. T., McDougle, C. J., Van Dyck, C. H., Scahill, L., Baldwin, R. M., Seibyl, J. P., et al. (1995). Beta-CIT SPECT imaging demonstrates increased striatal dopamine transporter binding in Tourette's syndrome. *American Journal of Psychiatry, 152,* 1359–1361.

Mayberg, H. S. (1993). Neuroimaging studies of depression in neurologic disease. In S. E. Starkstein & R. G. Robinson (Eds.), *Depression in neurologic disease* (p. 186). Baltimore: The Johns Hopkins University Press.

Patel, M. D., Filly, A., Hersh, D. R., & Goldstein, R. (1994). Isolated mild fetal cerebral ventriculomegaly: Clinical course and outcome. *Radiology, 192,* 759–764.

Peterson, B. S., Skudlarski, P., Anderson, A. W., Zhang, H., Gatenby, J. C., Lacadie, C. M., et al. (1998). A functional magnetic resonance imaging study of tic suppression in Tourette syndrome. *Archives of General Psychiatry, 55,* 326–333.

Pierce, K., Haist, F., Sedaghat, F., & Courchesne, E. (2006). The brain response to personally familiar faces in autism: Findings of fusiform activity and beyond. *Brain, 127,* 2703–2716.

Pine, D. S. (2006). A primer on brain imaging in developmental psychopathology: What is it good for? *Journal of Child Psychology and Psychiatry, 47*(10), 983–986.

Piven, J., Arndt, S., Bailey, J., & Andreasen, N. (1996). Regional brain enlargement in autism: A magnetic resonance imaging study. *Journal of the American Academy of Child and Adolescent Psychiatry, 35,* 530–536.

Plessen, K. J., Grüner, R., Lunervold, A., Hirsch, J. G., Xu, D., Bansal, R., et al. (2006). Reduced white matter connectivity in the corpus callosum of children with Tourette syndrome. *Journal of Child Psychology and Psychiatry, 47*(10), 1013–1022.

Rapoport, J. L., Giedd, J. N., Blumenthal, J., Hamburger, S., Jeffries, N., Fernandez, T., et al. (1999). Progressive cortical change during adolescence in childhood-onset schizophrenia: A longitudinal magnetic resonance imaging study. *Archives of General Psychiatry, 56,* 649–654.

Rauch, S. L., Bates, J. F., & Grachev, I. D. (1997). Obsessive-compulsive disorder. *Child and Adolescent Psychiatric Clinics of North America, 6,* 365–382.

Rubia, K., Overmeyer, S., Taylor, E., Brammer, M., Williams, S., Simmons, A., et al. (1996). Hypofrontality in ADHD during higher-order motor control: A study with functional MRI. *American Journal of Psychiatry, 156,* 891–896.

Santosh, P. J., & Baird, G. (1999). Psychopharmacotherapy in children and adults with intellectual disability [Seminar]. *Lancet, 354,* 231–240.

Steingard, R. J., Renshaw, P. F., Yurgelun-Todd, D., Appelmans, K. E., Lyoo, I. K., Shorrock, K. L., et al. (1996). Structural abnormalities in brain magnetic resonance images of depressed children. *Journal of the American Academy of Child and Adolescent Psychiatry, 35,* 307–311.

Wang, A. T., Lee, S. S., Sigman, M., & Dapretto, M. (2006). Neural basis of irony comprehension in children with autism: The role of prosody and context. *Brain, 129,* 932–943.

Wolf, S. S., Jones, D. W., Knable, M. B., Gorey, J. G., Lee, K. S., Hyde, T. M., et al. (1996). Tourette syndrome: Prediction of phenotypic variation in monozygotic twins by caudate nucleus D2 receptor binding. *Science, 273,* 1225–1227.

Zametkin, A., & Liotta, W. (1997). The future of brain imaging in child psychiatry. *Child and Adolescent Psychiatric Clinics of North America, 6,* 447–460.

7

The Concept and Development
of General Intellectual Ability

Mike Anderson

This chapter will argue that an understanding of the nature of general intelligence and how it influences cognitive development is vital to an understanding of the majority of developmental disorders. There are two main reasons for this: one is empirical and the other theoretical. The empirical reason, while dull, is very important. Most developmental disorders are diagnosed with reference to a discrepancy in levels of performance from that predicted by the general intellectual functioning of the child. This discrepancy criterion may be obscuring our understanding of these disorders for reasons that I will explain below (Dyck et al., 2004). The theoretical reason is anything but dull. If it is true, as I will argue in this chapter, that understanding developmental disorders requires models that explicitly represent the influence of general intelligence on specific cognitive functions, then this will necessitate a major shift in approach from most who currently investigate a particular disorder. A benefit of grasping this particular nettle, however, is that the comorbidity of developmental disorders, something that is the bane of those researchers who like things neat and tidy, might be put in its proper context.

This chapter has six main sections. In the first, I will sketch the principal lines of evidence that suggest that general intelligence, or g, is a biologically determined, possibly genetic, major dimension of intellectual abilities. If you do not need to be convinced of this, then you can skip this section altogether. In the second section, I will discuss what the information-processing basis of general intelligence might be. In the third, I will discuss the way that this might be construed in a developmental context. In particular, I will contrast two major hypotheses for the nature of g: One argues that it is based on differences in speed of processing and another argues that it is based on differences in executive functioning. I will conclude this section by arguing that in a special sense both are correct and that g has, in fact, two dimensions—one related to individual differences and the other to developmental change—and I will introduce a theory that embodies this distinction.

In the fourth section of this chapter I will change tack and present what we know about "low intelligence" as if it were just like any other developmental disorder (which it is not) presented in this book. In the fifth section, I will show how the theory presented in section 3 can not only make sense of the central features of "mental retardation" but also allows that particular condition to connect with the other developmental disorders. This will lead us to two complementary conclusions developed in the last section of the chapter. The first will be that we need to take account of general intelligence if we study just about any other developmental disorder (one of the things that make low intelligence a "special" case). The second will be that not only is it empirically desirable to account for general intelligence when our interests are really in some "other" developmental disorder, but that it is theoretically necessary. This is because general intelligence and many kinds of developmental disorders are functionally, and not just statistically, linked.

General Intelligence

The debate over whether or not general intelligence is "real" or just the result of statistical machinations seems to have been with us for more than a hundred years following Spearman's seminal paper on general intelligence or *g* (Spearman, 1904). While there are still those who maintain that the concept of general intelligence is a narrow, school-based construct that bears little or no resemblance to either how intellect functions in everyday life or, indeed, how the brain works (see, for example, Gardner, 1983), there is just about universal consensus in the field that general intelligence does indeed exist—the only debate that remains is what "it" is. It is not my intention to review that debate here as this has been done in a number of places (Anderson, 1992; Howe, 1990, 1997; Howe & Smith, 1988, Jensen, 1998; Nettelbeck, 1990; Richardson, 1999; Rose, 1998; Sternberg, 1988). Rather, I will state the main reasons for believing that general intelligence is "real," then quickly move on to some current hypotheses as to what it might correspond to psychologically.

At first blush, the evidence for the reality of *g* is overwhelming. If a battery of heterogeneous cognitive tests is given to a representative sample of the population then the intercorrelations between these tests will nearly all be significantly greater than zero (Jensen, 1998). A theory of intelligence that claims that there is no such thing as general intelligence, and rather that there are a number of independent abilities, would predict that the majority of these correlations would be zero. A look at the standardization sample from the Wechsler Adult Intelligence Scale (WAIS) reveals that of the 91 intercorrelations between the subtests, 50% of them are greater than 0.47 and none is less than 0.26. This "positive manifold" is perhaps the most important replicable finding in all of psychology. Yet the obvious hypothesis first advanced by Spearman that all intellectual tasks have something in common has been disputed in a number of ways.

The most celebrated line of attack on *g* has been from within psychometrics itself. In essence, the argument is that if you analyze a correlation matrix of ability tests appropriately, you will discover not one general ability common to all tests but a number of independent abilities each of which have a small degree of overlap. This residual overlap is a small price to pay for the clarity that such an analysis reveals because now the factors line up with clearly identifiable clusters of cognitive tests. It was Thurstone (1938) who first advocated this alternative version of factor analysis and named the resulting factors, Primary Mental Abilities. This was grist to the mill for those who would deny the reality of *g*. The chain of reasoning was then reversed with the claim that this analysis showed not only that there might be no *g* but that *g* was in any case a mere creation, or fabrication, of the statistical machinations in factor analysis itself. The greatest proponent of this view has been Stephen J. Gould, who said memorably: "Factor analysis is a fine descriptive tool; I do not think it will uncover the elusive (and illusory) factors, or vectors, of mind. Thurstone dethroned *g* not by being right with his alternative system, but by being equally wrong—and thus exposing the methodological errors of the whole enterprise" (Gould, 1981, p. 310).

So, said Gould, the fundamental mistake, made particularly by Arthur Jensen, was to "reify" Spearman's *g* as a thing, particularly as a biological or genetic thing, rather than an arcane, statistical artifact. But what kind of artifact could it be that would give such replicable results as this positive manifold (results that are denied by no one)? There are a number of usual suspects, each of which, in my view, does not stand up to any real degree of scrutiny. The main ones are:

(1)   *The positive manifold is an inevitable artifact of the way that items are selected for each subtest. Items that are uncorrelated with other items are simply not selected to be on a test in the first place.* While it is true that items that are uncorrelated with any other item would be ruled out at the item selection stage, it would be because we would have no reason to believe that such an item measures anything at all. However, it is possible that items that correlate with other items on one particular scale (and therefore would not be ruled out at the item selection stage) might not correlate with items from another scale. Moreover, the creators of at least one test battery (the British Ability Scales) were firm believers in a number of hypothetical specific abilities. The original British Abilities Scales were made up of 23 scales specifically designed to measure different abilities and conformed to the psychometric standard that each scale was itself "unidimensional" (Andrich, 1988). But like all omnibus tests of cognitive abilities before it, it still yielded a large general factor (Elliott, 1983).

(2)   *The positive manifold simply reflects the large differences in social circumstances that exist in society. The items from the tests are drawn from a largely white, middle-class culture so people from those backgrounds will necessarily have an edge. So a variable like social class will confer an advantage on tests of all kinds of different abilities, creating an artifactual g factor.* There are a number of refutations of this. The major ones are: (a) The construction of an intelligence test is a highly technical matter. A major component of test construction is to assemble scales with items that range on a scale of difficulty. There are no consistent differences in these items' characteristics across different social groups—something we would not expect if performance was so variable with social class or other social grouping variables. (b) In major social group contrasts (for example, Black Americans compared with White Americans) it turns out that the group differences

are *lower* on the items that might be considered a priori to be the most culturally loaded (for example, items from verbal subscales compared with nonverbal or performance items). (c) Consistent with this is the observation that two common nonverbal tests of intelligence, Raven's Progressive Matrices and the Cattell Culture Fair, load almost entirely on the *g* factor from omnibus intelligence tests and yet are usually considered to be among the least culturally loaded intelligence tests. While there are undoubtedly cultural effects on items in many different tests, those effects are largely sporadic, unsystematic, and small, and unable to account for the variance in *g* itself.

We are left then with the most likely hypothesis being one that starts from the proposition that *g* is psychologically real, rather than being either a test construction artifact or a reflection of cultural bias. The hypothesis that *g* is based on some biological, possibly genetically influenced, property of cognitive functioning is but one of the possible hypotheses. For example, *g* might be based on some motivational or attitudinal state. However, one hundred years of investigation has not produced more than a thimbleful of evidence for the alternatives. By contrast, there is ample evidence that *g* is based on some fundamental aspect of the information-processing system. The only real question is—which one?

The Information-processing Basis of General Intelligence

The dominant hypothesis of the past 40 years is that differences in speed of information processing are the fount of differences in general intelligence. This research program began in earnest in the 1970s with the studies of correlations between relatively simple measures of reaction time and IQ (Jensen, 1982). Following quickly on the heels of this work was the development of a speed measure, inspection time, which circumvents some of the interpretation difficulties of the reaction-time research because of the higher strategic components in reaction-time tasks (Longstreth, 1984). Because of the discussion later in the chapter on the role that inspection time plays in the speed of processing, it is worth considering the task in some more detail here.

In a typical inspection-time (IT) task, participants have to make a simple perceptual discrimination, usually whether two lines are of equal or unequal length or which of two lines is the longest. It is important that the perceptual discrimination is very easy, and under normal viewing conditions participants can make the discrimination with 100% accuracy. However, in the procedure the stimulus exposure duration is limited by the presence of a backward-masking stimulus whose onset prevents further processing of the IT stimulus. The stimulus onset asynchrony of the mask is systematically varied until an accuracy threshold (usually about 70%) is obtained for each participant. This threshold is an individual's inspection time and is taken to index their speed of information processing. Shorter inspection times therefore reflect higher speed of information processing. A number of reviews and meta-analysis have confirmed that the likely correlation between inspection time and IQ is around 0.5 in the general population

(Kranzler & Jensen, 1989; Nettelbeck, 1987). This is a very high correlation for a single task measure, and is one of the main lines of argument that supports the claim that variations in speed of processing cause individual differences in intelligence.

Because many cognitive psychologists were uninterested in the construct of general intelligence (see Anderson, 2005, for a discussion), research on the speed of the information-processing basis of general intelligence left much of mainstream cognitive psychology untouched, with the exception of those interested in the general processes of cognitive change in children (Fry & Hale, 1996; Hale, 1990; Kail, 1991a, 1991b, 1992; Kail & Park, 1994; Kail & Salthouse, 1994) and in the elderly (Salthouse, 1985, 1991, 1996). But meanwhile, an information-processing challenger to speed of processing as the basis of *g* was strutting its stuff on a different stage through the 1990s. This challenger comes in a variety of forms but can be categorized under the umbrella term "executive functioning." Executive functions can be broadly defined as those that afford the flow of control in information processing. The two main information-processing constructs central to both executive functions and what is now commonly called "fluid" intelligence (*g* by any other name, Gustafsson, 1984) are inhibition and working memory capacity.

Dempster (1991) argued that the ability to inhibit irrelevant task information may be a fundamental dimension of intelligence. He broadened this notion to say that resistance to interference in general subsumed particular processes of inhibition (Dempster & Corkill, 1999). Inhibitory processes have been measured using a great variety of tasks, including the Stroop color-naming task, go/no-go, negative priming and stop reaction-time tasks, the Wisconsin Card Sorting Test, and a variety of memory tasks designed to assess interference in memory. More recently, researchers have turned to working memory capacity as a possible basis of *g* (Blair, 2006; Engle, 2002). The present situation is even more complex with a current debate around whether working memory capacity itself depends on processes of inhibition or whether the situation is reversed and that individual differences in inhibitory tasks are themselves dependent on more fundamental individual differences in working memory capacity (Kane & Engle, 2002). Many studies have found a strong enough relationship between measures of inhibition, working memory capacity, and intelligence to lend substance to the claim that they might be the information-processing basis of *g*. Furthermore, the association of inhibition with executive functioning in general and the development of the frontal lobes of the brain have increased this momentum. This debate has played out more in the developmental literature, but before I turn to that I would like to turn to a radically different conception of both executive and frontal functioning that has unequivocally challenged the speed of processing theory of *g*. This is John Duncan's theory of fluid intelligence.

Duncan (1995; Duncan et al., 1996) has argued that Spearman's *g* and frontal processes are synonymous. The motive for his theory was provided by the paradox that while the frontal cortex of the brain has often been considered the seat of human intelligence, damage to the frontal regions often leave a patient's IQ unaffected. Certainly, the speed of processing view of general intelligence would not argue that there is anything special about frontal functions and so would be unsurprised by this finding. If it were not for the fact that the same patients usually have difficulties with problem solving in their everyday life, the matter might have been left there. Duncan's resolution of this paradox was to point out that IQ tests measure two important aspects of general intelligence, named by Cattell (1963) as crystallized and fluid *g*. Fluid *g* is the ability to solve problems in the here and now, whereas crystallized *g* is the knowledge depository of the application of fluid *g* to the real world. Cattell argued that these two kinds of *g* were differentially related to environmental and biological variables and have different developmental functions. Duncan's argument was that IQ tests are much more loaded on crystallized than fluid *g*, and that when patients with frontal damage are tested on IQ tests their crystallized knowledge masks the damage done to their fluid *g*. Indeed, an analysis of three patients with frontal damage showed that despite normal IQs, derived from an omnibus Wechlser test, their fluid intelligence, as measured by the Cattell Culture Fair test, was severely impaired (Duncan, Burgess, & Emslie, 1995). Duncan believes that this is because the frontal lobes of the brain are the areas responsible for instantiating cognitive routines for problem solving. These routines involve the establishing of hierarchies of task goals, maintaining those goals, and monitoring ongoing information processing in service of those goals: the core functions of what others call executive functioning. In a task designed to measure these functions, the goal-neglect task, Duncan not only showed that patients with frontal damage performed very poorly, but that performance on this task in individuals with no known brain damage is predicted by their levels of fluid *g*. So the current question is whether the basis of *g* is to be found in differences in speed of processing or in differences in executive functioning. The answer is both—as we shall see when we consider the development of general intelligence.

The Development of General Intelligence

We now have two alternative hypotheses to consider: (a) that *g* is caused by differences in speed of processing; and (b) that *g* is caused by differences in executive functioning. Before we consider the implications of each for understanding the development of general intelligence, we need to establish an important distinction when we consider general intelligence in a developmental context. The distinction is between intelligence as indexed by IQ and intelligence as indexed by mental age (MA). There are two reasons why this is important. The first is that the distinction is necessary for us to understand the concern of the next section: how low IQ affects developmental change. The second is that the distinction maps onto the two dimensions of *g* that will be the major hypothesis to emerge from the current section of the chapter.

The essence of the method invented by Binet to construct the first intelligence test or mental scale was to calculate the difficulty of any one ability test item (What is 2 + 2? Who is the president of the United States?) by determining the youngest age at which the average child passed the item. An easier item would be passed on average by a younger child than the average age of children who pass a more difficult item. It was Binet's genius to see that this empirical finding could be inverted so that we could now measure the child of whatever age against the mental-age scale of the items. So, if a child obtained a score that was typical of a 10-year-old on the new measurement scale, they recorded a mental age of 10. It was Stern (1912) who first quantified the alternative perspective on this score. If we know the child's mental age (derived from their test score), we can determine whether they are above or below average for their age. Stern realized that by calculating the ratio of mental age to chronological age, an intelligence quotient (IQ), indicating the relative intelligence of a child to his or her same-age peers, could be calculated. In developmental psychology, the notion of general intelligence that has dominated the field is that of mental age, with IQ regarded as some nonfunctional statistical artifact of the calculation of mental age. As we shall see, it was only in the context of investigating the development of children with mental retardation that IQ became a consideration in its own right.

Speed of processing and development

Given the strong association between speed of processing and IQ in adult research, it was a reasonable step for those interested in the development of intelligence to propose that perhaps this is underlain by changing speed of processing. At first blush, there is a great deal of evidence in favor of this idea: (a) The two major methods of measuring speed of processing, reaction time and inspection, both show substantial improvements with age (Fairweather & Hutt, 1978; Keating & Bobbitt, 1978; Nettelbeck & Wilson, 1985). (b) Brinley plots, where mean reaction times for many different kinds of information-processing conditions are compared across different age groups, seem to reveal amazingly linear functions, suggesting a common (or general) developmental factor that many have interpreted as changing speed of processing for both child development (Hale, 1990; Kail, 1986, 1991a, 1991b; Kail & Park, 1992; Kail & Salthouse, 1994) and cognitive decline in aging (Salthouse, 1985, 1991, 1996). However, I have long disputed this interpretation for both reaction-time and inspection-time data (Anderson, 1986, 1988, 1992) and for Brinley plots (Anderson, 1995).

In the case of reaction time and inspection time, I argued that both of these tasks might have processes that are unrelated to IQ in adults but are sensitive to developmental changes in children. For example, Anderson, Nettelbeck, and Barlow (1997) compared reaction times in 7- and 11-year-old children under two task conditions with different response-selection demands. In the low demand condition, children moved a single finger to a button located under a particular stimulus light (of which there were eight). In the high demand condition, children placed all eight of their fingers (thumbs were excluded!) on a separate response key. On the illumination of the light, children had to respond by pressing the appropriate response key and this involved choosing amongst alternative fingers. When speed estimates were derived from these tasks, Anderson et al. found that it was only the condition with high response-selection demands that showed apparent changes in speed with age. Even in inspection-time tasks, there are response-selection components that impose a relatively greater load on younger children (Anderson, 1989). I have argued, then, that what changes with age in children is not speed of processing per se, but response-selection processes that contribute more to task performance in children than they do in adults. In the case of the Brinley plot analyses that claim to show a single global speed function underlying developmental change, it has been shown that the method of analysis would be insensitive to specific processes that have different developmental functions (Anderson, 1995; Perfect 1994).

While it may be appealing to parsimony to argue that speed of processing underlies both individual differences in intelligence and developmental changes, the data are not conclusive. Moreover, there is a more interesting interpretation that reconciles the data on both speed of processing and executive functioning. Before I present that interpretation, let us consider the evidence that executive functioning undergoes large developmental changes and might be considered as the candidate process for the development of general intelligence.

The development of executive functioning

There is no doubt that the measures of the many facets of executive functioning—principally, working memory capacity, inhibition, error monitoring, goal setting and maintenance—undergo considerable developmental change. This makes executive functioning the prime candidate for the process underlying the development of general intelligence and carries with it the additional attraction to the goal of this chapter that it has been nominated as the process common to many different developmental disorders (Pennington & Ozonoff, 1996).

The notion of working memory capacity, so popular in developmental circles today, was predated by the older, more generic construct of processing capacity—offered as the driver of general developmental change by theorists such as Pascual-Leone (1970) and Halford (1993). Although quite different in detail, both theories argue that the development of intelligence involves the child's increasing ability to cope with the demands on cognitive capacity imposed by problems of increasing structural complexity. Halford's scheme in particular supposes that it is increases in cognitive capacity that enable the older child to hold in mind task representations of much higher complexity than that within the capabilities of a younger child. This increasing capacity, couched now in working memory terms, would allow the developing child to achieve much better executive control in many problem-solving situations (Engle, 2002).

While it may be the case that most developmentalists hold that some kind of changing cognitive capacity underlies development, some have argued that it is a particular "frontal function," namely inhibition (or resistance to interference in Dempster's terms), that causes this change in capacity. Again, it is not difficult to find research that demonstrates that older children appear to be better at inhibition in a number of the classic paradigms (Stroop, go/no-go, stop reaction time, and so on). Bjorklund and Harnishfeger (1990) in particular put great store in the development of inhibition as the general motor of developmental change. I too have argued that inhibitory processes may be core to developmental changes in fluid intelligence, although this argument has recently met with, at best, mixed empirical support (Michel & Anderson, in press).

Whatever the underlying cause, all agree that children can solve problems of increasing difficulty and that their apparent cognitive capacity increases during development. So, even if it is only at the level of description, it is uncontentious to regard the development of general intelligence as being concomitant with the development of executive functions. It is probably not worth spending much more time considering whether this can be best construed as caused by a changing ability to inhibit or by a changing working memory capacity, both of which are subserved by the development of the frontal cortices. That is, what we want to see is how the concept of general intelligence might be crucial for understanding both development in the mentally retarded and what role it might play in developmental disorders. To do this we need to cut to the chase and consider a theory that explicitly makes these links.

The theory of the minimal cognitive architecture

Anderson's theory of minimal cognitive architecture (Figure 7.1) is framed within a general theory of cognitive architecture proposed by Fodor (1983) that makes the distinction between central processes of thought and dedicated processing modules. Anderson (1992) argues that intelligence tests measure intelligence through assessing knowledge, but that knowledge itself is acquired through the two different routes proposed by Fodor. The major proposition is that these two processing routes are related to the two different dimensions of intelligence: one related to individual differences and the other to cognitive development.

The first route to knowledge is through *thought* (central processes). Thoughtful problem solving can be done either by verbalizing a problem (using language-like propositions to think) or by visualizing it (using visuospatial representations to think). In the theory, this is accomplished by having two different kinds of knowledge acquisition routines, each generated by one of two specific processors. The observed ability served by either specific processor is constrained by the speed of a basic processing mechanism—at slow speed only the simplest kinds of thoughts of either kind can be implemented (the speed of the basic processing mechanism can be measured using tasks such as inspection time and reaction time). It is this constraint that is the basis of individual differences in general intelligence and the reason why manifest specific abilities are correlated (giving rise to the g factor). A "differentiation" effect, where differences between specific abilities become more obvious at higher levels of intelligence (Anderson & Nelson, 2005; Rabbitt & Anderson, 2006) was built into this architecture. This means that the correlations between different abilities are lower in higher IQ groups and predicts, for example, that differences in different specific abilities are greater for high IQ children. To enable this effect, as speed of processing increases so the constraint on the specific processors decreases. Thus, at faster processing speed, the latent differences between the specific processors

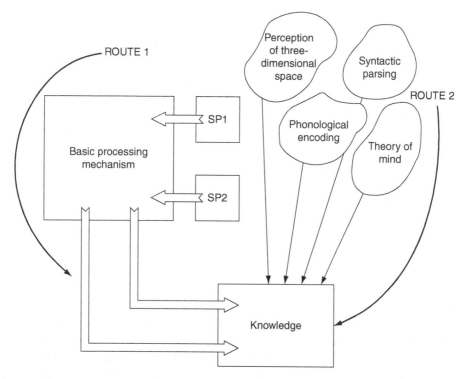

Figure 7.1 Anderson's model of minimal cognitive architecture.

become more manifest and correlations between tasks measuring these abilities should decrease. This makes speed of processing more important for "lower ability" groups, and in turn this would make the *g* factor stronger in low than in high groups. This predicts the differentiation of abilities (greater independence and importance of specific abilities) at higher levels of IQ (see Detterman & Daniel, 1989), and the complement: the pervasiveness and importance of difference in "general intelligence" at lower levels of IQ.

The second route for acquiring the knowledge that will influence intelligence test performance is through dedicated information-processing *modules*. Modules have evolved to provide information about the environment that could not be provided by central processes of thought (route 1 knowledge acquisition) in an ecologically useful time-frame. Examples of likely modules are various language acquisition devices, face recognition systems, the core computational procedures involved in acquiring a theory of mind, and the fetch and carry mechanisms of information processing (for example, inhibition) that might subserve "executive functions." In addition, modular processes can be acquired through extensive practice. The common features of both the acquired and the "innate" modules are that they operate automatically and independently of thought and are consequently unconstrained by the speed of the basic processing mechanism.

The theory of the *minimal cognitive architecture* argues, then, that there are two dimensions to *g*. The first is related to IQ differences within ages and is based on an unchanging speed of processing. The second is related to developmental changes in cognitive competence and is underpinned by the maturation and acquisition of modules. It is because modules function independently of variations in the speed of the basic processing mechanism that their operation is independent of differences in IQ. In turn, this means that individual differences and cognitive development represent two independent dimensions of intelligence. It also means that these complex cognitive functions are available to all nonbrain-damaged individuals with intellectual disabilities. In the next section, we shall see how this theory can be used to explain the developmental pattern we see in mental retardation. In the section following that we shall see how it explains why some developmental disorders should be independent of differences in general intelligence.

Low General Intelligence and Development

Understanding intelligence and understanding mental retardation have usually been regarded as complementary sides of the same coin, and understanding how children with mental retardation compare with typically developing children was once one of the most active research areas in developmental psychology—but no more I think. I believe the reason for this is the same as the reason why the modern developmental counterpart of this research—interest in developmental disorders—pays no heed to the idea of general intelligence. The reason, in short, is that it was thought that the notion of general intelligence added nothing much to our understanding of typical development and nothing at all to our understanding of specific developmental disorders. The dominant view was that children with mental retardation were pretty much just like their nonretarded younger counterparts, except in cases when mental retardation was caused by organic brain damage (Zigler & Balla, 1977), so they offered no special insight into the nature of developmental change. Equally, because mentally retarded children were poorer at everything by definition, studying their abilities was considered uninformative for those interested in specific developmental disorders. There were a few dissenting voices that claimed that the mentally retarded did develop differently and in ways functionally related to the cause of their retardation (Spitz, 1982). In my view these voices were correct: Mental retardation does influence the development of intelligence and in ways that throw light on the nature of many kinds of developmental disorders. So how is mental retardation diagnosed?

Unfortunately, mental retardation might be mistaken for a derogatory term, but in this chapter I use it in its technical sense because mental retardation is a well-known diagnostic category. DSM-IV lists a number of defining characteristics, the most pertinent and crucial of which is IQ less than 70 (two standard deviations below the population mean). However, to warrant the diagnosis, low IQ must be accompanied by deficits or impairments in adaptive functioning and onset must be before 18 years of age.

Mental retardation is further subdivided into a number of categories—mild, moderate, severe, and profound—directly related to decreasing levels of IQ.

When we look at the history of research into the effect of low IQ on development, there are two classic distinctions in the literature. The first is between two types of causes of retardation, and this is known as two groups theory (Zigler & Balla, 1977). This theory says that a distinction must be drawn between, on the one hand, mental retardation that is caused by organic brain damage and, on the other, mental retardation that represents the tail of the normal distribution of abilities—called, somewhat confusingly, cultural-familial retardation. The latter group is called cultural-familial because it is hypothesized that the normal distribution of intelligence is determined by both genetic and environmental factors and that, consequently, low intelligence within the normal distribution is caused either by poor genes or poor environment and most probably both. The basic idea is that in the former group brain damage results in a cognitive system that is likely to be abnormal in a whole host of ways and the development of these children cannot be similar to the development of typical children. However, in the latter case, the processes underlying cognition are not different but simply lie at the bottom end of a normal continuum, and so these children develop in the same way as normal children but do so more slowly.

Evidence that there are two such groups is fairly clear: (a) in some children with low IQ the source of brain damage is well known and easy to diagnose, but in many other children with low IQ there is no independent evidence of organic brain damage; (b) there is a "hump" in the tail of the normal distribution, indicating that there are more children of very low IQ (IQ 50 and below) than we would expect given only a normal distribution of intelligence; (c) the siblings of children with very low IQs are more likely to have higher IQs than the siblings of children with only mild to moderate mental retardation (Broman et al., 1987). This last piece of evidence is telling. It suggests that organic brain damage results in more severe retardation and that there is little reason to believe that it is familial. Less severe forms of retardation, on the other hand, show sibling relationships more consistent with familial transmission.

The second classic distinction in the literature is known as the development versus difference controversy. If you do not already know, you can probably guess how the advocates line up. The advocates of the developmental position argue that children with cultural-familial mental retardation go through the normal stages of cognitive development as do typically developing children; they just do so more slowly and perhaps in some cases stop at an earlier stage (Zigler, 1969). Proponents of the difference view, on the other hand, argue that children are mentally retarded because of some pervasive cognitive deficit that prevents retarded children ever being cognitively "normal" (Spitz, 1982). In short, the difference view, unlike the developmental view, holds that retarded children cannot ever be considered as cognitively equivalent to typical, albeit younger, children. My reading of the literature sees no real contest between these alternatives. The difference view was in the main correct: Mental retardation is usually caused by an information-processing deficit that is pervasive and unchanging, so a mentally retarded child cannot be cognitively equivalent to a nonretarded child no matter their respective ages. Yet there are some cognitive domains where development appears to be broadly unaffected by low IQ. Making sense of this requires turning our theoretical lens on this old material. But first, the basic logic of mental age-matching (MA-matching) needs to be explained, and the data considered in more detail.

The major prediction of the developmental position is that when retarded and non-retarded children are matched for mental age (overall they perform on intelligence tests at the same level), there should be no cognitive difference between the groups. This is because, on this view, the retarded children have reached the same cognitive stage as the nonretarded, they have just taken longer to get there. To understand the significance of this you need only realize that this would mean that MA-matching should leave no influence of IQ on performance. However, in nearly all studies comparing two MA-matched groups on some pertinent cognitive task the retarded (low IQ) group does worse than the younger, typically developing (normal IQ) group. The developmental theorists argue that this is because the retarded group have additional *noncognitive* problems that impair task performance. One example might be motivation, another learned helplessness. However, the difference theorists, Herman Spitz foremost among them, argue that the lack of cognitive equivalence has a pattern that reflects the differential loading of general intelligence on specific tasks. The difference that remains in performance on cognitive tasks between retarded and nonretarded MA-matched groups (called mental age-lag) is greatest on the most *g*-loaded subtests of intelligence tests (Spitz, 1982). And, of course, to achieve mental-age equivalence, the mentally retarded group performs better than their younger, typically developing counterparts on the least *g*-loaded subtests. In sum, what captures the different pattern is that *g*-loaded tests where the lag is greatest require more thinking and reasoning, whereas the other tests are more dependent on knowledge and experience—and this is where the older retarded children have an advantage.

However, it was a series of studies by Weisz and colleagues that finally settled this issue and generated in turn an interesting new twist to the story (Weiss, Weisz, & Bromfield, 1986). A series of meta-analyses looked at how MA-matched groups performed on a range of tasks subject to developmental change. Studies were analyzed that ranged over two kinds of groups with mental retardation, those with organic brain damage and those thought to be cultural-familial, and two kinds of task, Piagetian tasks and information-processing tasks. Although these analyses were very complex, two striking facts emerged. The mentally retarded group with known organic brain damage could not be considered to be cognitively equivalent to a normal-IQ, but MA-matched, typically developing group on either Piagetian or information-processing tasks. However, the cultural-familial mentally retarded group could be considered equivalent to their normal-IQ, MA-matched control children, but only when the task performance involved Piagetian tasks and not information-processing tasks. In the latter case, the mentally retarded still performed worse, demonstrating an effect of IQ over and above mental age. I have interpreted this effect as consistent with the idea that Piagetian tasks index broad-brush major conceptual changes in development that are largely independent of IQ, but not mental age. On the other hand, when the tasks require online information processing, performance shows the enduring effects of IQ differences. This may reflect the fact that MA-matching cannot equate for differences in speed of information processing, differences that are unchanging with cognitive development (Anderson, 1992, 1998, 2001). This brings us back to consider the data through the theoretical lens of the minimal cognitive architecture.

Let us first consider children who the literature would place within the cultural-familial group. They have low IQ because of the likely cojoint effects of genes and environment. In the theory of the minimal cognitive architecture (MCA), the primary cause of this kind of mental retardation is slow speed of processing. Further, because speed of processing is unchanging with development, this will represent an enduring cognitive deficit, even under conditions where retarded and nonretarded children are mental age-matched. Thus, this difference will be detected by any information-processing task that indexes speed of processing—most obviously by tasks that require thought. So, what of the findings that certain aspects of cognitive development seem spared the effect of IQ—at least when mental age is controlled? Clearly, this must mean that mental age itself includes development in processes that are independent of speed of processing.

There are two classes of process that this might be true for. To the extent that development is underpinned by the maturation or acquisition of modular processing, it should show independence from speed of processing and, therefore, IQ differences. One such category of processes might be those that themselves underpin the development of executive functioning. As I have already indicated, my favorite candidate was inhibition, but empirical tests of this have so far proved disappointing. But it may be other features of executive functioning, such as goal maintenance (Duncan et al., 1996), that hold the key to speed-independent cognitive change. The other class of processes may be where the development of knowledge itself reaches a particular state that intrinsic processes of reorganization, perhaps like those processes envisaged by Karmiloff-Smith (1992), lead to significant conceptual changes in children—such as might be measured by Piagetian tasks. If this knowledge state is best predicted by mental age, mentally retarded children might take longer to reach that state but when they do, cognitive change proceeds uninfluenced by their low IQ.

In the case of children whose mental retardation is caused by organic brain damage, the theory opens up a number of interesting possibilities. First, the organic brain damage may have the effect of lowering speed of information processing. Such cases of organic brain damage, while perhaps more severe, would not differ qualitatively from the cognitive pattern presented in mild to moderate cultural-familial mental retardation. Perhaps an example of such a case would be the pattern of abilities in children with Down syndrome. The second case would be where brain damage affects only one processing module. If that module has global effects on cognition, then we might see mental retardation in the presence of normal levels of speed of processing. This is the claim I would like to make for the cognitive pattern found in autism. According to MCA theory, it should also be the case that mental retardation caused by slow speed of processing, or mental retardation caused by damage to a module with global consequences, should nevertheless leave other modular processes intact. The next section will present some evidence consistent with this, and finally address how a consideration of general intelligence is necessary to understand many developmental disorders.

General Intelligence and Developmental Disorders

There are a number of hypothetical modules in the theory of the minimal cognitive architecture not all of which are likely to be implicated in developmental disorders. The modules themselves come in three categories. Modules Mark I are the full-blown computational devices, such as those supporting language acquisition and perception of space, built by evolution; Mark II are the fetch-and-carry mechanisms that make information processing possible, and Mark III are specialized computational devices acquired through extensive experience and task practice (Anderson, 1992). One of the principal lines of supporting evidence is to show that these hypothetical modules operate normally in people with mental retardation. While most of the evidence for modularity is to be found in the cognitive, neuroscience, and evolutionary psychology literature (e.g. the notion of a language module), the distinction has also received experimental support for both faces and ecological perception (Anderson & Miller, 1998; Moore, Hobson, & Anderson, 1995) and theory of mind. It is instructive that one developmental disorder, Williams syndrome, seems to represent the case where general intelligence is low but many aspects of language operate at normal levels. While it is clear that the linguistic abilities of Williams syndrome children are not "normal" (Karmiloff-Smith et al., 1997), they are nevertheless superior to those seen in children of similar IQs and therefore represent some kind of modular sparing from the effects of low IQ.

Table 7.1 gives a quick summary of the relationship between IQ, modularity, and three developmental disorders. According to MCA theory, developmental disorders that show no influence of general intelligence should have a modular basis. Consequently, which disorders are likely to fall into this category are most obvious when children with these disorders have normal IQs and perhaps the most obvious of these is dyslexia. Children with autism represent the opposite case. As already suggested, there are many indications that the autistic deficit in theory of mind is not a result of low IQ. This is because many of the control studies use children with low IQ as controls and they seem to find the problems that autistic children fail relatively easy. So it cannot be low IQ per se that causes problems with theory of mind. But why then do autistic children usually have low IQs? Is it simply that low IQ is *comorbid* with a theory of mind deficit? On the assumption that some brain damage underlying autism might damage the "systems" also underlying general intelligence, this is certainly possible. But a more interesting theoretical possibility is that in the case of autism it is the specific deficit in theory of mind that also causes low IQ. The global consequence of this specific deficit has been mooted before (Anderson, 1998; Frith & Happé, 1998). Further, Scheuffgen and colleagues (Scheuffgen, Happé, Anderson, & Frith, 2000), using an inspection-time task,

Table 7.1 A Summary of the Relationship between IQ, Modularity, and Three Developmental Disorders.

Developmental disorder	Basic processing mechanism	Module	Effect on IQ
Cultural-familial mental retardation	Impaired	Intact	Impaired
Autism	Intact	Specific module impairment leading to global effect	Impaired
Dyslexia	Intact	Specific module impairment leading to specific effect	Normal

have shown that children with autism had normal levels of speed of processing. This is also consistent with the fast speed of processing found in an autistic savant prime-number calculator reported by Anderson, O'Connor, and Hermelin (1998). Children with dyslexia, despite having normal levels of "intelligence," have a specific problem with reading and spelling—so their relationship to intelligence is quite different from children with autism, despite both problems being "modular." But there is an empirical quandary at the heart of looking for specific cognitive deficits only where intelligence is "normal."

Dyck et al. (2004) measured a number of ability dimensions (intelligence, language, motor coordination, empathic ability, and attentional control), all of which were hypothesized to be related to a variety of different developmental disorders. A variety of tests and tasks were used to measure these dimensions in a cohort of typically developing children ranging in age from 3 to 12 years. Most developmental disorders use some sort of criteria for diagnosis based on a discrepancy with intelligence; that is, a low ability score is only considered diagnostic for that disorder if it meets some criteria for being significantly lower than the score you would expect given a child's level of intelligence. Dyck et al. (2004) found two very important artifacts of using this method. The first is that the probability of finding a score that is deviant increases as a function of the intelligence test score. For purely statistical reasons, then, a child diagnosed with a developmental disorder is likely to have an above average IQ. The second artifact is that the probability of meeting this criterion varies with the size of the correlation between the ability dimension and intelligence. For example, age-standardized language scores correlated 0.66 with IQ scores whereas age-standardized motor control scores correlated 0.21. Only 2.6% of children had language scores more than 2 standard deviations lower than predicted from their intelligence, whereas 21% had motor scores that met the 2 standard deviation lower cut-off. Both groups of children who met the discrepancy criterion had mean IQs of 113 compared with a mean IQ of 100 in the groups who did not meet the criterion. This means that in our diagnostic schemes we have already "factored in" the fact that intelligence might be important to determining if a child has a disorder. But this simply leads to statistical artifacts of the kinds described and, without a model that explicitly accommodates what we mean by intelligence, it is likely that such factoring simply obscures attempts to understand the disorder.

In short, there is a confounding of the hypothetical role of general intelligence in any specific developmental disorder—for example, a reading disorder—simply because its very definition is not independent of general intelligence. Put another way, the definition rules out the possibility that a child with low intelligence *could also* have a specific reading disorder. However, according to the theory of the minimal cognitive architecture, it is equally likely that a child with low intelligence will have a reading disorder (if, for example, it is caused by a deficit in a module responsible for phonological awareness) as a child with normal or high intelligence. But how would we know it? None of this is to say that intelligence is irrelevant to understanding the disorder—far from it—but it is to say that we need a better understanding of the cognitive basis of the disorders that include an explicit role for general intelligence. That way, we could in principle distinguish the child with low IQ who also has a reading disorder from one with low IQ who hasn't. Equally, we might begin to understand how a child appears not to have disorder (i.e., passes a particular diagnostic task) because he or she has a certain level of general intelligence. Handwaving at the relationship is no longer good enough, especially when we come to grapple with comorbidity.

It should be clear by now that the problem in evaluating the role of "general intelligence" in developmental disorders is complicated by the fact that low IQ itself can have a number of different causes, and it is important theoretically to determine the cause of low IQ in each case. Equally, the case of autism also illustrates that while speed of processing may be the primary variable underlying individual differences in IQ, normal levels of speed of processing are not sufficient for normal levels of IQ. What is needed is a framework where these different theoretical options can be considered. This has been provided most recently by the causal modeling framework of Morton (2004).

General Intelligence Genetics and the Definition and Cause of Developmental Disorders

Morton's (2004) causal modeling framework recognizes that understanding developmental disorders requires us to do a number of things. The first is to clearly separate our observations and constructs into three different levels: the biological, the cognitive, and the behavioral. The second is to try to specify a model of the "cognitive phenotype" in such a way that the causal networks linking both biology and environment to behavioral outcomes make explicit the intervening roles of the various cognitive mechanisms. Figure 7.2 illustrates this for the case of autism. Essentially, the framework allows alternative cognitive theories of disorders to be compared in terms of their ability to explain the causal structure of the disorder. This is going to become increasingly "where the action is" as more and more theorists take on data about the genetics of disorders.

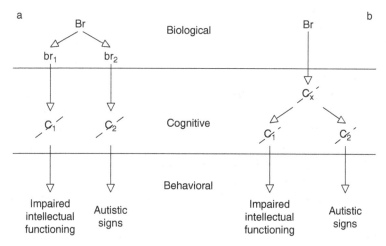

Figure 7.2 Morton's causal modeling framework. *Note.* Reproduced with permission from *Understanding developmental disorders: A causal modeling approach*, by J. Morton, 2004, Oxford: Blackwell.

Genetics, general intelligence, and developmental disorders

It is interesting that the genetic basis of general intelligence has long been the subject of a great deal of controversy, whereas the growing evidence that many developmental disorders have a genetic link is taken on board with barely a murmur of disapproval. Perhaps it is that we are prepared to accept that genes can be implicated when things go wrong but when things go right (high general intelligence) it is considered to be down to good education (or nurturing parents). But the data are well and truly in on general intelligence: There is a large genetic component to variation in general intelligence (Bouchard, Lykken, McGue, Segal, & Tellegen, 1990). Chapter 4 of this volume deals in detail with genetic influences on developmental disorders, so I will restrict myself to a few points to round out my case that understanding developmental disorders requires explicit representation of general intelligence in models of those disorders.

It is becoming clearer that developmental disorders like autism not only have a genetic component but may well have multiple genetic components. Moreover, the fact that there are multiple genetic components is now being used to argue that the disorder itself requires fragmentation into some more fundamental components (Happé, Ronald, & Plomin, 2006). Happé et al. (2006) argue that three genetic components in autism are causally related to each of the triad of core features of autism that were thought to be definitional for the disorder itself (social difficulty, communicative impairment, and rigid/repetitive behavior). However, they then rightly point out that we have to explain why those components co-occur so often as to attract single-cause theories in the first place. There are many ways that this can be attempted, overlapping genes being but one. But the issue of the co-occurrence of components of autism is but a microcosm of the issue of comorbidity itself.

Comorbidity is the increased probability that if a child is diagnosed with one developmental disorder they will be diagnosable with a second. The best known general case is the comorbidity between reading disorders and ADHD, something that is thought to be due to an overlap in genes implicated in both disorders. Pennington (2006) has described how he has moved from what he calls the single-cause model of a disorder to the multiple cognitive deficit model driven fundamentally not by the co-occurrence of a number of single causes but rather by the overlap of a number of risk factors, many of which will be genetic. Put together with the fractionation of single disorders like autism argued for by Happé et al., and we have a picture of developmental disorders that result from a smorgasbord of risk factors and causes, with cognitive sequelae that themselves can be combined in many different ways.

Such a move is consistent with other views stemming from our increased understanding of genetic influences on developmental disorders. For example, Bishop (2006) uses a risk-factor approach to look again at the cognitive basis of specific language impairment (SLI). She argues that different possible causes of SLI are differentially related to genetic and shared environmental variables and that for the cognitive components that show some heritability (phonologic and syntactic deficits) it is likely that different genes contribute to each. In reviewing these data, she makes the interesting observation that while the logic of dissociation has dominated research in developmental disorders (and dissociations are found), nevertheless *association* is more likely to be the norm. What is needed is not only to explain the crucial instances of dissociation but the occurrence of reliable associations between different types of impairments. While one way to do this is to regard the etiology of disorders as dependent on risk factors that may be correlated—sometimes for environmental reasons, sometimes for genetic reasons, and sometimes for brain reasons—there is another alternative that we may yet be wise to be sure to discount before we make such a fundamental conceptual shift. This alternative is that much of the apparent comorbidity may be due to the influence of different levels of "general intelligence." Representing what we believe general intelligence to be at the cognitive level might allow us to reinstate the simplicity of the single-cause model without violating all the new data on genetic risk factors. Leaving general intelligence out of the equation may well prove impossible anyway if modern genetic studies find that, after all this, it turns out that the genes implicated in specific developmental disorders and their comorbidity are the same genes implicated in variance in general intelligence. It is time for Cinderella to go to the ball.

A postscript on assessment

What does this theory and approach to understanding developmental disorders imply for assessment? First, it certainly does not argue that we should abandon standard approaches to intelligence testing. An omnibus intelligence test best typified by the Wechsler scales is probably always going to remain our single best estimate of the "intelligence" of a child. This is simply because intelligence tests work by sampling what individuals know, and what individuals know in turn is largely a function of the very mechanisms that we have been describing. However, in situations where we believe there may have been impoverished access to the conditions for typical knowledge acquisition then a more "knowledge-free" test of fluid intelligence (such as Raven's matrices) would give a better estimate of a child's capacity for thought rather than inferring that from an IQ derived from a Wechsler test. But, as I have argued before (Anderson, 1992), it is precisely because IQ-like tests are imperfect measures of the underlying constructs that they are of such practical use. They do pick up the additional variance provided by the child's social circumstances that makes them such useful educational predictors.

Second, when it comes to identifying developmental disorders, we pretty much face the same conundrum as before: Do we take "intelligence" itself into account in diagnosis and confront the issues highlighted by Dyck et al. (2004)? Clearly, one of the strengths of intelligence tests is that they are developmentally normed. There is a premium on developing tests of other developmental functions that have equivalent norms, allowing us to determine the presence or absence of a disorder by performance on that test alone (just as we detect mental retardation principally by identifying that an IQ is two standard deviations below the population norm). We would then be in a position to determine the *cause* of that deficit, and in most cases we may well decide it is because the general intelligence of the child has led to poor performance. But this is the appropriate logic of testing rather than using some apparent short-cut by diagnosing with respect to discrepancies with IQ that has all the attendant problems described above. Of course, as part of this subsequent process of determining cause, the development of more information-processing based *tests* of the hypothetical constructs may prove fruitful. At the moment, tasks such as inspection time are essentially experimental tools. We need to devote some energy to developing such tasks as measures, with reliabilities approaching those of psychometric tests, for them to be useful as assessment techniques. This applies just as much to tests of "inhibition" or "auditory sequencing" or the like as it does to speed of processing.

Acknowledgments

Thanks are due to Corinne Reid for her comments on drafts of this chapter, and to the Australian Research Council which supported this work through its discovery grant to the author (DP0665616) and colleagues, Allison Fox, Corinne Reid, and Dorothy Bishop.

References

Anderson, M. (1986). Understanding the cognitive deficit in mental retardation. *Journal of Child Psychology and Psychiatry, 27*, 297–306.

Anderson, M. (1988). Inspection time, information processing and the development of intelligence. *British Journal of Developmental Psychology, 6*, 43–57.

Anderson, M. (1989). Inspection time and the relationship between stimulus encoding and response selection factors in development. In D. Vickers & P. L. Smith (Eds.), *Human information processing measures, mechanisms and models* (pp. 509–516). Amsterdam: Elsevier Science.

Anderson, M. (1992). *Intelligence and development: A cognitive theory*. Oxford: Blackwell.

Anderson, M. (1995). Evidence for a single global factor of developmental change: Too good to be true? *Australian Journal of Psychology, 47*(1), 18–24.

Anderson, M. (1998). Individual differences in intelligence. In K. Kirsner, M. Maybury, C. Speelman, A. O'Brien-Malone, C. MacLeod, & M. Anderson (Eds.), *Implicit and explicit mental processes*. Hillsdale, NJ: Lawrence Erlbaum.

Anderson, M. (2001). Conceptions of intelligence. *Journal of Child Psychology and Psychiatry, 42*(3), 287–298.

Anderson, M. (2005). Cortex forum on the concept of general intelligence in neuropsychology. *Cortex, 41*, 99–100.

Anderson, M., & Miller, K. L. (1998). Modularity, mental retardation, and speed of processing. *Developmental Science, 1*, 239–245.

Anderson, M., & Nelson, J. (2005). Individual differences and cognitive models of the mind: Using the differentiation hypothesis to distinguish general and specific cognitive processes. In J. Duncan, P. McLeod, & L. Phillips (Eds.), *Measuring the mind: Speed, control and age* (pp. 89–113). Oxford University Press.

Anderson, M., Nettelbeck, T., & Barlow, J. (1997). Using reaction time measures of speed of information processing: Speed of response selection increases with age but speed of stimulus categorisation does not. *British Journal of Developmental Psychology, 15*, 145–157.

Anderson, M., O'Connor, N., & Hermelin, B. (1998). A specific calculating ability. *Intelligence, 26*(4), 383–403.

Andrich, D. (1988). *Rasch models for measurement*. Sage Series on Quantitative Applications in the Social Sciences, No. 07–068. Beverly Hills, CA: Sage.

Bishop, D. V. M. (2006). Developmental cognitive genetics: How psychology can inform genetics and vice versa. *Quarterly Journal of Experimental Psychology, 59*, 1153–1168.

Bjorklund, D. F., & Harnishfeger, K. K. (1990). The resources construct in cognitive development: Diverse sources of evidence and a theory of inefficient inhibition. *Developmental Review, 10*, 48–71.

Blair, C. (2006). Toward a revised theory of general intelligence: Further examination of fluid cognitive abilities as unique aspects of human cognition. *Behavioral and Brain Sciences, 29*, 145–153.

Bouchard, T. J., Lykken, D. T., McGue, M., Segal, N. L., & Tellegen, A. (1990). Sources of human psychological differences: The Minnesota study of twins reared apart. *Science Trends, 250*, 223–250.

Broman, S. H., Nicholas, P. L., Shaughnessy, P., & Kennedy, W. (1987). *Retardation in young children: A developmental study of cognitive deficit*. Hillsdale, NJ: Erlbaum.

Cattell, R. B. (1963). Theory of fluid and crystallized intelligence: A critical experiment. *Journal of Educational Psychology, 54*, 1–22.

Dempster, F. N. (1991). Inhibitory processes: A neglected dimension of intelligence. *Intelligence, 15*, 157–173.

Dempster, F. N., & Corkill, A. (1999). Neo-interference research and the development of intelligence. In M. Anderson (Ed.), *The development of intelligence* (pp. 215–243). Hove, East Sussex: Psychology Press.

Detterman, D. K., & Daniel, M. H. (1989). Correlations of mental tests with each other and with cognitive variables are highest for low IQ groups. *Intelligence, 13*, 349–359.

Duncan, J. (1995). Attention, intelligence, and the frontal lobes. In M. S. Gazzaniga (Ed.), *The cognitive neurosciences* (pp. 721–733). Cambridge, MA: MIT Press.

Duncan, J., Burgess, P., & Emslie, H. (1995). Fluid intelligence after frontal lobe lesions. *Neuropsychologic, 33*, 261–268.

Duncan, J., Emslie, H., Williams, P., Johnson, R., & Freer, C. (1996). Intelligence and the frontal lobe: The organization of goal-directed behaviour. *Cognitive Psychology, 30*, 257–303.

Dyck, M. J., Hay, D., Anderson, M., Smith, L. M., Piek, J., & Hallmayer, J. (2004). Is the discrepancy criterion for defining developmental disorders valid? *Journal of Child Psychology and Psychiatry, 45*, 979–995.

Elliott, C. D. (1983). *British ability scales: Technical handbook*. Windsor: NFER-Nelson.

Engle, R. W. (2002). Working memory capacity as executive attention. *Current Directions in Psychological Science, 11*, 19–23.

Fairweather, H., & Hutt, S. J. (1978). On the rate of gain of information in children. *Journal of Experimental Child Psychology, 26*, 216–229.

Fodor, J. A. (1983). *The modularity of mind*. Cambridge, MA: MIT Press.

Frith, U. & Happé, F. (1998). Why specific developmental disorders are not specific: On-line and developmental effects in autism and dyslexia. *Developmental Science, 1*, 267–272.

Fry, A. F., & Hale, S. (1996). Processing speed, working memory, and fluid intelligence: Evidence for a developmental cascade. *Psychological Science, 7*, 237–241.

Gardner, H. (1983). *Frames of mind: The theory of multiple intelligences*. London: Heinemann.

Gould, S. J. (1981). *The mismeasure of man*. New York: W. W. Norton.

Gustafsson, J. E. (1984). A unifying model for the structure of mental abilities. *Intelligence, 8*, 179–203.

Hale, S. (1990). A global developmental trend in cognitive processing speed. *Child Development, 61*, 653–663.

Halford, G. S. (1993). *Children's understanding: The development of mental models*. Hillsdale, NJ: Erlbaum.

Happé, F., Ronald, A., & Plomin, R. (2006). Time to give up on a single explanation for autism. *Nature Neuroscience, 9*, 1218–1220.

Howe, M. J. A. (1990). *The origins of exceptional abilities*. Oxford: Blackwell.

Howe, M. J. A. (1997). *IQ in question: The truth about intelligence*. London: Sage.

Howe, M. J. A., & Smith, J. (1988). Calendrical calculating in "idiots savants": How do they do it? *British Journal of Psychology, 79*, 371–386.

Jensen, A. R. (1982). Reaction time and psychometric g. In H. J. Eysenck (Ed.), *A model for intelligence* (pp. 93–132). Berlin: Springer Verlag.

Jensen, A. R. (1998). *The g factor: The science of mental ability*. Westport, CT: Praeger.

Kail, R. (1986). Sources of age differences in speed of processing. *Child Development, 57*, 969–987.

Kail, R. (1991a). Developmental change in speed of processing during childhood and adolescence. *Psychological Bulletin, 109*, 490–501.

Kail, R. (1991b). Processing time declines exponentially during childhood and adolescence. *Developmental Psychology, 27*, 259–266.

Kail, R. (1992). Processing speed, speech rate, and memory. *Developmental Psychology, 28*, 899–904.

Kail, R., & Park, Y.-S. (1992). Global developmental change in processing time. *Merrill-Palmer Quarterly, 4*, 525–541.

Kail, R., & Park, Y.-S. (1994). Processing time, articulation time, and memory span. *Journal of Experimental Child Psychology, 57*, 281–291.

Kail, R., & Salthouse, T. A. (1994). Processing speed as a mental capacity. *Acta Psychologica, 86*, 199–225.

Kane, M. J., & Engle, R. W. (2002). The role of prefrontal cortex in working-memory capacity, executive attention, and general fluid intelligence: An individual differences perspective. *Psychonomic Bulletin and Review, 9,* 637–671.

Karmiloff-Smith, A. (1992). *Beyond modularity: A developmental perspective on cognitive science.* Cambridge, MA: MIT Press.

Karmiloff-Smith, A., Grant, J., Berthoud, L., Davies, M., Howlin, P., & Udwin, O. (1997). Language and Williams syndrome: How "intact" is "intact?" *Child Development, 68,* 246–262.

Keating, D. P., & Bobbitt, B. L. (1978). Individual and developmental differences in cognitive processing components of mental ability. *Child Development, 49,* 155–167.

Kranzler, J. H., & Jensen, A. R. (1989). Inspection time and intelligence: A meta-analysis. *Intelligence, 13,* 329–347.

Longstreth, L. E. (1984). Jensen's reaction-time investigations of intelligence: A critique. *Intelligence, 8,* 139–160.

Michel, F., & Anderson, M. (in press). Do developmental changes in inhibitory ability underpin developmental changes in intelligence? *Developmental Science.*

Moore, D. G., Hobson, P., & Anderson, M. (1995). Person perception: Does it involve IQ-independent perceptual processing? *Intelligence, 20,* 65–86.

Morton, J. (2004). *Understanding developmental disorders: A causal modeling approach.* Oxford: Blackwell.

Nettelbeck, T. (1987). Inspection time and intelligence. In P. A. Vernon (Ed.), *Speed of information processing and intelligence* (pp. 295–346). Norwood, NJ: Ablex.

Nettelbeck, T. (1990). Intelligence does exist: A rejoinder to M. J. A. Howe. *The Psychologist, 3,* 494–497.

Nettelbeck, T. and Wilson, C. (1985). A cross sequential analysis of developmental differences in speed of visual information processing. *Journal of Experimental Child Psychology, 40,* 1–22.

Pascual-Leone, J. (1970). A mathematical model for the transition rule in Piaget's developmental stages. *Acta Psychologia, 32,* 301–345.

Pennington, B. F. (2006). From single to multiple deficit models of developmental disorders. *Cognition, 101,* 385–413.

Pennington, B. F., & Ozonoff, S. (1996). Executive functions and developmental psychopathology. *Journal of Child Psychology and Psychiatry, 37,* 51–87.

Perfect, T. J. (1994). What can Brinley plots tell us about cognitive aging? *Journal of Gerontology: Psychological Sciences, 49,* 60–64.

Rabbitt, P. M. A., & Anderson, M. (2006). The lacunae of loss? Aging and the differentiation of cognitive abilities. In F. Craik & E. Bialystok (Eds.), *Lifespan cognition: Mechanisms of change* (pp. 331–343). Oxford University Press.

Richardson, K. (1999). *The making of intelligence.* London: Weidenfeld & Nicolson.

Rose, S. (1998). *Lifelines: Biology beyond determinism.* Oxford University Press.

Salthouse, T. A. (1985). *A cognitive theory of aging.* Berlin: Springer Verlag.

Salthouse, T. A. (1991). *Theoretical perspectives in cognitive aging.* Hillsdale, NJ: Erlbaum.

Salthouse, T. A. (1996). The processing-speed theory of adult age differences in cognition. *Psychological Review, 103,* 403–428.

Scheuffgen, K., Happé, F., Anderson, M., & Frith, U. (2000). High "intelligence", low "IQ"? Speed of processing and measured IQ in children with autism. *Developmental Psychopathology, 12,* 83–90.

Spearman, C. (1904). "General intelligence", objectively determined and measured. *American Journal of Psychology, 15,* 201–293.

Spitz, H. H. (1982). Intellectual extremes, mental age, and the nature of human intelligence. *Merrill-Palmer Quarterly, 28*, 167–192.

Stern, W. (1912). *Die psychologische methoden der intelligenzprufung*. Leipzig: Barth.

Sternberg, R. J. (1988). Explaining away intelligence: A reply to Howe. *British Journal of Psychology, 79*, 527–533.

Thurstone, L. L. (1938). *Primary mental abilities*. University of Chicago Press.

Weiss, B., Weisz, J. R., & Bromfield, R. (1986). Performance of retarded and non-retarded persons on information processing tasks: Further tests of the similar structure hypothesis. *Psychological Bulletin, 100*, 157–175.

Zigler, E. (1969). Developmental versus difference theories of retardation and the problem of motivation. *American Journal of Mental Deficiency, 73*, 536–556.

Zigler, E., & Balla, D. (1977). *Mental retardation: The developmental difference controversy*. Hillsdale, NJ: Lawrence Erlbaum.

Part II
Theory of Neuropsychological Development

8

The Neuropsychology of Language Development

Frederic Dick, Robert Leech, and Fiona Richardson

At its most fundamental, language can be defined as a system composed of "words and the methods of combining them for the expression of thought" (*New Oxford American Dictionary*, 2005). In general, typically developing children will rapidly and comprehensively master at least one of the over 6,000 languages that exist around the globe. The complexity of these language systems, and the speed and apparent facility with which children master them, have been the topic of philosophical and scientific speculation for millennia. In AD 397, in reflecting upon his own acquisition of language, St. Augustine wrote "as I heard words repeatedly used in their proper places in various sentences, I gradually learnt to understand what objects they signified; and after I had trained my mouth to form these signs, I used them to express my own desires" (quoted in Wittgenstein, 1953). St. Augustine's intuitions notwithstanding, more recent thinking and research on children's language acquisition suggest that the problem facing a child is much more intricate than simply remembering the association between a sound and an object and learning to reproduce the word's sound. The rich and multitiered nature of this problem—and the many and varied paths to its solution (Bates, Bretherton, & Snyder, 1988)—make the process of language acquisition a unique window into multiple low and high level developmental processes. Indeed, studies of language development have provided unparalleled views into broad neural and behavioral change in response to input and consolidation, to injury, and the process of emergent organization and reorganization that unfolds over developmental time.

In this chapter, we will chart the multiple waves of change in language comprehension and production, beginning at birth with studies of speech perception, moving through babbling, phoneme and word discrimination into the dawn of word comprehension and production, and the subsequent emergence of syntactic and pragmatic abilities. We will also look at language's "fellow travelers," skills such as social cognition, gestural communication, and environmental sound recognition that appear to presage or accompany linguistic milestones. We will also consider the neural bases underlying early (mostly electrophysiological studies) and later language development (predominantly functional magnetic resonance imaging). In particular, recent neuro-imaging literature increasingly demonstrates the importance of experience and learning on the development of the neural correlates of language development, as well as the absence of any straightforward and task-independent, language-specific neural substrates. The section on typical development will focus, in part, on the impressive degree of individual differences in language learning—something that is of prime importance when evaluating language development in atypical populations. We will also highlight the importance of the structure and statistics of the input to multiple levels of language learning.

In the second half of the chapter, we turn to language acquisition in the face of disease, injury, or congenital disorder.[1] First, we review studies of "exogenous" challenges to children's language learning. These challenges include early exposure to neurotoxins or pathogens, as well as enforced sensory or social deprivation. The subsequent section presents a brief overview of the known effects of childhood traumatic brain injury (TBI) and surgical hemispherectomy on language learning. In the third section, we consider the trajectory of language development in four congenital developmental disorders (autism, Down syndrome, fragile-X syndrome, and Williams syndrome), with a special focus on the particular linguistic strengths and weakness observed in each population at different epochs of development. Finally, we survey the field of "specific" language impairment and its relationship to other developmental disorders. In all four sections, we explore the impact of genetic, neurological, and environmental influences on the developing system, showing how children's language acquisition can sometimes be dramatically delayed or deviant in the seeming absence of severe neurological, genetic, or environmental abnormality, but also how language acquisition is in some cases amazingly resilient to such insults. We close with a short overview of the literature on best clinical practice for the treatment of language disorders, and the potential directions for future research.

Language Acquisition in Typical Development

Precursors to language

The onset of language development is not signaled by the child's first word. Rather, even before birth infants are adapting to their language environment, mastering the necessary prelinguistic building blocks that support later language learning. As we will see in this section, over the first year of life children make huge strides in constructing the social, perceptual, and attentional tools that language needs to get off the ground.

---

[1] Please see also Chapter 5 of this volume for language and visuospatial development following perinatal focal lesions.

Even before and shortly after birth it is possible to see the effects of experience-dependent speech discrimination. For instance, the heartbeats of at-term fetuses tend to increase in response to hearing their mother's voice (Kisilevsky et al., 2003). Infants as young as 4 days old can use rhythm to discriminate between familiar and unfamiliar languages (Nazzi, Bertoncini, & Mehler, 1998); similar skills have also been noted in tamarin monkeys (Ramus, Hauser, Miller, Morris, & Mehler, 2000). Newborn infants also demonstrate evidence of phonetic categorical perception for the vowels and consonants from all human natural languages (Eimas, Siqueland, Juszcyk, & Vigorito, 1971; see Kuhl, 2004, for a review). Infants, like adults, classify sounds into different categories. That is to say, as some physical characteristic of a phonetic contrast varies along a continuum (such as voice-onset time), we do not hear gradual variation in the sounds but instead a sharp change from one sound to another. Again, this ability is not specific to humans: Monkeys (Kuhl & Padden, 1983) and chinchillas (Kuhl & Miller, 1975) demonstrate similar phonetic categorical perception as infants. One suggestion is that human phonetic categories have evolved around more general characteristics of mammalian sensory systems (Dick, Saygin, Moineau, Aydelott, & Bates, 2004; Kuhl, 1986; Smith & Lewicki, 2006; but see also Fitch & Hauser, 2004, and Tomasello, 1999, for evidence of more human-specific abilities that may play a part in language development).

Starting around the half-year mark, infants' ability to distinguish between all phonemes begins to disappear, so that by around the first year infants form a strong bias toward native language-specific phonetic perception, beginning with vowels and subsequently extending to consonants (for a review, see Werker & Desjardins, 1995). For instance, at 6 months an infant exposed to a Japanese-speaking environment can distinguish between the English /r/ and /l/ sounds, but by 12 months the same child discerns only a single phoneme, unlike an infant reared in an English-speaking environment. Furthermore, children's abilities to make such phonetic classifications in their native language at 7 months positively predicts language outcomes, such as word production, mean length of utterance (MLU), and sentence complexity between 14 and 20 months, whereas ability on non-native phonetic contrasts is inversely related to later language measures (Kuhl, Conboy, Padden, Nelson, & Pruitt, 2005).

What underlies these developmental changes in infants' auditory discrimination? There is growing evidence that in the second year of life, infants' phonetic discriminations in their native language increasingly rely on the stochastic distributional information available in natural speech. Although the actual examples of any given phoneme that an infant hears vary considerably along many acoustic dimensions, they tend to conform to general statistical distributions that the infant can use to identify the most informative boundaries for distinguishing phonemes (Juszcyk, Luce, & Charles-Luce, 1994; Kuhl, Williams, Lacerda, Stevens, & Lindblom, 1992; Maye, Werker, & Gerken, 2002; Saffran & Thiessen, 2003).

While infants do lose the ability to make discriminations for phonetic contrasts in all the world's languages at around the first birthday, this is not a straightforward example of a "critical" or "sensitive" period in brain maturation. An elegant combined behavioral and fMRI study by Pallier and colleagues demonstrated that Korean-speaking children who were adopted into French-speaking families between the ages of 3 and 8—importantly with no further exposure to Korean—did not differ from children born into French-speaking families when both were tested on phonetic contrasts in Korean and French as adults (Pallier et al., 2003).

In addition to learning to segment the speech stream into meaningful language, children are also faced with the task of producing meaningful speech themselves. The early precursors of productive language start with infants' preverbal vocalizations. From around 3 months, infants begin producing vowel sounds, and appear to be able to imitate adult-modeled vowel sounds (Kuhl & Meltzoff, 1996). From 6 to 8 months infants start *babbling*—making consonant–vowel combinations, for example, *ba, ata*. This early babbling is not obviously communicative, often occurring when the infant is on his or her own. As with phonetic perception, over the first year the sounds the infant produces move from being "universal" (with respect to all of the world's languages) to increasingly resembling the sounds of the language(s) spoken around them. Infants produce native language-specific vowel and consonant sounds before they produce their first words, thus internalizing the acoustical or phonetic patterns of the language they are exposed to (Boysson-Bardies, Halle, Sagart, & Durand, 1989; Boysson-Bardies & Vihman, 1991).

Although social development is not a direct precursor of word or syntax comprehension or production, it is entwined with language across early development. Indeed, the early beneficial effects of social context on language learning are evident in infants' vocalizations and phonetic discriminations. For instance, Bloom, Russell, and Wassenberg (1987) showed that turn-taking can alter very young infants' vocalizations, and Goldstein, King, and West (2003) showed that parental feedback increases infant vocalizations. In addition, Kuhl and colleagues (Kuhl, Tsao, & Liu, 2003) found that North American infants learned non-native Mandarin phonemic contrasts in the presence of a Mandarin speaker but not from a video recording of the same information.

At around 3–6 months, social cognition in infants is perhaps most evident in *gaze following*, first directed at nearby targets (D'Entremont, Hains, & Muir, 1997) and expanding to further targets by around the first birthday (Corkum & Moore, 1995). (As with other skills, this feature is not uniquely human, and is present in at least several other nonhuman primate species; Tomasello, Call, & Hare, 1998). Starting around 9 months, we also see a change from *dyadic* interactions (i.e., the infant interacting with another object or another person) to *triadic* interactions (i.e., the infant and a caregiver jointly attending to each other and an object; Trevarthen & Hubley, 1978).

From the end of the first year and beyond, children become increasingly adept at understanding and directing other people's attention, using this information to make the task of language learning more tractable (Bates, 2004). In a longitudinal study of infants from 9 to 15 months, Carpenter, Nagell, and Tomasello (1998) showed a linked progression of gesture and joint attention, from infants initially sharing attention, to subsequently following an adult's attention, to directing another's attention (for a detailed review, see Tomasello, Carpenter, Call, Behne, & Moll, 2005). Slightly older infants use an adult's communicative intent to rapidly attach meaning to novel words (for a review, see Tomasello, 2001). Given the prominence of joint attention and its relation to language development, it is not surprising that the quantity and type of joint attention between infant and caregiver predict children's early communicative abilities, with particular gains when the caregiver focuses on the object of the infant's attention (Carpenter et al., 1998; Tomasello & Todd, 1983).

First words

As the infant's native language discrimination improves, the child faces the daunting task of using these phonemes to segment speech into words, and attach some meaning to them. While adult listeners tend to perceive the speech stream as a series of discrete words presented one after another (at least in their native language), human speech actually affords no such luxury, in that there is generally no one-to-one mapping between pauses or silences and word boundaries. Despite this fact, by 7½ months, infants can detect words that they have been familiarized with from a stream of natural speech (Jusczyk & Aslin, 1995), and furthermore demonstrate longer-term memory for these words (Jusczyk & Hohne, 1997). The speech stream contains a number of different clues as to the location of word boundaries, such as *syllabic stress patterns* (Jusczyk, Houston, & Newsome, 1999) and *phonetic transitional probabilities* (i.e., the likelihood that one phonetic segment follows another; Saffran, Aslin, & Newport, 1996; see also Saffran, Johnson, Aslin, & Newport, 1999, and Hauser, Newport, & Aslin, 2001, for evidence of similar statistical pattern learning for nonspeech stimuli and in nonhuman primates). Infants use a combination of these different cues to segment speech into words, with the relative weighting of cues varying over development (Johnson & Jusczyk, 2001; Thiessen & Saffran, 2003).

The purpose of this segmentation is, of course, to identify the chunks of speech (words) to which meaning can be attached and/or extracted. Infants become increasingly rapid and skilful at forming these word-to-meaning associations. Indeed, by around 2 years (and possibly earlier), infants demonstrate *fast mapping* (Carey, 1978) whereby word-to-meaning mappings are learnt after a single exposure. As with previous examples, this skill is neither specific to language (Markson & Bloom, 1997) nor specific to humans (Kaminski, Call, & Fischer, 2004).

As any proud (yet weary) parent will attest, young children are not just consumers of language, but also use it increasingly productively to communicate their needs, desires, and interests with others. Whereas *word comprehension* typically starts around 9–10 months, *word production* typically follows several weeks later (Fenson et al., 1994). In general, the size of a toddler's early receptive vocabulary maintains a healthy numerical superiority over his or her productive vocabulary, although there is considerable individual variability in the extent of this relationship (Fenson et al., 1994). Infants' early productive vocabulary is mostly composed of nominal labels for objects or people, although they also produce non-nominal words (for instance, the relational label "up"). However, straightforward classifications of infants' language in terms of adult linguistic categories, such as verbs or nouns, are probably inaccurate. Since infant speech is driven primarily by the desire to communicate, Tomasello (2006) argues that many of the early one-word utterances are actually "holophrases"—expressing a holistic communicative function with a single label. For instance, an utterance such as "up" might serve as the infant's shorthand for an adult phrase such as "pick it up." Thus, the infant may be copying a part of the adult phrase as a way to express the communicative intent of the phrase as a whole.

Individual variability, developmental trajectories, and the vocabulary "burst"

As noted at the start of this chapter, in order to understand the mechanisms underlying both typical and atypical language development, it is vital to have an understanding of the trajectory of that development, both in the "average" child and in individual children. The MacArthur–Bates Communicative Development Inventory (CDI) provides an excellent and carefully normed method of tracing an individual child's linguistic developmental trajectory from the tentative start of meaningful communication around the first birthday (for the "average" child) through the advent of complex sentence production and comprehension. An instrument based on parental report (and validated through laboratory observation; Fenson et al., 2000), the CDI is extremely useful for comparing typical and atypical populations, and for assessing individual variation within a given sample.

One interesting finding of the initial MacArthur–Bates CDI norming studies (Fenson et al., 1994, 2000) is that there is *little overall difference between girls and boys* in terms of the trajectory of language development. Girls are on average one month ahead of boys, but this difference accounts for only 2% of the variation within and across age groups. Thus, these gender differences are relatively insignificant compared to the much greater variation between individuals. It is worth emphasizing how much *individual variation* there is between "typically" developing (TD) children—indeed, the idea of "typical" language development is something of a useful fiction. As an illustration of this, we reproduce here the cross-sectional growth curves from the Fenson et al. (1994) monograph showing the receptive and productive vocabulary size of children in the 10th, 25th, 50th, 75th, and 90th percentiles (Figures 8.1 and 8.2); we also show longitudinal growth curves for three different typically developing children for comparison (Figure 8.3).

The use of statistical averages to simplify complex and highly variable time series can sometimes mask more interesting phenomena. A case in point is the sudden acceleration at 16–20 months in a child's vocabulary, the so-called *vocabulary burst* that follows a period of very gradual increases in vocabulary size following the first few words. This vocabulary acceleration involves not just an increase in the total number of words a child produces, but also changes in the content of the words, with a shift to a greater proportion of adjectives and verbs (Bates et al., 1988; Fenson et al., 1994; Hampson & Nelson, 1993; Nelson, 1981; Tomasello, 2006). This sudden change in vocabulary size has often been considered an indicator of the onset of a new cognitive ability, such as

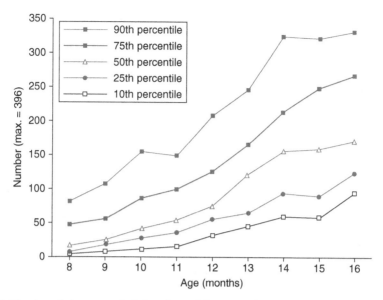

Figure 8.1 Number of phrases on the infant form of the MacArthur–Bates CDI reported to be understood by children at each month. Median values and percentile ranks are shown. *Note.* Reprinted with permission from "Variability in Early Communicative Development," by L. Fenson, P. Dale, J. Reznick, E. Bates, D. Thal, and S. Pethick, 1994, *Monographs of the Society for Research in Child Development,* 59. Oxford: Blackwell.

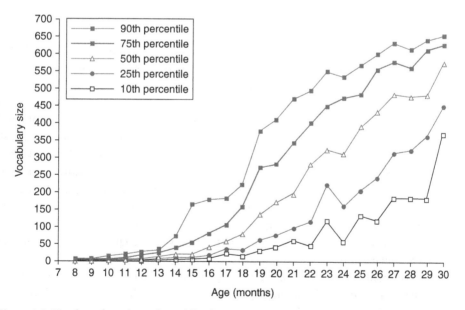

Figure 8.2 Number of words on the toddler form of the MacArthur–Bates CDI reported to be produced by children at each month. Median values and percentile ranks are shown. *Note.* Reproduced with permission from "Variability in Early Communicative Development," by L. Fenson, P. Dale, J. Reznick, E. Bates, D. Thal, and S. Pethick, 1994, *Monographs of the Society for Research in Child Development,* 59. Oxford: Blackwell.

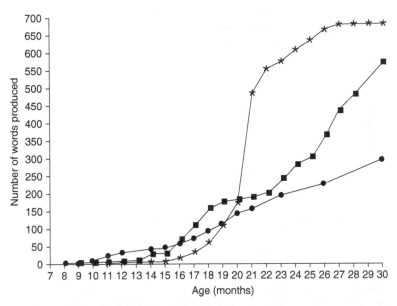

Figure 8.3 Longitudinal growth curves for the productive vocabulary of three different typically developing children, as measured by the MacArthur–Bates CDI. *Note.* From E. Bates, personal communication.

developing a "naming insight" (Dore, 1974). However, this "average" picture masks the wide gamut of individual developmental trajectories observed with the CDI for so-called "normal" children (i.e., children without obvious language problems).

There is wide individual variation in productive vocabulary size at the point when the "average" child launches his or her vocabulary burst. At this time in chronological development (~16 months), children in the highest 10th percentile produce about 180 words, whereas those in the lowest 10th percentile produce fewer than 10 words. It is very important to note that, despite this early variation, most of these children—including those in the 10th percentile who are slow getting language off the ground—will go on to have similar language outcomes as adults as their initially more able peers. There is also massive variation in the shape of the growth curves for different individuals' productive vocabulary with age. Some children show a recognizable burst, whereas others' vocabulary appears to grow at a much steadier pace, with still others advancing in a series of small successive bursts. A strong possibility is that the relationship between vocabulary size and age is inherently nonlinear, rather than the more frequently assumed form of one linear relationship giving way to another linear relationship with the onset of each new skill. Indeed, the variability across individual vocabulary growth curves can be captured most parsimoniously using nonlinear models (Bates & Carnevale, 1993; see also Elman et al., 1996, for a more general discussion of nonlinearity in development). Irrespective of the cause, recognizing the tremendous individual variability is paramount when assessing atypical populations and in understanding in what ways these children differ from typically developing infants.

Early language and its relationship to nonlinguistic abilities

Meaningful language production and comprehension develop in tandem with a raft of nonlinguistic cognitive and motor abilities, in particular gestural communication and environmental sound recognition. The close developmental relationship between gesture and language (see Bates & Dick, 2002, for a review) appears to begin from around 6 months with a correlation between the onset of babbling and the onset of rhythmic hand banging. Toward the end of the first year, first word comprehension tends to co-occur with the start of deictic gestures (e.g., pointing and showing gestures) and gestural routines (e.g., waving goodbye; Bates, Benigni, Bretherton, Camaioni, & Volterra, 1979). In a similar vein, the later onset of productive vocabulary also co-occurs with—or is slightly preceded by—early recognitory gestures, e.g., putting a phone to the ear, or a brush to hair (Volterra, Bates, Benigni, Bretherton, & Camaioni, 1979).

Infants' word comprehension also shares a similar developmental trajectory to their understanding of familiar environmental sounds (i.e., meaningful, nonlinguistic sounds such as a cow mooing or a car starting). Cummings, Saygin, Bates, and Dick (2007) found that 15 to 25-month-old infants' accuracy in comprehending environmental sounds and spoken phrases was roughly equivalent (with a slight advantage for environmental sound recognition early in development). These results suggest that in fact speech does not appear to start out as being "privileged" as an acoustical transmitter of referential information.

Over development, the relationship between language, environmental sound comprehension, and gesture production changes as the infant gains more linguistic experience. Recognitory gesture is eclipsed by the exponential increase in a child's productive vocabulary as language "wins custody" over gesture as the prime means of expressive communication (Bates & Dick, 2002). Similarly for environmental sound comprehension, infants with larger productive vocabularies show a significant accuracy advantage for comprehending spoken words over environmental sounds; this advantage for words over environmental sounds is not revealed when infants are grouped by chronological age. None the less, throughout the lifespan there remains a close relationship between language and gesture (Saygin, Dick, & Bates, 2005) and language and environmental sound (Borovsky et al., 2007; Cummings et al., 2006; Dick et al., in press; Saygin, Dick, Wilson, Dronkers, & Bates, 2003). In sum, language is not an isolated ability, "fenced off" from the rest of cognition. Instead, language appears to emerge from the interactions of many domain-general cognitive processes, including memory, attention, object recognition and categorization, social and emotional abilities, as well as the nonlinguistic motor and acoustical abilities just mentioned (Bates, Thal, Finlay, & Clancy, 2003). Language may be best described as "a new machine that Nature has constructed out of old parts" (Bates, 2004, p. 250).

Neural correlates of word learning

How is the child's brain reorganizing itself during this period of profound language development? A series of electrophysiological studies by Debra Mills and colleagues suggests that "cerebral specialization for language emerges as a function of learning, and to some extent depends on the rate of learning" (Mills & Sheehan, 2007). Mills and colleagues have shown that the relative lateralization of electrophysiological (EEG) components (P100, N200–400) in the first years of life is intimately related to language learning and expertise. In particular, the lateral distribution of the N200–400 component for known versus unknown words is related to the overall size of the infant's vocabulary in a particular language. Conboy and Mills (2006) showed that in 20-month-old bilingual toddlers classed as having high or low total vocabulary sizes, the N200–400 difference between known versus unknown words was lateralized only in children with higher vocabularies, and only in their dominant language. Conversely, this known versus unknown word N200–400 difference was bilaterally distributed in the nondominant language, and in the lower-total-vocabulary toddlers. (A similar finding was reported in a rapid-word-learning experiment by Mills, Plunkett, Prat, & Schafer, 2005.) Thus, changes in the large-scale topography of neural responses to words were driven by infants' expertise with words in general, as well as by their knowledge of specific word exemplars.

More generally, in their review of the infant and child EEG language literature, Mills and Sheehan point out that the relative lateralization of EEG components changes dynamically over the lifespan. As an example, they cite the case of the P1 component evoked in response to auditory stimuli, which shows an early left lateralization from 3 months to 3 years, a symmetrical distribution from 6 to 12 years, and a right-lateralized distribution from 13 years into adulthood. The existence of such complex developmental trajectories demonstrates that any putative "early lateralization" for speech or language stimuli—such as reported in neonates and 3-month-olds (Dehaene-Lambertz, Dehaene, & Hertz-Pannier, 2002; Peña et al., 2003)—must be understood in the context of changes over the lifespan. (For an alternative view of earlier neural commitment to language processing, as well as a very useful summary of recent results, see Friederici, 2005).

The relationship between vocabulary and grammar

The sudden acceleration in vocabulary growth is accompanied or followed by the first two-word combinations at 18–20 months. Early word combinations mark the start of a second "burst" in the child's abilities, this time in the realm of productive grammatical complexity.[2] As with previous language milestones, this rapid increase in syntactic

---

[2]   Note that in terms of comprehension, infants younger than 12 months can discriminate patterns analogous to simple grammars (Gomez & Gerken, 1999; Marcus, Vijayan, Bandi Rao, & Vishton, 1999).

sophistication does not occur in a vacuum. Rather, toddlers' burgeoning syntactic abilities during the middle of the second year are closely yoked to their productive vocabularies—that is, syntax is not independent of the lexicon (Bates & Goodman, 1997).

Bates et al. (1988) found significant positive correlations between productive vocabulary size at 20–28 months and *mean length of utterance* (MLU)[3] in the same period, with the strongest correlation between vocabulary at 20 months and MLU at 28 months when the "average" child's complex grammatical language is changing most rapidly. It is important to note that this tight synchronous and diachronous relationship between lexical size and grammatical complexity is not driven by a latent variable, like "maturation." In this vein, Bates and Goodman (1997) used data from the large CDI norming study (Fenson et al., 1994) to demonstrate that total vocabulary size correlates with grammatical complexity equally as strongly as grammatical complexity correlates with itself—and that this relationship held true when chronological age was partialled out. In fact, calculated over the entire CDI sample, hierarchical stepwise regressions revealed that age uniquely accounted for only 0.8% of the variance for grammatical complexity, while vocabulary size accounted for 32.3% of unique grammatical variance. These results suggest a law-like relationship whereby *total vocabulary size, irrespective of age, predicts grammatical complexity*. Furthermore, there is very little variability between individuals around this relationship—including in all but one clinical population where this question has been investigated (see Figure 8.4 and below).

Remarkably, the law-like relationship between grammar and the lexicon also appears to hold over languages, despite the fact that languages differ tremendously in terms of the morphosyntactic cues that provide "clues" to meaning. For example, in English the most reliable grammatical cue to agency ("who is doing what to whom") is word order, whereas for some other languages (for example, Italian), these sentential roles are often imparted through inflectional morphology. Prima facie, such languages show somewhat different grammatical developmental trajectories: For instance, in a highly inflected, regular, and transparent language like Turkish, the use of morphological particles is observed much earlier in development than in English (Slobin, 1985). This does not entail, however, that the relation between the lexicon and syntax need be fundamentally different. Indeed, the CDI has been used cross-linguistically to compare English and a language with rich inflectional morphology for tense, aspect, number, and gender—namely Italian. Despite the obvious differences in the languages, the same law-like predictive link between vocabulary size and grammatical complexity exists for Italian and English (Caselli, Casadio, & Bates, 1999), demonstrating the generality of

---

[3] MLU is a frequently used measure of grammatical complexity calculated by taking the average number of morphemes (the smallest units of meaning) per phrase. MLU is a somewhat problematic measure for comparing children's grammatical knowledge across ages and across languages (Bates et al., 1988). The CDI includes measures of grammatical complexity which have been normed across ages and languages, against benchmark laboratory studies, and so provide a more robust mechanism for investigating the grammar explosion seen in the third year.

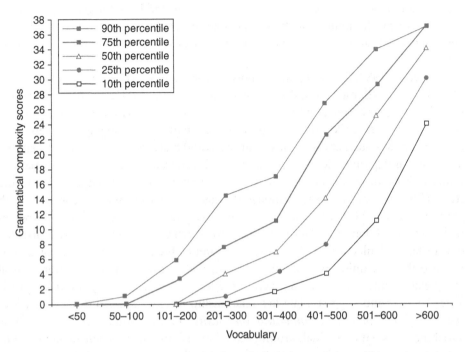

Figure 8.4 Relationship between grammar and vocabulary size: variation within each vocabulary level. *Note.* Reproduced with permission from "On the Inseparability of Grammar and the Lexicon: Evidence from Acquisition, Aphasia, and Real-time Processing," by E. Bates and J. Goodman, 1997, *Language and Cognitive Processes, 12,* 507–584.

this finding (see Figure 8.4). The implication of this work is that grammar is not a completely separate process from word learning, nor does grammar simply require some word knowledge to get started. Instead, grammar and the lexicon are interwoven throughout early development.

The nature of children's early grammar

One long-standing position in developmental psycholinguistics is that young children and adults fundamentally share the same syntactic "competence" (see Tomasello, 2000a, for a detailed critical review). This "continuity assumption" is one offshoot of the theory that all human languages are built upon a single innate universal grammar, with languages essentially differing only in the words they employ (Pinker, 1984, 1987, 1989).[4] An alternative developmental hypothesis postulates that children's early syntax

---

[4]   Please note, however, that there are many "flavors" of this basic proposal; for example, Clahsen and Felser (2006) and Crain and Pietroski (2001) to name but two.

is item based. That is, young children initially produce grammatical language not through the utilization of general and abstract linguistic structures (e.g., subject, verb, noun), but rather through reproduction and very conservative and gradual tweaking of individual and specific linguistic "constructions" that they have learnt from others' speech (Goldberg, 1995, 2006; Tomasello, 1992, 2000a, 2000b).

There is increasing evidence that at least some of young children's grammar is item based. A number of observational studies of children's early language production (Pizutto & Caselli, 1992, 1994; Tomasello, 1992) have revealed that children's early production of verbs does not reveal a systematic pattern of usage. Instead, young children produce many verbs in only a single form with no transfer of structure from verb to verb. For instance, for the verb *cut*, a child will only produce phrases of the form *cut—* (e.g., *cut apple* or *cut bread*). This phenomenon, termed the "verb island" hypothesis (Tomasello, 1992), has been reported cross-linguistically (e.g., Pizutto & Caselli, 1992, 1994; Rubino & Pine, 1998).

Experimental studies have also investigated the item-based nature of early syntax by considering how well children produce novel verb constructions. In a series of studies, Tomasello and colleagues (see Tomasello, 2000a, 2000b for reviews) investigated what linguistic forms a 2- to 3-year-old child produces when he or she is given a novel verb to use in a variety of linguistic situations. For instance, if a novel verb like "tam" is only modeled for the child in the intransitive form, will a child produce the transitive form of the verb given an appropriate context? These studies repeatedly demonstrate that before the age of about 3 years children will generally base their verb productions on the input that they have heard. In other words, children will not transfer the transitive structure to a novel verb that they encountered in the intransitive form, even when explicitly asked to do so. Akhtar (1999) demonstrated an even more extreme example of how the structure of the input determines children's linguistic productions. Exposing younger children (2- and 3-year-olds) to novel verbs in different word orders (i.e., subject, verb, object [SVO], SOV, and VSO) led to framing the novel verb in ways that reflected the exposed verb order—even for noncanonical English word orders like SOV and VSO. In contrast, older children (at 4 years) generalized from their knowledge of SVO word order and used the novel verb only in a "canonical" English way, thus suggesting that they were abstracting the verb away from its syntactic frame.

In general, these observational and experimental studies call into question the existence of abstract adult grammatical categories in children's early syntactic development. These novel verb production studies also indicate that early language is highly sensitive to statistical patterns in the ambient language; for example, the frequency of a word order, such as SVO, is a key determinant of its production by a child. Gradually, as the typical child develops, by 3–4 years of age he or she will be increasingly able to generalize to novel verbs using existing templates such as the transitive SVO structure. However, it is important to note that these word-order preferences are not immutable: Even college-age adults are exquisitely sensitive to changes in the relative frequency of word orders (Dick, Butler, St. John, Gernsbacher, & Ferreira, 2007).

Language development in older children

Children by the age of 3–4 years are increasingly proficient language users with large productive vocabularies, and are able to fluently use and comprehend complex grammatical constructions (Bates & Goodman, 1997). This milestone, however, does not mark the end of the development of language. Instead, children's language abilities keep gradually improving into adolescence and beyond (Nippold, 1998). One obvious area of improvement is vocabulary growth which continues throughout childhood, increasing by approximately 3,000 words per year (for a review, see Graves, 1986). Similarly, auditory and speech perception continues to improve into adolescence (Ceponiene, Rinne, & Naatanen, 2002). Most surprisingly, perhaps, syntactic abilities also continue to develop into later life.

As with infants, school-aged children remain sensitive to the frequency of syntactic constructions they hear. For instance, Huttenlocher and colleagues (Huttenlocher, Vasilyeva, Cymerman, & Levine, 2002) demonstrated that the proportion of complex syntactic constructions used by a child's primary school teacher predicts how well the child produces and understands difficult syntactic structures, over and above chronological age. Even approaching adolescence, children's syntactic comprehension can be demonstrated to vary from that of adults. Leech and colleagues (Leech, Aydelott, Symons, Carnevale, & Dick, 2007) explored children's (ages 5–17) and adults' (ages 18–51) comprehension of morphosyntactically diverse sentences under varying degrees of attentional demands, auditory masking, and semantic interference. The results indicated that perceptual masking of the speech signal has an early and lasting impact on comprehension, particularly for more complex sentence structures, and that young children's syntactic comprehension is particularly vulnerable to disturbance. This study not only demonstrated that syntax follows an elongated developmental trajectory, but that other more general attentional and perceptual skills continue to play an important role in syntactic processing across the lifespan (see also Hayiou-Thomas, Bishop, & Plunkett, 2004).

One of the advantages of working with older children is the possibility of investigating developmental changes in the neural underpinnings of language processing using fMRI. At least from the ages that are currently accessible with fMRI (about 5 years and up), the relatively small fMRI literature on language development does not show any simple maturational trends: For example, brain regions do not go "on-" and "offline" with increasing age. Rather, there are regionally specific increases and decreases in functional activation over development that tend to be nonlinear (Brown et al., 2005; Fair, Brown, Petersen, & Schlaggar, 2006; Schlaggar et al., 2002) and task-dependent (Saccuman et al., 2007a). For instance, in a comprehensive study of the development of overt verbal fluency from ages 7 to 32, Brown et al. (2005) showed "performance-independent" changes in 40 functionally defined brain regions, where 30 of 40 regions showed age-related decreases ("growing down"), and 10 showed age-related increases ("growing up"). The majority of the regions showing activation "growing down" were in bilateral occipital and temporal cortex, whereas the age-related increases were found in left frontal and parietal regions. Importantly, both the slope and shape of these increases and decreases in activation differed over regions.

Age-related increases in left frontal activation in word production tasks have also been observed by Gaillard et al. (2003) for word production and Saccuman et al. (2007b) for both word production and sentence comprehension (see also Koelsch, Fritz, Schulze, Alsop, & Schlaug, 2005, for similar frontal trends in the development of music perception). Saccuman et al. (2007a) also found "growing-down" regions in the development of auditory sentence comprehension in several left superior temporal and inferior frontal regions. The one relatively consistent finding over most developmental fMRI language studies is that of relatively early overall left lateralization of activation for production (Gaillard et al., 2003; Holland et al., 2001; Saccuman et al., 2007a) and comprehension (Saccuman et al., 2007a), although again some studies fail to find this effect, at least for auditory speech comprehension (Ulualp, Biswal, Yetkin, & Kidder, 1998). In sum, even the relatively small developmental fMRI literature confirms and extends the notion that the development of language-processing neural networks is an extended, variable, and nonlinear affair that continues well into the later school and adolescent years.

Language Acquisition in Developmental Disorders

The milestones of the "average" child's language development, as detailed in the previous section, constitute a necessary starting-point for considering how language learning and eventual language outcome is changed by atypical development. As we will show below, language learning can be disrupted by a wide variety of physical, social, and neural challenges to the developing child. However, each challenge tends to affect the trajectory of language acquisition at different points, and for different lengths of time. Historically, atypical development is often studied with a view to (a) the extent to which language learning in children with developmental disorders resembles the language of normally developing children; and (b) the changing patterns of language impairments between disorders. Such differences are usually described in terms of *delay* or *deviation* from the normal pathway, and permit us to establish relative strengths and weakness across subdomains of language, such as phonology, syntax, semantics, and pragmatics.

As noted above, the potential causes of delays or difficulties in language development are many, and diverse. For example, Down syndrome, Williams syndrome, and fragile-X syndrome are all defined in terms of genetic anomalies that are fairly well characterized at the molecular level. None the less, we must be particularly cautious in establishing mappings between genotype and phenotype; as we shall show, not only is there substantial phenotypic variability, but the behavioral phenotype changes over developmental time. In contrast to these genetic disorders, syndromes such as autism and specific language impairment are behaviorally defined, and are most likely the result of combinations of genetic and/or environmental factors (possibly including viral infection and disruptions during prenatal development). All of these developmental disorders are characterized by frequent co-occurring problems with working memory, balance, coordination, as well as perceptual differences and learning difficulties. In addition, social and behavioral problems may also be manifest, although it is unclear whether these are exacerbated by or contribute to ongoing language problems.

In the following sections we review the impact of four different challenges to the development of language. First, we sketch the effects of a number of "extrinsic" factors on language development, such as chronic disease or long-term sensory or social deprivation. Second, we briefly review the consequences of overt brain damage, disease, or malformation for language development (but see Chapter 5 of this volume for a thorough review of development following early focal brain injury). Third, we more thoroughly explore the trajectory of language development in a quartet of congenital developmental disorders—autism, Down syndrome, Williams syndrome, and fragile-X syndrome—that serve to demonstrate some of the "boundary conditions" of language learning. Finally, we discuss developmental language disorder (also known as "specific language impairment"; Leonard, Eyer, Bedore, & Grela, 1997), a behaviorally defined disorder where a child's language abilities are significantly lower than would be expected given his or her overall cognitive profile. We close the chapter by pointing the reader toward the latest guides for best practice in diagnosis and treatment of developmental language disorders.

Effects of extrinsic factors

As we have emphasized above, the child's environment plays a crucial role in language development. This is true not only for the kinds of "constructive" environmental influences we have discussed (such as structured language input, joint attention, and so forth), but also for "destructive" environmental effects, such as disease, toxins, and social or sensory deprivation. We review some of the complex consequences of these environmental factors in the following section.

Teratogenic and pathological influences on language development

Neurotoxins such as pesticides may have effects on language development, although there is a paucity of data on this topic. Eskenazi et al. (2006) showed significant negative, dose-related relationships between DDT blood serum levels and Bayley MDI scales (a global measure of early mental development that includes language abilities). Lead exposure has been tied to poorer phonological, lexical, and sentence processing even in randomly sampled asymptomatic adolescent boys, but only when tested on the more complex variants of each task (Campbell, Needleman, Riess, & Tobin, 2000). Indeed, growth curve analyses (Coscia, Ris, Succop, & Dietrich, 2003) suggest that children with higher lead levels show generally lower vocabulary abilities at 15 years of age, and also a slowed rate of vocabulary growth. Interestingly, this trend is not echoed in the development of perceptual organization abilities.

Fetal alcohol spectrum disorders (FASD) appear to have variable effects on language, which are modulated by concomitant factors that are difficult to parcel out in small samples (Cone-Wesson, 2005). None the less, as noted in a recent review by Riley and McGee (2005), children with prenatal exposure to alcohol are likely to show poorer profiles of language comprehension and production than their age-matched peers. This is perhaps unsurprising given these children's performance across a wide range of cognitive, emotional, and perceptual measures.

In contrast to what was originally feared, prenatal cocaine exposure does not appear to have severe deleterious effects on language development (Frank, Augustyn, Knight, Pell, & Zuckerman, 2001; Frank et al., 2005). Some studies have reported transient delays in expressive and/or receptive language development, but these effects are often difficult to tease apart from other comorbidities, which appear to have a significant and more lasting effect. For instance, Beeghly et al. (2006) found that, unlike prenatal cocaine exposure, exposure to violence or victimization predicted lower language scores, whereas preschool enrichment predicted greater language skill (see also below).

Chronic and/or severe infectious disease during early childhood may also cause delays in language acquisition, although there is relatively little research specifically on different aspects of language production and comprehension. None the less, several studies suggest effects of disease on language acquisition. For instance, Carter and colleagues (Carter, Murira, Ross, Mung'ala-Odera, & Newton, 2003) showed that Kenyan children who had undergone a severe bout of malaria early in life tended to have poorer comprehension and production scores years after their illness relative to matched control children. A further study by the same group (Carter et al., 2005) showed that cerebral malaria-induced epilepsy is particularly detrimental to language development. Abubakar and colleagues (2005) found that the productive vocabulary of Kenyan toddlers exposed to HIV in utero was almost half that of control children, when both were tested on an adaptation of the MacArthur–Bates CDI.

Social and sensory deprivation

As suggested by the results of Beeghly et al. (2006), chronic emotional neglect, physical mistreatment, or extreme stress during childhood may lead to significant, if possibly transient, delays in language development. In psycholinguistics, conclusions regarding the effect of social deprivation on language and cognition are often driven by a handful of case studies of extreme deprivation and/or abuse in early childhood (reviewed in Skuse, 1993). However, as summarized by Hough (2005), there is evidence from several fairly large group studies that severe neglect—as opposed to abuse alone—can cause serious delays in language comprehension and production (see also Allen & Oliver, 1982; Culp, Lawrence, Letts, Kelly, & Rice, 1991; Fox, Long, & Anglois, 1988).

The long-term effects on language development of early (orphanage) institutionalization are still in dispute, although a comprehensive survey by Frank, Klass, Earls, and Eisenberg (1996) suggests that deficits "in verbal skills and associated academic delays in reading seem to persist after early orphanage care into school age and adolescence, with the most severe deficits found in children institutionalized at the youngest ages for the longest amounts of time" (p. 572). A yet unpublished doctoral thesis on Eastern European adoptees from deprived orphanages (Hough, 2005) is perhaps the most thorough investigation of this question. Using a wide range of language measures, Hough showed that 29 of 44 Eastern European orphans adopted into North American families would be classed as overall language-impaired, although comprehension tended to be more resilient than other language skills.

It is important to note that the effect of institutionalization on language is likely to be contingent upon the quality and type of interactions between children and staff. In a multi-institution study, Tizard, Cooperman, Joseph, and Tizard (1972) showed that orphaned children in high-quality nurseries exhibited no overall impairment in their language abilities (in contrast to previous studies). However, they did show that the type of language and social interaction between staff and children had a significant effect upon the children's language comprehension skills, where the more interactive and informative the conversational style of the staff, the better the children's language comprehension tended to be. Similar findings were reported in a large study of very low birthweight (VLBW) children (Landry, Smith, & Swank, 2002). This eight-year longitudinal study showed that not only were VLBW children on average about 5–8 months delayed in their language development (particularly those with medical complications at birth), but that both full-term and VLBW children's language benefited from mothers who "built on their interests and topics of conversations" as opposed to simply directing those conversations (Landry et al., 2002, p. 199). These results presage those of Huttenlocher et al. (2002, discussed above), showing that the syntactic complexity of teachers' speech predicts that of their students. Landry et al. (2002) also found a very striking effect on language of socioeconomic status, above and beyond what would be predicted by the children's nonverbal abilities, thus suggesting that the conditions associated with extreme poverty may have a particularly pernicious effect on language development (see also Hart & Risley, 1995, for further discussion of this topic).

Language delays associated with early institutional privation or neglect may also be reversible, at least to some degree. For instance, Duyme, Dumaret, and Tomkiewicz (1999) showed that a group of low-IQ, neglected French children adopted later in childhood showed significant increases in verbal and performance IQ when retested as adolescents. Furthermore, the more "enriched" the adoptive home environment (as measured in terms of socioeconomic status), the greater the longitudinal increase in IQ. However, unlike matched early adoptees, who showed equivalent verbal and performance IQ outcomes, late adoptees' verbal IQ tended to lag behind performance IQ. Extrapolating from these results, the authors suggest that a "supportive environment will be especially valuable for VIQ at the time that language develops most rapidly, between age 1.5 and 4 years" (Duyme et al., 1999, p. 8792).

Auditory deprivation, in the form of early, severe, and untreated sensorineural hearing loss, has significant repercussions for the trajectory of language learning, although the longer-term effects of hearing loss require clarification. In a landmark study, Yoshinaga-Itano, Sedey, Coulter, and Mehl (1998) demonstrated that infants with severe or total hearing loss who were identified before 6 months of age showed significantly better language production and comprehension than those identified after 6 months of age. Indeed, the magnitude of the language advantage for the early intervention children (at least to 36 months) has prompted the implementation of quasi-universal hearing screening at birth in the United States.

Follow-up studies on these children and other samples should allow for a better understanding of long-term effects. Indeed, several studies of children with mild to moderate hearing loss (Briscoe, Bishop, & Norbury, 2001; Halliday & Bishop, 2006; Norbury, Bishop, & Briscoe, 2001) suggest that less severe hearing loss, while having an effect on some perceptual and metalinguistic skills, may not have a particularly significant effect on later language skills or literacy, at least for a majority of children with such hearing losses. In addition, the first studies of language outcomes in children with cochlear implants suggest that even very coarse auditory input may allow for good language development. In this regard, Geers (2004) found that a substantial minority of early implanted children (with implantation before 24 months) achieved language scores within the normal range. Spencer, Barker, and Tomblin (2003) found that language comprehension, reading comprehension, and writing accuracy scores for a sample of children with cochlear implants fell within one standard deviation of the mean for matched normal-hearing peers, although these children's expressive scores were significantly lower than would be expected in a normal-hearing sample. (Similar deficits were found in grammatical comprehension for children with cochlear implants; Nikolopoulos, Dyar, Archbold, & O'Donoghue, 2004.)

It is important to differentiate between the potential effects of more severe and permanent sensorineural hearing loss from those associated with transient periods of hearing difficulty, such as those caused by persistent otitis media with effusion (also known as glue ear). The standard clinical teaching is that children who have prolonged or numerous bouts of otitis media are at significantly elevated risk for language impairments or delay.[5] Despite this, there is strong evidence that there are minimal to no lasting effects on affected children's language or intellectual development, both in prospective studies—addressing causality—and when studies control for covariates such as socioeconomic status and schooling (Paradise et al., 2001, 2005). This does not necessarily mean that there are no possibly transient linguistic consequences of otitis media; for example, Rvachew, Slawinski, Williams, and Green (1999) report that children with persistent otitis media babble less than controls. However, the final language outcome for these children is very close or identical to that of unaffected children.

Effects of hemispherectomy and traumatic brain injury

A second variety of "extrinsic" factor that can radically change the course of language and cognitive development is acquired neurological damage as a result of traumatic brain injury or invasive surgery. In preface, we should note that there is a high degree

---

[5] For instance, see www.nhsdirect.nhs.uk/articles/article.aspx?articleId=178&sectionId=10822.

of variability in the etiology, comorbidities, and clinical sequelae of hemispherectomy and traumatic closed-head brain injury. Thus, it is very difficult to draw firm conclusions about brain and language development from these cases. None the less, hemispherectomy, in particular, is often cited in theoretical debates on language development as it relates to neural development and plasticity. As such, it is important to present what is currently known about language outcomes following closed-head brain damage or surgical removal of part of the brain.

Hemispherectomy

In the past decade, there has been considerable attention surrounding celebrated cases of extraordinary late language acquisition following removal of an entire cerebral hemisphere, such as the case of "Alex" who acquired fluent complex language following surgery at the age of 8 (Vargha-Khadem & Mishkin, 1997). Conversely, there are also many case studies of poor outcome following the procedure. Hemispherectomy is normally carried out in order to control untreatable epilepsy, meaning that hemispherectomy patients have usually received years of anti-seizure drug treatment, which may have dramatically altered the course of their development (Vargha-Khadem & Polkey, 1992). More importantly, the underlying etiology of the epilepsy is highly variable, including early onset epilepsies resulting from large-scale dysmorphologies in the laminar structure of the cortex, such as cortical dysplasias and hemimegalencephaly, congenital vascular disorders, such as Sturge–Weber syndrome, and disorders with much later onsets, for example, Rasmussen encephalitis. These etiological factors, combined with the small number and highly variable nature of the documented cases, confound a straightforward summary of the effects of hemispherectomy on language development (although, for recent medical reviews of cognitive and linguistic outcomes, see Jonas et al., 2004; Kossof, Buck, & Freeman, 2002; Pulsifer et al., 2004).

Language outcome following hemispherectomy is dependent on the extent to which the surviving hemisphere is unaffected, and thus varies massively with underlying etiology. Consequently, etiology appears to be the strongest predictor of postoperative language outcome: Children with cortical dysplasias and hemimegalencephaly perform far worse than those with Rasmussen encephalitis, while children with Sturge–Weber syndrome achieve the best linguistic outcome (with a sizable proportion of children in mainstream education; Kossof et al., 2002).

Etiology interacts substantially with the side of resection. Left hemispherectomy is only predictive of worse language outcome (as would be predicted by the adult language model) in the Rasmussen encephalitis children, who only present with seizures later in development, around 4 years, and so have followed a normal developmental trajectory till this point (Curtiss, de Bode, & Mathern, 2001; Pulsifer et al., 2004). Similarly, it is very hard to pull apart the differential effects of etiology, age of onset, and age of surgery upon language outcomes, since etiology strongly predicts symptom onset. Thus, given the current data, it is unwise to draw general conclusions about the positive or negative effects of early onset/surgery for language development.

Traumatic brain injury

Childhood closed-head traumatic brain injury (TBI)—as caused by traffic accidents, falls, sports injuries, or blows to the head—typically results in both multifocal injury and diffuse damage in the form of axonal shearing and long-term changes in neuro-transmitter function and balance (Ewing-Cobbs & Barnes, 2002). In general, most children with TBI do not show frank aphasic symptoms. However, there do tend to be lasting effects on lexical and sentential production and comprehension, particularly when the injury is suffered earlier in life. Much recent research has focused on the more overt disruption of discourse level processes in TBI children, such as difficulties in drawing inferences, understanding metaphors, and establishing links between different elements of a story. As summarized by Dennis and colleagues (Dennis, Purvis, Barnes, Wilkinson, & Winner, 2001), children with TBI have particular problems with "nonliteral" language use, including figurative expressions, humor, implicature, and idioms. Problems in "higher-level" language use, such as meta-cognition and inference, are particularly notable in children with severe injuries, particularly afflicting the frontal lobes (Dennis, Barnes, Wilkinson, & Humphreys, 1998). Our understanding of the neural sequelae of TBI and its effect on neural and cognitive development at various points during childhood should increase markedly in the coming years with the advent of richer and more precise neuroimaging methods (reviewed in Hurley, McGowan, Arfanakis, & Taber, 2004).

Congenital Language Disorders

In contrast to the case of acquired frank brain injury, the changes to brain structure and function that result from congenital developmental disorders tend to begin very early in development, and be more pervasive and yet more enigmatic. Language development in the face of neurodevelopmental disorder has been a topic of particular interest for both clinicians and psycholinguists, and the relative richness of the data on linguistic and nonlinguistic processing in congenital language disorders reflects this. Of particular import is the question: To what extent are cognitive abilities a limiting factor in the process of language development? Children with learning difficulties typically show a later onset of language learning, and the overall level of language ability that they achieve may be limited. Differential profiles of language ability across disorders may be attributed to (a) the social elements of communicative ability (e.g., joint attention); (b) the computational mechanisms that underpin language (e.g., audiomotor attention); and (c) the use of language in interacting with—and manipulating—other people and the environment (e.g., social pragmatics). These strengths and weaknesses can often be most easily identified in the early stages of development, although their impact upon language development may only be evident later "downstream" in development.

Early language learning

As in our description of typically developing children's language abilities, we will take a roughly chronological approach to developmental language disorders, highlighting the diverging developmental paths in Williams syndrome (WS), Down syndrome (DS), fragile-X syndrome (FXS), and autistic spectrum disorders (ASD), first in infancy and toddlerhood, and then into the school years and adolescence. An "early/late" comparison is particularly informative when exploring these disorders, in that the disorder-specific profile of relative strengths and weaknesses is not constant over development.

Problems with social cognition

In the section on typically developing children, we saw that early language is heavily dependent on social cognition to get off the ground, in particular the ability to share attention. Indeed, even in the first months of life, these important social precursors to language already distinguish between infants with developmental disorders and typically developing infants (TD). For example, TD infants show a preference for their mother's speech (Morse, 1972), whereas infants with ASD show no such preference, and seem to have very little interest in people and social interaction (Klin, 1991; Kuhl, Coffey-Corina, Padden, & Dawson, 2005). These infants, like those with FXS, show poor levels of eye contact and gaze following, and may even attempt to avoid the gaze of a caregiver (Cohen et al., 1988). In contrast, infants with WS are typified by their strong desire for social interaction and keen interest in faces. However, this preference also leads to poor gaze-following behavior through the tendency of infants with WS to prefer to look at the face of the caregiver rather than follow the direction of the gaze (Bellugi, Bihrle, Neville, Jernigan, & Doherty, 1992).

Infants with DS also enjoy interacting socially, though there is a delay in mutual eye contact, which may have an impact upon subsequent dyadic interactions between infant and caregiver (Berger & Cunningham, 1981; Jansow et al., 1988). Moreover, once these initial problems resolve, infants with DS seem to prefer to focus on the eyes, as opposed to visually exploring the facial features of the caregiver as TD infants do (Berger & Cunningham, 1981). Deviations in early interactive behavior can also be seen in more complicated triadic interactions between infant, caregiver, and object. For example, infants with WS struggle to switch their attention from the caregiver to an object. This problem with triadic interactions is thought to hinder acquisition of the conceptual knowledge of objects, contributing to a subsequent delay in vocabulary development (Laing et al., 2002; Mervis et al., 2003).

Precursors of expressive language in developmental disorders

Just as for social cognition, children with developmental disorders and TD infants diverge in terms of their prelinguistic productive abilities (e.g., babbling, gesturing). Although all the developmental disorders considered here are delayed in some way relative to TD infants, the exact patterns of these delays, and the mechanisms underlying them, may vary from population to population. For instance, for infants with DS, there is usually a delay in the onset of babbling by an average of two months. This delay in babbling and in subsequent phonological development may be due to the articulatory difficulties that frequently occur in conjunction with the disorder. They may also be due in part to the frequent problems DS children have with hearing loss due to chronic and severe otitis media (but see Shott, Joseph, & Heithaus, 2001, for work suggesting that early and aggressive medical treatment may stem almost all hearing loss due to infection).

In contrast to their profile with babbling, young children with DS produce far more communicative gestures than those seen in TD, a behavior that may serve as a compensatory mechanism for delayed and error-prone phonological production (Singer Harris, Bellugi, Bates, Jones, & Rossen, 1997).[6] In contrast, young children with ASD and WS gesture very little. In stark contrast to typical development, use of referential pointing in WS does not appear until after the naming explosion (Laing et al., 2002; Mervis & Bertrand, 1997).

Despite the differences between DS and WS, children with WS show a similar delay in the onset of babbling (Masataka, 2001). Furthermore, children with WS show early problems with speech segmentation (Nazzi, Paterson, & Karmiloff-Smith, 2003). For instance, toddlers with WS detect words with strong–weak stress patterns, but fail to detect weak–strong words, despite the fact that the average typically developing child accomplishes this feat at 10.5 months (Nazzi et al., 2003). These findings are somewhat surprising given the relative strengths of the language and phonological abilities of older children with WS, and highlight the fact that the pattern of deficits and relative strengths in the adult does not mean that these same deficits and strengths are present earlier on in development.

Word comprehension and production and early grammatical development

Just as prelinguistic expressive skills in developmental disorders are delayed, so is the onset of first word comprehension and production (Bates & Goodman, 1997; Singer Harris et al., 1997). Both WS and DS children are severely delayed in word production, reaching a vocabulary size of about 50 words about two years later than a TD child (who reaches this point at around 16 months). After reaching this critical vocabulary size, the language profiles of DS and WS children diverge. On the MacArthur–Bates CDI, WS follows the established law-like relationship between vocabulary size and grammatical complexity demonstrated by typically developing children, albeit one that is considerably delayed. In contrast, children with DS show an atypical relationship, with their grammatical complexity poor relative to their vocabulary (Rice, Warren, & Betz, 2005). Therefore, for WS—unlike DS—there is no obvious dissociation between

---

[6] Phonological difficulties are also shown by children with FXS (Dykins, Hodapp, & Leckman, 1994).

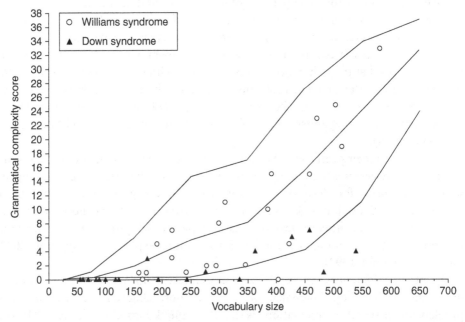

Figure 8.5 Grammar as a function of vocabulary size in children with Williams versus Down syndrome (lines = 10th, 50th, and 90th percentiles for typically developing children). *Note.* Reproduced with permission from "On the Inseparability of Grammar and the Lexicon: Evidence from Acquisition, Aphasia, and Real-time Processing," by E. Bates and J. Goodman, 1997, *Language and Cognitive Processes, 12,* 507–584.

lexical and grammatical ability at this point in development (see Figure 8.5). Indeed, children with WS are no better at a range of linguistic tasks than their mental age would predict (Vicari, Caselli, Gagliardi, Tonucci, & Volterra, 2002).

Furthermore, the types of construction produced by children with a developmental disorder also vary between populations. In DS, there is a varying rate of change in MLU, with a protracted two-word stage. Some DS children do not extend beyond this stage until 4 years of age, or as late as 5 or 6 years (Fowler, 1988). Moving beyond the two-word stage, the use of grammatical knowledge develops rapidly until an MLU of approximately 3.5 is reached. Subsequent grammatical development can be limited, particularly for those children with a low IQ (below 50) who may never develop complex language (Miller, 1988; Rice et al., 2005). Similar variability in the rate of change of MLU has also been seen for children with ASD. However, in contrast to DS, children with ASD may develop more complex language skills (Bellugi et al., 1992; Bellugi, Lichtenberger, Jones, Lai, & St. George, 2000).

By combining MLU with a more detailed measure of syntactic development—such as the index of productive syntax (Scarborough, 1990)—it is possible to compare syntactic abilities across populations in more detail. Importantly, one can determine whether children with disorders develop their knowledge of grammatical constructs in the same sequence as that observed in TD children. For children with DS and FXS, syntactic development is slow and does not generally result in these children consistently producing more complex forms. For at least some children with ASD, explanations for restricted growth in grammar point to the limited range of grammatical constructs used by these children, and their tendency to ask fewer questions. Overall, in spite of the differences in the rate of grammatical development, it has been suggested that children with disorders develop this knowledge in approximately the same sequence as TD children (Tager-Flusberg & Sullivan, 1998; see also Tager-Flusberg, Lord, & Paul, 2005).

Perhaps not surprisingly, there are profound differences in the ways in which children with these developmental disorders use language to communicate and interact within a social context. For example, both children with DS and WS generally enjoy the opportunity to interact within a social environment, and their use of language is motivated through social exchanges in conversation. By contrast, language in many children with ASD, although quite fluent and social, appears to lack a sense of reciprocity in conversational norms. Such a language profile is often linked to a significant discrepancy between verbal and nonverbal IQ (Tager-Flusberg & Joseph, 2003; this article is also a valuable overview of language abilities observed in several phenotypes of ASD). Children with FXS also show difficulty in communicating through conversation, exhibiting dysfluent, rapid speech that is described as cluttered (Dykins et al., 1994). Overall, communicative styles differ considerably between disorders.

Later language learning

We have seen how early language learning in atypically developing populations varies from that of TD children; however, the same patterns of strengths and weaknesses are not constant throughout the child's life. Instead, the relative strengths and weaknesses of early and late language abilities can be quite different as the multiple interacting factors underlying language acquisition unfold. For children with developmental disorders, the overall language ability attained in later childhood and into adolescence is predicted by a number of interacting factors. These include:

1. Mental age (traditionally assessed by standardized testing).
2. Severity of language impairment during the early stages of learning.
3. Influence of accompanying nonlanguage problems.
4. Frequency of communicative acts.
5. Ability to understand the thoughts and intentions of others.[7]

---

[7] It is important to note that there is not necessarily a unidirectional relationship between language development and theory-of-mind ability in either typically developing or autistic children. See Hale and Tager-Flusberg (2003) for a study showing that training on sentential complements improves TD children's performance on a false belief task.

With these factors in mind, it is worth revisiting the linguistic outcomes of the distinct developmental disorders in later life.

Williams syndrome

The main feature of language development in WS is *delay* (Brock, in press; Thomas et al., 2001, in press). In spite of this, relative to mental age-matched controls, these children may develop good semantic knowledge, an extensive vocabulary, and develop complex syntax, though their vocabulary skills generally exceed that of their syntactic ability in terms of mental age (Karmiloff-Smith et al., 1997). In this regard, Reilly, Losh, Bellugi, and Wulfeck (2004) showed that when narrating a picture-book story, children with WS show a very similar profile of slowed morphosyntactic development to children with specific language impairment (LI), with particular problems in inflectional morphology (but cf. Rice et al., 2005, for differing results). Interestingly, while Reilly et al. (2004) found that, by ages 10–12, children with WS (unlike LI) produced the same proportion of complex syntactic structures as typically developing controls, the children with WS failed to establish ties between episodic and thematic narrative events, whereas children with LI were very similar to typically developing children in this regard. Finally, as might be expected given their hypersocial nature, children with WS far outstripped even typically developing children in their use of socially engaging cues when telling a story.

Thomas and Karmiloff-Smith (2003) characterized two types of hypothesis regarding the developmental profile of WS: (a) a series of *imbalance hypotheses,* which accounts for the profile shown in WS as being due to some form of imbalance between phonological and semantic processing, and (b) a *conservative hypothesis,* which proposes that language development in WS is delayed but not fundamentally altered. Thus, the language profile of children with WS might be accounted for by the nonlinguistic characteristics of the disorder—such as a strong desire for social interaction and poor visuospatial skills (Brock, in press).[8]

Down syndrome

In general, children with DS show the same sequence of developmental "events" as do TD children, but are generally *very delayed.* For example, children with DS usually produce the same pattern of phonological errors produced by younger TD children (Stoel-Gammon, 1980). However, when we compare children with WS and those with DS across early and later childhood, we see a divergence of DS and WS developmental trajectories in different language domains. For instance, in early language development, both children with WS and those with DS have a similar level of vocabulary, but by adolescence the vocabulary of children with WS exceeds that of those with DS (Paterson, Brown, Gsödl, Johnson, & Karmiloff-Smith, 1999). Thus, the performance of children with DS appears to asymptote at a lower level.

---

[8] As with all atypically developing populations, it is important to keep in mind that there may be variability in terms of the relative strengths and weaknesses found in WS linguistic and cognitive skills (Porter & Coltheart, 2005).

Comparisons between children with DS and TD children suggest that the difficulty in DS may be associated with the encoding of verbal information, with children with DS showing better visuospatial than verbal encoding, a pattern opposite to that shown by TD children (Marcell & Weeks, 1988; Varnhagan, Das, & Varnhagan, 1987). Pragmatic abilities indicate that children with DS do have an awareness of the thoughts and intentions of others, though the strength of these pragmatic abilities is believed to be closely tied to mental age and IQ (Fowler, 1998).

Autistic spectrum disorders and fragile-X syndrome

In contrast to DS, children with ASD exhibit *severe pragmatic difficulties* in comparison to mental age-matched controls (Tager-Flusberg, 1981). Though children with ASD will use language to manipulate their environment, their use of language to engage in conversation or express thoughts and emotional states is limited. The pragmatic problems exhibited in ASD are thought to reflect a more general social-cognitive deficit related to theory of mind (Baron-Cohen, Tager-Flusberg, & Cohen, 1993), and it has been suggested that autistic children may actually use their language knowledge to bootstrap their understanding of mental states (Frith & Happé, 1994).

In terms of pragmatic ability, children with ASD struggle to understand figurative speech, such as "it's raining cats and dogs," taking literal meanings from such sentences (Singer Harris et al., 1997; Tager-Flusberg et al., 2005). Other characteristics of autistic speech include a flat pattern of intonation, and *echolalia*, where children repeat the verbal utterances of others (Prizant, 1983; Roberts, 1989). These may occur when the child is required to respond to a question or in the form of preconstructed speech during conversation. Children with FXS also exhibit echolalia, which is accompanied by further unusual pragmatic characteristics, such as perseveration, increased use of jargon, and poor conversational ability.

In sum, there are clear differences between disorders in terms of the level of language ability that may be achieved (and in terms of the mechanisms underlying these language problems) and the proficiency with which this language is used within a social context. From the example of WS, it is clear that complex language may be achieved in spite of cognitive limitations; however, this ability may be acquired through atypical means. Overall, language ability in these children may be restricted not only by general cognitive limitations, but also by characteristics of the disorder, which may or may not be language specific, but impede the ability of the child to develop effective communication skills. In the following section, we look at the trajectory of language development in a developmental disorder where language difficulties seem to occur in the absence of frank cognitive impairments, namely specific language impairment.

Specific Language Impairment

Specific language impairment (LI) is defined behaviorally as delay or abnormality in expressive and/or receptive language skills in the absence of overt neurological impairment, mental retardation, hearing loss, ASD, or severe social or emotional problems. Studies attempting to define the nature and specificity of the language deficit affecting these children have revealed problems in many areas, including phonological skills, lexical-semantic development, morphosyntax, and pragmatics (Johnston & Kamhi, 1984; Lahey & Edwards, 1999; Leonard, 1998; Leonard, Schwartz, Allen, Swanson, & Loeb, 1989; Schwartz & Leonard, 1985). Children with LI tend to produce their first words significantly later than normally developing children, and are slower and less accurate in retrieving lexical items (Lahey & Edwards, 1999; McGregor, Newman, Reilly, & Capone, 2002; Trauner, Wulfeck, Tallal, & Hesselink, 1995).

Grammatical morphology is an area of particular weakness. Children with LI have difficulty marking verb inflections, using the auxiliary system, and detecting grammatical violations (Bishop, 1994; Leonard et al., 1997; Marchman, Wulfeck, & Weismar, 1999; Marton, Abramoff, & Rosenzweig, 2005; Wulfeck, Bates, Krupa-Kwiatkowski, & Saltzman, 2004). The ability to use language effectively and flexibly in social contexts, and to use and understand figurative language may also be impaired (Marton et al., 2005; Norbury, 2004; Vance & Wells, 1994). These language difficulties hinder the development of reading and writing skills (Botting, Faragher, Simkin, Knox, & Conti-Ramsden, 2001; Stothard, Snowling, Bishop, Chipchase, & Kaplan, 1998), and the calculation skills of these children may also be affected (Cowan, Donlan, Newton, & Lloyd, 2005).

LI is also associated with accompanying nonlinguistic deficits, which have brought into question the label of *specific* in the strong sense (see Leonard, 1998, for an extensive review). These deficits include working memory problems, impairments in motor skill and speed (Schul, Stiles, Wulfeck, & Townsend, 2004), particularly those involving sequencing, timing, and balance (Hill, 2001), as well as poor auditory frequency discrimination, and sequential auditory processing (Hill, Hogben, & Bishop, 2005; McArthur & Bishop, 2005). Phonological memory problems, as assessed by nonword and sentence repetition, seem to be a particular point of difficulty for LI children (Briscoe, et al., 2001; Conti-Ramsden, Botting, & Faragher, 2001; Dollaghan & Campbell, 1998; Gathercole & Baddeley, 1990). However, the causal role of non-linguistic skills, especially auditory ones, in the emergence of language impairments is hotly debated, and has generated much interesting research (Benasich & Tallal, 2002; Bishop, Adams, Nation, & Rosen, 2005; Bishop, Adams, & Norbury, 2004; Bishop & McArthur, 2004, 2005; Choudhury, Leppanen, Leevers, & Benasich, in press; Halliday & Bishop, 2005, 2006; McArthur & Bishop, 2004a, 2004b; Mengler, Hogben, Michie, & Bishop, 2005; van der Lely, Rosen, & Adlard, 2004; Viding et al., 2004).

The profile of relative strengths and weaknesses in both linguistic and nonlinguistic skills in children with LI is highly variable, characterizing LI as a heterogeneous disorder. The prognosis for young children with LI is that they will develop functionally complex language, but with pervasive underlying difficulties in grammar and nonword repetition (Newbury, Bishop, & Monaco, 2005).

Although LI is a behaviorally defined disorder, there does appear to be a genetic component associated with language difficulties, indicated by twin studies and genomic screening (reviewed in Newbury et al., 2005; SLI Consortium, 2002, 2004). To date, loci on chromosomes 3 and 19, as well as a gene on chromosome 16, have all been implicated. Specifically, anomalies on chromosomes 3 and 16 are suspected to influence systems related to phonological short-term memory and articulation[9] (SLI Consortium, 2002, 2004), although the mechanisms by which this occurs remain to be clarified. These data indicate that multiple genetic factors may contribute to language difficulties.

In addition, a new, large-scale (556 twin pairs) study of the genetic and environmental influences on language skills showed that the same genetic and environmental factors underlie individual differences on a wide variety of language skills, such as receptive and expressive syntax, vocabulary and lexical semantics, and verbal memory (Hayiou-Thomas et al., 2006). These results suggest that the development of these disparate language abilities may rely upon the same underlying cognitive and perceptual mechanisms. However, in another large twin study, Bishop, Adams, and Norbury (2006) showed that the nonlinguistic task most associated with language impairments— nonword repetition—did not show much phenotypic or etiological overlap with verb-tense impairments, the other "gold standard" hallmark of LI (Rice et al., 2005).

A tantalizing link between quite severe language impairments and genetics was discovered in the KE family (Lai, Fisher, Hurst, Vargha-Khadem, & Monaco, 2001). Here, over half of the family members were affected by an expressive and receptive language and articulation disorder, one that is linked to mutations and deletions of the FOXP2 gene. Subsequent work in magnetic resonance imaging identified structural brain abnormalities in the preSMA/cingulate cortex and Broca's area, as well as both structural and functional abnormalities in the caudate nucleus, associated with FOXP2 gene mutations (Vargha-Khadem et al., 1998). However, it is extremely important to point out that subsequent studies have shown no involvement of FOXP2 in large-scale samples of language-impaired children, ruling this gene out as a unitary causal factor in language impairments more broadly.

Until recently, only a handful of studies (Gauger, Lombardino, & Leonard, 1997; Jernigan, Hesselink, Sowell, & Tallal, 1991; Trauner, Wulfeck, Tallal, & Hesselink, 2000) had attempted to delineate the neurological, neuroanatomical, or neurophysiological status of LI children revealing significant abnormalities. For example, anomalous asymmetries in prefrontal regions have been identified (Jernigan et al., 1991). Plante and colleagues (Plante, Boliek, Binkiewicz, & Erly, 1996; Plante, Swisher, Vance, & Rapcsak, 1991) found similar anomalies. Trauner and colleagues conducted extensive neurological examinations and observed a higher than normal occurrence of neurological "soft signs" in children with LI compared to control children, and a number of structural (MRI) abnormalities were identified (Trauner et al., 2000).

Two studies using quantitative analyses of structural MRI data have shed more light on the anatomical factors that might underlie language disorders. Herbert et al. (2004)

---

[9]   It is worth pointing out that LI is not necessarily comorbid with articulatory problems (see Shriberg, Tomblin, & McSweeny, 1999).

reported white-matter abnormalities in a group of 5- to 11-year-old children with a developmental language disorder. In particular, overall white-matter volume was found to be enlarged in impaired children compared to controls. The enlargement was observed in the radiate white-matter compartments, especially in later myelinating frontal and prefrontal regions, suggesting a process modulated by time rather than a disruption linked to specific circuits or processes. Abnormalities were also reported in gray matter. De Fosse et al. (2004) found patterns of reverse rightward asymmetry of cortical volume in the inferior frontal gyrus (pars triangularis and pars opercularis) in boys with LI. The asymmetry was correlated with verbal IQ scores, and not with non-verbal IQ. In sum, while these early studies have advanced our understanding of some of the global differences between TD children and children with LI, a great deal of work remains to be done in elucidating the neural bases of developmental language impairments.

Treatment of Language Disorders

Research on developmental language disorders is extremely useful for understanding how the brain develops to process language, but is primarily carried out with the intent to inform and develop new and better treatments. The literature on the treatment of language disorders is a vast field, and we will not attempt to survey it here. Rather, we point the reader to recent, government commissioned reviews on "best practice" principles and findings in the United States and Great Britain. In the US, Nelson, Nygren, Walker, and Panoscha (2006) conducted a systematic evidence review for the US Preventive Services Task Force on the efficacy of screening for speech and language delay in preschool children. This is an analysis of results from 745 articles published between 1966 and 2004 that reported results from either screening or intervention programs. A slightly earlier review by Law, Garrett, and Nye (2004), prepared for the UK-based Cochrane Collaboration, specifically analyzes the outcomes of speech and language interventions for children with language delays or disorders (see also the commentary on this meta-analysis by Johnston, 2005). Both surveys generally conclude that interventions and screening can be effective and valuable, but that much work remains to be done. The commentary by Johnston serves as a salutary reminder that it is nontrivial even to define what constitutes useful evidence for evaluating intervention and therapy programs.

Conclusion

Research into how the human child acquires language has come a long way over the past few decades, although this review demonstrates how much is still to be understood. We still know too little about the exact profiles and etiologies of developmental disorders, and the study of the neural bases of language development is only now beginning in earnest. Language development is inherently a process of change. Simple explanations in terms of static dissociations between developmental disorders are inevitably somewhat inadequate. Exploring the multiple and varied trajectories of language in both typically and atypically developing populations adds not only to our understanding of developmental disorders, but also provides us with insights into the development of more general cognitive processes.

Studies of language development have been particularly useful in helping us to understand the emergence of modularity and expertise, and the scale and flexibility of cognitive processes during learning. In exploring the mechanisms of language development, we cannot underestimate the multiple levels of interaction between the individual and his or her environment. Importantly, the environment should not be viewed as a static influence, but a force that itself may change in response to the child. In short, exploring the parameters affecting the trajectory of development will prove informative in terms of understanding not only developmental disorders but also the process of normal development itself.

Acknowledgments

All three authors contributed equally to this chapter. Work by Frederic Dick and Robert Leech is supported by an MRC New Investigator Award (G0400341) to Frederic Dick; Fiona Richardson is supported by an MRC Career Establishment Grant (GO300188) and British Academy Grant (SG-40400) awarded to Michael Thomas. We would like to acknowledge Cristina Saccuman, Courtenay Norbury, Annette Karmiloff-Smith, Shula Chiat, and Scott Miller for their advice and assistance with the chapter. Of course, any errors of commission or omission are our own.

References

Abubakar, A., Mithwani, S., Alcock, K., Espy, K., Sanders, E., Mutimba, S., et al. (2005). *Developmental outcomes of Kenyan children exposed to HIV prenatally: Preliminary findings.* Paper presented at the Conference on HIV and the Central Nervous System: Developed and Developing Countries, Frascati, Rome.

Akhtar, N. (1999). Acquiring basic word order: Evidence for data-driven learning of syntactic structure. *Journal of Child Language, 26,* 261–278.

Allen, R., & Oliver, J. (1982). The effects of child maltreatment on language development. *Child Abuse and Neglect, 6,* 299–305.

Baron-Cohen, S., Tager-Flusberg, H., & Cohen, D. J. (Eds.). (1993). *Understanding other minds: Perspectives from autism.* Oxford University Press.

Bates, E. (2004). Explaining and interpreting deficits in language development across clinical groups: Where do we go from here? *Brain and Language, 88,* 248–253.

Bates, E., Benigni, L., Bretherton, I., Camaioni, L., & Volterra, V. (1979). *The emergence of symbols: Cognition and communication in infancy.* New York: Academic Press.

Bates, E., Bretherton, I., & Snyder, L. (1988). *From first words to grammar: Individual differences and dissociable mechanisms.* Cambridge University Press.

Bates, E., & Carnevale, G. F. (1993). New directions in language development. *Developmental Review, 13,* 436–470.

Bates, E., & Dick, F. (2002). Language, gesture, and the developing brain. Special issue: Converging method approach to the study of developmental science. *Developmental Psychobiology, 40*(3), 293–310.

Bates, E., & Goodman, J. (1997). On the inseparability of grammar and the lexicon: Evidence from acquisition, aphasia, and real-time processing. *Language and Cognitive Processes, 12,* 507–584.

Bates, E., Thal, D., Finlay, B. L., & Clancy, B. (2003). Early language development and its neural correlates. In S. J. Segalowitz & I. Rapin (Eds.), *Handbook of neuropsychology,* Vol. 8, Pt. 2: *Child neuropsychology* (2nd ed., pp. 525–592). Amsterdam: Elsevier Science.

Beeghly, M., Martin, B., Rose-Jacobs, R., Cabral, H., Heeren, T., Augustyn, M., et al. (2006). Prenatal cocaine exposure and children's language functioning at 6 and 9.5 years: Moderating effects of child age, birthweight, and gender. *Journal of Pediatric Psychology, 31,* 98–115.

Bellugi, U., Bihrle, A., Neville, H., Jernigan, T., & Doherty, S. (1992). Language, cognition, and brain organization in a neurodevelopmental disorder. In M. Gunnar & C. Nelson (Eds.), *Developmental behavioral neuroscience* (pp. 201–232). Hillsdale, NJ: Erlbaum.

Bellugi, U., Lichtenberger, L., Jones, W., Lai, Z., & St. George, M. (2000). The neurocognitive profile of Williams syndrome: A complex pattern of strengths and weaknesses. *Journal of Cognitive Neuroscience, 12,* 7–30.

Benasich, A. A., & Tallal, P. (2002). Infant discrimination of rapid auditory cues predicts later language impairment. *Behavioural Brain Research, 136*(1), 31–49.

Berger, J., & Cunningham, C. (1981). The development of eye contact between mothers and norm versus Down syndrome infants. *Developmental Psychology, 17,* 678–689.

Bishop, D. V. M. (1994). Grammatical errors in specific language impairment: Competence of performance limitations? *Applied Psycholinguistics, 15,* 507–550.

Bishop, D. V. M., Adams, C. V., Nation, K., & Rosen, S. (2005). Perception of transient non-speech stimuli is normal in specific language impairment: Evidence from glide discrimination. *Applied Psycholinguistics, 26,* 175–194.

Bishop, D. V. M., Adams, C. V., & Norbury, C. F. (2004). Using nonword repetition to distinguish genetic and environmental influences on early literacy development: A study of 6-year-old twins. *American Journal of Medical Genetics, 129,* 94–99.

Bishop, D. V. M., Adams, C. V., & Norbury, C. F. (2006). Distinct genetic influences on grammar and phonological short-term memory deficits: Evidence from 6-year-old twins. *Genes, Brain and Behavior, 5,* 158–169.

Bishop, D. V. M., & McArthur, G. M. (2004). Immature cortical responses to auditory stimuli in specific language impairment: Evidence from ERPs to rapid tone sequences. *Developmental Science, 7,* 11–18.

Bishop, D. V. M., & McArthur, G. M. (2005). Individual differences in auditory processing in specific language impairment: A follow-up study using event-related potentials and behavioural thresholds. *Cortex, 41,* 327–341.

Bloom, K., Russell, A., & Wassenberg, K. (1987). Turn taking affects the quality of infant vocalizations. *Journal of Child Language, 14,* 211–227.

Borovsky, A., Saygin, A. P., Cummings, A., Trauner, D., Bates, E., & Dick, F. (2007). *The development of environmental sounds and language comprehension in typically developing children and children with peri-natal focal lesions or developmental language disorder*. Manuscript submitted for publication.

Botting, N., Faragher, B., Simkin, Z., Knox, E., & Conti-Ramsden, G. (2001). Predicting pathways of specific language impairment: What differentiates good and poor outcome? *Journal of Child Psychology and Psychiatry and Allied Disciplines, 42*(8), 1013–1020.

Boysson-Bardies, B. de, Halle, P., Sagart, L., & Durand, C. (1989). Across linguistic investigation of vowel formants in babbling. *Journal of Child Language, 16*, 1–17.

Boysson-Bardies, B. de, & Vihman, M. M. (1991). Adaptation to language: Evidence from babbling and first words in four languages. *Language, 67*, 297–319.

Briscoe, J., Bishop, D. V., & Norbury, C. F. (2001). Phonological processing, language, and literacy: A comparison of children with mild-to-moderate sensorineural hearing loss and those with specific language impairment. *Journal of Child Psychology and Psychiatry, 42*, 329–340.

Brock, J. (in press). Language abilities in Williams syndrome: A critical review. *Development and Psychopathology*.

Brown, R. (1973). *A first language*. Cambridge, MA: Harvard University Press.

Brown, T. T., Lugar, H. M., Coalson, R. S., Miezin, F. M., Petersen, S. E., & Schlaggar, B. L. (2005). Developmental changes in human cerebral functional organization for word generation. *Cerebral Cortex, 15*, 275–290.

Campbell, T. F., Needleman, L., Riess, J. A., & Tobin, M. (2000). Bone lead levels and language processing performance. *Developmental Neuropsychology, 18*, 171–186.

Carey, S. (1978). The child as word learner. In J. Bresnan, G. Miller, & M. Halle (Eds.), *Linguistic theory and psychological reality* (pp. 264–293). Cambridge, MA: MIT Press.

Carpenter, M., Nagell, K., & Tomasello, M. (1998). Social cognition, joint attention, and communicative competence from 9 to 15 months of age. *Monographs of the Society for Research in Child Development, 63*. Oxford: Blackwell.

Carter, J. A., Murira, G. M., Ross, A. J., Mung'ala-Odera, V., & Newton C. R. (2003). Speech and language sequelae of severe malaria in Kenyan children. *Brain Injury, 17*, 217–224.

Carter, J. A., Ross, A. J., Neville, B. G., Obiero, E., Katana, K., Mung'ala-Odera, V., et al. (2005). Developmental impairments following severe falciparum malaria in children. *Tropical Medicine and International Health, 10*, 3–10.

Caselli, C., Casadio, P., & Bates, E. (1999). A comparison of the transition from first words to grammar in English and Italian. *Journal of Child Language, 26*, 69–111.

Ceponiene, R., Rinne, T., & Naatanen, R. (2002). Maturation of cortical sound processing as indexed by event-related potentials. *Clinical Neurophysiology, 113*, 870–882.

Choudhury, N., Leppanen, P. H. T., Leevers, H. J., & Benasich, A. A. (in press). Assessing rapid auditory processing abilities in family history and control infants: Evidence from converging paradigms. *Developmental Science*.

Clahsen, H., & Felser, C. (2006). How native-like is non-native language processing? *Trends in Cognitive Sciences, 10*, 564–570.

Cohen, I. L., Fishch, G., Sudhalter, V., Wolf-Schein, E., Hanson, D., Hagerman, R., et al. (1988). Social gaze, social avoidance and repetitive behavior in fragile X males in a controlled study. *American Journal of Mental Retardation, 92*, 436–446.

Conboy, B. T., & Mills, D. L. (2006). Two languages, one developing brain: Event-related potentials to words in bilingual toddlers. *Developmental Science, 9*, 1–12.

Cone-Wesson, B. (2005). Prenatal alcohol and cocaine exposure: Influences on cognition, speech, language, and hearing. *Journal of Communication Disorders, 38*, 279–302.

Conti-Ramsden, G., Botting, N., & Faragher, B. (2001). Psycholinguistic markers for specific language impairment (SLI). *Journal of Child Psychology and Psychiatry, 42*, 741–748.

Corkum, V., & Moore, C. (1995). Development of joint visual attention in infants. In C. Moore & P. J. Dunham (Eds.), *Joint attention: Its origins and role in development* (pp. 61–83). Hillsdale, NJ: Erlbaum.

Coscia, J. M., Ris, M. D., Succop, P. A., & Dietrich, K. N. (2003). Cognitive development of lead exposed children from ages 6 to 15 years: An application of growth curve analysis. *Child Neuropsychology, 9*, 10–21.

Cowan, R., Donlan, C., Newton, E. J., & Lloyd, D. (2005). Number skills and knowledge in children with specific language impairment. *Journal of Educational Psychology, 97*, 732–744.

Crain, S., & Pietroski, P. (2001). Nature, nurture and universal grammar. *Linguistics and Philosophy, 24*, 139–186.

Culp, R., Lawrence, H., Letts, D., Kelly, D., & Rice, M. (1991). Maltreated children's language and speech development: Abused, neglected, and abused and neglected. *First Language, 11*, 377–389.

Cummings, A., Ceponiene, R., Koyama, A., Saygin, A. P., Townsend, J., & Dick, F. (2006). Auditory semantic networks for words and natural sounds. *Brain Research, 1115*, 92–107.

Cummings, A., Saygin, A. P., Bates, E., & Dick, F. (2007). *The development of linguistic and non-linguistic auditory comprehension from 15–25 months: A preferential looking study.* Manuscript submitted for publication.

Curtiss, S., de Bode, S., & Mathern, G. W. (2001). Spoken language outcomes after hemispherectomy: Factoring in etiology. *Brain and Language, 79*, 379–396.

De Fosse, L., Hodge, S. M., Makris, N., Kennedy, D. N., Caviness, V. S., Jr., McGrath, L., et al. (2004). Language-association cortex asymmetry in autism and specific language impairment. *Annals of Neurology, 56*, 757–766.

Dehaene-Lambertz, G., Dehaene, S., & Hertz-Pannier, L. (2002). Functional neuroimaging of speech perception in infants. *Science, 298*, 2013–2015.

Dennis, M., Barnes, M. A., Wilkinson, M., & Humphreys, R. P. (1998). How children with head injury represent real and deceptive emotion in short narratives. *Brain and Language, 61*, 450–483.

Dennis, M., Purvis, K., Barnes, M. A., Wilkinson, M., & Winner, E., (2001). Understanding of literal truth, ironic criticism, and deceptive praise following childhood head injury. *Brain and Language, 78*, 1–16.

D'Entremont, B., Hains, S. M. J., & Muir, D. W. (1997). A demonstration of gaze following in 3- to 6-month-olds. *Infant Behavior and Development, 20*, 569–572.

Dick, F., Butler, A. C., St. John, M., Gernsbacher, M. A., & Ferreira, V. (2007). *A change in distributional frequencies selectively ameliorates artificially induced agrammatism.* Manuscript submitted for publication.

Dick, F., Saygin, A. P., Galati, G., Pitzalis, S., Bentrovato, S., D'Amico, S., et al. (in press). What is involved and what is necessary for complex linguistic and non-linguistic auditory processing: Evidence from fMRI and lesion data. *Journal of Cognitive Neuroscience.*

Dick, F., Saygin, A. P., Moineau, S., Aydelott, J., & Bates, E. (2004). Language in an embodied brain: The role of animal models. *Cortex, 40*, 226–227.

Dollaghan, C., & Campbell, T. F. (1998). Nonword repetition and child language impairment. *Journal of Speech, Language, and Hearing Research, 41*(5), 1136–1146.

Dore, J. (1974). A pragmatic description of early language development. *Journal of Psycholinguistic Research, 4*, 423–430.

Duyme, M., Dumaret, A.-C., & Tomkiewicz, S. (1999). How can we boost IQs of "dull children?": A late adoption study. *Proceedings of the National Academy of Sciences, USA, 96*, 8790–8794.

Dykins, E., Hodapp, R., & Leckman, J. (1994). *Behavior and development in fragile X syndrome.* Thousand Oaks, CA: Sage.

Eimas, P. D., Siqueland, E. R., Jusczyk, P., & Vigorito, J. (1971). Speech perception in infants. *Science, 171*, 303–306.

Elman, J. L., Bates, E. A., Johnson, M. H., Karmiloff-Smith, A., Parisi, D., & Plunkett, K. (1996). *Rethinking innateness: A connectionist perspective on development.* Cambridge, MA: MIT Press.

Eskenazi, B., Marks, A. R., Bradman, A., Fenster, L., Johnson, C., Barr, D. B., et al. (2006). In utero exposure to dichlorodiphenyltrichloroethane (DDT) and dichlorodiphenyldichloroethylene (DDE) and neurodevelopment among young Mexican American children. *Pediatrics, 118*, 233–241.

Ewing-Cobbs, L., & Barnes, M. (2002). Linguistic outcomes following traumatic brain injury in children. *Seminars in Pediatric Neurology, 9*, 209–217.

Fair, D. A., Brown, T. T., Petersen, S. E., & Schlaggar, B. L. (2006). A comparison of analyses of variance and correlation methods for investigating cognitive development with functional magnetic resonance imaging. *Developmental Neuropsychology, 30*, 531–546.

Fenson, L., Bates, E., Dale, P., Goodman, J., Reznick, J., & Thal, D. (2000). Measuring variability in early child language: Don't shoot the messenger. *Child Development, 71*, 323–328.

Fenson, L., Dale, P., Reznick, J., Bates, E., Thal, D., & Pethick, S. (1994). Variability in early communicative development. *Monographs of the Society for Research in Child Development, 59*. Oxford: Blackwell.

Fitch, W. T., & Hauser, M. D. (2004). Computational constraints on syntactic processing in a non-human primate. *Science, 303*, 377–380.

Fowler, A. E. (1988). Determinants of rate of language growth in children with Down syndrome. In L. Nadel (Ed.), *The psychology of Down syndrome* (pp. 217–245). Cambrige, MA: MIT Press.

Fowler, A. E. (1998). Language in mental retardation: Associations with dissociations from general cognition. In J. A. Burack, R. M. Hodapp, & E. Zigler (Eds.), *Handbook of mental retardation and development* (pp. 290–333). Cambridge University Press.

Fox, L., Long, S., & Anglois, A. (1988). Patterns of language comprehension deficit in abused and neglected children. *Journal of Speech and Hearing Disorders, 53*, 239–244.

Frank, D. A., Augustyn, M., Knight, W. G., Pell, T., & Zuckerman, B. (2001). Growth, development, and behavior in early childhood following prenatal cocaine exposure: A systematic review. *Journal of the American Medical Association, 285*, 1613–1625.

Frank, D. A., Klass, P., Earls, F., & Eisenberg, L. (1996). Infants and young children in orphanages: One view from pediatrics and child psychiatry. *Pediatrics, 97*, 569–578.

Frank, D. A., Rose-Jacobs, R., Beeghly, M., Wilbur, M. A., Bellinger, D., & Cabral, H. (2005). Level of prenatal cocaine exposure and 48-month IQ: Importance of preschool enrichment. *Neurotoxicology and Teratology, 27*, 15–28.

Friederici, A. D. (2005). Neurophysiological markers of early language acquisition: From syllables to sentences. *Trends in Cognitive Sciences, 9*, 481–488.

Frith, U., & Happé, F. (1994). Autism: Beyond "theory of mind." *Cognition, 50*(1–3), 115–132.

Gaillard, W. D., Sachs, B. C., Whitnah, J. R., Ahmad, Z., Balsamo, L. M., Petrella, J. R., et al. (2003). Developmental aspects of language processing: fMRI of verbal fluency in children and adults. *Human Brain Mapping, 18*, 176–185.

Gathercole, S. E., & Baddeley, A. D. (1990). Phonological memory deficits in language disordered children: Is there a causal connection? *Journal of Memory and Language, 2*, 103–127.

Gauger, L. M., Lombardino, L. J., & Leonard, C. M. (1997). Brain morphology in children with specific language impairment. *Journal of Speech, Language, and Hearing Research, 40*(6), 1272–1284.

Geers, A. E. (2004). Speech, language, and reading skills after early cochlear implant. *Archives of Otolaryngology: Head and Neck Surgery, 130*, 634–638.

Goldberg, A. (1995). *Constructions: A construction grammar approach to argument structure.* University of Chicago Press.

Goldberg, A. (2006). *Constructions at work: The nature of generalization in language.* Oxford University Press.

Goldstein, M. H., King, A. P., & West, M. J. (2003). Social interaction shapes babbling: Testing parallels between birdsong and speech. *Proceedings of the National Academy of Sciences, USA, 100*, 8030–8035.

Gomez, R., & Gerken, L. (1999). Artificial grammar learnt by 1-year-olds leads to specific and abstract knowledge. *Cognition, 70*, 109–135.

Graves, M. F. (1986). Vocabulary learning and instruction. *Review of Research in Education, 13*, 49–89.

Hale, C. M., & Tager-Flusberg, H. (2003). The influence of language on theory of mind: A training study. *Developmental Science, 6*, 346–359.

Halliday, L., & Bishop, D. V. M. (2005). Frequency discrimination and literacy skills in children with mild to moderate sensorineural hearing loss. *Journal of Speech, Language, and Hearing Research, 48*, 1187–1203.

Halliday, L., & Bishop, D. V. M. (2006). Is poor frequency modulation detection linked to literacy problems? A comparison of specific reading disability and mild to moderate sensorineural hearing loss. *Brain and Language, 97*, 200–213.

Hampson, J., & Nelson, K. (1993). Relation of maternal language to variation in rate and style of language acquisition. *Journal of Child Language, 20*, 313–342.

Hart, B., & Risley, T. (1995). *Meaningful differences in the everyday experiences of young American children.* Baltimore: Paul Brookes.

Hauser, M. D., Newport, E. L., & Aslin, R. N. (2001). Segmentation of the speech stream in a non-human primate: Statistical learning in cotton-top tamarins. *Cognition, 78*, 53–64.

Hayiou-Thomas, M., Bishop, D. V. M., & Plunkett, K. (2004). Simulating SLI: General cognitive processing stressors can produce a specific linguistic profile. *Journal of Speech, Language, and Hearing Research, 47*, 1347–1362.

Hayiou-Thomas, M., Kovas, Y., Harlaar, N., Bishop, D. V. M., Dale, P., & Plomin, R. (2006). Common aetiology for diverse language skills in 4½-year-old twins. *Journal of Child Language, 33*, 339–368.

Herbert, M. R., Ziegler, D. A., Makris, N., Filipek, P. A., Kemper, T. L., Normandin, J. J., et al. (2004). Localization of white matter volume increase in autism and developmental language disorder. *Annals of Neurology, 55*, 530–540.

Hill, E. L. (2001). Non-specific nature of specific language impairment: A review of the literature with regard to concomitant motor impairments. *International Journal of Language and Communication Disorders, 36*, 149–171.

Hill, P. R., Hogben, J., & Bishop, D. V. M. (2005). Auditory frequency discrimination in children with specific language impairment: A longitudinal study. *Journal of Speech, Language, and Hearing Research, 48*, 1136–1146.

Holland, S. K., Plante, E., Weber Byars, A., Strawsburg, R. H., Schmithorst, V. J., & Ball, W. S. (2001). Normal fMRI brain activation patterns in children performing a verb generation task. *NeuroImage, 14*, 837–843.

Hough, S. D. (2005). *Language outcomes in school-aged children adopted from Eastern European orphanages.* Unpublished dissertation, University of Pittsburgh (available online).

Hurley, R. A., McGowan, J. C., Arfanakis, K., & Taber, K. H. (2004). Traumatic axonal injury: Novel insights into evolution and identification. *Journal of Neuropsychiatry and Clinical Neurosciences*, *16*(1), 1–7.

Huttenlocher, J., Vasilyeva, M., Cymerman, E., & Levine, S. (2002). Language input and child syntax. *Cognitive Psychology*, *45*, 337–374.

Jansow, W., Crown, C. L., Feldstein, S., Taylor, L., Beebe, B., & Jaffe, J. (1988). Coordinated interpersonal timing of Down-syndrome and non-delayed infants with their mothers: Evidence for a buffered mechanism of social interaction. *Biological Bulletin*, *174*, 355–360.

Jernigan, T. L., Hesselink, J. R., Sowell, E., & Tallal, P. A. (1991). Cerebral structure on magnetic resonance imaging in language- and learning-impaired children. *Archives of Neurology*, *48*, 539–545.

Johnson, E. K., & Jusczyk, P. W. (2001). Word segmentation by 8-month-olds: When speech cues count more than statistics. *Journal of Memory and Language*, *44*, 548–567.

Johnston, J. R. (2005). Re: Law, Garrett, & Nye (2004), "The efficacy of treatment for children with developmental speech and language delay/disorder: A meta-analysis." *Journal of Speech, Language, and Hearing Research*, *48*, 1114–1117.

Johnston, J. R., & Kamhi, A. G. (1984). Syntactic and semantic aspects of the utterances of language-impaired children: The same can be less. *Merrill-Palmer Quarterly*, *30*, 65–86.

Jonas, R., Nguyen, S., Hu, B., Asarnow, R. F., LoPresti, C., Curtiss, S., et al. (2004). Cerebral hemispherectomy: Hospital course, seizure, developmental, language, and motor outcomes. *Neurology*, *62*, 1712–1721.

Jusczyk, P. W., & Aslin, R. N. (1995). Infants' detection of the sound patterns of words in fluent speech. *Cognitive Psychology*, *29*, 1–23.

Jusczyk, P. W., & Hohne, E. A. (1997). Infants' memory for spoken words. *Science*, *277*, 1984–1986.

Jusczyk, P. W., Houston, D. M., & Newsome, M. (1999). The beginnings of word-segmentation in English-learning infants. *Cognitive Psychology*, *39*, 159–207.

Jusczyk, P. W., Luce, P. A., & Charles-Luce, J. (1994). Infants' sensitivity to phonotactic patterns in the native language. *Journal of Memory and Language*, *33*, 630–645.

Kaminski, J., Call, J., & Fischer, J. (2004). Word learning in a domestic dog: Evidence for "fast mapping." *Science*, *304*, 1682–1683.

Karmiloff-Smith, A., Grant, J., Berthoud, I., Davies, M., Howlin, P., & Udwin, O. (1997). Language and Williams syndrome: How intact is "intact?" *Child Development*, *68*, 246–262.

Kisilevsky, B. S., Hains, S. M. J., Lee, K., Xie, X., Huang, H., Ye, H. H., et al. (2003). Effects of experience on fetal voice recognition. *Psychological Science*, *14*, 220–224.

Klin, A. (1991). Young autistic children's listening preferences in regard to speech: A possible characterization of the symptom of social withdrawal. *Journal of Autism and Developmental Disorders*, *21*, 29–42.

Koelsch, S., Fritz, T., Schulze, K., Alsop, D., & Schlaug, G. (2005). Adults and children processing music: An fMRI study. *NeuroImage*, *25*, 1068–1076.

Kossoff, E. H., Buck, C., & Freeman, J. M. (2002). Outcomes of 32 hemispherectomies for Sturge–Weber syndrome worldwide. *Neurology*, *59*, 1735–1738.

Kuhl, P. K. (1986). Theoretical contributions of tests on animals to the special-mechanisms debate in speech. *Experimental Biology*, *45*, 233–265.

Kuhl, P. K. (2004). Early language acquisition: Cracking the speech code. *Nature Reviews Neuroscience*, *5*, 831–843.

Kuhl, P. K., Coffey-Corina, S., Padden, D., & Dawson, G. (2005). Links between social and linguistic processing of speech in preschool children with autism: Behavioral and electrophysiological measures. *Developmental Science*, *8*, F1–F12.

Kuhl, P. K., Conboy, B. T., Padden, D., Nelson, T., & Pruitt, J. C. (2005). Early speech perception and later language development: Implications for the "critical period." *Language Learning and Development, 1,* 237–264.

Kuhl, P. K., & Meltzoff, A. N. (1996). Infant vocalizations in response to speech: Vocal imitation and developmental change. *Journal of the Acoustical Society of America, 100,* 2425–2438.

Kuhl, P. K., & Miller, J. (1975). Speech perception by the chinchilla: Voiced–voiceless distinction in alveolar plosive consonants. *Science, 190,* 69–72.

Kuhl, P. K., & Padden, D. M. (1983). Enhanced discriminability at the phonetic boundaries for the place feature in macaques. *Journal of the Acoustical Society of America, 73,* 1003–1010.

Kuhl, P. K., Tsao, F. M., & Liu, H. M. (2003). Foreign-language experience in infancy: Effects of short-term exposure and social interaction on phonetic learning. *Proceedings of the National Academy of Sciences, USA, 100,* 9096–9101.

Kuhl, P. K., Williams, K. A., Lacerda, F., Stevens, K. N., & Lindblom, B. (1992). Language experience alters phonetic perception in infants by 6 months of age. *Science, 255,* 606–608.

Lahey, M., & Edwards, J. (1999). Naming errors of children with specific language impairment. *Journal of Speech, Language, and Hearing Research, 42,* 195–205.

Lai, C., Fisher, S., Hurst, J., Vargha-Khadem, F., & Monaco, A. (2001). A novel forkhead-domain gene is mutated in a severe speech and language disorder. *Nature, 413,* 465.

Laing, E., Butterworth, G., Ansari, D., Gsödl, M., Longhi, E., Panagiotaki, G., et al. (2002). Atypical development of language and social communication in toddlers with Williams syndrome. *Developmental Science, 5,* 233–246.

Landry, S. H., Smith, K. E., & Swank, P. R. (2002). Environmental effects on language development in normal and high-risk child populations. *Seminars in Pediatric Neurology, 9,* 192–200.

Law, J., Garrett, Z., & Nye, C. (2004). The efficacy of treatment for children with developmental speech and language delay/disorder: A meta-analysis. *Journal of Speech, Language, and Hearing Research, 47,* 924–943.

Leech, R., Aydelott, J., Symons, G., Carnevale, J., & Dick, F. (2007). The effect of semantic and attentional distractors on syntactic processing in typical development and adulthood. *Developmental Science, 10*(6), 794–813.

Leonard, L. B. (1998). *Children with specific language impairment.* Cambridge, MA: MIT Press.

Leonard, L. B., Eyer, J. A., Bedore, L. M., & Grela, B. G. (1997). Three accounts of the grammatical morpheme difficulties of English-speaking children with specific language impairment. *Journal of Speech, Language, and Hearing Research, 40,* 741–753.

Leonard, L. B., Schwartz, R. G., Allen, G. D., Swanson, L. A., & Loeb, D. F. (1989). Unusual phonological behavior and the avoidance of homonymy in children. *Journal of Speech, Language, and Hearing Research, 32,* 583–590.

Marcell, M. M., & Weeks, S. L. (1988). Short-term memory difficulties and Down's syndrome. *Journal of Mental Deficiency Research, 32,* 153–162.

Marchman, V. A., Wulfeck, B., & Weismer, S. E. (1999). Morphological productivity in children with normal language and SLI: A study of the English past tense. *Journal of Speech, Language, and Hearing Research, 42,* 206–219.

Marcus, G. F., Vijayan, S., Bandi Rao, S., & Vishton, P. M. (1999). Rule learning by seven-month-old-infants. *Science, 283,* 77–80.

Markson, L., & Bloom, P. (1997). Evidence against a dedicated system for word learning in children. *Nature, 385,* 813–815.

Marton, K., Abramoff, B., & Rosenzweig, S. (2005). Social cognition and language in children with specific language impairment (SLI). *Journal of Communication Disorders, 38,* 143–162.

Masataka, N. (2001). Why early linguistic milestones are delayed in children with Williams syndrome: Late onset of hand banging as a possible rate-limiting constraint on the emergence of canonical babbling. *Developmental Science, 4,* 158–164.

Maye, J., Werker, J. F., & Gerken, L. (2002). Infant sensitivity to distributional information can affect phonetic discrimination. *Cognition, 82,* 101–111.

McArthur, G. M., & Bishop, D. V. M. (2004a). Frequency discrimination deficits in people with specific language impairment: Reliability, validity, and linguistic correlates. *Journal of Speech, Language, and Hearing Research, 47,* 527–541.

McArthur, G. M., & Bishop, D. V. M. (2004b). Which people with specific language impairment have auditory processing deficits? *Cognitive Neuropsychology, 21,* 79–94.

McArthur, G. M., & Bishop. D. V. M. (2005). Speech and non-speech processing in people with specific language impairment: A behavioural and electrophysiological study. *Brain and Language, 94,* 260–273.

McGregor, K. K., Newman, R. M., Reilly, R. M., & Capone, N. C. (2002). Semantic representation and naming in children with specific language impairment. *Journal of Speech, Language, and Hearing Research, 45*(5), 998–1014.

Mengler, E. D., Hogben, J. H., Michie, P., & Bishop, D. V. M. (2005). Poor frequency discrimination is related to oral language disorder in children: A psychoacoustic study. *Dyslexia, 11,* 155–173.

Mervis, C., & Bertrand, J. (1997). Developmental relations between cognition and language: Evidence from Williams syndrome. In L. B. Adamson & M. A. Romski (Eds.), *Research on communication and language disorders: Contributions to theories of language development* (pp. 75–106). New York: Brookes.

Mervis, C., Morris, C., Klein-Tasman, B., Bertrand, J., Kwitny, S., Appelbaum, L., et al. (2003). Attentional characteristics of infants and toddlers with Williams syndrome during triadic interactions. *Developmental Neuropsychology, 23,* 243–268.

Miller, J. (1988). The developmental asynchrony of language development in children with Down syndrome. In L. Nadel (Ed.), *The psychobiology of Down syndrome* (pp. 167–198). Cambridge, MA: MIT Press.

Mills, D. L., Plunkett, K., Prat, C., & Schafer, G. (2005). Watching the infant brain learn words: Effects of language and experience. *Cognitive Development, 20,* 19–31.

Mills, D. L., & Sheehan, E. A. (2007). Experience and developmental changes in the organization of language-relevant brain activity. In D. Coch, K. W. Fischer, & G. Dawson (Eds.), *Human behavior, learning, and the developing brain: Typical development.* New York: Guilford.

Morse, P. (1972). The discrimination of speech and non-speech stimuli in early infancy. *Journal of Experimental Child Psychology, 1,* 173–183.

Nazzi, T., Bertoncini, J., & Mehler, J. (1998). Language discrimination by newborns: Towards an understanding of the role of rhythm. *Journal of Experimental Psychology: Human Perception and Performance, 24,* 756–766.

Nazzi, T., Paterson, S., & Karmiloff-Smith, A. (2003). Early word segmentation by infants and toddlers with Williams syndrome. *Infancy, 4*(2), 251–271.

Nelson, H. D., Nygren, P., Walker, M., & Panoscha, R. (2006). Screening for speech and language delay in preschool children: Systematic evidence review for the US Preventive Services Task Force. *Pediatrics, 117*(2), e298–e319.

Nelson, K. (1981). Individual differences in language development: Implications for development and language. *Developmental Psychology, 17,* 170–187.

New Oxford American Dictionary (2005). Second Edition (Erin McKean, Ed.). Oxford University Press.

Newbury, D. F., Bishop, D. V. M., & Monaco, A. P. (2005). Genetic influences on language impairment and phonological short-term memory. *Trends in Cognitive Sciences, 9*, 528–534.

Nikolopoulos, N. P., Dyar, D., Archbold, S., & O'Donoghue, G. M. (2004). Development of spoken language grammar following cochlear implantation in prelingually deaf children. *Archives of Otolaryngology: Head and Neck Surgery, 130*, 629–633.

Nippold, M. A. (1998). *Later language development: The school-age and adolescent years*. Austin, TX: Pro-Ed.

Norbury, C. F. (2004). Factors supporting idiom comprehension in children with communication disorders. *Journal of Speech, Language, and Hearing Research, 47*(5), 1179–1193.

Norbury, C. F., Bishop, D. V. M., & Briscoe, J. (2001). Production of English finite verb morphology: A comparison of SLI and mild–moderate hearing impairment. *Journal of Speech, Language, and Hearing Research, 24*, 165–178.

Pallier, C., Dehaene, S., Poline, J. B., LeBihan, D., Argenti, A. M., Dupoux, E., et al. (2003). Brain imaging of language plasticity in adopted adults: Can a second language replace the first? *Cerebral Cortex, 13*, 155–161.

Paradise, J. L., Campbell, T. F., Dollaghan, C. A., Feldman, H. M., Bernard, B. S., Colborn, D. K., et al. (2005). Effect of early or delayed insertion of tympanostomy tubes for persistent otitis media on developmental outcomes at age 6 years. *New England Journal of Medicine, 353*, 576–586.

Paradise, J. L., Feldman, H. M., Campbell, T. F., Dollaghan, C. A., Colborn, D. K., Bernard, B. S., et al. (2001). Early versus late tympanostomy tube placement for persistent otitis media: Developmental outcomes at age 3 years. *New England Journal of Medicine, 344*, 1179–1195.

Paterson, S. J., Brown, J. H., Gsödl, M. K., Johnson, M. H., & Karmiloff-Smith, A. (1999). Cognitive modularity and genetic disorders. *Science, 286*(5448), 2355–2358.

Peña, M., Maki, A., Kovacic, D., Dehaene-Lambertz, G., Koizumi, H., Bouquet, F., et al. (2003). Sounds and silence: An optical topography study of language recognition at birth. *Proceedings of the National Academy of Sciences, USA, 100*, 11702–11705.

Pinker. S. (1984). *Language learnability and language development*. Cambridge, MA: Harvard University Press.

Pinker, S. (1987). The bootstrapping problem in language acquisition. In B. MacWhinney (Ed.), *Mechanisms of language acquisition* (pp. 339–441). Hillsdale, NJ: Erlbaum.

Pinker, S. (1989). *Learnability and cognition*. Cambridge, MA: MIT Press.

Pizutto, E., & Caselli, C. (1992). The acquisition of Italian morphology. *Journal of Child Language, 19*, 491–557.

Pizutto, E., & Caselli, C. (1994). The acquisition of Italian verb morphology in a cross-linguistic perspective. In Y. Levy (Ed.), *Other children, other languages* (pp. 137–188). Hillsdale, NJ: Erlbaum.

Plante, E., Boliek, C., Binkiewicz, A., & Erly, W. K. (1996). Elevated androgen, brain development and language/learning disabilities in children with congenital adrenal hyperplasia. *Developmental Medicine and Child Neurology, 38*(5), 423–437.

Plante, E., Swisher, L., Vance, R., & Rapcsak, S. (1991). MRI findings in boys with specific language impairment. *Brain and Language, 41*(1), 52–66.

Porter, M. A., & Coltheart, M. (2005). Cognitive heterogeneity in Williams syndrome. *Developmental Neuropsychology, 27*(2), 275–306.

Prizant, B. (1983). Language acquisition and communication behaviour in autistic children. *Journal of Speech and Hearing Disorders, 46*, 241–249.

Pulsifer, M. B., Brandt, J., Salorio, C. F., Vining, E. P., Carson, B. S., & Freeman, J. M. (2004). The cognitive outcome of hemispherectomy in 71 children. *Epilepsia, 45*, 243–254.

Ramus, F., Hauser, M. D., Miller, C., Morris, D., & Mehler, J. (2000). Language discrimination by human newborns and by cotton-top tamarin monkeys. *Science, 288*, 349–351.

Reilly, J., Losh, M., Bellugi, U., & Wulfeck, B. (2004). "Frog, where are you?" Narratives in children with specific language impairment, early focal brain injury, and Williams syndrome. *Brain and Language, 88*, 229–247.

Rice, M. L., Warren, S. F., & Betz, S. K. (2005). Language symptoms of developmental language disorders: An overview of autism, Down syndrome, fragile X, specific language impairment, and Williams syndrome. *Applied Psycholinguistics, 26*, 7–27.

Riley, E., & McGee, C. L., (2005). Fetal alcohol spectrum disorders: An overview with emphasis on changes in brain and behavior. *Experimental Biology and Medicine, 230*, 357–365.

Roberts, J. M. A. (1989). Echolalia and comprehension in autistic children. *Journal of Autism and Developmental Disorders, 19*, 271–281.

Rubino, R., & Pine, J. (1998). Subject–verb agreement in Brazilian Portuguese: What low error rates hide. *Journal of Child Language, 25*, 35–60.

Rvachew, S., Slawinski, E. B., Williams, M., & Green, C. L. (1999). The impact of early onset otitis media on babbling and early language development. *Journal of the Acoustical Society of America, 105*, 467.

Saccuman, M. C., Dick, F., Bates, E., Müller, R. A., Krupa-Kwiatkowski, M., & Wulfeck, B. (2007a). *An fMRI comparison of language-impaired and typically developing children's language production and comprehension.* Manuscript in preparation.

Saccuman, M. C., Dick, F., Bates, E., Müller, R. A., Krupa-Kwiatkowski, M., & Wulfeck, B. (2007b). *Lexical access and sentence processing: A developmental fMRI study of language processing.* Manuscript submitted for publication.

Saffran, J., Aslin, R., & Newport E. (1996). Statistical learning by 8-month-old infants. *Science, 274*, 1926.

Saffran, J. R., Johnson, E. K., Aslin, R. N., & Newport, E. L. (1999). Statistical learning of tone sequences by human infants and adults. *Cognition, 70*, 27–52.

Saffran, J. R., & Thiessen, E. D. (2003). Pattern induction by infant language learners. *Developmental Psychology, 39*, 484–494.

Saygin, A. P., Dick, F., & Bates, E. (2005). An online task for contrasting auditory processing in the verbal and nonverbal domains and norms for college-age and elderly subjects. *Behavioral Research Methods, Instruments, and Computers. 37*, 99–110.

Saygin, A. P., Dick, F., Wilson, S. W., Dronkers, N. F., & Bates, E. (2003). Shared neural resources for processing language and environmental sounds: Evidence from aphasia. *Brain, 126*, 928–945.

Scarborough, H. (1990). Index of productive syntax. *Applied Psycholinguistics, 11*, 1–22.

Schlaggar, B. L., Brown, T. T., Lugar, H. M., Visscher, K. M., Miezin, F. M., & Petersen, S. E. (2002). Functional neuroanatomical differences between adults and school-age children in the processing of single words. *Science, 296*, 1476–1479.

Schul, R., Stiles, J., Wulfeck, B., & Townsend, J. (2004). How "generalized" is the "slowed processing" in SLI? The case of visuospatial attentional orienting. *Neuropsychologia, 42*(5), 661–671.

Schwartz, R. G., & Leonard, L. B. (1985). Lexical imitation and acquisition in language-impaired children. *Journal of Speech and Hearing Disorders, 50*, 141–149.

Shott, S. R., Joseph, A., & Heithaus, D. (2001). Hearing loss in children with Down syndrome. *International Journal of Pediatric Otorhinolaryngology, 61*(3), 199–205.

Shriberg, L. D., Tomblin, J. B., & McSweeny, J. L. (1999). Prevalence of speech delay in 6-year-old children and comorbidity with language impairment. *Journal of Speech, Language, and Hearing Research, 42*(6), 1461–1481.

Singer Harris, N. G., Bellugi, U., Bates, E., Jones, W., & Rossen, M. (1997). Contrasting the profiles of language development in children with Williams and Down syndromes. In D. Thal & J. Reilly (Eds.), Special issue: On the origins of communication disorders. *Developmental Neuropsychology, 13*(3), 345–370.

Skuse, D. (1993). Extreme deprivation in early childhood. In D. Bishop & K. Mogford (Eds.), *Language development in exceptional circumstances* (pp. 29–46). Hove, East Sussex: Psychology Press.

SLI Consortium. (2002). A genomewide scan identifies two novel loci involved in specific language impairment. *American Journal of Human Genetics, 70*, 384–398.

SLI Consortium. (2004). Highly significant linkage to the SLI1 locus in an expanded sample of individuals affected by specific language impairment. *American Journal of Human Genetics, 74*, 1225–1238.

Slobin, D. (1985). Crosslinguistic evidence for the language-making capacity. In D. I. Slobin (Ed.), *The crosslinguistic study of language acquisition.* Vol. 2: *Theoretical issues* (pp. 1157–1256). Hillsdale, NJ: Lawrence Erlbaum.

Smith, E. C., & Lewicki, M. S. (2006). Efficient auditory coding. *Nature, 239*, 978–982.

Spencer, L. J., Barker, B. A., & Tomblin, J. B. (2003). Exploring the language and literacy outcomes of pediatric cochlear implant users. *Ear and Hearing, 24*, 236–247.

Stoel-Gammon, C. (1980). Phonological analysis of four Down's syndrome children. *Applied Psycholinguistics, 1*, 31–48.

Stothard, S. E., Snowling, M. J., Bishop, D. V. M., Chipchase, B. B., & Kaplan, C. A. (1998). Language-impaired preschoolers: A follow-up into adolescence. *Journal of Speech, Language, and Hearing Research, 41*(2), 407–418.

Tager-Flusberg, H. (1981). Sentence comprehension in autistic children. *Applied Psycholinguistics, 2*, 5–24.

Tager-Flusberg, H., & Joseph, R. M. (2003). Identifying neurocognitive phenotypes in autism. *Philosophical Transactions of the Royal Society of London* (Series B), *358*, 303–314.

Tager-Flusberg, H., Lord, C., & Paul, R. (2005). Language and communication in autism. In F. Volkmar, R. Paul, A. Klin, & D. Cohen (Eds.), *Handbook of autism and pervasive developmental disorders* (3rd ed., pp. 335–364). New York: John Wiley.

Tager-Flusberg, H., & Sullivan, K. (1998). Early language development in children with mental retardation. In J. A. Burack, R. M. Hodapp, & E. Zigler (Eds.), *Handbook of mental retardation and development* (pp. 208–239). Cambridge University Press.

Thiessen, E. D., & Saffran, J. R. (2003). When cues collide: Use of stress and statistical cues to word boundaries by 7- to 9-month-old infants. *Developmental Psychology, 39*, 706–716.

Thomas, M. S. C., Dockrell, J. E., Messer, D., Parmigiani, C., Ansari, D., & Karmiloff-Smith, A. (in press). Speeded naming, frequency and the development of the lexicon in Williams syndrome. *Language and Cognitive Processes.*

Thomas, M. S. C., Grant, J., Barham, Z., Gsödl, M., Laing, E., Lakusta, L., et al. (2001). Past tense formation in Williams syndrome. *Language and Cognitive Processes, 16*, 143–176.

Thomas, M. S. C., & Karmiloff-Smith, A. (2003). Modelling language acquisition in atypical phenotypes. *Psychological Review, 110*(4), 647–682.

Tizard, B., Cooperman, O., Joseph, A., & Tizard, J. (1972). Environmental effects on language development: A study of children in long-stay residential nurseries. *Child Development, 43*, 337–358.

Tomasello, M. (1992). *First verbs: A case study in early grammatical development.* Cambridge University Press.

Tomasello, M. (1999). *The cultural origins of human cognition*. Cambridge, MA: Harvard University Press.

Tomasello, M. (2000a). Do young children have adult syntactic competence? *Cognition, 74*, 209–253.

Tomasello, M. (2000b). The item-based nature of children's early syntactic development. *Trends in Cognitive Sciences, 4*, 156–163.

Tomasello, M. (2001). Perceiving intentions and learning words in the second year of life. In M. Bowerman & S. C. Levinson (Eds.), *Language acquisition and conceptual development* (pp. 132–158). New York: Cambridge University Press.

Tomasello, M. (2006). Acquiring linguistic constructions. In D. Kuhn & R. Siegler (Eds.), *Handbook of child psychology* (pp. 1–48). New York: Wiley.

Tomasello, M., Call, J., & Hare, B. (1998). Five primate species follow the visual gaze of conspecifics. *Animal Behaviour, 55*, 1063–1069.

Tomasello, M., Carpenter, M., Call, J., Behne, T., & Moll, H. (2005). Understanding and sharing intentions: The origins of cultural cognition. *Behavioral and Brain Sciences, 28*, 675–691.

Tomasello, M., & Todd, J. (1983). Joint attention and lexical acquisition style. *First Language, 4*, 197–212.

Trauner, D., Wulfeck, B., Tallal, P., & Hesselink, J. (1995). *Neurologic and MRI profiles of language impaired children* (Tech. Rep. CND-9513). University of California at San Diego, Center for Research in Language.

Trauner, D., Wulfeck, B., Tallal, P., & Hesselink, J. (2000). Neurological and MRI profiles of children with developmental language impairment. *Developmental Medicine and Child Neurology, 42*(7), 470–475.

Trevarthen, C., & Hubley, P. (1978). Secondary intersubjectivity: Confidence, confiding and acts of meaning in the first year. In A. Lock (Ed.), *Action, gesture, and symbol: The emergence of language* (pp. 183–229). London: Academic Press.

Ulualp, S. O., Biswal, B. B., Yetkin, F. Z., & Kidder, T. M. (1998). Functional magnetic resonance imaging of auditory cortex in children. *Laryngoscope, 108*, 1782–1786.

van der Lely, H. K. J., Rosen, S., & Adlard, A. (2004). Grammatical language impairment and the specificity of cognitive domains: Relations between auditory and language abilities. *Cognition, 94*, 167–183.

Vance, M., & Wells, B. (1994). The wrong end of the stick: Language-impaired children's understanding of non-literal language. *Child Language Teaching and Therapy, 10*, 23–46.

Vargha-Khadem, F., & Mishkin, M. (1997). Speech and language outcome after brain damage in childhood. In I. Tuxhorn, H. Holthausen, & H. E. Boenigk (Eds.), *Paediatric epilepsy syndromes and their surgical treatment* (pp. 774–784). London: John Libbey.

Vargha-Khadem, F., & Polkey, C. E. (1992). A review of cognitive outcome after hemidecortication in humans. *Advances in Experimental Medicine and Biology, 325*, 137–151.

Vargha-Khadem, F., Watkins, K. E., Price, C. J., Ashburner, J., Alcock, K. E., Connelly, A., et al. (1998). Neural basis of an inherited speech and language disorder. *Proceedings of the National Academy of Sciences, USA, 95*, 12695–12700.

Varnhagan, C. K., Das, J. P., & Varnhagan, S. (1987). Auditory and visual memory span: Cognitive processing by TMR individuals with Down syndrome and other etiologies. *American Journal of Mental Deficiency, 91*(4), 398–405.

Vicari, S., Caselli, M. C., Gagliardi, C., Tonucci, F., & Volterra, V. (2002). Language acquisition in special populations: A comparison between Down and Williams syndromes. *Neuropsychologia, 40*(13), 2461–2470.

Viding, E., Spinath, F. M., Price, T. S., Bishop, D. V. M., Dale, P. S., & Plomin, R. (2004). Genetic and environmental influence on language impairment in 4-year-old same-sex and opposite-sex twins. *Journal of Child Psychology and Psychiatry, 45*, 315–325.

Volterra, V., Bates, E., Benigni, L., Bretherton, I., & Camaioni, L. (1979). First words in language and action: A qualitative look. In E. Bates, L. Benigni, I. Bretherton, L. Camaioni, & V. Volterra (Eds.), *The emergence of symbols: Cognition and communication in infancy* (pp. 141–222). New York: Academic Press.

Werker, J. F., & Desjardins, R. N. (1995). Listening to speech in the first year of life: Experiential influences on phoneme perception. *Current Directions in Psychological Science, 4*, 76–80.

Wittgenstein, L. (1953/2001). *Philosophical investigations.* Oxford: Blackwell.

Wulfeck, B., Bates, E., Krupa-Kwiatkowski, M., & Saltzman, D. (2004). Grammaticality sensitivity in children with early focal brain injury and children with specific language impairment. *Brain and Language, 88*(2), 215–228.

Yoshinaga-Itano, C., Sedey, A. L., Coulter, D. K., & Mehl, A. L. (1998). Language of early- and later-identified children with hearing loss. *Pediatrics, 102*(5), 1161–1171.

9

The Neuropsychology of Visuospatial and Visuomotor Development

Janette Atkinson and Marko Nardini

"Visual spatial development" has many definitions and levels of analysis with different perspectives from neuropsychology, developmental cognitive neuroscience, pediatric neurology and ophthalmology, education, and rehabilitation. It covers many areas, including brain processing related to spatial representations, an understanding of relative motion, of objects in space, the processes underpinning acts of mental rotation and location memory, reaching, grasping, and spatial attention. The neurobiological approach taken in this chapter will attempt to link findings from normal adults and patients with neurological damage, animal neurophysiology, and psychological studies on spatial development in infants and children, so as to identify relationships between changing behavior and brain function and to devise models of these processes.

In some areas, attempts have been made to separate "perception" from "cognition" in spatial development. For example, some developmental psychologists have defined cognitive acts as those in which infants demonstrate "intentionality," while "perception" is more automatic and less goal oriented. Some argue for limiting "visual perception" to lower centers in the eye and occipital lobes, while "cognition" is mediated by "higher centers"—parietal, temporal, and frontal cortices. Such divisions are somewhat artificial in that many visual spatial actions involve complex circuitry running from subcortical centers, such as the superior colliculus and basal ganglia, to occipitoparietal areas for spatial representations, including cortical and subcortical motor areas, specialist temporal lobe areas for object recognition, top-down attentional control from frontal areas, and feedback loops between all of these networks. In fact, it has been estimated that over half of the brain is involved in even simple spatial tasks such as pouring water from a jug into a glass. However, in many developmental studies there is an attempt to delineate and separate processes within a network by designing stimulus conditions with dimensions known to elicit responses in specific populations of tuned neurons within particular brain areas—these we might call "designer stimuli." Other studies have adapted tests for children and infants from adult visual spatial tasks, where failures have been related to specific locations of brain damage in the patient.

Of course, in human development, immaturity of processing in any one or more of these networks may limit behavioral performance on any specific visuospatial task. If analogies are found between infant and adult patient behavior, this does not necessarily mean that the cascading processes of human development follow the same course as the adult with specific brain damage. It can only be used as a first approximate step.

This chapter is divided into eight sections which consider:

1. Current neurobiological models of normal infant development of spatial vision.
2. Development of spatial selective attention for action in infancy.
3. Development of dorsal and ventral streams.
4. Development of action modules for reaching, grasping, and motor planning.
5. Development of action modules for locomotion and navigation.
6. Development of spatial localization in location memory tasks.
7. Summary of abnormal spatial development.
8. Summary of the developmental model of visual spatial development.

Examples of abnormality of development and their neurobiological underpinnings are briefly reviewed in each section, and are summarized in section 7.

1. Current Neurobiological Models of Normal Infant Development of Spatial Vision

For further details on much of this section see Atkinson (2000).

1.1. Two visual systems: subcortical and cortical

Early models of visual spatial development started from the idea of two visual systems, a phylogenetically older, retinotectal system and a newer, geniculostriate system. The tectal system defines *where* an object is located to trigger orienting, while cortical mechanisms define *what* is actually in the selected location (Schneider, 1969; Sprague & Meikle, 1965). Bronson's (1974) model for human visual development was based on this dual system. Since newborns orient by head and eye movements to conspicuous stimuli, but show little evidence of pattern discrimination, he proposed that vision is subcortically controlled for deciding *where* a stimulus was located, with the cortex maturing postnatally for deciding *what* was in the fixated location.

Extensive studies with typically developing infants have allowed more detailed models to be devised for these two systems. These studies have included behavioral measures (e.g., preferential looking) and electrophysiological measures of brain waves (EEGs, visual-evoked potentials or event-related potentials [VEP/ERP]). In Atkinson and Braddick's initial model (Atkinson, 1984; Braddick, Atkinson, & Wattam-Bell, 1989) distinct functional modules or channels for the different visual attributes for color, pattern, and motion were proposed, which had their underpinnings in populations of cortical neurons with distinct profiles of response to different visual stimuli.

The visual cortex undergoes very rapid development in neuronal selectivity in the first six months after birth, the beginning of a period during which the number of synapses in visual cortex increases dramatically (Huttenlocher, de Courten, Garey, & van der Loos, 1982), providing the rich connectivity on which the selective cortical processing proposed in the model depends. Atkinson and Braddick's VEP and behavioral studies with normal infants suggested that the various attributes of selectivity do not emerge together in this wiring-up of the cortex; rather, there is a clear developmental ordering. Mechanisms or channels for orientation for shape discrimination become functional closely after birth, followed by direction selectivity for visual motion, and then selectivity to binocular disparities for stereoscopic vision.

1.2. Magnocellular and parvocellular systems

Sensitivity to motion direction (directionality) and stereo depth information (binocularity) is associated with input to the cortex from the magnocellular pathway, and processing within the cortex by the dorsal stream (Livingstone & Hubel, 1988). The initial development of this pathway may be slower than that of the parvocellular ventral pathway which specializes in processing form (orientation or slant) and color (Atkinson, 1992). Motion and disparity processing both require the comparison of information between separated locations in the visual field and hence the establishment of relatively long, orderly, horizontal connections in cortex. The fact that, after the initial onset, there is a development of infants' directional sensitivity to progressively greater displacements (Wattam-Bell, 1992, 1996), and of binocular sensitivity to progressively greater disparities (Wattam-Bell, 1995), suggests that the range of these connections, increasing with age, may be a limiting factor in the development of these aspects of cortical selectivity.

1.3. Dorsal and ventral streams

Pioneering electrophysiology starting in the 1970s and 1980s mapped distinct brain areas beyond primary visual cortex containing neurons responding to particular visual attributes, including an area selective for motion information (V5/MT) and a color-specific area (V4; for reviews, see Felleman & Van Essen, 1991; Zeki, 1993). Ungerleider and Mishkin (1982) proposed two broad, functionally distinct, processing streams, the "dorsal" and "ventral" streams. The *dorsal* stream, including area V5/MT, transmits information to parietal lobe networks for localizing objects within a spatial array (*where*) and is intimately linked to eye-movement mechanisms of selective attention. The *ventral* stream processes information for the temporal lobe (including V4), concerned with the *what* aspects of objects, such as form, color, and face recognition. Supporting evidence came from other studies on primates (e.g., Boussaoud, Ungerleider, & Desimone, 1990; Merigan & Maunsell, 1993; Van Essen & Maunsell, 1983) and from

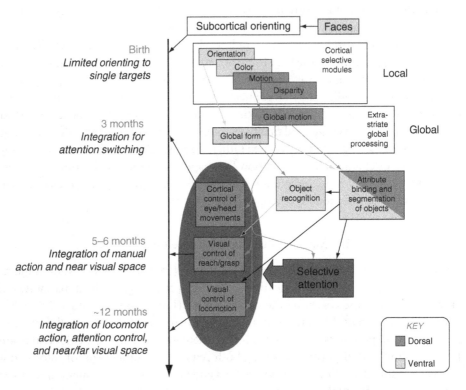

Figure 9.1 The Atkinson and Braddick model of visual spatial development of dorsal and ventral streams in infancy.

clinical observations of patients with specific deficits of spatial processing (e.g., Damasio & Benton, 1979), movement perception (Zihl, von Cramon, & Mai, 1983), or object recognition (Milner & Goodale, 1995).

Figure 9.1 shows the current model of Atkinson and Braddick, based on both developmental studies and neurophysiology from other species. In this figure, there are some additional divisions between onset of functioning in "local" and "global" processing (discussed below).

Milner and Goodale (1995; Goodale & Milner, 2003) suggested that the ventral and dorsal cortical streams have different functions in the visual control of behavior: The ventral stream is concerned with perceptual processing (including, for example, object recognition) and the dorsal with visual control of action. This is a functional description of the two streams rather than one based on the types of selectivity of cells.

1.4. Action modules in the dorsal stream

Substantial information now exists about many distinct action modules in primates. Figure 9.2 shows a schematic model of some of these dorsal circuits, drawing on the

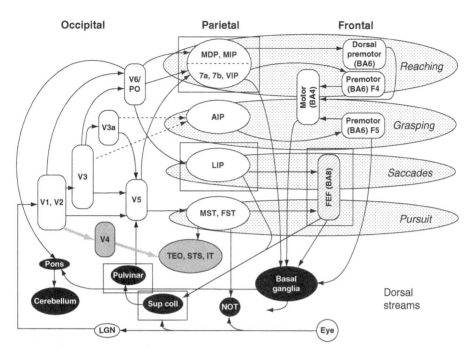

Figure 9.2 Schematic model of different action modules within the dorsal stream. *Abbreviations.* AIP, anterior intraparietal area; BA, Brodmann areas; FEF, frontal eye field; FST, fundal superior temporal; IT, inferior temporal areas; LGN, lateral geniculate nucleus; LIP, lateral intraparietal area; MDP, medial dorsal parietal area; MIP, medial intraparietal area; MST, medial superior temporal; PO, parietal occipital area; STS, superior temporal sulcus; TEO, temporal occipital area; V1, primary visual cortex; V2–V6, extrastriate visual cortical areas; VIP, ventral intraparietal areas.

extensive reviews of Milner and Goodale (1995) and Jeannerod (1997). For example, Jeannerod (1997) has argued that the dorsal stream, transmitting visual information to primary motor cortex (M1), has separate divisions for reaching and grasping.

Both dorsal and ventral streams project to prefrontal cortex, and in the mature brain the two systems are heavily interconnected. Visual spatial development can be divided into processes more dependent on dorsal stream functions, such as visual control of action, and those dependent on ventral, such as recognition. However, for many visuo-spatial tasks, processing across two or more modules must be combined. For example, in reaching for an object, the object must be identified as the correct object for the goal of the action using ventral stream networks before the appropriate action is planned using dorsal stream processing. In looking at development of the first stages of dorsal and ventral stream processing, stimuli have been designed to artificially separate one stream from the other, but even here there can be some debate about their separation.

The eye-movement control systems are the first to develop in young infants. These action systems control saccadic tracking and smooth pursuit of objects of interest and switches of attention involving head and eye movements to scrutinize different objects of interest sequentially. These two systems are schematized in Figure 9.2. However, before discussing development in each of these early action streams, mechanisms for controlling attention must be considered, as the action- and attention-processing systems are heavily interlinked in development.

1.5. Links between attention and spatial action

Mechanisms of attention play an essential role in perceptually "filtering out" irrelevant stimuli and enhancing those of interest. Traditionally, visual attention has been viewed as a unitary, supramodal mechanism subserved by anatomical systems separate from those involved in sensory and perceptual processing (e.g., LaBerge & Brown, 1989; Posner, 1980; Posner & Petersen, 1990). More recently, two attentional brain systems have been postulated, a posterior system that subserves spatial attention and an anterior system involved in various complex cognitive tasks related to executive function (Posner & Dehaene, 1994).

Effects of "covert attention" are seen in subjects' advantages in responding to a stimulus when they know where it will appear, even when they do not move their eyes to fixate the relevant place (Posner & Cohen, 1980). Attention has also been described as a mechanism that enables "selection for action" (e.g., Allport, 1989), the action being either an eye movement (a saccade to fixate the object) or a bodily movement such as a reach toward the object. Such motor acts have been taken as indicators of *overt* attention shifts. Rizzolatti and others (e.g., Berthoz, 1996; Rizzolatti, 1983; Rizzolatti & Camarda, 1987) have proposed a "premotor" theory of attention, according to which *covert* attention (without fixating the object of interest) exploits the same selection-for-action mechanism. In this theory, selective attention to a spatial location would involve a number of action modules. In Figure 9.2 areas related to selective attention overlapping with areas in the dorsal stream are highlighted in square boxes. This suggests considerable overlap between the attention and action systems. Whether or not the premotor theory can provide a complete account of adult attention, it is valuable in a developmental context where evidence for attention control comes from overt orienting acts. In the next section, development of these linked attention and action systems in early infancy is discussed.

2. Development of Spatial Selective Attention for Action in Infancy

The most basic visual spatial action system to develop in young infants involves the control of eye movements to track moving objects and people and to stabilize objects on the retina.

2.1. Newborn eye movements

With a large visual field of conspicuous vertical stripes, moving horizontally at a constant speed of around 10 deg/s, optokinetic nystagmus (OKN)—cycling eye movements, each cycle showing a brief period of smooth pursuit following in the direction of the motion, followed by a rapid saccadic return in the opposite direction—can be observed in new-borns. These stabilizing eye movements act to keep the head and eyes fixating on objects of interest in the real world. OKN is the first directional action system to operate in newborns, but does not seem to be one of which there is conscious awareness.

2.2. Smooth pursuit eye movements

Differences have also been found developmentally between newborns and 3-month-olds in the extent and gain of smooth pursuit, which implies that at least in human development, there are different stabilizing mechanisms for smooth pursuit, enabling targets to be tracked, and saccadic movements, enabling orienting. Detailed studies of the development of these stabilizing mechanisms in infants have been made by Claes von Hofsten and his colleagues (see, for example, von Hofsten & Rosander, 1996, 1997). They recorded smooth pursuit eye movements even in newborns, if targets of sufficient size and contrast were used and their velocity was kept relatively low. However, saccadic tracking is much more commonly observed than pursuit in the newborn. They also looked at the development of the initial coupling of eye and head movements, as the infant develops these stabilizing mechanisms. Fairly accurate coupling and a mature vestibular ocular response is achieved in the first few months of life, although many of the tracking eye movements observed in everyday situations in this period are saccadic, rather than continuous smooth pursuit. This changeover from passive saccadic tracking to smooth pursuit eye movements has been taken to imply anticipation of the end-point of the object in space and a planning mechanism used to control eye movements. Further evidence for this comes from the infant's ability to anticipate where an object will be in space when moving behind an occluder. There are extensive studies in this area concerning the factors, such as path trajectory, velocity, and target appearance, that will change this anticipatory behavior (for a review, see von Hofsten, 2005).

2.3. Eye/head movement systems for switching attention

For switching attention, there is general agreement that the newborn has a "where?" system, which is largely under subcortical control, and is used for orienting the head and eyes to abrupt and significant changes in the world. In the visual domain these are usually changes in luminance or movement. This system has been studied using the fixation shift paradigm (e.g., Atkinson & Braddick, 1985; Atkinson, Hood, Wattam-Bell, & Braddick, 1992). Newborn infants make a shift of the head and eyes from a central target to a target in the peripheral fields appearing at the moment when the central target disappears. The orienting system used when only one target is visible at one time (noncompetition) is likely to operate supramodally, across domains and sensory modalities, as a nonspecific alerting system. The superior colliculus is strongly implicated within this system, although there may be a number of subcortical circuits involved in different components of the responses (see Figure 9.2 for likely areas involved).

2.4.   Disengagement and switching attention when targets compete

The crude subcortical system, described above, will orient to a single salient target. However, it works much less effectively in the fixation shift paradigm when a peripheral stimulus appears but the central target remains visible. Responses to a peripheral stimulus when the central target continues to engage fixation require modulation and disengagement of this orienting system by cortical processes. Both right and left parietofrontal areas linked to subcortical eye-movement systems have been implicated as necessary for development of these attention-switching systems in infancy (Atkinson & Braddick, 1985; Atkinson & Hood, 1994; Atkinson et al., 1992). The cortical system appears to become functional around 3–4 months of age in normally developing infants. This modulation by the cortex can be mapped out by varying the interval between offset of one target and onset of another (Hood & Atkinson, 1993). In some infants who have suffered perinatal brain damage involving both cortical and subcortical areas (and in particular the basal ganglia) even the primitive orienting system may not be functional (Atkinson & Hood, 1994; Mercuri, Atkinson, Braddick, Anker, Cowan, et al., 1997; Mercuri et al., 1996; Mercuri, Atkinson, Braddick, Anker, Nokes, et al., 1997).

2.5.   Abnormalities of switching attention

The cortical contribution is vulnerable to brain damage, particularly in the parietal lobes. Two infants who underwent hemispherectomy (removal of one complete hemisphere), one at 4 months of age and the other at 8 months, to relieve intractable epilepsy, postoperatively failed to show disengagement and shifts of eyes and head from a centrally viewed target to one appearing in the periphery when the central target remained visible while the peripheral target appeared (i.e., fixation shift under competition). Failure to shift under competition was on the side of space opposite the removed hemisphere, but good shifts of gaze were made on the side controlled by the remaining functional hemisphere, and to either side when only one target was visible; that is, fixation shifts without competing targets (Braddick et al., 1992). In other studies, infants with either focal lesions or diffuse hypoxic-ischemic damage showed this "sticky fixation," an inability to easily switch visual attention from one target to another when two targets are present at once (Atkinson & Hood, 1994; Hood & Atkinson, 1990; Mercuri et al., 1996). This behavior resembles the problems often seen in adult stroke patients as part of a "visual neglect" syndrome.

In this section, the first spatial selective attention systems have been discussed. However, attention is not a unitary function. Besides neural systems controlling selective attention and switches of attention, there are those for sustaining attention and those for inhibiting actions and learning new ones (the latter sometimes being called "attentional control"). Many of these attentional systems mature in later childhood. Development of attention in spatial tasks in childhood will be considered later in the chapter, together with abnormalities in these component systems.

3. Development of Dorsal and Ventral Streams

3.1. Development of cortical motion systems: local and global processing

The first stage of development of the dorsal stream underpinning spatial development is the development of sensitivity to motion. Behavioral and VEP/ERP studies of infants and young children have been designed to distinguish "local" from "global" processing in the dorsal and ventral streams. Local motion processing can be defined as the sensitivity to direction in a small region of the image, such as a short segment of contour, while global motion processing allows the representation of motion over extended regions that may correspond to surfaces and objects. In adults and in other species, global processing has been identified with the integrative properties of neurons in visual area V5, while local processing is identified with neurons in V1 (Braddick & Qian, 2000).

Several aspects of infant performance indicate that global processes operate at an early stage of development. In a dot pattern containing a proportion of randomly moving dots, processing the motion of individual dots cannot yield the overall direction of motion; this requires integration of motion signals over many dots, a process that can be assessed in terms of the motion coherence threshold, the proportion of coherently moving dots required for detecting the global direction. Such thresholds can be measured using preferential looking where it can be shown that by about 3–4 months of age, a strip of coherently moving dots is preferred over an area of random motion; this closely follows the emergence of local direction discrimination at around 2 months (Wattam-Bell, 1994). These results suggest that very soon after local motion signals are first available in the developing brain, the processes that integrate them into global representations are operating quite efficiently. It may be that connectivity between V1 and extrastriate areas including V5, on which this integration is based, exists early at least in a crude form, awaiting the organization of local directional selectivity in V1—perhaps because the latter requires some minimum level of temporal precision before it can function. Deficits in global motion processing, which have been called "dorsal stream vulnerability," may originate in problems processing temporal information at these very early stages of motion processing.

3.2. Comparison of global form and global motion processing

The development of global motion processing—a function of extrastriate dorsal stream processing—can be compared with global processing of form in the ventral stream, where analogous thresholds can be measured. Here subjects must detect the organization of short line segments into concentric circles, with "noise" introduced by randomizing the orientation of a proportion of the line segments. Neurons responding to concentric organization of this kind have been reported in area V4 in macaques (Gallant, Braun, & Van Essen, 1993), an extrastriate area at a similar level in the ventral stream to V5 in the dorsal stream. In infants, form coherence discrimination is apparent from 4 to 5 months of age from preferential looking and VEP/ERP studies (Braddick, Curran, Atkinson, Wattam-Bell, & Gunn, 2002), with children's coherence thresholds reaching adult levels at around 7–8 years (Gunn et al., 2002). When dynamically rotating and static versions of the same circularly organized stimulus are compared, later maturity is found in children for the moving dynamic stimulus (*global motion coherence* stimulus) than the static stimulus (*global form coherence* stimulus). This is a reversal of earlier development in infancy where static global form detection appears to be earlier than global motion detection (Atkinson & Braddick, 2005).

Specific areas associated with form and motion coherence tasks have been identified for comparable stimuli in functional magnetic resonance imaging (fMRI) studies of normal adults (Braddick et al., 2001; Braddick, O'Brien, Wattam-Bell, Atkinson, & Turner, 2000). This work has shown that anatomically distinct circuits are activated in global processing of form and motion, although each circuit involves parts of both the parietal and temporal lobes, and cannot therefore be said to be strictly "dorsal" and "ventral" in the human brain. However, the activated areas do include dorsal stream areas V5 and V3A for motion, and anatomically ventral areas for form. It has also been found that brain activity measured on fMRI increases linearly with the degree of coherence in an area analogous to V5 (Rees, Friston, & Koch, 2000) and that areas in the lingual/fusiform gyrus, which may include V4, similarly show a linear response for form coherence (Braddick, O'Brien, Rees, et al., 2002).

In summary, although local orientation sensitivity emerges earlier in development than directional selectivity, global organization based on form, pattern, or orientation is found to be less effective in determining infant behavior than global organization based on motion. This may reflect the importance of global motion for segmentation and depth organization of the visual world for early spatial tasks. Such segmentation arises both from the independent movement of objects and from parallax due to self-motion; the latter is effective for infants (e.g., Kellman & Spelke, 1983), even though their self-motion is largely passive rather than actively controlled in the first six months. Later in childhood, sensitivity to form coherence attains adult levels rather earlier than sensitivity to motion coherence, and is less sensitive to developmental impairments; this "dorsal stream vulnerability" is discussed in the following section.

3.3. Abnormalities of dorsal and ventral stream development

The broad division between the functions of dorsal and ventral cortical streams is reflected in abnormal development. We have studied development of these functions in a number of groups of young children with atypical developmental profiles (children with Williams syndrome, autism, fragile-X syndrome, perinatal brain damage resulting in focal lesions and hemiplegia). Across all these groups, a general finding has been that in tasks designed to compare the two streams, the development of the dorsal action stream is more likely to be affected than the ventral. This has led us to a general hypothesis of "dorsal stream vulnerability" (Atkinson et al., 2001; Atkinson et al., 1999; Spencer et al., 2000). Children with Williams syndrome (or infantile hypercalcemia) typically show a very uneven profile of neuropsychological development, with relatively strong expressive language abilities combined with unusual semantics, good face recognition, but severely impaired spatial cognition (see, e.g., Bellugi, Bihrle, Trauner, Jernigan, & Doherty, 1990; Bellugi, Lichtenberger, Mills, Galaburda, & Korenberg, 1999; Bellugi, Sabo, & Vaid, 1988; Bellugi, Wang, & Jernigan, 1994; Bertrand, Mervis, & Eisenberg, 1997; Karmiloff-Smith, 1998; Klein & Mervis, 1999; Pezzini, Vicari, Volterra, Milani, & Ossella, 1999). They reach motor milestones later than typically developing children, are often delayed in learning to walk and in the development of fine motor skills, and on a standardized test of motor function (Movement ABC: Henderson & Sugden, 1992) they show an average delay of at least 2 years (Atkinson, Braddick, Anker, et al., 1996). Problems that persist into later life include uncertainty when negotiating stairs or uneven surfaces (Atkinson, Braddick, Anker, et al., 1996), awkward gait and joint con-tractures in some children (Kaplan, Kirsschner, Watters, & Costa, 1989), and difficulty with the use of everyday tools.

This neuropsychological profile is consistent with the possibility that ventral stream processes (e.g., face recognition) are relatively unimpaired, but dorsal stream function for visual control of action is developmentally abnormal. We have explored this possi-bility in several ways. First, we have compared tests of motion and form coherence which require global integration by extrastriate visual areas. Many children with Williams syndrome (WS) have considerable difficulty with the motion task relative to the form task (Atkinson, Braddick, Anker, Curran, & Andrew, 2003; Atkinson et al., 1997). In WS, these deficits are found across the age range from 3 years to adulthood (Atkinson, Braddick, Rose, et al., 2006). The same pattern is found in some younger, typically developing children (4–5 years) and so, although the results are in line with the "dorsal vulnerability" hypothesis, they suggest a more general delay with ability never approaching adult levels, but asymptoting at the 4–5 year level.

3.4. Use of motion information for more complex discriminations in infancy

In the previous section, the psychophysical sensitivity of infants to simple stimuli vary-ing in form, pattern, and motion has been measured. These abilities are useful to young infants for understanding the spatial world around them. For example, recognizing the pattern of motion of a human being rather than a rocking chair is fundamental to separating objects in space, and for separating one's own motion from the intrinsic motion of objects and people. Detecting three-dimensional (3-D) information from the distribution of optic flow information is also a necessary starting-point for seg-menting objects from their background.

A diverse range of studies have tested infants for complex discriminations for motion information in spatial tasks. Discrimination has been demonstrated between rigid and nonrigid transformations of a 3-D object (Walker, Owsley, Megaw-Nyce, Gibson, & Bahrick, 1980). Others have shown quite subtle discrimination of 3-D structure from motion (Arterberry & Yonas, 1988, 2000; e.g., the presence of an interior corner on a cube, represented by random dot kinematograms), and kinetic depth information leading to recognition of a 3-D shape subsequently provided through disparity cues. Infants' sensitivity to the temporal direction of apparently causal event sequences can be demonstrated (e.g., Leslie, 1984), and a preference has been reported for dynamic event sequences with simple shapes that adults categorize as social interactions (Rochat, Morgan, & Carpenter, 1997).

Infants have also shown sensitivity to the patterns of point-light motion that characterize biological motion (e.g., Bertenthal, Proffitt, Spetner, & Thomas, 1985; Booth, Pinto, & Bertenthal, 2002). Most of these discriminations have been in tests of 3- to 6-month-old infants, and none have been shown so early that they require us to revise the view that the general ability for directional discrimination emerges after 7 weeks of age. On the other hand, they demonstrate that, only a few weeks after infants acquire any ability to discriminate motion directions, they can exploit this ability in a wide variety of complex perceptual functions. Together with the findings on global motion, these results support the idea that the emergence of motion processing in development is constrained by the development of relatively low-level directional mechanisms, rather than by immaturity of processes that elaborate and integrate motion information.

3.5.   Dorsal and ventral pathways beyond extrastriate areas

The possibility of different courses of development for dorsal and ventral streams has already been mentioned, but there are also important developmental differences between different modules within a stream. The major milestones of exploratory head and eye movements, directed reaching and grasping, and locomotion each involves integrated function of a different spatial action module processing dorsal stream information. All these action programs must involve some spatial analysis of the visual layout, but the different systems need representations at different scales and with different frames of reference. For reaching and grasping, the infant only needs representation of space near to the body and an egocentric frame of reference to match object locations to hand actions. For locomotion, the child needs to represent the environment on a scale beyond arm's length, and with a reference frame that remains stable in space as the body moves. Next in this chapter, we will briefly describe studies on the development of reaching, grasping, and locomotion which are all underpinned by dorsal stream circuitry.

4.   Development of Action Modules for Reaching, Grasping, and Motor Planning

4.1.   Reaching and grasping in infancy

Typically developing infants usually start to reach and grasp successfully for objects in near distance at around 4–6 months of age. Two kinds of visual information must be processed within the visual action system controlling reaching and grasping. First, the location of the object, laterally and in distance, must be identified. Second, visual analysis is required to determine whether the object is a suitable target for reaching and grasping.

For the first, the coincidence in timing between the development of binocularity around 4 months (Braddick, 1996) and the emergence of visually guided reaching suggests that binocular disparity information, associated with convergence, is a key input to the visuomotor module for reaching. This is confirmed by the finding that binocular information is critical in determining the kinematics of infants' reaches (Braddick, Atkinson, & Hood, 1996).

From 6 to 9 months, reaching appears as a quite compulsive behavior for small objects presented within range. This behavior raises the question of the visual information by which an infant determines that an object is graspable and hence a suitable target for reaching.

4.2.   Preferential looking and preferential reaching

The development of distinct visuomotor modules, and their ultimate integration, is illustrated by experiments which combine preferential looking with preferential reaching (Newman, Atkinson, & Braddick, 2001). In preferential looking, infants make an orienting response of head and eyes toward the most salient object or region in the visual field. Presentation of paired stimuli allows the relative salience of these stimuli to be assessed. Depending on the development of various cortical modules, salience is a function of luminance, color, motion, or depth contrast, and of spatial structure defined by such contrast. It is also modulated by novelty (as in habituation tests) and by the special significance of certain stimuli such as faces. Salience, so defined, is the visual computation characteristic of the set of cortical modules which contribute to the orienting system (providing output through the superior colliculus). In the case where an infant is presented with two 3-D objects, similar in shape and surface but different in size, the infant tends to orient to the larger object (King, Atkinson, Braddick, Nokes, & Braddick, 1996; Newman et al., 2001).

However, reaching is only an appropriate response for objects that are small enough to be grasped. Thus the visual modules that provide information controlling this response need to compute, as well as the spatial direction for the reach, the size of the potential target. This computation is not necessarily possible for the infant at the age when the motor schema of reaching becomes available, but when it is possible, it will cause reaching to be preferentially directed to the smaller object of a pair, when the larger is beyond the span on the infant's hand.

Thus the two visuomotor dorsal stream systems for orienting and reaching may be driven by different visual information from the same pair of objects. The studies of King et al. (1996) and Newman et al. (2001) showed that these systems interact differently at different ages; a possible organization of the two systems at each stage is schematized in Figure 9.3. When infants first start to reach (up to 8 months), they do not show a significant reaching preference between large and small objects. However, their

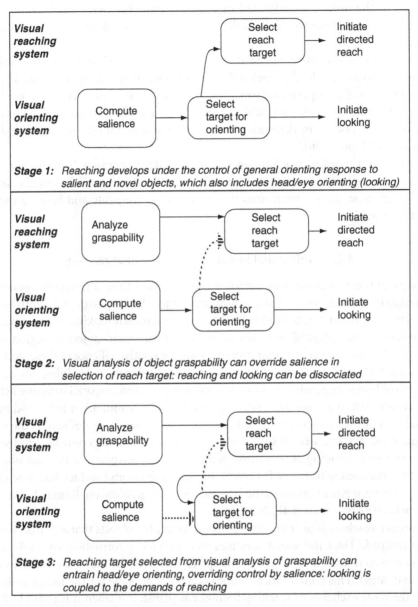

Figure 9.3 Schematic model of development of preferential looking and preferential reaching for objects in infancy.

reaching is predominantly directed to the object they initially fixate. We infer that processing of the specific visual attributes signifying graspability is not yet linked into a visuomotor module for reaching, and that at this stage there is a substantial coupling between the system controlling reaching and that determining orienting.

Between 8 and 12 months a strong preference emerges for reaching for the smaller object, which is within the span of the infant's hand. Thus an effective visual analysis of graspability has developed and serves as an input to the reaching control system. Infants at this age show a noticeable decoupling of reaching and initial orienting: They are more likely than younger or older infants to first fixate one object and then reach for another. This decoupling can be emphasized by manipulating visual salience: Marking a schematic face on one object increases preference for looking at that object, without altering its graspability and hence without a corresponding increase in the tendency for it to elicit reaching in competition (Newman et al., 2001).

After 12 months, reaching becomes less selective toward the smaller object, perhaps because it has become a less compulsive behavior, and also because the infant's grasp can encompass larger objects. At the same time, reaching and initial looking become more congruent again. It appears that the orienting and reaching systems can be integrated into a single piece of goal-directed behavior.

There is an extensive literature on factors affecting reaching in infants (for reviews, see Berthier & Keen, 2006; von Hofsten, 1991). A number of studies have found changes in development during the first two years of life in the kinematics, dependent on the size of the target (e.g., Fagard, 2000; Fagard & Jacquet, 1996). For example, in a recent study cubed objects were varied across a wide range of sizes (Braddick & Atkinson, 2003). For infants between 4 and 6 months, smaller objects elicited more grasping actions than nongrasp contacts. Between 6 and 10 months, the proportion of bimanual reaches for the larger objects increased, with different kinematics of the speed profiles in grasp compared to nongrasp reaches. Some of these differences in kinematics may reflect an understanding of the "graspability" of the object. This suggests that areas such as the anterior intraparietal area may be operating to identify salient object properties for guiding actions in the first year of life.

4.3. Bimanual coordination

Alongside reaching and grasping with one hand comes bimanual coordination for the many tasks requiring two hands to reach a goal. Early bimanual coordination patterns are typically similar for the two hands in that both hands reach or grasp synchronously and involve proximal control. With improvements in posture and visuomotor skill at around 6 months of age, the infant starts to explore objects placed in his or her hand and transfers the object from one hand to the other. These actions form the basis of later developing complementary bimanual patterns of coordination. In these early object explorations, only one hand is active at a time, but toward the end of the first year the two hands are capable of carrying out two different actions simultaneously; for example, lifting and holding open the lid of a box in order to retrieve a toy. The first bimanual attempts are often poorly timed and clumsy, but by 18 months of age the infants perform these tasks smoothly and efficiently with good spatial and temporal organization (e.g., Bruner, 1970; Diamond, 1991; Fagard, 1994). Bojczyk and Corbetta (2004) demonstrated that with repeated exposure (training) infants were able to develop well-coordinated bimanual actions by 8–9 months and thus outperform age-matched infants with no previous experience of the task.

4.4.   Visual information in motor planning: abnormalities in Williams syndrome

For everyday motor planning, many visual factors need to be taken into account. For example, for an object to be grasped, its distance, size, and orientation must be judged accurately. One experimental paradigm that gives insight into more complex visual control of action is the "postbox task" used by Goodale and colleagues (Goodale, Milner, Jakobsen, & Carey, 1991) to study a ventral stream impaired patient. Goodale and colleagues found a striking dissociation. This patient could accurately post a card through an oriented slot (dependent on dorsal-stream control of action) but failed on perceptual matching of the slot orientation (dependent on ventral-stream processing for perceptual judgments). On a task of this kind, children with Williams syndrome showed much greater inaccuracy in posting the card than in matching the card's orientation to that of the slot, compared with normally developing children (Atkinson et al., 1997). This supports the account of a dorsal-stream deficit, although again the degree of deficit was quite varied between individuals.

When picking up square shapes, children with WS were also impaired on adjusting grip aperture to target size, and made slower reaches, with more movement segments, suggesting that they were less able to program accurately the reach as a whole (Newman, 2001). There thus appears to be a continuing immaturity in WS children in the dorsal stream units controlling reaching and grasping. However, they also show poor performance on a matching test (judgment for the size of the squares without picking them up), indicating that problems in WS appear in both "ventral" and "dorsal" aspects of the task (Newman, 2001).

In the postbox task discussed above (Atkinson et al., 1997), children with WS often found their hands in awkward postures as they rotated the card, suggesting inefficiency in end-state planning, the ability to take into account the intended use or end-state of the object. End-state planning is likely to involve the integration of dorsal-stream information with prefrontal areas involved in inhibiting inappropriate actions and coordinating the elements of action sequences. An end-state planning deficit in WS was explicitly tested by Newman (2001) using a handle rotation task adapted from adult studies by Rosenbaum and colleagues (Rosenbaum, Vaughan, Barnes, & Jorgensen, 1992). Results from this study indicate that children with WS either do not attempt end-state planning or are unable to make the spatial transformations required to predict the end-state correctly.

Overall, these studies found subtle and variable deficits in the use of dorsal-stream information to control manual action, although these were not always dissociated from ventral-stream performance. The deficits were most striking beyond the early stages of visual processing for actions, in the use of visuospatial information for end-state planning. There may well be a "cascade" effect, with early abnormalities in more basic parts of the dorsal pathway affecting later development of complex feedback loops involved in visuomotor planning, which show deficits even if the lower level effects are overcome. The individual variability highlights the degree to which adaptive strategies may lead to differently configured systems even if there is a common initial developmental deficit.

5. Development of Action Modules for Locomotion and Navigation

The integration of different dorsal-stream modules is required when locomotion becomes part of the infant's behavioral repertoire. For instance, a desired object is processed in far space as a target for locomotion, and brought into near space as a target for reaching. The child must become able to switch attention from near to far, and to engage the visual processes required at these two scales. Other aspects of visual behavior also require such shifts; for example, joint attention invoked by an adult's pointing gesture, which is also achieved around the beginning of the second year (Butterworth & Grover, 1990). It remains a challenge for further research to characterize and understand these processes of integration and switching.

A key component of successful locomotion is balance. The use of visual information to maintain balance starts as young as 15 months (Lee & Aronson, 1974) and develops throughout childhood (Shumway-Cook & Woollacott, 1985). Real-world locomotion also depends on avoiding obstacles or accommodating movement to them (Patla, 1991). The visual decisions involved are: Can I step over this or should I walk round it? And, if I step over this, what height should I raise my feet to? These considerations are important when planning both single steps and longer routes.

We know that children avoid objects based on the visual information they have about their size. For example, the classic "visual cliff" experiment showed that young infants avoided crawling on an area they perceived to be dangerously deep (Gibson & Walk, 1960). Some new work considers how visual information is used to accommodate movements appropriately. This work shows that step descent is divided into "transport" and "placement" phases. The transition between phases is marked by the lead leg swinging in to contact the step. The vertical distance traveled by the knee during the transport phase increases in proportion to the step's riser height. This pattern is lost when vision is removed. Strikingly, this ability to scale movement to riser height is present in children as young as 3 years old. However, these children depend more than adults on online visual control to accomplish this (Cowie, 2007). These studies illustrate that children use vision to control accommodative processes as well as avoidance decisions.

Successful locomotion involves not only using visual information but also combining it with information about one's own locomotor abilities and current body state. Toddlers take locomotor decisions based on their own walking skill and experience (Kingsnorth & Schmuckler, 2000) and body dimensions (Adolph & Avolio, 2000). In a new "stepping stones" task children must choose to follow one of two paths of "stepping stones" across a pretend "river." Children as young as 3 years are influenced in their planning by their own body states—in this case the need to make anticipatory changes in foot position before the start of the task (Cowie, Smith, Braddick, & Atkinson, 2006a; Cowie, Smith, Braddick, Atkinson, & Nardini, 2006).

As with other visuomotor tasks, the visual control of locomotion is likely to be mediated by the dorsal stream. There is little work on this, but the patient D.F., with damage to the ventral stream but a spared dorsal stream, can accurately scale her stepping up movements (Patla & Goodale, 1996), though not her verbal estimates of step height; while young children with Williams syndrome, who show other dorsal-stream impairments, cannot scale stepping down movements in the task reported above (Atkinson, Braddick, Nardini, Cowie, et al., 2006; Cowie, Smith, Braddick, & Atkinson, 2006b).

6. Development of Spatial Localization in Location Memory Tasks

Further important aspects of spatial development depend on the systems underpinning accurate spatial localization in memory tasks. From studies of adults using psychophysics, brain imaging, and transcranial magnetic stimulation (TMS), and from animal lesion studies, dorsal stream parietal networks are the primary processing areas for basic spatial localization, while the hippocampus, parahippocampal gyrus, and entorhinal cortex are involved in more complex spatial memory tasks (see review by Stiles, Paul, Ark, & Akshoomoff, in press).

6.1. Location memory in infants

In the classic Piagetian "A not B" task, an object is repeatedly hidden at location A before a test trial on which it is hidden in novel location B. Infants aged around 9 months continue to search incorrectly in the "familiar location" (A); this is the "A not B" error. AB tasks have been used to test *object permanence*, that is, the infant's knowledge that objects exist independently over space and time. However, they also reveal the spatial framework that infants use to define the location of an object.

Children's ability to overcome the AB error depends on many factors. Self-locomotion reduces the likelihood of the error (Bertenthal & Campos, 1990; Horobin & Acredolo, 1986; Kermoian & Campos, 1988), and looking-time measures indicate that children are aware of the difference between the A and B locations before they are able to avoid the AB error in their reaching responses (e.g., Baillargeon & DeVos, 1991; Hofstadter & Reznick, 1996).

In nonhuman primates, bilateral lesions of dorsolateral prefrontal cortex disrupt AB performance, but bilateral lesions to parietal cortex (Diamond, 1991; Diamond, Werker, & Lalonde, 1994) or hippocampus (Diamond, Zola-Morgan, & Squire, 1989) have little effect. These findings suggest that children's solution of the task depends on frontal maturation. Further evidence from changes in frontal metabolic activity in the first year (Chugani, Phelps, & Mazziotta, 1987; Jacobs et al., 1995) supports this view, as do data from EEG and near infrared spectroscopy measures (Baird et al., 2002; Fox & Bell, 1990). Bell and Fox (1992) found increased anterior-posterior EEG coherence associated with improved performance on the AB task, suggesting that long-range axonal connections may contribute to the change in performance. As discussed earlier, these pathways may be critical for the control of reaching. Thus maturation of the anterior-posterior system may account for the differences in performance on reaching and looking tasks.

Infants make a related error when looking for an object after changing position. Infants aged 6–12 months old often search *egocentrically* after they have moved; that is, they seem not to appreciate that a target that was previously on their left is now on their right (e.g., Acredolo, 1978). As with the AB error, infant egocentrism is moderated by many factors. It can be overcome, particularly when a visual cue that directly indicates the target is available (e.g., Rieser, 1979). Crucial for mature navigation, however, is the later developing ability to use indirect landmarks, which do not directly indicate a target.

6.2. Development of location memory in childhood

Improvements in location memory in mid-childhood follow prefrontal, posterior parietal, and hippocampal maturation. Children's use of different spatial frames of reference to remember a location develops gradually. Egocentric representations, using the body as a reference, provide a good basis for immediate action toward objects. More robust representations are provided by encoding where objects are relative to stable landmarks (using an allocentric reference frame). This would enable objects to be found even when the viewer changes position. Another way to deal with a change of position is to track where an object is while the observer is moving ("updating" the egocentric representation as the observer moves); adults use these different frames of reference and updating processes in complementary ways.

Representations using external landmarks are reliably used for action by the second year (Huttenlocher, Newcombe, & Sandberg, 1994). At 16–36 months, children retrieve objects hidden in a sandbox after walking around to the other side (Newcombe, Huttenlocher, Bullock Drummey, & Wiley, 1998), showing coding relative to landmarks and/or spatial updating with self-motion. A more difficult problem is processing a change of viewpoint caused by the rotation of an object, rather than one's own displacement. In this case, the self-motion information that could be used to maintain an accurate egocentric representation while walking is not available. Judging what would be where if the viewer's viewpoint changed presents a "perspective problem" (Huttenlocher & Presson, 1973), potentially a test of children's ability to use a purely viewpoint-independent or allocentric frame of reference. Piaget and Huttenlocher's perspective-taking studies were not usually solved until around 10 years, although similar tasks have been solved earlier with a modified procedure (Newcombe & Huttenlocher, 1992).

Nardini and colleagues (Nardini, Burgess, Breckenridge, & Atkinson, 2006) tracked both egocentric coding, suitable for simple spatial recall, and allocentric codings, capable of solving the "perspective problem," in 3–6-year-olds within the same task. Children saw a toy hidden under one of 12 cups on a board with landmarks attached to two of its edges, and had to find it after a manipulation. The task systematically varied whether the same view of the board was seen at hiding and test (i.e., whether the toy kept its place relative to the *body*) and whether the array was rotated (i.e., whether the toy kept its place relative to the *room*). In 3–6-year-olds, as in adults (Wang & Simons, 1999), there were parallel, additive effects of both *body* and *room* frames of reference. The performance improvement when a familiar view allowed egocentric coding was already seen at 3 years. From 5 years, children showed successful recall after changes of viewpoint caused by rotation, which could only be solved by attending to the array and its local landmarks (a "perspective problem"). This ability may depend on codings relative to landmarks, supported by the hippocampus (O'Keefe & Burgess, 1996), and may also include mental rotation, which has elsewhere been demonstrated from 5 years (Kosslyn, Margolis, Barrett, Goldknopf, & Daly, 1990; Marmor, 1975), and shows activation including parietal areas (e.g., Booth et al., 2000) in children and adults.

A separate question concerns how children combine different kinds of visual information to maintain their sense of orientation. The human environment includes discrete landmarks, such as trees or buildings, which could be individuated by color or shape, as well as elements of layout, such as the shape of a room or a field, whose geometric aspects could be coded. Hermer and Spelke (1994, 1996) found that 18–24-month-olds, disoriented in sparsely featured enclosures, re-established their orientation using geometry (enclosure shape), but not the colors of the walls. They argued that early reorientation depends on a specialized geometric module "encapsulated" with respect to color, and that the eventual solution of the task depends on language (Hermer-Vazquez, Spelke, & Katsnelson, 1999).

Solution of the task by nonlinguistic animals (reviewed by Cheng & Newcombe, 2005), and children in larger enclosures (Learmonth, Nadel, & Newcombe, 2002), argues against this account. The ability of 18–24-month-olds to reorient using wall colors in small square enclosures (Nardini, Atkinson, & Burgess, 2008) also demonstrates that reorientation is not encapsulated with respect to color. Nevertheless, the early dominance of room geometry over color for spatial orientation, when both are available, remains an interesting phenomenon that has not been fully explained. Geometric judgments might be favored in small, but not large rooms, as relative wall lengths are easier to judge when standing at a corner (Sovrano & Vallortigara, 2006). In addition, children's poor use of color may not be specific to disorientation, but could represent a more general phenomenon. Oriented 18–24-month-olds searching in boxes on a table top were poor at using box color alone as a cue, and were especially likely to disregard colors when they had to be combined in memory with actions (Nardini et al., in press). At 30–36 months, children no longer showed this disregard for color, but did show it for monochromatic textures. "Disregard of color" may therefore be part of a more general developmental phenomenon linked to the uneven development of links between the dorsal and ventral visual streams and prefrontal mechanisms for working memory.

6.3. Impairments of spatial representation in memory in atypical development

Early focal cortical injury in the right hemisphere is associated with deficits in organizing spatial elements coherently, while left hemisphere injury is associated with poor encoding of detail in complex forms (Stiles, Stern, Trauner, & Nass, 1996; Stiles-Davis, Sugarman, & Nass, 1985). Although these patients often show remarkable recovery compared with those obtaining similar injuries in adulthood, fine-grained analysis indicates persistent deficits (Stiles, 2000).

Children born very premature, who show a range of cognitive deficits by school age (Bhutta, Cleves, Casey, Craddock, & Anand, 2002; Marlow, Wolke, Bracewell, Samara, & EpiCure Study Group, 2005), have especially marked deficits in the visuospatial and visuomotor domains (Atkinson, Braddick, Nardini, Anker, et al., 2006). On a spatial memory task assessing recall using different frames of reference, 6-year-olds born at 25–30 weeks' gestation had an average delay of more than one year across conditions (Nardini, Atkinson, et al., 2006). On average, this group's deficit was as large for external frames of reference (landmarks) as for egocentric recall. However, correlations with other cognitive and motor tests indicate subgroups with differential patterns of impairment. Impairments to spatial updating for changes of viewpoint produced by walking may be predicted by poor detection of coherent motion (related to visual processing of optic flow), while performance on the "perspective problem" (changes of viewpoint produced by movement of the array) is predicted by "frontal" tests of inhibition and response selection, suggesting that a "frontal" inhibition or selection process is involved in this task.

In addition to their visuomotor problems (Atkinson et al., 1997), children and adults with Williams syndrome (WS) show deficits on the purely perceptual task of egocentric localization for locations on a screen (Paul, Stiles, Passarotti, Bavar, & Bellugi, 2002; Vicari, Bellucci, & Carlesimo, 2006). Impairments to representations of location may therefore underlie their visuomotor and constructional difficulties. To compare the development of egocentric and landmark-based recall in Williams syndrome, we tested children and adults with WS on the "frames of reference" task. Overall, individuals with WS showed parallel, additive use of *body-* and *room-*based reference frames; however, these were combined anomalously in development, and performance in adulthood was not better than at 4 years in typical development (Nardini, Atkinson, Braddick, & Burgess, 2008). Crucially, adults with WS showed only marginal ability to use local landmarks to solve the "perspective problem," solved by typical children at 5 years. Visuomotor and constructional deficits in WS may thus be caused in part by the unusual integration of different frames of reference in development, and the poor ability to select local frames of reference even in adulthood.

7. Summary of Abnormal Spatial Development

Abnormalities of development have been seen in every aspect of spatial vision. Examples have already been given in each section of this chapter; these are summarized here together with a brief description of a number of relatively new tests for diagnosing spatial deficits in infants and very young children.

7.1. Deficits in the development of spatial attention linked to action

Earlier in the chapter, results from studies of infants who underwent hemispherectomy showed abnormal attentional control of actions, such as foveating or reaching for a target in peripheral vision on the side of space opposite the hemisphere lacking a normal cortex. This was only seen in conditions where two targets were competing for attention (Braddick et al., 1992). This failure to disengage and to make eye and head movements to a salient peripheral target when a central target is still visible is a common finding in many children with perinatal brain damage involving parietal and frontal areas. When damage extends to subcortical networks, then even without competition, shifts of gaze (and presumably attention) can be absent and/or slow.

7.2. Deficits in spatial attention in childhood

In school-aged children there are many studies of deficits related to attentional loss. In normally developing children there is considerable improvement in attentional capacities throughout childhood and adolescence. Three different components of attention have been identified from adult studies and patient populations, each with rather different neural underpinnings. The first component is linked to selective visual attention in visual search tasks. The second component is "sustained attention," which can be measured in vigilance tasks, and the third component involves inhibition of a prepotent response to switch and make a new association. Studies indicate that developmental trajectories differ for different attention components. Earlier maturity in selective attention (before 6–7 years), for example, contrasts with the continued development of sustained attention into adolescence, and rapid development of executive function between 7 and 11 years (Kelly, 2000; McKay, Halperin, Schwartz, & Sharma, 1994; Rueda et al., 2004). One test battery used to study attentional development is the Test of Everyday Attention for Children (TEACH; Manly et al., 2001), which examines components of attention between the ages of 6 and 16 years. Data from this battery support the notion that distinct components of this function exist in childhood, and suggest differential impairment of these components in clinical samples including ADHD (Heaton et al., 2001; Manly et al., 2001) and traumatic brain injury (Anderson, Fenwick, Manly, & Robertson, 1998).

A number of tasks have been developed to examine executive function in preschool children (e.g., Backen-Jones, Rothbart, & Posner, 2003; Gerstadt, Hong, & Diamond,

1994; Hood, 1995; Hughes & Russell, 1993; Kirkham, Cruess, & Diamond, 2003; Zelazo, Frye, & Rapus 1996); these show significant changes in the ability to inhibit prepotent responses and shift attention flexibly between the ages of 3 and 4 years. Many of these inhibitory tasks involving inhibition of a prepotent response are thought to have their underpinnings in frontal lobe circuitry. In one such test, "counterpointing," the child first points as rapidly as possible to a target which appears to either the left or right of a fixation spot. The rule is then changed and the child is asked to point as rapidly as possible to the opposite side to where the target appears. On this test, inhibitory control is achieved on average by 4 years of age in typically developing children, but can be considerably delayed in clinical populations (Atkinson et al., 2003). Measures have also emerged in recent years that allow for more formal assessment of selective and sustained attention in preschoolers, demonstrating improvement in these abilities between the ages of 3 and 6 years (Corkum, Byrne, & Ellsworth, 1995; Mahone, Pillion, Hoffman, Hiemenz, & Denckla, 2005; Prather, Sarmento, & Alexander, 1995).

Despite the clear changes in attention through the preschool age range, however, comprehensive batteries of attention measures are not generally available for children between 2 and 6 years. A new battery of attention measures is being developed for typically developing 3–6-year-olds and children in this mental age range, such as chronologically older children with Down syndrome or Williams syndrome (Breckenridge, 2007).

7.3. Deficits in development of the dorsal stream relative to ventral stream

The general hypothesis of "dorsal stream vulnerability" (Atkinson et al., 1999; Braddick, Atkinson, & Wattam-Bell, 2003; Spencer et al., 2000) was discussed in section 3.3. This refers to the general finding that across a number of clinical populations with very diverse etiologies (e.g., Williams syndrome, fragile-X syndrome, congenital cataract patients, autism, children with hemiplegia), when tasks are carefully designed to compare and isolate responses related to the dorsal and ventral streams, the development of the dorsal stream is more likely to be affected than the ventral (for a review, see Braddick et al., 2003).

7.4. Planning and execution of actions in spatial tasks

Taken together with a comparison of dorsal- and ventral-stream function in the post-box task (see section 4.4) and in other motor-planning tasks, Atkinson and Braddick have proposed that Williams syndrome is an example of broader dorsal stream vulnerability. Support for this relative deficit in dorsal-stream networks in WS comes from a structural MRI study with 2-year-olds (Mercuri, Atkinson, Braddick, Rutherford, et al., 1997) and from structural and functional MRI studies with WS adults (Meyer-Lindenberg et al., 2004; Reiss et al., 2004). Frontal executive functions have been found to be an additional area of deficit for WS, even relative to verbal IQ. The extent of this deficit depends on the nature of the task and is much greater when it requires inhibition of a prepotent spatially directed response, notably in counterpointing (see above) and also in a spatial detour task (Biro & Russell, 2001). Inhibition of a verbal response is considerably less affected. Thus the transmission of spatial information to frontal systems within the dorsal stream seems to be specifically disrupted in WS.

7.5.   New tests of spatial development

Shape-matching and block-construction copying tasks have been normalized and standardized as part of a battery (Atkinson Battery of Child Development for Examining Functional Vision [ABCDEFV]) to measure functional vision in children of mental ages between birth and 5 years (Atkinson, Anker, Rae, Hughes, & Braddick, 2002). All tests have been standardized with typically developing children, failure on a particular subtest usually corresponding to a score below the 15th percentile for the appropriate age. The battery is divided into tests of "core vision," requiring minimal saccadic tracking eye movement, including measures of acuity, refraction and field perimetry, and additional visuomotor, visuocognitive, and spatial tests (requiring minimum motoric skills of reaching and pointing or grasping with one hand). Some subtests measure spatial vision related to more ventral or more dorsal stream processing, whereas some involve integration across both processing streams.

The ABCDEFV has been used to test spatial development in a number of clinical populations. In a large-scale population infant vision screening program ($n = 5,000$) for detection of strabismus and refractive errors in 9-month-old infants and prevention of later onset strabismus and amblyopia through spectacle correction in infancy (Atkinson, Braddick, Bobier, et al., 1996), children who had significant hyperopia in the first year of life were significantly worse on many of the visuospatial ABCDEFV tests throughout the preschool years. However, none of the items on the Griffiths scales of pediatric development showed a difference, arguing against a general developmental delay in this clinical group. Overall, these results indicate mild deficits in the hyperopic group, concentrated in areas of visual perception and visuomotor control related to both dorsal and ventral stream development (Atkinson, Anker, Nardini, et al., 2002).

A second battery that has been developed is the Movement ABC (Henderson and Sugden, 1992), a standardized assessment of everyday visuomotor and spatial competence for 4–16-year-olds. The Movement ABC includes tasks to assess visuomotor development within three categories: manual dexterity, balance, and ball skills. At 3 and 5 years, children who had been significantly hyperopic as infants scored lower on these tests (Atkinson et al., 2005). The pattern did not show a subgroup of poorly performing children, but suggested a mild but widespread deficit in the formerly hyperopic group. There was no significant difference between children who had worn spectacles to correct refractive errors in infancy and those who had not, which suggests that there may not be a direct causal connection between poorer sensory vision in infancy and poorer preschool visuomotor and visuocognitive abilities, but rather that abnormal refraction and strabismus in infancy is a soft sign of poorer brain development, affecting not only specific eye–brain networks for sensory vision, but those of selective attention and spatial cognition involving temporal, parietal, and frontal lobe areas with links to subcortical networks.

In longitudinal studies of very premature infants (under 32 weeks' gestation), a comparison has been made between their visual spatial development, brain imaging at birth and term, and their general neurological and cognitive development over a period from birth to 5 years of age. Diffuse excessive high signal intensity (DEHSI) is a common feature of white matter abnormality in very premature infants when scanned around term. The presence and degree of white matter damage (DEHSI or periventricular leukomalacia) correlated with the measures of early attention on the fixation shift test, deficits in onset of cortical functioning measured with orientation-reversal VEPs, and deficits on spatial tasks in the ABCDEFV and preschool attentional tests of frontal lobe function (Atkinson & Braddick, 2007).

In a second cohort, children who were born very prematurely were intensively studied between 6 and 7 years of age. Across the group, deficits in visuomotor, visuospatial, and attention tasks are found, with relative sparing of verbal performance and language. From this analysis, an overall model of brain development for premature infants is that, as in other developmental disorders, there is vulnerability in the more dorsally controlled areas with attentional deficits arising from poor frontal lobe connections, whereas development of language and communication and ventral-stream function is relatively good (Atkinson & Braddick, 2007). For some children in the premature group these deficits are relatively mild, but many are likely to have subtle learning difficulties (e.g., mild ADHD) which persist and have cascading effects on later academic abilities.

8.   Summary of the Developmental Model of Visual Spatial Development

Figure 9.1 illustrates Atkinson and Braddick's (2003) account of the developmental sequence and the broad neural processes corresponding to it. From an initial subcortical stage, there is development of functioning in specific cortical channels, followed by development of integrative processes across channels within a single stream so that the infant can build up internal representations of objects and individuals. This aspect of the developing processes takes place largely in the ventral stream, with dynamic online information contributed from the dorsal stream to control orienting by eye and head movements. Of course, for objects to be represented, information about color, shape, and texture must be integrated with motion information at a relatively early stage so that objects can be segregated from each other and from their background. These processes provide object representations which must be integrated with dorsal-stream spatial information to allow, later, emergence of the visual action systems associated with reaching/grasping and with locomotion. These action systems are a combination of visual, attentional, and motor systems. It is over-simple, however, to show this as a linear sequence; there are likely to be important feedback loops, by which the consequences of a new development can affect the way in which earlier established processes work. Furthermore, a description of the sequence is only the start. We still cannot explain timing differences in functional onset and plasticity in one system as opposed to another: Why do some processes in certain networks start to function earlier than others? How far are we seeing the unfolding of a maturational sequence, and how far does the developmental trajectory depend on exposure to the environment, including the kinds of exposure made possible by earlier networks becoming functional? There are still many unanswered questions.

A model of deficits in spatial development has been suggested: "dorsal stream vulnerability." This is based on the general finding that tasks related to more dorsal stream areas show higher levels of deficit that those related to ventral across many different clinical conditions including children with developmental disorders related to genetic abnormalities such as Williams syndrome and fragile-X. We still need to find the basic cause of this difference in plasticity between dorsal stream and ventral stream modules. It may have its origin in very low-level timing mechanisms in subcortical or early cortical areas; it may depend on a misbalance between the number of functional magnocellular and parvocellular cells and their integration; or it may depend on integration of information from processing in many different occipital, parietal, and frontal areas before the planning and decision for action is taken. Of course, we do not know whether a deficit which seems similar behaviorally arises because of identical faults in its neural processing. It is to be hoped, with improved imaging methods and specific behavioral measures, that we may be able to answer these questions in the future and provide appropriate interventions, tuned to the individual, to alleviate spatial difficulties in children.

Acknowledgments

We would like to acknowledge the help and support of present and past members of the Visual Development Unit, in particular Oliver Braddick, Shirley Anker, Dee Birtles, Dorothy Cowie, and Kate Breckenridge. We also thank our collaborators for a number of studies cited in this chapter, in particular Eugenio Mercuri, Giovanni Cionni, Andrea Guzzetta, Ursula Bellugi, Joan Stiles, and the members of the Departments of Paediatrics and Neonatology and Brain Imaging, Hammersmith Hospital, namely Lily Dubowitz, David Edwards, Francis Cowan, Mary Rutherford, and Leigh Dyett. This work has been supported by grant G7908507 and previous program grants from the Medical Research Council, UK and the Williams Syndrome Foundation, UK.

References

Acredolo, L. P. (1978). Development of spatial orientation in infancy. *Developmental Psychology, 14*, 224–234.
Adolph, K. E., & Avolio, A. M. (2000). Walking infants adapt locomotion to changing body dimensions. *Journal of Experimental Psychology: Human Perception and Performance, 26*, 1148–1166.

Allport, A. (1989). Visual attention. In M. I. Posner (Ed.), *Foundations of cognitive science* (pp. 631–682). Cambridge, MA: MIT Press.

Anderson, V., Fenwick, T., Manly, T., & Robertson, I. (1998). Attentional skills following traumatic brain injury in childhood: A componential analysis. *Brain Injury, 12*, 937–949.

Arterberry, M. E., & Yonas, A. (1988). Infant's sensitivity to kinetic information for 3-dimensional object shape. *Perception and Psychophysics, 44*, 1–6.

Arterberry, M. E., & Yonas, A. (2000). Perception of three-dimensional shape specified by optic flow by 8-week-old infants. *Perception and Psychophysics, 62*, 550–556.

Atkinson, J. (1984). Human visual development over the first six months of life: A review and a hypothesis. *Human Neurobiology, 3*, 61–74.

Atkinson, J. (1992). Early visual development: Differential functioning of parvocellular and magnocellular pathways. *Eye, 6*, 129–135.

Atkinson, J. (2000). *The developing visual brain* (Oxford Psychology Series 32). Oxford University Press.

Atkinson, J., Anker, S., Braddick, O., Nokes, L., Mason, A., & Braddick, F. (2001). Visual and visuospatial development in young Williams syndrome children. *Developmental Medicine and Child Neurology, 43*, 330–337.

Atkinson, J., Anker, S., Nardini, M., Braddick, O., Hughes, C., Rae, S., et al. (2002). Infant vision screening predicts failures on motor and cognitive tests up to school age. *Strabismus, 10*, 187–198.

Atkinson, J., Anker, S., Rae, S., Hughes, C., & Braddick, O. (2002). A test battery of child development for examining functional vision (ABCDEFV). *Strabismus, 10*(4), 245–269.

Atkinson, J., & Braddick, O. J. (1985). Early development of the control of visual attention. *Perception, 14*, A25.

Atkinson, J., & Braddick, O. (2003). Neurobiological models of normal and abnormal visual development. In M. De Haan & M. Johnson (Eds.), *The cognitive neuroscience of development* (pp. 43–71). Hove, East Sussex: Psychology Press.

Atkinson, J., & Braddick, O. (2005). Dorsal stream vulnerability and autistic disorders: The importance of comparative studies of form and motion coherence in typically developing children and children with developmental disorders. *Cahiers de Psychologie Cognitive/Current Psychology of Cognition, 23*(1–2), 49–58.

Atkinson, J., & Braddick, O. (2007). Visual and visuocognitive development in children born very prematurely. In C. von Hofsten & K. Rosander (Eds.), *From action to cognition* (Progress in Brain Research, Vol. 164, pp. 123–149). Amsterdam: Elsevier.

Atkinson, J., Braddick, O., Anker, S., Curran, W., & Andrew, R. (2003). Neurobiological models of visuospatial cognition in children with Williams syndrome: Measures of dorsal-stream and frontal function. *Developmental Neuropsychology, 23*(1–2), 141–174.

Atkinson, J., Braddick, O., Anker, S., Ehrlich, D., Macpherson, F., Rae, S., et al. (1996). *Development of sensory, perceptual, and cognitive vision and visual attention in young Williams syndrome children.* Presentation and poster at the Seventh International Professional Conference on Williams Syndrome, King of Prussia, PA.

Atkinson, J., Braddick, O., Bobier, B., Anker, S., Ehrlich, D., King, J., et al. (1996). Two infant vision screening programmes: Prediction and prevention of strabismus and amblyopia from photo- and videorefractive screening. *Eye 10*(2), 189–198.

Atkinson, J., Braddick, O. J., Lin, M. H., Curran, W., Guzzetta, A., & Cioni, G. (1999). Form and motion coherence: Is there dorsal stream vulnerability in development? *Investigative Ophthalmology and Visual Science, 40*(4), S395.

Atkinson, J., Braddick, O. J., Nardini, M., Anker, S. E., Cowan, F. M., & Edwards, A. D. (2006). "Dorsal vulnerability" and patterns of visuo-cognitive deficit following very premature birth. *Perception*, 35(Suppl.), 3–4.

Atkinson, J., Braddick, O., Nardini, M., Cowie, D., Breckenridge, K., Anker, S., et al. (2006). *Spatial cognition, locomotion planning and problems of attention in Williams syndrome (WS): New tests developing the model of "dorsal stream vulnerability" in WS*. Presentation at Williams Syndrome Foundation Professional Meeting, Richmond VA, August.

Atkinson, J., Braddick, O., Rose, F. E., Searcy, Y. M., Wattam-Bell, J., & Bellugi, U. (2006). Dorsal-stream motion processing deficits persist into adulthood in Williams syndrome (Short Communication). *Neuropsychologia*, 44(5), 828–833.

Atkinson, J., & Hood, B. (1994). Deficits of selective visual attention in children with focal lesions. *Infant Behaviour and Development*, 17, 423.

Atkinson, J., Hood, B., Wattam-Bell, J., & Braddick, O. J. (1992). Changes in infants' ability to switch visual attention in the first three months of life. *Perception*, 21, 643–653.

Atkinson, J., King, J., Braddick, O. J., Nokes, L., Anker, S., & Braddick, F. (1997). A specific deficit of dorsal stream function in Williams syndrome. *NeuroReport*, 8, 1919–1922.

Atkinson, J., Nardini, M., Anker, S., Braddick, O., Hughes, C., & Rae, S. (2005). Refractive errors in infancy predict reduced performance on the Henderson Movement Assessment Battery for Children at 3.5 and 5.5 years. *Developmental Medicine and Child Neurology*, 47, 243–251.

Backen-Jones, L., Rothbart, M. K., & Posner, M. I. (2003). Development of executive attention in preschool children. *Developmental Science*, 6, 498–504.

Baillargeon, R., & DeVos, J. (1991). Object permanence in young infants: Further evidence. *Child Development*, 62, 1227–1246.

Baird, A. A., Kagan, J., Gaudette, T., Walz, K. A., Hershlag, N., & Boas, D. A. (2002). Frontal lobe activation during object permanence: Data from near-infrared spectroscopy. *NeuroImage*, 16, 1120–1125.

Bell, M. A., & Fox, N. A. (1992). The relations between frontal brain electrical activity and cognitive development during infancy. *Child Development*, 63, 1142–1163.

Bellugi, U., Bihrle, A., Trauner, D., Jernigan, T., & Doherty, S. (1990). Neuropsychological, neurological, and neuroanatomical profile of Williams syndrome children. *American Journal of Medical Genetics* (Suppl.), 6, 115–125.

Bellugi, U., Lichtenberger, L., Mills, D., Galaburda, A., & Korenberg, J. R. (1999). Bridging cognition, the brain, and molecular genetics: Evidence from Williams syndrome. *Trends in Neurosciences*, 22, 197–207.

Bellugi, U., Sabo, H., & Vaid, J. (1988). Spatial deficits in children with Williams syndrome. In J. Stiles-Davis, M. Kritchevsky, & U. Bellugi (Eds.), *Spatial cognition: Brain bases and development* (pp. 273–298). Hillsdale, NJ: Lawrence Erlbaum.

Bellugi, U., Wang, P. P., & Jernigan, T. L. (1994). Williams syndrome: An unusual neuropsychological profile. In S. H. Broman & J. Grafman (Eds.), *Atypical cognitive deficits in developmental disorders: Implications for brain function* (pp. 23–56). Hillsdale, NJ: Lawrence Erlbaum.

Bertenthal, B. I., & Campos, J. J. (1990). A systems approach to the organizing effects of self-produced locomotion during infancy. *Advances in Infancy Research*, 6, 1–60.

Bertenthal, B. I., Proffitt, D. R., Spetner, N. B., & Thomas, M. A. (1985). The development of infant sensitivity to biomechanical motions. *Child Development*, 56, 531–543.

Berthier, N., & Keen, R. (2006). Development of reaching in infancy. *Experimental Brain Research*, 169, 507–518.

Berthoz, A. (1996). Neural basis of decision in perception and the control of movement. In A. R. Damasio, H. Damasio, & Y. Christen (Eds.), *Neurobiology of decision making* (pp. 83–100). Berlin: Springer.

Bertrand, J., Mervis, C. B., & Eisenberg, J. D. (1997). Drawing by children with Williams syndrome: A developmental perspective. *Developmental Neuropsychology, 13*, 41–67.

Bhutta, A. T., Cleves, M. A., Casey, P. H., Craddock, M. M., & Anand, K. J. (2002). Cognitive and behavioral outcomes of school-aged children who were born preterm: A meta-analysis. *Journal of the American Medical Association, 288*, 728–737.

Biro, S., & Russell, J. (2001). The execution of arbitrary procedures by children with autism. *Development and Psychopathology, 13*, 97–110.

Bojczyk, K. E., & Corbetta, D. (2004). Object retrieval in the first year of life: Learning effects of task exposure and box transparency. *Developmental Psychology, 40*, 54–66.

Booth, A. E., Pinto, J., & Bertenthal, B. I. (2002). Perception of the symmetrical patterning of human gait by infants. *Developmental Psychology, 38*, 554–563.

Booth, J. R., MacWhinney, B., Thulborn, K. R., Sacco, K., Voyvodic, J. T., & Feldman, H. M. (2000). Developmental and lesion effects in brain activation during sentence comprehension and mental rotation. *Developmental Neuropsychology, 18*, 139–169.

Boussaoud, D., Ungerleider, L. G., & Desimone, R. (1990). Pathways for motion analysis: Cortical connections of the medial superior temporal and fundus of the superior temporal visual areas in the macaque. *Journal of Comparative Neurology, 296*, 462–495.

Braddick, O. (1996). Binocularity in infancy. *Eye, 10*, 182–188.

Braddick, O. J., & Atkinson, J. (2003). Top-down, bottom-up, and sideways in infants' development of visual object organisation. *Perception, 32*(Suppl.), 49–50.

Braddick, O., Atkinson, J., & Hood, B. (1996). Monocular vs binocular control of infants' reaching. *Investigative Ophthalmology and Visual Science, 37*, S290.

Braddick, O., Atkinson, J., Hood, B., Harkness, W., Jackson, G., & Vargha-Khadem, F. (1992). Possible blindsight in infants lacking one cerebral hemisphere. *Nature, 360*, 461–463.

Braddick, O. J., Atkinson, J., & Wattam-Bell, J. (1989). Development of visual cortical selectivity: Binocularity, orientation, and direction of motion. In C. von Euler (Ed.), *Neurobiology of early infant behaviour* (pp. 165–172). London: Macmillan.

Braddick, O., Atkinson, J., & Wattam-Bell, J. (2003). Normal and anomalous development of visual motion processing: Motion coherence and "dorsal stream vulnerability." *Neuropsychologia, 41*(13), 1769–1784.

Braddick, O., Curran, W., Atkinson, J., Wattam-Bell, J., & Gunn, A. (2002). Infants' sensitivity to global form coherence. *Investigative Ophthalmology and Visual Science 43*, E-Abstract 3995.

Braddick, O. J., O'Brien, J., Rees, G., Wattam-Bell, J., Atkinson, J., & Turner, R. (2002). *Quantitative neural responses to form coherence in human extrastriate cortex.* Presentation at the Society for Neuroscience, Program No. 721.9 (available online).

Braddick, O. J., O'Brien, J. M. D., Wattam-Bell, J., Atkinson, J., Hartley, T., & Turner, R. (2001). Brain areas sensitive to coherent visual motion. *Perception, 30*, 61–72.

Braddick, O. J., O'Brien, J. M. D., Wattam-Bell, J., Atkinson, J., & Turner, R. (2000). Form and motion coherence activate independent, but not dorsal/ventral segregated, networks in the human brain. *Current Biology, 10*, 731–734.

Braddick, O., & Qian, N. (2000). The organisation of global motion and transparency. In J. M. Zanker & J. Zeil (Eds.), *Motion vision* (pp. 86–112). Berlin: Springer Verlag.

Breckenridge, K. (2007). *The structure and function of attention in typical and atypical development.* Unpublished PhD thesis, University of London.

Bronson, G. W. (1974). The postnatal growth of visual capacity. *Child Development, 45,* 873–890.

Bruner, J. S. (1970). The growth and structure of skill. In K. Connolly (Ed.), *Mechanisms of motor skill development* (pp. 62–94). New York: Academic Press.

Butterworth, G., & Grover, L. (1990). Joint visual-attention, manual pointing, and preverbal communication in human infancy. In M. Jeannerod (Ed.), *Attention and performance XIII* (pp. 605–624). Cambridge, MA: MIT Press.

Cheng, K., & Newcombe, N. S. (2005). Is there a geometric module for spatial orientation? Squaring theory and evidence. *Psychonomic Bulletin and Review, 12,* 1–23.

Chugani, H. T., Phelps, M. E., & Mazziotta, J. C. (1987). Positron emission tomography study of human brain functional development. *Annals of Neurology, 22,* 487–497.

Corkum, P. V., Byrne, J. M., & Ellsworth, C. (1995). Clinical assessment of sustained attention in preschoolers. *Child Neuropsychology, 1,* 3–18.

Cowie, D. (2007). *The development of visually guided locomotion.* PhD thesis submitted to the University of Oxford.

Cowie, D., Smith, L., Braddick, O., & Atkinson, J. (2006a). Stepping stones across the river: Visually guided planning of locomotion in children and adults. *Perception, S35,* 95.

Cowie, D., Smith, L., Braddick, O., & Atkinson, J. (2006b). *Locomotor planning in Williams syndrome.* Paper presented to the Third Williams Syndrome Workshop, Reading.

Cowie, D., Smith, L., Braddick, O., Atkinson, J., & Nardini, M. (2006). The development of visually guided locomotor planning. *Cognitive Processing, 7*(S5), 123.

Damasio, A. R., & Benton, A. L. (1979). Impairment of hand movements under visual guidance. *Neurology, 29,* 170–178.

Diamond, A. (1991). Neuropsychological insights into the meaning of object concept development. In S. Carey & R. Gelman (Eds.), *Biology and knowledge: Structural constraints on development* (pp. 37–80). Hillsdale, NJ: Erlbaum.

Diamond, A., Werker, J. F., & Lalonde, C. (1994). Toward understanding commonalities in the development of object search, detour navigation, categorization, and speech perception. In K. W. Fischer & G. Dawson (Eds.), *Human behavior and the developing brain* (pp. 380–426). New York: Guilford.

Diamond, A., Zola-Morgan, S., & Squire, L. R. (1989). Successful performance by monkeys with lesions of the hippocampal formation on AB and object retrieval, two tasks that mark developmental changes in human infants. *Behavioral Neuroscience, 103,* 526–537.

Fagard, J. (1994). Manual strategies and interlimb coordination during reaching, grasping, and manipulating throughout the first year of life. In S. Swinnen, H. Heuer, J. Massion, & P. Casaer (Eds.), *Interlimb coordination: Neural, dynamical and cognitive constraints* (pp. 439–460). San Diego, CA: Academic Press.

Fagard, J. (2000). Linked proximal and distal changes in the reaching behaviour of 5- to 12-month-old human infants grasping objects of different sizes. *Infant Behaviour and Development, 23,* 317–329.

Fagard, J., & Jacquet, A. Y. (1996). Changes in reaching and grasping objects of different sizes between 7 and 13 months of age. *British Journal of Developmental Psychology, 14,* 65–78.

Felleman, D. J., & Van Essen, D. C. (1991). Distributed hierarchical processing in primate cerebral cortex. *Cerebral Cortex, 1,* 1–47.

Fox, N. A., & Bell, M. A. (1990). Electrophysiological indices of frontal lobe development: Relations to cognitive and affective behavior in human infants over the first year of life. *Annals of the New York Academy of Sciences, 608,* 677–704.

Gallant, J. L., Braun, J., & Van Essen, D. C. (1993). Selectivity for polar, hyperbolic, and Cartesian gratings in macaque visual cortex. *Science, 259*, 100–103.

Gerstadt, C. L., Hong, Y. J., & Diamond, A. (1994). The relationship between cognition and action: Performance of children 3½–7 years old on a Stroop-like day–night test. *Cognition, 53*, 129–153.

Gibson, E. J., & Walk, R. D. (1960). The "visual cliff." *Scientific American, 202*(April), 64–71.

Goodale, M. A., & Milner, A. D. (2003). *Sight unseen: An exploration of conscious and unconscious vision*. Oxford University Press.

Goodale, M. A., Milner, A. D., Jakobsen, L. S., & Carey, D. P. (1991). A neurological dissociation between perceiving objects and grasping them. *Nature, 349*, 154–156.

Gunn, A., Cory, E., Atkinson, J., Braddick, O., Wattam-Bell, J., Guzzetta, A., et al. (2002). Dorsal and ventral stream sensitivity in normal development and hemiplegia. *Neuroreport, 13*(6), 843–847.

Heaton, S. C., Reader, S. K., Preston, A. S., Fennell, E. B., Puyana, O. E., Gill, N., et al. (2001). The Test of Everyday Attention for Children (TEA-Ch): Patterns of performance in children with ADHD and clinical controls. *Child Neuropsychology, 7*, 251–264.

Henderson, S. E., & Sugden, D. A. (1992). *The movement ABC manual*. London: Psychological Corporation.

Hermer, L., & Spelke, E. (1994). A geometric process for spatial reorientation in young children. *Nature, 370*, 57–59.

Hermer, L. & Spelke, E. (1996). Modularity and development: The case of spatial reorientation. *Cognition, 61*, 195–232.

Hermer-Vazquez, L., Spelke, E. S., & Katsnelson, A. S. (1999). Sources of flexibility in human cognition: Dual task studies of space and language. *Cognitive Psychology, 39*, 3–36.

Hofstadter, M., & Reznick, J. S. (1996). Response modality affects human infant delayed-response performance. *Child Development, 67*, 646–658.

Hood, B. (1995). Gravity rules for 2–4 year olds. *Cognitive Development, 10*, 577–598.

Hood, B., & Atkinson, J. (1990). Sensory visual loss and cognitive deficits in the selective attentional system of normal infants and neurologically impaired children. *Developmental Medicine and Child Neurology, 32*, 1067–1077.

Hood, B., & Atkinson, J. (1993). Disengaging visual attention in the infant and adult. *Infant Behaviour and Development, 16*, 405–422.

Horobin, K., & Acredolo, L. (1986). The role of attentiveness, mobility history, and separation of hiding sites on Stage IV search behavior. *Journal of Experimental Child Psychology, 41*, 114–127.

Hughes, C., & Russell, J. (1993). Autistic children's difficulty with mental disengagement from an object: Its implications for theories of autism. *Developmental Psychology, 29*, 498–510.

Huttenlocher, J., Newcombe, N., & Sandberg, E. (1994). The coding of spatial location in young children. *Cognitive Psychology, 27*, 115–147.

Huttenlocher, J., & Presson, C. C. (1973). Mental rotation and the perspective problem. *Cognitive Psychology, 4*, 277–299.

Huttenlocher, P. R., de Courten, C., Garey, L. G., & van der Loos, H. (1982). Synaptogenesis in human visual cortex: Evidence for synapse elimination during normal development. *Neuroscience Letters, 33*, 247–252.

Jacobs, B., Chugani, H. T., Allada, V., Chen, S., Phelps, M. E., Pollack, D. B., et al. (1995). Developmental changes in brain metabolism in sedated rhesus macaques and vervet monkeys revealed by positron emission tomography. *Cerebral Cortex, 5*, 222–233.

Jeannerod, M. (1997). *The cognitive neuroscience of action*. Oxford: Blackwell.

Kaplan, P., Kirsschner, M., Watters, G., & Costa, M. T. (1989). Contractures in children with Williams syndrome. *Pediatrics, 84*(5), 895–899.

Karmiloff-Smith, A. (1998). Development itself is the key to understanding developmental disorders. *Trends in Cognitive Sciences, 2*, 389–398.

Kellman, P. J., & Spelke, E. S. (1983). Perception of partly occluded objects in infancy. *Cognitive Psychology, 15*, 483–524.

Kelly, T. P. (2000). The clinical neuropsychology of attention in school-aged children. *Child Neuropsychology, 6*, 24–36.

Kermoian, R., & Campos, J. J. (1988). Locomotor experience: A facilitator of spatial cognitive development. *Child Development, 59*, 908–917.

King, J. A., Atkinson, J., Braddick, O. J., Nokes, L., & Braddick, F. (1996). Target preference and movement kinematics reflect development of visuomotor modules in the reaching of human infants. *Investigative Ophthalmology and Visual Science, 37*, S526.

Kingsnorth, S., & Schmuckler, M. A. (2000). Walking skill versus walking experience as a predictor of barrier crossing in toddlers. *Infant Behaviour and Development, 23*, 331–350.

Kirkham, N. Z., Cruess, L., & Diamond, A. (2003). Helping children apply their knowledge to their behavior on a dimension-switching task. *Developmental Science, 6*, 449–476.

Klein, B. P., & Mervis, C. B. (1999). Contrasting patterns of cognitive abilities of 9 and 10-year-olds with Williams syndrome or Down syndrome. *Developmental Neuropsychology, 16*, 177–196.

Kosslyn, S. M., Margolis, J. A., Barrett, A. M., Goldknopf, E. J., & Daly, P. F. (1990). Age differences in imagery abilities. *Child Development, 61*, 995–1010.

LaBerge, D., & Brown, V. (1989). Theory of attentional operations in shape identification. *Psychological Review, 96*, 101–124.

Learmonth, A. E., Nadel, L., & Newcombe, N. S. (2002). Childrens' use of landmarks: Implications for modularity theory. *Psychological Science, 13*, 337–341.

Lee, D. N., & Aronson, E. (1974). Visual proprioceptive control of standing in human infants. *Perception and Psychophysics, 15*, 529–532.

Leslie, A. M. (1984). Spatiotemporal continuity and the perception of causality in infants. *Perception, 13*, 287–305.

Livingstone, M., & Hubel, D. H. (1988). Segregation of form, color, movement and depth: Anatomy, physiology and perception. *Science, 240*, 740–749.

Mahone, E. M., Pillion, J. P., Hoffman, J., Hiemenz, J. R., & Denckla, M. B. (2005). Construct validity of the auditory continuous performance test for preschoolers. *Developmental Neuropsychology, 27*, 11–33.

Manly, T., Nimmo-Smith, I., Watson, P., Anderson, V., Turner, A., & Robertson, I. H. (2001). The differential assessment of children's attention: The Test of Everyday Attention for Children (TEA-Ch), normative sample and ADHD performance. *Journal of Child Psychology and Psychiatry, 42*, 1065–1081.

Marlow, N., Wolke, D., Bracewell, M. A., Samara, M., & EpiCure Study Group (2005). Neurologic and developmental disability at six years of age after extremely preterm birth. *New England Journal of Medicine, 352*, 71–72.

Marmor, G. S. (1975). Development of kinetic images: When does the child first represent movement in mental images? *Cognitive Psychology, 7*, 548–559.

McKay, K. E., Halperin, J. M., Schwartz, S. T., & Sharma, V. (1994). Developmental analysis of three aspects of information processing: Sustained attention, selective attention, and response organization. *Developmental Neuropsychology, 10*, 121–132.

Mercuri, E., Atkinson, J., Braddick, O., Anker, S., Cowan, F., Rutherford, M., et al. (1997). Visual function in full term infants with hypoxic-ischaemic encephalopathy. *Neuropediatrics, 28*, 155–161.

Mercuri, E., Atkinson, J., Braddick, O., Anker, S., Nokes, L., Cowan, F., et al. (1996). Visual function and perinatal focal cerebral infarction. *Archives of Disease in Childhood, 75*, F76–F81.

Mercuri, E., Atkinson, J., Braddick, O., Anker, S., Nokes, L., Cowan, F., et al. (1997). Basal ganglia damage in the newborn infant as a predictor of impaired visual function. *Archives of Disease in Childhood, 77*, F111–F114.

Mercuri, E., Atkinson, J., Braddick, O., Rutherford, M., Cowan, F., Counsell, S., et al. (1997). Chiari I malformation and white matter changes in asymptomatic young children with Williams syndrome: Clinical and MRI study. *European Journal of Paediatric Neurology, 5*(6), 177–181.

Merigan, W. H., & Maunsell, J. H. R. (1993). How parallel are the primate visual pathways? *Annual Review of Neuroscience, 16*, 369–402.

Meyer-Lindenberg, A., Kohn, P., Mervis, C. B., Kippenhan, J. S., Olsen, R. K., Morris, C. A., et al. (2004). Neural basis of genetically determined visuospatial construction deficit in Williams syndrome. *Neuron, 43*, 623–631.

Milner, A. D., & Goodale, M. A. (1995). *The visual brain in action.* Oxford University Press.

Nardini, M., Atkinson, J., Braddick, O., & Burgess, N. (2006). The development of body, environment, and object-based frames of reference in spatial memory in normal and atypical populations. *Cognitive Processing, 7*, 68–69.

Nardini, M., Atkinson, J., Braddick, O., & Burgess, N. (2008). Developmental trajectories for spatial frames of reference in Williams syndrome. *Developmental Science* (published online January 10, 2008, doi: 10.1111/j.1467-7687.2007.00662.x).

Nardini, M., Atkinson, J., & Burgess, N. (2008). Children reorient using the left/right sense of coloured landmarks at 18–24 months. *Cognition, 106*, 519–527.

Nardini, M., Braddick, O., Atkinson, J., Cowie, D., Ahmed, T., & Reidy, H. (in press). Uneven integration for perception and action cues in children's working memory. *Cognitive Neuropsychology.*

Nardini, M., Burgess, N., Breckenridge, K., & Atkinson, J. (2006). Differential developmental trajectories for egocentric, environmental and intrinsic frames of reference in spatial memory. *Cognition, 101*, 153–172.

Newcombe, N., & Huttenlocher, J. (1992). Children's early ability to solve perspective-taking problems. *Developmental Psychology, 28*, 635–643.

Newcombe, N., Huttenlocher, J., Bullock Drummey, A., & Wiley, J. G. (1998). The development of spatial location coding: Place learning and dead reckoning in the second and third years. *Cognitive Development, 13*, 185–200.

Newman, C. (2001). *The planning and control of action in normal infants and children with Williams syndrome.* Unpublished PhD thesis, University of London.

Newman, C., Atkinson, J., & Braddick, O. (2001). The development of reaching and looking preferences in infants to objects of different sizes. *Developmental Psychology, 37*, 561–572.

O'Keefe, J., & Burgess, N. (1996). Geometric determinants of the place fields of hippocampal neurones. *Nature, 381*, 425–428.

Patla, A. E. (1991). Visual control of human locomotion. In A. E. Patla (Ed.), *Adaptability of human gait* (pp. 55–97). Amsterdam: Elsevier Science.

Patla, A. E., & Goodale, M. A. (1996). Obstacle avoidance during locomotion is unaffected in a patient with visual form agnosia. *NeuroReport, 8*(1), 165–168.

Paul, B. M., Stiles, J., Passarotti, A. M., Bavar, N., & Bellugi, U. (2002). Face and place processing in Williams syndrome: Evidence for a dorsal-ventral dissociation. *Neuroreport, 13*, 1115–1119.

Pezzini, G., Vicari, S., Volterra, V., Milani, L., & Ossella, M. T. (1999). Children with Williams syndrome: Is there a single neuropsychological profile? *Developmental Neuropsychology, 15,* 141–155.

Posner, M. I. (1980). Orienting of attention. *Quarterly Journal of Experimental Psychology, 32,* 3–25.

Posner, M. I., & Cohen, Y. (1980). Attention and the control of movements. In G. E. Stelmach & J. Requin (Eds.), *Tutorials in motor behavior* (pp. 243–258). Amsterdam: North Holland.

Posner, M. I., & Dehaene, S. (1994). Attentional networks. *Trends in Neurosciences, 17,* 75–79.

Posner, M. I., & Petersen, S. E. (1990). The attention system of the human brain. *Annual Review of Neuroscience, 13,* 25–42.

Prather, P. A., Sarmento, N., & Alexander, A. (1995). Development of vigilance in preschoolers. *Journal of the International Neuropsychological Society, 1,* 153.

Rees, G., Friston, K., & Koch, C. (2000). A direct quantitative relationship between the functional properties of human and macaque V5. *Natural Neuroscience, 3,* 716–723.

Reiss, A. L., Eckert, M. A., Rose, F. E., Karchemskiy, A., Kesler, S., Chang, M., et al. (2004). An experiment of nature: Brain anatomy parallels cognition and behavior in Williams syndrome. *Journal of Neuroscience, 24,* 5009–5015.

Rieser, J. J. (1979). Spatial orientation of six-month-old infants. *Child Development, 50,* 1078–1087.

Rizzolatti, G. (1983). Mechanisms of selective attention in mammals. In J. P. Ewwert, R. R. Capranica, & D. J. Ingle (Eds.), *Advances in vertebrate neuroethology* (pp. 261–297). Amsterdam: Elsevier.

Rizzolatti, G., & Camarda, R. (1987). Neural circuits for spatial attention and unilateral neglect. In M. Jeannerod (Ed.), *Neurophysiological and neuropsychological aspects of spatial neglect* (pp. 289–213). Amsterdam: Elsevier.

Rochat, P., Morgan, R., & Carpenter, M. (1997). Young infants' sensitivity to movement information specifying social causality. *Cognitive Development, 12,* 441–465.

Rosenbaum, D. A., Vaughan, J., Barnes, H. J., & Jorgensen, M. J. (1992). Time course of movement planning: Selection of handgrips for object manipulation. *Journal of Experimental Psychology: Learning, Memory and Cognition, 18*(5), 1058–1073.

Rueda, M. R., Fan, J., McCandliss, B. D., Halparin, J. D., Gruber, D. B., Lercari, L. P., et al. (2004). Development of attentional networks in childhood. *Neuropsychologia, 42,* 1029–1040.

Schneider, G. E. (1969). Two visual systems: Brain mechanisms for localization and discrimination are dissociated by tectal and cortical lesions. *Science, 163,* 895–902.

Shumway-Cook, A., & Woollacott, M. (1985). The growth of stability: Postural control from a developmental perspective. *Journal of Motor Behavior, 17,* 131–147.

Sovrano, V. A., & Vallortigara, G. (2006). Dissecting the geometric module. *Psychological Science, 17,* 616–621.

Spencer, J., O'Brien, J., Riggs, K., Braddick, O., Atkinson, J., & Wattam-Bell, J. (2000). Motion processing in autism: Evidence for a dorsal stream deficiency. *NeuroReport, 11,* 2765–2767.

Sprague, J. M., & Meikle, T. H. (1965). The role of the superior colliculus in visually guided behavior. *Experimental Neurology, 11,* 115–146.

Stiles, J. (2000). Neural plasticity and cognitive development. *Developmental Neuropsychology, 18,* 237–272.

Stiles, J., Paul, B., Ark, W., & Akshoomoff, N. (in press). The development of visuospatial processing. In C. A. Nelson & M. Luciana (Eds.), *Handbook of developmental cognitive neuroscience* (2nd ed.). Cambridge, MA: MIT Press.

Stiles, J., Stern, C., Trauner, D., & Nass, R. (1996). Developmental change in spatial grouping activity among children with early focal brain injury: Evidence from a modeling task. *Brain and Cognition, 31,* 46–62.

Stiles-Davis, J., Sugarman, S., & Nass, R. (1985). The development of spatial and class relations in four young children with right cerebral hemisphere damage: Evidence for early spatial-constructive deficit. *Brain and Cognition, 4,* 388–412.

Ungerleider, L. G., & Mishkin, M. (1982). Two cortical visual systems. In D. J. Ingle, M. A. Goodale, & R. J. W. Mansfield (Eds.), *Analysis of visual behavior* (pp. 549–586). Cambridge, MA: MIT Press.

Van Essen, D. C., & Maunsell, J. H. R. (1983). Hierarchical organization and functional streams in visual cortex. *Trends in Neurosciences, 6,* 370–375.

Vicari, S., Bellucci, S., & Carlesimo, G. A. (2006). Evidence from two genetic syndromes for the independence of spatial and visual working memory. *Developmental Medicine and Child Neurology, 48,* 126–131.

von Hofsten, C. (1991). Structuring of early reaching movements: A longitudinal study. *Journal of Motor Behavior, 23,* 280–292.

von Hofsten, C. (2005). The development of prospective control in looking. In J. J. Rieser, J. J. Lockman, & C. A. Nelson (Eds.), *Action as an organizer of learning and development* (Minnesota Symposia on Child Psychology, Vol. 33). Mahwah, NJ: Lawrence Erlbaum.

von Hofsten, C., & Rosander, K. (1996). The development of gaze control and predictive tracking in young infants. *Vision Research, 36,* 81–96.

von Hofsten, C., & Rosander, K. (1997). Development of smooth pursuit tracking in young infants. *Vision Research, 37,* 1799–1810.

Walker, A. S., Owsley, C. J., Megaw-Nyce, J., Gibson, E. J., & Bahrick, L. E. (1980). Detection of elasticity as an invariant property of objects by young infants. *Perception, 9,* 713–718.

Wang, R. F., & Simons, D. J. (1999). Active and passive scene recognition. *Cognition, 70,* 191–210.

Wattam-Bell, J. (1992). The development of maximum displacement limits for discrimination of motion direction in infancy. *Vision Research, 32,* 621–630.

Wattam-Bell, J. (1994). Coherence thresholds for discrimination of motion direction in infants. *Vision Research, 34*(7), 877–883.

Wattam-Bell, J. (1995). Stereoscopic and motion Dmax in adults and infants. *Investigative Ophthalmology and Visual Science, 36,* S910.

Wattam-Bell, J. (1996). The development of visual motion processing. In F. Vital-Durand, O. Braddick, & J. Atkinson (Eds.), *Infant vision* (pp. 79–84). Oxford University Press.

Zeki, S. (1993). *A vision of the brain.* Oxford: Blackwell.

Zelazo, P. D., Frye, D., & Rapus, T. (1996). An age-related dissociation between knowing rules and using them. *Cognitive Development, 11,* 37–63.

Zihl, J., von Cramon, D., & Mai, N. (1983). Selective disturbance of movement vision after bilateral brain damage. *Brain, 106,* 313–340.

10

The Neuropsychology of Children's Memory

Arthur MacNeill Horton, Jr. and Henry Soper

When we talk about memory, we have some conceptual problems. We have one term, and we even have definitions for the term. Then we have learning, and similar definitions. Are these really different things, or different aspects of the same thing? For example, Cohen (1997, p. 11) describes learning as "the process of acquiring new information," and memory as "the consolidation and retention of that acquired information…." At times, they appear to even merge into one word, "learningandmemory." What is learning and what is memory? In addition to the fact that both learning and memory are conceptually intermingled to a large degree, it is very hard to pin down an adequate definition as each is also really an array of concepts and processes. What is involved in the brain for iconic memory and very long-term olfactory memory are really quite different. To try to put them all together can cause conceptual problems. So we can conclude that there are really many different forms of memory—and of learning, for that matter. It is, however, useful to try some form of categorization, and the next section describes one such approach.

A Category System for Memory

The following is a categorization scheme for children's memory processes based primarily on temporal duration of the memory trace:

Categorization scheme	Problems
Iconic (echoic) memory—sensory memory	
Relatively large capacity, depending on how assessed (examples, visual, auditory)	
Rapid decay (order of milliseconds)	Encoding
Very short-term memory—primary memory	
Capacity of 7 ± 2	

Relatively rapid decay (order of second)	Storage

Short-term memory—secondary memory
  Larger capacity, working memory
  Slower decay (order of minutes)
	Storage/retrieval

Intermediate-term memory—secondary memory (ctd.)
  Large capacity
  Slow decay (order of hours, days, or months)
	Retrieval

Long-term memory—tertiary memory Very large capacity, relatively permanent	Retrieval
(Permanent memory—your name, birth date, etc.) (Maybe very good access)	Retrieval

Sensory memory

First, we have iconic memory, the sensory memory for vision. Here, using vision as an example, we are looking at the residuals from the changes on the retina from the visual stimuli. When you take a tachistoscope and it blinks a very fast visual stimulus, for a certain duration you can see the stimulus, which is on your eye for milliseconds. And then the decay for this iconic memory sets in very quickly, so you are unable to report much of what you saw. However, if you flash a large array and then flash a marker under the element to be retained, it turns out that this memory capacity is actually rather large, maybe 25 items, but the decay is very rapid.

Echoic memory is the same for the auditory modality except that it seems to be the impressions on the primary cortex that are retained for a short period of time. This is a tape-recorder phenomenon. Somebody says something to you and you were not paying close attention. You say, "What?" "You heard me." And you really are able to play it back. You cannot do it seconds or minutes later. But echoic memory is substantially larger and longer than iconic. Again, it fades fairly quickly. So these are the sensory memories. Can you really call it memory? Why not? But it may be begging the point a little bit. This kind of memory is particularly evident in young children, whose attention is often difficult to transfer to verbal information. You can watch them stop and replay the information and then respond appropriately. Very little is known about the sensory memory of children, but it would appear by its nature to be there from the beginning. The ability to interpret the contents would emerge later, but the basic form does not change over life.

Primary memory

So we have iconic and echoic memory, sensory memories with large capacity but with a very rapid decay. Then, we have a form of very short-term memory, sometimes called primary memory or attention and concentration. This is an electrical sensory form of memory. The information is converted so we can make sense of it, but it is in primary storage and lasts in the order of seconds. The problem again is storage. Someone gives you a phone number, 555–1234, and a couple of minutes from now it has gone from your memory, but the number does stay in your memory long enough to dial it or copy it down. This is Miller's famous seven plus or minus two, like a digit span. And so, the very short-term memory is still an electrical memory. Once you stop thinking about it, it goes away. Prior to object permanence there could be complications to this form of memory. The evidence from digit span indicates that this memory develops over early childhood, but that there is little improvement after early grammar school (approximately the age of 10).

Secondary memory—short term

Next, we have what most lay persons consider short-term memory, which some other people call secondary memory. At this point, the information is put in a form of storage such that the individual can think about something else and yet still retrieve the information later. It has a larger capacity and slower decay, in the order of minutes. Where did I put my glasses? What did I say a minute ago? And here the most common problem is that the information got in but it cannot be retrieved. The information was either not stored very effectively or it was not processed (encoded or learned) effectively.

With this form of memory one can recall the information minutes later. It has a much larger capacity than very short-term memory (i.e., attention and concentration) and slower decay. But the to-be-remembered information is still not there very long. Very young children, those who are in the here-and-now stages, are generally unable to organize information for later retrieval, even over the course of minutes. This ability develops through the toddler stages, but continues to develop to the school years and into adulthood.

Secondary memory—intermediate term

Next is intermediate-term memory, also considered a form of secondary memory. It has a still larger capacity. Information stored here will persist even after a blow to the head or ECT. The shorter-form secondary memory is still, to large extent, an electric memory. It has not converted from an electrical to a chemical storage basis necessary for long-term memory. It is still "reverberating" or being held in a nonpermanent memory storage area in the brain. If you interrupt somebody, the memories in the shorter secondary memory will likely be gone, but not always those within intermediate memory. At the intermediate level, the most common difficulty is retrieval. The information is there, but the person just has difficulty recalling it. The intermediate memory has a much larger capacity, a much slower decay, in the order of hours, or days, or possibly months. But it is not in permanent memory; it is not in long-term memory as that requires additional consolidation. For example, you can travel to San Francisco to a neuropsychology convention. You learn the names of streets that are there and recall them for a while. But after you return, the street names are gone from your memory. Are they there somewhere? Yes, if you went back to San Francisco you might be able at least to recognize, if not recall, the names. An additional example would be where you parked your car at the airport. This is the information you want to hold for a period of time, but then you want to throw it out when it is no longer relevant.

Tertiary memory—long term

Then there is long-term memory, or tertiary memory, which has a very large capacity, and is relatively permanent. As before, the primary problem with long-term memory is in retrieval of the information that has been encoded, consolidated, and stored in long-term memory. The information may be stored in your long-term memory but there may be difficulties in recalling the information quickly and efficiently. For example, you may wish, as an adult, to recall the name of your fifth-grade teacher. Curiously, sometimes the firing patterns for recognition will not work here. But if you looked at a list of teachers in the elementary school you attended for fifth grade, you might be able to recognize the name of your fifth-grade teacher. Thus, the information was stored in your long-term memory but could only be accessed through a recognition process.

Generally, the major problem of long-term memory is a question of retrieval. It is clear that this type of memory involves, among other brain areas, the temporal lobes and hippocampus structures. Although some people claim to be able to remember things back to the age of 2 (or some claim back to in utero), that is highly unlikely to be accurate. More likely, at the age of 3 they remember the incident at the age of 2, and at the age of 5 the memory of age 3, and so on. It is clear that some events from that time of life are accurately recalled, but it is just as true that many are mis-recalled. There is little evidence that would lead one to believe that the retrieval mechanisms of an adult would match the storage mechanisms of an infant. Clearly, long-term memory gets better as one gets older, but the changes in cognitive processing in the early years, along with here-and-now perception, make long-term memory for the earliest years of life questionable. Some people speak of permanent memory but that is perhaps an inaccurate term. There is information in long-term memory that is usually so well rehearsed that you will not forget it unless you become demented. This includes memories such as your name and your birth date. With frequent rehearsal there could be such good access to personal information memories that retrieval is unlikely to be a problem.

Luria's Model of Brain Function and Development

While there are a plethora of brain-functioning theories, one particularly insightful model for understanding brain functioning is based on the work of A. R. Luria, the famous Russian neurologist and neuropsychologist (Horton & Puente, 1986). The following comments are an oversimplified description of his theoretical paradigm but are offered for purposes of illustration.

Luria's model of brain functioning

A. R. Luria (1966, 1973) was a Russian neuroscientist who developed a conceptual model for understanding the organization of higher mental abilities such as memory and executive functioning. In essence, Luria's model of higher cortical functioning involved dividing brain anatomy into three major brain blocks. These were: (a) lower brain-stem structures, (b) the cerebral cortex posterior to the central sulcus or the fissure of Rolando, and (c) the cerebral cortex anterior to the central sulcus or the fissure of Rolando. Those major blocks, as conceptualized by Luria, make unique contributions to human brain functioning. Each will be briefly described.

Block One

The lower brain-stem structures, or block one in Luria's structure of the brain model, are responsible for maintaining the tone and energy supply of the cerebral cortex. In a way, a similar situation would be a personal computer and its electricity supply. For the personal computer to work in a reasonable fashion, it must have a supply of electricity and the level of supply must be constant. If the electricity supply or current voltage varies, then the memory banks of the personal computer will have difficulty working in an efficient manner. In a similar way, the lower brain-stem structures provide for the tone and energy level of the cerebral cortex in order for the higher-level areas to subserve memory and executive-functioning abilities.

Block Two

The area posterior to the central sulcus or the posterior cerebral cortex, which is block two in Luria's structure of the brain model, is the area into which sensory impressions of a visual, auditory, and tactile nature are identified, perceived, and organized for comprehension. The processes of perceiving the incoming sensory stimuli include the function of organizing and encoding sensory stimuli in such a way that the incoming sensory information can be understood by other areas of the cerebral cortex.

Block Three

This is the area anterior to the central sulcus, or block three on Luria's structure of the brain model. This area is involved in the initiation, production, monitoring, and evaluating of motor responses. The area of the anterior cerebral cortex is the area in which information from the posterior sensory impressions comes and where there is a formulation of intention planning and production of motor behaviors and monitoring and evaluation of the effects of motor behaviors. To carry the computer model mentioned above a little further: In block two, the input devices to the computer, which are like the keyboard or, in earlier days, a card reader, are models for the posterior cerebral cortex. Similarly, the anterior cerebral cortex is related to the arithmetic and logic unit and working memory area of the personal computer which makes decisions. The output of information by the printer or through some other output mechanism is planned by the anterior cerebral area.

Neuropsychological developmental stages

It might be noted that Luria (1966) postulated a number of stages by which neuropsychological functions are developed. These stages apparently interact with environmental stimuli. It might be noted that Luria's work to a large extent is based on Lev Vygotsky's cultural and historical theory (Horton, 1987). Vygotsky was a mentor to A. R. Luria and a major influence on Luria's thinking. Vygotsky developed a complex theory related to language and thought processes. He postulated that environmental/cultural influences were important in terms of interacting with neurological structures to develop higher-level mental abilities such as memory and executive functioning.

Vygotsky died of tuberculosis at a young age and he was unable to further develop his theories. Luria used Vygotsky's thinking as his major theoretical framework (Horton, 1987). Luria believed that the development of higher cortical functions required both the interaction of normal neurological development and specific environmental stimuli of a cultural, historical, and social nature to flourish. The result of the appropriate interaction of neurological development and the appropriate environmental stimuli would be the optimization of the higher cortical functions of language, memory, and executive functioning. The five stages in development proposed by Luria (1980) are related to Luria's conceptualization of the basic blocks of the brain.

As earlier noted, block one was related to the lower brain-stem structures, block two was related to the area posterior to the central sulcus, and block three was related to the area anterior to the central sulcus. Essentially, in the first stage, beginning in the first year of life, the brain-stem structures are primarily developed. These brain-stem structures in block one may be seen as involving the reticular activating system which was described earlier.

The second stage is related to the activation of the primary sensory areas for vision, hearing, and tactical perception and the primary motor areas for gross motor movement. To put it in terms of neuroanatomy, these would be areas immediately adjacent both posterior and anterior to the central sulcus. This particular stage relies primarily upon the unfolding of "hard wired" neurological structures.

The third stage focuses on single modalities in the secondary association areas of the brain. Often, this stage is associated with the movement of the child into preschool. The child at this stage recognizes and reproduces various symbolical/symbolic materials and is able to model various physical movements. The different modalities of learning may be separately accessed.

The fourth stage begins about the time of first or second grade. At this time, the tertiary areas of the parietal lobes become activated. The tertiary parietal lobe is the area in which the temporal, parietal, and occipital lobes come together. This enables a coordination of the three major sensory input channels. In order to help the child make sense of the sensor input coming in, environmental stimulation is particularly important. For instance, cultural, historical, and social influences are the major factors in shaping the crucial academic skills of reading, writing, and arithmetic which are the primary tasks for the child to learn in the early school years.

The fifth stage becomes activated during adolescence. In this stage, the frontal area, or the area anterior to the central sulcus, comes online in terms of mental functioning. As noted by others (Struss & Benson, 1984), the area anterior to the central sulcus is important for the development of working memory and executive functioning. Luria's model (1980) suggests that there are qualitative differences between children at different stages in neuropsychological development, and that children could use different functional systems to perform similar tasks. In addition, Luria's thinking suggests that there must be interaction between the child's level of neuropsychological development and the sorts of environmental stimulation that are crucial in terms of developing important human adaptive/vocational skills. Luria's model (1980) should be recognized as a unique, elegant, and efficient method by which to understand neuropsychological development and environmental stimuli/stimulation.

Luria's model of brain function was initially developed in work with children. Luria, at first, worked with Vygotsky and Alexei Leontiev, another Russian researcher, to validate Vygotsky's cultural-historical theory by studying how higher-level mental abilities developed as children got older (Horton, 1987). They were interested in how cultural tools that had been developed over time were used as mediators of mental abilities. Vygotsky had worked with mentally retarded children early in his career, when he was a school teacher, and had particular interest in the cognitive development of children (Homskaya, 2001). For example, a task Luria, Vygotsky, and Leontiev developed to study memory in children used pictures to assist memory (i.e., a picture of a sleigh is shown to the child to help him recall the word "horse" which was earlier shown to the child when the word "horse" was said; Luria, 1979). They demonstrated that young children did not use the picture to assist in recalling the word. As the child got older, the picture was used as an association but for the picture of a sleigh he or she might say "snow" as likely as "horse" because the process of using mediators was still external to the child (Luria, 1976). As the child reached the age of 10, internal mediation began and the child would begin to create his or her own reminders (Luria, 1979).

When Luria used similar memory procedures with brain-injured patients with localized brain injuries, he identified three neuropsychological syndromes of memory impairment: "modality-nonspecific and modality-specific dysfunction, and dysfunction of memory as a mnemonic activity" (Luria, 1976, pp. 72–73; Homskaya, 2001). The modality-nonspecific dysfunction involved "damage to deep structures located along the mesencephalic midline and is characterized by the preservation of gnosis, praxis, and speech in the patient, but with effects on all kinds of sensory (visual, auditory, kinesthetic and others) information processing and short-term memory traces" (Luria, 1976, p. 73; Homskaya, 2001). The second type of neuropsychological syndrome of memory dysfunction was related to modes of stimuli processing and involved "damage to the cortical analyzers and their subcortical constituents" (p. 73; Homskaya, 2001); in other words, selective impairment of auditory, verbal, or visual nonverbal memory processes. The third type of neuropsychological syndrome associated with memory dysfunction is mnemonic disturbance seen "with massive lesions of the frontal lobes and its symptoms were similar to the disturbance of any kind of psychological activity, in terms of its impact on the structure of voluntary behavioral regulation" (p. 73; Homskaya, 2001).

It is interesting to note how the three syndromes of neuropsychological dysfunction of memory with localized brain lesion described by Luria (1976) are similar to the three blocks of Luria's model of brain functioning described earlier (Horton, 1987). Put another way, each neuropsychological memory dysfunction syndrome describes the effects of brain damage localized to a single block of brain functioning in Luria's brain-functioning model (Luria, 1976). The neuropsychological memory syndromes may be seen as different in children relative to the stage of neuropsychological brain development as mental (and memory) functions develop and are internalized to a greater degree over time as the child gets older (Luria, 1979). As the earlier example of a mediated memory (i.e., showing the picture of a sleigh to assist recalling the word "horse") illustrated, memory functions are better mediated as the child gets older. Very young children are unable to use cues, older children use cues in an automatic manner, and adolescents internalize the use of cues to assist memory processes (Luria, 1976).

Organization of Memory

Rote memory and frontal memory

What most people call short-term memory is actually several categories of short-term memories. But let us simplify the concept. What we would like to do is to break short-term memory down into two subdivisions. One is rote memory, and this is a fairly mechanical memory. In some ways, it is probably closest to the tape recorder. People just remember information, without organizing the information or anything else. Luria (1968) writes of a mnemonist, who had an incredible rote memory.

At all ages but the youngest perhaps, there are people who are very good at rote memory and some who are not very good. One of us was testing a delightful 12-year-old girl once on a word list. On the first two trials, she got five and seven correct, but then she stopped and prior to the third trial she recited the list from the first to the last without any problem. She repeated them all in order on the rest of the regular trials and on the delay trials. She just had a tremendous rote memory. The evidence from digit span suggests that rote memory improves through childhood and then remains pretty stable.

There is another form of memory that is similar to rote memory in some ways. It can be called template memory. When asked to compare two rhythms, one simply holds the first rhythm as a chunk and then compares the second one to it. When asked to repeat sentences, this procedure is also often used. One simply echoes back the sequence of words with the same intonation and prosody, with only incidental thought to the meaning of the string of words. Developmentally, even very young children, certainly by the age of 4, are able to repeat sentences of several words, long before they comprehend those sentences.

In addition to rote memory and template memory, we have what can be called "frontal memory." This is generally described in the research literature as "working memory"

(Baddeley, 1986), and although this is a good term for it, it does not describe what is going on. What frontal memory does, through the executive functioning of the brain, is to initiate processing, to organize information for retention. For example, one way to retain a series of words is through repetition: say them over, over, over, and over again. Eventually, you will get them, or at least we hope so. Another way is to organize the words. One can group them into clothes and tools and such, or picture a farmer blowing a large nose with a handkerchief. One can think of a school curtain being drawn as a bell goes off. Similarly, one can organize the copying of a complex figure, which would make retention better. One can see how frontal or "working memory," as opposed to rote or template memory, is involved in our normal retention of information. By organizing the information, and making sense of it, retention is facilitated. Unfortunately, rote memory and working term memory are often assessed in the same way. In the case of rote memory, usually the exact same sequence is often used, and there is no or little coherence or deeper understanding of the information. Often primacy (first few items) and recency (last few items) are observed, especially early in the trials.

We have talked so far about template learning or retention, which is one form of short-term memory. This form of memory appears fairly early in the child; then comes rote memory, which seems to come in a bit later. Then there is the working memory. As the frontal association areas develop, children develop a better working memory. This continues to develop, and by high school their working memory skills approach that of the adult.

Detail versus gist

When remembering, what we try to do is to retain the gist of the story as well as the details. And then we recombine them and put them together. What happens to people? They tend to remember the beginning (primacy effect), they tend to remember the end (recency effect), and they tend to forget what is going on in the middle. Now with a patient who had right hemisphere brain injury there is not as much of a primacy and recency effect: They remember a few things, which they remember with great detail, but they do not remember the overall gestalt. There is no coherence or a framework to their story. They are just able to come up with bits and pieces. It is not curious that such individuals usually like slapstick comedy, but they do not like long, involved movies on television. Because they do not know where they are in the story, they are not able to appreciate coherence to the story; it does not make sense to them.

Many conceptualized "working memory" as having an auditory/verbal path on the left and a visual/spatial path on the right. That is not completely accurate because visual material can be processed analytically (successive) with the left hemisphere, and more gestaltically (simultaneous) verbal material can be processed with the right hemisphere. Most often, the details of a verbal story are processed with the left hemisphere, and the gist (or framework) of the story with the right hemisphere. Normally both forms of processing are integrated together to produce an accurate drawing or coherent story on free recall.

Let us give an example. The story might be: "The brown rabbit was looking for carrots. He went into a farmer's basement, and changed his mind and decided to eat the apples there." The person's right hemisphere might get the gist but miss the details, and come out with: "A small dark animal, maybe a rodent, was hungry and searching for food. It wound up in a hole or cellar or something, found something else and ate it." The person's left hemisphere might get the details but not appreciate the gist of the story, and come out with: "Farmer Brown was in his basement cooking a rabbit with some apples and carrots, but then he changed his mind." Normally, of course, both hemispheres would be working efficiently and the complete response would be produced. The limitations placed on development are the emergence of the analytic and gestaltic processing abilities, which mature through the early grammar school years (ages 5–10). Even here, though, the analytic, semantic aspects of verbal material, the meaning of the words, would be processed on the left. This would include chunking words for memory (all fruits, all clothes, and so on). Organizing the verbal information in an episodic manner or along the lines of the gist of the story would involve right hemisphere processing.

Dealing with irrelevant information

There is an aspect of memory that has been studied in the monkey, but not very much in the human. One of the important things we do is to throw something out of memory if it is no longer of use to us. For example, if you take a look at a stop light, you want to know the color. The important information is the color of the light. Less relevant is where it is, whether it is off to the side or in the middle of the street. Less important still is what the background of those lights looks like. Think of a stop light near your house. Is it a bunch of hexagons, is it a bunch of pentagons, is it by any chance a bunch of diagonal lines with little circles, or what? When we stop at a stop light, we do not think about what the back of the lens looks like. We throw that information out. It certainly got into the iconic memory. We could have looked. But for most of us the important information is the color of the light. That is all we care about. And so, as a result, we throw out all this irrelevant information. Similarly, you are driving through the valley and you are looking for Boise Street. On your course you read the names of many other streets, but you throw most of these names out as irrelevant. That is a good thing to do. Could you imagine what you would be like if you were unable to throw them out and were storing all of the irrelevant information you came in contact with during a day?

This is what it is like with an inferotemporal cortex lesion. People with damage to this area of the brain have difficulty throwing out irrelevant information. Preschool children also have difficulty throwing out irrelevant information, and as a result they often appear precocious because they can remember irrelevant things that adults do not. However, if you look closely, what they remember appears to be somewhat indiscriminate in that they remember a lot of trivia and not very much of the most important material. When you test people with brain trauma to the inferotemporal areas on the Wisconsin Card Sorting Test (WCST; Heaton, 1981) you get a strange set of results.

The WCST requires the patient to sort a deck of cards based on various criteria on target cards that are not given to the patient, but verbal feedback is given as to whether a card sort is correct. After a number of correct sorts, the criterion is changed without the patient being informed. The patient with brain trauma to the inferotemporal areas may get initial criteria shifts correct after a few errors, but after this, however, things are quite different. Subsequent responses to shifting criteria are slow and difficult, and the person frequently breaks set before achieving a complete set of correct responses. In this case, the brain-injured person is unable to consistently suppress the once but no longer relevant dimensions.

In children, this area is not as well developed, and you get what appears to be precocious memory. They remember a lot of irrelevant details that you have forgotten, but they also forget a lot of important facts that you remember. So you are driving along and this 4-year-old child says, "I remember this church." You were there at the same time they were, and yet you do not remember that church, because you threw it out as not relevant. You, as an adult with a fully functioning inferotemporal cortex, said this is a piece of information I will throw out. This goes with the trash heap, with the back of stop lights and everything else. All the stuff I do not need is thrown out because I can only pack so much into my memory. It is very important to know what to keep and what not to keep, and the inferotemporal cortex is involved in this. By the time the child gets to elementary school this ability to separate irrelevant from important facts appears to be developing well, but you can imagine the learning difficulty a child would have who cannot or has difficulty selecting what information to attend to and what information to throw out. Luria's (1968) mnemonist had difficulty with this and was distressed by his complete recall of irrelevant details.

Recall versus Recognition

There is another aspect of memory which we should talk about because it does become confusing. Here we speak of recall versus recognition. These are two different ways of assessing memory for information. Sometimes they are spoken of as if they were opposite sides of the same coin. They are totally different processes. They both involve the left and the right hemispheres. It is true that the temporal lobes, especially the anterior right temporal lobe, do seem to be involved in recognition and déjà vu types of phenomena. Those who experience Capgras syndrome, in which familiarity is impaired (though she looks like my wife, something, we do not know what, is missing, so it must be an imposter), are thought to have frontal involvement. But the trouble is that if you damage the anterior temporal lobe, you will probably damage the frontal lobe too.

Can you have recognition of information without recall of the same information with short-term memory? Yes, certainly, it happens all the time. You cannot remember what it was, but as soon as you hear the word, you recognize it. Can you have recall without recognition? Yes, you can, but only in unusual circumstances. How do you know somebody recognizes somebody or something? Basically, because they say they recognize it, and saying it involves the left hemisphere. Suppose your left hemisphere is isolated from your right hemisphere. This is exactly what happened in a series of patients studied by Roger Sperry (1961). Sperry conducted neuropsychological research with epilepsy patients who had undergone neurosurgical procedures for patients with severe refractory epilepsy. Each patient had been through a neurosurgical procedure that involved cutting the fibers connecting the two cerebral hemispheres. The theory underlying this surgical procedure was that refractory seizures will move from one cerebral hemisphere to another through these connecting fibers and that cutting the interconnecting fibers would reduce seizure frequency. Usually the treatment involved the corpus callosum, the largest set of interhemispheric connecting fibers. The corpus callosum, however, is not the only group of fibers connecting the cerebral hemispheres. There are also the anterior commissure, and the hippocampal commissure which also connect the cerebral hemispheres, but in smaller collections of fibers. As a general rule, as a result of severing these interhemispheric connecting fibers the patients were less troubled by their seizures. It might be mentioned that the research program of Roger Sperry was so successful and produced findings of such great importance that he later received the Nobel Prize in Medicine for his contributions.

Essentially, Sperry's research team found that while split-brain patients had few obvious consequences from the neurosurgical procedure there were none the less subtle neuropsychological changes. For example, information presented in the right visual field would go to the left cerebral hemisphere only and not be accessible to the right cerebral hemisphere (Gazzaniga, 1977). A fundamental experimental paradigm of Sperry's work was the presentation of stimuli to only one visual field of split-brain patients. An example of how this could work is to present a coin to a split-brain patient's right visual field. As the sensory stimuli are transmitted to the left cerebral hemisphere, the cerebral hemisphere specialized for speech and language, the split-brain patient is able to identify the object by name. On the other hand, or visual field, if the coin is presented to the left visual field, then sensory information is transmitted to the right cerebral hemisphere, which is specialized for visual-spatial perception and organization (Nebes, 1974). As a result, the split-brain patient is unable to name the coin but can match the coin when presented with alternatives (i.e., a dime is presented and a nickel, penny, and quarter are other options). Similarly, split-brain patients draw better with the left hand, and right cerebral hemisphere, regardless of their preneurosurgical dominance pattern (Gazzaniga, Steen, & Volpe, 1979).

One of Sperry's split-brain patients might verbally deny recognizing something seen only by the right hemisphere, yet be able to draw it with the left hand. It is therefore clear that recognition and recall really are different. Recognition does not require recall; recall does not technically require recognition, although most often it does occur. And so, recall and recognition tests tap into quite different memory abilities.

Recognition begins quite early in life, possibly as early as the prenatal period. Certainly, the language evidence indicates that long before semantic development, the infant is recognizing familiar sounds and voices and responds to them differentially. In order to demonstrate recall, the sensorimotor abilities must be adequately developed.

The generated speech sounds of late infancy indicate the beginnings of recall, and the development of language probably parallels the development of recall.

The Process of Memory

Let us talk a little bit about the processes of memory—what is involved in the memory process? Most people say that you have to encode information in order to store and recall the information; in other words, somehow the information has to get into your brain. The light has to get in, the feeling has to get in, the auditory sounds, or vibrations have to get in. And then this information has to be encoded (or learned) so that it makes sense. Next this encoded information has to be stored somehow. Sometimes, as for short-term memory, it does not have to be stored for very long. Here electrical reverberations will be sufficient to hold the information for later access. For long-term memory, the information has to be encoded into some kind of protein store for later recall.

Once the information has been stored, it has to be retrieved. Very often our memory problem is in our retrieval mechanisms. If we were able to put ourselves back into where we got all the cues, we would be able to retrieve more information than we could otherwise. So, there are many aspects to the memory processes involved in retrieval. The quality of encoding and storage are certainly important. Recall of information encoded while under the influence of alcohol is probably not as good as when sober.

For recall of information or the processes of memory so far we have encoding, storage, and retrieval. There is another aspect to talk about too. And that is how well you organize the information. Generally, important information is organized for retention. Under ideal conditions, it becomes organized so that it can be stored efficiently and it can be retrieved efficiently. So both encoding and storage include organizing the information. The frontal lobes are usually involved in this organization as the executive processes associated with the frontal lobes are necessary for initiating the organization, but in all likelihood multiple brain areas participate in executive functioning with the frontal lobes. Without the brain areas subserving executive functioning encoding and storing the information in memory, we are relegated to using rote forms of memory.

But retrieving, coding, and storage are all involved in executive functioning activities that develop as a person matures, and they are things all young children have great difficulty with until they become older. Improvement in working memory goes along with the substantial development of the frontal lobes in the pre- and early school years. Some, such as those who by chance are very good at rote memory, may have great difficulty switching to using their working memory skills to retain information. A part of this comes from habit. Some students, even in college, have a great deal of difficulty learning to organize information for retention. They will read the material, but they are not really studying it because they are not using their executive functioning abilities to reorganize the information into conceptual understandings of the information. This is clear even when teaching college sophomores. College students will come and say they have read the textbook, and when you ask if they have studied it, or just read it the way you read a novel, they respond they do not understand that there is a difference. The difference is, it is one thing to cast your eyes over the words, and it is another thing to sit there and study it (reorganize it into concepts) until you understand it. These students have no idea what you are talking about with respect to studying the material. They have never been trained to study.

The role of emotion in memory recall

Is executive functioning always needed for good retention? Not necessarily. If you have a gun go off near you, probably very little organization is needed for good retention. For most of us, however, that is not an everyday occurrence. No organizing is necessary when the emotional salience of information for survival is so strong; the important information goes right to a long-term memory store. In fact, some people who develop post-traumatic stress disorder have a dissociative reaction in which they block the traumatic event from conscious memory and are not able to recall it. They may go into a fugue state where they lose recall of what has happened. Then, a couple of years later, perhaps under hypnosis or in psychotherapy, they can recall the traumatic event. There was never any kind of conscious organization for retention as they never rehearsed the traumatic information. It was as if the memory of the traumatic event did not exist for that period of time. And yet a couple of years later, the traumatic memory comes back. It did not have to go through all the stages of memory; it did not have to be repeated over and over again to get into the long-term memory. On the other hand, somebody conveys information like a name when you are introduced at a social gathering, and if executive functioning skills are not used for encoding or storage of the name, the name is not retained in long-term memory.

The role of the hippocampus

At this point, the discussion will move to long-term memory and some of the ways it is broken down. An important case study of long-term memory was the patient known as H.M. He is now rather elderly, but at one time he was a young man who had severe epilepsy. He was heavily medicated and still had uncontrolled seizures. To achieve control of the seizures, neurosurgeons removed the epileptogenic brain tissue. The neurosurgeons removed the medial aspects of both temporal lobes. As a result of the neurosurgery, his epilepsy abated substantially, but H.M. was left with severe deficits in converting information from short-term memory to long-term memory. H.M. has been one of the most studied individuals in the history of clinical neuropsychology.

The brain structure known as the hippocampus appears to be involved in converting many forms of memory into long-term memories. Without the hippocampus, people tend to live in the here and now and not fully appreciate the past and future. Young children have an immature hippocampus, and tend to live in the here and now. As the hippocampus area develops, we develop the ability for analytic and gestaltic storage for the long term. At the other end of our lives, many of us with dementia also live in the here and now. We have not worked out all that is involved in converting information in short-term memory into long-term memory store, but for many aspects of transferring information from short-term to long-term memory the hippocampus is essential.

Semantic and episodic memory

There is also the dichotomy in short-term and long-term memory between semantic and episodic memory. Both semantic and episodic memories are ways in which information is organized and recalled. But episodic memory is more a question of information recall that occurs in a temporal or spatial context or what co-occurs at the same time and in what location. In other words, what is involved in an episode? Who is involved with whom and where? A child sees a neighbor in a store and comments that this man looks just like the neighbor. The child becomes adamant when told it is the same person that it cannot be, because the neighbor is in the house next to the child's, and cannot be in the store. One of the things we find about our dreams is that we have people from all facets of our lives, all adults or all children, all at the same time. The episodic memory seems to be disrupted here. But the semantic memory is categorically organized factual information that is independent of the temporal or spatial context. Who is this? What is the name of this? What is it? And what is it used for? And, less so, what is it associated with? So, for example, you show a patient with severe mental retardation a cake, and the patient when asked to identify the cake says "pie." The patient makes a semantic error if he or she, when shown a cake, calls the cake a pie. The concept of cake is a semantic category that is independent of a specific time or place. The patient's response is from a similar category to a cake because a pie is also within the category of a dessert, and looks round and is edible. But he or she does not correctly identify the cake, but says a pie. The mentally retarded patient makes a semantic error in responding because the basis of the error is inadequate categorization. On the other hand, if the patient when shown a cake says "birthday," then the patient makes an episodic error because the basis of the error is the temporal context when the patient last saw a cake. Similarly, another semantic error would be, when seeing an escalator, if the mentally retarded patient said "elevator." That is a semantic error, but if they said "department store" that would be an episodic error. Much of the child's early life involves procedural memory, but then, at about the age of 3–4, semantic memory takes predominance, and through that process vocabulary size explodes.

Implications for Assessment and Future Research

Future research questions regarding the neuropsychology of children's memory need to address the issue of the interaction of children's memory development and processes with the development and processes of children's executive functioning. As should be clear from the preceding pages, the development of attention and concentration underlie and support the processes of memory in children. As children develop, however, the processes of memory depend on executive functioning in terms of encoding and retrieving information (Baddeley, 1986). Similarly, Luria's (1976) conceptualization of neuropsychological syndromes of memory dysfunction with localized brain injuries and Luria's model of brain functioning (1980) would suggest that assessment of memory abilities requires assessment of all three blocks of Luria's brain-functioning model (1976, 1980).

Current test batteries designed to assess children's memory (Cohen, 1997; Reynolds & Bigler, 1994; Sheslow & Adams, 1990) all include measures of attention and concentration with measures of verbal and nonverbal recall, but none addresses the interaction of executive functioning and memory. Adding selected measures of executive functioning to memory test batteries for children could prove instructive in understanding how selected aspects of executive functioning may influence types of recall in the various memory abilities. Interestingly, inspection of a test battery for children's memory (Cohen, 1997) demonstrates moderate correlations between memory subtests and childhood executive functioning (Boll, 1993). Similarly, a recently published measure of executive functioning that includes children in its normative sample, the Test of Verbal Conceptualization and Fluency (Reynolds & Horton, 2006), reported moderate correlations with memory subtests of another test battery for children's memory (Reynolds & Bigler, 1994). Future research in children's memory development and processes may find the interaction of types of memory (Luria, 1976) and the various aspects of executive functioning (Reynolds & Horton, 2006) an exceptionally rich area for very important contributions to science.

The field of the clinical neuropsychology of children's memory is quite new and rests on an evolving research base. Moreover, the complex nature of clinical neuropsychology makes it a very difficult but rewarding area. This chapter has presented a very basic review of some selected elements of memory. It has addressed a categorization scheme for understanding memory, Luria's model of brain functioning and Luria's neuropsychological syndromes related to localized memory dysfunction, the role of the organization of memory, and implications for future research questions with children's memory. It is to be hoped that this chapter will be helpful in terms of facilitating the understanding of children's memory deficits and the delivery of neuropsychological services to the needy population of brain-injured children.

References

Baddeley, A. D. (1986). *Working memory*. New York: Oxford University Press.

Boll, T. J. (1993). *Children's category test*. San Antonio, TX: Psychological Corporation.

Cohen, M. (1997). *Children's memory scale: Professional manual*. New York: Psychological Corporation.

Gazzaniga, M. S. (1977). Consistency and diversity in brain organization. *Annals of the New York Academy of Sciences, 299*, 415–423.

Gazzaniga, M. S., Steen, D., & Volpe, B. T. (1979). *Functional neuroscience*. New York: Harper and Row.

Heaton, R. K. (1981). *Wisconsin card sorting test manual*. Odessa, FL: PAR.

Homskaya, E. D. (2001). *Alexander Romanovich Luria: A scientific biography* (D. Krotova, Trans.). New York: Kluwer Academic/Plenum.

Horton, A. M., Jr. (1987). Luria's contributions to clinical and behavioral neuropsychology. *Neuropsychology, 1*(2), 39–44.

Horton, A. M., Jr., & Puente, A. E. (1986). Behavioral neuropsychology for children. In G. Hynd & J. Obrzut (Eds.), *Child neuropsychology: Clinical practice* (vol. 2, pp. 299–316). Orlando, FL: Academic Press.

Luria, A. R. (1966). *Higher cortical functions in man.* New York: Basic Books.

Luria, A. R. (1968). *The mind of a mnemonist* (L. Solotaroff, Trans.). New York: Basic Books.

Luria, A. R. (1973). *The working brain: An introduction to neuropsychology.* New York: Basic Books.

Luria, A. R. (1976). *The neuropsychology of memory* (B. Haigh, Trans.). Washington, DC: V. H. Winston.

Luria, A. R. (1979). *The making of mind* (M. Cole, Trans.). Cambridge, MA: Harvard University Press.

Luria, A. R. (1980). *Higher cortical functions.* New York: Basic Books.

Nebes, R. W. (1974). Hemispheric specialization in commissurotomized man. *Psychological Bulletin, 81*, 1–14.

Reynolds, C. R., & Bigler, E. D. (1994). *Test of memory and learning: Examiner's manual.* Austin, TX: Pro Ed.

Reynolds, C. R., & Horton, A. M., Jr. (2006). *Test of verbal conceptualization and fluency: Professional manual.* Austin, TX: Pro Ed.

Sheslow, D., & Adams, W. (1990). *Wide range achievement of learning and memory.* Wilmington, DE: Jastak.

Sperry, R. W. (1961). Cerebral organization and behavior. *Science, 133*, 1949.

Struss, D. T., & Benson, D. F. (1984). Neuropsychological studies of the frontal lobes. *Psychological Bulletin, 95*(1), 23–38.

11

The Neuropsychology of Attention Development

Maxine Sinclair and Eric Taylor

We are constantly bombarded with more complex sensory information than our cognitive systems can fully process at one time. Although the sensory organs perform parallel processing, the capacity is severely limited and sensory information competes for representation in multiple brain systems. The ability to direct attention toward sensory events in the extrapersonal space is of crucial importance for adaptive behavior. Evidence based on imaging studies and studies of brain-lesioned organisms suggests that the human brain has the ability to select a limited subset of the available information for detailed processing, to filter out distracting, irrelevant information, and to switch this focus to some other part of the environment when necessary.

Whilst there is universal consensus that the brain has inherent limitations with regard to the amount of information it can simultaneously process, theorists have found agreement on an operational definition of attention, and the scope of the phenomena to which it applies, for the most part elusive. Attention has variously been regarded as an active mechanism that selects or binds (e.g., Treisman, 1988), a resource that is shared between competing processes (Norman & Bobrow, 1975), a factor that amplifies signals and improves sensitivity (Lu & Dosher, 1998), or a conglomeration of diverse mental functions (Driver, Vuilleumier, Eimer, & Rees, 2001). What is universally accepted is that attention is not a one-dimensional construct (i.e., a single resource process or mechanism), but complex, multidimensional processes involving several overlapping components (Heuer, 1996) that form the basis of, and are affected by, all cognitive activity.

In this review, we will consider current neurological and neuropsychological models of attention. We will consider in some detail the formal constructs of attention, providing definitions of each as well as evidence from functional neuroimaging studies that have enabled researchers to examine the neural basis of attention in the intact human brain with relatively high spatial resolution. Space does not allow us to catalogue the particular attention disturbances associated with every medical and neuropsychological condition associated with impaired attention. We will instead outline the core components of the development of attention, focusing on particular implications for attention deficit hyperactivity disorder.

This review will consider attentional mechanisms and development from an almost exclusively visual attention perspective. This correlates with the extant literature relating to attention which has focused almost exclusively on visual attentional processes, although theorists speculate that findings should and do generalize to other sensory modalites (Richards, 2003).

The Neuroanatomy of Attention

Contemporary cognitive neuroscience paradigms propose that attention involves a defined neural network that performs highly specific computations (Fuentes, Vivas, & Humphreys, 1999). In the most elaborated of these anatomical models proposed by Posner and Petersen (1990) and Mesulam (1981, 1990), attention is specified in terms of neural networks corresponding to brain regions activated during imaging tasks that require attention, and regions which, when damaged, produce attention deficits.

Mesulam's model has been influential in so far as it accentuates the anatomical specificity within the neural network, whilst Posner's model has dominated research conceptualization in this area because it emphasizes the cognitive functions performed by the subcomponents of the network (Webster & Ungerleider, 1998). Importantly, both models identify similar neural substrates for attention and are based on the traditional view of attention as a factor that amplifies signals, thereby enhancing the processing of the target stimuli.

Mesulam's distributed network for spatial attention

Mesulam (1999) suggests that at the psychological level attention refers to the preferential allocation of the limited processing resources and response channels to events that have become behaviorally relevant; and at the neurological level it is the reversible modulation in the selectivity, intensity, and duration of neuronal responses to such events. His model was informed by convergent findings from neuropsychological and brain imaging studies. Mesulam (1981) proposed that visuospatial attention was coordinated by a large-scale distributed network that includes three monosynaptically interconnected cortical areas. The epicenters of this neural network were the posterior parietal cortex around the intraparietal sulcus, the frontal eye fields in the premotor cortex, and the anterior cingulated cortex. These local networks have extensive interconnections with each other and the reticular activating system that together form the larger neural network for attention.

The parietal cortex
Mesulam identified the sulcus separating the superior and inferior parietal lobes as the primary anatomical region for attention within the parietal cortex. Its influence on

other areas within the attentional circuitry is explained in terms of reciprocal interconnections with the premotor cortex, the frontal eye fields, the superior colliculus and the paralimbic areas allowing for the potential for both top-down and bottom-up control of attention. Converging evidence from neuroimaging studies (Corbetta, Miezin, Shulman, & Petersen, 1993; Gittelman et al., 1999), behavioral analysis in neurological patients with focal cortical lesions (Posner & Dehaene, 1994), and neurophysiological recordings in nonhuman primates (Colby & Goldberg, 1999), implicate inferior and superior parietal regions neighboring the sulcus in the voluntary allocation of visuo-spatial attention. Experiments in the macaque have suggested that the parietal component of the attentional network is specialized for mapping the spatial location of salient sensory events and also for compiling motor strategies that would target such events for attentional behaviors (Andersen, 1995; Gottlieb, Kusunoki, & Goldberg, 1998; Robinson & Kertzman, 1995; Snyder, Batista, & Andersen, 1998).

The lateral prefrontal cortex/frontal eye fields
The frontal eye fields and surrounding premotor areas, on the other hand, appear to play a more prominent role in the selection, sequencing, and execution of attentional behaviors related to the foveation, scanning, exploring, reaching, and grasping of salient events (i.e., overt motor exploratory aspects of spatial attention; Goldberg & Bushnell, 1981). Tasks requiring shifts of attention without eye movements, as well as tasks requiring focused attention, activate the frontal cortex in the region of the frontal eye fields (Gitelman et al., 1999; Hopfinger, Buonocore, & Mangun, 2000). It is speculated that this region of the brain has a relative specialization for providing a mental map for the distribution of overt and covert exploratory behaviors. The cortical and subcortical inputs to the frontal eye fields and adjacent motor regions direct the eyes, head, and limbs, permitting exploration of the environment.

Cingulate gyrus
The cingulate gyrus is a major component of the "paralimbic belt." It provides a zone of cytoarchitectonic transition between core limbic areas and front parietal neocortex (Mesulam, 2000). The location of the cingulate gyrus within the limbic system contributes to the coordination of spatial attention by modulating the distribution of expectancy and emotional/motivational valence (Mesulam, 1981, 1990).

The relevance of the cingulate gyrus to spatial attention has been inferred from reports showing that damage to this part of the brain gave rise to contralesional neglect in monkeys and humans (Heilman, Watson, Valenstein, & Damasio, 1983; Watson, Heilman, Cauthen, & King, 1973). Anterior cingulotomy causes persistent impairments of focused and sustained attention. Cognitive research has demonstrated that the interference condition of the Stroop test elicits robust activation in the anterior cingulate region (Pardo, Pardo, Janer, & Raichle, 1990). Anterior, but not posterior, cingulate activation has been reported when subjects had to divide attention (Posner & Petersen, 1990; Taylor, Huang, Tandon, & Koeppe, 1998). The posterior cingulate gyrus, in contrast, monitors postsaccadic shifts in the direction of overt visual targets and promotes the speed of spatial target detection, especially when attentional shifts are influenced by such reflexive and volitional cue-induced anticipatory biases (Mesulam, Nobre, Kim, & Parrish, 2001).

Evidence from imaging, physiological, and behavioral investigations in nonhuman primates and humans suggests that each of these regions makes a differential contribution to spatial attention (Chedru, Lebranc, & Lhermitte, 1973; Mesulam, 1981, 1985, 1990; Posner, Walker, Friedrich, & Rafal, 1984). Accordingly, Mesulam's model posits the idea that effective apportionment of attention across the extrapersonal space requires the integrity of all three of these cortical areas, as well as their connections with each other and with specific subcortical regions in the thalamus and striatum. Damage to any one of these three cortical areas causes contralesional neglect (Heilman & van den Abell, 1980; Mesulam, 1981); that is, a loss of salience in the mental representation and conscious perception of contralateral space and a reluctance to direct orienting and exploratory behavior to the region. Lesions in only one component of this network are associated with partial unilateral neglect, whilst those that encompass more than one component result in more profound deficits (Mesulam, 1981). The evidence also indicates that lesions located within the right hemisphere produce more impairment than lesions within the left hemisphere. This led Mesulam to propose that the right hemisphere was more effective in the execution of attentional tasks; it appeared to coordinate attentional deployment across the entire extrapersonal space (spans both hemispheres). In contrast, the left hemisphere primarily contains the neural apparatus influencing contralateral orientation in the right hemi space (Mesulam, 1981).

Mesulam believed that this model was sufficient to explain all aspects of spatial attention regardless of modality of input or output. However, the exact functions of this network remain partially unspecified, though visual attention studies have suggested that one possible role of such a control network is to generate biases that influence activity in lower-level visual areas (Corbetta, Kincade, Ollinger, McAvoy, & Shulman, 2000).

Posner's model

The model of attention proposed by Posner and his colleagues incorporates the same brain regions as Mesulam's, but these are organized into different functional networks.

Posner and Petersen (1990) discuss three hypotheses about attention. First, the attention system of the brain is separate from the data-processing system. Second, attention is carried out by a network of anatomical areas. Third, the areas involved in attention carry out different functions that can be specified in cognitive terms. The whole network serves to enhance information that occurs at a selected location. Posner and Petersen (1990) propose that the sources of attention form a specific system of anatomical areas, which can be further broken down into three interrelated networks (Table 11.1).

Alerting network
The alerting or sustained attention system is responsible for providing an adequate level of arousal. The network is comprised of the mesencephalic reticular formation

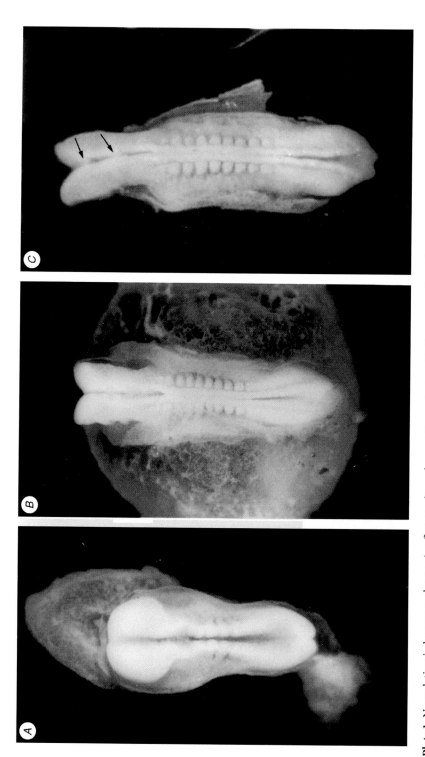

Plate 1 Neurulation in human embryos. *A*, a five-somite embryo at Carnegie stage 10; *B*, a ten-somite embryo at stage 10; *C*, another ten-somite embryo, in which the neural tube has closed at the future cervical level. Another initiation site of neural tube closure can be seen at the mesencephalic–rhombencephalic junction (lower arrow), whereas the medial walls of the mesencephalon appear to make contact with each other (upper arrow). *Note.* Reproduced with permission from "Neural Tube Closure in Human Initiates at Multiple Sites: Evidence from Human Embryos and Implications for the Pathogenesis of Neural Tube Defects," by T. Nakatsu, C. Uwabe, and K. Shiota, 2000, *Anatomica Embryologica (Berlin), 201,* 455–466.

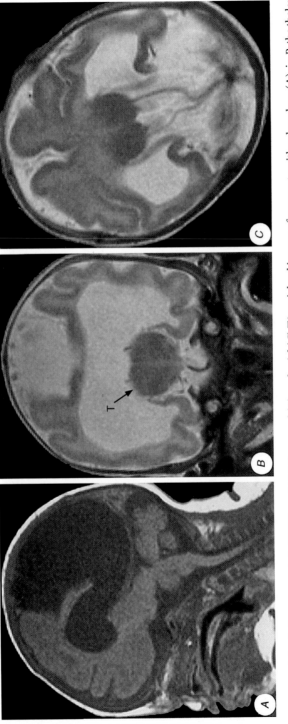

Plate 2 Semilobar holoprosencephaly (HPE): sagittal (*A*), coronal (*B*), and axial (*C*) T2-weighted images of a neonate with a dorsal sac (*A*); in *B*, the thalami (T) are separated below a single ventricle. *Note.* Images kindly provided by Ton van der Vliet, Nijmegen.

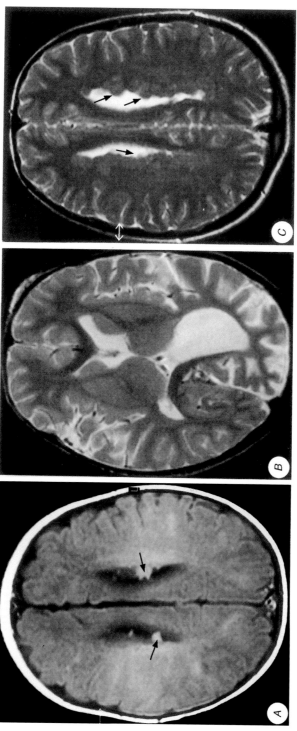

Plate 3 MRIs of some malformations of the cerebral cortex. *A*, tuberous sclerosis with subependymal tubers (arrows) in a 4-month-old girl; *B*, hemimegal-encephaly in a 5-year-old girl with neurofibromatosis with a unilaterally enlarged ventricle; *C*, X-linked bilateral periventricular nodular heterotopia in an 8-year-old girl presenting with seizures (arrows point at various nodules, lining the lateral ventricles);

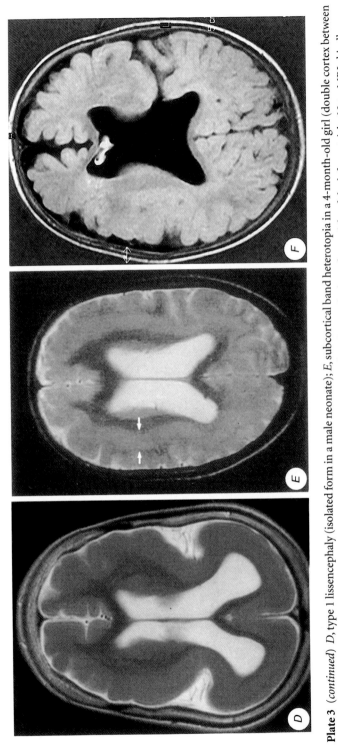

Plate 3 (*continued*) *D*, type 1 lissencephaly (isolated form in a male neonate); *E*, subcortical band heterotopia in a 4-month-old girl (double cortex between arrows); and *F*, schizencephaly in a 5-year-old girl: a complete cleft from the pial surface to the lateral ventricle of the left ventricle. *Note.* MRIs kindly provided by Berit Verbist, Leiden (*A, C, F*); Willy Renier, Nijmegen (*B, D*); and Henk Thijssen, Nijmegen (*E*).

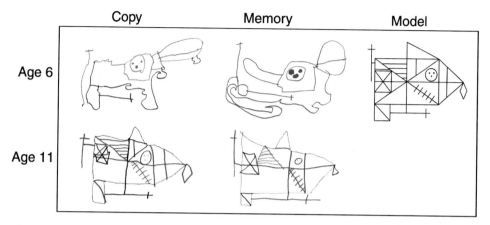

Plate 4 The Rey–Osterrieth figure: model and longitudinal data from a child with RPL on both the copy and memory conditions.

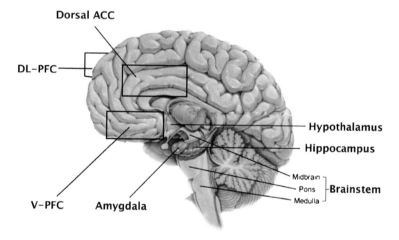

Plate 5 Frontal brain regions mediating emotion regulation processes. Our particular focus is on the V-PFC, which is the hub of ventral regulatory networks, and the ACC, which is the hub of dorsal control networks. The ACC is often co-activated with dorsolateral PFC and other frontal regions in effortful self-strategies.

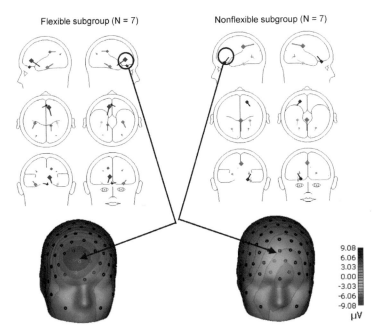

Plate 6 Antisocial children who showed the highest levels of behavioral flexibility in interactions with parents showed greater frontal scalp activations, associated with self-regulation, in a go/no-go task following a negative mood induction. Here we used patterns of scalp activation to model the cortical generators of the N2 for the seven most flexible and seven least flexible children in our sample. The model shows a source in the ACC region that is active only in the more flexible children.

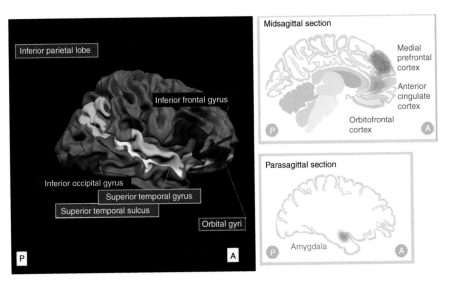

Plate 7 Brain regions involved in processing socially relevant stimuli. Medial and inferior frontal and superior temporal cortices, along with the amygdala, form a network of brain regions that implement computations relevant to social processes. *Note.* The image in the left panel was drawn using BrainTutor (www.brainvoyager.com/BrainTutor.html); the images in the right panel were adapted from "Autism: A Window onto the Development of the Social and the Analytic Brain," by S. Baron-Cohen and M. Belmonte, 2005, *Annual Review of Neuroscience, 28,* 109–126.

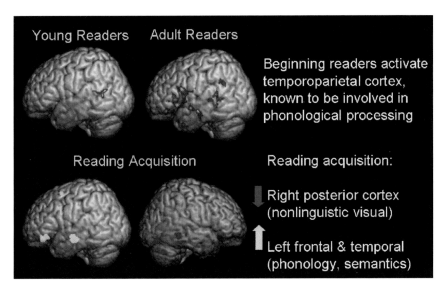

Plate 8 Brain areas involved in typical reading development measured with functional MRI. The images show the early reliance on left posterior superior temporal cortex in beginning readers and the expansive involvement of left parietal, temporal, and frontal cortices in adult readers (top). Correlations between brain activity during reading and reading ability (measured on standardized tests) demonstrate increased temporal and frontal involvement as reading develops (bottom). Right hemisphere activation declines as reading is acquired. *Note*. Reproduced from "Development of Neural Mechanisms for Reading," by P. E. Turkeltaub, L. Gareau, D. L. Flowers, T. A. Zeffiro, & G. F. Eden, 2003, *Nature Neuroscience*, 6(7), 767–73, courtesy of Guinevere Eden, Center for the Study of Learning, Georgetown University, Washington DC, USA.

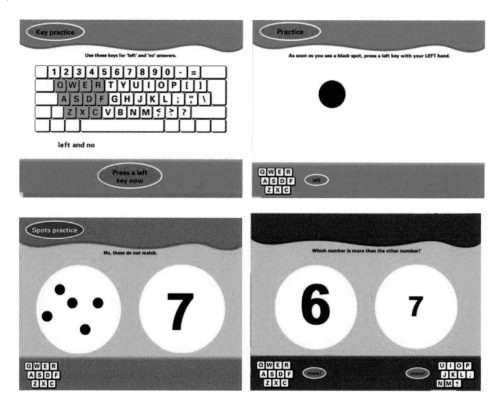

Plate 9 Capacity-test screen shots from the *Dyscalculia Screener* (Butterworth, 2003) showing keyboard response arrangement, simple reaction-time test where dot appears at random intervals and learner must press a key as quickly as possible, dot counting ("spots") where learner has to judge true or false, and number comparison where learner has to select left or right keys. *Note.* From *Dyscalculia Screener*, by B. Butterworth, 2003, London: NFER-Nelson.

Table 11.1 Posner and Petersen's Three Attentional Brain Networks and Suggested Functional Operations.

Neural system	Functional cognitive mechanism
Vigilance system alerting	Alerting
	Sustained attention
Posterior attention system	Reflexive orienting
	Early or perceptual selection
Anterior attention system	Strategic orienting
	Late or cognitive selection
	Conflict detection

Note. From "The Attention System of the Human Brain," by M. I. Posner & S. E. Petersen, 1990, *Annual Review of Neuroscience, 13*, 25–42.

and the amygdala, which are responsible for maintaining a state of alertness. The effect of different senses is weighted with respect to activating properties, and it is supposed that the system acts as a filter allowing the brain to concentrate only on those stimuli that are pertinent to the organism's activity at that particular time (select attention). The sensory stimuli, through multisynaptic chains of neurons, terminate in a group of nuclei located in the thalamus, which then relays the sensory impulses to the cerebral cortex. A descending pathway in the reticular system allows the cortical structures to "subordinate lower structures to the control of programs (axons) arising in the cortex and requiring modification and modulation of the state of waking for their performance" (Luria, 1974, p. 46).

Any disruption in the ascending or descending reticular activating system, or damage to the processes and structures that activate this functional unit, will result in an insufficient state of waking or cortical tone and subsequently will result in an organism that cannot sufficiently interact with its environment. Visual and acoustic stimuli activate the reticular activating system but bilateral damage or diffuse disruption to the reticular formation results in coma (Aston-Jones, Rajkowski, & Cohen, 1999). The patient is still capable of receiving sensory stimuli but there is no conscious processing of this information.

Posterior attention system

The neuroanatomy of the posterior or sensory orienting (facilitation of processing at specific locations in space), selective (filtering of information once a location is attended) attention network has been suggested by lesion studies (Posner, 1988; Sapir, Soroker, Berger, & Henik, 1999), evidence from neurophysiological research in animals, and from functional neuroimaging and electrophysiological techniques in man (Corbetta et al., 2000; Posner, Petersen, Fox, & Raichle, 1988). The results consistently implicate the superior parietal lobes, the midbrain, more specifically the lateral pulvinar nucleus, and the lateral posterior nucleus of the thalamus.

Sensory impulses travel from the reticular activating system through a distributed network that includes modalities within the posterior attentional network. The posterior attention system receives dense noradrenergic innervation from the locus coerulus (Bush et al., 1999). Noradrenalin functions to inhibit the spontaneous discharge of neurons, resulting in the enhancement of the signal-to-noise ratio of target cells, thus priming the posterior system to orient to and engage novel stimuli (Faraone & Biederman, 1998).

Anterior attention system

The anterior system is endowed with the responsibility for executive control of attention. This conceptualization is supported by neuroimaging studies that reveal increased activity in prefrontal and cingulate areas when there is an executive or decision-making component to attentional control, such as when attention must be divided across a number of different stimulus attributes (e.g., Corbetta, Miezin, Dobmeyer, Shulman, & Petersen, 1991).

The anterior network incorporates the frontal lobes (dorsolateral and ventromedial prefrontal cortex), anterior cingulated, and basal ganglia, and is activated when processing and/or responding requires cognitive control; for example, during tasks when conflict is present (requires suppression of a competing response choice or suppression of attention to a salient stimulus) and when the production of a nonhabitual (novel) response is necessary (Rothbart & Posner, 2001), that is, executive attention requires the mobilization of inhibitory attentional processes which are elements of "cognitive control" (Casey, 2001; Casey, Giedd, & Thomas, 2000).

Research suggests that the anterior attentional network exerts control by excitatory and inhibitory processes that are cooperatively engaged to enable the perceptual segregation of relevant and irrelevant information (Desimone, Wessinger, Thomas, & Schneider, 1990). Stuss and colleagues (Stuss, Shallice, Alexander, & Picton, 1995) postulate that this control is reflected in several types of attentional processes, including sustained attention, cognitive flexibility, inhibition, and divided attention. The purpose of this inhibitory pathway is to keep the system clamped down by inhibition to prevent stimulus-bound eye movements.

The priority network

Attention has been viewed as a mechanism for biasing the competitive interactions among mutually inhibitory sensory representations in cortex so that an attended object "wins" the competition and thereby comes to enter awareness. Attended objects thus produce more robust cortical activity than unattended objects. The attentional system is thought to have at least two subsystems that give rise to the attentional biasing signal that initiates the sensory enhancement of the selected stimulus. One is a bottom-up system involved in automatic and rapid shifts of "exogenous" (involuntary and stimulus driven, "attentional capture") attention to abrupt onsets that are sufficiently salient to divert attention from the current focus (Irwin, Colcombe, Kramer, & Hahn, 2000;

Jonides & Yantis, 1988; Remington, Johnson, & Yantis, 1992). The other is a top-down subsystem involved in volitional shifts of "endogenous" attention (goal directed and voluntary). The bottom-up subsystem is thought to involve circuitry in the superior colliculus (SC), and the top-down subsystem is thought to involve circuitry in the frontal lobe (Mesulam, 1981; Posner & Petersen, 1990). Both goal-directed and stimulus-driven mechanisms have ecological significance such that, under certain circumstances, attention in one or the other fashion has adaptive value. When processing demands are higher for the anterior task, the anterior attention network will modulate the action of the posterior attention network (Posner, Inhoff, Friedrich, & Cohen, 1987); the opposite occurs when detection of target location (i.e., the posterior task) has priority (Fuentes, 2004).

Normal Neuropsychological Development of Attention

The human attention system is immature at birth both anatomically and functionally, and goes through substantial changes, especially during the first few months of postnatal life. Development occurs in a hierarchical order. The critical period seems to vary in onset and duration between different brain regions. Subcortical regions mature earlier than cortical areas, and different functions emerge at different times and develop at different rates with an extended time period for executive attention underpinned by frontal lobes. The different developmental trajectories of the two attention systems potentially serve as the basis for marked individual difference in the rate and profile of attention development.

The differential time course of development of different cortical regions has been studied using positron emission tomography (PET; Chugani, Phelps, & Mazziotta, 1987). In infants under 5 weeks of age, glucose uptake is highest in sensorimotor cortex, thalamus, brain stem, and the cerebellar vermis, whereas by 3 months of age, there are considerable rises in activity in the parietal, temporal, and occipital cortices, basal ganglia, and cerebellar cortex. Maturational rises are not found in the frontal and dorsolateral occipital cortex until approximately 6–8 months of age, and the distribution of resting activity within and across brain regions does not approach adult levels until the end of the first year. As different subcortical and cortical modules are in differential states of maturation early in life, it seems likely that different properties of the attentional system will have primacy during these developmental transitions. Assuming that the same neural areas in adults are responsible for attentional control in infants, this maturational progression predicts attentional primacy that proceeds from the alerting network to the posterior network before ascendancy to the anterior network between 6–12 months.

Ruff and Rothbart (1996) hypothesized that the posterior and anterior attention systems could be developmentally conceptualized as (a) an early system in which attention is highly influenced by novelty of objects and events, and (b) a later one in which self-generated and goal-oriented schemes and tasks are a major incentive for sustained, focused attention. An important aspect of the transition should occur around 12 months as children begin to habituate more readily to novel objects and events, making novelty a less potent determinant of attention. Thus, the duration of attention based on the first system should decline from 12 months onward. However, the second, higher-level system of attention develops slowly with increasing cognitive sophistication and improved self-regulatory skills. As a result, attention may not be strongly governed by the second system until 6 or 7 years of age.

Colombo's model: development of alerting/arousal

This neural hierarchy is reflected in the conceptual framework for the development of visual attention in infancy advanced by Colombo (2001). This model, informed by recent advances in the research on visual attention in infancy, considers that the development of the alert state is the most fundamental attentional process in the neonate. The progression in the neonate from a sleep–wake cycle characterized by six distinct states, only two of which are in the alert phase, to being able to attain more extended periods of alertness (Berg & Berg, 1979) is seen as a prerequisite for other mental activity (Luria, 1974) including attention. Dahl (1996) describes sleep and arousal as the polar extremes of a single continuum where sleep is "a categorical diminution of awareness and responsiveness to the environment." In contrast, alerting is defined as achieving and maintaining a state of high sensitivity to incoming stimuli and is conceived as the initial component in the attention process. Colombo's (2001) ideas of the primacy of the alerting mechanism in the neonatal period concurs with the developmental imaging findings above that indicate greatest cortical activity within Posner and Petersen's (1990) alerting attentional system (the brain stem and thalamus) in infants under 5 weeks of age. This arousal/sustained alertness system permits attention and maintenance of an alert and vigilant state during periods of wakefulness in the neonate.

The reticular activating system's general arousal mechanism has an ascending influence on cortical areas that produces enhanced processing and arousal and a descending influence on heart rate through a parasympathetic outflow that decreases heart rate in infants and children, or decreases heart rate variability in adults. Research using neonates as subjects have used extended heart-rate slowing as an index of a state of general arousal in the brain. Investigators have found that stimuli that evoke heart-rate decreases in awake newborns have produced the reverse effects, heart-rate accelerations, during sleep (Clifton & Nelson, 1976; Pomerleau & Malcuit, 1981; Pomerleau-Malcuit & Clifton, 1973). Only in the awake state can newborns exhibit sustained decreases in heart rate (Graham, Anthony, & Zeigler, 1983). Further, stimulus complexity and intensity appear to interact in determining the direction of heart-rate responses in newborns. Simple auditory stimuli presented at 75–80 dB elicit heart-rate decelerations, while complex auditory stimuli, which require greater neural analysis, of equivalent intensity elicit heart-rate accelerations (Clarkson & Berg, 1983; Fox, 1979). The implication is that the neural substrate associated with complex analysis of the stimulus is insufficiently developed during this neonatal period. Also, heart-rate responses have been found to change with age. Infants are more likely to display heart-rate decelerations following stimulus exposure with increasing age across the first year of postnatal development which has been interpreted as reflecting the developing maturity of the attention system.

Development of the posterior attention system and orienting

In infancy, attention is typically parsed into two broad components: stimulus orienting and sustained attention (Cohen, 1973; Graham & Clifton, 1966; Ruff & Rothbart, 1996). Stimulus orienting occurs when individuals detect change or become aware of stimuli in their environment (also known as the orienting response, Sokolov, 1963, or "attention-getting," Cohen, 1973; Sokolov & Cacioppo, 1997). During this process, information on the importance, or the novelty, of the stimulus is encoded and a decision is made to maintain attention or disengage from the stimulus (Neisser, 1967; Sokolov, 1963).

The biophysiological data suggest that subcortical activity, including those areas that subserve the orienting or posterior attention circuitry, is high during early infancy. According to Posner's model, the act of shifting attention is achieved by a sequence of partially overlapping although separate operations. First, the target stimulus produces a general alerting state that interrupts ongoing activity; this is not spatially selective but works to potentiate other targets. The coordinates of the target stimulus are generated by the orienting system prior to the shift of attention, and orienting is achieved first by disengaging from the current task, next moving the "spotlight," and then engaging attention to the new location. Consequently, the allocation of visual attention or orienting is closely linked to the generation of saccadic eye movements (Corbetta et al., 1998; Kustov & Robinson, 1996) and the development of its neural substrates.

Correspondingly, the control of the eye has been used as a model system for studying the development of visual attention beyond the most basic arousal functioning. Over the first few weeks of life, most saccades generated by infants appear to be automatic, and are triggered in response to exogenous factors. The sudden appearance of the stimulus, which heightens its saliency, leads to the prepotency of the reflexive saccade. The short latency reflex saccade pathway is primarily subcortical and mature at birth (Schiller, 1985) and derives from a fast, reflexive pathway that initiates saccades to novel stimuli even when such saccades are inappropriate. These saccades are mediated by the parietal lobes which underlie the disengage function to facilitate engagement to the new coordinate or object.

Developmental changes consistent with neural maturational predictions in fixation and disengagement in infants have been examined in a number of studies. Visual behavior in 1–2-month-olds is characterized by a phenomenon called "obligatory attention" (Stechler & Latz, 1966) or "sticky fixation" (Hood, 1995); that is, during this period neonates have difficulty disengaging fixation from a central stimulus to orient to a new stimulus. Some have attributed this to the onset of competition between cortical and subcortical visuomotor pathways (Johnson, 1990). Other authors have compared obligatory attention with Balint's syndrome in adults (Hood, 1995). Patients with Balint's syndrome have acquired bilateral parietal cortex damage and experience similar difficulties in "disengaging" from one stimulus to another, indicating that immaturity of the parietal cortex in the infant has similar behavioral consequences. By 2–3 months of age, these markers of subcortical control are replaced by behavioral advances, such as acquiring the ability to disengage easily from one stimulus to orient to another, consistent with the maturation of regions of the parietal cortex and associated structures. Johnson and colleagues (Johnson, Dziurawiec, Ellis, & Morton, 1991) found that 4-month-olds showed a much greater propensity than 2- or 3-month-olds to disengage fixation from a central target in order to orient to a peripheral target. Similarly, the ability to make anticipatory saccades during a regular visual stimulus sequence has been demonstrated in 3-month-olds (Haith, Hazan, & Goldsmith, 1988) but not 2-month-olds (Canfield & Haith, 1991). Researchers have concluded that this pattern reflects the developmental improvements in disengagement resulting from brain maturation.

Johnson's model (1990, 1995), a synthesis of research on infant visual attention, oculomotor control, and neuroanatomical maturation, posits that developments in the layers of the primary visual cortex act as a limiting factor for visual attention controlled by neural systems. Influenced by Conel's (1939–1967) studies of cortical maturation in human infants, Johnson (1990) noted that cells in the early maturing layers 5 and 6 of primary visual cortex project only to subcortical structures, including the superior colliculus and the basal ganglia. Conel's research indicated that although cells in layers 2 and 3 (the major origin of associative and collosal fibers in the prefrontal cortex) eventually project to the prefrontal cortex, they would be insufficiently mature to contribute to information processing until infants are about 4–6 months of age. This led Johnson (1990; Johnson, Posner, & Rothbart, 1994) to conclude that frontally mediated oculomotor control, and therefore endogenous attention (subject directed), would not appear before this period, and attention control before the 4–6-month period must be under subcortical control. Subcortical control would simply allow visual stimuli to be detected, localized, and bought to the fovea but is controlled by exogenous (directed to salient characteristics of the environment) events and strongly governed by novelty.

Between 2 and 4 months of age, selectivity is influenced by the previous experience of the infant, and orienting is most associated with novelty. Around 9 months of age, there is evidence of a reduction in the orienting response to novel visual stimuli. It has been suggested that this decrease in orienting response may be important for the development of directed attention as it may help reduce distraction by irrelevant stimuli (Ruff & Rothbart, 1996).

Development of the anterior attention system: sustained attention, cognitive flexibility, and inhibitory control

Maturational changes in the neurophysiological organization of visual control between 3 and 6 months of age allow for voluntary shifting of attention (late selection) versus obligatory attention (Rothbart, Posner, & Boylan, 1990). Evidence from the work of

Rothbart and colleagues with infants indicates that 4-month-olds are capable of disengaging attention much more easily than younger infants, suggesting a developmental shift in attentional capacities at this age (Johnson, Posner, & Rothbart, 1991). This stage of development brings attention under volitional control and coincides with the maturation of the frontal lobes. The anterior system is responsible for saccades that are voluntary or planned. Correspondingly, developments at 4–6 months old, such as gaining the ability to inhibit reflexive saccades (Johnson, 1995) in order to sustain attention to a target stimulus and to make saccades in anticipation of a visual target being shown in a particular location (Csibra, Tucker, & Johnson, 2001; Gilmore & Johnson, 1995), have been associated with developments in the frontal cortex. Research evidence supports the proposition that these endogenous (internally directed) functions are mediated by frontal areas. Directed or voluntary attentional saccades are associated with the cingulate cortex in the medial frontal area (Posner, 1995; Posner & Petersen, 1990), and the maintenance of attention and inhibition of shifting have been linked with the frontal eye fields.

Whilst most theorists agree that there is a shift from predominantly subcortical to cortical control over saccades in early infancy, data collected in the 1990s have challenged the traditional views on the timing of the maturational status of the prefrontal cortex. Research utilizing intrastimulus shifting, associated with active and purposeful comparison of paired stimuli (therefore under endogenous control), reports that this ability is four times more likely to be observed in 4-month-old than 3-month-old infants (Colombo, Mitchell, Coldren, & Freeseman, 1991; Frick, Colombo, & Allen, 2000), whereas shifts in attention (cognitive flexibility) was more reliable in 7-month-olds than 4-month-olds across a one-week test/retest period suggestive of a critical period for endogenous control between 4 and 7 months.

Other researchers using different methodologies have reported endogenous attention abilities in much younger infants. Behavioral studies using the visual expectation paradigm (Canfield & Haith, 1991; Haith, Wentworth, & Canfield, 1993) and event-related potential data (Snyder, Batista, & Anderson, 2000; Wentworth & Haith, 1992) have reported evidence of predictive saccades (i.e., planned and voluntary interocular movements) in 3 to 3½-month-old infants. Also, sustained attention, which is dependent on the infant's ability to inhibit attentional shift (suppression of saccadic eye movement/antisaccade), has been demonstrated in infants as young as 8 weeks (Richards, 1989a). There is, however, considerable evidence that there are significant changes in the amount, depth, and frequency of sustained attention from this age compared to 3- and even 6-month-olds (Richards, 1989b; Richards & Casey, 1992). Richards found that maintained heart-rate decelerations, characteristic of sustained attention, occurred for longer durations in older infants than in younger infants. Furthermore, changes in sustained attention continue through to the latter half of the first year (Lansink, Mintz, & Richards, 2000; Ruff, Capozzoli, Saltarelli, & Dubiner, 1992), and well into the infant's second and third years (Ruff & Lawson, 1990). Taken together, these results suggest that the contributions of prefrontal cortex to endogenous attention control may emerge early in a rudimentary form but become increasingly differentiated and more efficient as the frontal lobes mature.

The period from 18 months through mid-adolescence is accompanied by an extended development of executive attention, but seems to undergo a particularly rapid development between 2 and 7 years of age. It has been traditionally believed that cognitive development during late childhood and adolescence is subserved primarily by the relatively late incorporation of the prefrontal cortex either by its intrinsic late structural maturation (Bourgeois, 1993; Sowell, Thompson, Holmes, Jernigan, & Toga, 1999) or by the maturation of other neocortical regions (Chugani, 1998; Rakic, 1995) that influence their functional integration with prefrontal cortex (Thatcher, Walker, & Giudice, 1987). Functional magnetic resonance imaging and positron emission tomography data demonstrate prolonged development in both the visual cortex and the frontal lobes which involve structural changes and maturation even in adulthood (Chugani et al., 1987; Sowell et al., 1999).

One aspect of executive attention is the ability to allocate resources in a way that is consistent with self-established goals and plans. The anterior circuitry enhances attention to the particular aspects of the environment that are consistent with these, and inhibits attention to other stimuli. Voluntary response suppression/inhibitory control and the ability to filter out distracters are both crucial for choosing a course of action based on a cognitive plan/goal-directed behavior over alternative task-irrelevant behaviors that hamper adaptive functioning (Bjorklund & Harnishfeger, 1995; Dempster, 1992). Voluntary response suppression has been found to develop throughout childhood (Fischer, Biscaldi, & Gezek, 1997; Luciana & Nelson, 1998; Munoz, Broughton, Goldring, & Armstrong, 1998) and adolescence (Ridderinkhof, Blanch, & Logan, 1999; Ridderinkhof, van der Molen, Band, & Bashore, 1997). The antisaccade task (Hallett, 1978) has been used successfully to characterize development of the ability to voluntarily suppress prepotent responses. The brain systems subserving performance on the antisaccade task have been well delineated in monkeys (Burman & Bruce, 1997) and adult humans (Doricchi et al., 1997; O'Driscoll et al., 1995). These areas include the frontal eye fields, supplementary eye fields, dorsolateral prefrontal cortex, posterior parietal cortex, anterior cingulate cortex, basal ganglia, thalamus, and superior colliculus.

Researchers (Casey, Castellanos, & Giedd, 1997; Casey, Trainor, et al., 1997; Luna et al., 2001) report both significant overlap and qualitative differences in the pattern and extent of brain activation across age groups, paralleling the enhanced voluntary control of behavior throughout adolescence. However, the presence of robust activation in several cortical regions in children indicates that these regions already participate in voluntary response suppression in childhood. Using other measures of response inhibition (go/no-go, stop tasks), researchers have also reported age-related increases in activation in frontal lobes, with children showing significantly greater intensity of activation than adults. Durston et al. (2002) showed that normally developing children aged 7 to 12 years activated regions in the frontal cortex more than adults and that activation was correlated with age. Schachar and Logan (1990) examined differences in both children and adults on another inhibition task (stop task). Findings indicated that normal inhibition is well developed early on, with children evidencing a similar rate of errors as adults

by the second grade. However, younger children had more variability in their responding rates and slower response times overall than did either older children or adults.

Theorists have concluded that this pattern is due to children being less efficient at
generating an inhibitory signal because of the immaturity of their frontal lobes.
Researchers suggest that although the capacity to suppress a response is present early
(all children could perform a correct antisaccade on at least one trial), as has been
seen in infancy (Johnson, 1995), efficiency (the ability to perform correct antisaccades
consistently) continues to improve into adolescence. Similarly, studies using dual task
paradigms indicate that top-down control over attention is still maturing during childhood and adolescence, even though the process of allocating attention is adult-like
quite early in childhood (Atkinson, Hood, Wattam-Bell, & Braddick, 1992; Karatekin,
Granholm, & Steinhaur, 2004). These data are consistent with the proposition that relatively automatic attentional processes develop earlier and complete their development
at a much younger age than anterior or cognitively demanding attentional processes,
commensurate with hypotheses that neural development proceeds along a posterior-
to-anterior gradient.

Attention Psychopathology Associated with Attention Deficit Hyperactivity Disorder

Attention deficit hyper⟨…⟩ity disorder is a neurodevelopmental condition characterized by persistent a⟨…⟩iate symptoms of attention, impulsivity, and hyperactivity. Behavior t⟨…⟩ulties with attention, difficulty sustaining attention
in tasks, bein⟨…⟩neous stimuli, and often having difficulty organizing tas⟨…⟩ia) are central components of attention deficit hy⟨…⟩r, the neurological basis of these behaviors
has n⟨…⟩onsensus exists regarding the behavioral
phenotyp⟨…⟩agnosis. The cognitive basis of this, however,
has resisted a⟨…⟩a single fundamental problem. Rather, there are
moderate associa⟨…⟩types of cognitive change.

Neuroanatomical correlates of ADHD

The neuroanatomical correlates of attention deficit hyperactivity disorder, the prefrontal
corticostriatopallidal pathways, approximately parallel Posner's anterior/executive
attention network. Specifically, volumetric reductions in total cerebral volume
(Castellanos, et al., 2001; Castellanos, Giedd, & Marsh, 1996; Castellanos, Lee, & Sharp,
2002; Filipek, Semrud-Clikeman, Steingrad, Kennedy, & Biederman, 1997), cerebellum
(Castellanos et al., 2001, 2002), prefrontal cortex (Castellanos et al., 1996; Filipek et al.,
1997; Hynd, Semrud-Clikeman, Lorys, Novey, & Eliopulos, 1990), striatal structures—
caudate and pallidum (Aylward et al., 1996, Castellanos et al., 1996, 2002), and the
splenium of the corpus callosum (Hynd, Lorys et al., 1991; Hynd, Semrud-Clikeman,

Lorys, Novey, & Eliopulos, 1991) have consistently implicated the right prefrontal corticostriatopallidal in the pathophysiology of ADHD (Barkley, 1998; Giedd, Blumenthal, Molloy, & Castellanos, 2001). Atypical structural volumes are assumed to relate to atypical function; however, the role of the deficits in brain morphology associated with ADHD remains unclear. Studies of cognitive function in ADHD have focused on different aspects of attentional processing in affected children.

Alerting in ADHD

There exists a plethora of methodologies for assessing alerting in children with ADHD, most of them relating to reaction time or physiological response in the first seconds after encountering a stimulus. Two different kinds of performance problem are consistent with an alerting deficit: slow and variable responses to fast tasks, and hasty, inaccurate responses to slow, careful tasks. Both kinds of response pattern have been described in children with ADHD (see Oosterlan, Logan, & Sergeant, 1998, for a meta-analysis; Sergeant & Scholten, 1985, for review; Leth-Steensen, Elbaz, & Douglas, 2000; Swanson et al., 2000, for randomized controlled trial). However, Huang-Pollock and Nigg's (2003) review of orienting studies did not find a dependable slow and variable response pattern even though most of the individual studies reported this effect. Further, EEG slow wave findings and early evoked response potential (ERP) are consistent with central nervous system (CNS) hypoarousal in a percentage of children with ADHD-C as well as ADHD-I (for a review of EEG, see Barry, Clarke, & Johnstone, 2003a; for ERP, Barry, Clarke, & Johnstone, 2003b).

Sustained attention in ADHD

The ability to maintain a state of alertness and wakefulness during "prolonged mental activity" (Weinberg & Harper, 1993) or sustained attention has been conceived as a central impairment in ADHD. Performance decrement (slower and more variable responses, more errors) over time is universal (Parasuraman, 1998); therefore, ADHD-related deficits in sustained attention should result in an excess decline over time versus controls, yielding a group-by-time interaction. However, the research does not support this notion. Whilst it is true that children with ADHD appear to lose interest in tasks quickly, they do not show a decline in accuracy (or in speed) over time on laboratory tasks (Sergeant, Oosterlaan, & van der Meere, 1999; Sergeant & Sholten, 1985; Sergeant & van der Meere, 1990). Typically, deficits in performance are evident from the very beginning of a task or response (Sergeant & van der Meere, 1990). This pattern suggests a problem in alerting or arousal, not sustained attention per se.

Posterior attention system in ADHD

In terms of Posner's attention network model, abnormalities of the neuroanatomical substrate of ADHD should implicate executive but not primary orienting and select attention which are under the control of the posterior attention system.

Orienting

Huang-Pollock and Nigg (2003) conducted a meta-analysis of the extant literature to determine the degree to which attention deficit hyperactivity disorder is associated with impaired attention. They reviewed 14 studies of visuospatial orienting in children with ADHD, as measured using Posner's (1980) Covert Orienting of Visuospatial Attention Task (COVAT). In the qualitative analysis reported by Huang-Pollock and colleagues (Huang-Pollock, Nigg, & Carr, 2005), group differences were found between children with ADHD and controls in each of the four endogenously cued studies (Carter, Krener, Chaderjian, Nortcott, & Wolfe, 1995; McDonald, Bennett, Chambers, & Castiello, 1999; Pearson, Yaffee, Loveland, & Norton, 1995; Tomporowski, Tinsley, & Hager, 1994) analyzed with some suggestion of right hemisphere anterior deficit but no replicated specific deficits were found. Huang-Pollock and her colleagues (2005) report that, despite intriguing single-study findings of weaknesses in the posterior disengage function in ADHD-C, meta-analytic effect sizes across studies have been small to nonexistent.

Select attention

Similarly, research does not support difficulties with perceptual select attention in ADHD (Berman et al., 1999; Sergeant & van der Meere, 1988). Nigg and colleagues (Nigg, Hinshaw, & Huang-Pollock, 2006) and Douglas (1999) have raised concerns regarding the validity of the conclusions that can be drawn from these investigations. The most significant reservation relates to the lack of systematic control of perceptual load; the omission is particularly critical given the contemporary theories of load and selection (Lavie, 1995). However, when perceptual load has been controlled more systematically using contemporary paradigms, no evidence of perceptual selection problems was evident in ADHD (with respect to combined type; Huang-Pollock et al., 2005).

There is a dearth of evidence concerning the ADHD predominantly inattentive subtype (ADHD-I) and attention mechanisms, despite the putative suggestion that underfocused selection in the posterior system might be implicated in the manifestation of this subtype. However, the limited data set on exogenous visual-spatial orienting in ADHD-I has not revealed impaired performance (Huang-Pollock & Nigg, 2003; Huang-Pollock et al., 2005), which would appear to negate dysfunctions within the posterior attention system. However, studies are so few that it might be premature at this stage to accept this conclusion.

Anterior attention system in ADHD

Neuropsychological research provides evidence of modest anterior attention dysfunction, although it is unclear whether these deficits are as robust or as large as might be needed for necessary and sufficient core deficit in ADHD.

Interference control ("late selection")

An inhibition deficit, including poor interference control (producing late selection), has been implicated as one of the core deficits in ADHD (Barkley, 1997a, 1997b).

Interference control is usually assessed using the Stroop Color–Word Interference Test and numerical Stroop test. An influential rationale for the increased Stroop effect in ADHD is a deficit in attentional modulation of the distributed parallel pathways processing, for example, word and color stimuli (Cohen, Dunbar, & McClelland, 1990; Peterson et al., 1999).

Qualitative (Nigg, 2001) and quantitative (Homack & Riccio, 2004; Van Mourik et al., 2005) reviews have concluded that Stroop interference is at most minimally impaired in ADHD-C in childhood. In the literature, studies employing the Stroop test have been considered as providing evidence for poor interference control in ADHD. However, most studies that report poor Stroop task performance have reported performance on the interference condition without controlling for performance on the color-naming condition. A recent meta-analysis shows that when noninterference aspects of the task are taken into account, children with ADHD do not demonstrate poor interference control on this task (Van Mourik et al., 2005). Van Mourik et al. (2005) concluded that the Stroop color test, in standard form, does not provide strong evidence for a deficit in interference control in ADHD. However, the Stroop color test may not be a valid measure of interference control in ADHD and alternative methodologies may be needed to test this aspect of the inhibitory deficit model in ADHD.

Set shifting

Classical measures of set shifting include trail making, Wisconsin Card Sorting Test (WCST), and Creature Counting (Test of Everyday Attention for Children). Computerized models include the switch task (Maudsley Attention and Response Suppression battery) and the Cambridge Neuropsychological Test Automated Battery (CANTAB). Empirical studies indicate evidence of rapid, controlled shifting deficits (Cepeda, Cepeda, & Kramer, 2000; Hollingsworth, McAuliffe, & Knowlton, 2001; Oosterlaan & Sergeant, 1998; Perchet, Revol, Fourneret, Mauguière, & Garcia-Larrea, 2001; Rubia & Smith, 2001; Schachar, Tannock, Marriott, & Logan, 1995), but studies to date are too few and varying in method to allow firm conclusions about the magnitude of the effect (Nigg et al., 2006).

These results suggest that the early maturing posterior attention network is intact in children with ADHD, whereas the later maturing executive or anterior attentional processes are implicated in its manifestation. However, its contribution is at best modest, representing perhaps secondary rather than primary etiological dysfunction. Meanwhile, arousal and related operations of the moderating noradrenergic vigilance network may well offer a promising candidate for a core within-child causal mechanism.

ADHD Case Study

Background

X is an 8-year-old, right-handed boy diagnosed with functional difficulties with attention, impulse control, and hyperactivity at home and at school. X's overactivity was first noticed when he was 2½ years old and had begun nursery school. At that time, there were no concerns about impulsivity or inattention. When he transferred to his reception class it was noted that he lacked motivation for academic activities. His inattentiveness and impulsive behaviors became more apparent in year 1, leading to his receiving an Individual Education Plan as these externalizing behaviors were interfering with his learning. Early infant milestones were unremarkable and there was no consanguinity and no other history of developmental disorders or learning disability within the family.

Hypothesis

Informed by the dominant neuropsychological models of ADHD, it was hypothesized that X would have:

1. Central impairment with behavioral inhibition.
2. Secondary impairment in working memory, planning, and attention.
3. Specific impairments in achievement tasks secondary to executive difficulties.

Behavioral observations

X's behavior during the assessment was certainly consistent with the primary behavioral characteristics of ADHD. Problems with attention were evident in his difficulty in sustaining attention to activities, careless errors, reluctance to engage in tasks that required sustained mental effort, and internal distractibility. He was restless and fidgety, especially in situations of low stimulation, and there was evidence of poor impulse control, especially anticipating failure before he had tried to solve a problem.

Measures

Together with tests of general cognitive ability (Wechsler Intelligence Scale for Children, fourth edition, UK [WISC IV^{uk}]) and academic attainment (Wechsler Individual Achievement Test II), the Test of Everyday Attention for Children (TEACH) and the Maudsley Attention and Response Suppression (MARS) battery were used to provide a profile of attentional capacity. The MARS battery is a computer-based research neuropsychological battery that provides measures of inhibitory and attentional control that are collectively considered to be components of executive functioning. An additional task looks at time perception.

Results

X's current general cognitive ability, as estimated by the WISC IV^{uk} Full Scale IQ, fell within the average range. He obtained FSIQ of 92 (confidence interval = 87–98). The indices were internally consistent, meaning that the Full Scale IQ provided a meaningful composite of his general intellectual ability.

Attention

X completed all nine subtests from the Test of Everyday Attention for Children (TEACH), which provides separate measures of selective (focused) attention, sustained attention, inhibition, and attentional control/switching. His scores ranged from the exceptionally low range to the high average range (from percentiles <0.2 to 79.8–87.7).

Selective attention: The Sky Search and Map Mission subtests measure selective attention. X's scores for the number of targets correctly identified and time-per-target were average for his age (percentile band 43.4–56.6).The time-per-target scaled score provides a measure of strategy efficiency indicating that X's use of a systematic left-right and top-down search strategy helped him find an above-average number of targets in a time that was appropriate for his age. When graphomotor speed is taken out of the equation to provide a purer measure of selective attention, X's attention score on Sky Search placed him in the high average range (percentile band 79.8–87.8). His performance on the analogous test of visual select attention Map Mission was average to high average (69.2–79.8) and commensurate with his performance on Sky Search.

Sustained attention: The Score, Score DT, Sky Search DT, and Code Transmission subtests measure sustained attention, which is the capacity to self-maintain an actively attentive stance to a task, goal, or one's own behavior despite there being little inherent stimulation for such continued processing. The Sky Search DT subtest is a dual task that involves the capacity to sustain attention on two tasks simultaneously and monitor one's allocation of attention to each task. Performance on this test is compared with performance on the earlier, simpler Sky Search subtest to determine the extent of any decrement in performance brought about by increasing the complexity of the task. X's dual task decrement score fell within the exceptionally low range (percentile band <0.2), indicating significantly greater decrement on this task when compared with others of his age. X found only 12 of the 20 visual targets and was successful in only one of the three auditory targets attempted, indicating difficulties on both components of the task.

X's score in the low ability range (percentile band 6.7–12.2) on the Score subtests indicates relative difficulties in actively maintaining attention to auditory stimuli/sound when this involves waiting for long periods before anything happens. He was similarly impaired on the Code Transmission subtest which, whilst deliberately monotonous, provides a consistently greater level of auditory stimulation than the Score subtest but is of considerably longer duration. His performance on the Score DT subtest, which incorporates a much more interesting auditory task to compete for the child's attention, was commensurate with his other sustained attention scores (percentile band 12.2–20.2). Task analysis indicated that X had a tendency to attend to the more interesting task. These results suggest that X's ability to maintain his attention to task will be greatly influenced by its ability to capture his attention.

Behavioral inhibition: The Walk/Don't Walk subtest provides a measure of sustained attention to one's own actions and intentions. To succeed on this task, one must actively resist an automatic, routine form of responding to facilitate a competing though less frequent response. X scored within the impaired range on this task (percentile band

<0.2), suggesting significant difficulty in inhibiting automatic responding compared with other young people of the same age. X found this activity particularly difficult and admitted to not putting any mental effort into the last five trials even though he agreed that it was a good task.

Attentional control/cognitive flexibility: The Creature Counting and Opposite Worlds subtests provide measures of X's ability to control his attention. X performed within the high average range for accuracy and was average on the timing element on the Creature Counting subtest, which was consistent with his performance within the average range on the Same World/Opposite World subtest.

Executive function

The Switch task of the MARS quantifies cognitive flexibility. When successive responses are governed by the same rule, X's response rate was indistinguishable from controls. However, his rate of responding was more variable than controls. His omission percentage indicates that this was not due to poor attention. His much larger switch effect, despite his percentage switch success, indicates significantly greater need for more processing time than controls to produce similar success.

The Stop task consists of two elements. Reaction time to go can be considered to be analogous to a behavioral activation system. X's responses are indistinguishable from controls, but his rate of responding, comparable to his performance on the Switch task, was more variable than controls. His much larger stop signal reaction time suggests difficulty with behavioral inhibition in that he needs longer than controls to successfully inhibit a preprogrammed/prepotent response.

Time perception

The timing task indicates that X has more problems with time perception than age-matched controls.

Conclusion

X is a right-handed, 8-year-old boy whose performance on assessment suggested specific impairment in some executive functions in the context of average intellectual functioning. X is developing along an age-appropriate trajectory with regards to his select attention and cognitive flexibility, but the cognitive control required for the latter was more variable than non-ADHD controls. He has relative difficulties with sustained attention but was most impaired on the tests of behavioral control and time perception.

Conclusion

Although we have focused on ADHD, it is worth noting that problems with inattention are implicated in a number of psychiatric and clinical conditions. Mirsky and Duncan

(2001) listed some 17 conditions associated with disordered attention, including schizophrenia, autism, fetal alcohol syndrome, and closed-head injury. To this list could be added other medical conditions and psychopathology: Tourette syndrome, anxiety disorders, depression, and obsessive compulsive disorder. Attention is a multidimensional process and not all such functions are equally affected across these various conditions. Thus, behavioral problems that appear as "inattention" may or may not be related to dysfunction in attentional mechanisms defined more formally. A range of causal mechanisms within the child could, in fact, be related to inattentive and otherwise dysregulated behavior (Nigg et al., 2006).

Furthermore, the cognitive changes in ADHD are by no means exhausted by the attentional changes considered here. Case-control studies have found alterations in accuracy of time perception (Smith, Taylor, Rogers, Newman, & Rubia, 2002), visuospatial memory (Rhodes, Coghill, & Mathews, 2005), delay discounting of reward (Sagvolden, Johansen, Aase, & Russell, 2005), delay aversion (Sonuga-Barke, 2005), and several tests of planning and foresight (Nigg et al., 2006). Each test considered singly shows a rather modest effect size (typically around 0.5 SD) for the discrimination. Combinations of tests, however, show much better discriminations, with specificity and sensitivity rising toward 80% (Solanto, Arnsten, & Castellanos, 2001). Individual children may show a large impairment on one test. Indeed, in clinical practice it is common to find that individual children show big discrepancies on tests such as speed of information processing or short-term memory. The implication is that cognitive testing does not (yet) make the diagnosis of ADHD, but may be very useful in delineating the strengths and weaknesses of an individual with a view to understanding the condition and advising educators.

The recent advances in the understanding of how attention develops have been striking and are likely to continue. The revolution of functional imaging is allowing the localization and study of progressively more subtle aspects. The mechanisms involved in the motivational and emotional control of attention will be particularly relevant for understanding psychopathology.

Several obstacles, however, still need to be overcome. At the level of basic understanding, the relatively weak temporal resolution of fMRI does not allow incisive analysis of how information is passed around different brain regions in the analysis of incoming information and the organization of response. Technical advances, such as those of electromagnetography, should contribute. The charting of normal developmental function has so far been done only for a limited number of functions and a limited range of ages. Further exploration is needed, especially of the functions most likely to be involved in pathology. Clinical application is severely limited by the lack of standardized tests that have been satisfactorily normed (TEACH and CANTAB are significant exceptions), but the field has advanced to the point where it should be possible to do this and to identify children on the basis of attentional change for behavioral investigation, rather than vice versa as at present in psychopathology. Standardization should advance to the point of understanding changes in people with intellectual disability, so that a concept of specific attentional disability could come to have operational meaning. The value of such analyses for remediation remains unknown: The training of attentional abilities is still a topic for the future. We can look forward to exciting and unpredictable changes.

References

Andersen, R. A. (1995). Encoding of intention and spatial location in the posterior parietal cortex. *Cerebral Cortex, 5*, 457–469.

Aston-Jones, G., Rajkowski. J., & Cohen, J. (1999). Role of locus coeruleus in attention and behavioral flexibility. *Biological Psychiatry, 46*, 1309–1320.

Atkinson, J., Hood, B. M., Wattam-Bell, J., & Braddick, O. J. (1992). Changes in infants' ability to switch attention in the first three months of life. *Perception, 21*, 643–653.

Aylward, E. H., Reiss, A. L., Reader, M. J., Singer, H. S., Brown, J. E., & Denckla, M. B. (1996). Basal ganglia volumes in children with attention deficit hyperactivity disorder. *Journal of Child Neurology, 11*, 112–115.

Barkley, R. A. (1997a). *ADHD and the nature of self-control*. New York: Guilford Press.

Barkley, R. A. (1997b). Behavioral inhibition, sustained attention, and executive function: Constructing a unified theory of ADHD. *Psychological Bulletin, 121*, 65–94.

Barkley, R. A. (1998). Attention-deficit hyperactivity disorder. *Scientific American, 279*, 66–71.

Barry, R. J., Clarke, A. R., & Johnstone, S. J. (2003a). A review of the electrophysiology in attention-deficit/hyperactivity disorder: I. Qualitative and quantitative electroencephalography. *Clinical Neurophysiology, 114*, 171–183.

Barry, R. J., Clarke, A. R., & Johnstone, S. J. (2003b). A review of the electrophysiology in attention-deficit/hyperactivity disorder: II. Event-related potentials. *Clinical Neurophysiology, 114*, 184–198.

Berg, W. K., & Berg, K. M. (1979). Psychophysiological development in infancy: State, sensory function, and attention. In J. D. Osofsky (Ed.), *Handbook of infant development* (pp. 283–243). New York: Wiley.

Berman, R. A., Colby, C. L., Genovese, C. R., Voyvodic, J. T., Luna, B., Thulborn, K. R., et al. (1999). Cortical networks subserving pursuit and saccadic eye movements in humans: An fMRI study. *Human Brain Mapping, 8*(4), 209–225.

Bjorklund, D. F., & Harnishfeger, K. K. (1995). The evolution of inhibition mechanisms and their role in human cognition and behavior. In F. N. Dempster & C. J. Brainerd (Eds.), *Interference and inhibition in cognition* (pp. 141–173). London: Academic Press.

Bourgeois, J. P. (1993). Synaptogenesis in the prefrontal cortex of the macaque. In B. de Boysson-Bardies (Ed.), *Developmental neurocognition: Speech and face processing in the first year of life* (pp. 31–39). Amsterdam: Kluwer.

Burman, D. D., & Bruce, C. J. (1997). Suppression of task-related saccades by electrical stimulation in the primate's frontal eye field. *Journal of Neurophysiology, 77*, 2252–2267.

Bush, G., Frazier, J. A., Rauch, S. L., Seidman, L. J., Whalen, P. J., & Jenike, M. A. (1999). Anterior cingulated cortex dysfunction in attention deficit hyperactivity disorder revealed by fMRI and the counting Stroop. *Biological Psychiatry, 45*, 1542–1552.

Canfield, R. L., & Haith, M. M. (1991). Young infants' visual expectations for symmetric and asymmetric stimulus sequences. *Developmental Psychology, 27*, 198–208.

Carter, C. S., Krener, P., Chaderjian, M., Nortcott, C., & Wolfe, V. (1995). Asymmetrical visual-spatial attention performance in ADHD: Evidence for right hemisphere deficit. *Biological Psychiatry, 37*, 789–797.

Casey, B. J. (2001). Disruption of inhibitory control in developmental disorders: A mechanistic model of implicated frontostriatal circuitry. In J. L. McClelland & R. S. Siegler (Eds.), *Mechanisms of cognitive development: Behavioral and neural perspectives* (Vol. 14, pp. 327–349). Mahwah, NJ: Erlbaum.

Casey, B. J., Castellanos, F. X., & Giedd, J. N. (1997). Implications of right frontostriatal circuitry in response inhibition and attention deficit/ hyperactivity disorder. *Journal of the American Academy of Child and Adolescent Psychiatry, 36,* 374–383.

Casey, B. J., Giedd, J. N., & Thomas, K. M. (2000). Structural and functional brain development and its relation to cognitive development. *Biological Psychiatry, 54,* 241–257.

Casey, B. J., Trainor, R. J., Orendi, J. L., Schubert, A. B., Nystrom, L. E., Giedd, J. N., et al. (1997). A developmental functional MRI study of prefrontal activation during performance of a go/ no-go task. *Journal of Cognitive Neuroscience, 9,* 835–847.

Castellanos, F. X., Giedd, J. N., Berquin, P. C., Walter, J. M., Sharp, W., & Tran, T. (2001). Quantitative brain magnetic resonance imaging in girls with attention-deficit/hyperactivity disorder. *Archives of General Psychiatry, 58,* 289–295.

Castellanos, F. X., Giedd, J. N., & Marsh, W. L. (1996). Quantitative brain magnetic resonance imaging in attention-deficit hyperactivity disorder. *Archives of General Psychiatry, 53,* 607–616.

Castellanos, F. X., Lee, P. P., & Sharp, W. (2002). Developmental trajectories of brain volume abnormalities in children and adolescents with attention-deficit/hyperactivity disorder. *Journal of the American Medical Association, 288,* 1740–1748.

Cepeda, N. J., Cepeda, M. L., & Kramer, A. F. (2000). Task switching and attention deficit hyperactivity disorder. *Journal of Abnormal Child Psychology, 28*(3), 213–226.

Chedru, F., Leblanc, M., & Lhermitte, F. (1973). Visual searching in normal and brain damaged subjects: Contribution to the study of unilateral inattention. *Cortex, 9,* 94–111.

Chugani, H. T. (1998). A critical period of brain development: Studies of cerebral glucose utilization with PET. *Preventive Medicine, 27,* 184–188.

Chugani, H. T., Phelps, M. E., & Mazziotta, J. C. (1987). Positron emission tomography study of human functional development. *Annals of Neurology, 22,* 487–497.

Clarkson, M. G., & Berg, W. K. (1983). Cardiac orienting and vowel discrimination in newborns: Crucial stimulus parameters of acoustic stimuli. *Child Development, 54,* 162–171.

Clifton, R. K., & Nelson, M. N. (1976). Developmental study of habituation in infants: The importance of paradigm response system state. In T. J. Tighe & R. N. Leaton (Eds.), *Habituation: Perspectives from child development, animal behavior and neurophysiology* (pp. 159–206). Hillsdale, NJ: Erlbaum.

Cohen, J. D., Dunbar, K., & McClelland, J. L. (1990). On the control of automatic processes: A parallel distributed processing account of the Stroop effect. *Psychological Review, 97,* 332–361.

Cohen, L. B. (1973). *Infant cognition: Predicting later intellectual functioning.* Newbury Park, CA: Sage.

Colby, C. L., & Goldberg, M. E. (1999). Space and attention in parietal cortex. *Annual Review of Neuroscience, 22,* 319–349.

Colombo, J. (2001). The development of visual attention in infancy. *Annual Review of Psychology, 52,* 337–367.

Colombo, J., Mitchell, D. W., Coldren, J. T., & Freeseman, L. J. (1991). Individual differences in infant attention: Are short lookers faster processors or feature processors? *Child Development, 62,* 1247–1257.

Conel, J. L. (1939–1967). *The post natal development of the human cerebral cortex* (vols. 1–8). Cambridge, MA: Harvard University Press.

Corbetta, M., Akbudak, E., Conturo, T. E., Snyder, A. Z., Ollinger, J. M., Drury, H. A., et al. (1998). A common network of functional areas for attention and eye movements. *Neuron, 21*, 761–773.

Corbetta, M., Kincade, J. M., Ollinger, J. M., McAvoy, M. P., & Shulman, G. L. (2000). Voluntary orienting is dissociated from target detection in human posterior parietal cortex. *Nature Neuroscience, 3*, 292–297.

Corbetta, M., Miezin, F. M., Dobmeyer, S., Shulman, G. L., & Petersen, S. E. (1991). Selective and divided attention during visual discrimination of shape, colour and speed: Functional anatomy by positron emission tomography. *Journal of Neuroscience, 11*, 2383–2402.

Corbetta, M., Miezin, F. M., Shulman, G. L., & Petersen, S. E. (1993). A PET study of visuospatial attention. *Journal of Neuroscience, 13*, 1202–1226.

Csibra, G. A., Tucker, L. A., & Johnson, M. H. (2001). Differential frontal cortex activation before anticipatory and reactive saccades in infants. *Infancy, 2*, 159–174.

Dahl, R. E. (1996). The regulation of sleep and arousal: Development and psychopathology. *Development and Psychopathology, 8*, 3–27.

Dempster, F. N. (1992). The rise and fall of the inhibitory mechanism: Toward a unified theory of cognitive development and aging. *Developmental Review, 12*, 45–75.

Desimone, R., Wessinger, M., Thomas, L., & Schneider, W. (1990). Attentional control of visual perception: Cortical and subcortical mechanisms. In *Cold Spring Harbor Symposium on Quantitative Biology* (Vol. 55, pp. 963–971). Cold Spring Harbor, NY: Cold Spring Harbor Laboratory Press.

Doricchi, F., Perani, D., Incoccia, C., Grassi, F., Cappa, S. F., Bettinardi, V., et al. (1997). Neural control of fast-regular saccades and antisaccades: An investigation using positron emission tomography. *Experimental Brain Research, 116*, 50–62.

Douglas, V. I. (1999). Cognitive control processes in ADHD. In H. C. Quay & A. E. Hogan (Eds.), *Handbook of disruptive behavior disorders* (pp. 105–138). New York: Kluwer Academic/Plenum.

Driver, J., Vuilleumier, P., Eimer, M., & Rees, G. (2001). Functional MRI and evoked potential correlates of conscious and unconscious vision in parietal extinction patients. *NeuroImage, 14*, 568–575.

Durston, S., Tyler, K. M., Yang, Y., Ulug, A. M., Zimmerman, R. D., & Casey, B. J. (2002). A neural basis for the development of inhibitory control. *Developmental Science, 5*, F9–F16.

Faraone, S., & Biederman, J. (1998). Neurobiology of attention deficit hyperactivity disorder. *Biological Psychiatry, 15*(10), 951–958.

Filipek, P. A., Semrud-Clikeman, M., Steingrad, R., Kennedy, D., & Biederman, J. (1997). Volumetric MRI analysis: Comparing subjects having attention-deficit hyperactivity disorder with normal controls. *Neurology, 48*(3), 589–601.

Fischer, B., Biscaldi, M., & Gezeck, S. (1997). On the development of voluntary and reflexive components in human saccade generation. *Brain Research, 754*, 285–297.

Fox, N. A. (1979). Psychophysiological correlates of emotional reactivity during the first years of life. *Developmental Psychology, 25*, 364–372.

Frick, J. E., Colombo, J., & Allen, J. S. R. (2000). The temporal sequence of global to local processing in 3-month-olds. *Infancy, 1*, 375–386.

Fuentes, L. J. (2004). Inhibitory processing in the attentional networks. In M. I. Posner (Ed.), *Cognitive neuroscience of attention* (pp. 45–55). New York: Guilford.

Fuentes, L. J., Vivas, A. B., & Humphreys, G. W. (1999). Inhibitory mechanisms of attention networks: Spatial and semantic inhibitory processes. *Journal of Experimental Psychology: Human Perception and Performance, 25*, 1114–1126.

Giedd, J. N., Blumenthal, J., Molloy, E., & Castellanos, F. X. (2001). Brain imaging of attention deficit/ hyperactivity disorder. *Annals of the New York Academy of Sciences, 931*, 33–34.

Gilmore, R. O., & Johnson, M. H. (1995). Working memory in infancy: Six-month-olds' performance on two versions of the oculomotor delayed response task. *Journal of Experimental Child Psychology, 59*, 397–418.

Gitelman, D. R., Nobre, A. C., Parrish, T. B., LeBar, K. S., Kim, Y. H., Meyer, J. R., et al. (1999). A large-scale distributed network for covert spatial attention: Further anatomical delineation based on stringent behavioral and cognitive controls. *Brain, 122*, 1093–1106.

Goldberg, M. E., & Bushnell, M. C. (1981). The role of the frontal eye fields in visually guided saccades. In A. F. Fuchs & W. Becker (Eds.), *Progress in oculomotor research* (pp. 49–52). Amsterdam: Elsevier.

Gottlieb, J. P., Kusunoki, M., & Goldberg, M. E. (1998). The representation of visual salience in monkey parietal cortex. *Nature, 391*, 481–484.

Graham, F. K., Anthony, B. J., & Zeigler, B. L. (1983). The orienting response and developmental processes. In D. Siddle (Ed.), *Orienting and habituation: Perspectives in human research* (pp. 371–430). Chichester: John Wiley.

Graham, F. K., & Clifton, R. K. (1966). Heart-rate changes as a component of the orienting response. *Psychological Bulletin, 65*, 305–320.

Haith, M. M., Hazan, C., & Goldsmith, G. S. (1988). Expectation and anticipation of dynamic visual events by 3.5 month-old babies. *Child Development, 59*, 467–479.

Haith, M. M., Wentworth, N., & Canfield, R. L. (1993). The formation of expectations in early infancy. *Advances in Infancy Research, 8*, 251–297.

Hallett, P. E. (1978). Primary and secondary saccades to goals defined by instructions. *Vision Research, 18*, 1279–1296.

Heilman, K. M., & van den Abell, T. (1980). Right hemisphere dominance for attention: The mechanism underlying hemispheric asymmetries of inattention (neglect). *Neurology, 30*, 327–330.

Heilman, K. M., Watson, R. T., Valenstein, E., & Damasio, A. R. (1983). Localization of lesions in neglect. In A. Kertesz (Ed.), *Localization in neuropsychology* (pp. 455–470). New York: Academic Press.

Heuer, H. (1996). Dual task performance. In O. Neuman & A. F. Sanders (Eds.), *Handbook of perception and action* (Vol. 3, pp. 113–153). London: Academic Press.

Hollingsworth, D. E., McAuliffe, S. P., & Knowlton, B. J. (2001). Temporal allocation of visual attention in adult attention deficit hyperactivity disorder. *Journal of Cognitive Neuroscience, 13*, 298–305.

Homack, S., & Riccio, C. A. (2004). A meta-analysis of the sensitivity and specificity of the Stroop color and word test with children. *Archives of Clinical Neuropsychology, 19*, 725–743.

Hood, B. (1995). Shifts of visual attention in the human infant: A neuroscientific approach. In C. Rover-Colloier & L. Lipsett (Eds.), *Advances in infancy research* (pp. 163–216). Norwood, NJ: Ablex.

Hopfinger, J. B., Buonocore, M. H., & Mangun, G. R. (2000). The neural mechanisms of top-down attentional control. *Nature Neuroscience, 3*, 284–291.

Huang-Pollock, C. L., & Nigg, J. T. (2003). Searching for the attention deficit in attention deficit hyperactivity disorder: The case of visuospatial orienting. *Clinical Psychology Review, 23*, 801–830.

Huang-Pollock, C. L., Nigg, J. T., & Carr, T. H. (2005). Deficient attention is hard to find: Applying the perceptual load of selective attention to attention deficit hyperactivity subtypes. *Journal of Child Psychology and Psychiatry, 46*, 1211–1218.

Hynd, G. W., Lorys, A. R., Semrud-Clikeman, M., Nieves, N., Huettner, M. I., & Lahey, B. B. (1991). Attention deficit disorder without hyperactivity: A distinct behavioral and neurocognitive syndrome. *Journal of Child Neurology, 6*, S37–S43.

Hynd, G. W., Semrud-Clikeman, M. S., Lorys, A. R., Novey, E. S., & Eliopulos, D. (1990). Brain morphology in developmental dyslexia and attention deficit/hyperactivity. *Archives of Neurology*, *47*, 919–926.

Hynd, G. W., Semrud-Clikeman, M., Lorys, A. R., Novey, E. S., & Eliopulos, D. (1991). Corpus callosum morphology in attention deficit-hyperactivity disorder: Morphometric analysis of MRI. *Journal of Learning Disorders*, *24*, 141–146.

Irwin, D. E., Colcombe, A. M., Kramer, A. F., & Hahn, S. (2000). Attentional and oculomotor capture by onset, luminance and color singletons. *Vision Research*, *40*, 1443–1458.

Johnson, M. H. (1990). Cortical maturation and the development of visual attention in early infancy. *Journal of Cognitive Neuroscience*, *2*, 81–95.

Johnson, M. H. (1995). The inhibition of automatic saccades in early infancy. *Developmental Psychobiology*, *28*, 281–291.

Johnson, M. H., Dziurawiec, S., Ellis, H. D., & Morton, J. (1991). Newborns' preferential tracking of face like stimuli and its subsequent decline. *Cognition*, *40*, 1–19.

Johnson, M. H., Posner M. I., & Rothbart, M. K. (1991). Components of visual orienting in early infancy: Contingency learning, anticipatory looking and disengaging. *Journal of Cognitive Neuroscience*, *3*, 335–344.

Johnson, M. H., Posner, M. I., & Rothbart, M. K. (1994). Facilitation of saccades toward a covertly attended location in early infancy. *Psychological Science*, *5*, 90–93.

Jonides, J., & Yantis, S. (1988). Uniqueness of abrupt visual onset in capturing attention. *Perception and Psychophysics*, *43*(4), 346–354.

Karatekin, C., Granholm, E., & Steinhaur, S. R. (2004). Development of attentional allocation in the dual task paradigm. *International Journal of Psychophysiology*, *15*, 7–21.

Kustov, A. A., & Robinson, D. L. (1996). Shared neural control of attentional shifts and eye movements. *Nature*, *384*, 74–77.

Lansink, J. M., Mintz, S., & Richards, J. E. (2000). The distribution of infant attention during object examination. *Developmental Science*, *3*, 163–170.

Lavie, N. (1995). Perceptual load as a necessary condition for selective attention. *Journal of Experimental Psychology: Human Perception and Performance*, *21*, 451–468.

Leth-Steensen, C., Elbaz, Z. K., & Douglas, V. I. (2000). Mean response times, variability and skew in responding of ADHD children: A response time distributional approach. *Acta Psychologica*, *104*, 167–190.

Lu, Z. L., & Dosher, B. A. (1998). External noise distinguishes attention mechanisms. *Vision Research*, *38*(9), 1183–1198.

Luciana, M., & Nelson, C. A. (1998). The functional emergence of prefrontally-guided working memory systems in four- to eight-year-old children. *Neuropsychologia*, *36*, 273–293.

Luna, B., Thulborn, K. R., Munoz, D. P., Merriam, E. P., Garver, K. E., Minshew, N. J., et al. (2001). Maturation of widely distributed brain function subserves cognitive development. *NeuroImage*, *13*(5), 786–793.

Luria, A. R. (1974). *The working brain*. Harmondsworth: Penguin.

McDonald, S., Bennett, K. M. B., Chambers, H., & Castiello, U. (1999). Covert orienting and focusing of attention in children with attention deficit hyperactivity disorder. *Neuropsychologia*, *37*, 345–356.

Mesulam, M. M. (1981). A cortical network for directed attention and unilateral neglect. *Annals of Neurology*, *10*, 309–325.

Mesulam, M. M. (1985). *Principles of behavioral neurology* (pp. 150–162). Philadelphia, PA: F. A. Davis.

Mesulam, M. M. (1990). Large-scale neurocognitive networks and distributed processing for attention, language, and memory. *Annals of Neurology, 28*, 597–613.

Mesulam, M. M. (1999). Spatial attention and neglect: Parietal, frontal, and cingulate contributions to the mental representation and attentional targeting of salient extrapersonal events. *Philosophical Transactions of the Royal Society Series B, 354*, 1325–1346.

Mesulam, M. M. (2000). Behavioral neuroanatomy: Large-scale networks, association cortex, frontal syndromes, the limbic system and hemispheric specialization. In M. M. Mesulam (Ed.), *Principles of behavioral and cognitive neurology* (pp. 1–120). New York: Oxford University Press.

Mesulam, M. M., Nobre, A. C., Kim, Y.-K., & Parrish, T. (2001). Heterogeneity of cingulate contributions to spatial attention. *NeuroImage, 13*, 1065–1072.

Mirsky, A. F., & Duncan, C. C. (2001). A nosology of disorders of attention. *Annals of the New York Academy of Sciences, 931*, 17–32.

Munoz, D. P., Broughton, J. R., Goldring, J. E., & Armstrong, I. T. (1998). Age related performance of human subjects on saccadic eye movement tasks. *Experimental Brain Research, 121*, 391–400.

Neisser, U. (1967). *Cognitive psychology*. New York: Appleton–Century–Crofts.

Nigg, J. T. (2001). Is ADHD a disinhibitory disorder? *Psychological Bulletin, 127*, 571–598.

Nigg, J. T., Hinshaw, S. P., & Huang-Pollock, C. (2006). Disorders of attention and impulse control regulation. In D. Vicetti & D. Cohen (Eds.), *Developmental psychology* (2nd ed., pp. 358–403). New York: Wiley.

Norman, D. A., & Bobrow, D. G. (1975). On data limited and resource limited processes. *Cognitive Psychology, 7*, 44–64.

O'Driscoll, G. A., Alpert, N. M., Matthysse, S. W., Levy, D. L., Rauch, S. L., & Holzman, P. S. (1995). Functional neuroanatomy of antisaccade eye movements investigated with positron emission tomography. *Proceedings of the National Academy of Sciences, USA, 92*, 925–929.

Oosterlaan, J., Logan, G. D., & Sergeant, J. A. (1998). Response inhibition in AD/HD, CD, comorbid AD/HD+CD, anxious, and control children: A meta-analysis of studies with the stop task. *Journal of Child Psychology and Psychiatry, 39*, 411–425.

Oosterlaan, J., & Sergeant, J. A. (1998). Response inhibition and response re-engagement in attention deficit hyperactivity disorder, disruptive, anxious and normal children. *Behavioural Brain Research, 94*, 533–543.

Parasuraman, R. (1998). *The attentive brain*. Cambridge, MA: MIT Press.

Pardo, J. V., Pardo, P. J., Janer, K. W., & Raichle, M. E. (1990). The anterior cingulate cortex mediates processing selection in the Stroop attentional conflict paradigm. *Proceedings of the National Academy of Sciences, USA, 87*, 256–259.

Pearson, D. A., Yaffee, L. S., Loveland, K. A., & Norton, A. (1995). Covert attention in children with ADHD: Evidence for developmental immaturity. *Developmental and Psychological Pathology, 7*, 351–364.

Perchet, C., Revol, O., Fourneret, P., Mauguière, F., & Garcia-Larrea, L. (2001). Attention shifts and anticipatory mechanisms in hyperactive children: An ERP study using the Posner paradigm. *Biological Psychiatry, 50*, 44–57.

Peterson, B. S., Skudlarski, P., Gatenby, J. C., Zhang, H., Anderson, A. W., & Gore, J. C. (1999). An fMRI study of Stroop word-color interference: Evidence for cingulate subregions subserving multiple distributed attentional systems—surface features, flat maps, and cytoarchitecture. *Biological Psychiatry, 45*, 1237–1258.

Pomerleau, A., & Malcuit, G. (1981). State effects on concomitant cardiac and behavioural responses to a rocking stimulus in human newborns. *Infant Behaviour and Development, 4*, 163–174.

Pomerleau-Malcuit, A., & Clifton, R. K. (1973). Neonatal heart rate response to tactile, auditory and vestibular stimulation in different states. *Child Development, 44,* 485–496.

Posner, M. I. (1980). Orienting attention. *Quarterly Journal of Experimental Psychology, 32,* 3–25.

Posner, M. I. (1988). Structures and functions of selective attention. In T. Boll & B. Bryant (Eds.), *Master lectures in clinical neuropsychology and brain function: Research, measurement, and practice* (pp. 171–202). Washington, DC: American Psychological Association.

Posner, M. I. (1995). Attention in cognitive neuroscience: An overview. In M. S. Gazzaniga (Ed.), *Cognitive neurosciences* (pp. 615–624). Cambridge, MA: MIT Press.

Posner, M. I., & Dehaene, S. (1994). Attentional networks. *Trends in Neuroscience, 17,* 75–79.

Posner, M. I., Inhoff, A. W., Friedrich, F. J., & Cohen, A. (1987). Isolating attentional systems: A cognitive anatomical analysis. *Psychobiology, 15,* 107–121.

Posner, M. I., & Petersen, S. E. (1990). The attention system of the human brain. *Annual Review of Neuroscience, 13,* 25–42.

Posner, M. I., Petersen, S. E., Fox, P. T., & Raichle, M. E. (1988). Localization of cognitive operations in the human brain. *Science, 240,* 1627–1631.

Posner, M. I., Walker, J. A., Friedrich, F. J., & Rafal, R. D. (1984). Effects of parietal lobe injury on covert orienting of visual attention. *Journal of Neuroscience, 4,* 1863–1874.

Rakic, P. (1995). The development of the frontal lobe: A view from the rear of the brain. In H. H. Jasper, S. Riggio, & P. S. Goldman-Rakic (Eds.), *Epilepsy and the functional anatomy of the frontal lobe* (pp. 1–8). New York: Raven Press.

Remington, R. W., Johnson, J. C., & Yantis, S. (1992). Involuntary attentional capture by abrupt onsets. *Perception and Physics, 51,* 279–290.

Rhodes, S. M., Coghill, D. R., & Mathews, K. (2005). Neuropsychological functioning in stimulant-naïve boys with hyperkinetic disorder. *Psychological Medicine, 35,* 1109–1120.

Richards, J. E. (1989a). Development and stability in visual sustained attention in 14–20- and 26-week-old infants. *Psychophysiology, 26,* 422–430.

Richards, J. E. (1989b). Sustained attention in 8-week-old infants. *Infant Behaviour and Development, 12,* 425–536.

Richards, J. E. (2003). Development of attentional systems. In M. De Hann & M. H. Johnson (Eds.), *The cognitive neurosciences of development* (pp. 73–98). Hove, East Sussex: Psychology Press.

Richards, J. E., & Casey, B. J. (1992). Development of sustained visual attention in the human infant. In B. A. Campbell, H. Hayne, & R. Richardson (Eds.), *Attention and information processing in infants* (pp. 30–60). Hillsdale, NJ: Erlbaum.

Ridderinkhof, K. R., Blanch, B. P. H., & Logan, G. D. (1999). A study of adaptive behavior: Effects of age and irrelevant information on the ability to inhibit one's action. *Acta Psychologica, 101,* 315–337.

Ridderinkhof, K. R., van der Molen, M. W., Band, G. P. H., & Bashore, T. R. (1997). Sources of interference from irrelevant information: A developmental study. *Journal of Experimental Child Psychology, 65,* 315–341.

Robinson, D. L., & Kertzman, C. (1995). Covert orienting of attention in macques: Contributions of the superior colliculus. *Journal of Neurophysiology, 74,* 713–721.

Rothbart, M. K., & Posner, M. I. (2001). Mechanism and variation in the development of attentional networks. In C. A. Nelson & M. Luciana (Eds.), *Handbook of developmental cognitive neuroscience* (pp. 353–363). Cambridge, MA: MIT Press.

Rothbart, M. K., Posner, M. I., & Boylan, A. (1990). Regulatory mechanisms in infant development. In J. Enns (Ed.), *The development of attention: Research and theory* (pp. 139–160). Amsterdam: Elsevier.

Rubia, K., & Smith, A. (2001). ADHD: Current findings and treatment. *Current Opinion of Psychiatry*, *4*, 309–316.

Ruff, H. A., Capozzoli, M., Saltarelli, L. M., & Dubiner, K. (1992). The differentiation of activity in infants' exploration of objects. *Developmental Psychology*, *28*, 851–861.

Ruff, H. A., & Lawson, K. R. (1990). Development of sustained, focused attention in young children during free play. *Developmental Psychology*, *26*, 85–93.

Ruff, H. A., & Rothbart, M. K. (1996). *Attention in early development: Themes and variations*. New York: Oxford University Press.

Sagvolden, T., Johansen, E. B., Aase, H., & Russell, V. A. (2005). A dynamic developmental theory of attention deficit hyperactivity disorder (ADHD) predominantly hyperactive/impulsive and combined subtypes. *Behavior Brain Science*, *28*, 397–419.

Sapir, A., Soroker, N., Berger, A., & Henik, A. (1999). Inhibition of return in spatial attention: Direct evidence for collicular generation. *Nature Neuroscience*, *2*, 1053–1054.

Schachar, R. G., & Logan, R. (1990). Impulsivity and inhibitory control in normal development and childhood psychopathology. *Developmental Psychology*, *26*, 710–720.

Schachar, R. G., Tannock, R., Marriott, H., & Logan, R. (1995). Deficient inhibitory control in ADHD. *Journal of Abnormal Child Psychology*, *23*, 411–437.

Schiller, P. H. (1985). A model for the generation of visually guided saccadic eye movements. In D. Rose & V. G. Dobson (Eds.), *Model of the visual cortex* (pp. 62–70). New York: John Wiley.

Sergeant, J. A., Oosterlaan, J., & van der Meere, J. (1999). Information processing and energetic factors in attention-deficit/hyperactivity disorder. In H. C. Quay & A. E. Hogan (Eds.), *Handbook of disruptive behavior disorders* (pp. 75–104). New York: Kluwer Academic/Plenum.

Sergeant, J. A., & Scholten, C. (1985). On data limitations in hyperactivity. *Journal of Child Psychology and Psychiatry*, *26*, 111–124.

Sergeant, J. A., & van der Meere, J. (1988). What happens after a hyperactive child commits an error? *Psychology Research*, *24*, 157–164.

Sergeant, J. A., & van der Meere, J. (1990). Additive factor method applied to psychopathology with special reference to childhood hyperactivity. *Acta Psychologica*, *74*, 277–295.

Smith, A., Taylor, E., Rogers, J. W., Newman, S., & Rubia, K. (2002). Evidence for a pure time perception deficit in children with ADHD. *Journal of Child Psychology and Psychiatry*, *43*, 529–542.

Snyder, L. H., Batista, A. P., & Andersen, R. A. (1998). Change in motor plan, without a change in the spatial locus of attention, modulates activity in posterior parietal cortex. *Journal of Neurophysiology*, *79*, 2814–2819.

Snyder, L. H., Batista, A. P., & Anderson, R. A. (2000). Intention-related activity in the posterior parietal cortex: A review. *Vision Research*, *40*, 1433–1441.

Sokolov, N. E. (1963). *Perception and conditioned reflex*. Oxford: Pergamon.

Sokolov, N. E., & Cacioppo, T. (1997). Orienting and defense reflexes: Vector coding and cardiac response. In P. J. Lang & M. Balaban (Eds.), *Attention and orienting: Sensory and motivational processes* (pp. 23–40). Mahwah, NJ: Lawrence Erlbaum.

Solanto, M. V., Arnsten, A. F. T., & Castellanos, F. X. (2001). The neuroscience of stimulant drug action in ADHD. In M. V. Solanto, A. F. T. Arnsten, & F. X. Castellanos (Eds.), *Stimulant drugs and ADHD: Basic and clinical neuroscience* (pp. 355–379). New York: Oxford University Press.

Sonuga-Barke, E. J. (2005). Causal models of attention deficit/hyperactivity disorder: From common simple deficits to multiple developmental pathways. *Biological Psychiatry*, *57*, 1231–1238.

Sowell, E. R., Thompson, P. M., Holmes, C. J., Jernigan, T. L., & Toga, A. W. (1999). In vivo evidence for post-adolescent brain maturation in frontal and striatal regions. *Nature Neuroscience*, *2*, 859–861.

Stechler, G., & Latz, E. (1966). Some observations on attention and arousal in the human infant. *Journal of the American Academy of Child Psychiatry, 5,* 517–525.

Stuss, D. T., Shallice, T., Alexander, M. P., & Picton, T. W. (1995). A multidisciplinary approach to anterior attentional functions. *Annals of the New York Academy of Sciences, 769,* 191–211.

Swanson, J., Oosterlaan, J., Murias, M., Moyzis, R., Schuck, S., Mann, M., et al. (2000). ADHD children with 7-repeat allele of the DRD4 gene have extreme behavior but normal performance on critical neuropsychological tests of attention. *Proceedings of the National Academy of Sciences, USA, 97,* 4754–4759.

Taylor, S. F., Huang, G., Tandon, R., & Koeppe, R. A. (1998). Letter naming among distracters activates anterior cingulate cortex in a selective attention task. *NeuroImage, 7,* S94.

Thatcher, R. W., Walker, R. A., & Giudice, S. (1987). Human cerebral hemispheres develop at different rates and ages. *Science, 236,* 1110–1113.

Tomporowski, P. D., Tinsley, V., & Hager, L. D. (1994). Visuospatial attentional shifts and choice responses of adults and attention deficit hyperactivity disorder and non-attention deficit hyperactivity disorder children. *Perceptual and Motor Skills, 79,* 1479–1490.

Treisman, A. (1988). Features and objects: The Fourteenth Bartlett Memorial Lecture. *Quarterly Journal of Experimental Psychology, 40,* 201–237.

Van Mourik, R., Oosterlaan, J., & Sergeant, J. A. (2005). The Stroop revisited: A meta-analysis of interference control in AD/HD. *Journal of Child Psychology and Psychiatry, 46,* 150–165.

Watson, R. T., Heilman, K. M., Cauthen, J. C., & King, F. A. (1973). Neglect after cingulectomy. *Neurology, 23,* 1003–1007.

Webster, M. J., & Ungerleider L. G. (1998). Neuroanatomy of visual attention. In R. Parasuraman (Ed.), *The attentive brain* (pp. 19–34). Cambridge, MA: MIT Press.

Weinberg, W. A., & Harper, C. R. (1993). Vigilance and its disorders. *Neurology Clinics, 11,* 59–78.

Wentworth, N., & Haith, M. M. (1992). Event specific expectation of 2- and 3-month-old infants. *Developmental Psychology, 28,* 842–850.

Yantis, S., & Jonides, J. (1984). Abrupt visual onsets and selective attention: Evidence from visual search. *Journal of Experimental Psychology: Human Perception and Performance, 10,* 601–621.

12

Executive Functions and Development

Claire Hughes and Andrew Graham

Each New Year finds many of us making mistakes when writing the date on letters or checks. This kind of "capture error," first described in William James's (1890) famous example of going upstairs to change and discovering himself in bed, supports cognitive psychologists' classical distinction between actions that require conscious effortful control and those that are executed automatically (e.g., Atkinson & Shiffrin, 1968; Schneider & Shiffrin, 1977). This distinction is not simply a contrast between simple and complex actions, as well-learned complex actions can be automatic (e.g., driving a car); nor between externally and internally driven actions, as the latter can be based on automatic processes (e.g., memory recall). Instead, the distinction between controlled and automatic actions hinges upon three key features: (a) the execution of *novel* versus familiar action sequences; (b) making a choice between *alternative* responses versus executing a single action sequence; and (c) the execution of acts that do versus those that do not require access to *consciousness*.

The term "executive function" (EF) therefore refers to a complex cognitive construct encompassing the whole set of processes underlying these controlled, goal-directed responses to novel or difficult situations. More specifically, EF is held to be necessary in situations that involve: (a) planning and decision-making; (b) error correction or troubleshooting; (c) initiation of novel sequences of actions; (d) danger or technical difficulty; or (e) the need to overcome a strong habitual response (Norman & Shallice, 1980, 1986; Shallice & Burgess, 1991). This view of EF as responsible for programming, monitoring, and regulating behavior has been expressed computationally in Shallice and Burgess's (1991) model of the supervisory attentional system (SAS) illustrated in Figure 12.1.

Alongside its functional definition described above, the term EF is often defined in structural terms: Clinical researchers typically view EF as essentially synonymous with the functioning of the prefrontal cortex (PFC), the regions of which are shown in Figure 12.2. From this clinical viewpoint, EF is most conspicuous by its absence

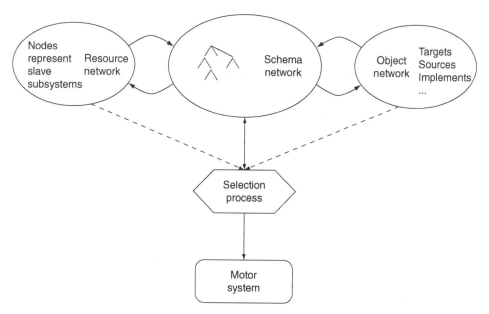

Figure 12.1 The Cooper and Shallice (2000) implementation of the "supervisory attentional system" model. At the center of the model is a hierarchically structured network of interactive action schemas that compete for activation. Schemas receive excitation and inhibition from various sources, including higher level schemas, the representation of the environment, and competing schemas. The model has been applied to a range of tasks, including preparing coffee and packing a lunchbox. *Note.* Reproduced with permission from "Contention Scheduling and the Control of Routine Activities," by R. Cooper and T. Shallice, 2000, *Cognitive Neuropsychology, 17,* 297–338.

in individuals with prefrontal lesions who, together with behavioral and personality changes, demonstrate impairments in functions such as planning or abstract thinking. The cognitive importance of the PFC first became apparent through studies of World War I veterans, which demonstrated that soldiers with frontal lobe injuries were unimpaired on routine tasks, but had difficulty mastering new tasks or grasping the whole of a complicated task (Goldstein, 1936, 1944). This led to the view that EF was important for abstract or high level thought, abilities only manifested in adulthood. Support for this view of EF as emerging late in development came from neuroanatomical work suggesting that the PFC only becomes functionally mature around adolescence (Golden, 1981). In addition, primate studies and early research on head injuries suggested that the consequences of juvenile lesions to the PFC did not become apparent until adulthood (the so-called "Kennard effect"). Together, the above factors led to a chronic neglect of EF in childhood for much of the past century.

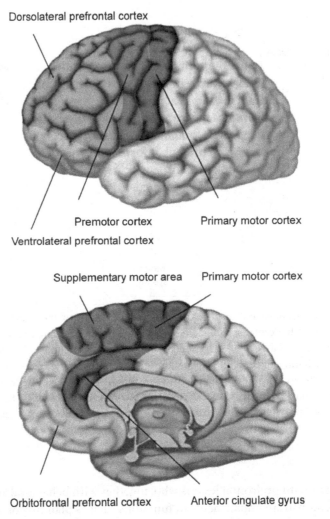

Figure 12.2 Surface and medial views of the brain, showing key regions of the prefrontal cortex.

Measurement: Problems and Solutions

In contrast with the consensus described above regarding the theoretical definition of EF, an operational definition of EF is much harder to establish. Despite its long history, EF research therefore continues to be riddled with practical challenges. The first obstacle to obtaining accurate, valid, and reliable measurements of EF is that the contrast between automatic and controlled actions is not absolute. Rather, these two types of actions are at the opposite ends of a continuum. Thus, the processes underlying an individual's performance on a novel task will shift gradually over time from controlled to automatic. In addition, small changes in task demands may lead to a collapse of automatic performance and a return to controlled performance. As a result, it is often difficult to distinguish "executive" from "nonexecutive" tasks. Indeed, re-administration of any particular test will never tap EF to the same extent as on the first presentation, leading to poor test/re-test reliability. In children, however, the shift from controlled to automatic processes is likely to be more extended, leading to greater stability in both underlying processes and overall performance. In other words, compared with adults, children may perceive (and process) a new task as novel for longer, so that both the validity of identifying a task as an EF test and the reliability of individual differences in task performance are potentially better in studies of children than in studies of adults.

A second obstacle stems from the complexity of standard EF tasks. This complexity means that measures of task performance often represent the pooled outcome of several distinct underlying processes. So, for example, an EF task may be presented as a "planning" task, but also involve other EF processes. Such complex tasks are also susceptible to problems of task impurity, in that their execution may trigger additional nonexecutive processes unrelated to the task at hand. Indeed, since everyday terms such as "planning" are poorly specified, there is no guarantee that the main psychological process actually underlying a "planning task" has any relationship to our folk notion of planning. Furthermore, for EF tasks that involve the simultaneous coordination of a variety of different processes (Kimberg & Farah, 1993), any attempt to isolate an index of a single functional process by applying classical experimental techniques to control task demands is unlikely to be successful.

However, in order to be developmentally appropriate for use with children, standard EF tasks need considerable simplification, and so problems of task impurity are likely to be reduced. Also, given children's relatively limited processing capacities, it is not necessary to tax several processes simultaneously in order to tap controlled processing. As a result, classical experimental techniques may be more successful. In addition, manipulating task parameters may be especially fruitful in studies of children, since their relatively limited processing capacity makes children more sensitive to effects of increased demands for particular functions. By enabling the components within a specific task to be manipulated directly, this approach provides an important step forward from studies that rely upon within-child correlations in performance across tasks. However, the corollary is that establishing standardized methodological procedures is especially important in studies of children.

A final obstacle for researchers is that of low process–behavior correspondence. Many psychological processes manifest themselves only in one narrow type of situation and not at all in others (e.g., the face recognition system is activated when a subject is shown photos of famous faces, but not a list of words). By contrast, executive processes manifest themselves in a range of different situations. This leads to a low correspondence between process and behavior: A specific process impairment can result in a variety of behaviors, and conversely a specific behavior can be caused by a variety of process impairments. However, compared with adults, children are more transparent in their behavior (e.g., they are more likely to "think aloud" and to make overt displays of response suppression), and so once again this problem may be less of an issue for research with children. In particular, EF studies of children may benefit particularly from combining *quantitative experimental measures* of task performance (e.g., percentage correct, time taken) with *qualitative observational ratings* of task behavior (e.g., frequency of rule violations, displays of frustration/distractibility). For example, one early method of studying rehearsal in children was to record overt signs such as lip movements and whispering. This approach indicated that children begin to use strategies of rehearsal around the age of 7 (Flavell, Beach, & Chinsky, 1966), confirming the results of more formal and inferential analyses in subsequent studies.

Thus, many of the difficulties in measuring EF in adult populations may, at least in part, be overcome when working with children, so that developmental studies of EF may provide special insights into the organization of EF. Nevertheless, researchers interested in charting the development of EF are confronted by a number of problems specific to childhood, particularly as a result of language limitations. For example, by taxing a child's verbal comprehension (e.g., via complex instructions) a task places demands upon peripheral functions that may well influence overall performance. In addition, fluent literacy emerges relatively late in development and so many adult EF tasks are inappropriate for children, simply because they depend upon over-learned (i.e., automatic) written language skills. Examples include: (a) the Stroop test, in which reading the word "blue" (say) written in a differently colored ink is assumed to be an automatic prepotent response; (b) the trail-making test, in which an alphabet sequence must be repeatedly interrupted to interleave a number sequence (and a tendency to complete either sequence is assumed); (c) random-sequence generation tasks, in which frequent letter/digit/word sequences (e.g., ABC) are again assumed to be automatic prepotent responses; (d) the FAS verbal fluency test, in which individuals are required to name as many words beginning with F, A, or S, and so a rudimentary spelling ability is assumed; and (e) the Hayling sentence completion task, in which an individual must complete a sentence in an unexpected way (so that, again, strong associations between certain word combinations are again assumed to be prepotent).

To minimize this load upon verbal comprehension, EF tests for young children must therefore be kept as simple as possible. A seminal figure who developed many classic EF tests suitable for use with children is the Soviet psychologist, Alexander Luria (1966). These tasks include the *go/no-go test* (in which the child must execute a response to stimulus A, but withhold this response when presented with stimulus B), and a variety of nonverbal Stroop tasks for children, including the picture-based *day/night task* (in which the child must say "day" for a picture of the moon, and "night" for a picture of the sun; Diamond & Taylor, 1996; Luria, Pribram, & Homskaya, 1964; Passler, Isaac, & Hynd, 1985), the *tapping game* (in which the child must tap once in reply to two taps, and twice in response to a single tap), or the *hand game* depicted in Figure 12.3.

In the same tradition, Frith (1972; Hughes, 1998a) devised a pattern-making task that required children to avoid simple repeats (e.g., dropping black [B] and white [W] marbles into a tube, but avoiding sequences such as BBB/WWW/BWBW). Child-friendly

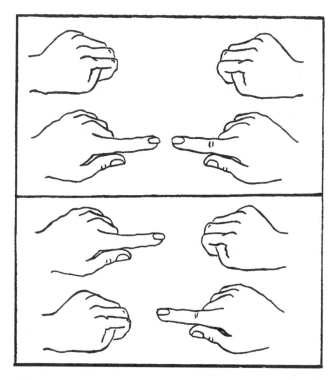

Figure 12.3 Luria's hand game. Above is the control "imitation" condition; below is the test "conflict condition" in which the child has to show a fist if presented with a finger, but point a finger if shown a fist. Performance is scored by the number of correct conflict trials (/12).

fluency tasks have also been devised: These involve generating names of objects in a particular category (e.g., animals/transport/clothes; White, Nortz, Mandernach, Huntington, & Steiner, 2001) rather than naming words beginning with a particular letter. Other EF tasks, simple enough even for infants, have also been developed. These tasks (described more fully later) include (a) Diamond's version of Piaget's *A-not-B* test; (b) the *object reversal* test in which an established reward contingency is reversed; and (c) object retrieval tasks that tap the ability to perform a means–end action, such as making a detour around a barrier to retrieve a desired object (Diamond, 1990; Diamond & Goldman-Rakic, 1989).

These simple tasks have also led to dramatic improvements in our understanding of the development of EF. For instance, it is now known that EF: (a) begins to emerge in the first few years of life; (b) shows stage-like, age-related changes; (c) becomes fully mature in late adolescence and declines with normal ageing; (d) subdivides in children and adults in similar ways (in each case the three most widely reported factors are *inhibitory control*, *attentional flexibility*, and *working memory/planning*); and (e) has important consequences for other cognitive functions. Below we discuss the fractionation and development of EF in more detail.

Neurological Substrate and Fractionation of Executive Function

It is widely accepted that EF is dependent on the functioning of the PFC, conventionally defined as the portion of the frontal cortex that receives projections from the mediodorsal nucleus of the thalamus. Based on the internal divisions of this nucleus, the prefrontal cortex may be further subdivided into three main regions: the orbitofrontal PFC, the dorsolateral PFC, and the frontal eye fields (the frontal eye fields are involved in the higher control of eye movements and will not be discussed further here). The PFC is also closely connected with neighboring brain regions such as the striatum, anterior cingulate cortex, and the limbic system, with these connections arranged to form a number of parallel circuits. In addition to these parallel anatomical systems, there are parallel neurochemical systems connecting to the PFC, chiefly ascending dopaminergic and serotoninergic pathways. There is some overlap between anatomical and neurochemical systems: Dorsolateral prefrontal cortex, for example, is particularly richly innervated by ascending dopaminergic neurons. A full account of the neuroanatomical and neurochemical evidence in support of a fractionated model of prefrontal function is beyond the scope of this chapter, but useful reviews can be found in Casey, Galvan, and Hare (2005) and Robbins (2005).

Working along these anatomical lines, clinical researchers into EF have repeatedly attempted to differentiate between the functions of the orbitofrontal PFC and the dorsolateral PFC. In brief, dorsolateral PFC is particularly connected with regions associated with motor control (e.g., the basal ganglia) and performance monitoring (e.g., the anterior cingulate cortex). Ventromedial PFC, by contrast, is reciprocally connected with regions involved in emotional processing (e.g., the amygdala) and memory (e.g., the hippocampus). In its simplest form, this amounts to a distinction between "hot" versus "cool" EF (i.e., emotional regulation and behavioral control versus affectively neutral higher order cognitive processes).

Exactly *how* the PFC supports EF is a matter of greater controversy. This is a rapidly expanding field of research, increasingly founded on novel, noninvasive techniques such as event-related potential (ERP) studies, electroencephalography (EEG), and functional imaging studies involving either magnetic resonance imaging (MRI) or positron emission tomography (PET). Many suggestions have been put forward, including Norman and Shallice's attentional control model, Duncan's adaptive coding model, Damasio's somatic marker hypothesis, and Goldman-Rakic's working memory model. At present, no consensus has been reached (for a comprehensive review of competing contemporary models of PFC function, see Wood & Grafman, 2003).

Within cognitive psychology, a multicomponential view of EF is attractive because it helps to avoid the philosophical problem of the homunculus or "ghost in the machine" (Ryle, 1949). Many psychologists have observed that the functions ascribed to the central executive such as "planning," "choosing," "deciding," and other "higher cognitive processes" are poorly defined and all too often imply some sort of conscious, overreaching system or entity making these plans, choices, and decisions. This has led investigators to decompose EF into smaller fragments—a collection of automatic tools, perhaps, rather than an engineer (Shallice & Burgess, 1991).

Empirically, the distinction between different components of EF is also important to developmental cognitive psychologists, for a number of reasons. First, interpreting the results from any EF task depends upon a precise specification of task demands, which in turn depends on a systematic outline of the components of EF. Second, in order to develop age-appropriate versions of adult EF tasks, it is desirable to simplify tasks along the lines of their natural components rather than in an ad hoc fashion. Third, given the variety of developmental disorders in which executive impairments are observed, a finer-grain level of analysis is required to draw useful distinctions between clinical groups and to advance hypotheses about the underlying mechanisms in each case. Here it is likely to be qualitative differences in *profiles* of EF performance, rather than differences in overall EF performance, that prove most informative. Nevertheless, studying the fractionation of EF in adult populations can be difficult, for a variety of reasons. In particular, fractionation may be either overestimated or underestimated, depending on which processes and behaviors are under investigation (Burgess, 1997).

Paradoxically, because of their relatively limited executive capacities, young children may be ideal candidates for evaluating theoretical predictions concerning the relationship between specific EFs. Compared with adults, tapping EF in children is less dependent upon demands for a *sequence* of acts, while experimental manipulations have a more pronounced effect; thus, interactive effects can be investigated directly using within-task designs. However, one should avoid the assumption that a specific EF task poses the same type of cognitive demands for children of different ages.

Normal Neuropsychological Development of Executive Function

What do we know about the development of EF in childhood? First, the onset of EF development is much earlier than was traditionally thought (e.g., by Golden, 1981; by Luria, 1973). This does, of course, depend on utilizing the appropriate tools to study EF at an early age. In particular, an impressive set of behavioral and comparative studies by Adele Diamond and colleagues has shown that the functioning of the dorsolateral PFC underpins the performance of infants on Piaget's A-not-B task (Piaget, 1976). In this task, a toy is conspicuously hidden in one place (A); the infant is then allowed to search for it. This is repeated for a few trials and then the object is visibly moved to location B. At this stage in the task, 8-month-old infants persist in searching at location A, but 12-month-olds search correctly at B on the first trial and show few if any perseverative errors on subsequent trials, even if a delay between concealment and search is introduced, making the task more difficult (Diamond, 1988). Support for the involvement of the dorsolateral PFC in this task comes from the finding (from a group of infants tested longitudinally between 7 and 12 months of age) that task performance is correlated with EEG activity and coherence in this brain region (Bell & Fox, 1992).

A second finding to emerge from several independent studies is that EF in children subdivides in a similar manner to adults. Using principal components analyses, Welsh and colleagues (Welsh, Pennington, & Groisser, 1991) showed that the performance of both 8- to 12-year-olds and adults on a battery of EF tasks displayed the same three-factor solution. Similarly, Levin and colleagues (1991) found that the performance of to 7- to 15-year-olds on a battery of EF tasks showed the same three-factor solution for all ages. Although the task loadings were not identical in the two studies, in both cases the first factor appeared to be a measure of *cognitive flexibility*, whilst the second factor tapped into problems of *inhibitory control* and the third factor captured *planning* (and working memory). A large-scale study of 537 school-aged children confirmed this three-factor structure (Pennington, 1997), which has also been extended to 3- and 4-year-olds in a study that employed simplified task variants that were adapted for preschoolers (Hughes, 1998a).

Together, these findings suggest remarkable continuity in the structure of EF from preschool to adulthood. However, as noted by Zelazo and Muller (2002), the story is more complicated than this commonality suggests: Correlations among tasks can result not only from similarities in the mechanisms underlying task performance, but also from shared method variance and shared sensitivity to individual differences at specific ages. Nevertheless, given the above consensus in findings, we shall in the remainder of this section present the key developmental changes for each of the three main factors identified above. For reasons of space, we shall not attempt an exhaustive review of EF tasks that have been used with children (the interested reader is referred to Zelazo & Muller, 2002, for a discussion of some of the tasks that are not reviewed here).

Cognitive flexibility

The most widely used measure of "cognitive flexibility" is Grant and Berg's (1948) Wisconsin Card Sorting Test (WCST), which involves a deck of picture cards (varying in color, shape, and number), and four target cards. Children are asked to place each card on one of the targets; through feedback on each trial they can, by a process of trial and error, deduce the sorting "rule" as to which dimension is salient. After six consecutively correct responses, the rule is changed (e.g., sort by shape to sort by color). Key measures from the WCST are the numbers of (a) rules deduced and (b) perseverative errors. Chelune and Baer (1986) reported a steady improvement in WCST performance from 6 years, achieving adult levels of performance by around 10 years of age (see also Levin et al., 1991; Welsh, Pennington, & Groisser, 1991). Unfortunately, like other traditional EF tasks, the WCST falls far short of providing a pure measure of cognitive flexibility. In particular, because the same cards are used for each rule (and the child is not told that the rule has changed), perseverative errors on the WCST may reflect either a genuine failure to shift mental set to the newly relevant dimension or simply a failure to inhibit a previously reinforced response to a specific exemplar (e.g., triangles). Thus, the WCST provides a sensitive but nonspecific index of EF impairment.

To rectify this problem of nonspecificity, a computerized variant of the WCST has been developed as part of the Cambridge Automated Neuropsychological Task Battery (CANTAB; Robbins et al., 1997). Two features of the ID/ED test (intradimensional/extradimensional shift test) from the CANTAB enable a finer grain of analysis: (a) a "total transfer" design (i.e., new exemplars are presented when the child achieves criterion on the key stages, alerting the child to the change in rule), and (b) graded multiple stages. Stage 1 tests rule learning; stage 2 tests rule reversal; stage 3 introduces distracter elements that in stage 4 become superimposed upon the salient shape; in stage 5, the rule is again reversed; in stage 6, the shapes and distracters are changed but the rule remains the same (this ID shift tests transfer of learning); in stage 7, the rule is again reversed; in stage 8, new exemplars are presented and the previously irrelevant distracters now become salient (this ED shift is crucial as it provides a relatively pure test of problems in set-shifting); in stage 9, the new rule is reversed.

Hughes, Russell, and Robbins (1994) showed that children with autism typically fail the ED stage of the ID/ED task, and this finding has recently been replicated in a large autistic sample (Ozonoff et al., 2004). Following this intriguing finding, which indicates a marked autistic impairment in higher order set-shifting, Luciana and Nelson (1998) found that most typically developing children did not succeed on the ED shift stage of the task before the age of 6 years. This highlights the importance of adopting developmentally appropriate EF tasks to investigate rudimentary EF skills in young clinical groups.

For example, total transfer set-shifting tasks that are failed by typically developing preschoolers (Hughes, 1998a) are too taxing to be sensitive to impairments in set-shifting among autistic preschoolers (Shearer, 2002); however, simpler rule-switching tasks, such as the Dimensional Change Card Sorting (DCCS) task do appear sensitive to autistic impairments in attentional flexibility (Colvert, Custance, & Swettenham, 2002; Zelazo, Jacques, Burack, & Frye, 2002). It should be noted that the authors of the DCCS view this task as a test of cognitive complexity rather than cognitive flexibility. Specifically, Zelazo and Frye (1997) argue that in order to switch between two rules, a child needs to be able to represent embedded if–if–then structures. According to this "cognitive complexity and control" (CCC) account, 3-year-olds fail the DCCS task because they are unable to distance themselves sufficiently from a particular way of conceptualizing a card so that they can select the right conceptualization when the time comes.

However, findings from a study by Perner and Lang (2002) challenge this view. Specifically, by systematically varying the component demands, Perner and Lang (2002) were able to show that 3-year-olds only displayed a performance deficit on a variant of the DCCS task that included *both* visual capture and an extradimensional shift. While they discuss this finding in terms of the questions it raises for both CCC and inhibitory control accounts, in the current context this interaction effect highlights the importance of a developmental perspective. That is, the 3-year-olds (but not the 4-year-olds) in Perner and Lang's study were clearly affected by both the novelty and pragmatic complexity of specific rule-switching tasks. This finding highlights the need to avoid the assumption that the same task poses the same type of cognitive demands for children of different ages.

Inhibitory control

Findings from both clinical and developmental research indicate that the construct of inhibitory control can itself be subdivided. In particular, there is a clear difference in demands between tasks that simply require the child to withhold a prepotent response (e.g., the stop task, or the go/no-go task) and tasks that require the child to withhold a prepotent response in order to execute a rule-guided action. With regard to the first type of task, recent findings suggest that the go/no-go task (widely used with school-aged children) also gives reliable and valid results with preschoolers (Mahone, Pillion, & Hiemenz, 2001). Specifically, 3-year-olds completed a computerized go/no-go task with few omission or commission errors, and from age 3 to age 6 there was a significant reduction in errors, response latency and variability (which correlated significantly with parental ratings of attentional problems).

The second, more complex, type of inhibitory control is tapped by nonverbal Stroop tasks (e.g., Luria's day/night, hand game, knock/tap) and by the detour-reaching task (Hughes & Russell, 1993). For example, Hughes and Russell (1993) reported that 3-year-olds and older children with autism (but not typically developing 4-year-olds) failed to retrieve a marble inside a box when this required not only the inhibition of a direct reach but also an indirect and arbitrary means–end action (flicking a switch before reaching into the box). Likewise, the majority of 3-year-olds (but not 4-year-olds) also fail the day/night task (Gerstadt, Hong, & Diamond, 1994), the hand game (Hughes, 1996, 1998a), and the knock/tap task (Perner & Lang, 2002). Significant improvements in both simple and complex inhibitory control are therefore evident across the preschool years. Developmental improvements in inhibitory control also continue throughout childhood, as demonstrated by findings from studies with school-aged children using the stop and go/no-go tasks and the Opposite Worlds Stroop task (e.g., Manly et al., 2001). Interestingly, findings from an fMRI study (Casey et al., 1997) suggest that children and adults show similar patterns of brain activation during the go/no-go task, and demonstrate a negative association between test indices for inhibitory control (e.g., errors of commission) and ventromedial PFC activity.

Planning

The most widely used paradigm for testing planning skills is the Tower of Hanoi task (Piaget, 1976), and its simplified variant, the Tower of London (Shallice, 1982). The differences between these two tasks are subtle, but important. In the Tower of Hanoi, a set of doughnut-like discs, graded in size to form a pyramid-like structure, must be moved from one of three equally sized pegs to another, following the following constraints: move only one disc at a time; move only the top disc on a peg; place no disc on top of a bigger disc. A "perfect" solution requires 2^n-1 moves, where n is the number of discs. So a very simple 2-disc problem would take 3 moves to solve, whereas a 6-disc problem would require a minimum of 63 moves. Performance is measured by the number of attempts the child (or adult!) requires to achieve a perfect solution: The Tower of Hanoi task therefore taps not only planning ability but also rule following and procedural learning.

The Tower of London provides a purer test of planning ability: Discs are replaced by three differently colored balls (removing much of the need for rule constraints); the pegs vary in length (reducing the size of the "problem space"); the full tower-to-tower transfer is replaced by a graded set of novel 2- to 5-move subproblems (minimizing practice effects). Key performance measures at each level include the number of perfect solutions and the mean number of extra moves. The computerized version of the Tower of London in the CANTAB also includes a yoked set of "follow" tasks; by subtracting individual response times for each of these from those on the corresponding full task, both thinking and execution times can be estimated. These modifications make the Tower of London a much more satisfactory test of planning than the Tower of Hanoi.[1] For reasons of space, we shall therefore restrict our report to findings from the Tower of London. Note that in a study using positron emission tomography (PET), the planning demands of the CANTAB Tower of London task were associated with activation of the dorsolateral PFC (Baker et al., 1996).

Using a manual version of the Tower of London, Hughes (1998b) found that 4- and 5-year-olds showed a steep drop in performance across problem levels: 62% produced perfect solutions to all three 2-move subproblems, as compared with 22% at the 3-move level, and just 16% at the 4-move level. Interestingly, overall scores correlated significantly with the children's performances on the detour-reaching task a year earlier. Together, these results indicate that the Tower of London is developmentally appropriate for preschool-aged children, and also highlight the magnitude and validity of early individual differences in planning ability. Finally, Luciana and Nelson (1998) demonstrated that developmental improvements in planning continue at a steady rate through the school years.

Abnormal Development

Impairments in EF are now thought to play a key role in a variety of developmental disorders, though the evidence is strongest for attention deficit hyperactivity disorder (ADHD) and autism (Pennington & Ozonoff, 1996). For reasons of space, and because the evidence for a *specific* EF impairment appears stronger for ADHD, we shall in this section only consider EF in relation to ADHD. This syndrome is relatively common, affecting 2–7% of school-aged children (mostly boys), but is difficult to diagnose before the age of 6, perhaps because its three cardinal symptoms (distractibility, hyperactivity, and impulsivity) tap what is often "normal" behavior in very young children. Children

---

[1] Nevertheless, planning ability clearly depends on several component executive skills (Goel & Grafman, 1995). According to Shallice (1982), success on the Tower of London involves focused and sustained attention, goal recognition/selection, generation of plans, and appropriate response to feedback.

with ADHD often show other comorbid problems such as oppositional defiant disorder, conduct disorder, reading disability, and (less frequently) depression or anxiety.

There is good evidence for PFC involvement in ADHD, in terms of both structure (e.g., delayed myelination of the PFC) and function (e.g., dopamine depletion). Increasingly, children with ADHD are medicated with amphetamine-based stimulants (most commonly, Ritalin) that affect the dopaminergic system and lead to improvements in both behavior and cognitive performance (e.g., Kempton et al., 1999). Group differences between children with ADHD and ability-matched controls show large effect sizes ($d \approx 1$) and are most evident on tasks that require inhibitory control (Barkley, 1997; Sergeant, 2000). Studies have also suggested that children with ADHD lack strategic flexibility, display poor planning and working memory, and are poor at monitoring their own behavior (Cepeda, Cepeda, & Kramer, 2000; Clark & Rutter, 1981), but none the less it is generally impairments in inhibitory control that are emphasized.

Impairment of attention in ADHD is clearly a diagnostic feature, although historically the nature of this impairment has been poorly specified. Manly et al. (2001) reported findings from 24 boys with ADHD (not yet receiving medication) tested on an age-normed battery of manual tests of attention and EF (the Test of Everyday Attention in Children). Compared with several comparison groups, the ADHD boys showed global deficits, but group differences were especially robust on the tests of sustained attention and suppression of prepotent responses. In contrast, a study using the CANTAB with a group of "hard to manage" 7-year-olds (Brophy, Taylor, & Hughes, 2002) showed no deficits on any of the formal task measures, despite significantly elevated rates of observed rule violations and perseverative errors whilst performing the tasks.[2] However, positive findings have been reported for another computerized battery, the Maudsley Attention and Response Suppression (MARS) battery which includes three response-inhibition tasks: go/no-go, stop, and rule reversal. Children with ADHD (aged 7–15 years, and off medication for at least 48 hours) performed significantly worse than IQ-matched psychiatric and typical controls on all three tasks (Rubia et al., 2001). Moreover, fMRI of a subset of participants during the response-inhibition tasks revealed reduced right prefrontal activation for the ADHD group.

The above findings support the conceptualization of ADHD as an executive disorder, in which inhibitory control is especially affected. However, an alternative view has also been posited, namely that the behaviors that typify ADHD may reflect deviance in motivational style rather than executive dysfunction (e.g., Haenlein & Caul, 1987; Johansen, Aase, Meyer, & Sagvolden, 2002; Zentall & Zentall, 1983). Specifically, children with ADHD appear motivated to avoid or escape delay, perhaps because of an altered perception of time (Sonuga-Barke, Houlberg, & Hall, 1994). If so, children

---

[2] This may be because the CANTAB software is programmed to ignore irrelevant responses in order to obtain "pure" measures of specific functions. Whilst clearly a laudable aim in adult studies, this design feature does appear to limit the use of CANTAB with younger children.

with ADHD may appear inattentive, overactive, or impulsive (and perform poorly on executive tasks) without any primary underlying executive impairments.

The true picture may be that ADHD is a heterogeneous disorder, and includes both executive and motivational deficits. In support of this "dual path" model (Sonuga-Barke, 2002), several experiments (Sonuga-Barke, Houlberg, & Hall, 1994; Sonuga-Barke, Taylor, Sembi, & Smith, 1992; Sonuga-Barke, Williams, Hall, & Saxton, 1996) demonstrate a double dissociation between preference for delayed rewards and inhibitory control; in addition, a recent multicenter study of children with ADHD (Solanto et al., 2001) revealed dual but unrelated impairments on a standard stop signal task (indicating poor inhibitory control) and a choice delay task (implicating motivational factors). Investigations of EF deficits may therefore be more informative at the level of symptoms than at that of diagnostic category.

Behavioral Genetics of Executive Function

The range of possible genetic influences on prefrontal function and EF is vast, and findings in this area are largely preliminary. In summary, there is good evidence that both general and specific genetic factors are involved in the determination of prefrontal function (Winterer & Goldman, 2003). Many of the general factors appear to play a wider role in the regulation of central nervous system function and are also implicated in the heritability of attributes such as general intelligence or processing speed. These general genetic factors are insufficient, however, to explain the heritability of more specific executive functions such as working memory.

Efforts to investigate the genetics of higher cognitive functions in more detail are constrained by the lack of an operational definition for EF, and studies to date have therefore concentrated, understandably, on either relatively narrow aspects of EF, such as the executive attention network (Fan, Wu, Fossella, & Posner, 2001), or the co-occurrence of EF impairment in heritable and operationally defined clinical disorders such as ADHD. For example, in individuals with ADHD, population-based twin studies show a highly significant overlap between ADHD symptoms/diagnosis and IQ, a co-association that appears to be almost entirely carried by shared genetic influences (Kuntsi et al., 2004). Similarly, structural equation modeling studies suggest a substantial overlap between the genetic liabilities to the disorder of ADHD, accompanying EF deficits, and comorbid conduct disorder or oppositional defiant disorder, although there is also support for additional genetic influences underlying EF variability independent of those shared with ADHD (Coolidge, Thede, & Young, 2000).

Perhaps the most specific genetic factor yet identified concerns polymorphisms in the gene for the enzyme catechol-O-methyltransferase (COMT), which is involved in the degradation of dopamine, and performance on tasks of working memory (Malhotra et al., 2002). In a significant proportion of individuals, the COMT gene contains a variation in its coding sequence at position 472, leading to a single amino acid substitution of methionine for valine. This substitution leads to a dramatic increase in the temperature lability of the enzyme, such that individuals with the *met* allele have only one-quarter of the enzyme activity of individuals with the *val* allele (Lachman et al., 1996). Remarkably, enzyme activity is in turn correlated with performance on a standard test of EF, the Wisconsin Card Sorting Test, individuals homozygous for the *val* allele showing the best performance, heterozygous *met/val* individuals showing intermediate performance, and individuals homozygous for the *met* allele showing the worst performance (Egan et al., 2001). Although studies screening further candidate genes for their influence on prefrontal function have so far yielded few clear results, this may in large part be due to a lack of power in early studies, a problem that is likely to be overcome by the rapid pace of methodological advances in the field of behavioral genetics.

Clinical Implications and Current Research

The rapid progress in our understanding of the basic development of EF has exciting consequences, and there are now several hot topics for research. First, impairments in the control of action contribute to the behavioral problems that set children on a trajectory towards deviance, delinquency, and antisocial conduct. For instance, in a study of "hard to manage" 3- and 4-year-olds, individual differences in EF were significantly associated with antisocial behavior (Hughes, White, Sharpen, & Dunn, 2000). Studies that deepen our understanding of normative age-related improvements in EF may therefore help to identify children with poor regulatory control who could benefit from intervention programs, and so has clear societal importance. Thus, interest in early EF is closely tied to the growth of the new discipline of *developmental neuropsychology*. In particular, impairments in EF are thought to play a key role in several childhood disorders, including attention deficit hyperactivity disorder (ADHD) and autism, though the latter is more controversial.

Second, studies with children offer the promise of differentiating the components of EF. In particular, the technique of manipulating task parameters may be especially fruitful in studies of children, since their relatively limited processing capacity makes them more sensitive to effects of increased demands for particular functions. This provides a direct solution to the low *discriminant validity* shown by traditional EF tasks. Because such tasks are typically complex and multicomponential, different clinical groups may perform equally poorly for different reasons. For example, ADHD and autism have quite different clinical presentations, and yet both groups show substantial EF deficits (scoring $\approx$ 1 *SD* below control groups). At first glance, one might therefore expect EF impairments to be rather nonspecific. However, studies that adopt an information-processing approach (involving simplified tasks that allow comparisons based on specific rather than global performance measures) have revealed both quantitative and qualitative distinctions between EF impairments in these two disorders.

Third, there is converging evidence for a functional link between EF and "theory of mind" (ToM) defined as the ability to attribute mental states to oneself and others.

This evidence includes: (a) pronounced impairments in both EF and ToM among children with autism; (b) the developmental synchrony of improvements in both EF and ToM among typically developing preschoolers; and (c) robust correlations between individual differences in EF and ToM, even with effects of age and IQ controlled. Since the topic of ToM continues to attract intense research interest, the nature and significance of its association with EF is a matter of considerable debate. Empirically, there is longitudinal evidence for a predictive association between individual differences in EF at age 4 and in ToM one year later (even controlling for initial ToM), but no association between early ToM and later EF (Hughes, 1998b). This asymmetry suggests a direction of influence (EF → ToM), but findings from intervention studies are needed to establish a causal path.

In addition, it may be that associations between EF and ToM are specific rather than global. For example, Carlson and Moses (2001) have reported particularly strong associations between inhibitory control and ToM. Further support for this view comes from the findings of several imaging studies, demonstrating that ToM tasks activate the ventromedial PFC (the subregion previously identified as important in inhibitory control). Since individuals with autism are known to show profound impairments in ToM, this finding suggests that research into EF impairments in autism should focus on EF tasks that are associated with the ventromedial PFC (previous research in this field has generally employed traditional EF tasks that are typically associated with the dorsolateral PFC). Thus, one positive consequence of the debate surrounding the relation between ToM and EF is the integration of brain-based research with studies of both normative and atypical development.

Methodological Challenges and Future Directions

Despite the various advances outlined above, it should be emphasized that EF research remains besieged by methodological problems. In particular, much more work is needed to achieve a fine-grained analysis of the distinct components of EF. This fractionated approach is also important as a solution to the *homunculus problem*, raised by terms such as "effortful control," since it allows EF to be compared with a set of automatic tools rather than an engineer. In addition, it is very difficult to design "pure" tests of EF, or even tasks that show good test/re-test reliability (an inherent problem with EF research is that any task is only truly novel once). Progress in our conceptual understanding of EF depends critically upon innovative and rigorous solutions to these methodological challenges.

The challenges for future research in the above areas are vast and varied. However, one that deserves special mention is the need to investigate whether contrasts in EF help explain differences in the form and severity of behavioral symptoms. Research on this topic may enable us to elucidate *specific* links between EF and behavior. Such links may be best described in terms of distinct behaviors, such as reactive versus proactive forms of aggression (for disruptive behavior disorders) or catastrophic responses to change versus ritualistic routines (for autism). Alternatively, links between EF and behavior may be clearest for specific contexts (e.g., peer interactions that are not scaffolded by familiar routines). Addressing the relation between variability in EF and in behavior also provides a promising alternative to simply comparing diagnostic groups, in that disorders with overlapping symptoms (e.g., ADHD and conduct disorder) may show relative rather than absolute differences in EF. For many reasons, then, research that combines innovative task manipulations with valid and reliable observational methods is vital.

References

Atkinson, R., & Shiffrin, R. (1968). Human memory: A proposed system and its control processes. In K. W. Spence and J. T. Spence (Eds.), *The psychology of learning and motivation: Advances in research and theory* (Vol. 2, pp. 89–195). New York: Academic Press.

Baker, S., Rogers, R., Owen, A. M., Frith, C., Dolan, R., Frackowiak, R., et al. (1996). Neural systems engaged by planning: A PET study of the Tower of London task. *Neuropsychologia, 34*, 515–526.

Barkley, R. A. (1997). Behavioral inhibition, sustained attention, and executive function: Constructing a unified theory of ADHD. *Psychological Bulletin, 121*, 65–94.

Bell, J. A., & Fox, N. (1992). The relations between frontal brain electrical activity and cognitive development during infancy. *Child Development, 63*, 1142–1163.

Brophy, M., Taylor, E., & Hughes, C. (2002). To go or not to go: Inhibitory control in "hard to manage" children. Special Issue on Executive Functions and Development. *Infant and Child Development, 11*, 125–140.

Burgess, P. (1997). Theory and methodology in executive function research. In P. Rabbitt (Ed.), *Methodology of frontal and executive function* (pp. 81–116). Hove, East Sussex: Psychology Press.

Carlson, S., & Moses, L. (2001). Individual differences in inhibitory control and children's theory of mind. *Child Development, 72*, 1032–1053.

Casey, B. J., Galvan, A., & Hare, T. A. (2005). Changes in cerebral functional organization during cognitive development. *Current Opinion in Neurobiology, 15*(2), 239–244.

Casey, B. J., Trainor, R. J., Orendi, J. L., Schubert, A. B., Nystrom, L. E., Giedd, J. N., et al. (1997). A developmental functional MRI study of prefrontal activation during performance of a go/no-go task. *Journal of Cognitive Neuroscience, 9*(6), 835–847.

Cepeda, N., Cepeda, M., & Kramer, A. (2000). Task switching and attention deficit hyperactivity disorder. *Journal of Abnormal Child Psychology, 28*, 213–226.

Chelune, G. J., & Baer, R. A. (1986). Developmental norms for the Wisconsin card sorting test. *Journal of Clinical and Experimental Neuropsychology, 8*, 219–228.

Clark, P., & Rutter, M. (1981). Autistic children's responses to structure and to interpersonal demands. *Journal of Autism and Developmental Disorders, 11*, 201–217.

Colvert, E., Custance, D., & Swettenham, J. (2002). Rule-based reasoning and theory of mind in autism: A commentary on the work of Zelazo, Jacques, Burack and Frye. Special Issue on Executive Functions and Development. *Infant and Child Development, 11*, 197–200.

Coolidge, F. L., Thede, L. L., & Young, S. E. (2000). Heritability and the comorbidity of attention deficit hyperactivity disorder with behavioral disorders and executive function deficits: A preliminary investigation. *Developmental Neuropsychology, 17*(3), 273–287.

Cooper, R., & Shallice, T. (2000). Contention scheduling and the control of routine activities. *Cognitive Neuropsychology, 17,* 297–338.

Diamond, A. (1988). Abilities and neural mechanisms underlying A not B performance. *Child Development, 59,* 523–527.

Diamond, A. (1990). Developmental time course in human infants and infant monkeys, and the neural bases of inhibitory control in reaching. *Annals of the New York Academy of Sciences, 608,* 637–706.

Diamond, A., & Goldman-Rakic, P. (1989). Comparison of human infants and rhesus monkeys on Piaget's A-not-B task: Evidence for dependence on dorsolateral prefrontal cortex. *Experimental Brain Research, 74,* 24–40.

Diamond, A., & Taylor, C. (1996). Development of an aspect of executive control: Development of the abilities to remember what I said and to "Do as I say, not as I do." *Developmental Psychobiology, 24,* 315–334.

Egan, M. F., Goldberg, T. E., Kolachana, B. S., Callicott, J. H., Mazzanti, C. M., Straub, R. E., et al. (2001). Effect of COMT Val108/158 Met genotype on frontal lobe function and risk for schizophrenia. *Proceedings of the National Academy of Sciences, USA, 98*(12), 6917–6922.

Fan, J., Wu, Y., Fossella, J. A., & Posner, M. I. (2001). Assessing the heritability of attentional networks. *BMC Neuroscience, 2,* 14.

Flavell, J., Beach, D., & Chinsky, J. (1966). Spontaneous verbal rehearsal in a memory task as a function of age. *Child Development, 37,* 283–299.

Frith, U. (1972). Cognitive mechanisms in autism: Experiments with colour and tone sequence production. *Journal of Autism and Childhood Schizophrenia, 2,* 160–173.

Gerstadt, C., Hong, Y., & Diamond, A. (1994). The relationship between cognition and action: Performance of children 3½–7 years old on a Stroop-like day–night test. *Cognition, 53,* 129–153.

Goel, V., & Grafman, J. (1995). Are the frontal lobes implicated in "planning" functions? Interpreting data from the Tower of Hanoi. *Neuropsychologia, 33,* 623–642.

Golden, C. J. (1981). The Luria–Nebraska children's battery: Theory and formulation. In G. W. Hynd & G. E. Obrzut (Eds.), *Neuropsychological assessment and the school-aged child* (pp. 277–302). New York: Grune & Stratton.

Goldstein, K. (1936). The modifications of behaviour consequent to cerebral lesions. *Psychiatric Quarterly, 10,* 586–610.

Goldstein, K. (1944). The mental changes due to frontal lobe damage. *Journal of Psychology, 17,* 187–208.

Grant, D. A., & Berg, E. A. (1948). A behavioural analysis of degree of reinforcement and ease of shifting to new responses in a Weigl-type card sorting problem. *Journal of Experimental Psychology, 38,* 404–411.

Haenlein, M., & Caul, W. (1987). Attention deficit disorder with hyperactivity: A specific hypothesis of reward dysfunction. *Journal of the American Academy of Child and Adolescent Psychiatry, 26,* 356–362.

Hughes, C. (1996). Control of action and thought: Normal development and dysfunction in autism. *Journal of Child Psychology and Psychiatry, 37,* 229–236.

Hughes, C. (1998a). Executive function in preschoolers: Links with theory of mind and verbal ability. *British Journal of Developmental Psychology, 16,* 233–253.

Hughes, C. (1998b). Finding your marbles: Does preschoolers' strategic behaviour predict later understanding of mind? *Developmental Psychology, 34,* 1326–1339.

Hughes, C., & Russell, J. (1993). Autistic children's difficulty with mental disengagement from an object: Its implications for theories of autism. *Developmental Psychology, 29*, 498–510.

Hughes, C., Russell, J., & Robbins, T. (1994). Evidence for central executive dysfunction in autism. *Neuropsychologia, 32*, 477–492.

Hughes, C., White, A., Sharpen, J., & Dunn, J. (2000). Antisocial, angry and unsympathetic: "Hard to manage" preschoolers' peer problems, and possible social and cognitive influences. *Journal of Child Psychology and Psychiatry, 41*, 169–179.

James, W. (1890). *The principles of psychology.* New York: Holt.

Johansen, E., Aase, H., Meyer, A., & Sagvolden, T. (2002). Attention deficit/hyperactivity disorder behaviour explained by dysfunctional reinforcement and extinction processes. *Behavioural Brain Research, 130*, 37–45.

Kempton, S., Vance, A., Maruff, P., Luk, E., Costin, J., & Pantelis, C. (1999). Executive function and attention deficit hyperactivity disorder: Stimulant medication and better executive function performance in children. *Psychological Medicine, 29*(3), 527–538.

Kimberg, D., & Farah, M. (1993). A unified account of cognitive impairments following frontal lobe damage: The role of working memory in complex, organized behaviour. *Journal of Experimental Psychology: General, 122*, 411–428.

Kuntsi, J., Eley, T. C., Taylor, A., Hughes, C., Asherson, P., Caspi, A., et al. (2004). Co-occurrence of ADHD and low IQ has genetic origins. *American Journal of Medical Genetics Part B: Neuropsychiatric Genetics, 124*(1), 41–47.

Lachman, H. M., Papolos, D. F., Saito, T., Yu, Y. M., Szumlanski, C. L., & Weinshilboum, R. M. (1996). Human catechol-O-methyltransferase pharmacogenetics: Description of a functional polymorphism and its potential application to neuropsychiatric disorders. *Pharmacogenetics, 6*(3), 243–250.

Levin, H., Culhane, K. A., Hartmann, J., Evankovich, K., Mattson, A. J., Harward, H., et al. (1991). Developmental changes in performance on tests of purported frontal lobe functioning. *Developmental Neuropsychology, 7*, 377–395.

Luciana, M., & Nelson, C. A. (1998). The functional emergence of prefrontally-guided working memory systems in four- to eight-year-old children. *Neuropsychologia, 36*, 273–293.

Luria, A. R. (1966). *Higher cortical functions in man.* New York: Basic Books.

Luria, A. R. (1973). *The working brain: An introduction to neuropsychology.* New York: Basic Books.

Luria, A. R., Pribram, K. H., & Homskaya, E. D. (1964). An experimental analysis of the behavioural disturbance produced by a left frontal arachnoidal endothelioma (meningioma). *Neuropyschologia, 2*, 257–280.

Mahone, E., Pillion, J., & Hiemenz, J. (2001). Initial development of an auditory continuous performance test for preschoolers. *Journal of Attention Disorders, 5*, 93–106.

Malhotra, A. K., Kestler, L. J., Mazzanti, C., Bates, J. A., Goldberg, T., & Goldman, D. (2002). A functional polymorphism in the COMT gene and performance on a test of prefrontal cognition. *American Journal of Psychiatry, 159*(4), 652–654.

Manly, T., Nimmo-Smith, I., Watson, P., Anderson, V., Turner, A., & Robertson, I. (2001). The differential assessment of children's attention: The test of everyday attention for children (TEA-Ch), normative sample and ADHD performance. *Journal of Child Psychology and Psychiatry, 42*(8), 1065–1081.

Norman, D., & Shallice, T. (1980). *Attention to action: Willed and automatic control of behavior* (Technical Report No. 99). San Diego: Center for Human Information Processing.

Norman, D., & Shallice, T. (1986). Attention to action: Willed and automatic control of behavior. In R. J. Davidson, G. E. Schwartz, & D. Shapiro (Eds.), *Consciousness and self-regulation: Advances in research and theory* (Vol. 4, pp. 1–18). New York: Plenum Press.

Ozonoff, S., Coon, H., Dawson, G., Joseph, R., Klin, A., McMahon, W. M., et al. (2004). Performance on CANTAB subtests sensitive to frontal lobe function in people with autistic disorder: Evidence from the CPEA network. *Journal of Autism and Developmental Disorders, 34,* 139–150.

Passler, M. A., Isaac, W., & Hynd, G. D. (1985). Neuropsychological development of behaviour attributed to frontal lobe functioning in children. *Developmental Neuropsychology, 1,* 349–370.

Pennington, B. (1997). Dimensions of executive functions in normal and abnormal development. In N. A. Krasnegor, G. R. Lyon, & P. S. Goldman-Rakic (Eds.), *Development of the prefrontal cortex: Evolution, neurobiology, and behavior* (pp. 265–281). Baltimore: Paul H. Brookes.

Pennington, B., & Ozonoff, S. (1996). Executive function and developmental psychopathology. *Journal of Child Psychology and Psychiatry, 37,* 51–87.

Perner, J., & Lang, B. (2002). What causes 3-year-olds' difficulty on the dimensional change card sorting task? Special Issue on Executive Functions and Development. *Infant and Child Development, 11,* 93–106.

Piaget, J. (1976). *The grasp of consciousness: Action and concept in the young child* (S. Wedgewood, Trans.). Cambridge MA: Harvard University Press (original work published 1974).

Robbins, T. (2005). Chemistry of the mind: Neurochemical modulation of prefrontal cortical function. *Journal of Comparative Neurology, 493*(1), 140–146.

Robbins, T., James, M., Owen, A., Sahakian, B., McInnes, L., & Rabbitt, P. (1997). A neural systems approach to the cognitive psychology of ageing using the CANTAB battery. In P. Rabbitt (Ed.), *Methodology of frontal and executive function* (pp. 215–238). Hove, East Sussex: Psychology Press.

Rubia, K., Taylor, E., Smith, A., Oksanen, H., Overmeyer, S., & Newman, S. (2001). Neuropsychological analyses of impulsiveness in childhood hyperactivity. *British Journal of Psychiatry, 179,* 138–143.

Ryle, G. (1949). *The concept of mind.* London: Hutchinson.

Schneider, W., & Shiffrin, R. (1977). Controlled and automatic human information processing: I. Detection, search and attention. *Psychological Review, 84,* 1–66.

Sergeant, J. (2000). The cognitive-energetic model: An empirical approach to attention-deficit hyperactivity disorder. *Neuroscience and Biobehavioral Reviews, 24,* 7–12.

Shallice, T. (1982). Specific impairments in planning. *Philosophical Transactions of the Royal Society of London, Series B, 298,* 199–209.

Shallice, T., & Burgess, P. (1991). Higher cognitive impairments and frontal lobe lesions in man. In H. Levin, H. Eisenberg, & A. Benton (Eds.), *Frontal lobe function and dysfunction* (pp. 135–138). New York: Oxford University Press.

Shearer, H. (2002). *Executive function and autistic symptomatology in very young children.* Unpublished PhD thesis, University of Durham.

Solanto, M. V., Abikoff, H., Sonuga-Barke, E., Schachar, R., Logan, G. D., Wigal, T., et al. (2001). The ecological validity of delay aversion and response inhibition as measures of impulsivity in AD/HD: A supplement to the NIMH Multimodal Treatment Study of AD/HD. *Journal of Abnormal Child Psychology, 29,* 215–228.

Sonuga-Barke, E. (2002). Psychological heterogeneity in AD/HD: A dual pathway model of behaviour and cognition. *Behavioural Brain Research, 130,* 29–36.

Sonuga-Barke, E., Houlberg, K., & Hall, M. (1994). When is impulsiveness not impulsive? The case of hyperactive children's cognitive style. *Journal of Child Psychology and Psychiatry, 35,* 1247–1253.

Sonuga-Barke, E., Taylor, E., Sembi, S., & Smith, J. (1992). Hyperactivity and delay aversion: I. The effect of delay on choice. *Journal of Child Psychology and Psychiatry, 33,* 387–398.

Sonuga-Barke, E., Williams, E., Hall, M., & Saxton, T. (1996). Hyperactivity and delay aversion: III. The effect on cognitive style of imposing delay after errors. *Journal of Child Psychology and Psychiatry, 37,* 189–194.

Welsh, M. C., Pennington, B. F., & Groisser, D. B. (1991). A normative-developmental study of executive function: A window on prefrontal function in children. *Developmental Neuropsychology*, *7*, 131–149.

White, D., Nortz, M., Mandernach, T., Huntington, K., & Steiner, R. (2001). Deficits in memory strategy use related to prefrontal dysfunction during early development: Evidence from children with phenylketonuria. *Neuropsychology*, *15*, 221–229.

Winterer, G., & Goldman, D. (2003). Genetics of human prefrontal function. *Brain Research Reviews*, *43*(1), 134–163.

Wood, J. N., & Grafman, J. (2003). Human prefrontal cortex: Processing and representational perspectives. *Nature Reviews Neuroscience*, *4*(2), 139–147.

Zelazo, P., & Frye, D. (1997). Cognitive complexity and control: A theory of the development of deliberate reasoning and intentional action. In M. Stamenov (Ed.), *Language structure, discourse, and the access to consciousness* (pp. 113–153). Amsterdam: John Benjamins.

Zelazo, P., Jacques, S., Burack, J., & Frye, D. (2002). The relation between theory of mind and rule use: Evidence from persons with autism-spectrum disorders. Special Issue on Executive Functions and Development. *Infant and Child Development*, *11*, 171–196.

Zelazo, P., & Muller, U. (2002). Executive function in typical and atypical development. In U. Goswami (Ed.), *Handbook of childhood cognitive development* (pp. 445–469). Oxford: Blackwell.

Zentall, S., & Zentall, T. (1983). A model of disordered activity and performance in normal and deviant children. *Psychological Bulletin*, *94*, 446–471.

13

Self-regulation in the Developing Brain

Rebecca M. Todd and Marc D. Lewis

The alarm rings, and Anne wakes up already jumpy. As she gets out of bed, she notices a steady hum of anxiety and, gradually, she remembers the reason for it—a difficult meeting scheduled with her boss. She takes a couple of deep yoga breaths and feels her muscles relax slightly, then reminds herself that it is not so bad—she has handled many difficult meetings, she is good at this kind of thing, and she has a basically good relationship with her boss. And, after work, as a reward, she will have the pleasure of dinner with an old friend she hasn't seen for months. She feels the anxiety subside to a bearable background level as she showers and makes coffee. On the subway she doesn't even notice her unconscious impulse to move away from a man who is subliminally threatening to her because of his race and clothing, nor does she notice herself suppressing that impulse out of subway politeness. She also doesn't notice herself inhibit the impulse to stare at an extremely attractive young man sitting nearby.

The meeting does not go well. Anne's boss is angry, blaming Anne for mistakes that Anne feels were not her fault. Anne bites back an angry counter-accusation (she is afraid that if she yells at or blames her boss she could lose her job) and suppresses the impulse to cry—tries to mask even the shadow of that impulse (if her boss thinks she's weak she will lose confidence in her). Instead, Anne counts to 10 and, calmer, thinks of a constructive solution to the problem, which she proposes in an even tone of voice. Her boss is pleased and the meeting ends on a positive note. None the less, Anne remains angry and hurt for the rest of the day, so she distracts herself from her feelings by becoming absorbed in her work. Then, when the time comes to meet her friend, she finds that all she wants to do is go home and curl up alone. Instead, she reminds herself how much pleasure she takes in her friend's company, and heightens her anticipation by recalling the way her friend always makes her laugh. Indeed, they have a wonderful time together, laughing about Anne's boss's unreasonableness. Anne doesn't want to end the evening, but at 11pm regretfully says goodbye to avoid being tired and hungover the next day, curtailing her present pleasure in the interests of preventing future pain.

As adults, we regulate our emotions and behavior to further our goals all the time, consciously and unconsciously, using simple or elaborate strategies. Yet we are not born with this ability. The capacity for self-regulation develops slowly, with experience and socialization, as children's brains mature to the point where they can support increasingly elaborate strategies in the service of more abstract and distant goals. Moreover, certain types of psychopathology are associated with the failure to develop effective self-regulation skills. For example, clinical levels of aggression are associated with the failure to suppress aggressive outbursts (e.g., Davidson, Putnam, & Larson, 2000), possibly because the fear of consequences is not strong enough to counteract the expression of anger. Furthermore, clinical levels of anxiety are associated with the compulsive tendency to ramp up fearfulness (e.g., Bradley, 2000). For example, if Anne were suffering from an anxiety disorder she might have woken up and listed the worst possible consequences of the meeting, dwelling only on negative outcomes, paralyzing her ability to deal with the situation effectively. Alternatively, she might have failed to employ the strategy she did use of regulating anxiety by deliberately putting the meeting in perspective. Finally, individual differences in regulatory style, as well as certain types of psychopathology, may be associated with specific patterns of brain activation. By better understanding brain processes underlying normative self-regulation in development, as well as the neurophysiological patterns that characterize emergent clinical trajectories, we can more effectively diagnose and treat psychopathologies as they arise.

In this chapter, we begin by defining key concepts in the study of self-regulation and briefly discuss the functional neuroanatomy of emotion processing. We then review evidence that two specific cortical regions, the ventral prefrontal cortex (V-PFC) and the anterior cingulate cortex (ACC), function as hubs of ventral and dorsal networks associated with different styles of regulatory processing. We proceed to further review empirical findings on the role of these regions in the normative development of self-regulation, as well as in the emergence of individual differences and childhood psychopathology. Finally, we discuss implications for the treatment of psychopathology as it emerges in development.

Self-regulation: Concepts and Definitions

For over a decade, the study of emotion regulation has generated a great deal of interest among developmental psychologists. It is not a unified field of study, however. Emotion regulation and self-regulation are complex and often ill-defined constructs that refer to a wide array of processes. For example, in different contexts, the term "emotion regulation" may be used to refer to both emotion as a regulator of attentional processes (the study of *emotion as regulator*, see Cole, Martin, & Dennis, 2004) and attentional processes that regulate emotional responses (the study of *emotion as regulated*). In this chapter, we focus on the development of brain processes by which emotion is *regulated*. Thus, the following working definition applies to the body of emotion regulation research that we will review: "Emotion regulation consists of the extrinsic and intrinsic processes responsible for monitoring, evaluating, and modifying emotional reactions, especially their intensive and temporal features, to accomplish one's goals" (Thompson, 1994, pp. 27–28).

Self-regulation is a more inclusive term, sometimes used interchangeably with *emotion regulation*, which refers to regulation of both emotional and behavioral responses. We will use the term self-regulation to refer to cognitive processes involved in response control; that is, the control of attention, thought, action impulses, and actions as well as regulation of the emotional states themselves. Although much of the emotion regulation literature focuses on inhibition of negative emotional responses, emotion regulation also involves the enhancement of positive responses (Thompson, 1994), as when Anne deliberately ramped up anticipation of her friend's company.

The term *extrinsic* emotion regulation refers to the scaffolding of regulation processes and socialization by caregivers (Fox & Calkins, 2003). Extrinsic emotion regulation includes circumstances in which an infant's distress is soothed by an adult, or a toddler's expression of anger is punished. In our example, Anne helped to regulate her boss's anger by calmly offering constructive solutions. Infants and very young children are largely reliant on extrinsic strategies, and rely increasingly on intrinsic strategies with development (Kopp, 1989). *Intrinsic* strategies are those employed by the individual to modulate his or her own emotional or behavioral responses. Specific intrinsic strategies may be either automatic or voluntary. They can include shifting attention away from a distressing object or event (e.g., Rothbart & Derryberry, 1981), as Anne did when she busied herself in work. They also include suppression of behaviors associated with approach, avoidance, or emotional display (Cole, Zahn-Waxler, & Smith, 1994; Fox, 1994; Fox & Calkins, 2003), as Anne did unconsciously on the subway and consciously in her meeting with her boss. They also include postponing immediate gratification for a more distant goal, as when Anne ended the evening to get a good night's sleep, as well as reinterpretation or reappraisal of events in order to modify one's emotional response (Gross, 1998), as Anne did in the morning as she prepared for work. Finally, they can include coping strategies such as problem-solving, as Anne did with her boss, or seeking support from others (Saarni, 1997), as she did in the evening with her friend.

As a way of parsing intrinsic strategies, Eisenberg (e.g., Eisenberg & Spinrad, 2004) proposes that self-regulation be categorized as either *reactive* or *effortful*. We will draw on this distinction to define *reactive control* processes (not to be confused with pure *emotional reactivity*, which we discuss later) as those that include implicit evaluations of objects or events as aversive or rewarding, and may be associated with automatically overriding tendencies to approach or withdraw. In contrast, we define *effortful* processes as those involving a wide range of voluntary strategies that include explicitly overriding a more automatic response (Rothbart & Bates, 1998) or consciously re-evaluating, or reappraising, a situation (e.g., Gross, 1998).

Defining emotion regulation also requires that one define emotion—that which is regulated in the first place—but such definitions are contentious as well. None the less, contemporary emotion theorists generally agree that emotion entails a combination of somatic emotional responses (for example, increased heart rate or increased levels of cortisol following a stressful event), as well as feeling states and action tendencies that are linked to cognitive appraisals. Appraisals can be either conscious or unconscious, and include appraisals of both an emotion-eliciting situation (as positive or negative) and include one's perception of one's own emotional response (for review, see Lewis, 2005a). It has been argued that because emotion itself comprises many regulatory and cognitive processes (Lewis & Stieben, 2004), it is difficult to know where emotion ends and regulation begins. Lewis (2005a) proposes that emotional events are embedded in what he calls "emotional interpretations" (EIs), which are amalgams of reciprocal emotional and appraisal processes that include emotion regulation.

Another important—and related—concept in the study of emotion regulation is that of temperament. The literature on temperament addresses individual differences in what gets regulated as well as how one regulates it. Kagan pioneered work in this area with investigations of individual differences in biologically pregiven *emotional reactivity* (what gets regulated). For example, Kagan and colleagues (Kagan, Reznick, Clarke, Snidman, & Garcia-Coll, 1984) identified certain infants, whom they classified as "inhibited," who showed high levels of fear in response to novel stimuli from birth. Inhibited infants were identified by differences in reactivity measured by behavioral responses and heart rate (e.g., Garcia-Coll, Kagan, & Reznick, 1984; Kagan et al., 1984), autonomic responses (e.g., Bornstein & Suess, 2000), and right hemisphere EEG activity (see Calkins & Fox, 2002). Subsequent research has shown that individual differences in fearful reactivity tend to remain stable over childhood (Fox, Henderson, Rubin, Calkins, & Schmidt, 2001; Kagan, Reznick, Snidman, Gibbons, & Johnson, 1988). Nevertheless, the degree to which an individual learns to regulate automatic responses is shaped by early experience, and influences whether he or she may be classified as behaviorally inhibited later in development (Fox et al., 2005). Rothbart and Derryberry's (1981) model of temperament proposes that individual differences in temperament are shaped by an individual's level of reactivity in combination with his or her capacity for self-regulation (Rothbart, 2004; Rothbart & Derryberry, 1981). Thus, a child's level of basic reactivity is thought to remain fairly constant, while multiple levels of regulatory strategy emerge with development (Calkins & Fox, 2002; Kopp, 1989).

With cognitive development, levels of regulatory strategy become increasingly elaborated, moving from limited stimulus-bound and temporally immediate responses to more deliberate and flexible strategies aimed at temporally distant goals (Zelazo & Cunningham, 2007). To a certain extent, each level of regulatory skill is thought to be dependent on development of the previous level (Calkins & Fox, 2002). Children with high levels of emotional reactivity or certain combinations of tendencies toward approach and avoidance (Fox, 1994), who do not develop appropriate regulatory skills, have been found to be at greatest risk for problems with aggression, anxiety, and depression—psychopathologies that are associated with dysfunction of self-regulation (Posner & Rothbart, 2000). In this chapter, we focus on the neural substrates of self-regulation processes in normative development as well as individual trajectories that contribute to individual personality style and psychopathology.

Neurobiology of Emotion Regulation

Developmental psychologists who study the *emotion-as-regulated* aspect of emotion regulation have distinguished emotional responses from regulatory ones, conceptualizing regulation as a second stage of activity that follows an initial stage of emotion activation (e.g., Cole et al., 2004). At the level of the brain, this distinction becomes somewhat problematic, however, as it can be difficult to distinguish systems that are regulated from those that regulate. Different neural subsystems are associated with emotional or regulatory responses at different levels of the brain, and these subsystems regulate each other in complex feedback cycles (see Lewis, 2005a; Lewis & Todd, 2007). Yet although emotional and regulatory processes are tightly intertwined, we can none the less describe certain cortical regions associated with particular regulatory processes. Such regulatory processes either enhance or inhibit rapid emotional reactivity in other brain regions.

Before we focus on particular cortical regions, however, we first need to review the functional neuroanatomy of the emotional brain. In doing so, we describe how emotional events can activate a hierarchy of systems ranging from evolutionarily older regions, such as the brain stem and hypothalamus, to the newer and more flexible cerebral cortex. We then focus on the role of the ventral prefrontal and anterior cingulate cortices in self-regulation processes before turning our attention to how such processes develop.

Functional anatomy of the emotional brain

Brain stem and hypothalamus

The brain stem is the most *caudal* (toward the tail) and evolutionarily oldest part of the brain. It contains nuclei, or clusters of cells, that mediate biologically pregiven, reflexive responses that include feeding, mating, defensive, and attack behaviors. For example, Panksepp (1998) proposes that basic emotional responses are associated with four basic circuits, primarily mediated by the brain stem and striatum, which he calls "Blue Ribbon, Grade A Emotional Systems." These are partially independent circuits that are common to all mammals and can be activated independently of any higher cortical systems. They include a *seeking* system, underlying appetitive approach behaviors, a *rage* system, which is triggered by frustrated goals, a *fear* system, and a counterintuitively named *panic* system, which underlies mammalian attachment behaviors. Thus, the brain stem can be seen as the primary seat of basic emotional responses and the action tendencies, or automatic behavioral responses, that accompany them. These brain-stem responses are prepackaged and inflexible—in themselves they do not change with learning and development. The brain stem is also the site of nuclei that produce neurochemicals, such as dopamine and norepinephrine, that influence activity in all other brain systems, including the cortex, and bodily responses that accompany emotion.

The hypothalamus, which sits just above the brain stem, is associated with the coordination of brain-stem activities as well as control of autonomic nervous system changes and the release of hormones into the bloodstream. It is the hub of the hypothalamic–pituitary–adrenal (HPA) axis, a system that produces cortisol, a stress hormone that has been associated with individual differences in anxiety and inhibition (see Kagan et al., 1988; Schmidt et al., 1997). Neuropeptides produced by the hypothalamus can set body and brain systems into coherent goal-directed states such as fighting for territory, seeking food, or courting a mate. Extended release of neuropeptides and accompanying goal-directed action tendencies may also contribute to maintenance of lasting emotional states or moods (Panksepp, 1998).

The hypothalamus not only triggers changes in the autonomic nervous system and bloodstream, it also receives information from these systems. It is optimally positioned to regulate the body's responses to relevant changes in the environment. Thus, the brain stem and hypothalamus can be seen to mediate biologically pregiven processes associated with emotional reactivity. In many studies of self-regulation, these processes are often measures of what is *regulated*.

The limbic system

The term *limbic system* refers to a series of structures between the brain stem and the cortex thought to mediate a number of emotional processes. Over the course of evolution, this rough semicircle of structures evolved hugely in mammals. Whereas lower structures are involved in controlling perception and action according to fixed "programs" that require no learning, these structures mediate learning and memory. The processing of sensory input and motor output is slowed down in the limbic system, so that responses can fit more precisely to the learned aspects of situations (Tucker, Derryberry, & Luu, 2000). Indeed, the limbic system mediates emotional states that orient attention and action to whatever is presently meaningful. For example, the amygdala (AM), a key limbic structure, is involved in tagging neutral stimuli with emotional content (LeDoux, 1995; Rolls, 1999), thereby creating chains of associations based on emotional experiences. Connections from the AM to lower (hypothalamic and brainstem) structures activate emotional response systems given current stimulus events, and connections from the AM up to the cortex harness perception, attention, and planned action to these events (Lewis, 2005a). The AM requires the participation of lower structures to produce emotional states, while the converse is not true (Panksepp, 1998). Individual differences in thresholds of AM activation are associated with differences in temperamental reactivity (Schwartz, Wright, Shin, Kagan, & Rauch, 2003), and in studies of self-regulation AM activation is used as another measure of what is *regulated*. Other limbic structures, including the septal and hippocampal structures, also support emotional behaviors (e.g., play, sex, nurturance) and organization of episodic memory and attention (e.g., MacLean, 1993).

The cerebral cortex

The layers of the cortex surround the limbic system, and the recently evolved cells that inhabit these layers mediate processes of cognition, perception, and attention. Mesulam (2002) describes the flexible and temporally extended functions of the cortex as allowing freedom from the "default mode" of stimulus-bound, reflexive responses, permitting us to override or harness them in the service of more distant goals. In particular, the prefrontal regions and related midline structures are associated with sophisticated perceptual and cognitive activities (including attention, monitoring, decision-making, planning, and working memory) that are recruited by (and that regulate) the emotional responses mediated by brain-stem and limbic structures (Barbas, 1995; Bechara, Damasio, & Damasio, 2000; Davidson & Irwin, 1999). For example, ventral prefrontal cortex (V-PFC) and dorsal anterior cingulate cortex (ACC) are associated with a host of self-regulation processes, which we describe in detail below. In addition, dorsolateral prefrontal cortex (DL-PFC) is associated with retrieving, maintaining, and using complex sets of rules (see Bunge, 2004, for review), and rostrolateral prefrontal cortex is associated with high order, abstract strategies for switching among sets of abstract rules (see Bunge & Zelazo, 2006). Moreover, sophisticated use of rule systems is involved in high order strategies associated with effective self-regulation in a complex social environment (Zelazo & Cunningham, 2007).

The hierarchy of brain levels is often construed in terms of domination or control of lower levels by higher levels, and this is how emotion regulation in the brain is often defined. Indeed, the cerebral cortex subordinates the more primitive functions of limbic system and brain stem in self-regulation. None the less, Tucker et al. (2000) emphasize that the downward flow of control and modulation—for example, from cortex to limbic system to brain stem—is reciprocated by an upward flow of synaptic activation and neurochemical stimulation. The brain stem and hypothalamus entrain limbic structures by means of neuromodulators and neuropeptides, locking in perceptual biases and associations, and they also recruit cortical activities in service of ancient mammalian and even reptilian agendas, which can be thought of as emotional *action tendencies*. Primitive agendas and requirements thus flow up the neuroaxis from its roots at the same time as executive attention, planning, and knowledge subordinate each lower level by the activities of the cortex. If not for the bottom-up flow, which can be seen as underlying motivated attention (*emotion as regulator*), the brain would have no energy and no direction for its activities. If not for the top-down flow, which underlies self-regulation processes (*emotion as regulated*), recently evolved mechanisms for perception, action, and integration would have no control over bodily states and behavior. It is the reciprocity of these upward and downward flows that links sophisticated cognitive processes with basic motivational mechanisms. Nevertheless, in our discussion of self-regulation we will limit our focus to the top-down processes by which cortical activation modulates limbic and brain-stem responses. To this end, we next discuss regions of prefrontal cortex that are key nodes in networks that mediate top-down control.

Two cortical systems are especially important for self-regulation processes as we have defined them: the ventral prefrontal cortex (V-PFC) and the anterior cingulate cortex (ACC). Both regions are at the outskirts of the prefrontal cortex. They are phylogenetically older and closer to the limbic system and are therefore called "paralimbic," and they play a role in cognitive activities relevant to emotional states (Barbas, 2000; Rolls, 1999). The V-PFC and ACC are highly interconnected, and both regions are important for the interaction of attention and emotion in general (Barbas, 1995; Lane et al., 1998), and self-regulation in particular (Davidson, Putnam, & Larson, 2000). Nevertheless, each is associated with a distinct "style" of processing. The V-PFC belongs to the ventral cortical trend, which has been characterized as the "what" system, attuned to the categorical properties of objects and people. Ventral prefrontal structures mediate attention to the environment rather than to anticipated actions (see Rolls, 2004). Their activity is stimulus bound, reactive rather than proactive, and allows the processing of perceptual information in great detail. It allows us to ascertain and anticipate the rewarding or punishing character of a given stimulus, and is flexible enough to mediate appropriate responses when the positive or negative aspects of a situation change (see Goldberg, 1985). To return to the distinction between reactive and effortful control, the V-PFC functions as a hub of a ventral trend associated with reactive control processes as we have defined them. By definition, such processes can unfold outside conscious awareness.

In contrast, the ACC is the hub of the dorsal cortical trend, which has been characterized as the "where" system, concerned with action, spatial location, and context (Goldberg, 1985). Dorsal systems appear to mediate the smooth, deliberate control of behavior, including emotional behavior, in a supervisory fashion, particularly in novel or challenging situations. In our model, it is associated with proactive, consciously explicit, effortful control of emotions and behavior. Thus, dorsal systems can be seen as more flexible than ventral systems in that they allow us to consciously select among a number of courses of action based on a range of anticipated consequences. We will now show how the differences in "cognitive style" that characterize these two trends can help map out the cortical terrain in a way that contributes to our understanding of reactive and effortful emotion regulation.

Ventral prefrontal cortex and reactive control

The V-PFC, including orbitofrontal and ventromedial prefrontal cortices, constitutes the most ventral regions of the prefrontal cortex (see Plate 5). The V-PFC has downward connections to the amygdala, hypothalamus, and brain-stem nuclei as well as upward connections to the ACC (for review, see Lewis, 2005a; Rolls, 2004). Its downward connections are integral to emotional states and its activity has been frequently implicated in the regulation of emotion through inhibition of AM activation (Davidson, Jackson, & Kalin, 2000; Hariri, Mattay, Tessitore, Fera, & Weinberger, 2003; Lévesque et al., 2003; Ochsner et al., 2004). It also has connections with the striatum that allow it to influence behavior quickly, without much thought. Furthermore, as we have mentioned, ventral prefrontal cortex activation is also implicated in approach activity associated with reward (Rolls, 2004).

Overall, V-PFC activity has been associated with assessing the emotional relevance of objects in the environment and adjusting responses accordingly (Rolls, 2004). More specifically, one well-documented activity of the V-PFC is its role in situations when one must change one's actions in response to changing cues in the environment

(Rolls, 2004), a process known as *response reversal*. For example, one of the most important changing social cues we encounter is facial expression. Different cells in the V-PFC are responsive to either the emotion or identity of a face (Rolls, 2004). Yet, unlike other face-responsive cells in the brain (e.g., in the fusiform gyrus), face-responsive cells in the V-PFC are sensitive to the reward value of faces as well. That is, they respond not just to emotion and identity but what a particular face or expression means to us based on our emotional histories. For example, we know (without having to consciously think about it) that the face of a parent or spouse belongs to a person we love, and we know that this person's smile means good things while a frown means our actions may have familiar negative consequences. This kind of implicit knowledge, based on personal history, is crucial to social learning and emotion regulation. Moreover, when a smile turns to a frown it can be a strong cue that we need to change our behavior. Blair (2004) refers to such behavior change in response to social cues as social reversal learning, a process that is mediated by specific regions in the V-PFC (see Kringelbach & Rolls, 2003).

The V-PFC is also implicated in decision-making processes associated with intuitive "gut" responses—as distinct from rational analysis of costs and benefits, a process that involves more dorsal and lateral regions of the prefrontal cortex (Bechara, 2004). Furthermore, V-PFC is involved in inhibiting or overriding impulsive emotional responses, including aggressive outbursts (Davidson, Putnam, & Larson, 2000). It is also activated when one overrides an impulse for immediate gratification to delay reward or avoid punishment (Clark, Cools, & Robbins, 2004). Finally, different areas of V-PFC may orchestrate different types of regulatory function. Happaney, Zelazo, and Stuss (2004) suggest that medial regions are associated with the initial evaluation of the reward value of a stimulus. In contrast, lateral regions are involved in shifting or reappraising the initial evaluation and modulating one's response accordingly. Rolls (2004) makes a slightly different distinction between regions, suggesting that medial regions are involved in tagging reward and lateral regions in tagging punishment.

The V-PFC receives a great number of projections from brain-stem nuclei that produce neuromodulators, and it is rich in receptors for dopamine and serotonin (Gabriel, Burhans, Talk, & Scalf, 2002), norepinephrine (Arnsten & Li, 2005), and endogenous opiates (Kolb, Pellis, & Robinson, 2004). Various neuromodulators play different roles in self-regulation processes. Dopamine is associated with approach behavior and reward-seeking (Depue & Collins, 1999; Luciana, 2001). Rolls (2004) suggests that in the V-PFC dopamine plays a role in determining whether an action is required in achieving reward or avoiding punishment. Luciana (2001) further proposes that dopamine provides a neural "gel" that links distributed regions in the performance of complex behaviors. In contrast, serotonin mediates functions associated with the capacity to control impulsive behavior (Clark et al., 2004; Davidson, Putnam, & Larson, 2000), as well as processes thought to facilitate relaxation (e.g., Lesch et al., 1996). Ventral prefrontal regions are also rich in receptors for endogenous opiates (Kolb et al., 2004) which contribute to feelings of well-being associated with getting (rather than seeking) rewards. Such rewards include those related to attachment and social bonding (Tucker, Luu, & Derryberry, 2005). For example, the sight of a parent's or spouse's smiling face can trigger the production of endogenous opiates. In turn, the opiate reward that comes along with such social approval is a strong motivator for regulating one's emotions or behavior appropriately.

Neuropsychological studies of patients with prefrontal damage provide additional evidence for the role of V-PFC in reactive regulation processes. Those suffering from ventral PFC damage tend to be impulsive and have trouble inhibiting their actions, find it hard to make advantageous decisions related to reward and punishment, and show impaired social understanding and difficulty changing their actions in response to changing social signals (Bechara, 2004; Eslinger, Flaherty-Craig, & Benton, 2004; Rolls, 2004). They also tend to show great rigidity in emotion regulation strategies (Eslinger et al., 2004). Yet patients who have lost PFC function in adulthood are generally able to give rational reasons for making advantageous decisions. They are simply unable to act on them. In terms of our model, what they lack is the capacity for the reactive control processes that entail direct, relatively automatic control of behavior.

Furthermore, abnormal patterns of ventral prefrontal activation are associated with forms of psychopathology that are characterized by deficits in self-regulation. For example, decreased V-PFC activation is associated with pathological aggression (Davidson, Putnam, & Larson, 2000). Conversely, anxious and depressed individuals show greater than normal activation in ventral systems (Drevets & Raichle, 1998; Mayberg et al., 1999). Overactivation of V-PFC in anxiety and depression is in part a function of its tight coupling with the amygdala, which makes it highly responsive to the emotional value of things in the world. Because the V-PFC (unlike the amygdala) also mediates *anticipated* reward and punishment, in anxious or depressed individuals the V-PFC and amygdala may work together in implicit anticipation of negative consequences. As we have seen, V-PFC systems mediate regulatory processes that are less flexible and deliberate than those mediated by dorsal systems. Thus, in the case of anxiety and depression, they can be seen as rigidly and "thoughtlessly" responding to the urgings of stimuli—either immediate or anticipated.

Dorsal systems and effortful control

The dorsal ACC is found on the medial surface of the posterior PFC. It has descending connections to the V-PFC, amygdala, hypothalamus, and brain stem, as well as multiple connections to motor cortex and numerous prefrontal regions, including the dorsolateral prefrontal cortex (DL-PFC; Gabriel et al., 2002). Whereas the ventral prefrontal cortex plays a key role in reactive control processes as we have defined them, the dorsal regulatory system mediates effortful control. The ACC is closely connected to the supplementary motor area, where new actions are formulated (Goldberg, 1985), and thus the ACC is associated with motor rather than sensory anticipation. Dorsal regions of the ACC are activated when we must direct attention to potential actions, evaluate their utility for intended outcomes, and select or generate a unitary stream of action (see Cardinal, Parkinson, Hall, & Everitt, 2002; Goldberg, 1985). The ACC is implicated in the generation of intentions (in interaction with other structures, including the hippocampus) and the dispatch of signals on to the motor areas for execution (Luu, Tucker, & Derryberry, 1998). Dorsal ACC activation has also been associated with monitoring and evaluating potential actions, monitoring and resolving conflicts (as in error detection), and selective attention more generally (Carter et al., 2000; Gehring, Goss, Coles, Meyer, & Donchin, 1993; van Veen, Cohen, Botvinick, Stenger, & Carter, 2001). The executive system mediated by the dorsal ACC is activated in contexts requiring voluntary choice as well as directed attention and learning (Frith, Friston, Liddle, & Frackowiak, 1991; van Veen et al., 2001), and, perhaps most notably, when we have to assert our will in uncertain or conflictual circumstances (Paus, 2001). Rainville (2002) has further suggested that ACC activation is associated with the feeling of mental effort that accompanies deliberate regulation processes. Like the V-PFC, the dorsal ACC is rich in dopamine, norepinephrine, and serotonin receptors (Arnsten & Li, 2005; Gabriel et al., 2002), though the two regions appear to respond differently to experimental perturbations (Kolb et al., 2004). Because dorsal ACC function appears to be central to deliberate and willed action, damage to this area can produce dissociation between actions and intentions (Luu et al., 1998).

As Posner and Rothbart (2000) point out, dorsal ACC networks are important in socialization processes, and key to the development of effortful emotion regulation. Whereas the dorsal ACC seems to be activated consistently in situations requiring explicit effortful attention, the frontal regions co-activated with it vary according to the nature of the regulation strategy (Fan, Flombaum, McCandliss, Thomas, & Posner, 2003). Neuroimaging studies of effortful emotion regulation strategies in adults have found the dorsal ACC to be activated during experiments that require deliberate reappraisal of negative stimuli (Ochsner et al., 2004) or performance of a demanding cognitive task to distract attention from a disturbing image (Hariri et al., 2003). In such experiments, the ACC has been activated in concert with other prefrontal regions, such as the DL-PFC, that mediate working memory and explicit planning. For example, Ochsner and colleagues (2004) conducted an experiment in which participants were shown emotionally evocative pictures and then asked to reappraise their responses. In some trials they were asked to down-regulate their emotions. In such trials, when faced with a disturbing image of a distressed-looking man in a hospital bed (for example), participants might be asked to provide an explanation that made the image seem less disturbing than it first appeared (perhaps the man has just been given medicine and will feel better very soon). On this type of trial, there was increased activation in dorsal ACC as well as in the right V-PFC and the dorsolateral prefrontal cortex. In contrast, activation in the amygdala *decreased*, suggesting that the ACC is instrumental in recruiting other frontal regions to decrease amygdala reactivity. In other trials, participants were asked to up-regulate their emotions by reappraising an image so that it seemed worse. (They might tell themselves that the man in the hospital bed was getting worse, that his agony would increase, and that he would die leaving his family devastated.) Again, in these trials the dorsal ACC and DL-PFC were active but amygdala activation *increased*. This finding suggests that the ACC was implicated in recruiting the frontal regions that, in this case, enhanced emotional reactivity.

In general, dorsal and ventral systems may either work in tandem or compete in the service of self-regulation. We are proposing a model in which dorsal systems, which are associated with conscious, volitional control, allow us either to elaborate on or override the relatively automatic approach and avoidance responses associated with V-PFC systems. For example, the capacity to override more reactive responses to immediate reward and punishment allow us to employ regulatory strategies in pursuing more long-term or abstract goals. The inability to harness dorsal ACC systems is associated with deficits in such regulatory strategies. For example, deficits in dorsal ACC function have been associated with ADHD (Bush et al., 1999), which may be linked to compromised dopamine and norepinephrine transmission (Arnsten & Li, 2005). Dorsal ACC deficits have also been linked to aggression (Davidson, Putnam, & Larson, 2000). Zelazo and Cunningham (2007) suggest that dorsal systems become active, in conjunction with ventral systems, in situations when relatively automatic ventrally mediated responses are not sufficient. Thus, in the case of ADHD and aggression, there may be suboptimal co-activation of dorsal and ventral systems to control impulsive behavior.

There is also evidence suggesting that in some circumstances dorsal prefrontal systems may *compete* with ventral ones for activation, with emotional demands turning off dorsal systems and activating ventral systems in their place (Bush, Luu, & Posner, 2000; Kolb et al., 2004). As we have mentioned, ventral dominance, along with deficits in dorsal activation, may be chronic in the case of anxiety disorders (Drevets & Raichle, 1998) and depression (Drevets, 1999; Mayberg et al., 1999). Anxious individuals show less dorsal ACC and less lateral prefrontal activation in response to threatening stimuli (Bishop, Duncan, Brett, & Lawrence, 2004). In the case of ventral dominance, reactive responses may overwhelm the capacity, mediated by dorsal systems, to pull attention away from distressing stimuli or employ other strategies that down-regulate amygdala activation (see Ochsner et al., 2004). At other times, V-PFC activation may "hijack" dorsally mediated processes of planning and reappraisal to increase rather than alleviate negative emotion (as in Ochsner et al., 2004).

Thus, there is evidence that we have two systems, subserving reactive and effortful control, which can either work together or compete when self-regulation is called for. But how do these systems come online? When and how do their functions emerge with development? Finally, how do individual differences in the patterns of dorsal/ventral co-activation or dominance emerge? We now turn to the neurophysiological and behavioral evidence behind models of self-regulation in development.

The Neural Substrates of Self-regulation in Development

We start life as tightly stimulus-bound creatures, reacting in the moment to pleasant and unpleasant events (e.g., Luciana, 2001). With social and cognitive development, we become better able to focus on distant goals, more planful, and better able to choose between competing strategies and responses in a contextually appropriate manner. In neurophysiological terms, the phylogenetically older brain-stem and midbrain systems underlying basic emotional reactivity mature relatively early in development (Chugani, Phelps, & Mazziotta, 1987). In contrast, the frontal cortical networks supporting self-regulation continue to develop through adolescence (Giedd et al., 2004; Gogtay et al., 2004). There is evidence that ventromedial prefrontal networks mature earlier than ventrolateral and dorsal networks (Gogtay et al., 2004). In fact, it has been suggested that the development of dorsally mediated self-regulation systems may be scaffolded by, and depend on, development of ventromedial systems (Kesek, Zelazo, & Lewis, in press) as well as by connectivity between dorsal and ventral prefrontal brain regions. Thus, the capacity for effortful control may depend in part on the development of reactive control.

As normative processes unfold, individual differences in self-regulation style consolidate. Indeed, our styles of interpreting and responding to events in the world can be seen as corticolimbic habits (Lewis, 2005b). As the neural connections underlying these habits become strengthened over development, personality style becomes entrenched— as do corticolimbic habits associated with psychopathology (Lewis, 2005b). In this section, we discuss both normative development and individual differences in the capacity for reactive and effortful self-regulation, as well as trajectories that can lead to disorders involving aggression, anxiety, and depression.

Until recently, little was directly known about the cortical changes that accompany behavioral milestones in effortful self-regulation. Even now, there are large gaps in our knowledge. None the less, a few recent developmental studies (e.g., Giedd et al., 1999; Gogtay et al., 2004; Paus, 2005) have added crucial information to our understanding of structural and functional development in the brain in general. Thus, we now know that phylogenetically older regions of the cortex mature earlier than more recent ones (Gogtay et al., 2004). Within the prefrontal cortex, there is evidence that the ventromedial PFC reaches adult levels of gray matter volume first, whereas lateral V-PFC and DL-PFC mature through adolescence (Gogtay et al., 2004). White matter volume matures into adulthood, as axons connecting distributed brain regions become myelinated, and thus more efficient (Nagy, Westerberg, & Klingberg, 2004). There is also evidence that the prefrontal cortex undergoes a major structural reorganization at puberty (Paus, 2005). Thus, the combination of increased emotional reactivity with the cognitive reorganization that accompanies frontal restructuring poses new challenges to self-regulation in adolescence (Kesek et al., in press).

Recent research also indicates that three basic trends characterize cortical development: increased frontalization, increased efficiency, and increased connectivity. Over time, children come to rely less on posterior/parietal regions and more on frontal networks to perform certain cognitive tasks (e.g., Rubia et al., 2000). To do so, they use smaller brain regions as they process information more efficiently (Bunge, Dudukovic, Thomason, Vaidya, & Gabrieli, 2002; Casey et al., 1997; Luna et al., 2001). At the same time, as axons connecting distant brain regions become increasingly myelinated, there is an increase in coordinated activity between brain regions (Luna et al., 2001). Indeed, evidence increasingly supports Johnson's (2000) hypothesis that the emergence of new skills arises not from the recruitment of new cortical regions but from the coupling of already functioning regions. As we have mentioned, such coordinated activity is necessary for effortful self-regulation. Zelazo and Cunningham (2007) have suggested that self-regulation strategies requiring more complex rule use are mediated by broader frontal networks. These include later developing regions of frontal cortex (e.g., Nagy et al., 2004). Thus, the capacity for complex regulation strategies, involving multiple context-dependent contingencies, long-term future planning, or elaborate reappraisal, may appear later in development because they require the coordination of later developing frontal regions with those that develop earlier (Zelazo & Cunningham, 2007). This principle of increasing connectivity helps us to think about the variety of systems connected with the dorsal ACC in the service of self-regulation.

Development of ventral self-regulation systems

Ventromedial systems mature earlier than ventrolateral and dorsal systems (Gogtay et al., 2004), and social understanding and reward-based regulatory behaviors mediated by the VM-PFC are thought to be shaped by early interactions between infants and caregivers (Schore, 1997). As we have reviewed, the V-PFC is active in implicit processes of labeling events with a positive or negative emotional charge, and its cells are sensitive to the salience of facial affect and identity. Schore (2003) has suggested that V-PFC development is shaped by face-to-face interactions between infants and caregivers. He proposes that, in the first year of life, development of dopamine receptors in this region is enhanced by positive interactions that create expectations of social reward. As a child becomes more mobile, however, parents increasingly express negative emotion in the course of socialization. First, children learn that positive interactions are rewarding, and these positive associations create expectancies of reward thought to be mediated by ventromedial PFC (Rolls, 2004). Then, by discovering that certain impulsive behaviors result in the loss of that reward, they develop the capacity to regulate those behaviors. Tronick and colleagues vividly describe just such a scenario in the following passage:

> A 6-month-old infant and his mother are playing a game and the mother leans in to nuzzle the baby. The infant takes hold of the mother's hair and when she pulls away he does not let go. In pain, the mother responds with an angry facial expression and vocalization. The infant immediately sobers and brings his hand up to his face in a defensive move. The mother pulls back, pauses, and then slowly approaches the infant again. The infant drops his hands and they resume their normal exchange. (Tronick et al., 1998, p. 293)

This ability to appraise social behavior, and the neural systems that support such appraisals, may need to be in place before children can learn to regulate impulsive actions.

Thus, during the first years, socialization processes are thought to tune some of the brain's ventral prefrontal systems associated with reactive control. This model is both plausible and intuitively appealing, as the skills that develop through social interaction in these years are known to be mediated by ventral prefrontal regions in adults, and they are precisely the skills that are lacking in frontal lobe patients. There is also a wide body of evidence connecting the quality of parent–child interactions to the capacity to inhibit aggressive and impulsive behavior and comply with parental demands (e.g., Calkins, Smith, Gill, & Johnson, 1998; Cole, Teti, & Zahn-Waxler, 2003)—again, all skills that are mediated by ventral prefrontal regions. To date, however, there is no direct empirical evidence linking early social interactions to the development of ventral systems in young children, and our model remains speculative.

At this point in time, there are few if any neuroimaging studies (positron emission tomography, or PET, and functional magnetic resonance imaging, or fMRI) that specifically localize brain regions tapping reactive emotion regulation in preschool-aged children. None the less, event-related potential (ERP) studies use less intrusive methods to tap differences in scalp activation between groups and conditions. ERPs are EEG waves, averaged across many trials, that show predictable patterns following a given stimulus or response. In our research, we have found preliminary neurophysiological data suggesting that ventral networks responsive to the valence of facial affect and identity are in place by the preschool years. For example, studies from our group found that, by the age of 4, children show ventral prefrontal responses to both facial affect and identity. These results suggest that V-PFC systems responsive to the valence of social information are in place and show adult-like activation patterns by 4 years (Todd, Evans, Lewis, & Taylor, 2007; Todd, Lewis, Meusel, & Zelazo, 2008). Yet, although these networks may be in place by the age of 4, the salience of specific aspects of facial identity and emotion may change with development (Carver et al., 2003). For example, our preliminary results suggest that preschool children are more tuned than older children to the reward value of mothers' expressions. In contrast, early school-aged children are more tuned than preschoolers or adults to threat associated with angry expressions on strangers' faces. The capacity to discriminate more fine-grained facial expression continues to develop through adolescence (see McLure, 2000) as connectivity between perceptual regions responsive to faces and frontal regions responsive to their significance increases. Thus, while ventral prefrontal networks that respond to the salience of social information may be in place by the age of 4, they continue to be tuned with experience.

By the age of 4, children also show frontal brain activation linked to social response shifting, a capacity associated with slower maturing ventrolateral prefrontal regions. For example, we found increased frontal scalp activity in a task where children had to override a reflexive impulse to either stop an action (Blair, Morris, Frith, Perret, & Dolan, 1999) or withdraw (Hare, Tottenham, Davidson, Glover, & Casey, 2005) in the presence of anger by pressing a button following the presentation of an angry face (Lewis, Todd, & Honsberger, 2007). Moreover, source models based on scalp activity suggested a V-PFC source for this activity. Thus, we can infer that children were able to draw on frontal regions to override a more reflexive response to stop when confronted with facial anger. In addition, behavioral data showed that response times were slower following angry faces than following happy or neutral ones, suggesting that children had to take more time to regulate emotional responses to facial anger before responding. Finally, in the same group of children, we also found individual differences in reactive control processes, with anxious children showing faster frontal neurophysiological responses following angry faces (Lewis, Todd, & Honsberger, 2007). Thus, more anxious children seemed quicker to harness regulatory processes following threatening stimuli. This rapid frontal response in more anxious children, which may be linked to a low threshold for amygdala activation, is consistent with findings of increased ventral prefrontal activity in anxious and depressed children (Fox et al., 2005).

Although there are only a few studies directly measuring neural correlates of reactive control processes, we can look at behavioral studies to make inferences about underlying brain development. We therefore review a number of behavioral studies that tap effortful behaviors that we believe, based on adult neuroimaging studies and lesion studies, to be mediated by ventral systems. For example, one reliable behavioral measure of ventrally mediated effortful control processes is the "disappointing gift task," which measures the capacity to inhibit emotional expression in accordance with social norms (e.g., Cole, Zahn-Waxler, & Smith, 1994). In this paradigm, a child is presented with a number of prizes and asked to rank them in order of preference. After some intervening tasks, the child is presented with the last choice prize. The child's affective response to the disappointment—both in the presence of an experimenter and when the child is alone—is then coded. The degree of modulation of negative expression in the experimenter's presence is used as a measure of the capacity for self-regulation (Cole et al., 1994). By the age of 3 years, children begin to be capable of successful performance in this task (Cole et al, 1994). Furthermore, performance on the disappointing gift task also marks individual differences associated with emerging behavior problems. Cole et al. (1994) found 4- and 5-year-old boys who were at risk of disruptive behavior disorders—disorders that are associated with dysregulation of ventral prefrontal systems—showed more negative emotion in the presence of the experimenter than boys who were not at risk.

One of the best studied manifestations of self-regulation associated with ventral systems is implicit reward-based decision-making. The Iowa Gambling Task is a behavioral measure designed to tap deficits shown by frontal lobe patients, and neuroimaging data suggest that it taps ventral prefrontal function in adults (e.g., Bechara, Damasio, & Damasio, 2000). In one study, the task was modified for preschoolers, who had to choose from two decks of cards showing either loss or gain of reward, as indicated by a smiling or frowning face (Kerr & Zelazo, 2004). Over a number of trials, disadvantageous decks provided an overall pattern of loss, whereas advantageous decks offered a pattern of gain. In a study of 3–5-year-olds, 3-year-olds (like frontal lobe patients) failed to learn to choose consistently from the advantageous decks, but 4- and 5-year-olds did learn to choose advantageously. In more complex versions of the task, performance on this task has been shown to improve steadily through adolescence and into adulthood (e.g., Crone, Bunge, Latenstein, & van der Molen, 2005; Hooper, Luciana, Conklin, & Yarger, 2004; Overman et al., 2004). Thus, there seems to be a rapid improvement of this capacity between the ages of 3 and 4, which may be associated with the maturation of ventral prefrontal systems. This burst of maturation may be followed by continued gradual development of more lateral regions of ventral prefrontal cortex through adolescence. Kesek et al. (in press) further suggest that such extended development of ventrally mediated functions may reflect increased connectivity between ventral prefrontal networks and other more dorsal regions. In childhood, poor performance on tasks marking ventral prefrontal function as it emerges is associated with vulnerability to aggressive behavior problems (Blair, 2004; Cole et al., 1994), as well as anxiety and depression (Fox et al., 2005). Indeed, more automatic patterns of control may need to be in place before effortful and deliberate behaviors can develop (Kesek et al., in press). Failure to develop circuits that mediate reactive control may limit the capacity to develop forms of effortful control subserved by dorsal systems. As we have seen, some forms of reactive control, mediated by early developing ventromedial systems, may come online quite early in development. These, in turn, may scaffold the explosion of both ventrolaterally and dorsal ACC-mediated skills that unfold over the preschool years.

Development of dorsal self-regulation systems

Very little is known about the development of the ACC and its connectivity to other systems through the preschool years. Posner and Rothbart (2000) have suggested that ACC maturation underlies milestones in executive function and effortful control achieved between the ages of 3 and 5 years, but there is little direct evidence supporting this hypothesis. We know a bit more about the development of systems that are co-activated with the ACC *later* in development, however. In prefrontal cortex, more caudal and lateral regions, such as DL-PFC, continue to mature through adolescence (Giedd et al., 1999; Gogtay et al., 2004). Connectivity between ACC and other prefrontal regions develops through adolescence as well. Correspondingly, the capacity for effortful and deliberate self-regulation strategies mediated by ACC networks also develops into adulthood. But although direct neurophysiological evidence on the development of dorsal ACC systems is limited, particularly in preschool-aged children, there is an abundance of behavioral evidence demonstrating that children reach a number of milestones in effortful self-regulation processes between the ages of 3 and 6. During this period children become better able to delay gratification (Prencipe & Zelazo, 2005; Thompson, Barresi, & Moore, 1997), effortfully control impulsive behavior (Jones, Rothbart, & Posner, 2003), and become capable of using higher order rule systems for decision-making (Zelazo & Müller, 2002). In this age range the capacity for intuitive, ventrally mediated social understanding is enhanced by the capacity for conscious perspective-taking, and children are able to understand explicitly that others may have knowledge or perspectives that differ from their own (Astington, 1994). Behavioral studies in older children and adolescents also suggest that the more complex the self-regulation task, and the more it taps complex rule use, the longer the developmental trajectory (Crone, Ridderinkhof, Worm, Somsen, & van der Molen, 2004; Kesek et al., in press). Thus, regulation strategies that involve long-term or contingent planning, or sophisticated reappraisal of context, take the longest to develop.

In order to address gaps in our understanding, several experimental paradigms have been developed to directly tap the neural correlates of regulatory processes in school-aged children and adolescents. These include "cool" cognitive tasks that tap dorsal ACC activation, such as Stroop tasks, in which participants are shown colored words and must override the impulse to read the word in order to respond to its color, and Flanker tasks, in which participants have to ignore misleading cues in order to identify the direction of a stimulus. Such tasks are thought to tap attentional processes important to self-regulation as reflected by activation of the dorsal ACC.

In emotionally charged contexts, however, dorsal ACC systems may work in tandem with V-PFC systems to regulate behavior (Kesek et al., in press). An example of a task that taps dorsal *and* ventral activation in adults and children (Bokura, Yamaguchi, & Kobayashi, 2001; Casey et al., 1997; van Veen & Carter, 2002) is a go/no-go task, in which participants must press a button but occasionally withhold a button press, over-riding the automatic impulse to press. In emotional versions of go/no-go, Stroop, and Flanker tasks, positively and negatively charged stimuli are presented within a task that requires effortful attention to either override a strong prepotent response or choose between conflicting responses. Emotional stimuli activate ventral systems, while dorsal systems are activated by the demands of the task (e.g., Pérez-Edgar & Fox, 2003, 2005). In order to successfully perform the task, children must recruit dorsal ACC systems either to harness or to override V-PFC systems. Such tasks are thought to tap emotion regulation processes because children must effortfully regulate their emotional reactions to respond to the task. Activation of dorsal ACC is used as a measure of the degree of *effortful* regulatory processes that are recruited.

One well-researched ERP component associated with effortful self-regulation is the N2. The N2 is a negative peak found roughly 200–400 ms (in adults) after the presentation of a stimulus (e.g., Bokura et al., 2001; van Veen & Carter, 2002). It is thought to be generated by sources in both the dorsal ACC (e.g., van Veen & Carter, 2002) and the right ventral prefrontal cortex (Bokura et al., 2001; Plizska, Liotti, & Woldorff, 2000). In children, the N2 has been associated with measures of prefrontally mediated executive function (Lamm, Zelazo, & Lewis, 2006), as well as behavioral indices of flexible emotion regulation skill (Lewis, Granic, & Lamm, 2006). A number of studies in our lab have used affectively charged stimuli within go/no-go tasks to elicit N2s thought to tap emotion regulation processes. For example, in a study of effortful self-regulation processes in 4–6-year-old children, we showed participants pictures of angry and happy faces as stimuli in a go/no-go task (Todd et al., 2008). After about one second, a frame appeared around the face. At that point, depending on the color of the frame, children pressed a button or withheld a response. When children pressed the button both the face and the frame disappeared. In right frontal regions, 4–6-year-old children showed the largest N2s following angry faces in no-go trials, suggesting that greater effortful regulation was required when children had to withhold the satisfying impulse to make the face go away, particularly when the face was angry. Models of cortical sources of scalp activation suggested that, although V-PFC regions were active in all conditions, it was a source in the region of the dorsal cingulate cortex that was most active following angry faces. This model is consistent with the conclusion that, by the age of 4, children are able to recruit dorsal cingulate systems to consciously override an impulsive response.

Furthermore, in a study of 5–16-year-olds that used an affectively charged go/no-go task, we found that N2 amplitudes decreased with age, suggesting greater efficiency in dorsal systems associated with effortful emotion regulation (Lewis, Lamm, Segalowitz, Zelazo, & Stieben, 2006). In this study, children had to perform a difficult, speeded version of a go/no-go task. The task was rigged so that in the middle block of trials children lost the points they needed to win a coveted prize. Thus, children had to regulate negative affect, triggered by the loss of reward, in order to maintain concentration on the difficult task. Our models of cortical sources suggested that both older and younger children showed activation contributing to the N2 in the region of the dorsal ACC as well as in right V-PFC regions. However, older children showed more anterior cingulate activity and younger children showed more posterior cingulate activity. Thus, while all children recruited dorsal systems, older children activated sources in more frontal ACC regions to perform the task more efficiently.

Taken together, results from both of these studies are consistent with the notion that, by 4 years of age, children can recruit dorsal ACC systems for effortful emotion regulation. The data further suggest a picture in which younger children tend to rely on simpler posterior and ventral systems of control, while older children increasingly recruit dorsal ACC systems—thus contributing to a body of evidence suggesting that frontal regions are increasingly activated in cognitive tasks over development (e.g., Bunge et al., 2002). Moreover, processes of frontalization, as well as trends toward increased efficiency and distributed activation, carry on into adolescence as children continue to refine their self-regulation skills. Other evidence suggests that activity in dorsal and lateral prefrontal regions associated with working memory, which are often co-activated with the dorsal ACC, has been shown to increase through adolescence (e.g., Kwon, Reiss, & Menon, 2002). Thus, we may conclude that activity in ACC networks subserving strategies requiring high levels of working memory, or complex strategies involving rule use, continues to develop into adulthood. Indeed, the *gradual* development of regions recruited by dorsal ACC networks, when juxtaposed with the *rapid* increases in emotional reactivity associated with puberty, may go a long way toward explaining many of the challenges adolescents face when they have to think their way through intense emotional experiences.

Emerging individual differences in effortful self-regulation style may also be linked to dorsal ACC activation. There is certainly a wealth of behavioral evidence that self-regulation style is associated with differences in children's social functioning. For example, children with better capacity for effortful self-regulation are better able to shift attention away from anger-inducing cues and use nonhostile verbal methods of problem-solving (Eisenberg, Fabes, Nyman, Bernzweig, & Pinuelas, 1994). The capacity for effortful control also contributes to the development of conscience in young school-aged children (Kochanska, Murray, & Coy, 1997), and children's emotion regulation fosters awareness of responsibility for their own actions and negative consequences for other people (Derryberry & Reed, 1996). Eisenberg et al. (1997) found associations between good effortful self-regulation and high-quality social functioning in conflict situations to be as strong in middle childhood as in the preschool period. Thus, behaviors that are at least partly associated with dorsal ACC systems play a large part in individual differences in social functioning in childhood.

There are, again, few direct data on individual differences in dorsal ACC activation patterns in development. None the less, our research has linked distinct patterns of cortical activation to differences in children's emotional behavior in social interactions. A recent study found that children who had larger N2s also showed more flexible emotional behavior in negative emotional interactions with parents (Lewis, Granic, & Lamm, 2006). In this study, which looked at the relationship between behavioral flexibility and N2 amplitudes in a group of children referred for treatment for antisocial behavior, parent–child interactions were videotaped in the home. The interactions included a discussion of an unresolved problem that was designed to elicit negative emotion. Videotapes were coded for affect, and measures of emotional flexibility within parent–child interactions were assessed for the problem-solving discussion. In the same children, the frontal N2 was elicited in the go/no-go task that included the loss of points described above. We then examined associations between behavioral flexibility in the problem-solving discussion and N2 amplitudes. Results showed that greater behavioral flexibility predicted larger amplitude N2s following the negative mood induction, suggesting greater recruitment of frontocortical control systems in children with more flexible self-regulation styles. Moreover, source models indicated a generator for the N2 in the midline region of the prefrontal cortex, corresponding to the dorsal ACC, but only for children showing the highest levels of flexibility (Plate 6). These results suggest greater dorsal ACC-mediated regulation of a response repertoire for children who manage to maintain flexible interpersonal interactions despite the experience of negative emotions. Additional behavioral evidence suggests that the *lack* of such dyadic flexibility may be associated with externalizing problems (Granic & Patterson, 2006; Hollenstein, Granic, Stoolmiller, & Snyder, 2004). Moreover, increases in flexibility have been linked to successful treatment for externalizing problems (Granic, O'Hara, Pepler, & Lewis, 2007).

As we have mentioned, clinically significant aggression and anxiety problems can be understood as disorders of emotion regulation (e.g., Bradley, 2000). Young children who are less able to voluntarily shift their attention and inhibit their emotional impulses have higher levels of aggression (Rothbart, Ahadi, & Hershey, 1994). Children with these problems have failed to develop the capacity to appropriately modulate their feelings of anger and anxiety and the behaviors that flow from them. There is some direct neurophysiological evidence that clinical aggression is linked to suboptimal patterns of dorsal activation in children. For example, an fMRI study by Sterzer and colleagues (Sterzer, Stadler, Krebs, Kleinschmidt, & Poutska, 2005) found that children with conduct disorders showed less dorsal ACC activation than controls. In terms of our model of co-activating/competing systems, this deficit in self-regulation may be linked simply to decreased activation in dorsal networks. Alternatively, it may be linked to the lack of co-activation between ventral and dorsal circuits mediating reactive and effortful control.

Anxiety problems have also been linked to ineffective effortful self-regulation. In the case of clinically significant anxiety and inhibition, however, research points to excessive and excessively rigid emotional controls. Anxious children are overly fearful and tend to amplify their fears by focusing on the stress-inducing stimuli rather than recruiting a repertoire of dorsally mediated coping strategies (e.g., problem-solving; Bradley, 2000). In a cued attention task, Pérez-Edgar and Fox (2005) found that temperamentally shy children showed larger amplitudes in ERPs which associated with preferential attention to negative cues—ERPs that are presumably tapping a *reactive* response. We can speculate that such reactive ERP responses suggest that children were less able to engage dorsally mediated effortful regulation processes to override an automatic bias toward negative stimuli. Thus, vigilance in the face of threatening cues prevents these children from flexibly allocating attention elsewhere (e.g., Kagan et al., 1984). Depression has also been linked to the combination of strong emotionality and deficits in effortful self-regulation (e.g., Compas, Connor-Smith, & Jaser, 2004). In terms of our model, we wondered: Are depressed children locked into ventral reactive control processes, and thus unable to recruit dorsal systems to flexibly shift attention, reinterpret events, or strategize effective solutions?

A recent ERP study in our lab attempted to address just such a question by examining differences in cortical activation patterns associated with pure aggression as well as with anxiety/depression in the group of antisocial children mentioned above. The study used the affectively charged go/no-go task described previously to investigate neural correlates of self-regulation in aggressive children and in a group of controls (Stieben, Lewis, Granic, Zelazo, & Segalowitz, 2007). Clinical children were further divided into two subgroups: The first group of pure externalizers showed clinical levels of aggression but subclinical internalizing scores (EXT), while the second group showed symptoms of anxiety or depression along with aggression (MIXED). ERP results showed that the MIXED children had significantly larger N2s than the EXT children following the negative mood induction. Source models of cortical activation, based on scalp results, suggested that control children showed a strong source in the region of the dorsal ACC, consistent with models of adult brain activity during performance monitoring. In contrast, EXT children showed activation in a posterior source in the region of the posterior cingulate cortex. MIXED children also demonstrated a posterior source and, importantly, a source in the region of the right OFC. These findings are consistent with our model of differences in neurocognitive mechanisms of emotion regulation. Whereas normal children appeared to utilize dorsal ACC circuits that mediate performance monitoring, EXT and MIXED children both failed to recruit these networks and relied instead on posterior systems associated with more primitive forms of attentional updating. Finally, in addition to these systems, MIXED children appeared to recruit ventral control processes consistent with their inflexible behavior and anxious symptoms following the negative emotion induction. This is consistent with the notion that V-PFC systems may sometimes compete with dorsal ACC systems, precluding more flexible effortful regulation.

Thus, there is a growing body of evidence that, by mid-childhood, children show specific patterns of cortical activation associated with self-regulation behaviors related to aggression, anxiety, and depression. Control children and aggressive children who show more flexible regulatory behaviors may also show relatively greater dorsal ACC activation. In contrast, pure aggression may be associated with reduced dorsal ACC activation, and internalizing disorders with relatively more ventral activation. These findings are consistent with research that finds reduced dorsal ACC activity in aggressive adults and increased ventral prefrontal activity in those who suffer from depression and anxiety.

Implications for Treatment

To summarize, current research suggests that the capacity for reactive self-regulation processes undergoes a rapid maturation prior to the preschool years, possibly mediated by early maturing medial V-PFC systems. This early burst of maturation is followed by more gradual maturation of the capacity for implicit decision-making and reappraisal mediated by more lateral regions of V-PFC. The capacity for dorsally mediated effortful control emerges somewhat later, and develops gradually into adulthood. Moreover, the growing capacity for dorsally mediated effortful self-regulation may be scaffolded by earlier developing, ventrally mediated responses to social stimuli. With development, differences in personality style—including those associated with psychopathology—become more entrenched. These differences may be associated with specific patterns of co-activation or competition between dorsal and ventral systems associated with effortful and reactive control. Individuals with a temperamental predisposition toward high levels of negative affect may be more vulnerable to conduct disorder, anxiety, or depression if early social interactions do not adequately scaffold self-regulation skills mediated by ventral and/or dorsal networks (e.g., Fox et al., 2005). Thus, the earlier that potentially pathological patterns of regulation are identified or treated, the better the chances of treatment success.

Cortical connections are highly plastic (Elbert, Heim, & Rockstroh, 2001), and to a certain extent neural circuitry can be "rewired" by changes in strategy and behavior. In the case of aggression, which is characterized by deficits in both V-PFC and dorsal ACC systems, treatment needs to address both systems. Thus habits of social evaluation may need to change while skills in effortful self-regulation are developed. Because childhood aggression has been strongly linked to parenting style and the quality of parent–child interactions, treatments such as parent management training (PMT) that address family interaction styles may be most effective forms of treatment for aggression (Granic et al., 2007). PMT directly targets family interactions and can "rewire" ventral systems underlying social evaluation and promote simple inhibitory control.

For example, PMT promotes positive parenting practices, such as skill encouragement, problem-solving, and monitoring (for review, see Granic et al., 2007) which can change patterns of social appraisal, mediated by medial V-PFC, for children who are biased toward negative interpretations of social interactions. It also can reinforce self-regulation processes by teaching the use of mild sanctions (e.g., time-out) that contingently target misbehavior and strengthen inhibitory control mediated by lateral V-PFC. Thus, PMT may strengthen ventral systems of reactive evaluation and inhibition, which in turn can scaffold more explicit and effortful regulatory strategies.

Effective effortful regulation allows us to deliberately override more automatic responses (e.g., Ochsner et al., 2004). For this reason, strategies for strengthening effortful regulation skills mediated by dorsal ACC systems, such as cognitive behavioral therapy (CBT), can also be effective for both childhood aggression and anxiety, particularly in conjunction with PMT (Barkley, 2000; see Granic et al., 2007). CBT targets aggressive behaviors through techniques such as behavior management, role-playing, modeling, problem-solving, cognitive restructuring, social and token reinforcements, contingent consequences, and generalization activities (Bloomquist & Schnell, 2002). Moreover, recent studies indicate that incorporating mindfulness meditation techniques into cognitive behavioral therapy can be effective in strengthening the capacity for effortful control mediated by dorsal ACC systems. Mindfulness techniques allow for increased awareness of emotional reactions and voluntary control of emotional responses, and thus reinforce dorsal ACC circuitry. These strategies have been shown to be particularly promising in treating anxiety (Bögels, Sijbers, & Voncken, 2006) and depression (Broderick, 2005; Ramel, Goldin, Carmona, & McQuaid, 2004; Williams, Duggan, Crane, & Fennell, 2006), conditions in which overactive ventral systems may "swamp" dorsal ACC systems. Thus, combinations of CBT and PMT may help develop the capacity for both reactive and effortful control in aggressive children, and strengthen the capacity for effortful processes to override reactive processes in those suffering from anxiety and depression. Mindfulness meditation techniques may also be effective in strengthening effortful processes in anxious and depressed children.

Conclusion

In this chapter, in order to investigate the development of brain processes underlying *emotion as regulated*, we have reviewed the functional neuroanatomy of the emotional brain and identified cortical regions associated with cortical control of emotional responses. Specifically, we distinguished ventral and dorsal paralimbic regions, each associated with a different processing and regulation style. V-PFC networks are associated with implicit evaluations of stimuli, social understanding, and regulation of responses associated with punishment and reward. Ventromedial prefrontal systems come online early in development, while lateral systems mature more slowly, and the capacity for reactive control continues to develop as ventral networks become more widely connected and efficient. Dorsal systems associated with deliberate and effortful self-regulation strategies may be recruited when automatic reactive responses are no longer sufficient.

We have proposed a model in which dorsal and ventral systems may be co-activated in the service of self-regulation, or they may compete so that one system may predominate. Both dorsal and ventral prefrontal systems develop into adulthood, and may involve increasingly wide networks of cortical regions with increasing complex cognitive strategies. Finally, deficits in both reactive and effortful control, and the neural systems underlying them, are associated with psychopathology. Whereas deficits in V-PFC as well as dorsal ACC systems are associated with aggressive and impulsive behavior, overactive V-PFC systems may override dorsal ACC systems in anxiety and depression. Thus, for aggression, treatment strategies that address the social scaffolding of reactive processes as well as effortful control of behavior are called for. In contrast, for anxiety and depression, strengthening more flexible dorsal ACC systems, in order to override rigid patterns of self-regulation mediated by V-PFC, may be most effective.

References

Arnsten, A. F. T., & Li, B. M. (2005). Neurobiology of executive functions: Catecholamine influences on prefrontal cortical functions. *Biological Psychiatry, 57,* 1377–1384.

Astington, J. W. (1994). *The child's discovery of the mind.* London: Fontana.

Barbas, H. (1995). Anatomic basis of cognitive-emotional interactions in the primate prefrontal cortex. *Neuroscience and Biobehavioral Reviews, 19,* 449–510.

Barbas, H. (2000). Connections underlying the synthesis of cognition, memory, and emotion in primate prefrontal cortices. *Brain Research Bulletin, 52,* 319–330.

Barkley, R. A. (2000). Commentary: Issues in training parents to manage children with behavior problems. *Journal of the American Academy of Child and Adolescent Psychiatry, 39,* 1004–1007.

Bechara, A. (2004). The role of emotion in decision-making: Evidence from neurological patients with orbitofrontal damage. *Brain and Cognition, 55,* 30–40.

Bechara, A., Damasio, H., & Damasio, A. R. (2000). Emotion, decision making and the orbitofrontal cortex. *Cerebral Cortex, 10,* 295–307.

Bishop, S., Duncan, J., Brett, M., & Lawrence, A. D. (2004). Prefrontal cortical function and anxiety: Controlling attention to threat-related stimuli. *Nature Neuroscience, 7,* 184–188.

Blair, R. J. R. (2004). The roles of orbital frontal cortex in the modulation of antisocial behavior. *Brain and Cognition, 55,* 198–208.

Blair, R. J. R., Morris, J. S., Frith, C. D., Perret, D. I., & Dolan, R. J. (1999). Dissociable neural responses to facial expressions of sadness and anger. *Brain, 122,* 883–893.

Bloomquist, M. L., & Schnell, S. V. (2002). *Helping children with aggression and conduct problems: Best practices for intervention.* New York: Guilford.

Bögels, S. M., Sijbers, G. F. V. M., & Voncken, M. (2006). Mindfulness and task concentration training for social phobia: A pilot study. *Journal of Cognitive Psychotherapy, 20,* 33–44.

Bokura, H., Yamaguchi, S., & Kobayashi, S. (2001). Electrophysiological correlates for response inhibition in a go/nogo task. *Clinical Neurophysiology, 112,* 2224–2232.

Bornstein, M. H., & Suess, P. E. (2000). Physiological self-regulation and information processing in infancy: Cardiac vagal tone and habituation. *Child Development, 71*, 273–287.

Bradley, S. (2000). *Affect regulation and the development of psychopathology*. New York: Guilford.

Broderick, P. C. (2005). Mindfulness and coping with dysphoric mood: Contrasts with rumination and distraction. *Cognitive Therapy and Research, 29*, 501–510.

Bunge, S. A. (2004). How we use rules to select actions: A review of evidence from cognitive neuroscience. *Cognitive, Affective, and Behavioral Neuroscience, 4*, 564–579.

Bunge, S. A., Dudukovic, N. M., Thomason, M. E., Vaidya, C. J., & Gabrieli, J. D. E. (2002). Immature frontal lobe contributions to cognitive control in children: Evidence from fMRI. *Neuron, 33*, 301–311.

Bunge, S., & Zelazo, P. D. (2006). A brain-based account of the development of rule use in childhood. *Current Directions in Psychological Science, 15*, 118–121.

Bush, G., Frazier, J. A., Rauch, S. L., Seidman, L. J., Whalen, P. J., Jenike, M. A., et al. (1999). Anterior cingulate cortex dysfunction in attention-deficit/hyperactivity disorder revealed by fMRI and the counting Stroop. *Biological Psychiatry, 45*, 1542–1552.

Bush, G., Luu, P., & Posner, M. I. (2000). Cognitive and emotional influences in anterior cingulate cortex. *Trends in Cognitive Sciences, 4*, 215–222.

Calkins, S. D., & Fox, N. A. (2002). Self-regulatory processes in early personality development: A multilevel approach to the study of childhood social withdrawal and aggression. *Development and Psychopathology, 14*, 477–498.

Calkins, S. D., Smith, C. L., Gill, K. L., & Johnson, M. C. (1998). Maternal interactive style across contexts: Relations to emotional, behavioral and physiological regulation during childhood. *Social Development, 7*, 350–369.

Cardinal, R. N., Parkinson, J. A., Hall, J., & Everitt, B. J. (2002). Emotion and motivation: The role of the amygdala, ventral striatum, and prefrontal cortex. *Neuroscience and Biobehavioral Reviews, 26*, 321–352.

Carter, C. S., MacDonald, A. M., III, Botvinick, M. M., Ross, L. L., Stenger, V. A., Noll, D., et al. (2000). Parsing executive processes: Strategic vs. evaluative functions of the anterior cingulate cortex. *Proceedings of the National Academy of Sciences, USA, 97*, 1944–1948.

Carver, L. J., Dawson, G., Panagiotides, H., Meltzoff, A. N., McPartland, J., Gray, J., et al. (2003). Age-related differences in neural correlates of face recognition during the toddler and preschool years. *Developmental Psychobiology, 42*, 148–159.

Casey, B. J., Trainor, R. J., Orendi, J. L., Schubert, A. B., Nystrom, L. E., Giedd, J. N., et al. (1997). A developmental functional MRI study of prefrontal activation during performance of a go/no-go task. *Journal of Cognitive Neuroscience, 9*, 835–847.

Chugani, H. T., Phelps, M. E., & Mazziotta, J. C. (1987). Positron emission tomography study of human brain functional development. *Annals of Neurology, 22*, 487–497.

Clark, L., Cools, R., & Robbins, T. W. (2004). The neuropsychology of ventral prefrontal cortex: Decision-making and reversal learning. *Brain and Cognition, 55*, 41–53.

Cole, P. M., Martin, S. E., & Dennis, T. A. (2004). Emotion regulation as a scientific construct: Methodological challenges for child development research. *Child Development, 75*, 317–333.

Cole, P. M., Teti, L. O., & Zahn-Waxler, C. (2003). Mutual emotion regulation and the stability of conduct problems between preschool and early school age. *Development and Psychopathology, 15*, 1–18.

Cole, P. M., Zahn-Waxler, C., & Smith, K. D. (1994). Expressive control during a disappointment: Variations related to children's behavior problems. *Developmental Psychology, 30*, 835–846.

Compas, B. E., Connor-Smith, J., & Jaser, S. S. (2004). Temperament, stress reactivity, and coping: Implications for depression in childhood and adolescence. *Journal of Clinical Child and Adolescent Psychology, 33*, 21–31.

Crone, E. A., Bunge, S. A., Latenstein, H., & van der Molen, M. W. (2005). Characterization of children's decision making: Sensitivity to punishment frequency, not task complexity. *Child Neuropsychology, 11*, 245–263.

Crone, E. A., Ridderinkhof, K. R., Worm, M., Somsen, R. J. M., & van der Molen, M. W. (2004). Switching between stimulus-response mappings: A developmental study of cognitive flexibility. *Developmental Science, 7*, 443–455.

Davidson, R. J., & Irwin, W. (1999). The functional neuroanatomy of emotion and affective style. *Trends in Cognitive Sciences, 3*, 11–21.

Davidson, R. J., Jackson, D. C., & Kalin, N. H. (2000). Emotion, plasticity, context, and regulation: Perspectives from affective neuroscience. *Psychological Bulletin, 126*, 890–909.

Davidson, R. J., Putnam, K. M., & Larson, C. L. (2000). Dysfunction in the neural circuitry of emotion regulation: A possible prelude to violence. *Science, 289*, 591–594.

Depue, R. A., & Collins, P. F. (1999). Neurobiology of the structure of personality: Dopamine, facilitation of incentive motivation, and extraversion. *Behavioral and Brain Sciences, 22*, 491–569.

Derryberry, D., & Reed, M. A. (1996). Regulatory processes and the development of cognitive representations. *Development and Psychopathology, 8*, 215–234.

Drevets, W. C. (1999). Prefrontal cortical-amygdalar metabolism in major depression. *Annals of the New York Academy of Sciences, 877*, 614–637.

Drevets, W. C., & Raichle, M. E. (1998). Reciprocal suppression of regional cerebral blood flow during emotional versus higher cognitive processes: Implications for interactions between emotion and cognition. *Cognition and Emotion, 12*, 353–385.

Eisenberg, N., Fabes, R. A., Nyman, M., Bernzweig, J., & Pinuelas, A. (1994). The relations of emotionality and regulation to children's anger-related reactions. *Child Development, 65*, 109–128.

Eisenberg, N., Fabes, R. A., Shepard, S. A., Murphy, B. C., Guthrie, I. K., Jones, S., et al. (1997). Contemporaneous and longitudinal prediction of children's social functioning from regulation and emotionality. *Child Development, 68*, 642–664.

Eisenberg, N., & Spinrad, T. L. (2004). Emotion-related regulation: Sharpening the definition. *Child Development, 75*, 334–339.

Elbert, T., Heim, S., & Rockstroh, B. (2001). Neural plasticity and development. In C. A. Nelson & M. Luciana (Eds.), *Handbook of developmental cognitive neuroscience* (pp. 191–202). Cambridge, MA: Bradford/MIT.

Eslinger, P. J., Flaherty-Craig, C. V., & Benton, A. L. (2004). Developmental outcomes after early prefrontal cortex damage. *Brain and Cognition, 55*, 84–103.

Fan, J., Flombaum, J. I., McCandliss, B. D., Thomas, K. M., & Posner, M. I. (2003). Cognitive and brain consequences of conflict. *NeuroImage, 18*, 42–57.

Fox, N. A. (1994). Dynamic cerebral processes underlying emotion regulation. *Monographs of the Society for Research in Child Development, 59*, 152–166.

Fox, N. A., & Calkins, S. D. (2003). The development of self-control of emotion: Intrinsic and extrinsic influences. *Motivation and Emotion, 27*, 7–16.

Fox, N. A., Henderson, H. A., Rubin, K., Calkins, S. D., & Schmidt, L. A. (2001). Continuity and discontinuity of behavioral inhibition and exuberance: Psychophysiological and behavioral influences across the first 4 years of life. *Child Development, 72*, 1–21.

Fox, N. A., Nichols, K. E., Henderson, H. A., Rubin, K., Schmidt, L., Hamer, D., et al. (2005). Evidence for a gene–environment interaction in predicting behavioral inhibition in middle childhood. *Psychological Science, 16,* 921–926.

Frith, C. D., Friston, K., Liddle, P. F., & Frackowiak, R. S. (1991). Willed action and the prefrontal cortex in man: A study with PET. *Proceedings of the Royal Society of London, Series B, 244,* 241–246.

Gabriel, M., Burhans, L., Talk, A., & Scalf, P. (2002). Cingulate cortex. In V. S. Ramachandran (Ed.), *Encyclopedia of the human brain* (Vol. 1, pp. 775–791). San Diego, CA: Academic Press.

Garcia-Coll, C., Kagan, J., & Reznick, S. J. (1984). Behavioral inhibition in young children. *Child Development, 55,* 1005–1019.

Gehring, W. J., Goss, B., Coles, M. G. H., Meyer, D. E., & Donchin, E. (1993). A neural system for error detection and compensation. *Psychological Science, 4,* 385–390.

Giedd, J. N., Blumenthal, J., Jeffries, N. O., Castellanos, F. X., Hong, L., Zijdenbos, A., et al. (1999). Brain development during childhood and adolescence: A longitudinal MRI study. *Nature Neuroscience, 2,* 861–863.

Giedd, J. N., Rosenthal, M. A., Rose, A. B., Blumenthal, J. D., Molloy, E., Dopp, R. R., et al. (2004). Brain development in healthy children and adolescents: Magnetic resonance imaging studies. In M. S. Keshaven, J. L. Kennedy, L. James, & R. M. Murray (Eds.), *Neurodevelopment and schizophrenia* (pp. 35–44). New York: Cambridge University Press.

Gogtay, N., Giedd, J. N., Lusk, L., Hayashi, K. M., Greenstein, D., Vaituzis, A. C., et al. (2004). Dynamic mapping of human cortical development during childhood through early adulthood. *Proceedings of the National Academy of Sciences, USA, 101*(21), 8174–8179.

Goldberg, G. (1985). Supplementary motor area structure and function: Review and hypotheses. *Behavioral and Brain Sciences, 8,* 567–616.

Granic, I., O'Hara, A., Pepler, D, & Lewis, M. D. (2007). A dynamic systems analysis of parent–child changes associated with successful "real-world" interventions for aggressive children. *Journal of Abnormal Child Psychology, 35,* 845–857.

Granic, I., & Patterson, G. I. (2006). Towards a comprehensive model of antisocial development: A dynamic systems model. *Psychological Review, 113,* 101–131.

Gross, J. J. (1998). Antecedent- and response-focused emotion regulation: Divergent consequences for experience, expression, and physiology. *Journal of Personality and Social Psychology, 74,* 234–237.

Happaney, K., Zelazo, P. D., & Stuss, D. T. (2004). Development of orbitofrontal function: Current themes and future directions. *Brain and Cognition, 55,* 1–10.

Hare, T. A., Tottenham, N., Davidson, M. C., Glover, G. H., & Casey, B. J. (2005). Contributions of amygdala and striatal activity in emotion regulation. *Biological Psychiatry, 57,* 624–632.

Hariri, A. R., Mattay, V. S., Tessitore, A., Fera, F., & Weinberger, D. R. (2003). Neocortical modulation of the amygdala response to fearful stimuli. *Biological Psychiatry, 53*(6), 494–501.

Hollenstein, T., Granic, I., Stoolmiller, M., & Snyder, J. (2004). Rigidity in parent–child interactions and the development of externalizing and internalizing behavior in early childhood. *Development and Psychopathology, 6,* 595–607.

Hooper, C. J., Luciana, M., Conklin, H. M., & Yarger, R. S. (2004). Adolescents' performance on the Iowa gambling task: Implications for the development of decision making and ventromedial prefrontal cortex. *Developmental Psychology, 40,* 1148–1158.

Johnson, M. H. (2000). Functional brain development in infants: Elements of an interactive specialization framework. *Child Development, 71,* 75–81.

Jones, L. B., Rothbart, M. K., & Posner, M. I. (2003). Development of executive attention in preschool children. *Developmental Science, 6,* 498–504.

Kagan, J., Reznick, S. J., Clarke, C., Snidman, N., & Garcia-Coll, C. (1984). Behavioral inhibition to the unfamiliar. *Child Development, 55,* 2212–2225.

Kagan, J., Reznick, J. S., Snidman, N., Gibbons, J., & Johnson, M. O. (1988). Childhood derivatives of inhibition and lack of inhibition to the unfamiliar. *Child Development, 59,* 1580–1589.

Kerr, A., & Zelazo, P. D. (2004). Development of "hot" executive function: The children's gambling task. *Brain and Cognition, 55,* 148–157.

Kesek, A., Zelazo, P. D., & Lewis, M. D. (in press). The development of executive function and emotion regulation in adolescence. In N. Allen & L. Sheeber (Eds.), *Adolescent emotional development and the emergence of depressive disorders.* New York: Cambridge University Press.

Kochanska, G., Murray, K., & Coy, K. C. (1997). Inhibitory control as a contributor to conscience in childhood: From toddler to early school age. *Child Development, 68,* 263–277.

Kolb, B., Pellis, S., & Robinson, T. E. (2004). Plasticity and functions of the orbital frontal cortex. *Brain and Cognition, 55,* 104–115.

Kopp, C. B. (1989). Regulation of distress and negative emotions: A developmental view. *Developmental Psychology, 25,* 343–354.

Kringelbach, M. L., & Rolls, E. T. (2003). Neural correlates of rapid reversal learning in a simple model of human social interaction. *NeuroImage, 20,* 1371–1383.

Kwon, H., Reiss, A. L., & Menon, V. (2002). Neural basis of protracted developmental changes in visuo-spatial working memory. *Proceedings of the National Academy of Sciences, USA, 99,* 13336–13341.

Lamm, C., Zelazo, P. D., & Lewis, M. D. (2006). Neural correlates of cognitive control in childhood and adolescence: Disentangling the contributions of age and executive function. *Neuropsychologia, 44,* 2139–2148.

Lane, R. D., Reiman, E. M., Axelrod, B., Yun, L., Holmes, A., & Schwartz, G. E. (1998). Neural correlates of levels of emotional awareness: Evidence of an interaction between emotion and attention in the anterior cingulate cortex. *Journal of Cognitive Neuroscience, 10,* 525–535.

LeDoux, J. E. (1995). In search of an emotional system in the brain: Leaping from fear to emotion and consciousness. In M. S. Gazzaniga (Ed.), *The cognitive neurosciences* (pp. 1049–1061). Cambridge, MA: MIT Press.

Lesch, K. P., Bengel, D., Heils, A., Sabol, S. Z., Greenberg, B. D., Petri, S., et al. (1996). Association of anxiety related traits with a polymorphism in the serotonin transporter gene regulatory region. *Science, 274,* 1527–1531.

Lévesque, J., Eugène, F., Joanette, Y., Paquette, V., Mensour, B., Beaudoin, G., et al. (2003). Neural circuitry underlying voluntary suppression of sadness. *Biological Psychiatry, 53,* 502–510.

Lewis, M. D. (2005a). Linking emotion theory and neurobiology through dynamic systems modeling. *Behavioral and Brain Sciences, 28,* 105–131.

Lewis, M. D. (2005b). Self-organizing individual differences in brain development. *Developmental Review, 25,* 252–277.

Lewis, M. D., Granic, I., & Lamm, C. (2006). Neurocognitive mechanisms of emotion regulation and behavioral flexibility in aggressive children. *Proceedings of the New York Academy of Sciences, USA, 1094,* 164–177.

Lewis, M. D., Lamm, C., Segalowitz, S. J., Zelazo, P. D., & Stieben, J. (2006). Neurophysiological correlates of emotion regulation in children and adolescents. *Journal of Cognitive Neuroscience, 18,* 430–443.

Lewis, M. D., & Stieben, J. (2004). Emotion regulation in the brain: Conceptual issues and directions for developmental research. *Child Development, 75,* 371–376.

Lewis, M. D., & Todd, R. M. (2007). The self-regulating brain: Cortical–subcortical feedback and the development of intelligent action. *Cognitive Development, 22,* 406–430.

Lewis, M. D., Todd, R. M., & Honsberger, M. (2007). ERP measures of emotion regulation in early childhood. *NeuroReport, 18,* 61–65.

Luciana, M. (2001). Dopamine-opiate modulations of reward-seeking behavior: Implications for the functional assessment of prefrontal development. In C. A. Nelson & M. Luciana (Eds.), *Handbook of developmental cognitive neuroscience* (pp. 647–661). Cambridge, MA: MIT Press.

Luna, B., Thulborn, K., Munoz, D. P., Merriam, E. P., Garver, K. E., Minshew, N. J., et al. (2001). Maturation of widely-distributed brain function subserves cognitive development. *NeuroImage, 13,* 786–793.

Luu, P., Tucker, D. M., & Derryberry, D. (1998). Anxiety and the motivational basis of working memory. *Cognitive Therapy and Research, 22,* 577–594.

MacLean, P. D. (1993). Perspectives on cingulate cortex in the limbic system. In B. A. Vogt & M. Gabriel (Eds.), *Neurobiology of cingulate cortex and limbic thalamus: A comprehensive handbook* (pp. 1–15). Boston: Brikhauser.

Mayberg, H. S., Liotti, M., Brannan, S. K., McGinnis, S., Mahurin, R. K., Jerabek, P. A., et al. (1999). Reciprocal limbic-cortical function and negative mood: Converging PET findings in depression and normal sadness. *American Journal of Psychiatry, 156,* 675–682.

McLure, E. (2000). A meta-analytic review of sex differences in facial expression and their development in infants, children and adolescence. *Psychological Bulletin, 126,* 424–453.

Mesulam, M. (2002). The human frontal lobes: Transcending the default mode through contingent encoding. In D. T. Stuss & R. T. Knight (Eds.), *Principals of frontal lobe function* (pp. 8–30). New York: Oxford University Press.

Nagy, Z., Westerberg, H., & Klingberg, T. (2004). Maturation of white matter is associated with the development of cognitive functions during childhood. *Journal of Cognitive Neuroscience, 16,* 1227–1233.

Ochsner, K. N., Ray, R. D., Cooper, J. C., Robertson, E. R., Chopra, S., Gabrieli, J. D. E., et al. (2004). For better or for worse: Neural systems supporting the cognitive down- and up-regulation of negative emotion. *NeuroImage, 23,* 483–499.

Overman, W. H., Frassrand, K., Ansel, S., Trawalter, S., Bies, B., & Redmond, A. (2004). Performance on the Iowa card task by adolescents and adults. *Neuropsychologia, 42,* 1838–1851.

Panksepp, J. (1998). *Affective neuroscience: The foundations of human and animal emotions.* New York: Oxford University Press.

Paus, T. (2001). Primate anterior cingulate cortex: Where motor control, drive and cognition interface. *Nature Reviews Neuroscience, 2,* 417–424.

Paus, T. (2005). Mapping brain maturation and cognitive development during adolescence. *Trends in Cognitive Sciences, 9,* 60–68.

Pérez-Edgar, K., & Fox, N. A. (2003). Individual differences in children's performance during an emotional Stroop task: A behavioral and electrophysiological study. *Brain and Cognition, 52*(1), 33–51.

Pérez-Edgar, K., & Fox, N. A. (2005). A behavioral and electrophysiological study of children's selective attention under neutral and affective conditions. *Journal of Cognition and Development, 6,* 89–118.

Plizska, S. R., Liotti, M., & Woldorff, M. (2000). Inhibitory control in children with attention-deficit/hyperactivity disorder: Event-related potentials identify the processing component and timing of an impaired right-frontal response-inhibition mechanism. *Biological Psychiatry, 48,* 238–246.

Posner, M. I., & Rothbart, M. K. (2000). Developing mechanisms of self-regulation. *Development and Psychopathology, 12,* 427–441.

Prencipe, A., & Zelazo, P. D. (2005). Development of affective decision-making for self and other: Evidence for the integration of first- and third-person perspectives. *Psychological Science, 16,* 501–505.

Rainville, P. (2002). Brain mechanisms of pain affect and pain modulation. *Current Opinion in Neurobiology, 12,* 195–204.

Ramel, W., Goldin, P. R., Carmona, P. E., & McQuaid, J. R. (2004). The effects of mindfulness meditation on cognitive processes and affect in patients with past depression. *Cognitive Therapy and Research, 28,* 433–455.

Rolls, E. T. (1999). *The brain and emotion.* Oxford: Oxford University Press.

Rolls, E. T. (2004). The functions of the orbitofrontal cortex. *Brain and Cognition, 55,* 11–29.

Rothbart, M. K., (2004). Commentary: Differentiated measures of temperament and multiple pathways to childhood disorders. *Journal of Clinical Child and Adolescent Psychology, 33,* 82–87.

Rothbart, M. K., Ahadi, S. A., & Hershey, K. L. (1994). Temperament and social behavior in childhood. *Merrill-Palmer Quarterly, 40,* 21–39.

Rothbart, M. K., & Bates, J. E. (1998). *Temperament.* Hoboken, NJ: John Wiley.

Rothbart, M. K., & Derryberry, D. (1981). Development of individual differences in temperament. In M. E. Lamb & A. L. Brown (Eds.), *Advances in developmental psychology* (pp. 37–86). Hillsdale, NJ: Erlbaum.

Rubia, K., Overmayer, S., Taylor, E., Williams, S. C. R., Simmons, A., Andrew, C., et al. (2000). Functional frontalization with age: Mapping neurodevelopmental trajectories with fMRI. *Neuroscience and Biobehavioral Reviews, 24,* 13–19.

Saarni, C. (1997). Coping with aversive feelings. *Motivation and Emotion, 21,* 45–63.

Schmidt, L. A., Fox, N. A., Rubin, K. H., Sternberg, E., Gold, P. W., Smith, C., et al. (1997). Behavioral and neuroendocrine responses in shy children. *Developmental Psychobiology, 35,* 119–135.

Schore, A. N. (1997). Early organization of the nonlinear right brain and development of a predisposition to psychiatric disorders. *Development and Psychopathology, 9,* 595–631.

Schore, A. N. (2003). *Affect regulation and the repair of the self.* New York: Norton.

Schwartz, C. E., Wright, C. I., Shin, L. M., Kagan, J., & Rauch, S. L. (2003). Inhibited and uninhibited infants "grown up": Adult amygdalar response to novelty. *Science, 300,* 1952–1953.

Sterzer, P., Stadler, C., Krebs, A., Kleinschmidt, A., & Poutska, F. (2005). Abnormal neural responses to emotional visual stimuli in adolescents with conduct disorder. *Biological Psychiatry, 57,* 7–15.

Stieben, J., Lewis, M. D., Granic, I., Zelazo, P. D., & Segalowitz, S. (2007). Neurophysiological mechanisms of emotion regulation for subtypes of externalizing children. *Development and Psychopathology, 19,* 455–480.

Thompson, C., Barresi, J., & Moore, C. (1997). The development of future-oriented prudence and altruism in preschoolers. *Cognitive Development, 12,* 199–212.

Thompson, R. A. (1994). Emotion regulation: A theme in search of definition. *Monographs of the Society for Research in Child Development, 59,* 25–52.

Todd, R. M., Evans, J. W., Lewis, M. D., & Taylor, M. J. (2007). *The changing face of emotion: fMRI responses to facial affect and identity in young children and adults.* Paper presented at the Annual Meeting of the Jean Piaget Society, Amsterdam, Netherlands.

Todd, R. M., Lewis, M. D., Meusel, L.-A., & Zelazo, P. D. (2008). The time course of social-emotional processing in early childhood: ERP responses to facial affect and familiarity in a Go-Nogo task. *Neuropsychologia, 46,* 595–613.

Tronick, E. Z., Burschweiler-Stern, N., Harrison, A. M., Lyons-Ruth, K., Morgan, A. C., Nahum, J. P., et al. (1998). Dyadically expanded states of consciousness and the process of therapeutic change. *Infant Mental Health Journal, 19,* 290–299.

Tucker, D. M., Derryberry, D., & Luu, P. (2000). Anatomy and physiology of human emotion: Vertical integration of brainstem, limbic, and cortical systems. In J. C. Borod (Ed.), *The neuropsychology of emotion* (pp. 56–79). London: Oxford University Press.

Tucker, D. M., Luu, P., & Derryberry, D. (2005). Love hurts: The evolution of empathic concern through the encephalization of nociceptive capacity. *Development and Psychopathology, 17*, 699–713.

van Veen, V., & Carter, C. S. (2002). The timing of action-monitoring processes in the anterior cingulate cortex. *Journal of Cognitive Neuroscience, 14*, 593–602.

van Veen, V., Cohen, J. D., Botvinick, M. M., Stenger, V. A., & Carter, C. S. (2001). Anterior cingulate cortex, conflict monitoring, and levels of processing. *NeuroImage, 14*, 1302–1308.

Williams, J. M. G., Duggan, D. S., Crane, C., & Fennell, M. J. V. (2006). Mindfulness-based cognitive therapy for prevention of recurrence of suicidal behavior. *Journal of Clinical Psychology, 62*, 201–210.

Zelazo, P. D., & Cunningham, W. A. (2007). Executive function: Mechanisms underlying emotion regulation. In J. Gross (Ed.), *Handbook of emotion regulation* (pp. 135–158). New York: Guilford.

Zelazo, P. D., & Müller, U. (2002). Executive function in typical and atypical development. In U. Goswami (Ed.), *Handbook of childhood cognitive development* (pp. 445–469). Oxford: Blackwell.

14

Social Neuroscience

Simon Baron-Cohen and Bhismadev Chakrabarti

In this chapter, we take a key concept in neuroscience, namely empathy, and consider it in terms of neurocognitive developmental mechanisms and in terms of individual differences. The first part of the chapter deals with the development of empathy; the second part presents some empirical evidence on a quantitative trait measure of empathy. Trait empathy is intrinsically connected with our perception of, and response to, others' emotions. We therefore briefly review the literature on emotion processing from neuroimaging studies that suggest that discrete basic emotions are subserved by different neural regions and networks (Panksepp, 1998). Finally, we describe a recent study that investigates whether and how an individual's level of empathy affects the way in which their brain processes discrete emotions.

What is Empathizing?

Empathizing is the drive to identify another person's emotions and thoughts, and to respond to these with an appropriate emotion (Davis, 1994). We use the term "drive" but recognize that it also overlaps with the concept of a skill or ability. We also focus on the definition of empathy given by Davis (1994), whilst recognizing that other authors may have a slightly different definition. Empathizing does not just entail the cold calculation of what someone else thinks and feels (or what is sometimes called "mind-reading"). Psychopaths can do that much. Empathizing is also about having an appropriate emotional reaction inside you, an emotion triggered by the other person's emotion. Empathizing is done in order to understand another person, to predict their behavior, and to connect or resonate with them emotionally. Imagine you could recognize that "Jane is in pain" but this left you cold, or detached, or happy, or preoccupied. This would not be empathizing. Now imagine you do not only see Jane's pain, but you also automatically feel concern, wincing yourself, and feeling a desire to run across and help alleviate her pain. That is empathizing. And empathizing extends to recognizing and responding to any emotion or state of mind, not just the more obvious ones, like pain. Empathy is a skill (or a set of skills). As with any other skill, such as athleticism or mathematical or musical ability, we all vary in it. In the same way that we can consider why someone is talented or average or even disabled in these other areas, so we can think about individual differences in empathy.

Empathy is a defining feature of human relationships. Empathy stops you doing things that would hurt another person's feelings. Empathy also stops you inflicting pain on a person or animal. Empathy allows you to tune into someone else's world, setting aside your own world—your perception, knowledge, assumptions, or feelings. It allows you to see another side of an argument easily. Empathy drives you to care for, or offer comfort to, another person, even if they are unrelated to you and you stand to gain nothing in return. Empathy also makes real communication possible. Talking "at" a person is not real communication. It is a monologue. Real conversation is sensitive to this listener at this time. Empathy also provides a framework for the development of a moral code. Moral codes are built out of fellow-feeling and compassion.

Fractionating Empathy

Philosophical (Stein, 1989) and evolutionary (Brothers, 1990; Levenson, 1996; Preston & de Waal, 2002) accounts have suggested that empathizing is not a unitary construct. Possible constituent "fractions" of empathy include (a) "emotional contagion/affective empathy," (b) "cognitive empathy," and (c) sympathy. Cognitive empathy is involved in explicit understanding of another's feelings and switching to take their perspective. Piaget referred to empathy as "decentering" or responding non-egocentrically (Piaget & Inhelder, 1956). More recent developmental psychologists refer to this aspect of empathy in terms of using a "theory of mind" or "mindreading" (Astington, Harris, & Olson, 1988; Whiten, 1991). Essentially, the cognitive component of empathizing entails setting aside your own current perspective, attributing a mental state (sometimes called an "attitude") to the other person, and then inferring the likely content of their mental state, given their experience. The cognitive element also allows you to predict the other person's mental state or behavior.

The second aspect to empathy is the "affective" component (Hobson, 1993). A similar component in other accounts has been called "emotional contagion," defined as the tendency to automatically mimic and synchronize facial expressions, vocalizations, postures, and movements with those of another person, and, consequently, to converge emotionally (Hatfield, Cacioppo, & Rapson, 1992). This may be the most primitive component of empathy. For example, if, when witnessing someone else in a state of fear, you "catch" a similar state of fear, this acts as a quick and easy route to alerting you to environmental dangers without having to face the dangers yourself. A third component involves a "concern mechanism" (Nichols, 2001) often associated with a prosocial/altruistic component, also termed "sympathy." This is distinct from emotional contagion as it does not necessarily involve matched states between the observer and the person experiencing the emotion, and is possibly specific to a certain class of emotions (sadness and pain, but not disgust or happiness) in the other person. It represents a case where the observer feels both an emotional response to someone else's distress and a desire to alleviate their suffering.

Development of Empathy

In 1994, Baron-Cohen proposed a model to specify the neurocognitive mechanisms that comprise the "mindreading system" (Baron-Cohen, 1994, 1995). "Mindreading" is defined as the ability to interpret one's own or another agent's actions as driven by mental states. The model was proposed in order to explain (a) the ontogenesis of a theory of mind, and (b) the neurocognitive dissociations that are seen in children with or without autism. The model is shown in Figure 14.1 and contains four components: ID, or the intentionality detector; EDD, or the eye direction detector; SAM, or the shared attention mechanism; and, finally, ToMM, or the theory of mind mechanism.

ID and EDD build "dyadic" representations of simple mental states. ID automatically represents or interprets an agent's self-propelled movement as a desire or goal-directed movement, a sign of its agency, or an entity with volition (Premack, 1990). For example, ID interprets an animate-like moving shape as "it wants x" or "it has goal y." EDD automatically interprets or represents eye-like stimuli as "looking at me" or "looking at something else." That is, EDD picks out that an entity with eyes can perceive. Both ID and EDD are developmentally prior to the other two mechanisms, and are active early in infancy, if not from birth.

SAM is developmentally more advanced. SAM automatically represents or interprets whether the self and another agent are (or are not) perceiving the same event. SAM does this by building "triadic" representations. For example, where ID can build the

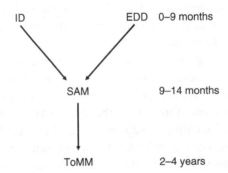

Figure 14.1 Baron-Cohen's 1994 model of mindreading. ID, intentionality detector; EDD, eye direction detector; SAM, shared attention mechanism; ToMM, theory of mind mechanism. *Note.* From "The Mindreading System: New Directions for Research," by S. Baron-Cohen, 1994, *Current Psychology of Cognition, 13*, 724–750.

dyadic representation "Mother wants the cup" and where EDD can build the dyadic representation "Mother sees the cup," SAM can build the triadic representation "Mother sees that I see the cup." As is apparent, triadic representations involve embedding or recursion. (A dyadic representation ["I see the cup"] is embedded within another dyadic representation ["Mother sees the cup"] to produce this triadic representation.) SAM takes its input from ID and EDD, and triadic representations are made out of dyadic representations. SAM typically functions from 9 to 14 months of age, and allows "joint attention" behaviors such as protodeclarative pointing and gaze monitoring (Scaife & Bruner, 1975).

ToMM is the jewel in the crown of the 1994 model of the mindreading system. It allows epistemic mental states to be represented (e.g., "Mother thinks this cup contains water" or "Mother pretends this cup contains water"), and it integrates the full set of mental state concepts (including emotions) into a theory. ToMM develops between 2 and 4 years of age, and allows pretend play (Leslie, 1987), understanding of false belief (Wimmer & Perner, 1983), and understanding of the relationships between mental states (Wellman, 1990). An example of the latter is the seeing-leads-to-knowing principle (Pratt & Bryant, 1990) where the typical 3-year-old can infer that if someone has seen an event, then they will know about it.

The model shows the ontogenesis of a theory of mind in the first four years of life, and justifies the existence of four components on the basis of developmental competence and neuropsychological dissociation. In terms of developmental competence, joint attention does not appear possible until 9–14 months of age, and joint attention appears to be a necessary but not sufficient condition for understanding epistemic mental states (Baron-Cohen, 1991; Baron-Cohen & Swettenham, 1996). There appears to be a developmental lag between acquiring SAM and ToMM, suggesting that these two mechanisms are dissociable. In terms of neuropsychological dissociation, congenitally blind children can ultimately develop joint (auditory or tactile) attention (i.e., SAM), using the amodal ID rather than the visual EDD route. They can therefore go on to develop ToMM. Children with autism appear able to represent the dyadic mental states of seeing and wanting, but show delays in shared attention (Baron-Cohen, 1989b) and in understanding false belief (Baron-Cohen, 1989a; Baron-Cohen, Leslie, & Frith, 1985)—that is, in acquiring SAM and ultimately ToMM. It is this specific developmental delay that suggests that SAM and ToMM are dissociable from EDD.

The 1994 model of the mindreading system was revised in 2005 because of certain omissions and too narrow a focus. The key omission is that information about affective states, available to the infant perceptual system, has no dedicated neurocognitive mechanism. In Figure 14.2, the revised model (Baron-Cohen, 2005) is shown and now includes a new, fifth component: TED, or the emotion detector. But the concept of mindreading (or theory of mind) makes no reference to the affective state in the observer triggered by recognition of another's mental state. This is a particular problem for any account of the distinction between autism and psychopathy. For this reason, the model is no longer of "mindreading" but is of "empathizing," and the revised model also includes a new sixth component, TESS, or the empathizing system. (TESS is spelt as it is to playfully populate

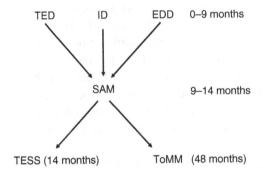

Figure 14.2 Baron-Cohen's 2005 model of empathizing. TED, the emotion detector; ID, intentionality detector; EDD, eye direction detector; SAM, shared attention mechanism; TESS, the empathizing system; ToMM, theory of mind mechanism. *Note.* From "The Empathizing System: A Revision of the 1994 Model of the Mindreading System," by S. Baron-Cohen, 2005, in B. Ellis and D. Bjorklund (Eds.), *Origins of the social mind* (pp. 468–492). New York: Guilford.

the mindreading model with apparently anthropomorphic components.) Where the 1994 mindreading system was a model of a passive observer (because all the components had simple decoding functions), the 2005 empathizing system is a model of an observer impelled toward action (because an emotion is triggered in the observer which typically motivates the observer to respond to the other person).

Like the other infancy perceptual input mechanisms of ID and EDD, the new component of TED can build dyadic representations of a special kind, namely, it can represent affective states. An example would be "Mother—is unhappy," or even "Mother—is angry—with me." Formally, we can describe this as agent—affective state—proposition. We know that infants can represent affective states from as early as 3 months of age (Walker, 1982). As with ID, TED is amodal, in that affective information can be picked up from facial expression or vocal intonation, "motherese" being a particularly rich source of the latter (Field, 1979). Another's affective state is presumably also detectable from their touch (e.g., tense versus relaxed), which implies that congenitally blind infants should find affective information accessible through both auditory and tactile modalities. TED allows the detection of the basic emotions (Ekman & Friesen, 1969). The development of TED is probably aided by the simple imitation that is typical of infants (e.g., imitating caregiver's expressions) which in itself would facilitate emotional contagion (Meltzoff & Decety, 2003).

When SAM becomes available, at 9–14 months of age, it can receive inputs from any of the three infancy mechanisms, ID, EDD, or TED. Here, we focus on how a dyadic representation of an affective state can be converted into a triadic representation by SAM. An example would be that the dyadic representation "Mother is unhappy" can be converted into a triadic representation "I am unhappy that Mother is unhappy" or "Mother is unhappy that I am unhappy," and so on. Again, as with perceptual or volitional states, SAM's triadic representations of affective states have this special embedded or recursive property.

TESS in the 2005 model is the real jewel in the crown. This is not to minimize the importance of ToMM, which has been celebrated for the past 20 years in research in developmental psychology (Leslie, 1987; Whiten, 1991; Wimmer, Hogrefe, & Perner, 1988). ToMM is of major importance in allowing the child to represent the full range of mental states, including epistemic ones (such as false belief), and is important in allowing the child to pull mentalistic knowledge into a useful theory with which to predict behavior (Baron-Cohen, 1995; Wellman, 1990). But TESS allows more than behavioral explanation and prediction (itself a powerful achievement). TESS allows an empathic reaction to another's emotional state. This is, however, not to say that these two modules do not interact. Knowledge of the mental states of others made possible by ToMM could certainly influence the way in which an emotion is processed and/or expressed by TESS. TESS also allows for sympathy. It is this element of TESS that gives it the adaptive benefit of ensuring that organisms feel a drive to help each other.

To see the difference between TESS and ToMM, consider this example: I see you are in pain. Here, ToMM is needed to interpret your facial expressions and writhing body movements in terms of your underlying mental state (pain). But now consider this further example: I am devastated—that you are in pain. Here, TESS is needed since an appropriate affective state has been triggered in the observer by the emotional state identified in the other person. And where ToMM employs M-representations ("M" stands for "mental"; Leslie, 1994) of the form agent—attitude—proposition (e.g., Mother—believes—Johnny took the cookie), TESS employs a new class of representations, which we can call E-representations ("E" stands for "empathy") of the form self—affective state—(self—affective state—proposition); for example, "I feel sorry that—Mother feels sad about—the news in the letter" (Baron-Cohen, 2003). The critical feature of this E-representation is that the self's affective state is appropriate to, and triggered by, the other person's affective state. Thus, TESS can represent "I am horrified—that you are in pain," or "I am concerned—that you are in pain," or "I want to alleviate—that you are in pain," but it cannot represent "I am happy—that you are in pain." At least, it cannot do so if TESS is functioning normally. One could imagine an abnormality in TESS leading to such inappropriate emotional states being triggered, or one could imagine them arising from other systems (such as a competition system or a sibling rivalry system), but these would not be evidence of TESS per se.

Before leaving this revision of the model, it is worth discussing why the need for this has arisen. First, emotional states are an important class of mental states to detect in others, and yet the earlier model focused only on volitional, perceptual, informational, and epistemic states. Second, when it comes to pathology, it would appear that in autism TED may function, although this may be delayed (Baron-Cohen, Spitz, & Cross, 1993; Baron-Cohen, Wheelwright, & Joliffe, 1997; Hobson, 1986), at least in terms of detecting basic emotions. Even high functioning people with autism or Asperger syndrome have difficulties both in ToMM (when measured with mental-age appropriate tests; Baron-Cohen, Joliffe, Mortimore, & Robertson, 1997; Baron-Cohen, Wheelwright, Hill, Raste, & Plumb, 2001; Happé, 1994) and TESS (Attwood, 1997; Baron-Cohen,

O'Riordan, Jones, Stone, & Plaisted, 1999; Baron-Cohen, Richler, Bisarya, Gurunathan, & Wheelwright, 2003; Baron-Cohen, & Wheelwright, 2004; Baron-Cohen, Wheelwright, Stone, & Rutherford, 1999). This suggests that TED and TESS may be fractionated.

In contrast, the psychiatric condition of psychopathy may entail an intact TED and ToMM, alongside an impaired TESS. The psychopath (or sociopath) can represent that you are in pain, or that you believe that he is the gasman, thereby gaining access to your house or your credit card. The psychopath can go on to hurt you or to cheat you without having the appropriate affective reaction to your affective state. In other words, he or she does not care about your affective state (Blair, Jones, Clark, & Smith, 1997; Mealey, 1995). Lack of guilt or shame or compassion in the presence of another's distress are diagnostic of psychopathy (Cleckley, 1977; Hare et al., 1990). Separating TESS and ToMM thus allows a functional distinction to be drawn between the neurocognitive causes of autism and psychopathy.

Developmentally, one can also distinguish TED from TESS. We know that at 3 months of age, infants can discriminate facial and vocal expressions of emotion (Trevarthen, 1989; Walker, 1982), but that it is not until about 14 months that they can respond with appropriate affect (e.g., a facial expression of concern) to another's apparent pain (Yirmiya, Kasari, Sigman, & Mundy, 1990) or show "social referencing." Clearly, this account is skeletal in not specifying how many emotions TED is capable of recognizing. Our recent survey of emotions identifies that there are 412 discrete emotion concepts that the adult English-language user recognizes (Golan, & Baron-Cohen, 2006). How many of these are recognized in the first year of life is not clear. It is also not clear exactly how empathizing changes during the second year of life. We have assumed that the same mechanism that enables social referencing at 14 months old also allows sympathy and the growth of empathy across development. This is the most parsimonious model, though it may be that future research will justify further mechanisms that affect the development of empathy.

Sex Differences in Empathizing

Some of the best evidence for individual differences in empathizing comes from the study of sex differences, where many studies converge on the conclusion that there is a female superiority in empathizing. Sex differences are best viewed as summated individual differences on multiple dimensions that include genetic and epigenetic factors. Some of the observed behavioral differences are reviewed here:

1. *Sharing and turn-taking.* On average, girls show more concern for fairness, whilst boys share less. In one study, boys showed fifty times more competition, whilst girls showed twenty times more turn-taking (Charlesworth & Dzur, 1987).
2. *Rough and tumble play* or "rough housing" (wrestling, mock fighting, and so on). Boys show more of this than girls do. Although there is a playful component, it can hurt or be intrusive, so it needs lower empathizing to carry it out (Maccoby, 1999).

3.   *Responding empathically to the distress of other people.* Girls from 1 year old show greater concern through more sad looks, sympathetic vocalizations, and comforting. More women than men also report frequently sharing the emotional distress of their friends. Women also show more comforting, even of strangers, than men do (Hoffman, 1977).

4.   *Using a "theory of mind."* By 3 years old, girls are already ahead of boys in their ability to infer what people might be thinking or intending (Happé, 1995). This sex difference appears in some but not all studies (Charman, Ruffman, & Clements, 2002).

5.   *Sensitivity to facial expressions.* Women are better at decoding nonverbal communication, picking up subtle nuances from tone of voice or facial expression, or judging a person's character (Hall, 1978).

6.   *Questionnaires measuring empathy.* Many of these find that women score higher than men (Davis, 1994).

7.   *Values in relationships.* More women value the development of altruistic, reciprocal relationships, which by definition require empathizing. In contrast, more men value power, politics, and competition (Ahlgren & Johnson, 1979). Girls are more likely to endorse cooperative items on a questionnaire and to rate the establishment of intimacy as more important than the establishment of dominance. Boys are more likely than girls to endorse competitive items and to rate social status as more important than intimacy (Knight, Fabes, & Higgins, 1989).

8.   *Disorders of empathy* (such as psychopathic personality disorder or conduct disorder) are far more common among males (Blair, 1995; Dodge, 1980).

9.   *Aggression,* even in normal quantities, can only occur with reduced empathizing. Here again, there is a clear sex difference. Males tend to show far more "direct" aggression (pushing, hitting, punching, etc.), whilst females tend to show more "indirect" (or "relational," covert) aggression (gossip, exclusion, bitchy remarks, etc.). Direct aggression may require an even lower level of empathy than indirect aggression. Indirect aggression needs better mindreading skills than does direct aggression because its impact is strategic (Crick & Grotpeter, 1995).

10.   *Murder* is the ultimate example of a lack of empathy. Daly and Wilson (1988) analyzed homicide records dating back over 700 years from a range of different societies. They found that "male on male" homicide was 30–40 times more frequent than "female on female" homicide.

11.   *Establishing a "dominance hierarchy."* Males are quicker to establish these. This, in part, may reflect their lower empathizing skills because often a hierarchy is established by one person pushing others around to become the leader (Strayer, 1980).

12.   *Language style.* Girls' speech is more cooperative, reciprocal, and collaborative. In concrete terms, this is also reflected in the ability of girls to keep a conversational exchange with a partner going for longer. When girls disagree, they are more likely to express their different opinion sensitively, in the form of a question, rather than an assertion. Boys' talk is more "single-voiced discourse" (the speaker presents their own perspective alone). The female speech style is more "double voiced discourse" (girls spend more time negotiating with the other person, trying to take the other person's wishes into account; Smith, 1985).

13. *Talk about emotions.* Women's conversation involves much more talk about feelings, whilst men's conversation with each other tends to be more object or activity focused (Tannen, 1991).

14. *Parenting style.* Fathers are less likely than mothers to hold their infant in a face-to-face position. Mothers are more likely to follow through the child's choice of topic in play, whilst fathers are more likely to impose their own topic. And mothers fine-tune their speech more often to match what the child can understand (Power, 1985).

15. *Face preference and eye contact.* From birth, females look longer at faces, and particularly at people's eyes, and males are more likely to look at inanimate objects (Connellan, Baron-Cohen, Wheelwright, Ba'tki, & Ahluwalia, 2001).

16. Finally, females have also been shown to have better *language ability* than males. It seems likely that good empathizing would promote language development (Baron-Cohen, Baldwin, & Crowson, 1997) and vice versa, so these may not be independent.

Leaving aside sex differences as one source of evidence for individual differences, one can see that empathy is normally distributed within the population. Figure 14.3 shows the data from the Empathy Quotient (EQ), a validated, 60-item, self-report questionnaire (Baron-Cohen & Wheelwright, 2004). It has been factor analyzed in two independent studies (Lawrence, Shaw, Baker, Baron-Cohen, & David, 2004; Muncer & Ling, 2006) to suggest the existence of three distinct components, which roughly correspond

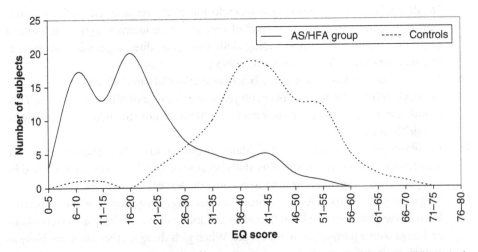

Figure 14.3 The normal distribution of empathy in the population (dotted line). Also shown is the distribution of empathy scores from people with Asperger syndrome (AS) or high functioning autism (HFA). *Note.* From "The Empathy Quotient (EQ): An Investigation of Adults with Asperger Syndrome or High Functioning Autism, and Normal Sex Differences," by S. Baron-Cohen and S. Wheelwright, 2004, *Journal of Autism and Developmental Disorders, 34,* 163–175.

to the three-component model of empathy. Scores on the EQ show a continuous distribution in several populations, with scores from people with autism spectrum conditions (ASC) clustering toward the lower end (see Figure 14.3). The EQ is associated with significant sex differences (Goldenfeld, Baron-Cohen, Wheelwright, Ashwin, & Chakrabarti, 2007).

The search for the neural correlates of empathy has had two traditions of research, one focusing on theory of mind studies (largely involving intention attribution or emotion attribution) and another focusing on action understanding. The latter has gained considerable importance in recent years since the discovery of mirror neurons (Rizzolatti, Fadiga, Gallese, & Fogassi, 1996).

On finding increasing evidence of sex differences in the EQ in the "normal" population, we sought to investigate the neural correlates of this trait measure of empathizing across the population. Since trait empathy, by definition, influences how we perceive and respond to emotions, we attempted to marry the two fields of emotion perception and empathizing. The following section briefly introduces the current state of the literature on the neural bases of basic emotions as well as the different processes that contribute to the development of empathy. We then discuss a recent neuroimaging study from our laboratory that explicitly addresses this question.

Neuroimaging Studies of Empathizing and Emotion

Neuroimaging studies, conducted mostly on adults, have implicated the following different brain areas for performing tasks that tap components of the model of empathy proposed above, presented in order of their development (see Plate 7).

(1) Studies of emotional contagion have demonstrated involuntary facial mimicry (Dimberg, Thunberg, & Elmehead, 2000), as well as activity in regions of the brain where the existence of "mirror" neurons has been suggested; for example, the inferior frontal gyrus, the inferior parietal lobule, and the superior temporal sulcus (Carr, Iacoboni, Dubeau, Mazziotta, & Lenzi, 2003; Jackson, Meltzoff, & Decety, 2005; Wicker et al., 2003). Dapretto and colleagues (2006) have recently demonstrated that children with ASC show a lower response in inferior frontal gyrus both during observation and explicit imitation of facial expressions of emotion, when compared to typically developing controls.

(2) ID has been tested in a PET study in a task involving attribution of intentions to cartoon characters versus predicting physical causality using the same set of characters (Brunet, Sarfati, Hardy-Bayle, & Decety, 2000). Significantly activated regions included the right medial prefrontal (BA 9) and inferior frontal (BA 47) cortices, superior temporal gyrus (BA 42), and bilateral anterior cingulate cortex. In an elegant set of experiments that required participants to attribute intentions to animations of simple geometric shapes (Castelli, Happé, Frith, & Frith, 2000), it was found that the "intentionality" score attributed by the participants to individual animations was positively correlated to the activity in the superior temporal sulcus (STS), the temporoparietal

junction, and the medial prefrontal cortex. In a subsequent study (Castelli, Frith, Happé, & Frith, 2002), a group difference in activity in the same set of structures was demonstrated between people with ASC and typical controls.

(3)   EDD has been studied in several neuroimaging studies on gaze direction perception (Calder et al., 2002; Grosbras, Laird, & Paus, 2005; Pelphrey, Singerman, Allison, & McCarthy, 2003), and have implicated the posterior STS bilaterally. This evidence, taken together with similar findings from primate literature (Perrett & Emery, 1994), suggests that this area is a strong candidate for the anatomical equivalent of the EDD.

(4)   A recent imaging study (Williams, Waiter, Perra, Perrett, & Whiten, 2005) investigated the neural correlates of SAM and reported bilateral activation in anterior cingulate (BA 32, 24) and medial prefrontal cortex (BA 9, 10) and the body of caudate nucleus in a joint attention task, when compared to a control task involving non-joint attention (Frith & Frith, 2003).

(5)   Traditional "theory of mind" (cognitive empathy) tasks have consistently shown activity in the medial prefrontal cortex, the superior temporal gyrus, and the temporoparietal junctions (Frith & Frith, 2003; Saxe, Carey, & Kanwisher, 2004). This could be equated to the brain basis of ToMM.

(6)   Sympathy has been relatively less investigated, with one study implicating the left inferior frontal gyrus, among a network of other structures (Decety & Chaminade, 2003). Work on "moral" emotions has suggested the involvement of a network comprising the medial frontal gyrus, the medial orbitofrontal cortex, and the STS (Moll et al., 2002).

Neuroimaging of Discrete Emotions

An increasing body of evidence from lesion, neuroimaging, and electrophysiological studies suggests that these affect programs might have discrete neural bases (Calder, Lawrence, & Young, 2001). Fear is possibly the most well-investigated emotion. Passive viewing of fear expressions as well as experiencing fear (as induced through recalling a fear memory or seeing fear stimuli) reliably activates the amygdala, orbitofrontal cortex, and the anterior cingulate cortex (Blair, Morris, Frith, Perrett, & Dolan, 1999; Hariri, Mattay, Tessitore, Fera, & Weinberger, 2003). There is considerable evidence from nonhuman primates (Kalin, Shelton, & Davidson, 2001) and rats (LeDoux, 2000) to suggest a crucial role for these regions in processing fear. Passive viewing of disgust faces as well as experiencing disgust oneself is known to evoke a response in the anterior insula and globus pallidus as reported in several studies (Calder et al., 2001; Phillips et al., 1997; Wicker et al., 2003). An increasing consensus on the role of the ventral striatum in processing reward from different sensory domains (receiving food rewards: O'Doherty, Deichmann, Critchley, & Dolan, 2002; viewing funny cartoons: Mobbs, Greicius, Abdel-Azim, Menon, & Reiss, 2003; remembering happy events: Damasio et al. 2000) concurs well with studies that report activation of this region in response to viewing happy faces (Lawrence et al., 2004; Phillips, Baron-Cohen, & Rutter, 1998; Phillips et al., 1998).

Perception of angry expressions has been shown to evoke a response in the premotor cortex and the striatum (Grosbras & Paus, 2006) as well as the lateral orbitofrontal cortex (Blair & Cipolotti, 2000; Blair et al., 1999). The results of studies on the processing of sad expressions are comparatively less consistent. Perception of a sad face and induction of a sad mood are both known to be associated with an increased response in the subgenual cingulate cortex (Liotti et al., 2000; Mayberg et al., 1999), the hypothalamus in humans (Malhi et al., 2004) and in rats (Shumake, Edwards, & Gonzalez-Lima, 2001), as well as in the middle temporal gyrus (Eugene et al., 2003). There have been very few studies on the passive viewing of surprise. One study by Schroeder and colleagues (2004) reported bilateral activation in the parahippocampal region, which is known for its role in novelty detection from animal literature.

While the discrete emotions model holds well for these relatively "simple" emotions, the dimensional models (Rolls, 2002) become increasingly relevant as we consider the more socially complex emotions—for example, pride, shame, and guilt—since it would not be economical to have discrete neural substrates for the whole gamut of emotions. These two models, however, need not be in conflict, since the more complex emotions can be conceptualized as being formed from a combination of the basic ones (i.e., with each of the "basic" emotions representing a dimension in emotion space).

Two major meta-analytic studies of neuroimaging literature on emotions highlight the role of discrete regions in primarily visual processing of different basic emotions (Murphy, Nimmo-Smith, & Lawrence, 2003; Phan, Wager, Taylor, & Liberzon, 2002). Some studies using other sensory stimuli (olfactory: Anderson et al., 2003; gustatory: Small et al., 2003; auditory: Lewis, Critchley, Rothstein, & Dolan, 2005) have shown the possibly dissociable role of the amygdala and the orbitofrontal cortex in processing emotions along the two dimensions of valence and arousal.

The relative absence of neuroimaging studies of "complex" emotions could be possibly due to the increased cultural variability of the elicitors, as well as the display rules that these expressions entail. Among the few exceptions, guilt and embarrassment have been investigated by Takahashi and colleagues (2004), who reported activation in the ventromedial prefrontal cortex, the left superior temporal sulcus, and higher visual cortices when participants read sentences designed to evoke guilt or embarrassment. This, taken together with the areas underlying the ToMM system, suggests an increased role of "theory of mind" to make sense of these emotions.

Empathizing with Discrete Emotions

Returning to the concept of individual differences in empathizing, this poses an interesting question for the brain basis of perception of discrete emotions. Do we use a centralized "empathy circuit" to make sense of all emotions? If so, can one detect differences in how discrete emotions are processed among individuals at different points on the EQ continuum?

A direct approach to investigating individual differences in empathizing has been to test for sex differences in the perception of emotions. Using facial electromyography, one study (Helland, 2005) observed that females tend to show increased facial mimicry to facial expressions of happiness and anger when compared to males. In a meta-review of neuroimaging results on sex differences in emotion perception, Wager and colleagues (Wager, Phan, Liberzon, & Taylor, 2003) report that females show increased bilaterality in emotion-relevant activation compared to males, though this is not always found (Lee et al., 2002; Schienle, Shafer, Stark, Walter, & Vaitl, 2005). One of the reasons for this might be the fact that sex differences are summated individual differences. Instead of such a broad category-based approach (as in sex-difference studies), an approach based on individual differences in self-report personality scores (Canli, Sivers, Whitfield, Gotlib, & Gabrieli, 2002) or genetic differences (e.g., Hariri et al., 2002)) may be more finely tuned.

To test this model of individual variability, we asked whether an individual's score on the EQ predicted his or her response to four basic emotions (happy, sad, angry, disgust). If empathizing was modulated by a unitary circuit, then individual differences in empathizing would correlate with activity in the same structures for all basic emotions. Twenty-five adult volunteers (13 female, 12 male), selected across the EQ space, were scanned in a 3T fMRI scanner on a passive viewing task using dynamic facial expressions as stimuli. It was found that activity in different brain regions correlated with EQ scores for different basic emotions (Chakrabarti, Baron-Cohen, & Bullmore, 2005).

Using a whole-brain analysis with permutation-based techniques (XBAMM, www-bmu.psychiatry.cam.ac.uk/software/docs/xbamm/), we found that different regional responses were correlated with the EQ for different emotions. Specifically, for the perception of happy faces, a parahippocampal-ventral-striatal cluster response was positively correlated with the EQ. The role of this region in reward processing is well known (O'Doherty, 2004). This suggests that the more empathic a person is, the higher is his or her reward response to a happy face. Interestingly, the response from the same region correlated negatively with the EQ during the perception of sad faces. This fits perfectly with the earlier results; that is, the more empathic a person is, the lower is his or her reward response to a sad face.

For happy and sad faces, therefore, empathizing seems to involve mirroring. The higher a person's EQ, the stronger the reward response to happy faces and vice versa for sad faces. This is in concordance with suggestions from earlier studies on pain (Singer et al., 2004) and disgust perception (Wicker et al., 2003), where observation and experience have been shown to be mediated by the same set of structures. One of the issues with the previous studies is a possible confound between "personal distress" and empathizing. The novel element in our study is that we explicitly tested for the personality trait of empathizing in relation to the perception of specific emotions.

However, empathizing does not appear to be purely an index of mirroring. For the perception of angry faces, EQ correlated positively to clusters centered on the precuneus/inferior parietal lobule, the superior temporal gyrus, and the dorsolateral prefrontal cortex. The posterior cingulate region is known to be involved in self/other distinction (Vogt, 2005), and the superior temporal gyrus is known for its role in ToM tasks (Saxe et al., 2004). This suggests that higher EQ corresponds to higher activation in areas related to the distinction of self versus other, as well as those that are recruited to determine another person's intentions. The dorsolateral prefrontal cortex is known for its role in decision-making and context evaluation (Rahm et al., 2006). Higher EQ would therefore predict better evaluation of the threat from an angry expression. Since expressions of anger are usually more socially urgent for attention than those of either sadness or happiness, it is essential that highly empathic persons do not merely "mirror" the expression. A high empathizer's perception of an angry face would therefore need to be accompanied by an accurate determination of the intentions of the person as well as an evaluation of the posed threat.

In response to disgust faces, a cluster containing the dorsal anterior cingulate cortex and medial prefrontal cortices is negatively correlated with EQ, suggesting that the areas involved in the attribution of mental states (primarily required for deciphering the "complex" emotions) are selectively recruited less by people of high EQ. This is what might be expected, since disgust as an emotion is less interpersonal than anger or sadness, so resources for decoding complex emotional signals need not be utilized. Another cluster that includes the right insula and inferior frontal gyrus (IFG) is negatively correlated with EQ. Given the well-established role of this region in processing disgust, this was a surprising result. We expected that an increased ability to empathize would result in an increased disgust response to facial expressions of disgust. The negative correlation suggests that people with high EQ had a lower insula-IFG response to disgust expressions. A re-examination of the behavioral literature on disgust sensitivity reveals a similar result since Haidt, McCauley, and Rozin (1994) suggested that increased socialization leads to lower disgust sensitivity. Individuals with high EQ may socialize more than those with low EQ.

The results suggest that empathizing with different basic emotions involves distinct brain regions. While some of the emotions involve more "mirroring" (the same areas show activation during recognition and experience; e.g., the striatal response to happy faces correlating positively with EQ), others require an increased distinction between one's own emotional state and another's (e.g., the superior temporal gyrus and precuneus/inferior parietal lobule response to angry faces correlating with EQ). While this explanation fits the discrete emotions model, it did not explicitly test whether there was any region that was common to all four correlation maps. To explore this, we performed a conjunction analysis for all four (emotion-neutral) versus EQ correlation plots. Using a hypothesis-driven region of interest analysis, we found a significant overlap in the left IFG-premotor cortex. This region was positively correlated with EQ for all four (emotion-neutral) contrasts.

The IFG-premotor cortex is a fundamental part of the "mirror systems" discussed earlier (Keysers & Perrett, 2004; Rizzolatti & Craighero, 2004). Several studies have shown involvement of "mirror systems" during perception of facial expressions (Buccino et al., 2001; Carr et al., 2003; Dapretto et al., 2006) and actions (Johnson-Frey et al., 2003; Molnar-Szakacs, Iacoboni, Koski, & Mazziotta, 2005) in humans. This fits well with predictions from heuristic models that integrate perception and action (Hurley, 2005). The lower IFG-premotor response to all expressions as a function of trait empathy corroborates similar findings (Dapretto et al., 2006; Nishitani, Avikainen, & Hari, 2004). However, some studies (Carr et al., 2003; Dapretto et al., 2006) have used paradigms involving perception and explicit imitation of facial expressions and did not report any analysis for possible differences between emotions. Our analysis takes these possible differences into account and the IFG-premotor cluster emerges as a candidate region that correlates with empathy, independent of which emotion is being perceived.

This result provides a putative biomarker for empathy, a trait distributed continuously across the general population, with people with autism spectrum conditions (ASC) clustering toward the low end (Baron-Cohen & Wheelwright, 2004).

Common and Discrete Neural Substrates of Empathy

Comparing the results from the conjunction analysis (showing a common neural substrate of EQ across different emotions) with those from the whole-brain analysis (showing varying spatial patterns of correlation of EQ with different emotions) shows that there are both common regions that underlie empathy across different emotions and regions specific to certain emotions.

We interpret this using a model of face processing (Haxby, Hoffman, & Gobbini, 2000) applied to a discrete-emotions framework (see Figure 14.4a). At its simplest, the model proposes a core visual system for face perception. This constitutes the inferior occipital gyrus (IOG, for low level facial feature analysis), the lateral fusiform gyrus (FG, for higher order invariant aspects of faces such as identity), and the superior temporal sulcus (STS, for variable aspects of faces, such as lip movement and speech comprehension). This then interacts with an extended system, which involves different structures for different emotions (Haxby, Hoffman, & Gobbini, 2002). Focusing specifically on the perception of dynamic facial expressions of emotion, we propose that an intermediate module for action perception is involved, in line with similar suggestions from others (Gallese, 2003; Keysers & Perrett, 2004; Preston & de Waal, 2002; Rizzolatti & Craighero, 2004; see Figure 14.4b).

Focusing on the left of the dotted line in Figure 14.4b shows the processes that are equally influenced by trait empathy across all emotions. This includes the regions involved in face perception and the fundamental "mirror systems" used for action perception. This is revealed by the conjunction analysis, which shows a cluster that includes the IFG-premotor cortex. The common element in different facial expressions of emotion is the fact that they involve movement of eyes and mouth, which are possibly coded for by the generic "mirror systems" used for action perception. However, on investigating the interaction of each emotion with empathy, we move over to the right-hand side of the dotted line, which gives us emotion-specific correlation maps, in accordance with the discrete emotions model. We interpret these in light

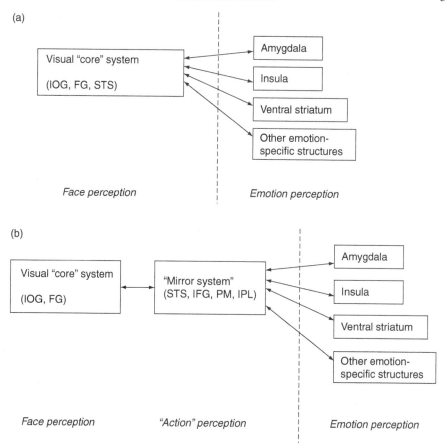

Figure 14.4 (a) The original model for face perception proposed by Haxby et al. (2000) applied to a discrete-emotions framework. (b) Suggested modifications to the model, specifically for perception of facial expressions of emotion, incorporating a module for "action perception." IOG, inferior occipital gyrus; FG, fusiform gyrus; STS, superior temporal sulcus; IFG, inferior frontal gyrus; PM, premotor cortex; IPL, inferior parietal lobule.

of their evolutionary function. It is worth noting, though, that we do not propose a strict temporal sequence of activation from left to right of this model; nor do we represent subcortical pathways from the visual areas to the emotion-related structures. As in the original model, several of these regions are reciprocally connected and the temporal progression of activation could be mediated through reafferent projections (Iacoboni et al., 2001). These can be investigated through methods that allow better temporal resolution (e.g., magnetoencephalography) and forward-model-based connectivity analysis (e.g., dynamic causal modeling: Friston, Harrison, & Penny, 2003).

This study reveals how empathy at the neural level is subtle and complex: Neural networks activated by perception of discrete emotions depend on the observer's EQ.

At the molecular level, empathy is likely to be determined by other individual differences, such as fetal testosterone (Castelli et al., 2000; Knickmeyer, Baron-Cohen, Raggatt, & Taylor, 2005), genetic variation (Chakrabarti, Kent, Suckling, Bullmore, & Baron-Cohen, 2006; Skuse et al., 1997), as well as early care or neglect (Fonagy, Steele, Steele, & Holder, 1997). We conclude that more basic research into the neuroscience of empathy will enrich our understanding of this most fundamental human quality.

Acknowledgments

Simon Baron-Cohen was supported by the Medical Research Council and the Lurie Marks Family Foundation during the period of this work. Bhismadev Chakrabarti was supported by Trinity College, Cambridge. Parts of this chapter are taken from elsewhere (Baron-Cohen, 2005; Chakrabarti, Bullmore, & Baron-Cohen, 2006; Goldenfeld et al., 2007).

References

Ahlgren, A., & Johnson, D. W. (1979). Sex differences in cooperative and competitive attitudes from the 2nd to the 12th grades. *Developmental Psychology, 15,* 45–49.

Anderson, A., Christoff, K., Stappen, I., Panitz, D., Ghahremani, D., Glover, G., et al. (2003). Dissociated neural representations of intensity and valence in human olfaction. *Nature Neuroscience, 6,* 196–202.

Astington, J., Harris, P., & Olson, D. (1988). *Developing theories of mind.* New York: Cambridge University Press.

Attwood, T. (1997). *Asperger's syndrome.* London: Jessica Kingsley.

Baron-Cohen, S. (1989a). The autistic child's theory of mind: A case of specific developmental delay. *Journal of Child Psychology and Psychiatry, 30,* 285–298.

Baron-Cohen, S. (1989b). Perceptual role taking and protodeclarative pointing in autism. *British Journal of Developmental Psychology, 7,* 113–127.

Baron-Cohen, S. (1991). Precursors to a theory of mind: Understanding attention in others. In A. Whiten (Ed.), *Natural theories of mind* (pp. 233–251). Oxford: Blackwell.

Baron-Cohen, S. (1994). The mindreading system: New directions for research. *Current Psychology of Cognition, 13,* 724–750.

Baron-Cohen, S. (1995). *Mindblindness: An essay on autism and theory of mind.* Boston: IT Press/ Bradford.

Baron-Cohen, S. (2003). *The essential difference: Men, women and the extreme male brain.* London: Penguin.

Baron-Cohen, S. (2005). The empathizing system: A revision of the 1994 model of the mindreading system. In B. Ellis & D. Bjorklund (Eds.), *Origins of the social mind* (pp. 468–492). New York: Guilford.

Baron-Cohen, S., Baldwin, D., & Crowson, M. (1997). Do children with autism use the speaker's direction of gaze (SDG) strategy to crack the code of language? *Child Development, 68,* 48–57.

Baron-Cohen, S., & Belmonte, M. (2005). Autism: A window onto the development of the social and the analytic brain. *Annual Review of Neuroscience, 28,* 109–126.

Baron-Cohen, S., Joliffe, T., Mortimore, C., & Robertson M. (1997). Another advanced test of theory of mind: Evidence from very high functioning adults with autism or Asperger syndrome. *Journal of Child Psychology and Psychiatry, 38*, 813–822.

Baron-Cohen, S., Leslie, A. M., & Frith, U. (1985). Does the autistic child have a "theory of mind?" *Cognition, 21*, 37–46.

Baron-Cohen, S., O'Riordan, M., Jones, R., Stone, V., & Plaisted, K. (1999). A new test of social sensitivity: Detection of faux pas in normal children and children with Asperger syndrome. *Journal of Autism and Developmental Disorders, 29*, 407–418.

Baron-Cohen, S., Richler, J., Bisarya, D., Gurunathan, N., & Wheelwright, S. (2003). The systemising quotient (SQ): An investigation of adults with Asperger syndrome or high functioning autism and normal sex differences. Special issue on Autism: Mind and Brain. *Philosophical Transactions of the Royal Society, Series B, 358*, 361–374.

Baron-Cohen, S., Spitz, A., & Cross, P. (1993). Can children with autism recognize surprise? *Cognition and Emotion, 7*, 507–516.

Baron-Cohen, S., & Swettenham, J. (1996). The relationship between SAM and ToMM: The lock and key hypothesis. In P. Carruthers & P. Smith (Ed.), *Theories of theories of mind* (pp. 158–168). Cambridge University Press.

Baron-Cohen, S., & Wheelwright, S. (2004). The empathy quotient (EQ): An investigation of adults with Asperger syndrome or high functioning autism, and normal sex differences. *Journal of Autism and Developmental Disorders, 34*, 163–175.

Baron-Cohen, S., Wheelwright, S., Hill, J., Raste, Y., & Plumb, I. (2001). The "reading the mind in the eyes" test revised version: A study with normal adults, and adults with Asperger syndrome or high-functioning autism. *Journal of Child Psychology and Psychiatry, 42*, 241–252.

Baron-Cohen, S., Wheelwright, S., & Joliffe, T. (1997). Is there a "language of the eyes"? Evidence from normal adults and adults with autism or Asperger syndrome. *Visual Cognition, 4*, 311–331.

Baron-Cohen, S., Wheelwright, S., Stone, V., & Rutherford, M. (1999). A mathematician, a physicist, and a computer scientist with Asperger syndrome: Performance on folk psychology and folk physics test. *Neurocase, 5*, 475–483.

Blair, R. J. (1995). A cognitive developmental approach to morality: Investigating the psychopath. *Cognition, 57*, 1–29.

Blair, R. J., & Cipolotti, L. (2000). Impaired social response reversal: A case of "acquired" sociopathy. *Brain, 123*, 1122–1141.

Blair, R. J., Jones, L., Clark, F., & Smith, M. (1997). The psychopathic individual: A lack of responsiveness to distress cues? *Psychophysiology, 34*, 192–198.

Blair, R. J., Morris, J., Frith, C., Perrett, D. I., & Dolan, R. J. (1999). Dissociable neural responses to facial expressions of sadness and anger. *Brain, 122*, 883–893.

Brothers, L. (1990). The neural basis of primate social communication. *Motivation and Emotion, 14*, 81–91.

Brunet, E., Sarfati, Y., Hardy-Bayle, M.-C., & Decety, J. (2000). A PET investigation of the attribution of intentions with a non-verbal task. *NeuroImage, 11*, 157–166.

Buccino, G., Binkofski, F., Fink, G., Fadiga, L., Fogassi, L., Gallese, V., et al. (2001). Action observation activates premotor and parietal areas in a somatotopic manner: An fMRI study. *European Journal of Neuroscience, 13*, 400–404.

Calder, A. J., Lawrence, A. D., Keane, J., Scott, S. K., Owen, A. M., Christoffels, I., et al. (2002). Reading the mind from eye gaze. *Neuropsychologia, 40*, 1129–1138.

Calder, A. J., Lawrence, A. D., & Young, A. W. (2001). Neuropsychology of fear and loathing. *Nature Reviews Neuroscience, 2*, 352–363.

Canli, T., Sivers, H., Whitfield, S. L., Gotlib, I. H., & Gabrieli, J. D. (2002). Amygdala response to happy faces as a function of extraversion. *Science, 296*, 2191.

Carr, L., Iacoboni, M., Dubeau, M.-C., Mazziotta, J., & Lenzi, G. (2003). Neural mechanisms of empathy in humans: A relay from neural systems for imitation to limbic areas. *Proceedings of the National Academy of Sciences, USA, 100*, 5497–5502.

Castelli, F., Frith, C., Happé, F., & Frith, U. (2002). Autism, Asperger syndrome and brain mechanisms for the attribution of mental states to animated shapes. *Brain, 125*, 1839–1849.

Castelli, F., Happé, F., Frith, U., & Frith, C. (2000). Movement and mind: A functional imaging study of perception and interpretation of complex intentional movement patterns. *NeuroImage, 12*, 314–335.

Chakrabarti, B., Baron-Cohen, S., & Bullmore, E. T. (2005). *"Empathizing" with discrete emotions: An fMRI study.* Paper presented at the Annual Conference of the Society for Neuroscience, Washington, DC.

Chakrabarti, B., Bullmore, E. T., & Baron-Cohen, S. (2006). Empathising with basic emotions: Common and discrete neural substrates. *Social Neuroscience, 1*, 364–384.

Chakrabarti, B., Kent, L., Suckling, J., Bullmore, E. T., & Baron-Cohen, S. (2006). Variations in human cannabinoid receptor (CNR1) gene modulate striatal response to happy faces. *European Journal of Neuroscience, 23*, 1944–1948.

Charlesworth, W. R., & Dzur, C. (1987). Gender comparisons of preschoolers' behavior and resource utilization in group problem-solving. *Child Development, 58*, 191–200.

Charman, T., Ruffman, T., & Clements, W. (2002). Is there a gender difference in false belief development. *Social Development, 11*, 1–10.

Cleckley, H. M. (1977). *The mask of sanity: An attempt to clarify some issues about the so-called psychopathic personality.* St. Louis, MO: Mosby.

Connellan, J., Baron-Cohen, S., Wheelwright, S., Ba'tki, A., & Ahluwalia, J. (2001). Sex differences in human neonatal social perception. *Infant Behavior and Development, 23*, 113–118.

Crick, N. R., & Grotpeter, J. K. (1995). Relational aggression, gender, and social-psychological adjustment. *Child Development, 66*, 710–722.

Daly, M., & Wilson, M. (1988). *Homicide.* New York: Aldine de Gruyter.

Damasio, A. R., Grabowski, T. J., Bechara, A., Damasio, H., Ponto, L. L. B., Parvizi, J., et al. (2000). Subcortical and cortical brain activity during the feeling of self-generated emotions. *Nature Neuroscience, 3*, 1049–1056.

Dapretto, M., Davies, M., Pfeifer, J., Scott, A., Sigman, M., Bookheimer, S., et al. (2006). Understanding emotions in others: Mirror neuron dysfunction in children with autism spectrum disorders. *Nature Neuroscience, 9*, 28–30.

Davis, M. H. (1994). *Empathy: A social psychological approach.* Boulder, CO: Westview Press.

Decety, J., & Chaminade, T. (2003). Neural correlates of feeling sympathy. *Neuropsychologia, 41*, 127–138.

Dimberg, U., Thunberg, M., & Elmehead, K. (2000). Unconscious facial reactions to emotional facial expressions. *Psychological Science, 11*, 86–89.

Dodge, K. (1980). Social cognition and children's aggressive behaviour. *Child Development, 51*, 162–170.

Ekman, P., & Friesen, W. (1969). The repertoire of non-verbal behavior: Categories, origins, usage, and coding. *Semiotica, 1*, 49–98.

Eugene, F., Levesque, J., Mensour, B., Leroux, J.-M., Beaudoin, G., Bourgouin, P., et al. (2003). The impact of individual differences on the neural circuitry underlying sadness. *NeuroImage, 19*, 354–364.

Field, T. (1979). Visual and cardiac responses to animate and inanimate faces by term and preterm infants. *Child Development, 50*, 188–194.

Fonagy, P., Steele, H., Steele, M., & Holder, J. (1997). Attachment and theory of mind: Overlapping constructs? *ACPP Occasional Papers, 14*, 31–40.

Friston, K., Harrison, L., & Penny, W. (2003). Dynamic causal modelling. *NeuroImage, 19*, 1273–1302.

Frith, U., & Frith, C. (2003). Development and neurophysiology of mentalizing. *Philosophical Transactions of the Royal Society, 358*, 459–473.

Gallese, V. (2003). The roots of empathy: The shared manifold hypothesis and the neural basis of intersubjectivity. *Psychopathology, 36*, 171–180.

Golan, O., & Baron-Cohen, S. (2006). Systemizing empathy: Teaching adults with Asperger's syndrome/high functioning autism to recognize emotions using interactive multimedia. *Development and Psychopathology, 18*, 591–617.

Goldenfeld, N., Baron-Cohen, S., Wheelwright, S., Ashwin, C., & Chakrabarti, B. (2007). Empathizing and systemizing in males, females and autism: A test of the neural competition theory. In T. Farrow & P. Woodruff (Eds.), *Empathy and mental illness* (pp. 322–334). Cambridge University Press.

Grosbras, M.-H., Laird, A. R., & Paus, T. (2005). Cortical regions involved in eye movements, shifts of attention and gaze perception. *Human Brain Mapping, 25*, 140–154.

Grosbras, M.-H., & Paus, T. (2006). Brain networks involved in viewing angry hands or faces. *Cerebral Cortex, 16*, 1087–1096.

Haidt, J., McCauley, C., & Rozin, P. (1994). Individual differences in sensitivity to disgust: A scale sampling seven domains of disgust elicitors. *Personality and Individual Differences, 16*, 701–713.

Hall, J. A. (1978). Gender effects in decoding nonverbal cues. *Psychological Bulletin, 85*, 845–858.

Happé, F. (1994). An advanced test of theory of mind: Understanding of story characters' thoughts and feelings by able autistic, mentally handicapped, and normal children and adults. *Journal of Autism and Developmental Disorders, 24*, 129–154.

Happé, F. (1995). The role of age and verbal ability in the theory of mind: Task performance of subjects with autism. *Child Development, 66*, 843–855.

Hare, R. D., Harpur, T. J., Hakstian, A. R., Forth, A. E., Hart, S. D., Newman, J. P., et al. (1990). The revised psychopathy checklist: Reliability and factor structure. *Psychological Assessment, 2*, 338–341.

Hariri, A. R., Mattay, V. S., Tessitore, A., Fera, F., & Weinberger, D. R. (2003). Neocortical modulation of the amygdala response to fearful stimuli. *Biological Psychiatry, 53*, 494–501.

Hariri, A. R., Mattay, V. S., Tessitore, A., Kolachana, B., Fera, F.,Goldman, D., et al. (2002). Serotonin transporter genetic variation and the response of the human amygdala. *Science, 297*, 400–403.

Hatfield, E., Cacioppo, J. T., & Rapson, R. (1992). Emotional contagion. In M. Clark (Ed.), *Review of personality and social psychology: Emotion and behavior* (pp. 151–177). Newbury Park, CA: Sage.

Haxby, J. V., Hoffman, E. A., & Gobbini, M. I. (2000). The distributed human neural system for face perception. *Trends in Cognitive Sciences, 4*, 223–233.

Haxby, J. V., Hoffman, E. A., & Gobbini, M. I. (2002). Human neural systems for face recognition and social communication. *Society of Biological Psychiatry, 51*, 59–67.

Helland, S. (2005). *Gender differences in facial imitation.* Unpublished BA thesis, University of Lund.

Hobson, R. P. (1986). The autistic child's appraisal of expressions of emotion. *Journal of Child Psychology and Psychiatry, 27*, 321–342.

Hobson, R. P. (1993). *Autism and the development of mind.* Hillsdale, NJ: Lawrence Erlbaum.

Hoffman, M. L. (1977). Sex differences in empathy and related behaviors. *Psychological Bulletin, 84*, 712–722.

Hurley, S. L. (2005). Active perception and perceiving action: The shared circuits hypothesis. In T. Gendler & J. Hawthorne (Ed.), *Perceptual experience* (pp. 205–259). New York: Oxford University Press.

Iacoboni, M., Koski, L., Brass, M., Bekkering, H., Woods, R., Dubeau, M., et al. (2001). Reafferent copies of imitated actions in the right superior temporal cortex. *Proceedings of the National Academy of Sciences, USA, 98*, 13995–13999.

Jackson, P., Meltzoff, A., & Decety, J. (2005). How do we perceive the pain of others? A window into the neural processes involved in empathy. *NeuroImage, 24*, 771–779.

Johnson-Frey, S., Maloof, F., Newman-Norlund, R., Farrer, C., Inati, S., & Grafton, S. (2003). Actions or hand-object interactions? Human inferior frontal cortex and action observation. *Neuron, 39*, 1053–1058.

Kalin, N. H., Shelton, S. E., & Davidson, R. J. (2001). The primate amygdala mediates acute fear but not the behavioral and physiological components of anxious temperament. *Journal of Neuroscience, 21*, 2067–2074.

Keysers, C., & Perrett, D. I. (2004). Demystifying social cognition: A Hebbian perspective. *Trends in Cognitive Science, 8*, 501–507.

Knickmeyer, R., Baron-Cohen, S., Raggatt, P., & Taylor, K. (2005). Foetal testosterone, social cognition, and restricted interests in children. *Journal of Child Psychology and Psychiatry, 46*, 198–210.

Knight, G. P., Fabes, R. A., & Higgins, D. A. (1989). Gender differences in the cooperative, competitive, and individualistic social values of children. *Motivation and Emotion, 13*, 125–141.

Lawrence, E. J., Shaw, P., Baker, D., Baron-Cohen, S., & David, A. S. (2004). Measuring empathy: Reliability and validity of the empathy quotient. *Psychological Medicine, 34*, 911–919.

LeDoux, J. (2000). Emotion circuits in the brain. *Annual Review of Neuroscience, 23*, 155–184.

Lee, T., Liu, H.-L., Hoosain, R., Liao, W.-T., Wu, C.-T., Yuan, K., et al. (2002). Gender differences in neural correlates of recognition of happy and sad faces in humans assessed by functional magnetic resonance imaging. *Neuroscience Letters, 333*, 13–16.

Leslie, A. M. (1987). Pretence and representation: The origins of "theory of mind." *Psychological Review, 94*, 412–426.

Leslie, A. M. (1994). ToMM, ToBY, and agency: Core architecture and domain specificity. In L. A. Hirschfeld & S. A. Gelman (Eds.), *Mapping the mind: Domain specificity in cognition and culture* (pp. 119–148). Cambridge University Press.

Levenson, R. (1996). Biological substrates of empathy and facial modulation of emotion: Two facets of the scientific legacy of John Lanzetta. *Motivation and Emotion, 20*, 185–204.

Lewis, P., Critchley, H. D., Rothstein, P., & Dolan, R. J. (2005). *Processing valence and arousal in affective words.* Paper presented at the SFN Annual Conference, Washington DC, USA.

Liotti, M., Mayberg, H., Brannan, S., McGinnis, S., Jerabek, P., & Fox, P. (2000). Differential limbic-cortical correlates of sadness and anxiety in healthy subjects: Implications for affective disorders. *Biological Psychiatry, 48*, 30–42.

Maccoby, E. (1999). *The two sexes: Growing up apart, coming together.* Cambridge, MA: Harvard University Press.

Malhi, G., Lagopoulos, J., Ward, P., Kumari, V., Mitchell, D., Parker, G., et al. (2004). Cognitive generation of affect in bipolar depression: An fMRI study. *European Journal of Neuroscience, 19*, 741–754.

Mayberg, H., Liotti, M., Brannan, S., McGinnis, M. Y., Mahurin, R., Jerabek, P., et al. (1999). Reciprocal limbic-cortical function and negative mood: Converging PET findings in depression and normal sadness. *American Journal of Psychiatry, 156*, 675–682.

Mealey, L. (1995). The sociobiology of sociopathy: An integrated evolutionary model. *Behavioral and Brain Sciences, 18*, 523–599.

Meltzoff, A. N., & Decety, J. (2003). What imitation tells us about social cognition: A rapprochement between developmental psychology and cognitive neuroscience. *Philosophical Transactions of the Royal Society, 358*, 491–500.

Mobbs, D., Greicius, M. D., Abdel-Azim, E., Menon, V., & Reiss, A. L. (2003). Humor modulates the mesolimbic reward centres. *Neuron, 40*, 1041–1048.

Moll, J., de Oliveira-Souza, R., Eslinger, P., Bramati, I., Mourao-Miranda, J., Andreiuolo, P., et al. (2002). The neural correlates of moral sensitivity: A functional magnetic resonance imaging investigation of basic and moral emotions. *Journal of Neuroscience, 22*, 2730–2736.

Molnar-Szakacs, I., Iacoboni, M., Koski, L., & Mazziotta, J. C. (2005). Functional segregation within pars opercularis of the inferior frontal gyrus: Evidence from fMRI studies of imitation and action observation. *Cerebral Cortex, 15*(7), 986–994.

Muncer, S., & Ling, J. (2006). Psychometric analysis of the empathy quotient (EQ) scale. *Personality and Individual Differences, 40*, 1111–1119.

Murphy, F. C., Nimmo-Smith, I., & Lawrence, A. D. (2003). Functional neuroanatomy of emotions: A meta-analysis. *Cognitive, Affective and Behavioral Neuroscience, 3*, 207–233.

Nichols, S. (2001). Mindreading and the cognitive architecture underlying altruistic motivation. *Mind and Language, 16*, 425–455.

Nishitani, N., Avikainen, S., & Hari, R. (2004). Abnormal imitation-related cortical activation sequences in Asperger's syndrome. *Annals of Neurology, 55*, 558–562.

O'Doherty, J. (2004). Reward representations and reward-related learning in the human brain: Insights from neuroimaging. *Current Opinion in Neurobiology, 14*, 769–776.

O'Doherty, J., Deichmann, R., Critchley, H. D., & Dolan, R. J. (2002). Neural responses during anticipation of a primary taste reward. *Neuron, 33*, 815–826.

Panksepp, J. (1998). *Affective neuroscience: The foundations of human and animal emotions.* New York: Oxford University Press.

Pelphrey, K. A., Singerman, J. D., Allison, T., & McCarthy, G. (2003). Brain activation evoked by perception of gaze shifts: The influence of context. *Neuropsychologia, 41*, 156–170.

Perrett, D. I., & Emery, N. (1994). Understanding the intentions of others from visual signals: Neurophysiological evidence. *Current Psychology of Cognition, 13*, 683–694.

Phan, K. L., Wager, T., Taylor, S. F., & Liberzon, I. (2002). Functional neuroanatomy of emotion: A meta-analysis of emotion activation studies in PET and fMRI. *NeuroImage, 16*, 331–348.

Phillips, M. L., Bullmore, E. T., Howard, R., Woodruff, P. W. R., Wright, I. C., William, S. C. R., et al. (1998). Investigation of facial recognition memory and happy and sad facial expression perception: An fMRI study. *Psychiatry Research Neuroimaging, 83*, 127–138.

Phillips, M. L., Young, A., Senior, C., Brammer, M., Andrew, C., Calder, A., et al. (1997). A specific neural substrate for perceiving facial expressions of disgust. *Nature, 389*, 495–498.

Phillips, W., Baron-Cohen, S., & Rutter, M. (1998). Understanding intention in normal development and in autism. *British Journal of Developmental Psychology, 16*, 337–348.

Piaget, J., & Inhelder, B. (1956). *The child's conception of space.* London: Routledge and Kegan Paul.

Power, T. G. (1985). Mother– and father–infant play: A developmental analysis. *Child Development*, *56*, 1514–1524.

Pratt, C., & Bryant, P. (1990). Young children understand that looking leads to knowing (so long as they are looking into a single barrel). *Child Development*, *61*, 973–983.

Premack, D. (1990). The infant's theory of self-propelled objects. *Cognition*, *36*, 1–16.

Preston, S. D., & de Waal, F. B. M. (2002). Empathy: Its ultimate and proximate bases. *Behavioural and Brain Sciences*, *25*, 1–72.

Rahm, B., Opwis, K., Kaller, C., Spreer, J., Schwarzvald, R., Seifritz, E., et al. (2006). Tracking the subprocesses of decision-based action in the human frontal lobes. *NeuroImage*, *30*(2), 656–667.

Rizzolatti, G., & Craighero, L. (2004). The mirror-neuron system. *Annual Review of Neuroscience*, *27*, 169–192.

Rizzolatti, G., Fadiga, L., Gallese, V., & Fogassi, L. (1996). Premotor cortex and the recognition of motor actions. *Cognitive Brain Research*, *3*, 131–141.

Rolls, E. T. (2002). Neural basis of emotions. In N. Smelsner & P. Baltes (Ed.), *International encyclopedia of the social and behavioral sciences* (pp. 4444–4449). Amsterdam: Elsevier.

Saxe, R., Carey, S., & Kanwisher, N. (2004). Understanding other minds: Linking developmental psychology and functional neuroimaging. *Annual Review of Psychology*, *55*, 87–124.

Scaife, M., & Bruner, J. (1975). The capacity for joint visual attention in the infant. *Nature*, *253*, 265–266.

Schienle, A., Schafer, A., Stark, R., Walter, B., & Vaitl, D. (2005). Gender differences in the processing of disgust- and fear-inducing pictures: An fMRI study. *Neuroreport*, *16*, 277–280.

Schroeder, U., Hennenlotter, A., Erhard, P., Haslinger, B., Stahl, R., Lange, K., et al. (2004). Functional neuroanatomy of perceiving surprised faces. *Human Brain Mapping*, *23*, 181–187.

Shumake, J., Edwards, E., & Gonzalez-Lima, F. (2001). Hypermetabolism of paraventricular hypothalamus in the congenitally helpless rat. *Neuroscience Letters*, *311*, 45–48.

Singer, T., Seymour, B., O'Doherty, J., Kaube, H., Dolan, R., & Frith, C. (2004). Empathy for pain involves the affective but not sensory components of pain. *Science*, *303*, 1157–1167.

Skuse, D. H., James, R. S., Bishop, D. V. M., Coppins, B., Dalton, P., Aamodt-Leeper, G., et al. (1997). Evidence from Turner's syndrome of the imprinted x-linked locus affecting cognitive function. *Nature*, *287*, 705–708.

Small, D., Gregory, M., Mak, Y., Gitelman, D., Mesulam, M., & Parrish, T. (2003). Dissociation of neural representation of intensity and affective valuation in human gustation. *Neuron*, *39*, 701–711.

Smith, P. M. (1985). *Language, the sexes and society*. Oxford: Blackwell.

Stein, E. (1989). *On the problem of empathy (1917)*. Washington, DC: ICS.

Strayer, F. F. (1980). Child ethology and the study of preschool social relations. In H. C. Foot, A. J. Chapman, & J. R. Smith (Ed.), *Friendship and social relations in children* (pp. 235–266). New York: John Wiley.

Takahashi, H., Yahata, N., Koeda, M., Matsuda, T., Asai, K., & Okubo, Y. (2004). Brain activation associated with evaluative process of guilt and embarrassment: An fMRI study. *NeuroImage*, *23*, 967–974.

Tannen, D. (1991). *You just don't understand: Women and men in conversation*. London: Virago.

Trevarthen, C. (1989). The relation of autism to normal socio-cultural development: The case for a primary disorder in regulation of cognitive growth by emotions. In G. Lelord, J. Muk, & M. Petit (Ed.), *Autisme et troubles du développement global de l'enfant*. Paris: Expansion Scientifique Française.

Vogt, B. (2005). Pain and emotion interactions in subregions of the cingulate gyrus. *Nature Reviews Neuroscience, 6*, 533–544.

Wager, T., Phan, K. L., Liberzon, I., & Taylor, S. (2003). Valence gender and lateralization of functional brain anatomy: A meta-analysis of findings from neuroimaging. *NeuroImage, 19*, 513–531.

Walker, A. S. (1982). Intermodal perception of expressive behaviours by human infants. *Journal of Experimental Child Psychology, 33*, 514–535.

Wellman, H. (1990). *Children's theories of mind*. Bradford: MIT Press.

Whiten, A. (1991). *Natural theories of mind*. Oxford: Blackwell.

Wicker, B., Keysers, C., Plailly, J., Royet, J.-P., Gallese, V., & Rizzolatti, G. (2003). Both of us disgusted in *my* insula: The common neural basis of seeing and feeling disgust. *Neuron, 40*, 655–664.

Williams, J. H. G., Waiter, G. D., Perra, O., Perrett, D. I., & Whiten, A. (2005). An fMRI study of joint attention experience. *NeuroImage, 25*, 133–140.

Wimmer, H., Hogrefe, J., & Perner, J. (1988). Children's understanding of informational access as a source of knowledge. *Child Development, 59*, 386–396.

Wimmer, H., & Perner, J. (1983). Beliefs about beliefs: Representation and constraining function of wrong beliefs in young children's understanding of deception. *Cognition, 13*, 103–128.

Yirmiya, N., Kasari, C., Sigman, M., & Mundy, P. (1990). Facial expressions of affect in autistic, mentally retarded, and normal children. *Journal of Child Psychology and Psychiatry, 30*, 725–735.

15

Reading

Usha Goswami

Literacy encompasses both reading and spelling. It is essentially the ability to comprehend and communicate using language expressed in visual form. The visual form may comprise an alphabet, a code in which individual speech sounds are represented by individual symbols, as in English or Russian. The visual form may comprise characters, which may represent whole words or individual syllables in the spoken form, as in Chinese or Japanese. In either case, the visual symbols represent speech written down. To become literate, the child must learn the code used by their culture for representing spoken language visually.

Accordingly, the neuropsychological development of reading is highly dependent on competent visual and auditory processing. A child who is blind needs a specially adapted script in order to read, a script that can be decoded using another sensory system (such as Braille). A child who is deaf may struggle to attain a reading age or spelling skills in line with chronological age because of oral language problems. For children without gross sensory impairments of this nature, individual differences in reading and spelling development are mainly governed by phonological skills, and not by visual skills. Although originally conceived as a visual disorder, believed to involve letters reversing themselves on the page (Hinshelwood, 1896), developmental dyslexia across languages and scripts is usually a *phonological* disorder. The child with developmental dyslexia has a serious and specific difficulty with the neural representation of the sounds that make up words.

In this chapter, I will first discuss the development of phonological representations in typically developing children. I will demonstrate how phonological skills determine and are then shaped by literacy acquisition across languages. The focus will be on data gathered by cognitive developmental psychologists. To date, there is very little genetic and imaging data concerning the development of reading in typically developing children. Most genetic and imaging data have come from studies of adults with developmental dyslexia. I will thus first discuss developmental dyslexia within the cognitive framework developed for typical reading development, and then discuss associated imaging and genetic studies. As will become clear, the view that individual differences in literacy development are governed by individual differences in a child's awareness of phonology is accepted across languages and cultures.

Typical Neuropsychological Development of Reading across Languages

The phonological structure of language

The child's awareness of the phonological structure of their language, measured before schooling, is the strongest predictor that we have of how well a particular child will learn to read and to spell. The construct of "phonological awareness" is usually defined as the ability to detect and manipulate component sounds in words. Component sounds can be defined at a number of different linguistic levels or "grain sizes." For example, a single word can comprise a number of syllables (*caterpillar* has four syllables, *wigwam* has two syllables). One word can rhyme with another. A word like *fountain* rhymes with *mountain* because the words share their phonology after the first sound (this sound is called the *onset*). A word like *street* rhymes with *eat* even though *street* has an onset made up of three sounds before the part of the word that rhymes with *eat*. This onset comprises three *phonemes*. The rhyming part of the syllable is called the *rime* by linguists. There are two shared rimes in *fountain* and *mountain*, the sounds *ount* and *ain*. There is one shared rime in *street* and *eat*, the sound *eet*. Phonemes are the smallest units of sound in words that change meaning. For example, *street* differs in meaning from *treat* because it has one extra phoneme (the phoneme /s/). Phonemes usually correspond to alphabetic letters: The alphabet is a code that works primarily at the phoneme level of phonology. However, the primary phonological processing unit across most of the world's languages is the syllable.

In most languages of the world, syllables follow what linguists call a simple structure. Syllables consist of a consonant (C) and a vowel (V). The CV syllable structure characterizes spoken languages as diverse as Finnish, Italian, and Chinese. Clearly, not all languages with a CV syllable structure use the alphabet as their visual code, although many do. Cross-language research suggests that it is easier to become phonologically aware in languages like Spanish and Italian. This is because dividing a syllable into its component sounds is relatively easy. Most syllables contain two sounds, an onset comprising a single phoneme, and a rime comprising a single phoneme. In fact, for languages with a CV syllable structure, there is no distinction between phonemes, onsets, and rimes. This makes it easier to become phonologically aware.

For English monosyllables, only 5% follow the CV pattern (De Cara & Goswami, 2002). Examples are words like *sea* and *go*. The majority of monosyllables in English (43%) follow a CVC structure (*dog, soap, hill*). The next most frequent structure, CVCC, accounts for an additional 21% of monosyllables (*last, felt, jump*). A further 15% of monosyllables follow a CCVC structure (*trip, clap, broom*). Dividing up complex syllables like these into their constituent sounds is more challenging for young children. Even for CVC syllables, there are two phonemes in the rime. Consonant clusters pose particular difficulties (*jump, trip, street, spring*); some clusters may contain three phonemes. These aspects of English phonology make it more challenging for English-speaking children across English-speaking countries to develop phonological awareness.

The development of phonological awareness across languages

Most theorists assume that phonological awareness develops from the phonological representations that underpin spoken language. During the first four or five years of their linguistic development, children are acquiring spoken language, not written language. Their focus is communication, and not phonological awareness, and they know about phonology at an implicit level, by being competent users of their language. Whereas the average 1-year-old might have a productive vocabulary of around 100 words, by the age of 6 it is estimated that the average child's vocabulary contains around 14,000 words (Dollaghan, 1994). All of these words need to be represented as phonologically distinct from each other. Clearly, most children achieve this, as typically developing children seldom produce the wrong word during communication, apart from slips of the tongue (which adults produce as well). A pre-reading child in fact recognizes phonological similarities that, as literate adults, we no longer notice. For example, a pre-reading child will judge correctly that *chair* and *train* share more phonological similarity at onset than *train* and *tip* (Read, 1986). As literate adults, we have lost this insight. This is because orthography tells us that *train* and *tip* begin with the same phoneme, /t/.

There seems to be a universal sequence in the development of phonological awareness, even though the phonology of languages differs. Despite the differences in syllable structure and in the absolute number of phonemes found in the phonological inventories of different languages (e.g., 44 phonemes in English compared to 21 phonemes in Finnish), children in all languages so far studied appear to follow a similar developmental pathway in terms of phonological awareness. Children first become aware of relatively *large* sounds in words, such as syllables. They then become aware of the onset/rime division of the syllable (*str-eet, j-ump, tr-ip*). Awareness of phonemes develops later in children learning to speak languages with a complex phonology, such as English and German. Pre-readers in English and German are aware of onsets and rimes, but they cannot recognize or manipulate phonemes (Goswami, Ziegler, & Richardson, 2005). However, pre-readers in languages like Italian and Spanish do not have a problem. For them, onsets and rimes are also phonemes because of the simple phonology of the CV syllable. The hierarchical organization of syllable structure is shown in Table 15.1.

The development of phonological awareness appears to respect this hierarchical organization. Empirical data for a developmental progression comes from studies that measure children's phonological skills at different points in development in different languages. Some of these studies have also demonstrated longitudinal

Table 15.1 Hierarchical Phonological Structure for the Early Acquired Word "Girl" in English and Italian.

Linguistic level	English		Italian		
Word	Girl		Ragazza		
Syllable	Girl		Ra	ga	za
Onset/rime	G	irl	Ra	ga	za
Phoneme[a]	G	ir l	Ra	ga	za

[a] The phoneme represented as "ir" is phonetically a single vowel.

connections between phonological awareness measured at time 1, and reading measured at time 2. These longitudinal connections have been found across languages. A few studies have demonstrated that the connection between phonological awareness and literacy is a causal one. These studies involve training children's phonological skills, and demonstrating an impact on literacy. As space precludes a thorough discussion of the relevant empirical data, a more comprehensive review can be found in Ziegler and Goswami (2005).

The sequence of phonological development

A large variety of tasks has been invented to measure the development of phonological awareness in young children. For example, children may be asked to monitor and correct speech errors (e.g., *sie* to *pie*), to select the "odd word out" in terms of sound (e.g., which word does not rhyme: *cat, bat, sit*), to make a judgment about sound similarity (e.g., do these two words share a syllable? *compete, repeat*), to count sounds in words by tapping with a stick (e.g., tap out the component sounds in *soap* = 3 taps), and to blend sounds into words (e.g., *d-ish* or *d-i-sh* to make *dish*; see, for example, Bradley & Bryant, 1983; Chaney, 1992; Liberman, Shankweiler, Fischer, & Carter, 1974; Metsala, 1999; Treiman & Zukowski, 1991). These different tasks also make differing cognitive demands on young children. For example, "same–different" judgments (*compete–repeat* = same) are often considered to be easier than oddity tasks (see Treiman & Zukowski, 1991). The best way to investigate the *sequence* of phonological development is to equate the cognitive demands of the chosen task across linguistic level. For example, an oddity task or a same–different judgment task can be used to compare both onset/rime and phoneme levels of awareness (see Goswami et al., 2005; Treiman & Zukowski, 1991).

Surprisingly, it is rare to find research studies that have used the same cognitive task to study the emergence of phonological awareness at the different linguistic levels of syllable, onset/rime, and phoneme. The most comprehensive studies in English are those conducted by Anthony and his colleagues (Anthony & Lonigan, 2004; Anthony et al., 2002; Anthony, Lonigan, Driscoll, Phillips & Burgess, 2003). For example, Anthony et al. (2003) used blending and deletion tasks at the word, syllable, onset/rime, and phoneme level. They studied a large group of more than 1,000 children, and included a much wider age range than many studies (2–6 years). Anthony et al. (2003) found that the development of children's phonological awareness followed the hierarchical model shown in Table 15.1. English-speaking children generally mastered word-level skills before they mastered syllable-level skills; they mastered syllable-level skills before onset/rime-level skills; and they mastered onset/rime-level skills before phoneme skills.

This developmental progression from syllable awareness via onset/rime awareness to phoneme awareness has been mirrored by many other studies conducted in English using a broad variety of tasks (see Goswami & Bryant, 1990, for a survey). Counting and oddity tasks have been particularly useful for comparisons across languages. Focusing usually on syllable versus phoneme awareness (because of the typical CV syllable structure), such studies demonstrate that syllable awareness emerges prior to phoneme awareness in children learning all languages so far studied. For example, Cossu and colleagues studied the development of syllable versus phoneme awareness in Italian preschoolers and school-aged children using a counting task (comparing groups of 4-year-olds, 5-year-olds, and 7–8-year-olds). Syllable awareness was shown by 67% of the 4-year-olds, 80% of the 5-year-olds, and 100% of the school-aged sample (Cossu, Shankweiler, Liberman, Katz, & Tola, 1988). Phoneme awareness was shown by 13% of the 4-year-olds, 27% of the 5-year-olds, and 97% of the school-aged sample. A similar study was carried out by Liberman and her colleagues (1974) with American children. Children aged from 4 to 6 years were asked to tap once for words that had either one syllable or phoneme (*dog, i*), twice for words that had two syllables or phonemes (*dinner, my*), and three times for words that had three syllables or phonemes (*president, book*). Syllable awareness was shown by 46% of the 4-year-olds, 48% of the 5-year-olds, and 90% of the 6-year-olds. The 4- and 5-year-olds were pre-readers, and the 6-year-olds had been learning to read for about a year. Phonemic awareness was shown by 0% of the 4-year-olds, 17% of the 5-year-olds, and 70% of the 6-year-olds. Liberman et al. (1974) concluded that whereas syllabic awareness was present in pre-readers, phonemic awareness was dependent on learning to read. This finding for English has now been replicated many times (see Ziegler & Goswami, 2005).

Longitudinal connections between phonological awareness and reading

The existence of a longitudinal connection between individual differences in children's phonological awareness measured prior to schooling and their later progress in reading and spelling was first demonstrated in a seminal study in Danish carried out by Lundberg, Olofsson, and Wall (1980). Similar results were reported for English by Bradley and Bryant (1983), who demonstrated the importance of onset/rime awareness measured in pre-readers for subsequent reading development using the oddity task. Longitudinal studies in other languages are also finding significant relationships between phonology and reading (e.g., German: Schneider, Roth, & Ennemoser, 2000; Norwegian: Hoien, Lundberg, Stanovich, & Bjaalid, 1995; Chinese: Ho & Bryant, 1997). I will only describe the study in English by Bradley and Bryant here.

In their study, oddity tasks at the onset and rime level were administered to 400 preschoolers when they were aged 4 and 5 years. The same children's progress in reading and spelling was then measured 2–3 years later. Examples of the oddity tasks are *sun, sock, rag* (onset) or *pin, win, sit* (rime). Bradley and Bryant reported that onset/rime awareness was a significant predictor of the children's progress in reading and spelling when measured at 8 and 9 years of age. This longitudinal correlation remained significant even when other factors such as IQ and socioeconomic status were controlled in multiple regression equations. It was also specific to reading, as no significant longitudinal correlations were found for development in mathematics. Subsequently, MacLean, Bryant, and Bradley (1987) reported a significant connection for English between rhyming skills at the age of 3 measured via nursery rhyme knowledge and single word reading at 4 years and 6 months. When the same sample was followed up two years later, Bryant, MacLean, Bradley, and Crossland (1990) found a significant relationship between nursery rhyme knowledge at the age of 3 and success in reading and spelling at the ages of 5 and 6. This relationship was significant even after factors such as social background and IQ were controlled in multiple regression equations.

While these controls for possible intervening variables are very important, however, they do not in themselves guarantee that the longitudinal connection between phonology at time 1 and reading at time 2 is a causal one. In order to demonstrate a causal connection, a training study is required. If early phonological awareness has a direct effect on how well a child learns to read and spell, then training children to discover and attend to the phonological structure of language should have a measurable impact on their reading progress. In fact, Bradley and Bryant (1983) included a training component in their longitudinal study. They selected for training the 60 children in their cohort of 400 who had performed most poorly in the oddity task at 4 and 5 years of age. The children were given two years of intervention, which largely comprised grouping words on the basis of sounds by using a picture sorting task. The children were taught to group words by onset, rime, vowel, and coda (syllable-final) phonemes (for example, placing pictures of a *hat*, a *rat*, a *mat*, and a *bat* together for grouping by rime). A control group learned to sort the same pictures into semantic categories (e.g., farmyard animals). In addition, half of the experimental group also learned to match plastic letters to the shared phonological units in the words in the pictures; for example, making the spelling unit *at* for words like *hat, rat,* and *mat*.

Following the intervention, the children in the experimental group which had had plastic letters training were 8 months further on in reading than the children in the semantic control group, and 12 months further on in spelling, even after adjusting post-test scores for age and IQ. A second control group was "unseen," comprising children who had spent the intervening period receiving normal classroom teaching without an additional intervention. Compared to these children, the experimental group was a remarkable 24 months further on in spelling, and 12 months further on in reading. Positive effects of intervention have also been reported by large-scale training studies with Danish children (Lundberg, Frost, & Petersen, 1988) and German children (Schneider, Kuespert, Roth,

Vise, & Marx, 1997). In both the English and German studies, particularly strong effects of phonological training were reported for progress in spelling.

In summary, cross-sectional, longitudinal, and training studies conducted across languages have shown that the links between phonological awareness and literacy appear to be language-universal. In all languages so far studied, phonological awareness progresses from an awareness of large units of sound, such as syllables and rimes, to an awareness of small units of sound—phonemes. In all languages so far studied, including character-based scripts, individual differences in phonological awareness are predictive of individual differences in literacy. Finally, in all languages so far studied, providing children with training in phonological awareness which is coupled with training in how letters represent sounds has a measurable positive impact on progress in literacy. Let us now consider how differences in the phonological structure of different languages might affect the ways in which early phonological awareness can support the acquisition of literacy.

The acquisition of reading and spelling skills across languages

As noted at the beginning of this chapter, the primary phonological unit in language is the syllable. Furthermore, many of the world's languages have a simple syllabic structure, comprising largely CV syllables. For children learning to speak these languages, the onset/rime level of phonological structure and the phoneme level represented by the alphabet are the same. Other languages, like English and German, have a complex phonological structure. These languages allow syllables to contain clusters of consonant phonemes. These clusters can be either before the vowel (*spray, street*), after the vowel (*jump, sand*), or both (*stamp, clasp*). For languages like these, the onset/rime level of phonological structure and the phoneme level are not the same. In languages like these, children typically arrive in school with good onset/rime awareness, but lacking phoneme awareness (Goswami & Bryant, 1990; Goswami et al., 2005). Phoneme awareness must be learned, and it is usually learned via letters.

Learning letters helps to develop phoneme awareness in all languages. This is easily shown by cross-language studies demonstrating phoneme awareness in pre-readers versus readers of different ages (see Ziegler & Goswami, 2005). A few studies have also demonstrated that illiterate adults, who have never learned to read, lack phoneme awareness (e.g., Morais, Cary, Alegria, & Bertelson, 1979). However, for most European languages, acquisition of phoneme awareness is very rapid once children begin learning to read. For English-speaking children, it is not. The reasons appear to be twofold. It is relatively easy to learn about phonemes when your language has a CV syllable structure, and a transparent orthography. It is relatively difficult to learn about phonemes when your language has a complex syllable structure, and an ambiguous orthography. Unfortunately for English-speaking children, cross-language analyses show that English is particularly ambiguous with respect to both spelling-to-sound and sound-to-spelling relations (Ziegler, Stone, & Jacobs, 1997). In English, a single letter or letter cluster can have multiple pronunciations (e.g., the letter *a* in *car, cat, cake, call*; the cluster *ough* in *cough, bough, through*). A phoneme can also have multiple spellings (consider the vowel sound in *hurt, dirt,* and *Bert*; or the sound /f/ in *photo* versus *off* versus *cough*). Some languages, like Italian, are remarkably consistent in both directions. Other languages, like German, have a complex phonology but an orthography that is transparent for reading, although not for spelling.

Cross-language studies of literacy acquisition show that these factors have systematic effects on the acquisition of reading. Children who are learning to read a language with a simple CV syllable structure and a transparent orthography, like Finnish, learn to read simple words efficiently within weeks of arriving in school (Seymour, Aro, & Erskine, 2003). Children learning to read English take much longer to become competent at decoding, despite their earlier start. In England, we begin to teach reading at the age of 4 years. In some European countries, such as the Scandinavian countries, reading instruction can commence as late as 7 years. Nevertheless, children in such countries become highly efficient at decoding quite rapidly following the onset of teaching. This was shown, for example, by the largest and most consistent cross-language study of early reading acquisition to date, the study reported by Seymour et al. (2003). They reported the outcome of a 14-language study carried out by scientists participating in the European Concerted Action on Learning Disorders as a Barrier to Human Development.[1] These scientists developed a matched set of simple real words and nonwords across languages that were given to children to read during their first year of schooling in the different EU member states. Participating schools all used a "phonics-based" instructional approach to reading. A summary of the results is reported in Table 15.2.

As is clear from Table 15.2, decoding accuracy approached ceiling levels in many European languages during the first year of schooling (Greece, Finland, Italy, Spain). All of these languages have a transparent spelling system. It was not close to ceiling in four languages: French, Portuguese, Danish, and English. All of these languages have less transparent spelling systems. English, in particular, has a very inconsistent orthography, as described above. The English-speaking children (a Scottish sample—Scotland traditionally has strong phonics teaching for early reading) performed particularly poorly, reaching 34% accuracy for real word reading and 29% accuracy for simple nonsense words (like *eb* and *fip*). It is interesting to compare the performance of the English children with that of the German children, as English and German have the same linguistic root. In fact, many of the words in English and German are the same words (*wine/Wein, mouse/Maus, garden/garten*). Nevertheless, German has a consistent orthography. The German children attained 98% accuracy for real word reading, and 94% accuracy for nonsense word reading. These differences in reading acquisition by

---

[1] National representatives of this action were: H. Wimmer, T. Reinelt (Austria), J. Alegria, J. Morais, J. Leybaert (Belgium), C. Elbro, E. Arnbak (Denmark), H. Lyytinen, P. Niemi (Finland), J.-E. Gombert, M.-T. Le Normand, L. Sprenger-Charolles, S. Valdois (France), A. Warnke, W. Schneider (Germany), C. Porpodas (Greece), V. Csepe (Hungary), H. Ragnarsdottir (Iceland), C. Cornoldi, P. Giovanardi Rossi, C. Vio, P. Tressoldi, A. Parmeggiani (Italy), C. Firman (Malta), R. Licht, A. M. B. De Groot (Netherlands), F.-E. Tonnessen (Norway), L. Castro, L. Cary (Portugal), S. Defior, F. Martos, J. Sainz, X. Angerri (Spain), S. Stromqvist, A. Olofsson (Sweden), P. Seymour, P. Bryant, U. Goswami (United Kingdom).

Table 15.2 Data (% correct) from the COST A8 Study of Grapheme–Phoneme Recoding Skills for Monosyllables in 14 European Languages.

Language	Familiar, real words	Nonwords
Greek	98	92
Finnish	98	95
German	98	94
Austrian German	97	92
Italian	95	89
Spanish	95	89
Swedish	95	88
Dutch	95	82
Icelandic	94	86
Norwegian	92	91
French	79	85
Portuguese	73	77
Danish	71	54
Scottish English	34	29

Note. Adapted from "Foundation Literacy Acquisition in European Orthographies," by P. H. K. Seymour, M. Aro, and J. M. Erskine, 2003, *British Journal of Psychology, 94*, 143–174.

English versus German children have also been demonstrated in smaller studies with careful cognitive matching of the participants (Frith, Wimmer, & Landerl, 1998; Wimmer & Goswami, 1994).

Clearly, the normal neuropsychological development of reading differs depending on the language that you are learning to read. The same cognitive factor underpins successful reading acquisition in all languages so far studied, namely phonological awareness. However, phonological skills interact with orthographic transparency. Children who are learning to read languages with a simple phonological structure and a transparent orthography do particularly well (Finnish, Spanish). Children who are learning to read languages with a complex phonological structure but a transparent orthography also do well (German, Welsh—not in Table15.2, but see Ellis & Hooper, 2001). Children who are learning to read a language like English, which has a complex phonological structure and a particularly inconsistent orthography, take longer to acquire efficient decoding skills. But for typically developing children, this longer learning process is easily explained. Literacy is a more difficult "learning problem" in a language like English. By the age of around 10 years, and sometimes earlier, differences in decoding efficiency between English children and those learning to read in other languages have disappeared (e.g., Goswami, Gombert, & de Barrera, 1998). In fact, the better English readers have done rather well in recent international comparisons. We turn now to consider children who have specific difficulties with reading, children with developmental dyslexia. For these children, having to learn to read a language like English has rather different consequences.

Atypical Neuropsychological Development of Reading across Languages

The cognitive framework developed above to explain the typical neuropsychological development of reading across languages makes some clear predictions regarding atypical development. One key prediction is that a specific difficulty in representing the phonological structure of words should manifest itself differently in reading depending on the language that you are learning to read. For example, if you are learning to read a language like Italian, which has a simple CV syllable structure and a transparent orthography, having a specific difficulty with phonology might not have a very large impact on your reading. Once you learn about letters, the 1:1 relationship between these letters and sounds might help you to improve your deficient phonological representations. The highly predictable relationship between spelling and sound also enables reading accuracy, as children with developmental dyslexia are of average intelligence. They can learn letter–sound relationships if the relationships are 1:1, even if they do so rather slowly. If you are learning to read a language like German, which has a complex syllable structure but a transparent orthography, having a specific difficulty with phonology might also have a relatively minor impact on your eventual ability to read. Again, the 1:1 relationship between letters and sounds should help to improve your phonological abilities and enable accurate reading. However, if you are learning to read a language like English, which has a complex syllable structure and a highly inconsistent orthography, a specific difficulty with phonology might have rather profound consequences. Learning letters will not be particularly helpful for phonological awareness, and recoding letters to sound seems likely to remain problematic given the highly variable relationships that will be encountered. The research base in developmental dyslexia supports exactly this picture of atypical development.

Phonological awareness in developmental dyslexia

Cognitive studies across languages demonstrate that children with developmental dyslexia in all languages so far studied have difficulties with phonological awareness tasks. They find it difficult to count syllables, to recognize rhyme, to decide whether words share phonemes, and to substitute one phoneme for another (e.g., Korean: Kim & Davis, 2004; German: Wimmer, 1996; Greek: Porpodas, Pantelis, & Hantziou, 1990; Hebrew: Share & Levin, 1999; see Ziegler & Goswami, 2005, for a comprehensive review). Numerous studies in English, in particular, have shown that children with developmental dyslexia remain poor at tasks such as deciding whether words rhyme (Bradley & Bryant, 1978), making accurate judgments in counting, or same–different judgment tasks at the different linguistic levels of syllable, onset/rime, and phoneme (Swan & Goswami, 1997), making oddity judgments about phonemes (Bowey, Cain, & Ryan, 1992), and Spoonerism tasks (Landerl, Wimmer, & Frith, 1997). These difficulties persist into the teenage years (e.g., Bruck, 1992).

However, for dyslexic children who are learning to read transparent orthographies, reading has an impact on phonological awareness. Learning consistent letter–sound relationships appears to help children to specify phonological similarities and differences between words. For example, German dyslexic children show age-appropriate phonological skills in some phonological awareness tasks (those that can be solved using letters) by the age of 10 years. A Spoonerism task is an example of a phonological awareness task that can be solved using orthography. In Spoonerism tasks, the child has to swap onsets in words (like Reverend Spooner, who told students "You have hissed all my mystery lectures"). For example, the child may have to say "Dob Bylan" instead of "Bob Dylan." German dyslexic children eventually became able to do such tasks as well as control children (Wimmer, 1993). However, when German dyslexic children are compared to matched English dyslexic children, the Germans perform much better in Spoonerism tasks (Landerl et al., 1997).

Acquisition of literacy skills in developmental dyslexia

Despite measurable phonological difficulties in children with developmental dyslexia across languages, for most of the world's languages, differences in the accuracy of decoding print compared to age-matched peers is only found in the very earliest stages of reading. Studies of young Greek and German children who later turned out to have specific reading difficulties showed that word and nonsense word reading was significantly poorer than that of age-matched controls in the first year of reading instruction, but this difference soon disappeared (Porpodas, 1999; Wimmer, 1993). Although difficulties with phonology remain for children learning to read transparent orthographies, they do not impede reading accuracy. Rather, they impede reading *speed* and *spelling* accuracy. Developmental dyslexia in most languages other than English is usually diagnosed on the basis of extremely slow and effortful reading, and strikingly poor spelling.

For English children, however, developmental dyslexia is characterized by both inaccurate and effortful reading and by inaccurate spelling. Even dyslexic adults in English remain poor at decoding words accurately (Bruck, 1992). Hence the same cognitive deficit can manifest differently in different languages. In fact, English children with developmental dyslexia perform significantly more poorly in tasks such as nonsense word reading compared to German children with developmental dyslexia, even when they are trying to read the same items (e.g., nonsense words like *grall*, see Landerl et al., 1997). This demonstrates the pervasive effects of learning to read an inconsistent orthography on reading development. The consequences of having a phonological deficit are more profound in developmental terms for literacy in English.

Behavioral genetics

The phonological deficit that characterizes dyslexia across languages appears to be heritable. The heritability of dyslexia has been demonstrated by a number of family and twin studies, particularly in English (e.g., Gayan & Olson, 2001; Gayan et al., 1999). Linkage studies have been used to try to determine where in the human genome the critical genes for dyslexia are located. The most promising findings so far concern the short arm of chromosome 6, and sites on chromosome 15 (e.g., Grigorenko et al., 1997). These studies depend on definitions of the dyslexic phenotype that are based on deficits in phonological awareness tasks and single or nonsense word reading. The dyslexic "phenotype" is defined in terms of phonology. Of course, there cannot be a "gene" for dyslexia in the sense that there is a gene for eye color, as reading is a culturally determined activity. Individuals at genetic risk for dyslexia who develop in a favorable early environment as far as reading is concerned (for example, children whose carers actively develop their phonological awareness via language games, nursery rhymes, and so on; and who read books to them and model and encourage literacy activities by reading and writing extensively themselves) may be able to compensate to some extent for their genetic predisposition to dyslexia. Other individuals with a lower degree of risk but relatively adverse early environments may be more handicapped. Nevertheless, no candidate gene so far identified can be described as a "gene for reading." Levels of association reported so far in behavioral and molecular genetics are not strong enough to translate into reliable predictors of risk for a single individual (Fisher & Francks, 2006).

Neuroimaging of Typical and Atypical Readers

Reading and phonological processing in adults depends on a left-lateralized network of frontal, temporoparietal, and occipitotemporal regions. Studies of aphasia long ago revealed the importance of Broca's area (inferior frontal gyrus) and Wernicke's area (posterior superior temporal gyrus) for the motor production and receptive aspects of speech, respectively, and these areas appear to be recruited along with visual and frontal areas by literacy. In normally reading adults, remarkable overlap is found in the neural networks underpinning reading, whether the adult has learned to read a consistent orthography like Italian, an inconsistent orthography like English, or a character-based orthography like Chinese (Paulesu et al., 2001; Siok, Perfetti, Jin, & Tan, 2004). This has led researchers such as Paulesu to propose that a common neurological network underpins dyslexia across languages. Studies of adults with developmental dyslexia suggest that phonological mechanisms are localized in the temporoparietal junction (see Eden & Zeffiro, 1998, for review). When performing tasks like rhyme judgment, rhyme detection, and word and nonsense word reading, dyslexic adults show reduced activation in temporal and parietal regions, particularly within the left hemisphere.

Work by Turkeltaub and colleagues has explored the neural underpinning of phonological processing in children (Turkeltaub, Gareau, Flowers, Zeffiro, & Eden, 2003; see Plate 8). Phonological awareness appears to depend on a network of areas in the left posterior superior temporal cortex. Activity in this region is modulated by the level of children's phonological skills. The rapid output of phonological information appears to depend on a different, bilateral network, including right posterior superior temporal gyrus, right middle temporal gyrus, and left ventral inferior frontal gyrus. The left posterior temporal sulcus is also the primary area recruited by young children at the beginning of reading development. As reading skills develop, an area termed the "visual word form area" becomes more engaged (Cohen & Dehaene, 2004). This area is also active for nonsense word reading, hence it probably stores orthography–phonology connections at different grain sizes (Goswami & Ziegler, 2006). Children with developmental dyslexia show reduced activation in the normal left hemisphere sites, and atypical engagement of right temporoparietal cortex. If targeted remediation is provided, usually via intensive tuition in phonological skills and in letter–sound conversion, activity in the left temporal and parietal areas appears to normalize (e.g., Simos et al., 2002). These studies have all been carried out with dyslexic children learning to read in English. Studies with children learning to read in other languages have yet to be done.

Implications of Current Research

Research suggests that while brains are similar across languages, orthographies are not. In all languages so far studied, one aspect of language acquisition is the development of phonological awareness. Individual differences in phonological awareness determine individual differences in the development of reading and spelling. Literacy, in turn, results in the further development of phonological awareness. Indeed, the demonstration of the importance of phonological awareness for literacy has been hailed as the success story of developmental psychology (see Adams, 1990; Lundberg, 1991; Stanovich, 1992). Specific characteristics of this developmental relationship vary with language, but the variation is systematic, depending on phonological complexity and orthographic consistency. One important factor is the "grain size" or unit of analysis (e.g., the syllable is a large grain size, the phoneme is small grain size). There are predictable developmental differences in the ease with which phonological awareness at different grain sizes emerges across orthographies, in the grain size of lexical representations across orthographies, and in developmental reading strategies across orthographies (see Ziegler & Goswami, 2005). Future research in additional languages using this "psycholinguistic grain size" framework will be very useful in pinpointing universal causal mechanisms for literacy.

The importance of phonology for reading and spelling means that clinical assessments of reading and reading difficulties rely on phonological tests. One of the most widely used test batteries is the Phonological Assessment Battery (PhAB), which provides standardized age norms for different measures of phonological awareness such as rhyme fluency and Spoonerisms (Fredrickson, Frith, & Reason, 1997). Other tests which purport to measure a wider range of skills, such as the Dyslexia Early Screening Test (Nicolson & Fawcett, 1996) also rely heavily on phonological subtests. The development of single word reading, spelling, and reading comprehension skills can also be measured by a range of standardized tests, such as the British Ability Scales (Elliott, 1996) and the Neale Analysis of Reading Ability (Neale, 1989). In terms of intervention, the most successful interventions remain those that work directly on the component skills of phonology and letter–sound relationships. Although claims are sometimes made for interventions based on remediating motor skills (e.g., the Dyslexia Dyspraxia Attention Deficit Treatment [DDAT]; Reynolds, Nicolson, & Hambly, 2003) or disturbances of the visual system (e.g., Irlen lenses), research on their effectiveness remains equivocal (e.g., Snowling & Hulme, 2003). Most children who present in the clinic with developmental dyslexia are best served by systematic teaching of phonological skills, letter–sound relationships, and the larger orthographic patterns that enable consistency in English spelling–sound relations.

References

Adams, M. J. (1990). *Beginning to read: Thinking and learning about print*. Cambridge, MA: MIT Press.

Anthony, J. L., & Lonigan, C. J. (2004). The nature of phonological awareness: Converging evidence from four studies of preschool and early grade school children. *Journal of Educational Psychology, 96*, 43–55.

Anthony, J. L., Lonigan, C. J., Burgess, S. R., Driscoll, K., Phillips, B. M., & Cantor, B. G. (2002). Structure of preschool phonological sensitivity: Overlapping sensitivity to rhyme, words, syllables, and phonemes. *Journal of Experimental Child Psychology, 82*, 65–92.

Anthony, J. L., Lonigan, C. J., Driscoll, K., Phillips, B. M., & Burgess, S. R. (2003). Phonological sensitivity: A quasi-parallel progression of word structure units and cognitive operations. *Reading Research Quarterly, 38*(4), 470–487.

Bowey, J. A., Cain, M. T., & Ryan, S. M. (1992). A reading-level design study of phonological skills underlying fourth grade children's word reading difficulties. *Child Development, 63*, 999–1011.

Bradley, L., & Bryant, P. E. (1978). Difficulties in auditory organization as a possible cause of reading backwardness. *Nature, 271*, 746–747.

Bradley, L., & Bryant, P. E. (1983). Categorising sounds and learning to read: A causal connection. *Nature, 310*, 419–421.

Bruck, M. (1992). Persistence of dyslexics' phonological awareness deficits. *Developmental Psychology, 28*, 874–886.

Bryant, P. E., MacLean, M., Bradley, L. L., & Crossland, J. (1990). Rhyme and alliteration, phoneme detection, and learning to read. *Developmental Psychology, 26*, 429–438.

Chaney, C. (1992). Language development, metalinguistic skills and print awareness in 3-year-old children. *Applied Psycholinguistics, 13*, 485–514.

Cohen, L., & Dehaene, S. (2004). Specialization within the ventral stream: The case for the visual word form area. *NeuroImage, 22*, 466–476.

Cossu, G., Shankweiler, D., Liberman, I. Y., Katz, L., & Tola, G. (1988). Awareness of phonological segments and reading ability in Italian children. *Applied Psycholinguistics, 9*, 1–16.

De Cara, B., & Goswami, U. (2002). Statistical analysis of similarity relations among spoken words: Evidence for the special status of rimes in English. *Behavioural Research Methods and Instrumentation, 34*(3), 416–423.

Dollaghan, C. A. (1994). Children's phonological neighbourhoods: Half empty or half full? *Journal of Child Language, 21*, 237–271.

Eden, G. F., & Zeffiro, T. A. (1998). Neural systems affected in developmental dyslexia revealed by functional neuroimaging. *Neuron, 21,* 279–282.

Elliott, C. D. (1996). *British ability scales II.* Windsor: NFER-NELSON.

Ellis, N. C., & Hooper, A. M. (2001). Why learning to read is easier in Welsh than in English: Orthographic transparency effects evinced with frequency-matched tests. *Applied Psycholinguistics, 22,* 571–599.

Fisher, S. E., & Francks, C. (2006). Genes, cognition and dyslexia: Learning to read the genome. *Trends in Cognitive Sciences, 10*(6), 250–257.

Fredrickson, N., Frith, U., & Reason, R. (1997). *Phonological assessment battery.* Windsor: NFER-NELSON.

Frith, U., Wimmer, H., & Landerl, K. (1998). Differences in phonological recoding in German- and English-speaking children. *Scientific Studies of Reading, 2,* 31–54.

Gayan, J., & Olson, R. K. (2001). Genetic and environmental influences on orthographic and phonological skills in children with reading disabilities. *Developmental Neuropsychology, 20,* 483–507.

Gayan, J., Smith, S. D., Cherny, S. S., Cardon, L. R., Fulker, D. W., Kimberling, W. J., et al. (1999). Large quantitative trait locus for specific language and reading deficits in chromosome 6p. *American Journal of Human Genetics, 64,* 157–164.

Goswami, U., & Bryant, P. E. (1990). *Phonological skills and learning to read.* Hillsdale, NJ: Erlbaum.

Goswami, U., Gombert, J. E., & de Barrera, L. F. (1998). Children's orthographic representations and linguistic transparency: Nonsense word reading in English, French, and Spanish. *Applied Psycholinguistics, 19*(1), 19–52.

Goswami, U., & Ziegler, J. C. (2006). A developmental perspective on the neural code for written words. *Trends in Cognitive Sciences, 10*(4), 142–143.

Goswami, U., Ziegler, J. C., & Richardson, U. (2005). The effects of spelling consistency on phonological awareness: A comparison of English and German. *Journal of Experimental Child Psychology, 92*(4), 345–365.

Grigorenko, E. L., Wood, F. B., Meyer, M. S., Hart, L. A., Speed, W. C., Shuster, A., et al. (1997). Susceptibility loci for distinct components of developmental dyslexia on chromosomes 6 and 15. *American Journal of Human Genetics, 60,* 27–39.

Hinshelwood, J. A. (1896). A case of dyslexia: A peculiar form of word-blindness. *Lancet, 2,* 1451.

Ho, C. S.-H., & Bryant, P. (1997). Phonological skills are important in learning to read Chinese. *Developmental Psychology, 33,* 946–951.

Hoien, T., Lundberg, L., Stanovich, K. E., & Bjaalid, I. K. (1995). Components of phonological awareness. *Reading and Writing, 7,* 171–188.

Kim, J., & Davis, C. (2004). Characteristics of poor readers of Korean Hangul: Auditory, visual and phonological processing. *Reading and Writing, 17*(1–2), 153–185.

Landerl, K., Wimmer, H., & Frith, U. (1997). The impact of orthographic consistency on dyslexia: A German–English comparison. *Cognition, 63,* 315–334.

Liberman, I. Y., Shankweiler, D., Fischer, F. W., & Carter, B. (1974). Explicit syllable and phoneme segmentation in the young child. *Journal of Experimental Child Psychology, 18,* 201–212.

Lundberg, I. (1991). Phonemic awareness can be developed without reading instruction. In S. A. Brady & D. P. Shankweiler (Eds.), *Phonological processes in literacy: A tribute to Isabelle Liberman* (pp. 47–53). Hillsdale, NJ: Erlbaum.

Lundberg, I., Frost, J., & Petersen, O. (1988). Effects of an extensive programme for stimulating phonological awareness in pre-school children. *Reading Research Quarterly, 23,* 163–284.

Lundberg, I., Olofsson, A., & Wall, S. (1980). Reading and spelling skills in the first school years predicted from phonemic awareness skills in kindergarten. *Scandinavian Journal of Psychology*, *21*, 159–173.

MacLean, M., Bryant, P. E., & Bradley, L. (1987). Rhymes, nursery rhymes and reading in early childhood. *Merrill-Palmer Quarterly*, *33*, 255–282.

Metsala, J. L. (1999). Young children's phonological awareness and nonword repetition as a function of vocabulary development. *Journal of Educational Psychology*, *91*, 3–19.

Morais, J., Cary, L., Alegria, J., & Bertelson, P. (1979). Does awareness of speech as a sequence of phones arise spontaneously? *Cognition*, *7*, 323–331.

Neale, M. D. (1989). *Neale analysis of reading ability: Revised*. Windsor: NFER-NELSON.

Nicolson, R. I., & Fawcett, A. J. (1996). *The dyslexia early screening test*. London: Psychological Corporation.

Paulesu, E., Démonet, J.-F., Fazio, F., McCrory, E., Chanoine, V., Brunswick, N., et al. (2001). Dyslexia: Cultural diversity and biological unity. *Science*, *291*(5511), 2165–2167.

Porpodas, C. D. (1999). Patterns of phonological and memory processing in beginning readers and spellers of Greek. *Journal of Learning Disabilities*, *32*, 406–416.

Porpodas, C. D., Pantelis, S. N., & Hantziou, E. (1990). Phonological and lexical encoding processes in beginning readers: Effects of age and word characteristics. *Reading and Writing*, *2*, 197–208.

Read, C. (1986). *Children's creative spelling*. London: Routledge and Kegan Paul.

Reynolds, D., Nicolson, R. I., & Hambly, H. (2003). Evaluation of an exercise-based treatment for children with reading difficulties. *Dyslexia*, *9*, 48–71.

Schneider, W., Kuespert, P., Roth, E., Vise, M., & Marx, H. (1997). Short- and long-term effects of training phonological awareness in kindergarten: Evidence from two German studies. *Journal of Experimental Child Psychology*, *66*, 311–340.

Schneider, W., Roth, E., & Ennemoser, M. (2000). Training phonological skills and letter knowledge in children at-risk for dyslexia: A comparison of three kindergarten intervention programs. *Journal of Educational Psychology*, *92*, 284–295.

Seymour, P. H. K., Aro, M., & Erskine, J. M. (2003). Foundation literacy acquisition in European orthographies. *British Journal of Psychology*, *94*, 143–174.

Share, D., & Levin, I. (1999). Learning to read and write in Hebrew. In M. Harris & G. Hatano (Eds.), *Learning to read and write: A cross-linguistic perspective* (pp. 89–111). New York: Cambridge University Press.

Simos, P. G., Fletcher, J. M., Bergman, E., Breier, J. I., Foorman, B. R., Castillo, E. M., et al. (2002). Dyslexia-specific brain activation profile becomes normal following successful remedial training. *Neurology*, *58*, 1203–1213.

Siok, W. T., Perfetti, C. A., Jin, Z., & Tan, L. H. (2004). Biological abnormality of impaired reading is constrained by culture. *Nature*, *431*, 71–76.

Snowling, M. J., & Hulme, C. (2003). A critique of claims from Reynolds, Nicolson & Hambly (2003) that DDAT is an effective treatment for children with reading difficulties: "Lies, damned lies and (inappropriate) statistics?" *Dyslexia*, *9*, 127–133.

Stanovich, K. E. (1992). Speculations on the causes and consequences of individual differences in early reading acquisition. In P. B. Gough, L. C. Ehri, & R. Treiman (Eds.), *Reading acquisition* (pp. 307–342). Hillsdale, NJ: Erlbaum.

Swan, D., & Goswami, U. (1997). Phonological awareness deficits in developmental dyslexia and the phonological representations hypothesis. *Journal of Experimental Child Psychology*, *66*, 18–41.

Treiman, R., & Zukowski, A. (1991). Levels of phonological awareness. In S. Brady & D. Shankweiler (Eds.), *Phonological processes in literacy* (pp. 67–83). Hillsdale, NJ: Erlbaum.

Turkeltaub, P. E., Gareau, L., Flowers, D. L., Zeffiro, T. A., & Eden, G. F. (2003). Development of neural mechanisms for reading. *Nature Neuroscience, 6*(7), 767–73.

Wimmer, H. (1993). Characteristics of developmental dyslexia in a regular writing system. *Applied Psycholinguistics, 14,* 1–33.

Wimmer, H. (1996). The nonword reading deficit in developmental dyslexia: Evidence from children learning to read German. *Journal of Experimental Child Psychology, 61,* 80–90.

Wimmer, H., & Goswami, U. (1994). The influence of orthographic consistency on reading development: Word recognition in English and German children. *Cognition, 51*(1), 91–103.

Ziegler, J. C., & Goswami, U. C. (2005). Reading acquisition, developmental dyslexia and skilled reading across languages: A psycholinguistic grain size theory. *Psychological Bulletin, 131*(1), 3–29.

Ziegler, J. C., Stone, G. O., & Jacobs, A. M. (1997). What's the pronunciation for -OUGH and the spelling for /u/? A database for computing feedforward and feedback inconsistency in English. *Behavior Research Methods, Instruments, and Computers, 29,* 600–618.

16

Developmental Dyscalculia

Brian Butterworth

As learners go through school, the difference between achieved and expected levels in mathematics gets worse. In the UK, at the end of Key Stage 1, 90% of all learners have achieved the expected Level 2, while by Key Stage 2, only 75% achieve the expected Level 4, and at Key Stage 5 it is even worse: Only 54% achieve the expected A*–C grades in GCSEs (DfES, 2006). This means that very many learners and their parents may seek specialist advice on poor levels of achievement in mathematics.

Parents and children are right to be worried. Low numeracy skills are a more severe handicap than most people, let alone most clinicians, realize. A study of the effects of low numeracy (about 8% of the population) shows that it is more of a handicap in the workplace than poor literacy (Bynner & Parsons, 1997). Men and women aged 30, with poor numeracy, are more likely to be unemployed, more likely to be depressed, and more likely to be arrested (Bynner & Parsons, 2005). Low numeracy in learners is a cause of distress, low self-esteem, stigmatization, and disruptive behavior in class (Butterworth, 2005a). It is therefore a major social, educational, and clinical problem.

A focus group study of 9-year-old children with developmental dyscalculia (Bevan & Butterworth, 2007, quoted in Butterworth, 2005a) revealed that they suffered considerable anguish during the daily mathematics lesson:

Focus group 1 (verbatim transcripts):
CHILD 5: It makes me feel left out, sometimes.
CHILD 2: Yeah.
CHILD 5: When I like—when I don't know something, I wish that I was like a clever person and I blame it on myself—
CHILD 4: I would cry and I wish I was at home with my mum and it would be—I won't have to do any maths.

Focus group 2:
MODERATOR: How does it make people feel in a math lesson when they lose track?

CHILD 1:   Horrible.
MODERATOR: Horrible? ... Why's that?
CHILD 1:   I don't know.
CHILD 3 (WHISPERS):   He does know.
MODERATOR: Just a guess.
CHILD 1:   You feel stupid.

More able learners, of course, are well aware of this and often tease or stigmatize classmates with developmental dyscalculia:

CHILD 1:   She's like—she's like all upset and miserable, and she don't like being teased.
CHILD 4:   Yeah, and then she goes hide in the corner—nobody knows where she is and she's crying there.

A major cause of low numeracy is developmental dyscalculia (DD), which, according to the current best estimates, affects 6–7% of the population (see below). The usual presenting symptoms of DD are poor performance in school math tests, failing to understand numerical concepts, losing track in math lessons, often in the presence of good marks in other school subjects, and inability to deal with numbers in everyday life situations, such as shopping, telling the time, and remembering phone numbers. However, these can be symptoms with other causes, including poor or inappropriate math teaching, missing lessons, anxiety about numbers and mathematics, behavioral problems, poor working memory, attentional problems, and some language-related impairments including dyslexia. Mathematics seems particularly vulnerable to any kind of stress on learning, perhaps because of the cumulative structure of its content: Failing to understand one concept can mean that the learner will fail to understand concepts that depend on it (though this has not been systematically investigated). I will deal with these issues in more detail in what follows.

DD also persists into adulthood. In a six-year prospective follow-up study, of the learners diagnosed as having DD at the age of 11, over 40% were still in the DD category (here two years behind chronological age-matched controls) at 17, and 95% were still in the lowest quartile of their age group (Shalev, Manor, & Gross-Tsur, 2005).

Defining Dyscalculia

Despite being as prevalent as dyslexia (according to the more rigorous criteria for dyslexia), and despite being at least as much of a handicap in everyday life, DD is not widely recognized. The first mention that I can find in a document of the UK Department of Education and Skills comes in 2001 (DfES, 2001), and it is only very recently that information appeared on an official website (see www.standards.dfes.gov.uk/primary/faqs/inclusion/56233/). One reason for this lack of recognition reminds us why dyslexia remained unrecognized for a long time. The lay and, to a considerable extent, the expert account of the cause of the inability to learn to read was stupidity. This is still the case for DD, as we will see, and while being good at reading is not regarded as an indicator of high intelligence, being good at mathematics often is.

The situation is not helped by the variety of terms and definitions used to characterize difficulties in acquiring numerical skills. For example, *The Diagnostic and Statistical Manual of Mental Disorders*, fourth edition, gives the following diagnostic criteria for "Mathematics Disorder" (American Psychiatric Association, 1994, section 315.1):

A. Mathematical ability, as measured by individually administered standardized tests, is substantially below that expected given the person's chronological age, measured intelligence, and age-appropriate education.

B. The disturbance in Criterion A significantly interferes with academic achievement or activities of daily living that require mathematical ability.

C. If a sensory deficit is present, the difficulties in mathematical ability are in excess of those usually associated with it.

This is a discrepancy criterion, which rules out by definition the possibility that someone can have both a mathematics disorder and low general cognitive ability; and it presumably implies that low measured intelligence is sufficient to cause the symptoms of "mathematics disorder."

The World Health Organization's *International Classification of Diseases: 10* (1994, section 8.21) defines a "Specific disorder of arithmetical skills" as involving "a specific impairment in arithmetical skills that is not solely explicable on the basis of general mental retardation or of inadequate schooling. The deficit concerns mastery of basic computational skills of addition, subtraction, multiplication, and division rather than of the more abstract mathematical skills involved in algebra, trigonometry, geometry, or calculus." This is subtly different from the DSM-IV definition in that it allows for the possibility of both dyscalculia and low cognitive ability, and moreover begins to use a qualitative approach that is focused on numerical abilities, rather than other aspects of mathematics.

However, both definitions depend explicitly or implicitly on poor performance on standardized tests of *arithmetic*. Of course, there may be many causes of poor arithmetical performance besides "inadequate schooling," as I have noted above, and no explanation is offered why, despite the advantages of good intelligence and "age-appropriate education," the person may suffer from this selective handicap. The UK's Department for Education and Skills offered a suggestion in its definition of "dyscalculia" as "A condition that affects the ability to acquire arithmetical skills." "Dyscalculic learners may have difficulty understanding simple number concepts, lack an intuitive grasp of numbers, and have problems learning number facts and procedures. Even if they produce a correct answer or use a correct method, they may do so mechanically and without confidence" (DfES, 2001). Here the focus is on the intuitive grasp of simple number concepts. This is not, unfortunately, explained further.

These definitions therefore create a big explanatory gap: Why should individuals of cognitive ability who experience adequate and age-appropriate education fail to learn basic arithmetic? In trying to find an explanation, it is important to attend to critical differences among the studies carried out so far. As usual with developmental categories, the operational definition of the target group is critical. For DD, the problem is exacerbated by widely different populations considered by different investigators. These range from 3 to 7% of the cohort using a mathematics age to chronological age discrepancy of two years (Gross-Tsur, Manor, & Shalev, 1996; Lewis, Hitch, & Walker, 1994), while others have considered the lowest quartile (Koontz & Berch, 1996; Shalev & Gross-Tsur, 2001; Siegel & Ryan, 1989), or a standard score of less than 90 (e.g., Mazzocco & McCloskey, 2005). In some studies, the exact criterion for the DD group is not provided at all (Rubinsten & Henik, 2005). Koontz and Berch (1996) use the term "arithmetic learning disabilities" (ALD) and include learners below the 25th percentile on the Iowa Test of Basic Skills. Most learners so classified would fall between 0.67 and 1.18 *SD* below the expected mean, and could thus be regarded as in the low average or even the average range. The terminology of these authors, as well as their criteria, make it clear that they are considering a range of causes for low mathematics achievement, not just the clinical condition of dyscalculia.

In general, there appears to be a basic distinction between prevalence studies, which give these low prevalences, and experimental studies, which use a much broader criterion. Geary and Hoard (2005, p. 254), in a review of learning disabilities in arithmetic, note that "5% to 8% of school age learners have some form of MD [mathematical disability]" but base their analysis of the causes on studies, especially their own, which use a 30th percentile criterion (the exception being the study by Landerl, Bevan, & Butterworth, 2004, where learners who were 3 *SD* worse than controls were in the DD sample).

The larger the proportion of the cohort used in a study, the more heterogeneous it is likely to be. This will mean that information-processing deficits affecting schooling achievement generally, such as poor language skills including dyslexia, low IQ, poor working memory, and behavioral problems, are likely to differentiate the average of the DD group in comparison with normally achieving (NA) controls on tasks that call upon a wide range of capacities, skills, and learning experiences.

This is precisely the case with mathematics. Even school arithmetic is complex, with a diverse collection of facts and procedures prescribed by the curriculum. In the UK, for example, the following are prescribed for Year 4 (age 9 years):

- Use symbols correctly, including less than (<), greater than (>), equals (=).
- Round any positive integer less than 1,000 to the nearest 10 or 100.
- Recognize simple fractions that are several parts of a whole, and mixed numbers; recognize the equivalence of simple fractions.
- Use known number facts and place value to add or subtract mentally, including any pair of two-digit whole numbers.
- Carry out column addition and subtraction of two integers less than 1,000, and column addition of more than two such integers.

- Know by heart facts for the 2, 3, 4, 5, and 10 multiplication tables.
- Derive quickly division facts corresponding to the 2, 3, 4, 5, and 10 multiplication tables. Find remainders after division.
- Choose and use appropriate number operations and ways of calculating (mental, mental with jottings, pencil and paper) to solve problems.

Because even 9- and 10-year-olds have so many different kinds of facts and skills to acquire, it is not surprising that the reported symptoms of dyscalculia are diverse. The following arithmetical symptoms are frequently cited (e.g., Butterworth, 2005a; Geary, 1993):

- Poor memory for arithmetical facts (e.g., number bonds and multiplication tables).
- Reliance on immature strategies (e.g., adding and multiplying using fingers).
- Poor grasp of arithmetical procedures (e.g., borrowing and carrying).
- Poor grasp of arithmetical laws (e.g., commutativity of addition).

Is Developmental Dyscalculia a Domain-general or Domain-specific Deficit?

A key question for the clinician is whether poor arithmetical performance—for example, low scores on a standardized test—is due to cognitive characteristics that affect other domains. For example, poor working memory or poor language skills are linked to reading difficulties and their educational sequelae. Low cognitive ability, as measured by standard IQ tests, correlates significantly with educational attainment (e.g., Wainwright, Wright, Geffen, Luciano, & Martin, 2005). Behavioral and emotional problems, including attention deficit hyperactivity disorder (ADHD), can have wide-ranging effects on education. A further complicating factor is that DD often co-occurs with these conditions (Shalev & Gross-Tsur, 2001; Shalev, Manor, & Gross-Tsur, 1997).

However, we can pose this question more generally and more theoretically: Is it possible to have a selective deficit in learning arithmetic, one that is not caused by a deficit in domain-general capacities? To get a handle on this, we should consider what cognitive tools the learner might bring to acquiring normal arithmetical skills. The toolbox will contain the following: memory tools, reasoning tools, and language tools. It may be the case that the usual tools we bring to learning school subjects will do equally well for learning arithmetic, and that if any of them are not working efficiently, then we will be in trouble to a greater or lesser extent.

On the other hand, will the toolbox also contain tools specialized for processing numbers? If so, what would these be like? Just as it is possible to screw a screw into a plank of wood without a screwdriver, by using, for example, pliers or a wrench, it won't be easy, it won't be quick, and it won't be the way that most people do it. So we may not be looking for absolute inabilities—perhaps in the way that some people are unable to discriminate red and green—but rather slow, difficult, and abnormal ways of dealing with numbers.

Domain-general explanations

Now there have been a variety of attempts at domain-general explanations.

General intelligence

The most obvious explanation for both expert and layperson alike lies in intelligence or reasoning ability. Thus, 9-year-old children with DD ascribe their inability to learn math to their own stupidity, and their more able classmates frequently stigmatize them for being stupid as well (Bevan & Butterworth, 2007; Butterworth, 2005a).

However, very poor number skills can coexist with high cognitive ability. This is certainly true in cases of acquired dyscalculia (e.g., C.G. in Cipolotti, Butterworth, & Denes, 1991; D.R.C. in Warrington, 1982). Developmental cases have also been reported (e.g., "Charles" in Butterworth, 1999). More recently, we have studied B. D., an English major at a leading US university with very rigorous entry requirements, whose arithmetic was disastrous. Here is an example of her ability in multiplication:

EXPERIMENTER: Can you please tell me the result of nine times four?
B.D.: Yes, well, looks difficult. Now, I am very uncertain between fifty-two and forty-five ...
I really cannot decide: it could be the first but could be the second as well.
EXPERIMENTER: Make a guess then.
B.D.: Okay ... uhm ... I'll say forty-seven.
EXPERIMENTER: Good, I'll write down forty-seven. But you can still change your answer, if you want. For example, how about changing it with thirty-six?
B.D.: Bah, no ... it does not seem a better guess than forty-seven, does it? I'll keep forty-seven.
(unpublished data from Dr. B. Losiewicz and Dr. E. Rusconi)

It is difficult to get useful measures of the relationship between intelligence and DD, since studies typically exclude learners with low IQ. For example, Geary, Hoard, and Hamson (1999) and Shalev et al. (1997) exclude learners with an IQ below 80; Landerl et al. (2004) exclude learners below the 50th percentile on an IQ measure, and Koontz and Berch (1996) exclude learners "below normal IQ" (their sample had an average IQ of 102). However, this does mean that low general cognitive ability in itself cannot be the explanation for DD. It also means that additional effects of low cognitive ability on DD, if there are any, cannot be assessed.

Memory explanations

One of the usual suspects for poor cognitive performance is the low capacity of working memory (WM). As we know from the work of Baddeley and his colleagues (see Baddeley, 1986, for a review), WM is a complex construct with components for storage (the phonological buffer and the associated articulatory loop for rehearsal, and visuo-spatial sketchpad) which are slave systems for the "central executive," a system responsible for attentional and inhibitory control of information processing. Geary and Hoard (2005) implicate poor functioning of the "central executive," but also deficits in the "language system" (the phonological buffer) for representing and manipulating information in arithmetical fact storage and retrieval of arithmetical facts and also the "visuospatial system" which could play a role in columnar arithmetic. Note that WM is intended by Baddeley (1986) and others as a domain-general system that supports a wide range of cognitive tasks, including speech processing and comprehension, reasoning, and immediate memory (verbatim serial recall). The standard signature of WM is digit span length or, more generally, accurate serial recall of any unrelated verbal items.

Although the idea that impaired working memory could be the cause of DD has considerable plausibility given the apparent role of WM in calculation, there is in fact very little evidence to support this. Unfortunately, the standard test of WM is digit span, and this may be affected by an inability to code or interpret the digits. What is needed is a measure of WM capacity that does not rely on digit span, and a correlation between its functioning in non-numerical and numerical tasks. Typically, it is found that children and adults with an arithmetical deficit perform less well on both types of WM task. Thus, Siegel and Ryan (1989) found that learners with DD did less well than controls on a working memory task involving counting and remembering digits, but not on a non-numerical working memory task. McLean and Hitch (1999) found no difference on a non-numerical task testing phonological working memory (nonword repetition), suggesting that children with DD do not have reduced phonological working memory capacity in general, although they may have a specific difficulty with working memory for numerical information. Temple and Sherwood (2002) found no differences between groups on any of the working memory measures (forward and backward digit span, word span, and the Corsi blocks) and no correlation between measures of WM and measures of arithmetical ability. In the study by Landerl et al. (2004) of 9-year-olds, the DD and NA groups were matched on span, so it was unlikely that a WM deficit could explain differences between groups.

Geary (1993) has argued that WM deficits could have knock-on effects for long-term memory. If an arithmetical fact cannot be maintained in WM long enough, its transfer to long-term memory will be affected, resulting in "difficulty in the representation and retrieval of arithmetic facts from long-term semantic memory" (Geary, 1993, p. 346). However, Temple found no evidence that the subjects with poor memory for arithmetical facts had weak short-term memory spans on any span measure, nor that short-term memory spans related to arithmetical fact skills (Temple & Sherwood, 2002). Moreover, if poor memory for arithmetical facts is, as Geary and Hoard (2005) and Geary (1993) claim, a failure of (semantic) memory, this should apply to all forms of factual or semantic memory, but this has never been demonstrated in DD.

Moreover, Geary's basic proposition that access to long-term memory depends on routing through working memory is inconsistent with 35 years' research demonstrating the neural and functional independence on these systems (e.g., Butterworth, Cipolotti, & Warrington, 1996; Butterworth, Shallice, & Watson, 1990; McCarthy & Warrington, 1990; Warrington, 1982).

Space

Geary (1993, p. 346) noted that "a disruption of the ability to spatially represent numerical information ... appears to affect both functional skills (e.g., columnar alignment in complex arithmetic problems) and the conceptual understanding of the representations (e.g., place value)." The idea that space and number are cognitively related has had many supporters, and the role of the parietal lobes in both space and number has been noted by researchers since Gerstmann (1940). The representation of numerical magnitudes spatially as a kind of a mental number line has frequently been proposed (e.g., Dehaene, Piazza, Pinel, & Cohen, 2003; Fias, Lammertyn, Reynvoet, Dupont, & Orban, 2003; Galton, 1880; Spalding & Zangwill, 1950), and it would seem plausible that deficits in spatial representation ability could affect a sense of numerical magnitude. However, even severe unilateral spatial neglect where the patient neglects one side of space may affect the mental number line, but leaves arithmetic entirely spared (Zorzi, Priftis, & Umilta, 2002).

While being unable to maintain a mental representation of multidigit numbers in the correct columnar organization leads in neurological patients to "spatial acalculia" (Hécaen, Angelergues, & Houillier, 1961), such a condition has been rarely, if ever, reported as a pure symptom. It has never, to my knowledge, been reported in DD, and does not appear to affect the grasp of basic numerical concepts.

Domain-specific accounts

Koontz and Berch (1996, p. 2) asked "whether the mathematical difficulties experienced by ALD learners may stem in part from slower and less efficient cognitive processing of numerical information at an even more basic level than has heretofore been examined."

Research on infants suggests that we are born with an ability to recognize small numerosities, that is, the number of objects in a set (Antell & Keating, 1983; Starkey & Cooper, 1980), and carry out mental manipulations on representations of numerosities (e.g., Simon, Hespos, & Rochat, 1995; Wynn, 1992; Wynn, Bloom, & Chiang, 2002; see Gelman & Butterworth, 2005, for a review). Moreover, chimpanzees can learn numerosities and associate them with numerals (Matsuzawa, 1985), numerical ordering quickly (Kawai & Matsuzawa, 2000), and monkeys can select the numerically larger of two visual arrays of objects (Brannon & Terrace, 1998). It has recently been established that monkeys use parietal brain areas homologous to those used by humans in a matching to numerosity task (Nieder, Freedman, & Miller, 2002; Sawamura, Shima, & Tanji, 2002). This evidence suggests that there is a domain-specific mechanism for detecting, comparing, and manipulating "the numerosity parameter" of environmental stimuli (Dehaene et al., 2003) in human infants and primates.

So we may have inherited this capacity from an ancestral version in the common ancestor to humans and monkeys, which in turn implies that there are genes in the human genome that code for building a domain-specific brain system (presumably in

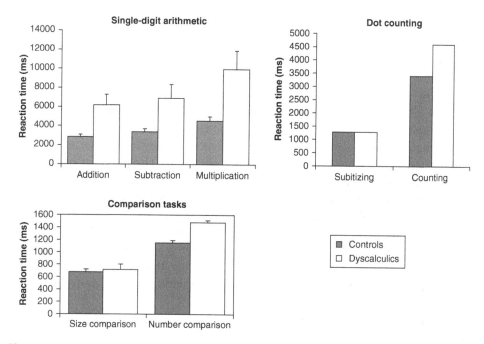

Figure 16.1 Dyscalculic 9-year-olds' performance (white) compared with matched controls (gray) on single-digit arithmetic, dot counting, and comparison tasks. All differences were significant except for size comparison. *Note*: Adapted from "Developmental Dyscalculia and Basic Numerical Capacities: A Study of 8–9 year old students," by K. Landerl, A. Bevan, & B. Butterworth, 2004, *Cognition*, *93*, 99–125.

the parietal lobes) that carries out simple numerical information processing, such as detecting and comparing numerosities. This capacity may therefore function as a kind of starter kit for understanding numbers and arithmetic. Selective deficits will arise, on this view, when the specialized capacity, or number tool, fails to develop normally. This is what I have called "the defective number module hypothesis" (see Butterworth, 2005a, for an elaboration of this hypothesis). The core competence in this module is a capacity to estimate accurately the number of objects in a set, and to order or rank numerosities by magnitude. Accordingly, DD should be formally diagnosable using very simple tests of processing numerosities, such as enumerating small sets of objects or ordering numerosities.

This was the approach used by Landerl et al. (2004). They took a sample of 9-year-old learners identified by their teacher as having severe difficulties with mathematics, and with timed arithmetic performance more than 3 *SD* worse than controls. The DD sample were equivalent to controls on IQ, digit span, language (as measured by a color-naming test), and comparing sizes. However, they were significantly worse at estimating the number of dots in a set and in comparing numbers (see Figure 16.1). Similarly, Koontz and Berch (1996) found their ALD learners to be slower at estimating dots and slower to retrieve the meaning of numerals.

Diagnosing Dyscalculia

The study by Landerl and colleagues (2004) led to the development of a test for use in school standardized for learners aged 6 to 14 years, the *Dyscalculia Screener* (Butterworth, 2003). This is a computerized test that measures the reaction times for each trial on two capacity tests (dot estimation and number comparison) and one attainment test (single-digit addition, plus single-digit multiplication for older learners). It also adjusts these reaction times according to a measure of each learner's simple reaction time, so that the test is not simply sensitive to slow responders. The program calculates an inverse efficiency measure for each test (median adjusted reaction time/proportion correct) and compares this with a standardized inverse efficiency measure derived from a representative English sample of the testee's age group. The *Screener* automatically assigns a learner to the diagnostic category DD if the learner is in the bottom two sta-nines (about 11%) on *both* capacity tests. If a learner is poor or very poor on attain-ment, but not on the capacity tests, then the *Screener* says that the learner does not have DD, but that there must be some other reason for their difficulty learning arithmetic (see Plate 9).

The *Dyscalculia Screener* has several advantages over existing methods of diagnosing dyscalculia.

1. It is designed for the purpose, whereas other methods depend on general-purpose standardized arithmetic tests, and setting a criterion such as two years behind age level or 2 *SD* below age level.
2. It is relatively independent of education since it tests dot counting and number comparison.
3. It is standardized against a representative national sample.
4. It is theoretically motivated.
5. It is easy to use. The learner sits at the computer with onscreen instructions and a voiceover to guide the testing. Computation of standardized scores is automatic, and diagnosis with pictures and a narrative is produced by the program. The diagnosis can be printed out and given to the testee at the end of the session.

An independent evaluation of the *Dyscalculia Screener* can be found at www.school zone.co.uk/resources/evaluations/evaluation.asp?p=GRAN-7446104.

Brain systems for arithmetic and dyscalculia

Many studies have shown that the anterior intraparietal sulcus plays a special role in processing numerosities (e.g., Castelli, Glaser, & Butterworth, 2006; Dehaene et al., 2003; Eger, Sterzer, Russ, Giraud, & Kleinschmidt, 2003). There is some evidence that in subjects with low numeracy skills the intraparietal sulcus may be abnormal, either in having less gray matter (Isaacs, Edmonds, Lucas, & Gadian, 2001) or in having an atypical formation and activation pattern (Molko et al., 2003). However, the subjects in these studies were not necessarily typical of the majority of those with DD. In the study of Isaacs and colleagues (2001), these were adolescents with very low birthweight, and in the study of Molko et al. (2003), the subject had Turner's syndrome.

The genetics of dyscalculia

An implication of the defective number module hypothesis is that DD will be congenital, and in many cases due to a genetic anomaly. Family studies support a genetic basis in at least some cases. If one twin has DD, then 58% of monozygotic co-twins and 39% of dizygotic co-twins also have DD (Alarcon, Defries, Gillis Light, & Pennington, 1997); and nearly half of the siblings of dyscalculics are also dyscalculic (five to ten times greater risk than controls; Shalev et al., 2001). Although a substantial proportion of the variance in a twin study of mathematics can be attributed to some general factor (e.g., *g* or "generalist genes"), nevertheless something like a third of the variance seems to be specific to mathematical ability, though not exclusively numerical ability (Kovas, Harlaar, Petrill, & Plomin, 2006).

Various X-chromosome disorders seem to affect numeracy more than other cognitive functions (see Mazzocco & McCloskey, 2005; Rovet, Szekely, & Hockenberry, 1994). Interestingly, Turner's syndrome subjects are slower on a dot-estimation task (Bruandet, Molko, Cohen, & Dehaene, 2004; Butterworth et al., 1999). Bruandet et al. (2004, p. 293) note that they are slower even with two dots: "This suggested that many of the patients were counting within the range in which controls normally subitize. Indeed, the increase in response time from 3 to 4 dots was 237 ms in the patients, close to the value observed in the counting range, where it was only 72 ms in the controls, a significance difference." Particularly poor number skills are also found in fragile-X syndrome (Mazzocco & McCloskey, 2005), Klinefelter's syndrome, and other extra X conditions (Semenza, personal communication).

Prevalence

Estimates of prevalence are clearly going to depend on criteria for inclusion in the DD category. Table 16.1 lists some of the prevalence studies carried out, and the criteria used. As I have previously noted (Butterworth, 2005a, p. 457):

> standardized math tests are not sufficient for prevalence studies, as any a priori criterion will simply define a particular proportion of the population as DDs if the criterial dimension is normally distributed. Thus, a criterion of one standard deviation below the population mean (which is equivalent to a standard score of less than 85) entails that approximately 16% of those tested will be classified as DD. When a minimum IQ level is used to create a discrepancy criterion, for example, 90 or above, this means that about 12% of those tested will meet the criterion. (Notice that these are the criteria used by Lewis et al. (1994), and, strangely, they found not 12% of their cohort with "specific arithmetical difficulties" but only 3.4%.) Therefore, a different approach needs to be found.

Table 16.1 Prevalence Estimates, Sample Size, and Methodologies from Three Studies.

Study (author/date, location, sample size)	Estimate of learning disability	Test and criterion	Sample with literacy disorder (%)
Gross-Tsur et al. (1996) *Israel* (*n* = 3029)	6.5% "dyscalculia"	Two grades below chronological age on standardized battery	17% reading disorder
Kosc (1974) *Czechoslovakia* (*n* = 300+)	6.4% "developmental dyscalculia"	Special test battery	N/A
Lewis et al. (1994) *England* (*n* = 1056)	3.6% "specific arithmetic difficulties"	<85 on arithmetic test, >90 on NVIQ	64% reading difficulties

The approach taken in the *Dyscalculia Screener* (Butterworth, 2003) defines DD as falling into the bottom two stanines on both capacity tests: that is, the intersection of two sets each representing about 11% of the sample. So the prevalence is an empirical matter and not one trivially defined by the criteria. This is the approach taken by a very large-scale study in Havana, Cuba, using dot counting and number comparison reaction-time tests very similar to the *Dyscalculia Screener*, standardized against the population of 7–14-year-olds in Havana Centro municipality. From an initial sample of over 11,000 learners, nearly 1,400 were tested. The prevalence found was 6.8% (Reigosa et al., 2004).

Subtyping

The problem of subtyping has typically been investigated in terms of comorbidity with other developmental disorders, such as dyslexia (e.g., Landerl et al., 2004; Lewis et al., 1994) or ADHD (Shalev et al., 1997). However, Temple and colleagues have identified forms of developmental disorder affecting different components of arithmetical skill as such, here as defined in the model of McCloskey and colleagues (e.g., McCloskey & Lindemann, 1992; Sokol, McCloskey, Cohen, & Aliminosa, 1991). They distinguished between memory for arithmetical facts and knowledge of arithmetical procedures.

Temple has identified selective deficits in both fact retrieval and arithmetical processes (e.g., Temple, 1991). In this study, Temple also looked at speed of access to lexical representations outside the realm of numbers. While it was true that learners with slow number fact retrieval overall were also slower in naming colors and objects, Temple was careful not make the causal link. First of all, there was no systematicity in the relationship between naming and retrieval. One subgroup was as fast as controls on multiplication fact retrieval, but not on addition. Second, it was not clear that the DD subjects were actually retrieving facts rather than trying to calculate the answers. Temple concludes that "The results are consistent with modular accounts, in which there is a specialized system for the storage and retrieval of arithmetical facts" (Temple & Sherwood, 2002, p. 1).

More recently, Rousselle and Noël (2007) have suggested that DD is due to an inability to link verbal symbols to numerical concepts ("5" to the concept of fiveness). Their evidence is that learners with DD can be unimpaired on estimating the numerosity of sets, yet impaired on comparing "5" and "3." Their DD learners are in the bottom 15% of their school sample, and this is more than twice the usual prevalence rate (of 6–7%, see above). Their sample may therefore be more heterogeneous than more rigorously defined samples of DD, and this leaves open the possibility that there are two kinds of severe arithmetical learning difficulties: DD as characterized by both Landerl et al. (2004) and Butterworth (2005a) as a defective number module, that is, an abnormally weak sense of numerosity.

Since most of arithmetic, or at least school arithmetic, is communicated through language, and because people often speak of the "language of mathematics," it is reasonable to infer that linguistic skills are intimately linked to arithmetical competence. Indeed, two specific theoretical claims have been advanced about the centrality of language coding to arithmetic. First, in Dehaene and Cohen's "Triple Code" model (e.g., Dehaene & Cohen, 1995), arithmetical facts are stored in a verbal form. By implication, then, weakness in language coding should have effects on the storage and retrieval of the verbally coded facts. Second, Carey (2004) and other researchers have claimed that the representation of the concepts of exact numbers beyond three require the "integer list" of number words, *one, two, three*, etc. Both claims have recently been challenged (Gelman & Butterworth, 2005). Another important possibility is that verbal counting is a significant component in the *practice* of enumeration and manipulating sets of objects, both of which are stages in the development of arithmetical skills (Butterworth, 2005b).

One critical test is whether learners with specific language impairment (SLI) have deficits in arithmetic, especially deficits in understanding concepts of numbers bigger than three and in arithmetical fact retrieval. Learners with SLI are certainly poorer in verbal counting than chronological age-matched controls, but nevertheless understand counting principles, including the "cardinal principle" that the last number counted indicates the cardinality of the set counted (see Donlan, 2003, for a review, and also Cowan, Donlan, Newton, & Lloyd, 2005). However, Donlan, Bishop, and Hitch (1998) report that SLI learners seem to perform at normal levels. Normally, the time it takes to select the larger of two numbers depends on numerical "distance" between them. Learners with SLI show this normal distance effect when comparing two digits, for example, 2 and 8. Interestingly, an articulatory suppression task, which presumably interferes with the phonological coding of the input, did not affect the distance effect. However, a recent and very thorough study of SLI by Donlan and colleagues (Donlan, Cowan, Newton, & Lloyd, 2007) shows that SLI is linked to significantly poorer performance in tasks that depend critically on education—such as calculation, reading, and comparing multidigit numbers, and story tasks—but they did not investigate basic numerical concepts.

Intervention

Our focus group study with 9-year-olds (Bevan & Butterworth, 2007) makes it clear that children with DD fail to understand even simple concepts. In the context of the UK National Curriculum daily numeracy hour, this means that the concepts introduced at the beginning of the lesson are rarely grasped, with the consequence that the rest of the lesson is essentially wasted (verbatim transcripts of recordings):

> CHILD 5:   Oh, there's this really hard thing, about when you're doing times—Miss S__ says you can't take away this number, but I keep on taking away, I don't understand one single bit of it.
> CHILD 2:   I sometimes don't understand whatever she (the teacher) says.

Even when they think they understand something, the slightest distraction causes them to lose track:

> CHILD 3:   When you listen to the teacher, then you turn your head and you don't know nothing … If I remember something, and then the teacher says "stop for a second, just listen to me" then as soon as she talks, yeah, and we come back, we do work, and I say "what do I have to do?" I always forget.
> CHILD 1:   I don't forget it, I don't even know what she's saying.

We take the view that the key to progress is that the learner moves on only when he or she has properly grasped a concept. This may mean that the learner has to go back to working with manipulables until basic numerosities and the ten-based system is properly mastered before going on to work with numerals and other symbols (Butterworth & Yeo, 2004). Unfortunately, there is as yet no properly evaluated method for helping children with DD specifically, but a good review of the current research into training methods for learners with low numeracy was produced for the UK Department of Education and Skills by Dowker (2004).

Conclusion

Developmental dyscalculia is a selective and congenital inability to acquire arithmetic. The core cognitive deficit is a poor grasp of basic numerical concepts, especially numerosities, which makes the subsequent attempt to understand and develop more complex arithmetical concepts extremely difficult. It seems plausible that an abnormality in the intraparietal sulcus, the key region for processing numerosities, is implicated. This abnormality may arise from environmental stressors, though this has not been investigated, or from abnormality in the X-chromosome. Little is known about how best to treat this condition, which is a serious concern, since DD affects a large number of people, and is a serious handicap in everyday life as well as in education.

It is worth noting that DD may arise as a legal issue. The UK Disability Discrimination Act of 1995 states that "A disabled person is someone who has a physical or mental impairment that has a substantial and long term adverse effect on his or her ability to carry out normal day to day activities." At least one of the following areas must be badly affected: "memory or ability to concentrate, learn or understand." DD would certainly seem to fall under this Act.

References

Alarcon, M., Defries, J., Gillis Light, J., & Pennington, B. (1997). A twin study of mathematics disability. *Journal of Learning Disabilities, 30*, 617–623.

Antell, S. E., & Keating, D. P. (1983). Perception of numerical invariance in neonates. *Child Development, 54*, 695–701.

American Psychiatric Association (1994). *Diagnostic and statistical manual of mental disorders* (4th ed.). Washington, DC: American Psychiatric Association.

Baddeley, A. (1986). *Working memory*. Oxford: Clarendon Press.

Bevan, A., & Butterworth, B. (2007). *The responses to maths disabilities in the classroom* (www.mathematicalbrain.com/pdf/2002BEVANBB.PDF).

Brannon, E. M., & Terrace, H. S. (1998). Ordering of the numerosities 1 to 9 by monkeys. *Science, 282*, 746–749.

Bruandet, M., Molko, N., Cohen, L., & Dehaene, S. (2004). A cognitive characterization of dyscalculia in Turner syndrome. *Neuropsychologia, 42*, 288–298.

Butterworth, B. (1999). *The mathematical brain*. London: Macmillan.

Butterworth, B. (2003). *Dyscalculia screener*. London: NFER-Nelson.

Butterworth, B. (2005a). Developmental dyscalculia. In J. I. D. Campbell (Ed.), *The handbook of mathematical cognition* (pp. 455–467). Hove, East Sussex: Psychology Press.

Butterworth, B. (2005b). The development of arithmetical abilities. *Journal of Child Psychology and Psychiatry, 46*(1), 3–18.

Butterworth, B., Cipolotti, L., & Warrington, E. K. (1996). Short-term memory impairments and arithmetical ability. *Quarterly Journal of Experimental Psychology, 49A*, 251–262.

Butterworth, B., Granà, A., Piazza, M., Girelli, L., Price, C., & Skuse, D. (1999). Language and the origins of number skills: Karyotypic differences in Turner's syndrome. *Brain and Language, 69*, 486–488.

Butterworth, B., Shallice, T., & Watson, F. L. (1990). Short-term retention without short-term memory. In G. Vallar & T. Shallice (Eds.), *Neuropsychological impairments of short-term memory* (pp. 187–214). Cambridge University Press.

Butterworth, B., & Yeo, D. (2004). *Dyscalculia guidance*. London: NFER-Nelson.

Bynner, J., & Parsons, S. (1997). *Does numeracy matter?* London: Basic Skills Agency.

Bynner, J., & Parsons, S. (2005). *Does numeracy matter more?* London: National Research and Development Centre for Adult Literacy and Numeracy, Institute of Education.

Carey, S. (2004). Bootstrapping and the origin of concepts. *Daedulus*, 59–68.

Castelli, F., Glaser, D. E., & Butterworth, B. (2006). Discrete and analogue quantity processing in the parietal lobe: A functional MRI study. *Proceedings of the National Academy of Sciences, USA, 103*(12), 4693–4698.

Cipolotti, L., Butterworth, B., & Denes, G. (1991). A specific deficit for numbers in a case of dense acalculia. *Brain, 114*, 2619–2637.

Cowan, R., Donlan, C., Newton, E., & Lloyd, D. (2005). Number skills and knowledge in children with specific language impairment. *Journal of Educational Psychology, 97*, 732–744.

Dehaene, S., & Cohen, L. (1995). Towards an anatomical and functional model of number processing. *Mathematical Cognition, 1,* 83–120.

Dehaene, S., Piazza, M., Pinel, P., & Cohen, L. (2003). Three parietal circuits for number processing. *Cognitive Neuropsychology, 20,* 487–506.

DfES (Department for Education and Skills). (2001). *Guidance to support pupils with dyslexia and dyscalculia* (No. DfES 0512/2001). London: Department for Education and Skills.

DfES (Department for Education and Skills). (2006). *Press Notice 2006/0119.* London: Department for Education and Skills.

Donlan, C. (2003). The early numeracy of children with specific language impairments. In A. J. Baroody & A. D. Dowker (Eds.), *The development of arithmetic concepts and skills: Constructing adaptive expertise* (pp. 337–358). Mahwah, NJ: Lawrence Erlbaum.

Donlan, C., Bishop, D. V. M., & Hitch, G. J. (1998). Magnitude comparisons by children with specific language impairments: Evidence of unimpaired symbolic processing. *International Journal of Language and Communication Disorders, 33,* 149–160.

Donlan, C., Cowan, R., Newton, E. J., & Lloyd, D. (2007). The role of language in mathematical development: Evidence from children with specific language impairments. *Cognition, 103,* 23–33.

Dowker, A. D. (2004). *What works for children with mathematical difficulties?* (No. 554). London: Department for Education and Skills.

Eger, E., Sterzer, P., Russ, M. O., Giraud, A., & Kleinschmidt, A. (2003). A supramodal number representation in human intraparietal cortex. *Neuron, 37,* 719–725.

Fias, W., Lammertyn, J., Reynvoet, B., Dupont, P., & Orban, G. A. (2003). Parietal representation of symbolic and nonsymbolic magnitude. *Journal of Cognitive Neuroscience, 15,* 47–56.

Galton, F. (1880). Visualised numerals. *Nature, 21,* 252–256.

Geary, D. C. (1993). Mathematical disabilities: Cognition, neuropsychological and genetic components. *Psychological Bulletin, 114,* 345–362.

Geary, D. C., & Hoard, M. K. (2005). Learning disabilities in arithmetic and mathematics: Theoretical and empirical perspectives. In J. I. D. Campbell (Ed.), *Handbook of mathematical cognition* (pp. 253–268). New York: Psychology Press.

Geary, D. C., Hoard, M. K., & Hamson, C. O. (1999). Numerical and arithmetical cognition: Patterns of functions and deficits in children at risk for a mathematical disability. *Journal of Experimental Child Psychology, 74,* 213–239.

Gelman, R., & Butterworth, B. (2005). Number and language: How are they related? *Trends in Cognitive Sciences, 9*(1), 6–10.

Gerstmann, J. (1940). Syndrome of finger agnosia: Disorientation for right and left, agraphia and acalculia. *Archives of Neurology and Psychiatry, 44,* 398–408.

Gross-Tsur, V., Manor, O., & Shalev, R. S. (1996). Developmental dyscalculia: Prevalence and demographic features. *Developmental Medicine and Child Neurology, 38,* 25–33.

Hécaen, H., Angelergues, R., & Houillier, S. (1961). Les variétés cliniques des acalculies au cours des lésions rétro-rolandiques: Approche statistique du problème. *Revue Neurologique, 105,* 85–103.

Isaacs, E. B., Edmonds, C. J., Lucas, A., & Gadian, D. G. (2001). Calculation difficulties in children of very low birthweight: A neural correlate. *Brain, 124,* 1701–1707.

Kawai, N., & Matsuzawa, T. (2000). Numerical memory span in a chimpanzee. *Nature, 403,* 39–40.

Koontz, K. L., & Berch, D. B. (1996). Identifying simple numerical stimuli: Processing inefficiencies exhibited by arithmetic learning disabled children. *Mathematical Cognition, 2*(1), 1–23.

Kosc, L. (1974). Developmental dyscalculia. *Journal of Learning Disabilities, 7,* 159–162.

Kovas, Y., Harlaar, N., Petrill, S. A., & Plomin, R. (2006). "Generalist genes" and mathematics in 7-year-old twins. *Intelligence, 35*(5), 473–489.

Landerl, K., Bevan, A., & Butterworth, B. (2004). Developmental dyscalculia and basic numerical capacities: A study of 8–9 year old students. *Cognition, 93*, 99–125.

Lewis, C., Hitch, G., & Walker, P. (1994). The prevalence of specific arithmetic difficulties and specific reading difficulties in 9- and 10-year-old boys and girls. *Journal of Child Psychology and Psychiatry, 35*, 283–292.

Matsuzawa, T. (1985). The use of numbers by a chimpanzee. *Nature, 315*, 57–59.

Mazzocco, M. M. M., & McCloskey, M. (2005). Math performance in girls with Turner or Fragile X syndrome. In J. I. D. Campbell (Ed.), *Handbook of mathematical cognition* (pp. 269–297). New York: Psychology Press.

McCarthy, R. A., & Warrington, E. K. (1990). *Cognitive neuropsychology: A clinical introduction.* London: Academic Press.

McCloskey, M., & Lindemann, A. M. (1992). Mathnet: Preliminary results from a distributed model of arithmetic fact retrieval. In J. I. D. Campbell (Ed.), *The nature and origins of mathematical skills* (pp. 365–409). Amsterdam: Elsevier.

McLean, J. F., & Hitch, G. J. (1999). Working memory impairments in children with specific arithmetical difficulties. *Journal of Experimental Child Psychology, 74*, 240–260.

Molko, N., Cachia, A., Rivière, D., Mangin, J.-F., Bruandet, M., Le Bihan, D., et al. (2003). Functional and structural alterations of the intraparietal sulcus in a developmental dyscalculia of genetic origin. *Neuron, 40*, 847–858.

Nieder, A., Freedman, D. J., & Miller, E. K. (2002). Representation of the quantity of visual items in the primate prefrontal cortex. *Science, 297*, 1708–1711.

Reigosa, V., Valdés Sosa, M., Torres, P., Santos, E., Estevez, N., Hernádez, D., et al. (2004). *Prevalence study of developmental dyscalculia in Havana City Municipality.* Havana, Cuba: Cuban Neurosciences Centre.

Rousselle, L., & Noël, M.-P. (2007). Basic numerical skills in children with mathematics learning disabilities: A comparison of symbolic vs non-symbolic number magnitude processing. *Cognition, 102*, 361–395.

Rovet, J., Szekely, C., & Hockenberry, M.-N. (1994). Specific arithmetic calculation deficits in children with Turner syndrome. *Journal of Clinical and Experimental Neuropsychology, 16*, 820–839.

Rubinsten, O., & Henik, A. (2005). Automatic activation of internal magnitudes: A study of developmental dyscalculia. *Neuropsychology, 19*, 641–648.

Sawamura, H., Shima, K., & Tanji, J. (2002). Numerical representation for action in the parietal cortex of the monkey. *Nature, 415*, 918–922.

Shalev, R. S., & Gross-Tsur, V. (2001). Developmental dyscalculia: Review article. *Pediatric Neurology, 24*, 337–342.

Shalev, R. S., Manor, O., & Gross-Tsur, V. (1997). Neuropsychological aspects of developmental dyscalculia. *Mathematical Cognition, 3*(2), 105–120.

Shalev, R. S., Manor, O., & Gross-Tsur, V. (2005). Developmental dyscalculia: A prospective six year follow up. *Developmental Medicine and Child Psychology, 47*(2), 121–125.

Shalev, R. S., Manor, O., Kerem, B., Ayali, M., Badichi, N., Friedlander Y., et al. (2001). Developmental dyscalculia is a familial learning disability. *Journal of Learning Disabilities, 34*(1), 59–65.

Siegel, L. S., & Ryan, E. B. (1989). The development of working memory in normally achieving and subtypes of learning disabled children. *Child Development, 60*, 973–980.

Simon, T. J., Hespos, S. J., & Rochat, P. (1995). Do infants understand simple arithmetic? A replication of Wynn (1992). *Cognitive Development, 10*, 253–269.

Sokol, S. M., McCloskey, M., Cohen, N. J., & Aliminosa, D. (1991). Cognitive representations and processes in arithmetic: Inferences from the performance of brain-damaged subjects. *Journal of Experimental Psychology: Learning, Memory, and Cognition, 17,* 355–376.

Spalding, J. M. K., & Zangwill, O. L. (1950). Disturbance of number-form in a case of brain injury. *Journal of Neurology, Neurosurgery and Psychiatry, 13,* 24–29.

Starkey, P., & Cooper, R. G., Jr. (1980). Perception of numbers by human infants. *Science, 210,* 1033–1035.

Temple, C. M. (1991). Procedural dyscalculia and number fact dyscalculia: Double dissociation in developmental dyscalculia. *Cognitive Neuropsychology, 8,* 155–176.

Temple, C. M., & Sherwood, S. (2002). Representation and retrieval of arithmetical facts: Developmental difficulties. *Quarterly Journal of Experimental Psychology, 55A,* 733–752.

Wainwright, M., Wright, M., Geffen, G., Luciano, M., & Martin, N. (2005). The genetic basis of academic achievement on the Queensland core skills test and its shared genetic variance with IQ. *Behavior Genetics, 35*(2), 133–145.

Warrington, E. (1982). The fractionation of arithmetical skills: A single case study. *Quarterly Journal of Experimental Psychology, 34A,* 31–51.

World Health Organization. (1994). *International classification of diseases: 10* (10th ed.). Geneva: World Health Organization.

Wynn, K. (1992). Addition and subtraction by human infants. *Nature, 358,* 749–751.

Wynn, K., Bloom, P., & Chiang, W. C. (2002). Enumeration of collective entities by 5-month-old infants. *Cognition, 83*(3), B55–B62.

Zorzi, M., Priftis, K., & Umilta, C. (2002). Brain damage: Neglect disrupts the mental number line. *Nature, 417*(6885), 138–139.

Part III
Practice

17

Neuropsychological Assessment in a Neurological Setting

Ingram Wright and Peta Sharples

Clinical neuropsychology serves two primary functions within a pediatric neurology service. First, where cognitive, behavioral, and other observable symptoms are strongly suggestive of underlying neuropathology, a neuropsychological assessment may support the diagnostic process. Second, once neuropathology is clearly identified or diagnosed, a neuropsychological assessment addresses corresponding cognitive and behavioral symptoms and, on this basis, informs future management of the condition. The aim of this chapter is to address how a neuropsychological service enhances the health care of children with acquired brain injuries in a pediatric neurology setting. We will first describe the dominant practical challenges in such settings before illustrating the specific application of clinical neuropsychology to common neurological problems.

General Issues

The distinction between developmental and acquired neuropathology is important from both theoretical and service delivery perspectives. This distinction is widely recognized as having important implications for functional outcome. Furthermore, because of the demand for correspondingly specialist expertise, services tend to be divided along these lines. Neurodevelopmental services are offered to children who have identifiable or suspected neuropathology from birth or very early in development (e.g., cerebral palsy or Down syndrome) or to children with recognized developmental syndromes with distinct cognitive and behavioral features or phenotypes (e.g., attention deficit hyperactivity disorder [ADHD] or conduct disorder). Acquired brain injury services accommodate children with infections (e.g., meningitis, encephalitis), cerebrovascular accidents (stroke), and neoplastic tumors in addition to traumatic brain injuries. The clarity of distinction between developmental and acquired brain injury is challenged by some conditions—for example, acquired perinatal injuries which, in terms of outcome, have much in common with developmental disorders—or developmental tumors which, although present from birth, have symptoms (e.g., epilepsy) which may be manifest much later in life. However, the distinction is important as the developmental timing of an injury is an important moderator of outcome and has important consequences for rehabilitation (see Chapters 2 and 5).

Neuropsychological assessment has a key role in determining the relevance of cognitive and behavioral symptoms alongside broader diagnostic investigations. Specific cognitive symptoms and general changes in rates of cognitive development are of diagnostic significance in a range of childhood neurological conditions including focal epilepsy, neurometabolic disorder, viral infections, and other forms of acquired brain injury. Where such symptoms exist, it may be insufficient to rely on educational and parental reports, and a neuropsychological assessment may therefore assist in providing objective evidence of underlying cognitive dysfunction.

Children with neurological conditions commonly present with behavioral and emotional disturbance and may find it difficult to access appropriate services if the relationship between the neurological condition and the behavioral symptoms is unclear. Recent studies reported a 37% prevalence of psychiatric disorder in children with epilepsy, 61% in children with congenital hemiplegia, and 22–36% in those with traumatic brain injury (Davies, Heyman, & Goodman, 2003; Goodman & Graham, 1996; Schwartz et al., 2003). Most studies report a general association between the severity of the neurological condition and the severity or likelihood of significant mental health problems. However, further identification of underlying cognitive deficits also accounts for a large proportion of the residual variance in mental health status and is more useful with respect to intervention (see Chapter 18). Whether or not neurological and cognitive factors are seen as the primary cause of mental health problems, children's access to effective treatment is mediated by a thorough diagnostic process that clarifies the relationship between this underlying neurological condition and the child's emotional and behavioral symptoms. Furthermore, at a group level, our increased understanding of cognitive *endophenotypes* for many behavioral disorders suggests a role for individual cognitive assessment in guiding diagnosis and effective intervention (see also Chapter 18; Coghill, Nigg, Rothenberger, Sonuga-Barke, & Tannock, 2005).

Supporting Neurological Management

In the context of a known neurological condition, an assessment: (a) helps to clarify the relationship between the identified pathology and associated cognitive and behavioral symptoms, and (b) has an important role in guiding medical management. A relatively rare but useful illustrative example is in children with adrenoleukodystrophy (ALD). X-linked ALD is an inherited metabolic disorder and one of the most common variants of this disorder is childhood cerebral ALD. Cerebral involvement is identified by neuroimaging, coupled with neurological examination and neuropsychological assessment. If undetected and untreated, cerebral ALD follows a rapid progression and death typically occurs 2–3 years after the onset of cerebral symptoms. Identification of cerebral involvement via neuropsychological assessment therefore supports timely intervention such as bone marrow transplant to stabilize, or even reverse, cerebral degeneration at the early stages of disease progression (Ronghe et al., 2002).

ALD provides a powerful illustration of the role of neuropsychology in guiding neurological intervention. Clarification of the severity and nature of cognitive symptoms linked to neuropathology is important in guiding further intervention which may itself be associated with significant morbidity and mortality. More aggressive treatment may be considered only if cognitive symptoms are sufficiently severe to have a marked impact on a child's quality of life or educational attainment. In this regard, neuropsychological assessment is particularly important in considering the risks and potential benefits of surgical intervention for epilepsy. With the advent of innovative neurosurgical techniques such as deep brain stimulation, presurgical cognitive assessment provides important guidance as to the individual benefits of surgery.

Assessment of change

A common referral request for neuropsychology with respect to diagnosis and treatment concerns assessment of change in cognitive functioning. Rare but serious conditions associated with developmental regression warrant objective assessment to determine the rate of decline. Assessment of general intellectual development or progressive deterioration or specific focal effects of neuropathology is also an important consideration in the management of many childhood neurological conditions. Changes to medication or options for surgical treatment may be considered on the basis of evidence for impoverished development, poor educational progress, or deteriorating attention. Furthermore, highlighting a relative decline in a child's ability may form the basis for proactive intervention to avoid corresponding educational failure and disengagement or behavioral problems emerging as a consequence of mismatched parental expectations.

Assessment of change in children is more technically challenging than in adults, primarily due to natural skill development and the restricted age range for many psychometric tests. Following an acquired brain injury, it is typical for children to exhibit a reduced rate of learning or developmental progress. Over time, this change is manifest as a progressive reduction in IQ. Such numerical declines in IQ do not necessarily imply regression or loss of skills but reflect a failure to learn at the same pace as healthy peers. These changes in IQ can appear dramatic, and are most prominent at developmental stages where peers exhibit rapid relative improvement in performance. For example, a child whose development stagnates at 8 years would have an IQ of 84 at the age of 10, and 70 at the age of 12 years.

Absolute declines in skill, although unusual, are of critical significance in identifying progressive encephalopathy or brain disease. It is important in such cases to minimize extraneous sources of test error or uncertainty; for example, performance variability due to fatigue, motivation, use of different testing materials, and so on. Careful selection and use of test materials can result in greater sensitivity to the assessment of change. Key determinants of suitable tests for such purposes include (a) sensitivity to the cognitive construct of the underlying pathological process, (b) adequate test/re-test reliability, and (c) validity across the likely age range for monitoring. Tests frequently selected for monitoring purposes include attention, memory, and executive tests as changes in the corresponding aspects of functioning are linked to common neurological conditions. However, these tests, while adequately sensitive, typically have poorer test/re-test reliability, as they are equally sensitive to extraneous sources of performance variability. A guide when selecting tests is to examine the standard error due to test/re-test reliability and compare this to the minimum clinically significant change that is required to be detected. Corresponding adjustments to the threshold for detecting change can subsequently be made to achieve appropriate sensitivity and specificity (Loong, 2003).

"Actuarial" assessment

Neuropsychological assessment is frequently requested as a precursor to planned changes in medical management or as a prelude to necessary surgical intervention. The results of such tests may not necessarily change the course of medical management or response to surgery but allow the monitoring of the change associated with a treatment. In the case of surgical resection, the intervention is irreversible and such assessment therefore has an "actuarial" quality; that is, in clinical audit of surgical procedures and/or medical management, it assists in the management of surgical risks for future patients or provides objective evidence of the consequences of surgery for a particular aspect of functioning. Postsurgical assessments also have a vital role in addressing educational and parental expectations and informing intervention. A subtle but significant change in memory or attentional function following tumor resection may be too subtle to immediately attract the attention of parents or educational services. Similarly, positive but focal cognitive changes following a change in medication may not be manifest in global cognitive improvement for many months. None the less, early identification facilitates the delivery of appropriate support or fine-tuning of medical management.

Informing and delivering rehabilitation

Neuropsychological services provide an important starting-point for effective rehabilitation informing other aspects of therapeutic intervention, including hospital-based education and nursing management. In the acute recovery phase of an acquired brain injury, assessment of evident cognitive deficits or screening for hidden cognitive problems is helpful in monitoring the pace of recovery and promoting an understanding of any cognitive basis for behavioral and emotional symptoms. In the longer term, there is a clear need to address apparent deficits and guide environmental adaptations to account for such deficits. There is a growing evidence base for cognitive rehabilitation in adults, but very limited evidence for the efficacy of specific strategies employed in childhood (Limond & Leeke, 2005; Wright & Limond, 2004).

The organization of services poses a problem for clinical neuropsychologists attempting to deliver rehabilitation from specialist regional settings. Although close working with colleagues in educational psychology and child mental health settings is likely to be beneficial for the child, alongside intensive intervention with families, limited resources and geographical factors often impede the development of such services (Braga, Da Paz, & Ylvisaker, 2005; Ylvisaker et al., 2005).

Assessment of specific conditions

In a typical child neuropsychology service (serving a 750,000 population and 150,000 children), one would expect neurologists to be managing 68 patients with moderate to severe head injuries, 600 children with epilepsy, 102 of these proving to have a complex or intractable condition, and 8 new cases of malignant brain tumor (British Psychological Society, 2004; Eriksson & Koivikko, 1997). These conditions represent the most commonly occurring source of referrals for specialist neuropsychological assessment and rehabilitation. Each of the conditions poses distinct challenges for neuropsychological assessment and rehabilitation, depending upon the pattern of emergence of cognitive deficits over time alongside the evolution and management of the neurological condition.

Traumatic Brain Injuries

It is estimated that each year 280 per 100,000 children have a traumatic brain injury (TBI) of sufficient severity to warrant admission to hospital (Hawley, Ward, Long, Owen, & Magnay, 2003). Of these, 232 will have a mild brain injury, 25 moderate, and 19 severe. Traumatic brain injury is the most common cause of death and acquired disability in childhood, and is most likely to be caused by falls and road traffic accidents (RTAs) as pedestrians (Sharples, Storey, Aynsley-Green, & Eyre, 1990). Children under 2 years of age account for 20% of all childhood TBIs, usually due to falls, nonaccidental injuries (NAIs), or being dropped (NAIs). Falls remain common in the under 5s, while for those over 10 years, RTAs are the most common cause (Hawley et al., 2003). Premorbid child and family factors make a recognized contribution to the epidemiology of childhood TBI and also influence the subsequent recovery and adaptation processes. Injuries are most common in children with lower socioeconomic status, and premorbid attention and learning difficulties are particularly common (Gerring et al., 1998; Sharples et al., 1990). Premorbid levels of ADHD are around 20% in the TBI population relative to around 4% in the general population (Gerring et al., 1998).

Assessment issues

A key issue in neuropsychological assessment of traumatic brain injuries is the decision about when to conduct an assessment relative to the time of injury and discharge from hospital. Parents and clinicians are naturally keen to have early indicators of prognosis and guidance as to rehabilitation needs in the post-acute phase. However, early assessment results are potentially confounded by transient states, such as post-traumatic amnesia (PTA), and rapidly resolving neurological conditions, such as elevated intracranial pressure. Early assessments have relatively poor predictive validity with respect to long-term outcome (Kay & Warschausky, 1999). Despite the large number of studies addressing the prognostic value of physiological measures of severity, such as Glasgow Coma Score (GCS), length of coma or PTA, in addition to premorbid and sociodemographic factors, very few studies give indicators of the prognostic value of early formal cognitive assessment.

Despite the questionable long-term validity of early assessment results, decisions about schooling and appropriate levels of parental support and supervision necessitate some understanding of cognitive deficits following TBI. Such information may be required prior to discharge, only weeks after medical stabilization and emergence from coma and PTA. Measures of nonverbal intellectual ability, processing speed, working memory, and attentional function are particularly sensitive indicators of the severity of head injury, but are equally sensitive to the rather unpredictable recovery trajectory. Consideration of when to assess should therefore include early assessments to inform diagnostic issues and to support therapeutic involvement, and later follow-up to estimate likely prognosis and guide rehabilitation and reintegration.

Assessment in the acute phase

Disorientation, inattention, and anterograde amnesia are commonly reported features of the acute phase of recovery following traumatic brain injury. This constellation of symptoms has been labeled post-traumatic amnesia or PTA. The underlying mechanisms governing the evolution and resolution of PTA are poorly understood but plausibly include a range of transient metabolic and neurochemical factors, which also contribute to chronic secondary effects of TBI. In the absence of further secondary injury or infection, one would ordinarily expect such causes to resolve within weeks of the initial injury.

Assessment of PTA has historically focused on interviews to elicit memories around the time of the incident. Criticism of the subjective nature of such assessment led to the development of standardized scales (such as the Galveston Orientation and Amnesia Test and Westmead scales, in addition to children's analogues, e.g., Children's Orientation and Amnesia Test [COAT]; Forrester, Encel, & Geffen, 1994). Detailed examination of the cognitive features of PTA and the order of resolution of attentional, memory, and orientation features has led to a suggested reconceptualization of PTA as an acute confusional state or post-traumatic disorientation with attentional features assuming a more central role in the condition (Stuss et al., 1999).

Despite conceptual uncertainties, assessment of PTA has an important role in guiding the commencement of other therapeutic interventions and the management of risk. The safety of hospital discharge and reintegration into education is clearly dependent upon the prior recovery of memory systems. The duration of PTA symptoms is the most robust predictor of long-term outcome, superior to GCS and imaging variables, and thus provides useful information about long-term rehabilitation needs (Brown et al., 2005; Dawson, Levine, Schwartz, & Stuss, 2004).

Assuming that assessment of post-traumatic cognitive symptoms is a valuable exercise, there are a number of conceptual and psychometric challenges in assessing PTA. There are relatively few comparative studies to identify the merits of different scales in adults and still fewer in the pediatric population (Tate, Pfaff, & Jurjevic, 2000). Scales specifically equipped to assess PTA in children include the COAT and the Westmead PTA scale. Assessment of younger children is problematic due to the increased population variability of attentional and memory performance, compounded by limited normative data for children and those with premorbid cognitive difficulties. A number of adapted scales have been proposed but these necessarily cover only narrow age ranges or are based on a traditional "adult" construct of PTA that does not have established validity in young children (Fernando, Eaton, Faulkner, Moodley, & Setchell, 2002; Ruijs, Keyser, & Gabreels, 1992).

Over-reliance on psychometric tools may lead to erroneous judgments about the length of PTA. A prevalent clinical challenge is to consider possible chronic memory and attentional problems in addition to developmental expectations and evidence of premorbid functioning. Making a valid judgment regarding the length of PTA involves detailed knowledge of the limitations of the scales used, estimates of premorbid functioning, and an understanding of the biological plausibility of continued PTA versus chronic inattention or amnesia.

Estimation of premorbid functioning

Distinguishing between pre-existing and acquired cognitive impairments is of crucial importance in the assessment of an acquired brain injury. As noted above, determining whether or not a cognitive deficit is "new" will dictate the need for further adaptation and adjustment in the family and educational settings (Anderson, Catroppa, Haritou, Morse, & Rosenfeld, 2005). Furthermore, premorbid cognitive factors, alongside global family functioning, may interact with acquired cognitive impairments and behavioral factors. The form of any adaptation or intervention and the likely prognosis will depend crucially on whether a deficit is acquired or recognized as pre-existing (Donders & Strom, 1997).

Estimation of premorbid functioning in adults often utilizes algorithms based on social and demographic or employment factors. Such algorithms are not valid when applied to children. Alternative approaches include "hold/don't hold" methods which rely on the finding that some tests appear invulnerable with respect to brain injury. The use of all such methods in the pediatric population is problematic due to increased variability of functioning between individuals and reduced associations between hold-tests (e.g., reading ability) and IQ. Furthermore, while demographic factors are useful in predicting adult IQ, childhood IQ is less readily predicted and some factors (e.g., employment history) are not available (Wright, 2005; Yeates & Taylor, 1997). The difficulty in utilizing adult methods in the child population is mitigated by the often abundant availability of school-based tests to provide estimates of premorbid functioning. Such tests are readily available for indicators of academic progress such as literacy and numeracy but also, increasingly, for factors such as reasoning ability which are highly correlated with traditional IQ tests (Wright, 2005).

Epilepsy

Epilepsy is the most common cause of chronic neurological disability, and its peak incidence is in early to mid-childhood. For most children with epilepsy, seizures are well controlled by the first-line treatment. However, learning difficulties, behavioral disturbance, and mental health problems are common in the epilepsy population (Davies et al., 2003; Hauser, Annegers, & Anderson, 1983). Epilepsy is best regarded as a group of syndromes, each with distinct etiology and specific prognosis. A number of epilepsy syndromes have been identified, each with a specific etiology, although a specific cause is identified in only 25% of cases. Seizures are symptomatic of underlying neurological abnormalities, which may be transient or follow a chronic course. Common transient cases include febrile seizures, associated with high temperature, metabolic imbalances, or acute brain infections. In such cases, once the underlying condition remits, the seizures will often do so as well. However, when epilepsy proves difficult to control, this is often the result of an underlying developmental lesion or acquired brain injury or genetic abnormality. Genetic causes for epilepsy are increasingly being identified, often provoking epilepsy via metabolic imbalances (Guerrini & Parmeggiani, 2006).

Optimal treatment of epilepsy involves minimizing the frequency of overt seizures while also minimizing the behavioral and cognitive side-effects of medication. An appropriate choice and dosage of medication is based on an accurate diagnosis of the underlying syndrome. Although control of overt seizures is often the primary indicator of successful treatment, quality of life and cognitive development are important considerations (Guerrini & Parmeggiani, 2006).

The role of the clinical neuropsychologist

The association between epilepsy and learning difficulties defines a clear role for the clinical neuropsychologist in the medical management of these children. Significant cognitive problems are associated with many epilepsy syndromes, with 65% of parents reporting schooling difficulties, and 31% of children having documented learning difficulties (Besag, 2002). Determining the source of learning problems is a particularly common clinical challenge as a plausible cause of cognitive problems includes a combination of seizures themselves, underlying brain abnormalities, and the side-effects of medication. The role of the clinical neuropsychologist in the management of epilepsy also includes a contribution to diagnosis, medical management, and the consideration of other treatments including surgery, and informing educational intervention or parental behavioral management.

The diagnosis of epilepsy is fraught with difficulty. Specific challenges include the rapid change and evolution of epilepsy syndromes over time, the prevalence of non-epileptic seizures, and the difficulties of obtaining prolonged EEG recordings to "catch" relatively rare clinical events. Neuropsychological assessment may assist in the diagnosis of marginal cases by addressing the validity of cognitive and behavioral symptoms associated with underlying seizures. Nonepileptic seizures are common and are also prevalent alongside genuine seizure disorders (Ferrie, 2006).

In cases of difficult-to-control epilepsy, regular monitoring of cognitive performance and development is an important component in optimizing medical management, while also ensuring that educational support is appropriately tuned to children's general abilities and any specific deficits. If development is adversely affected by seizure activity, then more aggressive medical treatment, such as steroids or benzodiazepines, may be considered. In such cases, careful monitoring of the efficacy of treatment, including cognitive functioning, is vital.

If epilepsy remains difficult to control with several different medications, then further treatment such as neurosurgery may be considered. Surgical treatment of epilepsy commonly relies on identifying the underlying eleptogenic focus in the brain via EEG and corresponding pathology via neuroimaging techniques, such as MRI, PET, and SPECT. Neuropsychological assessment at this stage assists in confirmatory evidence concordant with the location of the lesion and the damaging effects of seizures on cognitive function, as well as providing an opportunity to revisit diagnostic issues. A crucial further aspect of the presurgical assessment is to determine the likely risks and benefits of a surgical resection. In this case, neuropsychological assessment may ascertain whether adequate cognitive function can be supported by the nonresected brain regions and that the target of the resection is relatively "nonfunctional." Neuropsychological input and associated functional neuroimaging is particularly important where surgical resection is close to areas of "eloquent cortex"; that is, those that are vital and anatomically localized to cognitive functions such as language and memory (Cross et al., 2006).

Effects of epilepsy on learning

Making a useful contribution to medical, surgical, and educational consideration requires a detailed understanding of the combinatorial effects of seizures, medication, and underlying neuropathology on cognitive development. Seizures themselves can have a profound independent impact on cognitive development, particularly if prolonged or frequent, via disruption to neuronal development or anoxic damage to previously intact but vulnerable structures (Thompson & Duncan, 2005).

The effects of medication are relatively poorly understood as there have been few comparative trials of medication in children, and particularly with reference to the new generation of medication: Eight new antiepileptic drugs have been introduced in the past 10–15 years alone. However, most studies suggest that the effects of commonly employed drugs are modest, dose related, and "reversible." Medication effects make a smaller contribution than other factors such as the epilepsy syndrome itself (Mandelbaum & Burack, 1997). None the less, medication effects are controllable and may have an influence on children's learning at a crucial period in development (Loring & Meador, 2004).

Underlying lesions are common in intractable epilepsy and potentially exert an independent effect on the course of cognitive development. Such lesions may provoke focal epilepsy, which originates from a specific, well-defined area of the brain and has a corresponding effect on cognitive development; for example, frontal seizures tend to result in impairments on tests of working memory, attention, and executive function, while seizures originating in the mesial temporal lobe tend to effect memory functioning. Developmental evidence suggests that unilateral lesions can provoke interhemispheric reorganization of function given a healthy homologous brain area in the opposite hemisphere to the lesion. Such reorganization is most likely if seizures start relatively early in development, while seizures of later onset are likely to lead to corresponding specific deficits with limited capacity for reorganization (Cormack et al., 2007; Rankin & Vargha-Khadem, 2007).

In conducting an assessment, it is important to give due consideration to the relationship between seizures, an underlying lesion, and the effects of medication. Due consideration should be given to age at onset and the subsequent evolution of seizures, alongside a history of cognitive development. It is equally important to note any history of prolonged seizures (>10 minutes), a description of current seizures (types, frequency, duration, pre- and postseizure behavior), current medication, and any variability in reported functioning or behavior alongside seizures.

A prevalent challenge for both medical management and neuropsychological assessment concerns subtle seizures. Such seizures, while minimally disruptive to everyday life, can have marked cognitive effects if they are particularly frequent and exert a cumulative effect on educational progress (Aldenkamp & Arends, 2004). So-called transient cognitive impairment is associated with subtle, brief EEG abnormalities, which may well be regarded as interictal or subclinical episodes. Evidence for transient cognitive impairment is growing, alongside evidence that subtle or interictal abnormalities can be effectively treated (Aldenkamp & Arends, 2004; Staden, Isaacs, Boyd, Brandl, & Neville, 1998).

Choosing appropriate assessment tools is vital to conducting useful neuropsychological assessments in epilepsy. As discussed earlier in this chapter, measures that are stable and therefore possess good test/re-test reliability are often insufficiently sensitive to be useful in guiding medical management or assessing the impact of subtle seizures on learning. In such cases, single case methods should be used as a framework for the analysis of serial assessments of less stable functions such as attention or information processing. Advances in technology support the use of web-based assessment tools to facilitate convenient repeated assessment or may facilitate detailed analysis of correlates of EEG abnormalities and cognitive function (Berger, 2006; Collie, Darby, & Maruff, 2001).

Conclusion

In this chapter, we have outlined the work of the neuropsychologist in a pediatric neurological setting. The neuropsychologist's role includes involvement in diagnosis, medical, and surgical management of common neurological conditions such as epilepsy. With reference to the broad spectrum of acquired brain injury, we have illustrated the role of the neuropsychologist in illuminating the relationship between underlying neuropathology and specific cognitive deficits. An understanding of this relationship forms the basis for advising colleagues about the need for medical treatment or benefits of educational intervention.

Neuropsychologists face specific challenges when working in this setting. The theoretical basis for assessment is complex given the frequent lack of a clear distinction between acquired and developmental aspects of a child's functioning or cognitive deficits. Corresponding methodological challenges include assessment of premorbid functioning in acquired brain injury and assessment of post-traumatic amnesia following traumatic injuries. The limited availability and constrained validity and reliability of assessment tools demand careful test selection and usage in order to provide meaningful assessment results for any neurological condition.

Theoretical and technological advances in developmental neuroscience have enhanced the role of the neuropsychologist in a specialist clinical setting. The use of neuroimaging and cognitive testing alongside neurophysiological techniques (EEG and ERP studies) has bolstered traditional cognitive assessment techniques.

References

Aldenkamp, A., & Arends, J. (2004). The relative influence of epileptic EEG discharges, short nonconvulsive seizures, and type of epilepsy on cognitive function. *Epilepsia, 45*(1), 54–63.

Anderson, V. A., Catroppa, C., Haritou, F., Morse, S., & Rosenfeld, J. V. (2005). Identifying factors contributing to child and family outcome 30 months after traumatic brain injury in children. *Journal of Neurology, Neurosurgery and Psychiatry, 76*(3), 401–408.

Berger, M. (2006). Computer assisted clinical assessment. *Child and Adolescent Mental Health, 11*(2), 64–75.

Besag, F. M. C. (2002). Childhood epilepsy in relation to mental handicap and behavioural disorders. *Journal of Child Psychology and Psychiatry and Allied Disciplines, 43*(1), 103–131.

Braga, L. W., Da Paz, A. C., & Ylvisaker, M. (2005). Direct clinician-delivered versus indirect family-supported rehabilitation of children with traumatic brain injury: A randomized controlled trial. *Brain Injury, 19*(10), 819–831.

British Psychological Society. (2004). *Services for children with acquired brain damage.* Leicester: British Psychological Society, Division of Neuropsychology.

Brown, A. W., Malec, J. F., McClelland, R. L., Diehl, N. N., Englander, J., & Cifu, D. X. (2005). Clinical elements that predict outcome after traumatic brain injury: A prospective multicenter recursive partitioning (decision-tree) analysis. *Journal of Neurotrauma, 22*(10), 1040–1051.

Coghill, D., Nigg, J., Rothenberger, A., Sonuga-Barke, E., & Tannock, R. (2005). Whither causal models in the neuroscience of ADHD? *Developmental Science, 8*(2), 105–114.

Collie, A., Darby, D., & Maruff, P. (2001). Computerised cognitive assessment of athletes with sports related head injury. *British Journal of Sports Medicine, 35*(5), 297–302.

Cormack, F., Cross, J. H., Isaacs, E., Harkness, W., Wright, I., Vargha-Khadem, F., et al. (2007). The development of intellectual abilities in pediatric temporal lobe epilepsy. *Epilepsia, 48*(1), 201–204.

Cross, J. H., Jayakar, P., Nordli, D., Delalande, O., Duchowny, M., Wieser, H. G., et al. (2006). Proposed criteria for referral and evaluation of children for epilepsy surgery: Recommendations of the subcommission for pediatric epilepsy surgery. *Epilepsia, 47*(6), 952–959.

Davies, S., Heyman, I., & Goodman, R. (2003). A population survey of mental health problems in children with epilepsy. *Developmental Medicine and Child Neurology, 45*(5), 292–295.

Dawson, D. R., Levine, B., Schwartz, M. L., & Stuss, D. T. (2004). Acute predictors of real-world outcomes following traumatic brain injury: A prospective study. *Brain Injury, 18*(3), 221–238.

Donders, J., & Strom, D. (1997). The effect of traumatic brain injury on children with learning disability. *Pediatric Rehabilitation, 1*(3), 179–184.

Eriksson, K. J., & Koivikko, M. J. (1997). Prevalence, classification, and severity of epilepsy and epileptic syndromes in children. *Epilepsia, 38*(12), 1275–1282.

Fernando, K., Eaton, L., Faulkner, M., Moodley, Y., & Setchell, R. (2002). Development and piloting of the starship posttraumatic amnesia scale for children aged between four and six years. *Brain Impairment, 3*(1), 34–41.

Ferrie, C. D. (2006). Preventing misdiagnosis of epilepsy. *Archives of Disease in Childhood, 91*(3), 206–209.

Forrester, G., Encel, J., & Geffen, G. (1994). Measuring post-traumatic amnesia (PTA): An historical review. *Brain Injury, 8*(2), 175–184.

Gerring, J. P., Brady, K. D., Chen, A., Vasa, R., Grados, M., Bandeen-Roche, K. J., et al. (1998). Premorbid prevalence of ADHD and development of secondary ADHD after closed head injury. *Journal of the American Academy of Child and Adolescent Psychiatry, 37*(6), 647–654.

Goodman, R., & Graham, P. (1996). Psychiatric problems in children with hemiplegia: Cross sectional epidemiological survey. *British Medical Journal, 312*(7038), 1065–1069.

Guerrini, R., & Parmeggiani, L. (2006). Practitioner review: Use of antiepileptic drugs in children. *Journal of Child Psychology and Psychiatry, 47*(2), 115–126.

Hauser, W. A., Annegers, J. F., & Anderson, V. E. (1983). Epidemiology and the genetics of epilepsy. *Research Publications of the Association for Research in Nervous and Mental Disease, 61*, 267–294.

Hawley, C. A., Ward, A. B., Long, J., Owen, D. W., & Magnay, A. R. (2003). Prevalence of traumatic brain injury amongst children admitted to hospital in one health district: A population-based study. *Injury, 34*(4), 256–260.

Kay, J. B., & Warschausky, S. (1999). Wisc-iii index growth curve characteristics following traumatic brain injury. *Journal of Clinical and Experimental Neuropsychology, 21*(2), 186–199.

Limond, J., & Leeke, R. (2005). Practitioner review: Cognitive rehabilitation for children with acquired brain injury. *Journal of Child Psychology and Psychiatry, 46*(4), 339–352.

Loong, T. W. (2003). Understanding sensitivity and specificity with the right side of the brain. *British Medical Journal, 327*(7417), 716–719.

Loring, D. W., & Meador, K. J. (2004). Cognitive side effects of antiepileptic drugs in children. *Neurology, 62*(6), 872–877.

Mandelbaum, D. E., & Burack, G. D. (1997). The effect of seizure type and medication on cognitive and behavioral functioning in children with idiopathic epilepsy. *Developmental Medicine and Child Neurology, 39*(11), 731–735.

Rankin, P. M., & Vargha-Khadem, F. (2007). Neuropsychological evaluation: Children. In J. Engel & T. A. Pedley (Eds.), *Epilepsy: A comprehensive textbook* (2nd ed., pp. 1067–1076). Philadelphia, PA: Lippincott Williams & Wilkins.

Ronghe, M. D., Barton, J., Jardine, P. E., Crowne, E. C., Webster, M. H., Armitage, M., et al. (2002). The importance of testing for adrenoleucodystrophy in males with idiopathic Addison's disease. *Archives of Disease in Childhood, 86*(3), 185–189.

Ruijs, M. B., Keyser, A., & Gabreels, F. J. (1992). Assessment of post-traumatic amnesia in young children. *Developmental Medicine and Child Neurology, 34*(10), 885–892.

Schwartz, L., Taylor, H. G., Drotar, D., Yeates, K. O., Wade, S. L., & Stancin, T. (2003). Long-term behavior problems following pediatric traumatic brain injury: Prevalence, predictors, and correlates. *Journal of Pediatric Psychology, 28*(4), 251–263.

Sharples, P. M., Storey, A., Aynsley-Green, A., & Eyre, J. A. (1990). Causes of fatal childhood accidents involving head injury in northern region, 1979–86. *British Medical Journal, 301*(6762), 1193–1197.

Staden, U., Isaacs, E., Boyd, S. G., Brandl, U., & Neville, B. G. (1998). Language dysfunction in children with rolandic epilepsy. *Neuropediatrics, 29*(5), 242–248.

Stuss, D. T., Binns, M. A., Carruth, F. G., Levine, B., Brandys, C. E., Moulton, R. J., et al. (1999). The acute period of recovery from traumatic brain injury: Posttraumatic amnesia or posttraumatic confusional state? *Journal of Neurosurgery, 90*(4), 635–643.

Tate, R. L., Pfaff, A., & Jurjevic, L. (2000). Resolution of disorientation and amnesia during post-traumatic amnesia. *Journal of Neurology, Neurosurgery and Psychiatry, 68*(2), 178–185.

Thompson, P. J., & Duncan, J. S. (2005). Cognitive decline in severe intractable epilepsy. *Epilepsia, 46*(11), 1780–1787.

Wright, I. (2005). Estimation of premorbid general cognitive abilities in children. *Educational and Child Psychology, 22*(2), 100–107.

Wright, I., & Limond, J. (2004). A developmental framework for memory rehabilitation in children. *Pediatric Rehabilitation, 7*(2), 85–96.

Yeates, K. O., & Taylor, H. G. (1997). Predicting premorbid neuropsychological functioning following pediatric traumatic brain injury. *Journal of Clinical and Experimental Neuropsychology, 19*(6), 825–837.

Ylvisaker, M., Adelson, P. D., Braga, L. W., Burnett, S. M., Glang, A., Feeney, T., et al. (2005). Rehabilitation and ongoing support after pediatric TBI: Twenty years of progress. *Journal of Head Trauma Rehabilitation, 20*(1), 95–109.

18

Neuropsychological Assessment in Child Mental Health Contexts

Ian Frampton

Why might neuropsychology be relevant to child mental health services? Surely such specialist assessment methodologies and neurorehabilitation strategies are the preserve of that rare and rarefied creature, the developmental neuropsychologist? While acknowledging that there are very real pressures on clinical staff to take account of the complex psychosocial contexts that children inhabit and to see a lot of children, it is possible to argue that there is a vital role for the neuropsychological assessment of children with mental health difficulties for three related reasons.

First, neuropsychological assessment is helpful because there are known relationships between neuropsychological and psychological functioning, the so-called *brain to behavior* relationship. Nunn (1997) reviews the neurobiological bases of psychiatric disorders in making his case for all practitioners working in child mental health services to adopt a developmental neuropsychiatric approach, even if we have not been formally trained in this area. Nunn argues that there are consistent and identifiable relationships between neurobiological functioning (what is happening in the child's brain) and psychiatric disorder (what is happening to the child's behavior). The remainder of this chapter adopts Nunn's recommendation in exploring the potential neurobiological basis for a range of child mental health problems.

Second, adopting a developmental neuropsychological perspective in child mental health helps us to keep in mind a *when not where* heuristic. Although beyond the scope of the present chapter, there is ample empirical evidence from a range of childhood disorders that increasing neuropsychological disturbance is associated with an earlier disruption of the brain in fetal or postnatal life (Yates, Williams, Frampton, & Crum-Lindqvist, 2005). This heuristic reverses previous thinking embodied in the Kennard principle that it is generally best to get your brain damage or disruption out of the way as early as possible in life. It also challenges adult-oriented neuropsychological thinking that relates specific patterns of deficits to specific brain regions (so, for example, visual perceptual deficits index right hemisphere damage in right-handed adults, whereas in children similar deficits are associated with early rather than late acquired damage;

Frampton, 2004). Thus, from a developmental neuropsychological perspective, patterns of deficit might index temporal (early versus late) rather than the spatial (right versus left) dimensions of adult neuropsychology.

Third, it is implicit in this approach that *assessment is the start not the end of the process*. As discussed elsewhere in this book, a neuropsychological assessment can only be of any value to a child, and to a child mental health service, if it contributes to our understanding of his or her needs, and ultimately to treatment planning and an improved quality of life. This strategy of viewing the assessment as an opportunity to test tentative hypotheses about the potential contribution of neurobiological factors to the child's psychological presentation might help us to get away from a tendency to produce the universal definitive assessment.

The tendency of neuropsychologists to deliver vast tomes detailing every nuance of the child's profile is clearly unhelpful in a busy, frontline child mental health service, where the key question concerns the *implications* of the assessment for the child's functioning and treatment. A parallel from neurophysiology might be helpful to illuminate this point: Although a vast amount of EEG data is collected in order to make an assessment, as a clinician all I need is the single-line report about whether the overall pattern is abnormal and indicative of epilepsy or not. Drilling down into more detail, it is then helpful to know whether the focus of abnormal activity is in the temporal or frontal region, since this will predict the different patterns of problems that the child is likely to have. What is not needed in order to use these assessments is a highly complex, second by second description of exactly what was recorded at each probe.

In this chapter, this pragmatic approach will be adopted to consider why neuropsychological assessment might be helpful in a child mental health context. Following a brief review of some useful theoretical models, a summary is presented of neuropsychological functioning and its implications in a range of disorders commonly seen in children's services, including anxiety disorders (especially obsessive compulsive disorder, where elaborate models have been developed), depression, early psychosis, and Tourette syndrome. Attention deficit and autistic spectrum disorders are considered in detail elsewhere in this book, along with pediatric head injury and epilepsy, and so are omitted from this discussion. The chapter concludes with some thoughts on how to conduct an assessment in a child mental health setting.

The Function of Neuropsychological Assessment in Child Mental Health

Why, then, might it be helpful to conduct a neuropsychological assessment in a child mental health setting? At a most basic level, the summary scores from the assessment will make it possible to establish a level of cognitive functioning in order to support diagnosis and treatment planning. For example, a contributory factor for a child with a school phobia may be a learning disability masked by a good verbal presentation (Humphrey, 2006). In a similar way, an assessment can help to identify specific learning difficulties and their impact on emotional and behavioral functioning (see Chapter 19 for more details).

Neuropsychological assessment can also help to identify potential neurodevelopmental factors contributing to mental health problems and to test hypotheses (see Table 18.1 for a case example). Detailing a neuropsychological profile can contribute to treatment planning (for example, children with early-onset anorexia nervosa are more likely to have a chronic course if they are significantly impaired on more than two domains of neuropsychological functioning; Hamsher, Halmi, & Benton, 1981) or to identify whether a child fits into one of the hypothesized theoretical models for a range of disorders (for example, the nonverbal learning disability syndrome; Rourke, 1989).

Importantly, an assessment may help to set a baseline for future assessment, since for children with developing brains, change is a unit of measurement (Fletcher & Taylor, 1984). In order to explore whether a child is making the expected rate of change in the future, we need to establish their overall level of functioning at this time in their life, and to identify their unique pattern of neuropsychological strengths and weaknesses to begin tracking their progress across time.

Finally, neuropsychological assessment in the child mental health context can contribute to the research effort, either by reporting on single cases (a classical approach in neuropsychology) or to collect case series with related difficulties. For those of us working in busy clinical services with little dedicated time for research or professional development, the opportunity to reflect on and write up individual children we see can contribute to our engagement with the science.

Table 18.1 Case Example of a Hypothesis-testing Approach.

Carole, aged 12, has been referred to the local child mental health service by her family doctor at the request of her parents. Since early childhood, she has been fearful of coming down stairs, and this has progressed to the point where she is unable to use any unfamiliar stairs. She describes being afraid of falling and hurting herself. She is able to crawl up and down the stairs at home, but will not use the stairs anywhere else and is now refusing to go to school. The only developmental history of note is that Carole was premature and suffered an intraventricular hemorrhage with hydrocephalus at birth and has a shunt fitted. As well as completing a thorough functional analysis of her difficulties, consider the following hypotheses:

Hypothesis	Assessment strategy
Carole has a specific deficit in depth perception caused by brain damage associated with her hydrocephalus.	Assess visual perceptual skills, including figure-ground and depth perception.
Carole has impaired balance associated with her early brain damage.	Assess balance and gross motor skills.
Carole has a phobia for heights and/or stairs associated with a nonspecific neurodevelopmental process secondary to her early brain damage.	Assess verbal and nonverbal reasoning skills to look for evidence of nonverbal learning disability, a nonspecific factor in anxiety disorders.

Theoretical Models

Of course, there is nothing as practical as a good theory, and arguably when time is short in a busy community context, adopting a theoretical approach to neuropsychological assessment may become even more important. In basing assessment on a theoretical model of developmental functioning, we can predict the important neuropsychological domains to sample and avoid a lengthy and exhaustive "carpet bombing" approach to testing.

This perspective begs the question of which theories of cognitive and neurodevelopment might be relevant in child mental health settings to help guide assessment. Piaget remains a crucially important influence on developmental psychologists, not least because his theories predict that higher cognitive functions develop from the concrete operations of the child on the world in a predictable and lawful way (see Donaldson, 1984, for the definitive digestible guide to Piaget's sometimes complex theorizing). The work of Luria, Vygotsky, and, more recently, Feuerstein (Sharron, 1987) helps us to understand how processes of learning involve interactions between child and an adult caregiver, and so inform us about the impact of impaired attachment relationships on cognitive development.

More recently, the neuropsychiatric theories of Nunn (1997) and Gillberg (1995) have challenged the view that psychological distress in children is primarily caused by environmental factors such as neglect or parental mental health difficulties. In posing the disarmingly simple question "why this child and not another who has grown up in a similarly adverse environment?" these theorists have promoted a profound shift in neuropsychiatric theorizing to consider what *intrinsic* or neuropsychological factors might make *this* child vulnerable to the adverse effect of this particular environment when others do not suffer in similar circumstances. The converse is equally important and arguably better articulated by our colleagues in health psychology: "What are the protective factors that have supported *this* child in adverse circumstances to avoid psychological distress?" Thus, the analysis of coping mechanisms, and therefore a preventive approach to child mental health, might be more helpful to time-pressed services than an expectation of psychopathology as an inevitable consequence of environmental stressors (Lovering, Frampton, Crowe, Moseley, & Broadhead, 2006).

Finally, Damasio (1994) has argued convincingly that an adequate assessment of child neuropsychological functioning must be referenced to the neuroanatomical structures on which those functions depend. The intimate relationship between brain structure and function does require us to develop our knowledge of the complex microstructure of the brain, which is a challenge to those of us working in child mental health settings without the luxury of time to learn all the Latin names.

My suggested solution is to adopt Nunn's (1997) approach to distinguishing between a child's functioning in relation to his or her external environmental context and his or her *intrinsic capabilities*. Nunn suggests that we should consider the child's ability to cope with a specific demand at any given point in development as a hierarchy of *organizational levels*, each of which depends on the integrity of the system below. He suggests that the subtle, higher level functions, such as planning, judgment, and insight, are the most likely to be disrupted by more basic intrinsic system dysfunction. This suggests that a developmental neuropsychological approach needs to make sense of higher level functioning problems through the assessment of the integrity of the underlying basic systems supporting these functions.

A Neuropsychological Perspective in Childhood Mental Health

Before exploring some strategies to conduct such an assessment in a community setting, this section explores how a developmental neuropsychological perspective can be helpful in child mental health services, illustrated using a range of disorders.

The neurobiological basis of mental health disorders: obsessive compulsive disorder

We should be seeing quite a lot of children with anxiety problems in specialist mental health services. Catchment area studies have reported prevalence rates of 3.7% for generalized anxiety disorder (GAD) in nonreferred teenagers aged 14–17 (Whitaker, Johnson, Shaffer, & Rapoport, 1990), and 4.6% in 7–11-year-olds (Benjamin, Costello, & Warren, 1990). Epidemiological studies in the UK suggest that the prevalence of anxiety disorders overall in the UK for 5–15-year-olds is 3.8% (Meltzer, Gatward, & Goodman, 2000).

For the purposes of this analysis, obsessive compulsive disorder (OCD) can be considered as a special case of an anxiety disorder with a well-described neurobiological basis. The overall prevalence of OCD in young people aged 5–15 years has been established as 0.25%, with prevalence rising exponentially with increasing age to adult rates of approaching 1% at puberty (Heyman et al., 2001).

Neuroimaging studies show that children with OCD have significantly larger ventricular to brain ratios relative to age- and sex-matched controls (Behar, Rapoport, & Berg, 1984), and Luxenberg and colleagues (Luxenberg, Swedo, & Flamant, 1988) found significantly smaller caudate volumes in late adolescent and young adult male patients with OCD compared with controls. These differences in brain structure suggest that there may be underlying neurobiological factors contributing to the disorder.

Turning to brain functioning, the majority of functional imaging studies in OCD have shown changes in regional blood flow and oxygenation in specific parts of the brain, including the caudate, anterior cingulate, thalamus, putamen, and orbitofrontal cortex (Rauch et al., 1994). All these parts of the brain are linked in a circuit of pathways called the CSPT (cortico-striatal-palladial-thalamic) network. One theory is that this neuronal network normally has a resting level of activity which is reduced in OCD, allowing the emergence of automatic thoughts (obsessions) or behaviors (compulsions) that are normally inhibited in healthy individuals (Graybiel & Rauch, 2000).

OCD may thus be associated neurobiologically with impairment in mechanisms of *inhibitory control*. In this model, compulsions could emerge first developmentally (as a failure of gating mechanisms that normally prevent us from constantly performing behavioral repertoires evolutionarily important for survival, such as grooming, checking, and other environmental monitoring). These "evolutionarily preserved" behavioral repertoires were predicted by Rapoport, Swedo, and Leonard (1992) to be important in the genesis of OCD. Thus, the child who has a neurodevelopmental predisposition to produce these kinds of compulsive behaviors in response to anxiety-inducing situations may then begin to generate thought content to account for them (so the reason I am washing my hands all the time must be because I am afraid of being contaminated by germs), rather than the other way round.

In this developmental model, the direction of effect between obsessions and compulsions is the reversal of the adult cognitive behavioral therapy (CBT) model posited by Rachman and Hodgson (1980) in which obsessions come first and compulsions act to reduce the resultant anxiety. From a clinical perspective, the value of a neuropsychological assessment of children presenting to a mental health service with OCD would be to establish whether they exhibit the cluster of impaired inhibition and set-shifting skills in stop and go/no-go tasks, Stroop interference inhibition, and inhibition of irrelevant stimulus–response associations in set-shifting tasks (Chamberlain, Blackwell, Fineberg, Robbins, & Sahakian, 2005; Woolley et al., 2008) that have been shown to characterize a neurodevelopmental subtype of the disorder. Clinically, this group does appear to have a more chronic and difficult to treat form of the disorder (I. Heyman, personal communication).

The relationship between developmental neuropsychology, neurobiology, and psychopathology: a model for early psychosis

Childhood-onset psychosis is usually defined as onset by the age of 12 years, and is fortunately extremely rare. While no large-scale epidemiological studies have been conducted, it has been estimated that the prevalence of childhood-onset schizophrenia may be fifty times less than that of adult-onset (Karno & Norquist, 1989).

Neuroimaging studies of adolescents with schizophrenia or schizophreniform disorder (mean age 16.5 years) demonstrated significant increases in ventricular volume in the clinical group relative to both normal controls and a contrast group of borderline patients, with greater increases in ventricular/brain ratio being related to poorer treatment response (Schulz et al., 1983). A longitudinal structural magnetic resonance imaging (MRI) study of the National Institute of Mental Health childhood-onset schizophrenia sample has shown that, consistent with studies of adult schizophrenia, enlarged basal ganglia volumes normalize after patients are started on atypical antipsychotic medication (Frazier et al., 1996). Functional neuroimaging studies using positron emission tomography (PET) in childhood-onset schizophrenia have demonstrated similar patterns of reduced frontal activation during a continuous performance task as seen in adults (Jacobson et al., 1998).

The link between these neurobiological abnormalities, neuropsychological functioning, and psychopathology has been elegantly constructed by Frith (1996). In his model, the positive symptoms of hallucinations and delusional beliefs result from the patient attributing his or her own actions to an external agency. This error is due to an inability to distinguish between external events in the outside world (such as hearing another's voice) and the internal perceptual changes caused by our own actions. Frith suggests that the basis of this failure in turn could be a functional *disconnection* between frontal brain areas concerned with the initiation and monitoring of action and posterior brain areas concerned with perception.

This idea that schizophrenia could be a kind of disconnection syndrome has had important treatment implications. The kinds of executive functioning deficits predicted by Frith's frontal model have proved modifiable by cognitive remediation, using training approaches derived from the treatment of adults with acquired brain injury (Wykes & Reeder, 2005).

How understanding the neuropsychology can help to make treatment decisions: depression and Tourette syndrome

In reviewing the neuropsychological and cognitive theory and therapy literature related to depression, Crews and Harrison (1995) suggest that evidence from the neurosciences can account for the effectiveness of some treatments and not others. For example, difficulties with set-shifting can be mirrored by the problems young people with depression develop in all or nothing thinking and reduced cognitive flexibility. This suggests that, at least in the acute stages of depression, a young person may simply not be able to access alternative ways of thinking about their situation required by cognitive therapies in reality-testing approaches. Rather, young people at this stage may need a much more behavioral approach to activity scheduling and increasing opportunities for mood-enhancing engagement.

In the case of Tourette syndrome (TS), Yeates and Bornstein (1994) note that there is a very high frequency of comorbidity between TS and both OCD and attention deficit hyperactivity disorder (ADHD). Both OCD and ADHD are significantly more common than expected in children with TS, with up to 50% having comorbid OCD and/or ADHD. In their sample, children with TS and ADHD demonstrated significant deficits in aspects of attention, including encoding, sustaining, and focusing, as well as in academic attainment, compared to controls with just TS.

Yeates and Bornstein (1994) suggest that TS might therefore be associated with specific impairments in subcortical–cortical motor circuits, whereas ADHD implicates a more distributed network comprising striatal, thalamic, brain stem, and limbic structures, along with their associated cortical afferents. From a treatment perspective, this theory helps to account for the fractal nature of tics (Peterson & Leckman, 1998), meaning that while it may be possible to alter the distribution of tic productions (through mass practice or "tic time"), the overall amount of tics that are produced across a day, a week, a year, and a lifetime follows a common frequency distribution of an initial "ramping up" phase, followed by an intensive performance phase, followed by a refractory phase.

These bursts, and bursts of bursts, are compelling evidence of the neurobiological basis of tics in striatal systems, and in clinical terms suggests that it might be helpful for the child with TS in school to be given a task that takes them out of the classroom several times a day, so that they can perform the tics that have been suppressed in structured lesson time. It also accounts for the tendency of children with TS to have explosive outbursts at the end of the school day, the release of the tension associated with suppressing tics contributing to a behavioral outburst.

Research findings have also shown that children with comorbid TS and ADHD have more significant executive functioning deficits (Harris, Schuerholz, Singer, & Reader, 1995), and so may be good candidates for a more detailed assessment of their organization and planning skills, as well as remedial help in these domains.

Getting beyond the environmental factors: a neuropsychological model of early-onset anorexia nervosa

What has the brain got to do with eating disorders? Surely (predominantly) young women develop eating disorders as a result of the psychosocial pressures to be thin and attractive, and as a means of taking control of some aspect of their lives? However, since not all young females go on to develop anorexia nervosa, we need to invoke some kind of intrinsic factor (just as Nunn, 1997, suggests) to account for why this particular child presents with an eating disorder, when the external pressures are by definition universal.

Beginning from this starting-point, empirical studies have "gone fishing" (an honorable tradition in neuroscience) to collect accounts of the nature and extent of neuropsychological deficits in young people with eating disorders. In a recent systematic review of the literature, Ryan and colleagues (Ryan, Frampton, Overas, & Lask, 2007) have identified no fewer than 117 studies that explore neuropsychological functioning and anorexia nervosa. Emerging from all these studies is a consensus that some young people and adults with anorexia nervosa have consistent patterns of neuropsychological deficits (primarily in visual-spatial functioning and set-shifting) that appear to endure even when they are weight-recovered and no longer unwell.

The recent development of sophisticated neuroimaging techniques has allowed for detailed investigation of brain structure and function in anorexia nervosa that might contribute to a potential neurobiological basis for the disorder alongside these reliable neuropsychological findings. Structural neuroimaging has consistently shown ventricular enlargement which decreases with refeeding, both in mixed populations of adults and adolescents (Palazidou, Robinson, & Lishman, 1990) and in early-onset anorexia nervosa (Katzmann, Zipursky, Lambe, & Mikulis, 2003). The findings suggest that the changes are most likely to be due to neuronal damage secondary to malnutrition, with possible regeneration of myelin accounting for the general reversibility (Artmann, Grau, Adelmann, & Schleiffer, 1985).

There have been very few functional imaging studies of brain activity in early (prepubertal) onset anorexia nervosa. Some studies using single photon emission computerized tomography (SPECT) to measure regional cerebral blood flow (rCBF;

Chowdhury et al., 2003; Gordon, Lask, Bryant-Waugh, Christie, & Timimi 1997; Lask et al., 2005) have demonstrated unilateral reduction of blood flow in the temporal region in about 75% of patients with early-onset anorexia nervosa that persists even after treatment.

These studies demonstrate that there is a relationship between neurobiological abnormalities and impaired neuropsychological functioning in anorexia nervosa: It is unlikely that unilateral and regional hypoperfusion would result from the short-term effects of starvation. The persistence of reduced rCBF at follow-up, independent of such variables as previous or current nutritional status and eating disorder psychopathology (Rastam et al., 2001), suggests that the brain abnormality is either a primary phenomenon or a result of starvation that is slow to reverse, or is actually irreversible. The combination of reduced rCBF in the temporal region and its association with impairment of neuropsychological functioning, independent of nutritional status, point to both cortical and subcortical components, indicating a systemic neural network rather than a focal abnormality.

This suggests the possibility that an underlying neurobiological vulnerability may be a predisposing factor in making some children more likely to develop an eating disorder than others in the context of precipitating factors such as adolescence and family functioning difficulties. This theory is difficult to prove experimentally since it would require serial scanning of huge numbers of children from an early age before a very few of them went on to develop an eating disorder. Nevertheless, it does suggest the possibility that neurobiological factors could constitute a vulnerability to the later development of a range of mental health problems.

Conducting Neuropsychological Assessment in a Child Mental Health Setting

The major constraints on conducting a neuropsychological assessment in a child mental health setting are likely to be time and available assessment tools. Both these constraints implicate a hypothesis-testing rather than battery approach to assessment, which aims to use the smallest number of highest quality measures to address a specific question. Chapter 21 makes recommendations about assessment approaches; Table 18.2 records some assessments that might be useful additions to a child mental health service test cupboard.

It is always important to take a full developmental history since this will inform the generation of potential hypotheses. Rarely will parents volunteer information about previous head injuries unless you specifically ask. A useful checklist is the *Child Neuropsychological Questionnaire* (Melendez, 1984), which, although not normed, consists of 42 items to elicit standard information from parents about their child's perinatal history, developmental milestones, medical events, psychosocial development, and educational history. It is also helpful to have some other measures of psychological functioning, such as the Strength and Difficulties Questionnaire (SDQ; Goodman, 2001) or the Child Behavior Checklist (CBCL) to help in developing hypotheses about the potential brain–behavior relationships between neuropsychological and psychological functioning.

Table 18.2 Cognitive Domains and Indicative Tests for a Neuropsychological Assessment.

Cognitive domain	Indicative test
Global cognitive ability	Wechsler Abbreviated Scale of Intelligence
Executive functioning	Delis–Kaplan Executive Functioning System
Attention and concentration	Test of Everyday Attention for Children
Language	Clinical Evaluation of Language Functioning
Motor functioning	Movement ABC
Visual spatial analysis	Wide Range Assessment of Visual Motor Ability
Learning and memory	Test of Memory and Learning
Academic achievement	Wechsler Individual Attainment Test

As Table 18.2 suggests, it is usually worth making a brief assessment of overall cognitive ability (unless this has recently been conducted in another setting), particularly to take into account differences between verbal and nonverbal reasoning skills, for two reasons. First, the child may have an undetected significant discrepancy between (enhanced) verbal reasoning and (impaired) nonverbal reasoning skills, often a nonspecific marker of early abnormalities in brain development (Frampton, 2004; Rourke, 1989). This can be an important finding in so far as teachers (and to some extent parents) tend to base their expectations of a child's ability on their verbal presentation. A child with good verbal skills but a significant neurodevelopmental impairment in processing visual-spatial information may be having unexpected problems with processing complex social situations and other simultaneous processing tasks contributing to a nonverbal learning disability. On the other hand, a child may have undiscovered strengths in nonverbal reasoning, suggesting subtle language or sequential processing problems, pointing toward potential cognitive remediation strategies using their strengths in simultaneous processing and gestalt strategies such as mind mapping.

Second, a sense of overall level of cognitive functioning will help to clarify whether general expectations for academic and social performance are simply pitched too high for this particular child, especially in a high-achieving family setting where older (or even younger) siblings are forging ahead academically. Although it is not always fashionable in the UK, knowing the child's overall general cognitive ability helps us to make sense of their progress in literacy, and so to detect whether specific reading and/ or spelling difficulties could be contributing to their emotional or behavioral functioning (Humphrey, 2006).

With limited time and budget, it may be prudent to focus on a small number of assessments that have a good pedigree and sample a range of cognitive systems. The NEPSY (Korkman, Kirk, & Kemp, 1997), which has measures of attention, executive functioning, language, visual-spatial, sensory-motor and memory and learning in children aged 3–12 years, can be used as a good overall screener. For older children, subscales of the Delis–Kaplan Executive Functioning System (D-KEFS; Delis, Kaplan, & Krameret, 2001) can be used to rapidly screen developmental components of executive functioning, including fluency (verbal fluency), inhibition (color–word interference), and planning (tower test). Although expensive, with careful planning this test can be shared with adult colleagues since it is normed from 8 to 89 years.

Since the ability to inhibit responses and switch between response set appears to be crucial to so many aspects of psychological dysfunction (including ADHD, OCD, TS, anxiety, and depression), tests of these domains such as go/no-go from the Test of Everyday Attention for Children (TEACH; Manly, Robertson, Anderson, & Nimmo-Smith, 1998) are useful to probe verbal and motor inhibition. The availability of additional measures will be constrained by time and cost, but classics such as the Rey–Osterrieth Complex Figure yield rich clinical data, especially if you watch closely how the child approaches the task, and have enhanced scoring systems for interpreting children's productions, including their planning approach to the task (Holmes Bernstein & Waber, 1999).

Conclusion

It is clear that most neuropsychological assessment in child mental health service settings will necessarily be conducted and interpreted by clinical child psychologists who have not had additional post-qualification training. For example, in the UK, commissioning advice from the British Psychological Society recommends that one full-time consultant child neuropsychologist should be appointed for a population of 750,000 people (British Psychological Society, 2004); clearly not enough capacity to do all the assessment needed across children's service. My personal view is that this a good thing, since it means that most assessment will be conducted by clinicians working in local services who remain closely linked to the clinical needs of the child, rather than becoming an academic exercise divorced from the immediate concerns and questions for *this* child and *this* family.

As put so clearly by Apley in his seminal study of pediatrics, *One Child*: "The Cartesian split of human creatures into 'psyche' and 'soma' has had a profoundly bad influence on the medical care of children" (Apley & Ounsted, 1982, p. 2). Applying a parallel dichotomy to child mental health, we have become very sophisticated in our understanding and assessment of the psychological consequences of environmental influences on child mental health (in terms of parental mental health, family functioning, and so on); a more complete understanding requires that we assess and take into account how neuropsychological factors operating within the brain might also be contributing to *this* child's distress to support positive therapeutic change.

References

Apley, J., & Ounsted, C. (1982). *One child* (Clinics in Developmental Medicine No. 80). London: Heinemann.

Artmann, H., Grau, H., Adelmann, M., & Schleiffer, R. (1985). Reversible and non-reversible enlargement of cerebrospinal fluid space in AN. *Biological Psychiatry, 23*, 377–387.

Behar, D., Rapoport, J. L., & Berg, C. J. (1984). Computerized tomography and neuropsychological test measures in adolescents with OCD. *American Journal of Psychiatry, 141*, 363–369.

Benjamin, R. S., Costello, E. J., & Warren, M. (1990). Anxiety disorders in a pediatric sample. *Journal of Anxiety Disorders, 4*(4), 293–316.

British Psychological Society (2004). *Commissioning child neuropsychology services*. Leicester: British Psychological Society.

Chamberlain, S. R., Blackwell, A. D., Fineberg, N. A., Robbins, T. W., & Sahakian, B. J. (2005). The neuropsychology of obsessive compulsive disorder: The importance of failures in cognitive and behavioural inhibition as candidate endophenotypic markers. *Neuroscience Biobehaviour Reviews, 29*(3), 399–419.

Chowdhury, U., Gordon, I., Lask, B., Watkins, B., Watt, H., & Christie, D. (2003). Early-onset anorexia nervosa: Is there evidence of limbic system imbalance? *International Journal of Eating Disorders, 33*, 388–396.

Crews, W. D., & Harrison, D. W. (1995). The neuropsychology of depression and its implications for cognitive therapy. *Neuropsychology Review, 5*(2), 81–123.

Damasio, A. (1994). *Decartes' error*. London: Macmillan.

Delis, D. C., Kaplan, E., & Krameret, J. H. (2001). *Delis–Kaplan executive functioning system: Manual*. Hove, East Sussex: Harcourt International.

Donaldson, M. (1984). *Children's minds*. Harmondsworth: Penguin.

Fletcher, J. M., & Taylor, H. G. (1984). Neuropsychological approaches to children: Towards a developmental neuropsychology. *Journal of Clinical Neuropsychology, 6*(1), 39–56.

Frampton, I. (2004). Research in pediatric neuropsychology: Past, present and future. *Pediatric Rehabilitation, 7*, 31–36.

Frazier, J. A., Giedd, J. N., Kayson, D., Albus, K., Hamburger, S., Alaghband-Rad, J., et al. (1996). Brain magnetic resonance imaging rescan after two years of clozapine maintenance. *American Journal of Psychiatry, 153*, 564–566.

Frith, C. (1996). Neuropsychology of schizophrenia: What are the implications of intellectual and experimental abnormalities for the neurobiology of schizophrenia? *British Medical Bulletin, 52*, 618–626.

Gillberg, C. (1995). *Clinical child neuropsychiatry*. Cambridge University Press.

Goodman, R. (2001). Psychometric properties of the strengths and difficulties questionnaire. *Journal of the American Academy of Child and Adolescent Psychiatry, 40*, 1337–1345.

Gordon, I., Lask, B., Bryant-Waugh, R., Christie, D., & Timimi, S. (1997). Childhood-onset anorexia nervosa: Towards identifying a biological substrate. *International Journal of Eating Disorders, 22*(2), 159–165.

Graybiel, A. M., & Rauch, S. L. (2000). Toward a neurobiology of obsessive-compulsive disorder. *Neuron, 28*(2), 343–347.

Hamsher, K. S., Halmi, K. A., & Benton, A. L. (1981). Prediction of outcome in anorexia nervosa from neuropsychological status. *Psychiatry Research, 4*, 79–88.

Harris, E. L., Schuerholz, L. J., Singer, H. S., & Reader, M. E. (1995). Executive function in children with Tourette syndrome and/or attention deficit hyperactivity. *Journal of the International Neuropsychological Society, 1*, 511–516.

Heyman, I., Fombonne, E., Simmons, H., Ford, T., Meltzer, H., & Goodman, R. (2001). Prevalence of obsessive-compulsive disorder in the British nationwide survey of child mental health. *British Journal of Psychiatry, 179*, 324–329.

Holmes Bernstein, J., & Waber, D. (1999). *Developmental scoring system for the Rey–Osterrieth complex figure*. Lutz, FL: PAR-Inc.

Humphrey, A. (2006). Children behaving badly: A case of misunderstanding? *The Psychologist, 19*(8), 494–495.

Jacobson, L. K., Giedd, J. N., Castellanos, F. X., Vaituzis, C. A., Hamburger, S. D., Kumra, S., et al. (1998). Progressive reduction of temporal lobe structures in childhood onset schizophrenia. *American Journal of Psychiatry, 155,* 678–685.

Karno, M., & Norquist, G. S. (1989). Schizophrenia: Epidemiology. In H. I. Kaplan & B. J. Sadock (Eds.), *Comprehensive textbook of psychiatry* (5th ed., pp. 1110–1116). Baltimore: Williams and Wilkins.

Katzmann, D. K., Zipursky, R. B., Lambe, E. K., & Mikulis, D. J. (1997). A longitudinal magnetic resonance imaging study of brain changes in adolescents with AN. *Archives of Paediatric Adolescent Medicine, 151,* 793–797.

Korkman, M., Kirk, U., & Kemp, S. (1997). *NEPSY: A developmental neuropsychology assessment.* Lutz, FL: PAR-Inc.

Lask, B., Gordon, I., Christie, D., Frampton, I., Chowdhury, U., & Watkins, B. (2005). Functional neuroimaging in early-onset anorexia nervosa. *International Journal of Eating Disorders, 37*(Suppl.), S49–S51, discussion S87–S89.

Lovering, K., Frampton, I., Crowe, B., Moseley, A., & Broadhead, M. (2006). Community-based early intervention for children with behavioural, emotional and social problems: Evaluation of the Scallywags Scheme. *Emotional and Behavioural Difficulties, 11*(2), 83–104.

Luxenberg, J. S., Swedo, S. E., & Flamant, M. (1988). Neuroanatomical abnormalities in OCD detected with quantitive X-ray computed tomography. *American Journal of Psychiatry, 145,* 1089–1093.

Manly, T., Robertson, I., Anderson, V., & Nimmo-Smith, I. (1998). *Test of everyday attention for children.* Oxford: Harcourt.

Melendez, F. (1984). *Child neuropsychological questionnaire.* Lutz, FL: PAR-Inc.

Meltzer, H., Gatward, R., & Goodman, R. (2000). *Mental health of children and adolescents in Great Britain.* London: HMSO.

Nunn, K. P. (1997). How to approach neuropsychiatric problems when you are not a neuropsychiatrist: An hierarchical formulation. *Clinical Child Psychology and Psychiatry, 2*(1), 11–26.

Palazidou, E., Robinson, P., & Lishman, A. W. (1990). Neuroradiological and neuropsychological assessment in anorexia nervosa. *Psychological Medicine, 20,* 521–527.

Peterson, B. S., & Leckman, J. (1998). The temporal dynamics of tics in Gilles de la Tourette syndrome. *Biological Psychiatry, 44*(12), 1337–1348.

Rachman, S., & Hodgson, R. (1980). *Obsessions and compulsions.* Englewood Cliffs, NJ: Prentice Hall.

Rapoport, J. L., Swedo, S. E., & Leonard, H. L. (1992). Childhood obsessive compulsive disorder. *Journal of Clinical Psychiatry, 54*(4), 11–16.

Rastam, M., Bjure, J., Vestergren, E., Uvebrant, P., Gillberg, I., Wentz, E., et al. (2001). Regional cerebral blood flow in weight-restored anorexia nervosa: A preliminary study. *Developmental Medicine and Child Neurology, 43,* 239–242.

Rauch, S. L., Jenike, M. A., Alpert, N. M., Baer, L., Breiter, H. C. R., & Fischman, A. J. (1994). Regional cerebral blood flow measured during symptom provocation in obsessive-compulsive disorder using oxygen 15-labeled carbon dioxide and positron emission tomography. *Archives of General Psychiatry, 51*(1), 62–70.

Rourke, B. P. (1989). *Non-verbal learning disabilities: The syndrome and the model.* New York: Guilford.

Ryan, J., Frampton, I. Overas, M., & Lask, B. (2007). *The Ravello profile: Neuropsychological assessment in anorexia nervosa.* Poster presentation at the 2007 Eating Disorders Research Conference, London.

Schulz, S. C., Koller, M. M., Kishore, P. R., Hamer, R. M., Gehl, J. J., & Friedel, R. O. (1983). Ventricular enlargement in teenage patients with schizophrenia spectrum disorder. *American Journal of Psychiatry, 154,* 1459–1461.

Sharron, H. (1987). *Changing children's minds: Feuerstein's revolution in the teaching of intelligence.* Birmingham: Imaginative Minds.

Whitaker, A., Johnson, D., Shaffer, J. L., & Rapoport, K. (1990). Uncommon troubles in young people: Prevalence estimates of selected psychiatric disorders in a nonreferred adolescent population. *Archives of General Psychiatry, 47,* 487–496.

Woolley, J., Heyman, I., Brammer, M., Frampton. I., McGuire P., & Rubia, K. (2008). Reduced activation during inhibitory control in task-specific brain regions in paediatric OCD. *British Journal of Psychiatry, 192,* 25–31.

Wykes, T., & Reeder, C. (2005). *Cognitive remediation therapy for schizophrenia: Theory and practice.* London: Guilford.

Yates, P., Williams, H. W., Frampton, I., & Crum-Lindqvist, A. (2005). A six year follow-up study of neuropsychological functioning in school children who sustained a mild head injury under five years of age. *Brain Impairment, 6*(2), 118.

Yeates, K., & Bornstein, R. (1994). Attention-deficit disorder and neuropsychologic functions in children with Tourette's syndrome. *Neuropsychology, 8,* 65–74.

19

Applications of Neuropsychology in Schools

Sue Harrison and Jane Hood

Education professionals are concerned with understanding how to optimize all children's learning and performance. While it is clear that the brain is responsible for human learning and actions, its role in the process of learning has rarely been considered in educational settings. There may be huge potential benefits in understanding more about how the brain contributes to children's performance and learning, and those working in educational contexts ignore the brain at their peril. At the very least, educational practice should be consistent with what is known about the brain.

Whilst neuropsychological assessment of children is currently the preserve of child neuropsychologists trained in neuroscientific concepts and techniques, educational professionals are increasingly showing an interest in brain functioning. This is beginning to lead to greater possibilities for neuropsychology and neuropsychological assessment to be applied more widely and creatively in educational settings.

Most children progress through school without difficulties. However, a significant proportion will require some additional help to do well, and a small group of those may have difficulties as a result of abnormal brain activity or development. These include children with hypoxia-related birth injuries, head injury, developmental tumors or dysplasias, hydrocephalus and spina bifida, cerebral infections such as meningitis or encephalitis, metabolic and endocrine disorders such as phenylketonuria, and young people with epilepsy. For children with neurological problems, who may have potentially complex, serious, but poorly understood sequelae, it is imperative that they undergo detailed assessment and intervention based on neuroscientific knowledge and principles so that their needs are understood and met as they progress through educational settings.

Breuer (1997) has claimed that it is "a bridge too far" to make any links between neuroscience and education. In a similar vein, Stanovich (1998) has argued that, while interesting, brain research does not have much to offer the understanding of academic tasks such as reading, and is not necessarily relevant to education. However, more recently, the case for the educational relevance of neuroscience has been made persuasively, initially in the United States (Byrnes, 2001; Byrnes & Fox, 1998), and subsequently in the United Kingdom (Blakemore & Frith, 2005; Goswami, 2004; Hall, 2005). Many other writers agree (Geary, 1998; Mayer, 1998; O'Boyle & Gill, 1998; Schunk, 1998; Wittrock, 1998).

Even if the benefits of links between the disciplines are accepted, the application of neuropsychological knowledge is not straightforward. Even within neuroscience, understanding of how brains work is still far from complete, and the links between established neuroscientific knowledge and education are not well developed. Those interested in making such links need to have time to review the research and the academic skills to review its worth critically, skills that may be challenging to use and apply for educators (Byrnes, 2001). Even if it is possible to identify sound and relevant studies, much neuroscientific research, whilst interesting and important, is not yet at a stage for implications to be drawn from it (Blakemore & Frith, 2005).

Another problem, once relevant and ready-to-translate research is identified, is transforming the findings into educationally relevant practice. All the authors mentioned above have presented strong arguments for the future potential of this, but there are few current examples. This picture may well be different when a further 20 years of neuroscientific work has been done, and more educationalists, including teachers and psychologists working in schools, are better informed.

Incidence of Neurological Problems in Educational Contexts

As noted above, the number of children experiencing neurological problems is small. Some problems, such as brain cancers or cerebral infection, are thankfully rare. Nevertheless, it is important to acknowledge that the brain can be vulnerable and, unfortunately, in some children it will be compromised. In this situation, as Lincoln and Gibbs (2005, p. 6) argue, "there will be an inevitable need for knowledgeable and skilful professional work with either the injured child or those with primary responsibility for the child's recovery and education." Even where a condition is rare, it may have a large impact, and its very rarity means that it is likely to be poorly understood.

It is difficult to give precise figures for all possible neurological disorders. However, to give some examples, it has been estimated that the prevalence of children with head injury is around 200 per 100,000 or 1 in 500 (Bozic & Morris, 2005; Tiret, Hausherr, & Tlhicoipe, 1990). The incidence of children with epilepsy is 1 in 200 (Anderson, Northam, Hendy, & Wrennall, 2001). Medical advances in the past 30 years have meant that three times as many infants and children who would have died because of pregnancy and birth problems or traumatic brain injury are now surviving to school age, but with concomitant neurological damage (Mackay, 2005). From these figures alone, it is clear that at least 1 child in every 200 is likely to have a neurological problem even before those with neurodevelopmental disorders, such as attention deficit hyperactivity disorder (ADHD) and autism, are taken into account.

Of course, the presence of a neurological difficulty is not an inevitable passport to problems. For example, many premature children and young people with epilepsy grow up to flourish and function extremely well. However, there are also many with such difficulties who experience problems ranging from major disability to subtle but far-reaching impairments in a number of cognitive domains. These children and young people need to have their neuropsychological profiles investigated and supported.

A child with a neurological difficulty is inevitably going to spend a large proportion of his or her time in an educational setting. However, there are concerns that educational professionals lack training and knowledge concerning the needs of such children (Bozic & Morris, 2005; McCusker, 2005) and that the needs of the children are not always being met (Farrell et al., 2006).

Current Links between Neuropsychology and Education

Very little literature exists that addresses the practicalities of how neuropsychology can be applied in educational contexts, although there have been attempts to set up such services; for example, Hood (2003) calls for more links between neuropsychology and education and describes the development of an "educational neuropsychology service" that integrates neuropsychology and educational psychology. Other writers have called for the development of a new discipline—that of "learning science" which should be interdisciplinary and populated by practitioners from neurophysiology, psychology, and education (Blakemore & Frith, 2005).

The increasing interest in making links between neuropsychology and education was expressed in a special issue of *Educational and Child Psychology* (issue 22, 2005) which was devoted entirely to neuropsychology, reflecting the growing awareness of the relevance of neuropsychology to those working in education. However, just three of the nine articles make explicit links between neuropsychology and education: MacKay's article on the relationship between the two, a description of how to manage head injury in schools (McCusker, 2005), and a paper reporting a questionnaire study of the roles that psychologists in schools currently take in the recovery of children with head injury (Bozic & Morris, 2005). The early stages of the links between neuropsychology and education are further evident in the fact that, of the 25 contributors, most were academic psychologists or clinical neuropsychologists, and just one was a psychologist working in schools.

Barriers to the Relationship between Neuropsychology and Education

The relationship between neuropsychology and education is currently patchy and tenuous. This is partly a function of the different ways that education and neuropsychology have been conceptually divided which does not make for easy bridges or links. Cognitive psychologists and neuropsychologists have understood the human brain partly in terms of individual aspects of cognitive performance, namely intellect, memory, attention, language, and perception. It would be difficult to argue against the fundamental importance of these domains to learning and education; however, teachers and psychologists working in classrooms tend to understand the child as a learner in terms of different aspects of performance. Many of these are curriculum areas: reading, spelling, and numeracy, although language ability, motivation, and concentration are also often referenced. It can be very challenging to map these two different domains of thought onto each other and explain how they relate.

Child neuropsychologists and education personnel may also work according to different values and paradigms. In education, there may be a reluctance to focus on deficit-based descriptions of children's functioning in the place of positive descriptions of what the child is able to achieve and how he or she responds to adjustments to the curriculum or learning environment. Psychometric testing, particularly IQ testing, has been controversial and at times associated with labeling, reductionism, and limiting opportunities for children. Many teachers and school psychologists, particularly in the United Kingdom, have preferred to focus on opportunities and context rather than individual differences which can appear limiting and contrary to equality of opportunity.

However, the different paradigms of assessment and orientation of traditional neuropsychological and educational services need not be incompatible; rather, they can be seen as complementary, with each having valuable things to offer in different situations and for different children. The differences can be bridged by multiprofessional meetings and liaison work and by mutual respect and understanding of the different models and the idea that they both have something to offer.

Another issue that may make it difficult for education and neuropsychology to integrate is the practical consideration of the time taken to conduct a full neuropsychological assessment. Administering a comprehensive assessment may take 6–8 hours. This time is not generally available for psychologists working in schools, whose opportunity for in-depth case work may be limited compared with that of child neuropsychologists. However, neuropsychologists would argue that children need and deserve to have their cognitive profiles understood. This is the case for all children with complex needs, not just those with identified brain damage or disease. While it is important to see the child in the context of his or her environment and experiences, specific cognitive deficits can have very different impairments depending on how these are managed.

Although there has not yet been any formal evaluation of attempts in the UK to integrate educational and neuropsychological services, in the United States more progress is being made to this end. The term "ecological neuropsychology" is used by D'Amato and colleagues (D'Amato, Crepeau-Hobson, Huang, & Geil, 2005) to refer to attempts to link neuropsychology and interventions. D'Amato has expressed concern that the traditional models of neuropsychology do not make any attempt to measure a child's potential for change. Ecological neuropsychology is based on the Response to Instruction (RTI) model (Fuchs, Mock, Morgan, & Young, 2003; Vaughn & Fuchs, 2003), which is similar to Dynamic Assessment in looking at children's potential for change. D'Amato aims to use the information from traditional neuropsychological assessments to see how children learn and for rehabilitative purposes, rather than simply for identifying pathology. As neuropsychologists are becoming more aware of how the brain interacts with environmental factors, ecological neuropsychology aims to take a more dynamic approach (Work & Hee-Sook, 2005) and propose interventions within the context of the whole child. The ecological neuropsychological model integrates multiple sources of information, including those more traditionally used such as psychosocial systems, with multiple information-gathering methods, such as interview, observation, and objective measures.

Beyond Individual Assessment: Applying Neuropsychology with Groups of Children

There are some studies that are beginning to show how neuropsychological assessments of groups of children in schools can be used to obtain useful information about subtle difficulties that are preventing them learning. For example, Morgan, Singer-Harris, Bernstein, and Waber (2000) studied a group of children who were shown to be of average ability on psychometric assessments but who were failing to progress at school. They hypothesized that they would show similar neuropsychological profiles to children who were failing to achieve in at least one academic area. They administered a number of executive and attention measures with these children and a control group of children with specific learning difficulties and found that the experimental group had problems dealing with complexity and had decreased automaticity (executive function problems) that were similar to, although not as severe as, the control group. They presented as having problems adapting to their environment. The authors concluded that, since these measures were quick and easy to administer and provided simple examples of how to alleviate the difficulties these children were experiencing, they might provide more ecological validity than more traditional measures of ability. Other studies have also shown links between executive and attention skills and academic attainment (e.g., Commodari & Guarnera, 2005; St. Clair-Thompson & Gathercole, 2006) rather than IQ alone.

Links have also been found between classroom performance and significant learning difficulties, such as specific executive or language weaknesses. Language difficulties, particularly expressive language, were found to be a problem for a group of excluded pupils studied by Ripley and Yuill (2005). Amongst the younger members of their experimental group, they found additional auditory working memory problems. They concluded that language problems should be assessed early in children with conduct difficulties, but also commented on the fact that language difficulties did not account for a large proportion of the group's conduct problems.

Mattison, Hooper, and Carlson (2006) assessed a group of 35 primary school-aged children who were misbehaving to a significant extent. Of these pupils, 54% were found to have significant difficulties, at or below the 2nd percentile on at least one domain of the NEPSY (Korkman, Kirk, & Kemp, 1998), a developmental neuropsychological measure, chiefly either language or attention/executive functions.

They commented on the fact that the additional learning difficulties of children with emotional and conduct problems are not routinely investigated. They concluded that specialist teachers of these children would benefit from having access to information about their specific difficulties, so that the teachers could adapt the curriculum accordingly; for example, to prevent children acting out because they had misunderstood the language being used.

Psychologists are aware of the benefits of early intervention for children who are seen to have difficulties that are likely to impact on their educational and social development, but it is important to be able to identify the specific nature of their difficulties in order to be able to target help appropriately. It is also important to determine whether early individual differences will persist to affect future learning as there is a tendency with younger children to "wait and see" how they progress during their first few years at school, particularly where children have subtle or specific difficulties.

Neuropsychological assessments have recently been shown to help in the identification of preschool children who are likely to go on to have academic difficulties. Espy and colleagues (2004) examined whether they could show a link between children's executive functioning ability and their mathematical ability, as both are related to activation within the prefrontal cortex. They found that inhibitory control accounted for variance in their emergent mathematical skills. Working memory difficulties, both visuospatial and verbal, have a lasting impact on mathematical computational skills (Wilson & Swanson, 2001) and early identification of these difficulties would ensure that interventions are instigated that support the specific areas of weakness rather than simply repeating unsuccessful teaching methods. Waber and colleagues (Waber, Gerber, Turcios, Wagner, & Forbes, 2006) assessed 91 primary school-aged children from inner-city schools and low-income families and found that early executive function difficulties featured highly in this group and that they accounted for a significant degree of the variance in their academic attainments.

Neuropsychology and Educational Intervention and Rehabilitation

In terms of using neuropsychological measures to inform intervention, a few studies have emerged. Attempts have been made to link specific approaches—for example, approaches to manage children's conduct—with assessments of their effect on neuropsychological processes. For example, the PATHS (Promoting Alternative Thinking Skills) Curriculum (Kusche & Greenberg, 1994) has been well validated as an effective means of reducing aggression and promoting social competence in children with significant difficulties relating to their conduct (Greenberg, Kusche, Cook, & Quamma, 1995). Riggs and colleagues (Riggs, Greenberg, Kusche, & Pentz, 2006) examined the role of neuropsychology in the children's social functioning. They found that the PATHS program was effective in improving inhibitory control and verbal fluency (executive functions) and helped children to use inhibitory control to affect their actions. They urged the developers of social-emotional programs to ensure that they support the development of children's executive skills, verbal processing skills, and emotional awareness. They argued that such programs should be delivered to coincide with known periods of neurocognitive development to maximize their impact and permanence.

While the studies described above indicate that there might be a useful role for conducting neuropsychological assessments on children with complex, albeit subtle, learning difficulties, it is the link between assessment and intervention that crucially needs to be established at the outset. Both the Response to Instruction and the Dynamic Assessment models are based on similar principles in terms of the individual nature of interventions provided. If these interventions are generated following the administration of a neuropsychological assessment, it would introduce a completely different element. The majority of interventions are task specific: For example, poor readers are taught better ways of breaking down words; children with poor sustained attention are provided with environmental or material changes that help reduce distractions. However, there have yet to be convincing group studies to determine whether areas of specific deficit can be improved upon by direct teaching and, more importantly, whether these improvements are generalizable; for example, whether children with verbal working memory problems can train specifically to improve their working memory such that it affects their mental arithmetic performance (Rankin & Hood, 2005).

Hood and Rankin (2005; Rankin & Hood, 2005) have developed an account of children's memory which also links neuropsychological knowledge with education. The way in which children's different memory difficulties may present in the classroom is clearly described and specific rehabilitation techniques to address these difficulties are outlined. They use case studies to describe children's neuropsychological difficulties, and interventions were generated to address the difficulties not just in educationally meaningful terms but also in terms of robust neuroscientific models. This has the potential to stimulate education professionals to think about the use of evidence-based practice at the level of suggesting interventions. However, whilst this work could be beneficial in raising awareness of memory problems, the identification of such memory disorders is presented as a complex task requiring the assessment skills of a clinical neuropsychologist. Thus, the robust model of memory assessment and intervention in education may not be easily accessible to those working in education until they have access to the clinical skills necessary to conduct a full memory assessment.

The links between assessment and intervention need to be made in a practical way; that is, generating interventions for specific difficulties that can be proved to have a positive impact on children's learning and/or conduct. For example, children with executive functioning difficulties may be those children observed in class to have problems initiating activities, generating ideas, organizing their work, and so on. They are likely to struggle with academic tasks such as open-ended activities and project work. Any intervention program needs to provide strategies that they are able to use to enable them to initiate and complete activities independently, such as teaching them to use specific prompts to commence a task, providing them with visual information depicting the steps that they need to take to reach an end-point, and providing an example of the end-point. An illustration of applying this approach to a task could be training children to use an essay template. The template provides specific prompts to help children to generate and sequence ideas in order to structure their essay. When they have become accustomed to using the template independently, their implicit memory for the task should be assessed. For example, are they able to use the template automatically, without direct reference to it? And are they able to generalize its use; for example, alter the structure of the essay according to task demands?

Similarly, if a child has working memory difficulties that are impacting on their ability to carry out mental arithmetic calculations, such as short multiplications, they might be encouraged to use written times tables to solve problems, the theory being that this will improve their computational skills and limit the impact of their poor working memory skills (Hood & Rankin, 2005). What remains to be seen is whether this method enables them to improve their implicit memory for their tables through the use of what amounts to an errorless learning technique.

Linking Neuroscience to Education: A Role for Child Neuropsychologists

Child neuropsychologists are very well placed to make use of neuroscientific information and neuropsychological knowledge in their everyday practice and "translate" it into relevant educational advice and recommendations. When working with individuals, in line with Bernstein's (2000) and Anderson et al.'s (2001) systemic models of assessment, child neuropsychologists collect qualitative and quantitative information about a child relating to his or her background history, family and school setting, current developmental stage, and current concerns. Written and verbal reports of concerns are obtained from parents, schools, medical personnel, and from the child. Information about neurological status is obtained from medical reports, from neurological examination, imaging studies such as MRI, fMRI, PET, or other scans, and electroencephalogram (EEG) investigations (which involve recording patterns of electrical activity in the brain from electrodes on the scalp). Standardized psychometric and neuropsychological tests are used to provide evidence of the child's cognitive status and identify domains in which the child exhibits particular strengths or weaknesses. The cognitive domains of intellectual function, language, memory, executive function, perception, motor function, and emotional conduct are examined. However, it is not the administration of neuropsychological tests per se that makes an assessment neuropsychological, rather the interpretation of these tests integrated with knowledge about the child's socioeducational background and neurological status. After neuropsychological interpretation of strengths and difficulties, the child neuropsychologist can then suggest appropriate interventions that fit both the child's unique cognitive profile and unique socioeducational situation.

The following case illustrates how neuropsychological assessment carried out in a hospital setting may have a beneficial impact on a child's educational context. The child's name has been changed.

Case Study

Daniela experienced a left middle cerebral artery territory stroke at the age of 18 months, in the context of hemolytic uremic syndrome (a rare genetic condition causing children to experience kidney failure and blood clotting problems). Following her stroke, MRI scans showed extensive damage to the left hemisphere. Daniela developed a right hemiplegia. She had a limp and poor balance, tired easily, and found it difficult to run or walk for long distances, especially on rough terrain. She had very limited use of her right hand, with no finger function. She needed help with most two-handed activities including dressing, cutting food, and carrying books or trays.

Daniela was referred for a neuropsychological assessment by her neurologist in the light of her transfer to secondary school. When she was aged 10 years, Daniela's mother and mainstream primary school were concerned about her social and emotional function and her self-control. Daniela was characterized as a highly emotional girl who could easily become irritable, distressed, and angry. This had an impact on her social interactions. Although she could make friends, she had difficulties compromising and seeing others' points of view, and often had stormy on-and-off relationships. Daniela could also become very upset in lessons she found difficult, particularly mathematics, and would leave angrily or feign illness as an avoidance technique. Daniela's mother was also concerned that her daughter was not performing at the levels she was capable of at school and that she had particular problems with mathematics and writing. She was said to be haphazard, unable to set work out on a page neatly, and often to "lose her place" in textbooks or the board. Daniela's main concerns were friendships and how to maintain them, and the difficulties that she experienced in arithmetic and with "making" in science and design and technology.

It was notable that Daniela's IQ scores were lower at her current assessment than when she was 6 years old (see Table 19.1). Close analysis of the two assessments showed that she had not deteriorated; rather, her rate of progress had slowed, particularly in the area of nonverbal intellect. She still continued to show average verbal intellect and this, along with her well-developed memory and reading skills, indicated she had the capacity to make good progress at school. The most significant finding of the assessment was the discrepancy that Daniela now showed between her well-developed verbal abilities and her much poorer nonverbal intellect. It was explained to Daniela's mother that this was likely to be a natural consequence of her brain's compensation for her early injury. Her undamaged right hemisphere, as well as continuing to subserve visuospatial functions, had probably taken over the language functions of the damaged left hemisphere. As young people with extensive unilateral damage become older, a "crowding" effect may be seen with the unaffected hemisphere not able to perform optimally because it

Table 19.1 Neuropsychological Test Data from Assessment of Daniela at Age 6:0 and 10:10 Years.

Domain		Age 10:10 years	Age 6:0 years
Emotional function and conduct		*Parent and school*	
Strengths and Difficulties Questionnaire	Emotional symptoms	High	
	Behavior difficulties	High	
	Hyperactivity	High	
	Peer relationships	High	
	Prosocial behavior	Normal	
	Total difficulties	High	
Intellectual ability		*Current*	*Previous*
Wechsler Intelligence Scale for Children, 3rd ed.	Verbal IQ	93	111
	Performance IQ	73	116
	Full-scale IQ	81	115
Memory			
Children's Memory Scale	Verbal immediate index	106	
	Verbal delayed index	91	
	Visual immediate index	100	
	Visual delayed index	97	
Visuomotor			
Motor-free Visual Perception Test, 2nd ed.	Perceptual quotient	106	
Developmental Test of Visual Motor Integration, 4th ed.	Visual perception	109	
	Motor coordination	79	
	Visual motor integration	78	
Annett Pegboard Test of Fine Motor Speed	Score (left hand only)	<10th percentile	
Literacy			
Wechsler Objective Reading Dimensions	Basic reading	100 (11:3 yrs)	
	Spelling	81 (8:6 yrs)	
	Reading comprehension	106 (11:6 yrs)	
Numeracy			
Wechsler Objective Numerical Dimensions	Mathematics reasoning	92 (10:0 yrs)	
	Numerical operations	77 (8:3 yrs)	

is effectively doing an extra job. Verbal abilities are usually spared at the expense of higher-order visuospatial abilities such as visuomotor integration (Muter & Vargha-Khadem, 2000). Daniela's current, relatively poor nonverbal intellect and her poor visuomotor integration scores are consistent with this.

These poor skills underlie Daniela's problems with spelling, a visuomotor activity, and her difficulties with copying from the board and setting out her work neatly on the page. It was recommended that she take part in a visuomotor spelling program, and receive support for her writing difficulties, including the use of double-spaced, lined paper, extra time, a sloping board to write on, and alternative recording methods such as a Dictaphone and laptop. It was suggested that Daniela would need to avoid copying from books or the board; it would be more effective for her to receive a typed copy of teacher notes to highlight. It was suggested that Daniela's nonverbal intellectual difficulties would mean that lessons that tap visuospatial skills, such as design and technology, art, and geometry, would be especially challenging for her. Teaching situations where the interpretation of line and form was needed, such as interpreting or making maps, drawings, charts, diagrams, and tables should be avoided for Daniela. Where unavoidable, they would need to be supplemented with verbal "translations" or descriptions of the visuospatial material so that Daniela could use her better verbal skills as compensation. Daniela's scores on mathematical assessment suggested that she had good mathematical reasoning ability and thus the potential to do well, but that she had poor knowledge of specific numerical operations. It was felt that this was probably related to her anxiety about this subject and her history of avoiding lessons she found difficult, thus missing out on the teaching of specific techniques.

It was explained that children with hemiplegia were likely to show a constitutionally higher level of irritability than their peers (Muter & Vargha-Khadem, 2000) and that this was something Daniela would always struggle with. It was also highlighted that difficulties with nonverbal intellect and visuospatial processing can be associated with social problems because of difficulties with "reading" body language and facial expression (Rourke, 1995). The family was already linked to local clinical child mental health services and this was felt to be useful for Daniela and her mother. Daniela's school was advised to provide specific pastoral support, including social skills training and individual support with negotiating friendships.

Daniela's mother attended the hospital for a feedback session, and she and the current and impending schools received a copy of the neuropsychological report. A school visit was made soon after Daniela transferred to her new school at the age of 11. A meeting was held with Daniela's teachers and mother in order to explain her profile and make suggestions for her management. The school was very aware of her physical disability and had put in place a great deal of support for this. However, her physical disability, and the fact that she struggled with producing work in many lessons, meant that her school saw her as a girl with mild general learning difficulties. They were unaware of her well-developed abilities in verbal intellect and memory and unaware of her nonverbal difficulties (or even that a child's learning could be conceptualized in terms of verbal and nonverbal difficulties). By attending the meeting, it was possible to paint a picture of Daniela that captured her strengths and clearly identified her difficulties. Advice was given about how poor nonverbal intellect may manifest, and suggestions were made as noted above.

Effective Neuropsychology–Education Links in Individual Casework

The first of many important issues that arise when considering effective links between neuropsychology and education is the value to the child, family, and school of having specific neuropsychological difficulties recognized. The explanatory power of a good assessment should not be underestimated. As Anderson et al. (2001, p. 350) state, "an accurate explanation of the child's functional difficulties ... can result in acknowledgement, understanding and support." In educational contexts, the reluctance to label a child, and the emphasis of focusing on what a child can do rather than what they cannot do, can lead to parents feeling in the dark about how their child is actually doing. Simply having clear information about where a child is, and what the difficulties are, can improve the family's and the school's attitude to the child's difficulties and facilitate appropriate management of these difficulties. For many parents who have struggled with a child's perplexing problems in the context of a brain illness or injury, it is a welcome relief to know exactly the nature and magnitude of the issues that they and their child are facing. Furthermore, explanations of difficulty in terms of neuropsychological domains can help conceptualize a child's difficulties more helpfully (for example, difficulties with impulse control rather than naughtiness) and provide suggestions for remediation (for example, frequent breaks and self-regulation strategies; Hale, Fiorello, & Brown, 2005).

Education professionals such as teachers and psychologists working in schools are often very competent at recognizing children who are struggling, but they may not have the time or assessment skills to identify specific problems with crucial cognitive domains such as intellect, memory, and language. Thus they may, as in Daniela's case, miss some of the most salient difficulties altogether, or even misattribute them to context factors. With clear information about the nature of Daniela's difficulties, they were able to put in place specific adaptations to the curriculum and everyday life, and to teach her compensation strategies.

Neuropsychological assessments traditionally use many psychometric tests. They can be criticized as irrelevant and difficult to translate into everyday school practice. Daniela's case shows how an effective neuropsychological assessment must give weight and significance to the most salient aspects of the test results, placing less emphasis on others. It must also explain how particular test scores fit with the child's socioeducational context and presenting problems, and discuss test findings in terms of how they may manifest in the child's day-to-day functioning at home and at school. In Daniela's case, the most important finding was not the drop in her IQ scores, but the discrepancy between her current verbal and nonverbal IQ. Her school was interested to hear how this discrepancy could manifest at school and relieved to understand how it explained some of her difficulties.

A child may have a difficulty that does not translate easily into a low score on a single test; for example, Daniela's difficulty with copying from the board and keeping her place. It may be that there is no test that picks up their difficulty or that their difficulty is a result of a combination of factors that show up on several tests: in Daniela's case her performance on tests of nonverbal intellect and visuomotor function.

Risks of Conducting Neuropsychological Assessments in Schools

As mentioned above, most commentators call for more links between neuroscience and education, and recommend an increase in the knowledge and skills of everyone in terms of neuropsychological problems and how to understand them. However, there may be a danger in over-interpreting neuroscientific information and in over-applying small amounts of neuropsychological knowledge without appropriate training and supervision. There are concerns that just because psychologists may be trying to practice neuropsychology in schools, they are not necessarily doing so appropriately (Pelletier, Hiemenz, & Shapiro, 2004). The practice of neuropsychology includes using a range of standardized assessments. However, it is the inferences and interpretation of the neuropsychological tests within the wider knowledge of the child's context and neurological investigations that constitute the neuropsychological expertise. For example, a child may perform poorly on a memory test because they have a severe memory difficulty. However, poor performance on a memory test may also be because a child has language difficulties and has not understood the task properly, because they have attention problems and have not encoded the information accurately, or because they have expressive language difficulties and cannot describe the information they have recalled. While enthusiasm for expanding neuropsychological knowledge should be maintained, it must be balanced with caution about using and interpreting tests in an incorrect or misleading way due to lack of knowledge, training, and experience.

Future Directions for Links between Neuropsychology and Education

As Goswami (2004) states, "bridges need to be built" and psychologists need to take the initiative by "thinking outside the box" about how to link neuropsychological knowledge with educational contexts. Currently, neuropsychology is mainly practiced by a small number of individuals in hospital settings. There is evidence that some of these neuropsychologists do try to extend their practice to link with education (Hood, 2003; McCusker, 2005).

Child neuropsychologists can influence the educational context in many ways and at many levels. Child neuropsychologists who are "education aware" are able to link an individual child's neuropsychological profile of strengths and weaknesses to their educational (and social and family) situations. Neuropsychologists can help by liaising with schools directly about individual children, by making school visits, and being involved in the drawing up of educationally meaningful learning strategies, targets, and programs based on robust neuropsychological models. This could be at the level of discussing the right type of educational environment (best type of school, size of class, level and type of extra help) or modifications to the curriculum taught (for example, dropping a subject or prioritizing subjects), or employing technology or accommodations such as computers, diaries, and so on, or teaching strategies, such as the use of a timer, errorless learning techniques, or coaching.

Neuropsychologists can link with local school psychologists and may provide training, supervision, and specialist input to education professionals. A few psychologists have worked innovatively to develop links at the level of educational psychology services (e.g., Calver, 2004; Hood, 2003), but in general the level of knowledge and understanding of neuropsychology is at a very early stage and links are few.

However, it is heartening to see such a high level of interest in building more bridges. There have been calls for more training for psychologists who can cross the boundaries of neurology, psychology, and education (Bozic & Morris, 2005). Modules and even specialist degrees in neuropsychology are now offered to psychologists studying at postgraduate level. The popularity of courses and conferences on neuropsychology among educational professionals is testament to the desire to understand more about this area. There are journals dedicated to the study of issues relating to brain illness and disease in children (e.g., *Developmental Neuropsychology, Child Neuropsychology, Pediatric Rehabilitation*) and special issues of child and educational psychology journals concerning neuropsychology (*Educational and Child Psychology*, 22, 2005). Special interest groups for brain research and education have been established between psychology and education groups in the United States and the United Kingdom (Atherton, 2005; Goswami, 2006).

Neuropsychology is also beginning to have applications at a group level by showing how neuropsychological assessment of cognitive functions with groups of young children can provide ecologically valid early identification of learning potential and learning problems. In the future, such an application of neuropsychological assessment techniques has the potential to become a more widely applied and useful tool in the screening of groups of children in educational settings.

Conclusion

Even though the number of children with neurological illness or injury remains small, the impact of neuropsychological assessment in educational contexts is important both at the level of the individual child and more widely. There is currently very little evidence for any interventions that are recommended to support children's learning in schools, in terms of their effect on the child's educational progress and on the child's neuropsychological development. Comprehensive initial assessment of children's difficulties, the application of specifically targeted interventions, and the instigation of rigorous follow-up of children, including the use of quantitative neuropsychological measures, would provide the information for psychologists to begin to answer some of the essential questions about children's learning and brain development discussed in this chapter.

References

Anderson, V., Northam, E., Hendy, J., & Wrennall, J. (2001). *Developmental neuropsychology: A clinical approach*. Hove, East Sussex: Psychology Press.

Atherton, M. (2005). *Applying the neurosciences to educational research: Can cognitive neuroscience bridge the gap?* Paper presented at the Annual Meeting of the American Educational Research Association, Montreal, Canada (available online at www.tc.umn.edu/~athe007/BNEsig/papers/EducationandNeuroscience.pdf).

Bernstein, J. H. (2000). Developmental neuropsychological assessment. In K. O. Yeates, D. O. Ris, & H. G. Taylor (Eds.), *Pediatric neuropsychology: Research, theory and practice* (pp. 405–438). New York: Guilford.

Blakemore, S. J., & Frith, U. (2005). *The learning brain: Lessons for education*. Oxford: Blackwell.

Bozic, N., & Morris, S. (2005). Traumatic brain injury in childhood and adolescence: The role of educational psychology services in promoting effective recovery. *Educational and Child Psychology, 22,* 7–18.

Breuer, J. T. (1997). Education and the brain: A bridge too far. *Education Research, 26,* 4–16.

Byrnes, J. P. (2001). *Minds, brains and learning: Understanding the psychological and educational relevance of neuroscientific research*. New York: Guilford.

Byrnes, J. P., & Fox, N. A. (1998). The educational relevance of research in cognitive neuroscience. *Educational Psychology Review, 10,* 297–342.

Calver, A. (2004). *Setting up neuropsychology assessment in a local education authority: A model of collaboration between NHS clinical neuropsychology and LEA educational psychology services.* Paper presented at University College London Educational Psychology Leading Edge Psychology Day, Neuropsychology and Educational Psychology Practice, London.

Commodari, E., & Guarnera, M. (2005). Attention and reading skills. *Perceptual and Motor Skills, 100,* 375–386.

D'Amato, R. C., Crepeau-Hobson, F., Huang, L. V., & Geil, M. (2005). Ecological neuropsychology: An alternative to the deficit model for conceptualizing and serving students with learning disabilities. *Neuropsychology Review, 15,* 97–103.

Espy, K. A., McDiarmid, M. M., Cwik, M. F., Stalets, M. M., Hamby, A., & Senn, T. E. (2004). The contribution of executive functions to emergent maths skills in preschool children. *Developmental Neuropsychology, 26,* 465–486.

Farrell, P., Woods, K., Lewis, S., Rooney, S., Squires, G., & O'Connor, M. (2006). *A review of the functions and contribution of educational psychologists in England and Wales in light of "Every Child Matters: Change for Children."* Research Brief No. RB792 for the Department for Education and Skills (DfES), London.

Fuchs, D., Mock, D., Morgan, P. L., & Young, C. L. (2003). Responsiveness-to-intervention: Definitions, evidence and implications for the learning disabilities construct. *Learning Disabilities Research and Practice, 18,* 157–171.

Geary, D. C. (1998). What is the function of mind and brain? *Educational Psychology Review, 10,* 379–389.

Goswami, U. (2004). Neuroscience and education. *British Journal of Educational Psychology, 74,* 1–14.

Goswami, U. (2006). Neuroscience and education: From research to practice? *Nature Reviews Neuroscience, 7,* 406–413.

Greenberg, M. T., Kusche, C. A., Cook, E. T., & Quamma, J. P. (1995). Promoting emotional competence in school-aged children: The effects of the PATHS Curriculum. *Development and Psychopathology, 7,* 117–136.

Hale, J. B., Fiorello, C. A., & Brown, L. L. (2005). Determining medication treatment effects using teacher ratings and classroom observations of children with ADHD: Does neuropsychological impairment matter? *Educational and Child Psychology, 22,* 39–62.

Hall, J. (2005). *Neuroscience and education. A review of the contribution of brain science to teaching and learning.* Scottish Council for Research in Education (SCRE), Research Report No. 121.

Hood, J. (2003). Neuropsychological thinking within educational psychology. *Debate, 105,* 8–12.

Hood, J., & Rankin, P. M. (2005). How do specific memory disorders present in the school classroom? *Pediatric Rehabilitation, 8,* 272–282.

Korkman, M., Kirk, U., & Kemp, S. (1998). *NEPSY: A developmental neuropsychological assessment manual.* San Antonio: Psychological Corporation.

Kusche, C. A., & Greenberg, M. T. (1994). *The PATHS Curriculum.* Seattle: Developmental Research and Programs.

Lincoln, N., & Gibbs, S. (2005). Editorial. *Educational and Child Psychology, 22,* 5–7.

MacKay, T. (2005). The relationship of educational psychology and clinical neuropsychology. *Educational and Child Psychology, 22,* 7–18.

Mattison, R. E., Hooper, S. R., & Carlson, G. A. (2006). Neuropsychological characteristics of special education students with serious emotional/behavioural disorders. *Behavioural Disorders, 31,* 176–188.

Mayer, R. (1998). Does the brain have a place in educational psychology? *Educational Psychology Review, 10,* 419–426.

McCusker, C. G. (2005). An interacting subsystems approach to understanding and meeting the needs of children with acquired brain injury. *Educational and Child Psychology, 22,* 18–29.

Morgan, A. E., Singer-Harris, N., Bernstein, J. H., & Waber, D. P. (2000). Characteristics of children referred for evaluation of school difficulties who have adequate academic achievement scores. *Journal of Learning Disabilities, 33,* 489–501.

Muter, V., & Vargha-Khadem, F. (2000). Neuropsychology and educational management. In B. Neville & R. Goodman (Eds.), *Congenital hemiplegia* (pp. 179–194). London: MacKeith Press.

O'Boyle, M. W., & Gill, H. S. (1998). On the relevance of research findings in cognitive neuroscience to educational practice. *Educational Psychology Review, 10,* 397–410.

Pelletier, S., Hiemenz, J., & Shapiro, M. (2004). The application of neuropsychology in the schools should not be called school neuropsychology. *The School Psychologist, 58,* 17–24.

Rankin, P. M., & Hood, J. (2005). Designing clinical interventions for children with specific memory disorders. *Pediatric Rehabilitation, 8,* 283–297.

Riggs, N. R., Greenberg, M. T., Kusche, C. A., & Pentz, M. A. (2006). The mediational role of neurocognition in the behavioural outcomes of a socio-emotional prevention program in elementary school students: Effects of the PATHS curriculum. *Prevention Science, 7,* 91–102.

Ripley, K., & Yuill, N. (2005). Patterns of language impairment and behaviour in boys excluded from school. *British Journal of Educational Psychology, 75,* 37–50.

Rourke, B. P. (1995). *Syndrome of nonverbal learning disabilities: Neurodevelopmental manifestation.* New York: Guilford.

Schunk, D. H. (1998). An educational psychologist's perspective on cognitive neuroscience. *Educational Psychology Review, 10*, 419–426.

Stanovich, K. E. (1998). Cognitive neuroscience and educational psychology: What season is it? *Educational Psychology Review, 10*, 413–417.

St. Clair-Thompson, H. L., & Gathercole, S. E. (2006). Executive functions and achievements in school: Shifting, updating, inhibition and working memory. *Quarterly Journal of Experimental Psychology, 59*, 745–759.

Tiret, L., Hausherr, E., & Tlhicoipe, M. (1990). The epidemiology of head trauma in Aquitaine, France 1988: A community based study of hospital admissions and deaths. *International Journal of Epidemiology, 19*, 133–140.

Vaughn, S., & Fuchs, L. S. (2003). Redefining learning disabilities as inadequate response to instruction: The promise and potential problems. *Learning Disabilities Research and Practice, 18*, 137–146.

Waber, D. P., Gerber, E. B., Turcios, V. Y., Wagner, E. R., & Forbes, P. W. (2006). Executive functions and performance in high-stakes testing in children from urban schools. *Developmental Neuropsychology, 29*, 459–477.

Wilson, K. M., & Swanson, H. L. (2001). Are mathematics disabilities due to a domain-general or a domain-specific working memory deficit? *Journal of Learning Disabilities, 34*, 237–249.

Wittrock, M. C. (1998). Comment on "The educational relevance of research in cognitive neuroscience." *Educational Psychology Review, 10*, 427–430.

Work, L. P., & Hee-Sook, C. (2005). Developing classroom and group intervention programs based on neuropsychological principles. In R. C. D'Amato, E. Fletcher-Janzen, & C. R. Reynolds (Eds.), *The handbook of school neuropsychology* (pp. 663–683). New York: Wiley.

20

Neuropsychological Assessment in Medical Contexts

Sarah Helps

The aim of neuropsychology within a medical context is first to determine how diseases of organs or systems induce impairment in cognitive functioning (Butters, Beers, & Tarter, 2001). Second, medical neuropsychology as a subspecialty has emerged in response to increasing evidence that cognitive functioning can be significantly influenced by the medical regimens used to treat medical conditions (Tarter, Van Thiel, & Edwards, 1988).

Early research with children with medical conditions tended to compare a global estimate of cognitive ability with a healthy population. More recently, as the field of pediatric neuropsychology has developed, and the impact of medical conditions and their treatment has become better understood, research has moved from assessing a child's overall cognitive ability to looking in detail at specific patterns of neurocognitive strengths and weakness. The aim of this chapter is to address how neuropsychological assessment adds to the care and understanding of a child in a medical setting.

Children with medical conditions are well known to be at increased risk for emotional, behavioral, and educational difficulties (e.g., Wallander, Thompson, & Alriksson-Schmidt, 2003). Families of children with chronic health conditions are also well known to be affected by the illness, resulting in increased rates of maternal anxiety and depression, marital distress, and sibling adjustment problems. There is burgeoning research on how the quality of life of children with medical conditions is affected by their condition. Cognitive ability, neuropsychological functioning, and academic attainment are important factors in determining quality of life.

There are few medical conditions that have not received attention regarding their cognitive sequelae. This chapter will use a small number of health conditions as examples, and will discuss evaluation, treatment, and research. It will conclude with a discussion of practice issues. The chapter will not address the assessment or treatment of children with neurological conditions such as epilepsy, traumatic brain injury, or brain infection. This is dealt with in chapter 17.

Diabetes

Children with diabetes have received considerable attention in the literature regarding their neurocognitive status, and information from neuropsychological research has influenced treatment practice. The evidence is mixed in terms of whether, and to what extent, diabetes directly affects neurocognitive abilities.

Type 1 diabetes mellitus (T1DM) is one of the most prevalent chronic health conditions in children under the age of 18 years. T1DM is caused by autoimmune destruction of pancreatic beta cells where the hormone insulin, which is essential for glucose metabolism, is produced. If insulin is lacking, glucose accumulates in the bloodstream and the urine, and the body literally starves. The brain is particularly susceptible to damage, as it cannot store glucose in its cells and thus requires a continuous supply from the vascular system (Desrocher & Rovert, 2004).

Patients with diabetes are thought to be at increased risk of impaired cognitive functioning due to the subtle brain changes associated with chronic (typically mild) aberrations in levels of glucose. For example, Northam et al. (2001) carried out a longitudinal follow-up of 90 children with T1DM and found that, six years after onset, children with T1DM performed more poorly than controls on measures of intelligence, attention, processing speed, long-term memory, and executive skills. Attention, processing speed, and executive skills were particularly affected in children with onset of the disease before 4 years of age, whereas severe hypoglycemia was associated with lower verbal and full-scale intelligence quotient scores. They concluded that the neuropsychological profiles were consistent with subtle compromise of anterior and medial temporal brain regions.

McCarthy and colleagues (McCarthy, Lindgren, Mengeling, Tsalikian, & Engvall, 2002) concluded that children in their sample performed no worse and, in fact, performed better than their healthy siblings in some areas of academic performance. McCarthy et al. (2002) argued therefore that subtle neurocognitive deficits often associated with type 1 diabetes may not significantly affect the functional academic abilities of these children over time.

Children with a history of severe hypoglycemia have been found to have more neuropsychological impairments (especially in short-term memory and phonological processing), as well as more learning difficulties, and to require more additional educational help than those without such a history (Hannonen, Tupola, Ahonen, & Riikonen, 2003). However, Wysocki et al. (2003) reported no adverse effects on neurocognitive ability of severe hypocalcemia.

In their detailed review of the neurocognitive correlates of diabetes in children, Desrocher and Rovert (2004) emphasize that the key variables in diabetes that impact on outcome are disease onset, presence of hypoglycemia, chronicity of effects (duration), and hyperglycemia at around the time of puberty. Desrocher and Rovert (2004) present evidence for four key relationships: (a) early onset T1DM and motor and visuospatial deficits; (b) hypoglycemia and attention and memory deficits; (c) hyperglycemia and

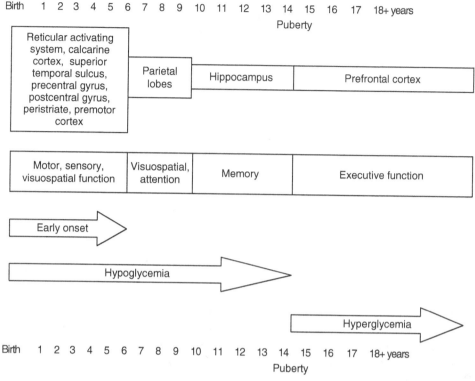

Figure 20.1 Model of the relationship between diabetes variables and neurocognitive development. *Note.* Reproduced from "Neurocognitive Correlates of Type 1 Diabetes," by M. Desrocher & J. Rovert, 2004, *Child Neuropsychology, 10*(1) 36–52, with the permission of Psychology Press.

verbal and executive function deficits; and (d) puberty and executive function deficits (see Figure 20.1). This model proposed by Desrocher and Rovert needs to be tested thoroughly using multicenter longitudinal studies, but it is a useful starting-point and is clinically helpful in planning assessments for children who present with difficulties. It is also useful in alerting clinicians to potential difficulties that might need exploration at different stages in the patient's journey.

Evaluating treatment efficacy

Neuropsychological assessment has been of huge benefit in evaluating the effects of different medical treatment regimens, such as intensive insulin therapy versus standard care for young people and adults with diabetes. For example, in the Diabetes Control and Complications Trial (DCCT, 1994, 1996) participants were administered a comprehensive battery of neuropsychological assessments. The primary concern of the trial was to evaluate whether intensive insulin provision would be associated with an increased risk of hypoglycemia which might lead to an increased incidence of brain damage. The secondary concern of the trial therefore involved patient safety. The results of the longitudinal study showed that, despite the increased incidence of hypoglycemia, intensive therapy was not associated with a corresponding increase in cognitive dysfunction. Results therefore provided reassurance for staff and patients alike that the potential side-effects of intensive insulin therapy did not include cognitive compromise.

Sickle Cell Disease

Sickle cell disease is a good example of a condition where disease characteristics are likely to have a significant impact on cognitive functioning. It is also a good example of a condition where neurocognitive data have affected the kind and the timing of medical treatments provided.

Sickle cell disease (SCD) is a genetic disorder with an autosomal recessive pattern of inheritance. There are numerous subgroups of SCD, the three most common genotypes being HbSS, often regarded as the most severe form of the disease; HbSC, a heterozygous condition associated with a more benign presentation; and HbSB-thalassemia, also regarded as a milder form. The majority of families affected are Afro-Caribbean and West African in origin, but others are from the Mediterranean, Middle East, and Asia.

Children with SCD are at increased risk of the development of cognitive and learning problems, although the majority of children with SCD function well within the normal range. Early work by Swift et al. (1989) reported that children and young people with SCD had lower full-scale IQs as measured by the Wechsler Intelligence Scales Revised (Wechsler, 1974), and performed more poorly on a battery of other neurocognitive tests, compared with nonaffected siblings, although no specific pattern of dysfunction was noted. In a meta-analysis of cognitive outcome data, Midence and colleagues (Midence, McManus, Fuggle, & Davies, 1996) estimated that children with SCD showed a five-point IQ deficit compared with their nonaffected peers.

Research progressed to an evaluation of the specific domains in which children with SCD had difficulties, and Brown, Armstrong, and Eckman (1993) reported that children with SCD had impairments in sustained attention and in some aspects of academic achievement compared to nonaffected siblings, and these deficits were significantly, if mildly, predicted by hemoglobin levels. Similar findings have been reported by Steen and colleagues (Steen, Xiong, Mulhern, Langston, & Wang, 1999) who reported that IQ scores were found to be a function of hematocrit levels (the percentage by volume of packed red blood cells in a given sample of blood after centrifugation) so that those with a hematocrit of <27% had significantly lower psychometric test scores, and significantly lower gray matter T1 on magnetic resonance imaging.

Children with sickle cell anemia (HbSS) are at significant risk of cerebral vascular accident (CVA; Adams, 2000) and by the age of 20, 6–12% of children with HbSS will have sustained a stroke (Ohene-Frempong et al., 1998). This is due to occlusion of the blood vessels in the central nervous system, which may lead to cerebral vascular accidents, microvascular infarction, or cerebral hemorrhaging. Without medical intervention, children who have one stroke are highly at risk of another (Gribbons,

Zahr, & Opas, 1995). Medical interventions in SCD aim at decreasing the risk of CVA by transcranial Doppler screening for increased flow velocity. When high flow velocity is detected, chronic transfusion therapy is used to keep the HbS level below 30%.

Bonner, Gustafson, Shumacher, and Thompson (1999) highlighted the short- and longer-term sequelae of CVA as including deficits related to memory, aphasia, apraxia, mathematical computation/reasoning, and spatial functioning, as well as motor ability. R. T. Brown et al. (2000) showed that children with overt CVA tend to struggle more with tasks requiring sustained attention. Armstrong et al. (1996) found children who had sustained overt CVAs to have poorer scores on full-scale IQ, mathematics achievement, verbal knowledge and language abilities, and visual-motor and spatial organization and integration.

In addition to overt strokes, children with HbSS are at risk of "silent infarcts," defined as abnormal magnetic resonance imaging without neurologic deficit. These silent strokes are thought to be the most frequent cause of neurocognitive impairment for children with HbSS. Indeed, the designation of infarcts as "silent" has now been questioned because those affected have been shown to have minor, but measurable neuropsychological abnormalities (Armstrong et al., 1996; Bernaudin et al., 2000; Craft, Schatz, Glauser, Lee, & DeBaun, 1993; Pegelow et al., 2002).

In a study of 266 children with HbSS, aged between 6 and 19 years, Pegelow et al. (2002) found that while the prevalence of overt stroke was around 11%, the prevalence of "silent infarcts" was around 21.8%, a little higher than previously been reported (Moser et al., 1996). Most lesions happened in girls before the age of 6 years, but boys remained at risk until they were 10. Children with HbSC were found to be at much lower risk of silent infarct and stroke.

In order to try to find ways of limiting the neurocognitive effects of silent strokes, new trials are beginning (i.e., the silent infarct transfusion trial) to determine whether regular blood transfusions will decrease the likelihood of progressive neurological and neuropsychological complications (Kirkham et al., 2006). Here, it seems likely that if the neuropsychological data show benefits for transfusion, or a lack of progression of the disease, then regular blood transfusions may become a much more widely used treatment for these children.

In looking more at functional outcomes for children with SCD, Schatz and colleagues (Schatz, 2004; Schatz, Brown, Pascual, Hsu, & DeBaun, 2001) examined the relationship between academic attainment (e.g., grade scores, repeating a grade, and the need for special educational needs services) and achievement (cognitive ability) in children with SCD compared with demographically matched peers. Attainment problems were more frequent in children with SCD than in controls. Cognitive ability was a strong predictor of both attainment and achievement. Illness-related school absences predicted academic attainment but not achievement. Schatz and colleagues concluded that academic attainment was affected by SCD, and tests of academic attainment were meaningful predictors of functional impairments for children with SCD. They suggest that illness frequency may have an impact on academic attainment that is somewhat independent of academic achievement skills.

Clinical implications

While the painful episodes and overt strokes that are experienced by children with SCD are easily identified and require urgent management, the more subtle neurocognitive changes that may occur are less often identified and treated (Routhieaux, Sarcone, & Stegenga, 2005). It is nevertheless important to recognize them in order to provide holistic and remedial care for children. Routine screening and assessment for neuro-cognitive deficits in children who have had a stroke or are at risk of, or identified as having, silent infarcts are now commonplace in most SCD clinics to identify children at risk.

Routhieaux et al. (2005) encourage medical practitioners to listen carefully to parents' observations about subtle changes in their child's behavior or academic performance, as it is these observations that may indicate the need for thorough assessment. Also recommended is training for schools that have children with SCD in their care. The results of assessments should be communicated to children's schools, and training should be provided for teachers educating children with SCD. Furthermore, educating parents that SCD may give rise to subtle behavioral and cognitive deficits is helpful in highlighting the need to be observant for these changes.

As comprehensive neuropsychological evaluation is resource heavy and time-con-suming, many clinics are starting to develop screening tools to distinguish children with no neurocognitive difficulties from those who require more detailed assessment. For example, Brown, Davis et al. (2000) report that frontal lobe impairments are very common and suggest that neuropsychological assessment of children who are thought to be at risk of cognitive impairments may be a practical (and likely cost-effective) way of selecting children who require more detailed medical evaluation. They conclude that measures of attention and concentration are valuable additional indices to identify children with possible cerebral infarcts.

White et al. (2006) identified a small number of variables from their comprehensive cognitive battery of 30 variables that might be most useful in screening for silent in-farcts. They found that the learning slope from the California Verbal Learning Test, Children's version and the Block Design from the Wechsler Abbreviated Scale of Intelligence was 75% accurate and 75% specific in distinguishing children who had suffered silent infarcts from those who had not. One implication of this is that brief targeted screening batteries could then be administered in the course of the child's routine clinic appointment, so as not to increase the burden of attending hospital appointments on children and their families.

Human Immunodeficiency Virus

Advances in medical care have led to human immunodeficiency virus (HIV) being seen not as an acute, lethal, life-threatening disease but as a chronic disease with long-term developmental consequences (Fishkin et al., 2001) where children may well live to their teenage years and beyond (Lewis, 2001).

Children with HIV are at particular risk of psychological disturbance due to both the direct effects of HIV infection on brain structures involved in the regulation of emotion, behavior, and cognition, and indirect effects relating to coping with the medical, psychological, and social stressors associated with the condition (Browers, Moss, Wolters, & Schmitt, 1994; L. K. Brown, Lourie, & Pao, 2000; Coscia et al., 2001). Indeed, approximately 25% of children with HIV exhibit clinically significant emotional or behavioral problems (Bachanas et al., 2001).

Neuroimaging studies have demonstrated a high incidence of structural brain abnormalities in children with symptomatic HIV-1 infection, including cortical atrophy, white matter abnormalities and calcifications (DeCarli, Civitello, Brouwers, & Pizzo, 1993). A variety of specific deficits have been identified for children who are HIV positive. For example, Wolters, Brouwers, Civitello, and Moss (1997) reported that expressive language was impaired in their group of symptomatic HIV children and suggested that global measures of cognitive ability may mask differential changes in specific brain functions. Bisiacchi, Suppiej, and Laverda (2000) reported that executive function abilities were affected, whereas language and overall intelligence abilities were not, in a group of 42 HIV-positive asymptomatic children.

Fishkin et al. (2001) reported that in their study of 40 preschool children with HIV, gross cognitive deficits were not found relative to matched controls. However, some focal deficits were identified: Specifically, the HIV group scored significantly lower on the Block Design task of the WPPSI-R than did the controls. They hypothesized that, although expected differences in frontal functions were not found, the result may reflect the multiple functions assessed by the Block Design task (involving processing speed, visual-motor integration, sustained attention, motor speed, and coordination), and that these functions are usually associated with the frontal cortex and developing connecting structures. The authors call for further investigation of these functions in older children.

Clinical implications

Neuropsychological assessment in children with HIV can be useful clinically to identify the particular pattern of strengths and weaknesses in the child. Measures of neuropsychological and motor function have also been found to be useful in predicting long-term outcomes; for example, longevity (Pearson et al., 2000). Pearson and colleagues (2000) conclude that global neuropsychological, neurological, and motor markers (e.g., verbal and performance IQs) were indeed found to provide information beyond that which came from traditional surrogate markers of disease progression (e.g., CD4 count and HIV RNA levels). Pearson et al. suggest that neuropsychological evaluation should routinely be considered in the initial evaluation of patients with HIV infection and should be repeated during treatment.

General Implications for Neuropsychological Testing in Medical Settings

In their review of the utility of neuropsychological assessment in evaluating treatment effects for medical disorders, Ryan and Hendrickson (1998) argue that the benefits of a neurocognitive assessment arm in treatment trials are incontrovertible, and suggest that neuropsychological assessment ought to be routinely included in medical trials. They highlight the importance of demonstrating that such assessments are both beneficial and cost-effective, and suggest informed patient choice, in terms of making decisions about the potential risk and benefits of a specific treatment, as one particular benefit.

Clinically, psychologists working within medical contexts need a thorough understanding of conditions that affect the children with whom they work. This is not only to be able to understand the possible effect of the condition on the brain, but also to be able to actively contribute within the multidisciplinary setting. It is also helpful in order to communicate with parents (and sometimes older children) who are often increasingly well informed about the condition. As well as understanding the physical aspects of the condition, the psychologist needs to be aware of the psychological and psychosocial aspects of the condition that may affect child and family. All neuropsychological data should be put into the context of the wider child and family picture, and, indeed, their social and cultural setting. It is noteworthy that although patients and their carers are increasingly well informed about their condition, the diagnosis of cognitive difficulties may still come as a shock, and the presentation of the results needs to be carried out as any other "bad news" should be delivered.

Children with chronic medical conditions are faced with frequent hospital outpatient appointments. Therefore it will be very important to ensure that appointments with the pediatric neuropsychologist are arranged to fit in with these, so as to reduce the burden placed on the child and the family and the amount of time that is required away from school and work. Having said this, the timing of the assessment is also important and needs to be considered in relation to any particular exacerbation of the condition, or the receiving of bad medical news, which might affect the child's ability to complete the assessment to the best of their ability.

It is unlikely that clinicians working in community settings in general clinics will have sufficient knowledge or experience to conduct in-depth assessments of children with uncommon conditions. Referral of such children to specialist centers is therefore likely to be of benefit. If this is not possible, the accessing of specialist knowledge via supervision and consultation will be of benefit to both clinician and patient.

In an ideal world, regular screening and assessment of all children with medical conditions would be a useful addition to the medical team's repertoire. However, in the current climate of the challenge to provide cost-effective services, justifying the cost is difficult. Therefore, the development of brief screening batteries that are sensitive and specific enough to identify those children in greatest clinical need of more detailed neuropsychological/medical assessment is urgently needed.

The provision of adequate training for teachers and appropriate educational interventions are of paramount importance in ensuring the best possible outcomes for children with neuropsychological effects of medical conditions. Certainly in the UK, where resources are stretched in education, children with subtle difficulties may struggle to get their needs addressed. The role of the pediatric neuropsychologist is therefore vital in liaising with educators, and in producing short, practice-oriented reports, specifying clearly what the child's strengths and weaknesses are, and how these are affected by his or her physical condition, and giving concrete recommendations that can be easily applied with few extra resources.

Just as there is now an awareness that children with medical conditions are at increased risk of psychological difficulties, there is also awareness that medical conditions and their treatment can give cognitive effects. Of course, there will be interactions between the psychological well-being of a child and his or her cognitive profile, which should be considered. However, all too often in clinical practice children with medical conditions are thought to have psychological/adjustment difficulties when they actually/also have significant neurocognitive impairments that have heretofore been undiagnosed, and it is these deficits that are at least part of the cause of the psychological difficulties. Access to screening and comprehensive assessment and treatment in both areas should be available in order to improve and maintain the child's quality of life and that of his or her family.

References

Adams, R. (2000). Lessons from the stroke prevention trial in sickle cell anaemia (STOP) study. *Journal of Child Neurology, 15*(5), 344–349.

Armstrong, F. D., Thompson, R. J., Wang, W., Zimmerman, R., Pegelow, C. H., Miller, S., et al. (1996). Cognitive functioning and brain magnetic resonance imaging in children with sickle cell disease. Neuropsychology Committee of Cooperative Study of Sickle Cell Disease. *Pediatrics, 97*(6), 864–870.

Bachanas, P. J., Kullgren, K., Suzman Schwartz, K., Lanier, B., McDaniel, S., Smith, J., et al. (2001). Predictors of psychological adjustment in school-aged children infected with HIV. *Journal of Pediatric Psychology, 26*(6), 343–352.

Bernaudin, F., Verlhac, S., Fréard, F., Roudot-Thoraval, F., Benkerrou, M., Thuret, I., et al. (2000). Multi-center prospective study of children with sickle cell disease: Radiographic and psychometric correlation. *Journal of Child Neurology, 15*, 333–343.

Bisiacchi, P. S., Suppiej, A., & Laverda, A. (2000). Neuropsychological evaluation of neurologically asymptomatic HIV-infected children. *Brain and Cognition, 43*(1–3), 49–52.

Bonner, M. J., Gustafson, K. E., Shumacher, E., & Thompson, R. J. (1999). The impact of sickle cell disease on cognitive functioning and learning. *School Psychology Review, 28*(2), 182–193.

Browers, P., Moss, H., Wolters, P., & Schmitt, F. A. (1994). Developmental deficits and behavioural changes in pediatric AIDS. In I. Grant & A. Marin (Eds.), *Neuropsychology of HIV infection* (pp. 310–338). New York: Oxford University Press.

Brown, L. K., Lourie, K. J., & Pao, M. (2000). Children and adolescents living with HIV and AIDS: A review. *Journal of Child Psychology and Psychiatry and Allied Disciplines, 41*(1), 81–96.

Brown, R. T., Armstrong, F. D., & Eckman, J. R. (1993). Neurocognitive aspects of pediatric sickle cell disease. *Journal of Learning Disabilities, 26*(1), 33–45.

Brown, R. T., Davis, P. C., Lambert, R., Hsu, L., Hopkins, K., & Eckman, J. (2000). Neurocognitive functioning and magnetic resonance imaging in children with sickle cell disease. *Journal of Pediatric Psychology, 25*(7), 503–513.

Butters, M. A., Beers, S. R., & Tarter, R. E. (2001). Perspective for research on neuropsychological assessment of medical disease. In R. E. Tarter, M. Butters, & S. R. Beers (Eds.), *Medical neuropsychology* (2nd ed.). New York: Kluwer Academic/Plenum.

Coscia, J. M., Christensen, B. K., Henry, R. R., Wallston, K., Radcliffe, J., & Rutstein, R. (2001). Effects of home environment, socioeconomic status and health status on cognitive functioning in children with HIV-1 infection. *Journal of Pediatric Psychology, 26*(6), 321–329.

Craft, S., Schatz, J., Glauser, T. A., Lee, B., & DeBaun, M. R. (1993). Neuropsychologic effects of stroke in children with sickle cell anaemia. *Journal of Pediatrics, 123*, 712–717.

DCCT (Diabetes Control and Complications Trial Research Group). (1994). A screening algorithm to identify clinically significant changes in neuropsychological functions in the Diabetes Control and Complications Trial. *Journal of Clinical and Experimental Neuropsychology, 16*, 303–316.

DCCT (Diabetes Control and Complications Trial Research Group). (1996). Effects of intensive diabetes therapy on neuropsychological function in adults in the Diabetes Control and Complications Trial. *Annals of Internal Medicine, 124*, 379–388.

DeCarli, C., Civitello, L. A., Brouwers, P., & Pizzo, P. A. (1993). The prevalence of computed axial tomographic abnormalities in the cerebrum in 100 consecutive children symptomatic with the human immunodeficiency virus. *Annals of Neurology, 34*, 198–205.

Desrocher, M., & Rovert, J. (2004). Neurocognitive correlates of type 1 diabetes. *Child Neuropsychology, 10*(1), 36–52.

Fishkin, P. E., Armstrong, F. D., Routh, D. K., Harris, L., Thompson, W., Miloslavich, K., et al. (2001). Brief report: Relationship between HIV infection and WPPSI-R performance in pre-school age children. *Journal of Pediatric Psychology, 25*(5), 347–351.

Gribbons, D., Zahr, L., & Opas, S. (1995). Nursing management of children with sickle cell disease: An update. *Journal of Pediatric Nursing, 10*(4), 232–242.

Hannonen, R., Tupola, S., Ahonen, T., & Riikonen, R. (2003). Neurocognitive functioning in children with type-1 diabetes with and without episodes of severe hypoglycaemia. *Developmental Medicine and Child Neurology, 45*, 262–267.

Kirkham, F. J., Lerner, N. B., Noetzel, M., DeBaun, M. R., Datta, A. K., Rees, D. C., et al. (2006). Trials in sickle cell disease. *Pediatric Neurology, 34*(6), 450–458.

Lewis, S. Y. (2001). Commentary. Coping over the long haul: Understanding and supporting children and families affected by HIV disease. *Journal of Pediatric Psychology, 26*(6), 359–361.

McCarthy, A. M., Lindgren, S., Mengeling, M. A., Tsalikian, E., & Engvall, J. (2002). Effects of diabetes on learning in children. *Pediatrics, 109*, 9–19.

Midence, K., McManus, C., Fuggle, P., & Davies, S. (1996). Psychological adjustment and family functioning in a group of British children with sickle cell disease: Preliminary empirical findings and a meta-analysis. *British Journal of Clinical Psychology, 35*(3), 439–450.

Moser, F. G., Miller, S. T., Bello, J. A., Pegelow, C. H., Zimmerman, R. A., Wang, W. C., et al. (1996). The spectrum of brain MR abnormalities in sickle-cell disease: A report from the Cooperative Study of Sickle Cell Disease. *American Journal of Neuroradiology, 17*, 985–972.

Northam, E. A., Anderson, P. J., Jacobs, R., Hughes, M., Warne, G. L., & Werther, G. A. (2001). Neuropsychological profiles of children with type 1 diabetes 6 years after disease onset. *Diabetes Care, 24*(9), 1541–1546.

Ohene-Frempong, K., Weiner, S. J., Sleeper, L. A., Miller, S. T., Embury, S., Moohr, J. W., et al. (1998). Cerebrovascular accidents in sickle cell disease: Rates and risk factors. *Blood, 91*, 288–294.

Pearson, D. A., McGrath, N. M., Nozyce, M., Nichols, S. L., Raskino, C., Brouwers, P., et al. (2000). Predicting HIV disease progression in children using measures of neuropsychological and neurological functioning. *Pediatrics, 106*, 76–86.

Pegelow, C. H., Macklin, E. A., Moser, F., Wang, W. C., Bello, J. A., Miller, S. T., et al. (2002). Longitudinal changes in brain magnetic resonance imaging findings in children with sickle cell disease. *Blood, 99*(8), 3013–3018.

Routhieaux, J., Sarcone, S., & Stegenga, K. (2005). Neurocognitive sequelae of sickle cell disease: Current issues and future directions. *Journal of Pediatric Oncology Nursing, 22*(3), 160–167.

Ryan, C. M., & Hendrickson, R. (1998). Evaluating the effects of treatment for medical disorders: Has the value of neuropsychological assessment been fully realised? *Applied Neuropsychology, 5*(4), 209–219.

Schatz, J. (2004). Brief report: Academic attainment in children with sickle cell disease. *Journal of Pediatric Psychology, 29*(8), 627–633.

Schatz, J., Brown, R. T., Pascual, J. M., Hsu, L., & DeBaun, M. R. (2001). Poor school and cognitive functioning with silent cerebral infarcts and sickle cell disease. *Neurology, 56*, 1109–1111.

Steen, R. G., Xiong, X., Mulhern, R. K., Langston, J. W., & Wang, W. C. (1999). Subtle brain abnormalities in children with sickle cell disease: Relationship to blood hematocrit. *Annals of Neurology, 45*(3), 279–286.

Swift, A. V., Cohen, M. J., Hynd, G. W., Wisenbaker, J. M., McKie, K. M., & Makari, G. (1989). Neuropsychologic impairment in children with sickle cell anaemia. *Pediatrics, 84*(6), 1077–1085.

Tarter, R. E., Van Thiel, D. H., & Edwards, K. L. (1988). *Medical neuropsychology: The impact of disease on behavior.* New York: Plenum.

Wallander, J. L., Thompson, R. J., Jr., & Alriksson-Schmidt, A. (2003). Psychosocial adjustment of children with chronic physical conditions. In M. C. Roberts (Ed.), *Handbook of pediatric psychology* (3rd ed., pp. 141–158). New York: Guilford.

Wechsler, D. (1974). *Wechsler intelligence scale for children: Revised.* New York: Psychological Corporation.

White, D. A., Moinuddin, A., McKinstry, R. C., Noetzel, M., Armstrong, M., & DeBaum, M. (2006). Cognitive screening for silent cerebral infarctions in children with sickle cell disease. *Journal of Pediatric Hematology/Oncology, 28*(3), 166–169.

Wolters, P. L., Brouwers, P., Civitello, L., & Moss, H. A. (1997). Receptive and expressive language function of children with symptomatic HIV infection and relationship with disease parameters: A longitudinal 24-month follow-up study. *AIDS, 11*(9), 1135–1144.

Wysocki, T., Harris, M. A., Mauras, N., Fox, L., Taylor, A., Craig Jackson, S., et al. (2003). Absence of adverse effects of severe hypoglycemia on cognitive function in school-aged children with diabetes over 18 months. *Diabetes Care, 26*(4), 1100–1105.

21

A Clinician's Guide to Child Neuropsychological Assessment and Formulation

Jody Warner-Rogers and Jonathan Reed

As the various chapters in this book make clear, an understanding of the brain and its functioning has been critical to increasing our appreciation of how various cognitive processes develop throughout childhood. However, for many children, the pathway from infancy through childhood to adolescence and young adulthood will not be straightforward. For some, the developmental course will be peppered from the outset with neurodevelopmental obstacles that may only become evident with the passage of time as the demands of their environment begin to outstrip their capacity to meet them. For others, their expected trajectories will be suddenly thrown off track by illness, disease, or damage. Parents, professionals—perhaps even the children themselves—will seek to understand what has gone (or might go) wrong and why. Neuropsychological evaluation has a key role to play in this journey of understanding.

Of course, one would never expect a neuropsychologist to be the only one involved in the assessment and treatment process. Professionals from a wide variety of disciplines contribute to the understanding and management of children. What unique contribution does the pediatric neuropsychologist have to offer to a multidisciplinary approach to children's difficulties? This is not just a theoretical question. In the increasingly business-like environment of hospital and educational settings, justifying the relevance and expense of various assessment procedures or treatment options is becoming ever more necessary. Demonstrating value for money, engaging in evidence-based practice, and monitoring effectiveness of outcome are all now essential components of service delivery. Pediatric neuropsychologists must be aware of these issues and embed their clinical practice in reality.

How does one go about collecting and interpreting "neuropsychological" data and sharing this information with others in a "useful" manner, understanding that "usefulness" may be defined differently by the various players involved in any given assessment (i.e., service user, referrer, service purchaser, other professionals). This chapter aims to answer that question by providing a template for neuropsychological assessment and formulation that can be applied across settings and problem areas and audited for the purposes of clinical governance and service monitoring.

Neuropsychological Assessment: A Valuable Endeavor?

When it comes to understanding the difficulties children experience, we believe that possessing the clearest possible understanding of the brain's contribution to "what's wrong" and "why" puts everyone in a better position to work toward improving or overcoming the obstacles they face. When there is a "brain basis" for a child's difficulties, neuropsychologists are well positioned to examine what is going on for these children "on the surface"—that is, their cognitive, behavioral, social, emotional, and adaptive functioning—and link any identified problems to aspects of brain functioning, developmental issues, and environmental factors. It is the integration across domains—brain, development, and context—that characterizes the practice of pediatric neuropsychology (Holmes Bernstein, 2000).

Academically, the field of pediatric neuropsychology is built upon the theories and research of developmental and cognitive psychologists. Understanding any "difficulties" requires an appreciation of how the issues being assessed *differ* or *deviate* from what would be expected during the course of "normal" development. In other words, a firm grounding in "normal" child development is the foundation of any efforts to evaluate and (most importantly) improve those situations in which developmental progress has not proceeded smoothly. Clinically, the profession is characterized by the application of this knowledge to children who present "with cognitive, behavioural or educational change in the context of actual or suspected neurological illness or injury" (British Psychological Society, 2004, p. 3). From its very early days as a fledgling discipline, pediatric neuropsychologists emphasized that consideration of brain-based difficulties could only be achieved "by thorough understanding of the child and their development" (Fletcher & Taylor, 1984, p. 52).

In his seminal textbook *Introduction to Neuropsychology*, Beaumont (1983, p. 4) noted that "to understand human behaviour we need to understand the human brain." This statement reflects a critical core belief in neuropsychology. For the practitioner, this is a core belief that underpins three key assumptions:

- If one is to evaluate and treat childhood difficulties effectively, then one must consider brain functioning (because the two are inexorably linked).
- If one is to *understand* any concept or phenomenon, then one must be able to measure it systematically, reliably, and validly.
- If a neuropsychological assessment is to be clinically relevant, then the emphasis must rest not on the *methods* of data gathering, but rather on the *interpretation and integration* of all available data and the extent to which they enhance the appreciation of the various factors impinging on the child's behavior.

In our view, it is these three assumptions that drive the true goal of any neuropsychological assessment: the establishment of a clinically relevant, theoretically valid, and effectively communicated case formulation. In this formulation rests the true value of a neuropsychological evaluation. The formulation can enhance the understanding of the child's current difficulties, inform subsequent treatment or management decisions, and form the basis of prognostications. A neuropsychologically informed case formulation, which has, at its center, the brain–behavior relationship, is truly the unique selling point of the assessment.

The Building Blocks of Case Formulation

As evidenced throughout this book, the brain–behavior relationship is a complex and bidirectional one. It is a relationship that is programmed, in part, from conception. It is in action before birth, influenced by a myriad of factors both intrinsic and extrinsic, and will play out in a continuous fashion throughout the lifespan of an individual. But brains do not operate in a vacuum. Clinicians must consider brain functioning, but not limit their formulations to it. The sirens of neurocentricity must be avoided. Clinicians must remain holistic in their thinking about children, the environments in which they live and learn, and the vast range of factors (genetic, organic, contextual) that can influence behavior and the timing of their impact (historical, concurrent) as this is the hallmark of good practice.

If we are to understand the human brain, we must be able to index its functioning. If we are to consider behavior in a scientific way, we must be able to operationalize it and assess it reliably. There are many ways to measure brain activity, including electroencephalograms (EEGs) and magnetic resonance imaging (MRI). If one believes that all behavior is, to some degree, brain-based, then studying overt behavior is yet another way of measuring brain functioning. This is a defining characteristic of clinical neuropsychology, described by Lezak and colleagues as "an applied science concerned with the behavioral expression of brain dysfunction" (Lezak, Howieson, & Loring, 2004, p. 3). Neuropsychologists have long been in the business of studying and observing behavior in a systematic manner. The advent of psychometric theory allowed the development of standardized assessment measures, which led to the wide range of commercially available tools the clinician has at his or her disposal which, theoretically, tap into many different neuropsychological processes. Tests afford the opportunity to sample behavior under standardized conditions and to compare the results obtained against large databases. Such comparisons allow psychologists to comment upon the level of performance (average, superior, impaired) as well as the statistical significance of any variability. These tests provide a way of measuring neuropsychological processes, such as attention and memory, by making covert brain activity overt, observable and, most important, measurable. However, as Baron (2004, p. 5) reminds us, "neuropsychological assessment is only one component of neuropsychological practice."

Indeed, it is the next step, the linking of this information to the integrity of the individual's central nervous system (CNS) that differentiates a neuropsychological evaluation from other forms of clinical or intellectual assessment. This is where one finds the third assumption in operation. Elaborating upon the test data and observations by combining them with other evidence of CNS functioning (in addition to information regarding the other, environmental or historical, factors thought to impact upon the child) is the step that puts the "neuro-" prefix onto a psychological assessment. Lezak puts it succinctly: "Regardless of whether a behavioural study is undertaken for clinical or research purposes, it is neuropsychological as long as the questions that prompted it, the central issues, the findings or the inferences drawn from them ultimately relate to brain function" (Lezak et al., 2004, p. 15). Note that *no mention of methodology* is made in Lezak's definition of a neuropsychological assessment. A quick scan through any catalogue of the major test publishers generally reveals a section entitled "neuropsychology." It is important to remember that administration of "neuropsychological tests" is not necessarily synonymous with the concept of a "neuropsychological evaluation." Neuropsychological assessments have less to do with how you collect the data (as long as valid and reliable means are employed) and everything to do with how you interpret it and combine it with other pieces of information, particularly data related to CNS functioning. This process of combining and integrating culminates in the actual product of neuropsychological evaluation: the clinical formulation.

The Assessment Process

Imagine the scene. You have a 2 o'clock appointment with an 8-year-old child. You have booked a 2-hour slot for today's session and are armed with the tools of the trade: pencils, a stopwatch, ratings scales, developmental history form, perhaps some stickers, and a cupboard full of assessment devices and record forms. This child is experiencing difficulties in several areas and your task is to consider the relative role brain functioning might play in the manifestation of these difficulties. The outcome measure for your efforts?: a valid clinical formulation that draws together all the various factors, including, but not limited to, those related to CNS integrity, that may be operating to impact upon the expression of this child's difficulties. How will you proceed and extract the most "value for money" from the resources at your disposal?

As clinicians, we faced that scene many times and were guided implicitly by our clinical judgments and intuition. But as supervisors, we needed to steer our trainees through the scene as well, and saw the need to create a model that would render the clinical decision-making process more explicit. In addition to addressing our training demands, we recognized that a clear operational definition of the evaluation process would enhance our ability to audit our service in a more systematic, effective manner.

A variety of assessment models are already well established in clinical practice. Holmes Bernstein (2000) identifies these as:

1. *Fixed batteries* (standardized administration of a pre-established set of assessment procedures).
2. *Eclectic batteries* ("idiosyncratic" batteries chosen by clinicians based upon their theoretical stances, and employing a variety of tasks selected to answer a particular question).

3. *Qualitative batteries* (focused upon describing patterns of cognitive performance).
4. *Process approaches* (in which emphasis is placed on microanalysis of how the individual earned a particular score, rather than focusing on the scores themselves).
5. *Functional evaluations* (takes into account poor ecological validity of test results and attempts to examine "real-life" skills).

These models focus on the procedures for collecting and examining data by informing the clinician's answer to the questions: "Which tools am I going to use?" and "What emphasis am I going to put on the scores?" Whilst these are critical questions, they do not sufficiently cover the wider assessment process, which must encompass questions such as "Why has this child been referred for neuropsychological assessment" and "What value will assessment add to the management of this child's difficulties?"

A Five-step Template

To address these needs, we developed the following five-step model which, on a theoretical level, we based on Holmes Bernstein's (2000) tripartite model of brain–development–context. Her model helps the clinician focus from the outset on brain-based processes, but reminds one to consider the dynamic nature of both the brain (a developing organ) and the cognitive processes it underpins (trajectories of skill emergence). On a practical level, we turned to the discussion of the various components of neuropsychological assessment outlined by Anderson and colleagues (Anderson, Northam, Hendy, & Wrennall, 2001). Ultimately, we based our template on the views of Baron (2004), who suggests: "a basic consideration is not which testing model one phil-osophically endorses, but whether one follows a logical and justifiable path to best answer a referral question and comprehensively understand the range of psychological, medical, and sociocultural issues impacting on the individual being assessed" (Baron, 2004, p. 16).

Collectively, these writers contributed to our own five-step template, which is outlined as follows:

1. Clarification
2. History and assessment
3. Formulation
4. Communication
5. Monitoring and reassessment

A "Gold Standard" of Assessment?

This template offers a *guide* to the process of child neuropsychological assessment. This is different from a *prescriptive manual* for "perfect" evaluation. Like many clinicians, we believe no such "gold standard" exists. Ultimately, clinicians should aim to design and produce evaluations that are useful—and "usefulness" must always remain a context-dependent concept. What is extremely helpful in one situation might be quite useless in another. For example, the most lengthy and comprehensive of evaluations might not actually provide the highest utility if it is overly inclusive or obtusely written. As noted earlier, multiple approaches to assessment exist within the field of neuropsychology and each has its own supporters, perhaps even a few zealots. What is lacking, however, is a body of empirical evidence demonstrating the superiority of one style over the other.

Very good reasons underlie the fact that no "gold standard" has yet to emerge. After all, one cannot imagine a research psychologist planning the procedures for a particular project with the premise: "I'm not sure what I'm after here, so I'm going to give them everything I've got! This will take hours and with all the fascinating data that will be pouring in, I am sure I'll find something significant and of interest!" The selection of a test battery for research purposes is governed by the hypotheses under investigation. The same principles should be applied in clinical practice. Clinical assessments are prompted by a wide range of referral concerns and thus naturally will be conducted for a whole host of different reasons. Some concerns may require hours of clinical time in order to be fully addressed. Others might lend themselves to concise, idiosyncratic measures of specific aspects of functioning. In addition to the referral questions, local policies, availability of equipment and expertise, constraints on the allocation of resources, and even the compliance of the child may play a role in determining the nature and extent of any individual evaluation. Clinical neuropsychological assessments can be construed as $n = 1$ research projects because specific hypotheses can be explored, the data collected and summarized systematically, and the results interpreted in the context of the extant literature.

So what makes a good neuropsychological assessment? Assessments are "good" if they can answer, as far as possible, the questions that prompted them. We would argue that in most *clinical* situations, a goal-oriented, individually tailored assessment that has been carefully planned according to the specific referral question(s), developmental level and stamina of the child, and informed by our knowledge regarding important neuropsychological correlates of the presenting difficulties, represents the best value for time and money. We mention money yet again because specialist evaluations of any sort are expensive commodities. Neuropsychologists in clinical practice must be able to demonstrate value for money. If clinicians focus on the product of assessment (i.e., clinical formulation) from the outset (i.e., clarification of referral issues), and have a framework for tracking time spent in each component of the assessment, then they will be in a better position to audit the process. They can examine the extent to which they are providing a "useful" service whose product—the case formulation—is informing and improving the ultimate management of the child. In our view, "management" is a concept that must include both a shared understanding of the problems as well as the recommendations, strategies, and treatments put in place to minimize the impact of these problems.

Step 1 Clarification: What, Why, Why Now?

Establishing how and why a neuropsychological assessment might be useful is essential at the start of the evaluation process. Typically, a referral is prompted by a particular problem or constellation of concerns. Understanding who has referred this child and why is key to designing an appropriate assessment. It is not uncommon for initial referral letters to be somewhat obscure in the descriptions of the relevant issues. It is also not uncommon for different people to have different views on the problems. We have found working through the following series of specific queries very helpful. The responses obtained allow us to clarify and expand upon the concerns that prompted the referral and to lay the initial scaffolding for our formulations:

- What is the child doing (or not doing) that is worrying?
- Who else shares these worries?
- If it wasn't for these worries, would anyone be seeking help from professionals for any other reasons? (This is often useful to uncover other, additional—or comorbid—problems.)
- Does this child have a neurological or medical condition that is known to impact upon brain functioning? If so, is their current presentation (across domains) consistent with what (if anything) is expected based on the research literature?
- Are there any settings in which the difficulties are relatively less apparent? (This is useful to establish extent of pervasiveness; it also identifies situations where either (a) minimal demands are being placed upon the child's weaknesses or (b) the setting is sufficiently supportive to minimize the impact of these weaknesses.)
- Why are you seeking assistance for these difficulties right now? (This helps to identify any possible triggers that might have exacerbated an underlying weakness.)
- What do you (parent/child/school/referrer) hope to gain from this assessment? (This identifies any inappropriate expectations, and helps to identify key areas to include in formulation.)

Ultimately, this line of questioning helps everyone involved in the child's ongoing management to shift their focus onto the potential *outcomes* of the evaluation. Agreeing discrete end-product goals can inform decisions at other stages in the process. Importantly, it allows one to evaluate the ability of the assessment findings to actually meet these goals, and immediately flags up the possibility that a neuropsychological assessment may not be the best method for working toward those goals or answers.

To clarify the referral concerns in our own practice, we developed a referral form which outlines some common reasons neuropsychological assessments are requested. Feedback from the consultants who tap into our service indicated that this format provided a useful tool which allowed them to concentrate their thinking and utilize scarce neuropsychological resources more effectively. The form also helped all parties identify inappropriate referrals at an earlier stage and redirect them to more suitable services. The most common reasons for referral included:

- Establish a baseline level of functioning before a change in treatment (commencement of medication, surgery).
- Document changes following an acquired brain injury.
- Track deterioration in conditions associated with loss of capacities.
- Identify profile of neurocognitive strengths and weaknesses to inform educational remediation or as precursor to rehabilitation planning.
- Evaluate the efficacy of intervention.

It is important to note that our service is embedded in a department of pediatric neurosciences, so all referrals were from consultant pediatric neurologists. Services that are linked to other disciplines (e.g., psychiatry) or located within other agencies (e.g., education) might have a different profile of intake issues.

Step 2 History and Assessment

Developmental history

Taking a thorough developmental history is time-consuming, but time well spent. This is true irrespective of whether the issue at hand involves damage in the context of normal development (where information on premorbid functioning is particularly important) or developmental difficulties (in which consideration of how the difficulties have impacted upon the processes of change are key). Establishing the child's developmental trajectories across the different functional domains (motor, language, social, behavioral, emotional) allows one to begin to generate hypotheses for specific investigation. In particular, it is important to establish whether trajectories across domains have been relatively even, or whether there is evidence of global delay in development (i.e., across many different domains of functioning), or alternatively, whether progress within specific modalities has been differentially affected or at risk.

Integrating the medical condition (if applicable)

Specific neurological information
At this early stage in the evaluation process, if the child already has a diagnosable neurological or neurodevelopmental disorder, one can bring in the medical data (e.g., EEG or MRI results) particular to that child and the research literature pertinent to the problem area. However, this is where adult models based on neuropsychology lose their relevance. If the other CNS investigations identify specific areas of structural impairment (e.g., specific lesions), one would not immediately focus one's efforts on cognitive capacities localized to that region. Rather, one would draw on the concepts more

relevant to pediatric neuropsychology, specifically those of plasticity, crowding, and reorganization. The hypotheses would focus more on how the processes of change may have been impacted by the damage recorded on the other means of investigation.

Consulting the literature

At this stage, reviewing the literature to establish what is known in general about the impact on CNS functioning of any medical conditions or treatments is a good starting-point (*Pediatric Neuropsychology* edited by Yeates, Ris, & Taylor, 2000, and *The Development of Psychopathology* by Pennington, 2002, are helpful in this regard). If, for example, the child is on any medications (e.g., certain pharmacological interventions for epilepsy) that are associated with slowness in processing speed, then it would be useful to include measures of this aspect of neuropsychological functioning in the assessment protocol. The neuropsychological phenotypes of certain disorders that affect the CNS (e.g., phenylketonuria) are well documented, and determining the extent to which the difficulties experienced by the individual at the focus of your particular assessment do or do not fit the "usual" pattern seen with that disorder can be a useful starting-point for the formulation.

Unpicking the presenting concerns

Elaborating upon the response to the earlier query "What is the child doing (or not doing) that is worrying?" helps to elucidate potential targets for formal psychometric assessment. Ideally, this should involve developing a list from the parents and/or school of the exact types of *functional impairments* on the observable level. In other words, what is the child actually doing (or not doing) that is impacting upon his or her functioning. This should encompass functioning in five key domains: (a) behavioral, (b) social, (c) emotional, (d) cognitive/learning, and (e) adaptive. This list can some-times be divided into two: One is a list that reflects a *lack of progress or absence of skills* (e.g., not concentrating sufficiently, not learning to read, not making friends, not keeping up with peers with regard to x); the other a record of *behavior excesses* (e.g., too boisterous, temper tantrums). Each point on the lists helps clinicians to: (a) consider which cognitive processes might underpin the behavior; (b) provide a focal point for observations during the assessment itself (e.g., he does x in the classroom—was it also evident in the test room?); and (c) identify potential targets for later intervention/monitoring.

Establishing rapport and gaining consent

Before any tests can be administered, the clinician must be able to engage the child. Rapport is an essential component to any assessment with children. Many children are only too happy to engage one on one with a friendly adult who is encouraging them to try various puzzles and tasks. But this is not always the case and rapport can be a tenu-ous and transient phenomenon. Some children are avoidant or even oppositional, refusing to apply themselves or comply with instructions. It is important to remember that such children may actually be finding the tasks too difficult, and therefore it may be helpful to restart at an easier level. Conveying the message "I'm not doing it" may be easier than admitting "I can't do it."

How long should an assessment last? There is some debate about this. We tend to limit our assessment sessions to two hours, with breaks as necessary. One argument for having longer assessment sessions is that it stresses the child's brain which will expose any subtle difficulties and also that it replicates what happens in a school environment. But at what point might the standardization and validity start to break down? Although it is not always clear from the technical manuals, the majority of tests were likely normed either on their own or with a comparison test. Chances are they were not normed as part of a very long battery of tests.

Conducting the "assessment"

We would argue that the assessment process itself actually starts from the very moment one begins to contemplate the referral issues. However, in this section, the term "assessment" is used to denote the administration of psychometric tests of various neuropsychological constructs and cognitive capacities. We believe that assessments should encompass five key areas of functioning: (a) behavioral, (b) cognitive/learning, (c) emotional, (d) social, and (e) adaptive. In practice, protocols of psychometric tests will consist predominantly of those focusing on the cognitive/learning aspect, as these are the ones that are most commercially available and empirically validated.

An assessment protocol can be developed that outlines the areas to be targeted and the methods via which these areas will be indexed. Such protocols should be individualized based on the unique questions that prompted the referral. In general, most assessments will include some index of general intellectual ability and a reference to academic attainment. Table 21.1 presents an overall list of the possible areas that might be targeted.

Table 21.1 Targets for Neuropsychological Assessment: Sample Form for Collating the Evidence from Different Sources.

Area of functioning	Developmental history	School reports	Questionnaires	Results of psychometric assessment (include scores)	Behavioural observations during testing
General intellectual ability					
Attention					
Sustained					
Selective					
Divided					
Switching					

Table 21.1 (*Continued*)

Area of functioning	Developmental history	School reports	Questionnaires	Results of psychometric assessment (include scores)	Behavioural observations during testing
Inhibition					
Executive functioning					
Planning					
Flexibility					
Time management					
Self-monitoring					
Problem-solving					
Organizing					
Memory					
Working memory					
Verbal					
Immediate recall					
Delayed recall					
Recognition					
Visual					
Immediate recall					
Delayed recall					
Recognition					
Semantic and episodic					
Language					
Vocabulary					
Grammar					
Expressive					
Receptive					
Discourse/pragmatics					
Visual					

Table 21.1 (*Continued*)

Area of functioning	Developmental history	School reports	Questionnaires	Results of psychometric assessment (include scores)	Behavioural observations during testing
Perceptual					
Visuomotor					
Configural processing					
Spatial processing					
Visual attention					
Academic attainment					
Phonological processing					
Reading					
Spelling					
Comprehension					
Calculations					
Math					
Reasoning					
Numerosities					
Handwriting					
Emotions and behavior					
Reactive and proactive regulation					
Social functioning					
Theory of mind					
Empathy					
Adaptive functioning					

General intellectual ability

The majority of neuropsychological protocols will include at least a basic screen of general intellectual ability (IQ). In adult neuropsychology, this is typically used as a baseline against which to compare performance on other tests of specific neuropsychological abilities. This is based on the assumption that in adults IQ has already developed and is stable. One has to be more cautious about this use in child neuropsychology assessments. For adults, one might look for dissociations with key modular cognitive functions; in childhood, however, structural or functional abnormalities have the potential to exert a much more diffuse impact on global functioning. This also depends on the age at which the injury occurred. As Anderson reminds us in Chapter 7 of this volume, at its best an IQ score reflects the overall integrity of brain functioning because it taps into different functions simultaneously. This results in IQ scores having a predictive utility in terms of academic attainment and, as a result, also employment prospects (Neisser et al., 1996). It is important to emphasize that the normative data on the vast majority of neuropsychological assessment devices were collected on individuals who fall within the average range intellectually. If initial intellectual assessment flags up the presence of a global cognitive impairment (i.e., IQ < 70), then clinicians must tread carefully when interpreting performance on other measures. In our view, however, it is still useful to proceed with neuropsychological assessment because it often will flag up specific strengths and vulnerabilities even in the context of global delay.

Academic ability
A key indicator of neuropsychological disability in children is found in their performance of school-based tasks. We would argue that it is important to get a key measure of some academic indices as part of any neuropsychological assessment as this is a key functional outcome for any developing child. If there are concerns in terms of literacy development, as discussed by Goswami in Chapter 15, it is vital to assess phonological ability as this is the key skill required in developing reading. It is also useful to have an up-to-date normative measure of reading, spelling, and comprehension. In terms of numeracy, the key disability will be dyscalculia and it is important to assess for basic understanding of number and the ability to recognize numerosities (i.e., the number of objects in a set) as described by Butterworth in Chapter 16. Again, some normative measure of ability to undertake numerical calculation or mathematical reasoning is desirable.

Neuropsychological domains
The key focus here is capturing the essence of the variety of different modular functions, such as memory, executive function, language, and so on. A comprehensive review of all areas is beyond the scope of this chapter, and the reader is referred to other current textbooks which outline in greater detail the actual tests and methods available for tapping into these functions. In particular, Anderson and colleagues (2001) and Baron (2004) provide comprehensive lists of assessment tools.

What is it important to assess in terms of what we know about the development of brain and behavior? The various chapters contained in the present volume provide a contemporary insight from key researchers in the field. In terms of key points, with regard to language development, Frederic Dick and colleagues highlight in Chapter 8 the importance of the development of vocabulary in relation to lateralization and for subsequent language development. Another key developmental marker is the use of grammar. As Judy Reilly and colleagues point out in Chapter 5, early brain injury can affect language development but improvements often occur over time, highlighting the importance of a longitudinal approach to language assessment. They also point out that one of the functions most sensitive to injury is the child's use of language, which seems to be particularly affected in right-sided injury, and therefore it is particularly helpful to consider pragmatic use of language and discourse.

In terms of visuomotor and visuospatial functioning, as Janette Atkinson and Marko Nardini discuss in Chapter 9, in development there is a need to consider both basic visual processing and perception (e.g., form and recognition) based on ventral stream function and visual-motor tasks (e.g., head and eye movements and reaching and grasping) based on dorsal stream function. In particular, it is important to hold in mind the developmental sequence in visual-motor function from gross motor development, such as reaching and grasping, to motor tasks requiring more complex end-state planning, such as shape-posting tasks. It is also important to think about the interaction between visual-motor development with spatial processing and developments in attention. Judy Reilly and colleagues (Chapter 5) show the importance of considering configural visual-motor processing requiring integration of different parts in tasks such as copying a house or Rey–Osterrieth figure which is based on right brain function.

In terms of executive function, it would be important to focus on the three subdivisions highlighted in the research discussed by Claire Hughes and Andrew Graham in Chapter 12, namely cognitive flexibility, inhibitory control, and planning/ working memory. Arthur MacNeill Horton and Henry Soper (Chapter 10) underline a number of factors to consider when assessing memory. Overall, they show that it is important to assess the extent to which the child is organizing material to be remembered rather than relying on rote memory. Other important factors to consider are whether the child is able to remember both detail and gist as these are processed by different hemispheres. It is also important to assess whether the child is able to discard irrelevant material. From a process perspective, it is helpful to distinguish recall and recognition processes, semantic and episodic memory, and to be able to identify retrieval problems.

As Maxine Sinclair and Eric Taylor show in Chapter 11, it is important to distinguish the alerting, posterior, and anterior attention systems. The posterior system is associated with orienting, select attention, and the ability to disengage. As was also seen in Chapter 9, a particular difficulty with disengaging is seen in children with damage to the parietal area. The anterior system is associated with divided attention, inhibition, and attention switching. Some of these anterior functions can be disrupted in children with attention deficit hyperactivity disorder (ADHD).

Social and emotional function
Assessment of these areas tends to rely on interview, observation, and rating scales. There is also a great deal of cross-over with mental health services. From a neuropsychological point of view, it is important to keep in mind the brain–behavior relationships. As shown in Chapter 14 by Simon Baron-Cohen and Bhismadev Chakrabarti, it is possible to dissociate the various components involved in the development of social

behavior. It is important to consider the processes involved in the development of both theory of mind and the empathizing system. Baron-Cohen and Chakrabarti also show the association between different emotions with different brain systems.

In terms of further assessing emotional brain–behavior function, as discussed in Chapter 13 by Rebecca Todd and Marc Lewis, it is important to distinguish the development of reactive stimulus-bound processes associated with the ventral prefrontal cortex from the later developed, more proactive processes associated with the anterior cingulated cortex. As Todd and Lewis point out, this distinction has important implications for treatment.

Interpreting the scores: a cautionary tale

The extent to which performance on actual psychometric tests reflects "performance" in real life is often variable. This must be kept in mind at all times when interpreting test scores. For a whole host of reasons, a score within the "normal" range does not necessarily predict "normal" functioning outside the test room. Neuropsychological tests are not intended to be diagnostic nor anatomically specific. Psychometric assessment measures are designed to provide standardized means of sampling behavior. Take, for example, a child who presents with "concentration difficulties." On the behavioral level, these might manifest in a variety of ways, such as failure to complete tasks, or directing their gaze at irrelevant aspects of the environment (e.g., out of the window instead of toward the teacher when he or she is speaking). For this child, we might be interested in evaluating the cognitive construct of sustained attention, and choose to administer a task that purports to measure sustained attention. As suggested in Chapter 11, we might recall that sustained attention is subserved anatomically by the cerebellum and alerting attention system. Now, suppose the child scores poorly on our test of sustained attention. How do we interpret this? Tests do not directly tap anatomical areas nor, as Sattler (2001) notes, do they directly index traits or capacities. Rather, they allow us to make inferences about such things. These inferences must never be made in isolation and always in relation to other pieces of data (observations, clinical history, other test scores). A low score on a test of sustained attention would allow us to make an inference about the cognitive processes that underpin the behavior observed in other settings.

But what would happen if that same child performed in the average or even above-average range on our test of sustained attention? Are they choosing to switch off their attention in class? Do they really have a "concentration" problem? For some children, their actual behavioral difficulties might not be driven by lack of skill, but a lack of drawing on that skill at the right time and in the right place. As such, they do not have skills deficits, but rather implementation deficits. Again, Sattler (2001, p. 9) is useful here in prompting us to remember to "interpret scores by asking yourself what they suggest about the child's competencies." If a child is scoring in a certain range, but performing on a functional level below that range, one must ask oneself why the environment is failing to function as a discriminative stimulus—one that should be triggering the production of a particular behavior (or skill) at a specific time. This is not an infrequent phenomenon and one that lends itself neatly to psychological intervention. The take-home message is that profiles of scores show what a child is capable of doing in the unique—and frankly quite artificial—test environment. What is of paramount importance is how the child applies his or her repertoire of skills and capacities in real life. Test performance is interesting, but functional ability is the key.

Step 3   Formulation

This step involves pulling all the sources of data together and integrating them into a coherent whole. This requires building upon the descriptions of the presenting problems, summarizing the performance on psychometric tests of cognitive abilities, combining this information with data from other sources, and mapping all of this onto the child's day-to-day functioning. In other words, what does everything gathered in Steps 1 and 2 tell us about how a child is functioning across different domain areas? In particular, how does the relationship between brain functioning (as deduced from performance on tests of cognitive functions and interpreted in the context of developmental and contextual factors) and behavior play out? By linking brain–behavior relationships to day-to-day functioning, one sheds light on the impact of the specific deficits (be they at the skill or implementation level). By understanding the impact, one holds the key to intervention planning.

Step 4   Communication: Sharing Formulations, Improving Understanding

How does one best communicate case formulations? Often, this formulation is embedded in the reports that document the findings of the assessment. On the whole, however, referrers have neither the time nor inclination to trawl through lengthy tomes outlining the step-by-step analysis of neuropsychological testing data. In our experience, referring clinicians welcome pithy and direct responses to their concerns; parents want considerably more. Compiling a report that will inform such a diverse audience, however, can be quite a challenge.

In our own practice, we write two separate reports: one for referrers where we directly answer the referral question and may include some details as to how we arrived at our opinion; we write a second report for parents and for schools, which is basically a summary of the findings without any discussion of how we arrived at those findings. Depending on the issue at hand, we outline recommendations in the reports. Reports have a clearly demarcated "formulation" section.

Verbal discourse also has a role, and extended case discussions certainly have their place in clinical management. Parents and children, on the other hand, have particular needs, and it is important to put aside time to discuss the results of the assessment with the family. It is important to be as clear as possible and try not to be too technical. A face-to-face feedback session is often essential to ensure adequate parental understanding of what the neuropsychological assessment and formulation aimed to communicate.

Effective management of children's brain-based difficulties often necessitates multi-agency collaboration, as the effects of any such difficulties are likely to be pervasive across many settings. Thus, allocating time to meet or consult with relevant professionals, particularly school professionals, is essential. In our experience, the usefulness of neuropsychological reports grows exponentially if they are backed up with individual discussion.

Step 5   Monitoring and Reassessment

Children's brains are dynamic and developing organs. A single assessment provides a "snapshot" of that child's capacities at the time of evaluation. Ensuring that snapshot is a reliable and valid one is an obvious hallmark of good practice. But what does the future hold? Based on data from longitudinal studies one can, from the snapshot, prognosticate about future functioning, but at the level of the individual such predictions would remain only hypothetical. The forces of change, compensation, remediation and reorganization, and other aspects of their environment will undoubtedly exert their impact upon an individual child's unique trajectory. *There is no substitution for formal re-evaluation at later stages of development.* Perhaps, like fresh food, reports that document children's abilities should have a sell-by date. Out-dated reports on children no longer serve their original purpose.

Conclusion

The practice of pediatric neuropsychology has its academic roots in basic neurosciences, as well as cognitive and developmental psychology. A solid grounding in normal child development, combined with an understanding of brain development and cognitive processes, places the practicing clinician in a unique position with regard to understanding and managing childhood difficulties. We hope that this book helps clinicians to develop this understanding.

This chapter has outlined a particular template that can be used to structure pediatric neuropsychological assessments. It is not the only template, but it is one that we have found useful for practice and teaching. We place a heavy emphasis on the clinician's ability to develop and share neuropsychologically informed formulations with everyone involved in managing a child's difficulties. Indeed, we view neuropsychological case formulations as the "unique commodity" of clinical assessments—a product valued both by service users and purchasers.

References

Anderson, V., Northam, E., Hendy, J., & Wrennall, J. (2001). *Developmental neuropsychology: A clinical approach*. Hove, East Sussex: Psychology Press.

Baron, I. S. (2004). *Neuropsychological evaluation of the child*. New York: Oxford University Press.

Beaumont, J. G. (1983). *Introduction to neuropsychology*. New York: Guilford.

British Psychological Society. (2004). *Commissioning child neuropsychology services*. Leicester: British Psychological Society.

Fletcher, J., & Taylor, H. G. (1984). Neuropsychological approaches to children: Towards a developmental neuropsychology. *Journal of Clinical Neuropsychology, 6*, 39–56.

Holmes Bernstein, J. (2000). Developmental neuropsychological assessment. In K. O. Yeates, M. D. Ris, & H. G. Taylor (Eds.), *Pediatric neuropsychology: Research, theory and practice* (pp. 405–438). New York: Guilford.

Lezak, M., Howieson, D. B., & Loring, D. W. (2004). *Neuropsychological assessment* (4th ed.). New York: Oxford University Press.

Neisser, U., Boodoo, G., Bouchard, T. J., Wade Boykin, A., Brody, N., Ceci, S. J., et al. (1996). Intelligence: Knowns and unknowns. *American Psychologist, 51*(2), 77–101.

Pennington, B. F. (2002). *The development of psychopathology*. New York: Guilford.

Sattler, J. M. (2001). *Assessment of children: Cognitive applications* (4th ed.). La Mesa, CA: Sattler.

Yeates, K. O., Ris, M. D., & Taylor, H. G. (Eds.). (2000). *Pediatric neuropsychology: Research, theory and practice*. New York: Guilford.

Index